T0245492

In a day when "global Christianity" is frequently spoken of as a mono[...] *Christianity*, brings out a beautiful and variegated overview of the chur[...] She highlights not just the four major Christian traditions but the di[...] Christian movements all across the globe. This is an invaluable resourc[...] [...] guide for anyone who wants to have a better understanding of the surprisingly diverse expressions and faces of Christianity in the 21st century.

> **Timothy C. Tennent**, PhD, president and professor of World Christianity
> at Asbury Theological Seminary

From Pentecost onward, Christianity has been a global faith. We hold to the same Christ, but a Christian in Afghanistan is in a far different context from one in Alabama or Australia. This book is a thorough, accessible guide to understanding the way Christians live, believe, and worship, country by country and region by region.

> **Russell Moore**, public theologian at *Christianity Today*,
> director of *Christianity Today*'s Public Theology Project

Dr. Gina Zurlo's *Global Christianity* is a comprehensive, essential, and valuable book in the study of World Christianity. She covers four major Christian traditions and provides trends, declines, growth, and vital information about these traditions around the globe. Each country covered includes a map, graphs, statistics, facts, culture, comparative charts, and other pertinent data. This book is accessible and a rich resource for students, churches, and anyone interested in global Christianity. I highly recommend it.

> **Grace Ji-Sun Kim**, professor of theology at Earlham School of Religion,
> author of *Spirit Life*, *Invisible*, and *Hope in Disarray*

Global Christianity brings the world to our doorstep. Using simple language, the latest statistics, and clear charts and maps, this book opens up the panorama of Christianity—the world's largest religion—country by country. It works! I looked up unfamiliar countries and within minutes could surmise the status and scope of Christianity in that country and continent across various traditions. This long-awaited volume is for *everyone* to grasp Jesus's magnificent gospel spreading in the nations!

> **Mary Ho**, international executive leader at All Nations

Global Christianity by Zurlo demonstrates how Christianity is lived in various localities, in all its beautiful diversity. A go-to-resource—there's plentiful wisdom here beyond demographic statistics, interpretation of trends, and a sample of persecution, as Zurlo offers information that can be tools for decision-making and prayer. Unbeknownst to most, the last century has witnessed a tectonic shift in global Christianity, and this one-stop publication is for all who are interested in the state of the largest religion in the world.

> **Rev. Dr. Casely Baiden Essamuah**, secretary to the Global Christian Forum

GLOBAL CHRISTIANITY

GLOBAL CHRISTIANITY

A Guide to the World's Largest Religion
from Afghanistan to Zimbabwe

GINA A. ZURLO

ZONDERVAN ACADEMIC

Global Christianity
Copyright © 2022 by Gina Zurlo

Requests for information should be addressed to:
Zondervan, *3900 Sparks Dr. SE, Grand Rapids, Michigan 49546*

Zondervan titles may be purchased in bulk for educational, business, fundraising, or sales promotional use. For information, please email SpecialMarkets@Zondervan.com.

Library of Congress Cataloging-in-Publication Data

Names: Zurlo, Gina A., 1986– author.
Title: Global Christianity: a guide to the world's largest religion from Afghanistan to Zimbabwe / Gina A. Zurlo.
Description: Grand Rapids: Zondervan, 2022.
Identifiers: LCCN 2022009713 (print) | LCCN 2022009714 (ebook) | ISBN 9780310113614 (paperback) | ISBN 9780310113638 (ebook)
Subjects: LCSH: Christianity. | Church history. | Missions. | BISAC: RELIGION / Christianity / Denominations | RELIGION / Reference
Classification: LCC BR121.3 .Z87 2022 (print) | LCC BR121.3 (ebook) | DDC 270.8/3—dc23/eng/20220502
LC record available at https://lccn.loc.gov/2022009713
LC ebook record available at https://lccn.loc.gov/2022009714

Cover design: Emily Weigel
Cover art: © Suriya Sising / Shutterstock
Interior illustrations: Peter F. Crossing and Bryan Nicholson
Interior typesetting: Kait Lamphere

Printed in the United States of America

22 23 24 25 26 27 28 29 30 31 32 33 /TRM/ 15 14 13 12 11 10 9 8 7 6 5 4 3 2 1

For my parents,

Mark and Renée Zurlo

Contents

Acknowledgments

This book represents my long-standing desire to continue the outward dissemination of research from the Center for the Study of Global Christianity. The center's founder, David B. Barrett (1927–2011), pioneered a new way to understand changes in the religious/nonreligious world. In doing so, he paved the way for research that could be accessible to both scholarly and lay audiences. Despite the common critique that such work is too expensive, hidden away in costly reference works and subscription databases, we are committed to partner with high-quality, reputable publishers and scholars, without losing sight of Barrett's vision to also produce materials for the benefit of Christians around the world. As a result, I'd like to acknowledge Zondervan for having the first vision of this book. Madison Trammel envisioned a popular reference work that could be disseminated far and wide for the benefit of the church in the United States. I'd also like to thank Ryan Pazdur and Kait Lamphere for helping me further focus the content and design of this book, as well as thanks to Kim Tanner for her careful reading and helpful commentary on the text.

This book was supported by my wider team at the Center for the Study of Global Christianity, including our host institution, Gordon-Conwell Theological Seminary, and its president, Scott Sunquist. My codirector, Todd Johnson, supported this project from the beginning and assisted me in every way to ensure its success. Peter Crossing, data analyst for the *World Christian Database*, produced the graphs and tables in this book. Nothing is possible at the Center without Peter's careful calculations and beautiful spreadsheets, ready for analysis. Thanks also goes to Christopher Guidry, who helped with the initial layout and design, and our cartographer, Bryan Nicholson, for creating the maps. I'd also like to thank the Center's research assistants from 2020–2022, who were always ready to help with tasks big or small: Nadia Andrilenas, Shela Chan, Danielle DeLong, Sharon Ellis, Alejandra Fontecha, David Hannan, Noah Karger, Jane Kyong Chun, and Renzo Meza. This was a talented group of students. Finally, I would like to thank Michael Hahn—research associate, editor, proofreader, and friend.

This book builds on the research conducted for the *World Christian Encyclopedia* (Edinburgh University Press, 2019), which has been condensed and updated to the contemporary global situation of 2020–2021. As a result, hundreds of church leaders, Christian workers, missionaries, and scholars have previously interacted with some of the material that appears in this book. Their names are listed in the Collaborators & Contributors pages in the *World Christian Encyclopedia*. I am deeply indebted to this global network of colleagues who help sustain the work of the Center for the Study of Global Christianity.

I wrote the majority of this book during the COVID-19 restrictions and quarantines of 2020 and 2021 while working full time and parenting my two young daughters, Elisa and Ashley. This book would not exist without the endless support of my husband, Christopher Bodecker, who entertained the children in lockdowns, took on all kinds of additional responsibilities, helped me carve out the time and space needed to pursue this work, and presumably enjoyed playing the game "Guess what country we are in today!" Thank you.

Introduction

Global Christianity provides an accessible entryway to understand contemporary trends in the world's largest religion. This book serves as a quick global reference to bring together relevant, well-researched information on the status of Christianity and world religions to American churches, Christian organizations, and individuals. This book can be used to answer some of the most frequently asked questions about World Christianity, such as:

> How many Christians are in the world?
> Is Christianity growing or declining?
> What is Christian life like in other places around the world?
> Where are the most challenging places to be a Christian today?

Christianity is no longer a Western-majority faith, as most Christians today live in Asia, Africa, and Latin America. With many adherents in the United States unaware of this shift in Christianity's center of gravity, this book is designed to be a companion for readers interested in learning more about how Christianity has changed over the twentieth century and continues to change today. This book provides readers a framework for understanding the state of Christianity around the world, with information on Christianity on six continents, in four major Christian traditions, within two Christian movements, and in 234 countries. Each entry features text that includes a brief history of Christianity, general religious trends, and important information on Christian life in that area. Next, a "Facts to Consider" bullet list of current events and salient information offers a wider socio-political-religious understanding of Christianity in its specific context. This list typically includes information on other religious communities, political conflicts or church-state relations, the status of religious freedom, and challenges related to gender equality, climate change, health, education, or economics.

Christianity by Continent

These pages cover trends in World Christianity by continent: Africa, Asia, Europe, Latin America, North America, and Oceania.

Christianity by Tradition and Movement

This book divides World Christianity into four major traditions: Catholic, Orthodox, Protestant, and Independents. The last category, Independents, includes individual Christians and major denominations that do not self-identify as Catholic, Orthodox, or Protestant, such as many African Independent Churches (AICs). It also includes churches outside traditional Christian orthodoxy that still self-identify as Christian, such as the Church of Jesus Christ of Latter-day Saints (Mormons). World Christianity is further distinguished by two movements: Evangelicals and Pentecostals/Charismatics.

Christianity by Country

There are three kinds of country layouts. Generally, countries with the largest Christian populations (over 5 million; 67 countries) are presented in a two-page spread, countries with medium-sized Christian populations (between 100,000 and 4.9 million; 108 countries) occupy a single page, and countries with small Christian populations (under 100,000; 59 countries) are closer to half a page.

Data

This book relies on the United Nations demographic database for general population information on the world's countries (233 countries, plus Kosovo). They are arranged alphabetically from Afghanistan to Zimbabwe. The Republic of the Congo and the Democratic Republic of the Congo are listed in the C's under Congo and Congo, DR. The Methodology and Sources section includes definitions of terms and explanations of data sources, including data on Bible translation, churches, missionaries, and gospel access.

The main sources for demographic data and analysis presented in this book are Todd M. Johnson and Gina A. Zurlo, eds., *World Christian Database* (Leiden: Brill, 2021) and Todd M. Johnson and Gina A. Zurlo, *World Christian Encyclopedia*, 3rd ed. (Edinburgh: Edinburgh University Press, 2019). These resources are produced by the Center for the Study of Global Christianity at Gordon-Conwell Theological Seminary (South Hamilton, Massachusetts, USA), which has been producing quantitative data on Christianity and other religions for over 55 years. The Center for the Study of Global Christianity is an academic research center that monitors worldwide demographic trends in Christianity, including outreach and mission. The center provides a comprehensive collection of information on the past, present, and future of Christianity in every country of the world. Their data and publications help churches, mission agencies, and nongovernmental organizations (NGOs) to be more strategic, thoughtful, and sensitive to local contexts. For more information, please visit www.globalchristianity.org or contact a researcher at info@globalchristianity.org.

Methodology and Sources

Methodology

The starting point of quantifying religious affiliation of all kinds is the United Nations 1948 Universal Declaration of Human Rights, Article 18: "Everyone has the right to freedom of thought, conscience and religion; this right includes freedom to change his religion or belief, and freedom, either alone or in community with others and in public or private, to manifest his religion or belief in teaching, practice, worship and observance." Variations on this statement have been incorporated into the state constitutions of many countries around the world. This fundamental doctrine also includes the right to claim the religion of one's choice and the right to be called a follower of that religion and to be counted as such. Utilizing the United Nations Universal Declaration of Human Rights as a foundation, this book uses the term *Christian* to mean all those who profess to be Christians in government censuses or public opinion polls, that is, those who declare or identify themselves as Christians, who say "I am a Christian" or "We are Christians" when asked the question "What is your religion?" Self-identification—meaning, a person's ability to choose their own religion—is the foundation of the statistics presented in this book.

Affiliated Christians are those known to the churches or known to the clergy and claimed in their statistics, that is, those enrolled on the churches' books or records. This usually means all known baptized Christians and their children. This definition of *Christian* is what the churches usually mean by the term, and statistics on affiliated Christians are what the churches themselves collect and publish. In all countries, it may be assumed with confidence that the churches know better than the state how many Christians are affiliated to them. Unaffiliated Christians are people who consider themselves Christians but do not belong to any church or denomination. Doubly affiliated Christians are those who are affiliated to two or more churches or denominations, such as individuals who were baptized Catholic as infants but switched to Protestantism later in life.

Population figures for the United Nations regions and countries, and for the world as a whole, were obtained from *World Population Prospects: The 2017 Revision*, prepared by the Population Division of the Department of Economic and Social Affairs of the United Nations Secretariat. Figures may not add to 100% due to rounding.

Religion

The *World Christian Database* includes 16 categories of religion: Christians, Muslims, Hindus, Buddhists, Chinese folk religionists, ethnic religionists, New Religionists, Sikhs, Spiritists, Jews, Daoists, Confucianists, Baha'is, Jains, Shintoists, and Zoroastrians; plus two categories of nonreligion: agnostics and atheists. Ethnic religion is also referred to as indigenous religion or traditional religion. The glossary includes definitions of these terms. The line graphs in this book show religious change over time from 1900–2050. Each graph include two lines, one for the continent or country's Christian population and the other for the second-largest religion (or nonreligion). For these graphs, atheists and agnostics have been combined and labeled as nonreligious.

Christian Traditions

This book organizes World Christianity into four major Christian traditions: (1) Catholics, (2) Orthodox (both Eastern and Oriental), (3) Protestants (including Anglicans), and (4) Independents. The first three are largely known and understood, but the fourth requires more explanation. There are many large churches and denominations that do not define themselves as Catholics, Orthodox, or Protestant and sometimes reject those terms. Zion churches in South Africa, for example, do not consider themselves as part of European Protestantism; neither do Jehovah's Witnesses self-identify as Protestants; and Old Catholics reject affiliation with Roman Catholicism.

Consequently, Independent Christianity refers to the many churches or movements that self-identify as Christian but are independent of historic Christianity. This category includes a broad range of movements, including African Independent Churches (AICs); many Pentecostal and Charismatic churches; nontraditional house and cell churches, many nondenominational churches; Independent Baptists; schisms from Orthodoxy; Old Catholics and other autocephalous Catholic churches; and Christians distinguished from mainline Christianity that claim a second, supplementary, or ongoing source of divine revelation in addition to the Bible, either a new revealed book or angelic visitations. Thus, Independent Christianity also includes Unitarians, Jehovah's Witnesses, Christian Scientists, the Church of Jesus Christ of Latter-day Saints (Mormons), and other more recent movements.

The Christian tradition charts that appear in this book represent a country or continent's affiliated Christian population, from 1900–2050, which includes Catholics, Orthodox, Protestants, and Independents. The charts exclude the unaffiliated and doubly affiliated. Each chart has two lines, one for the tradition's share of the continental population, and the other for the tradition's share of all Christians.

Christian Movements

Evangelicalism and Pentecostal/Charismatic Christianity are considered movements within Catholic, Protestant, Orthodox, and Independent Christianity. The four major traditions are mutually exclusive—a Christian cannot be both a Protestant and a Catholic (unless doubly affiliated). However, movements are found within the major traditions and are not mutually exclusive. For example, a Christian can be an Evangelical Protestant or a Catholic Charismatic or an Evangelical Charismatic Independent. The Christian movement charts include two lines, one for the percent of the global population, the other for the percent of all Christians.

Christian Families

Although the four traditions are a logical way to organize World Christianity, another layer of traditions immediately below this is readily recognizable and is useful to organize the faith—Christian families. Within the Catholic tradition, families further distinguish among Catholic rites, Roman, Byzantine, etc. Within the Orthodox tradition, families distinguish between the Eastern churches from the Oriental Orthodox. But it is within the Protestant and Independent traditions that denominational families are most recognizable. Protestants and Independents can be combined to produce a number for groups such as Anglicans, Baptists, Lutherans, Methodists, Presbyterians, and others. These families offer a more detailed look at the global Christian church.

Global North and Global South

Global North is defined in a geopolitical sense by five current United Nations regions: Eastern Europe (including Russia), Northern Europe, Southern Europe, Western Europe, and North America. Global South is defined as the remaining 17 current UN regions: Eastern Africa, Middle Africa, Northern Africa, Southern Africa, Western Africa, Eastern Asia, Central Asia, South Asia, Southeastern Asia, Western Asia, the Caribbean, Central America, South America, Australia/New Zealand, Melanesia, Micronesia, and Polynesia.

Sources

Individuals self-identify as a particular religion (or nonreligion) in a variety of ways. The estimates for religious affiliation and nonaffiliation in this book are from Todd M. Johnson and Gina A. Zurlo, eds., *World Christian Database* (Leiden: Brill, 2021) and Todd M. Johnson and Gina A. Zurlo, *World Christian Encyclopedia*, 3rd edition (Edinburgh: Edinburgh University Press, 2019). These resources are produced by the Center for the Study of Global Christianity at Gordon-Conwell Theological Seminary (South Hamilton, Massachusetts, USA). The *World Christian Database* contains best estimates for religious affiliation in all countries and known Christian denominations. Data are collected from governmental censuses, social scientific surveys and polls, and from religious communities themselves. Data are triangulated with other information on religions by ethnic people groups and reconciled with country population figures from the United Nations.

Estimates related to religious beliefs, practices, and attitudes from surveys are sourced from Pew Research Center reports, including Religion in Latin America (2014), Attitudes of Christians in Western Europe (2018), and Religious Belief and National Belonging in Central and Eastern Europe (2017). Contemporary information on the political status of religion and issues related to religious freedom are largely sourced from the US State Department Religious Freedom Reports of 2019 and 2020. Issues related to human rights are sourced from the US State Department Human Rights Reports 2020, Open Doors USA, and various organizations of the United Nations (Refugee Agency, Women, Human Development Report, etc.).

Data

Many different socioeconomic, health, and gender indicators could have been chosen for inclusion in this book to provide broader context for the Christian situation. The Human Development Index, physicians per 1,000 population, and a gender gap index were chosen to represent overall national development, access to health resources, and gender equality. Other variables can be found online in the *World Christian Database*. Below are explanations and sources of data found in the continent and country entries.

Map. A country locator map provides the immediate geographic context for each country or continent including shading of provinces by percentage Christian. Minimal detail is provided, including a capital city and the names of some surrounding countries. An inset continental map gives the broader context of where each country is located.

Population (2020). The population of this continent or country in 2020 (United Nations).

% under 15 years. The percent of the general population that are children (under 15 years) (United Nations).

Capital city. The capital city of the country and population of the urban agglomeration according to the United Nations. In some countries, the United Nations definition of the extent of the capital is different from that identified by governmental and other national entities. Urban agglomerations are defined as of 2,500 or more inhabitants, generally with population densities of 1,000 people per square mile.

% urban dwellers. The percent of the continent or country's population that lives in urban areas and the rate of change in percent per year (United Nations).

Official language(s). The official state or national language(s) defined for general use in the country's administration. Some countries do not have an official language.

Largest language. Language names and their scope are defined by the International Standards Organization either as a macrolanguage (such as Arabic, which consists of several individual languages) or as individual languages included in the ISO 639-3 standard.

Largest people. The largest ethnolinguistic people group as defined by ethnicity and language (rather than by social or caste characteristics).

Largest culture. The largest culture when the population of ethnolinguistic people groups are summed by just the cultural component, regardless of language.

Development. The continent or country's ranking on the United Nations Human Development Index (2018), where 1 is the lowest score (least developed) and 100 is the highest (most developed). This is a composite index that measures average achievement in three areas: (1) a long and healthy life, (2) knowledge, and (3) a decent standard of living. A higher value represents greater human development in this continent or country.

Physicians per 1,000. The number of physicians (both generalists and specialists) per 1,000 of the continent or country's population (World Health Organization 2017).

Gender gap. The gap between female Human Development Index (HDI) and male HDI (as a percentage of male HDI). Negative numbers indicate that female HDI is greater than male HDI (United Nations Human Development Report 2018). A high positive number means women are disadvantaged at higher rates than men.

Bible translations

- **Languages.** The number of languages (as defined by the ISO) identified by the *World Christian Database* as being in the continent or country in 2020.
- **Full Bible.** The number of languages in the continent or country that had a full Bible translation available in 2020.

Churches

- **Denominations.** The number of denominations (as defined in the glossary) in the continent or country in 2020.
- **Congregations.** The number of congregations (as defined in the glossary) in the continent or country in 2020.

Missionaries

- **Received.** The number of long-term (two years or more) foreign missionaries received by the continent or country in 2020.
- **Sent.** The number of long-term (two years or more) indigenous missionaries sent to other countries by the continent or country in 2020.

Gospel Access

Also known as "evangelization," which measures the extent to which the Christian message has been spread, or the extent of awareness of Christianity, Christ, and the Christian message.

- **Very low:** 0–20% of the population has access
- **Low:** over 20% but less than 40%
- **Medium:** over 40% but less than 60%
- **High:** over 60% but less than 80%
- **Very High:** over 80% of the population has access to the gospel

CHRISTIANITY BY CONTINENT

—

World Christianity

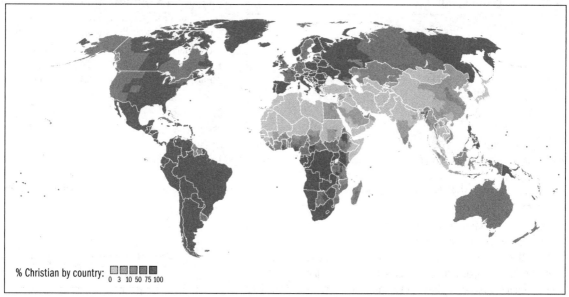

% Christian by country: 0 3 10 50 75 100

Christianity is the world's largest religion; with over 2.5 billion members, it comprises 32% of the global population. It is a massively diverse religion, found in thousands of languages, ethnic groups, geographic regions, and cultures worldwide. Some may argue that this diversity makes it difficult to talk about "World Christianity" as a unified whole—how can there be one singular thing called "Christianity" when beliefs, practices, and attitudes toward the faith vary widely from one place to another? However, the other side of that coin is the beauty of its diversity. Christianity is highly adaptable and makes itself at home in any culture and language. Any person or community in the world can be a part of the global Christian family regardless of ancestry, background, or language. Among other things, Christians around the world are bound together by the biblical mandate for followers of Jesus to be his witnesses to the ends of the earth. They accomplish this in a variety of ways—in their worship and evangelism in local congregations and communities, in their service to society through providing health care and education, in their academic contexts as theologians and scholars, and as people inspired by their faith to be political, environmental, and gender equality activists. Christianity is a truly global religion, not just because there are Christians in every country of the world but because of the indigenous-led contextualization of the faith and meaningful Christian engagement with humanity.

One of the major features of World Christianity is its shift from the global North (Europe and North America) to the global South (Asia, Africa, Latin America, Oceania). In 1900, 82% of Christians lived in the North. By 2020 this figure had dropped dramatically to just 33%. Today 26% of Christians in the world live in Africa alone, the highest percentage of any continent (11% of Christians live in North America). By the year 2050, an estimated 77% of Christians will live in the global South (39% in Africa). Another feature of this global shift is the rise of Pentecostal/Charismatic Christianity, which at less than 1% of Christians in 1900 was at 26% in 2020 and is estimated to be at 30% by 2050. The future of World Christianity is largely in the hands of Christians in the global South, where most Christians practice very different kinds of the faith compared to those in the North.

Christians by Continent

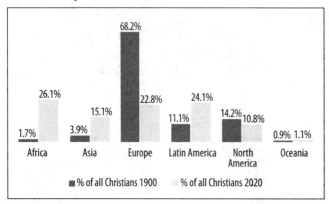

% of all Christians 1900 — % of all Christians 2020

Christianity has shifted from a tradition that was once majority global North to one that is majority global South. In 1900, 18% of Christians lived in Asia, Africa, Latin America, and Oceania. By 2020, this had changed dramatically to 67%, and this shift is poised to continue in the future. The most dramatic reversal has been in Europe, where 68% of all Christians lived in 1900, down to 23% by 2020. Significant gains were made in Africa, growing from less than 2% of all Christians in 1900 to 26% in 2020.

Countries with the Most Christians

Country	1900	Country	2020
United States	73,712,000	United States	244,313,000
Russia	62,545,000	Brazil	193,859,000
Germany	41,533,000	Mexico	128,229,000
France	40,731,000	Russia	117,848,000
United Kingdom	37,125,000	China	106,030,000
Italy	32,903,000	Philippines	99,577,000
Ukraine	28,501,000	Nigeria	95,358,000
Poland	22,050,000	DR Congo	85,120,000
Spain	18,795,000	Ethiopia	67,491,000
Brazil	17,319,000	India	67,356,000

The shift of Christianity to the global South has also changed the countries with the most Christians from 1900 to 2020. In 1900, nine of the ten countries were in the global North. This completely reversed by 2020, where in 2020, there were only two countries in the top ten: the United States and Russia.

Indicators & Demographic Data

Population (2020)...........7,795,482,000
% under 15 years 25%
Largest city (pop.). . Tokyo, Japan (37,393,000)
% urban dwellers..........56% (2.00% p.a.)
Largest language......12% Mandarin Chinese
Largest people .. 12% Han Chinese (Mandarin)
Development.........................70
Physicians..........................18.0
Gender gap..........................8%

Religion in the World

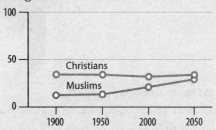

The percentage of the world that is Christian has dropped slightly over the last 120 years, at 34% of the world's population in 1900 and 32% in 2020. However, the world Christian movement grew from 558 million to 2.5 billion, with most of that growth occurring in the global South. Islam is the second largest religion in world, which grew from 12% of the global population in 1900 to 24% in 2020. Demographically, the gap is closing between Christianity and Islam. By 2050, it is expected that Christians will be 35% and Muslims will be 29% of the world's population.

Alongside the growth of the world's two largest religions has been an increase in nonreligious populations. Atheists and agnostics together were only 0.2% of the world's population in 1900; by 2020, they were 12%.

Bible Translations		Churches		Missionaries		Gospel Access	
Languages	7,490	Denominations	44,800	Received	425,000	1900	Medium
Full Bible	600	Congregations	4,059,000	Sent	425,000	2020	High

Facts to Consider

- Positive Christian engagement in religiously diverse societies, as in those throughout Asia, is increasingly important today and for the future. Many countries are becoming more religiously and ethnically diverse, such as in Europe, where migration is changing the continent's religious composition.
- Christianity is largely growing in places where, overall, people have a much lower quality of life than in the global North. Christians in the South deal with a series of issues related to poverty, proper health care, and lack of educational opportunities, especially for women and girls.
- While women make up the majority of Christian congregations around the world, they are frequently excluded from official positions of leadership. Women are highly active in service to church and society, but nowhere in the world do they have complete physical safety. Rape, abuse, and domestic violence are widespread, even in majority Christian contexts.
- Christianity around the world is just as much about theology and particular beliefs as it is history, culture, and politics. Many people choose to join or leave a church not only for theological reasons, but also for sociological reasons (race, class, family status, gender, ethnicity, and so on).

Christian Traditions in the World

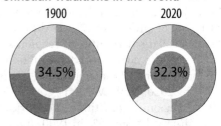

1900 | 2020

34.5% | 32.3%

☐ Independent ☐ Protestant ▨ Catholic ▩ Orthodox ■ Christian

In 1900, World Christianity was 51% Catholic, 26% Protestant, 22% Orthodox, and 2% Independent. In 2020, Catholic and Protestant shares of World Christianity dropped slightly (50% and 23% respectively), and the Orthodox share dropped much further to 12%. The major internal change to Christianity was the rise of Independent Christianity, which grew to represent 16% of Christians by 2020.

Christian Families in the World

Family	Population 2020	%	Trend	Change
Latin-rite Catholic	1,219,604,000	15.6	↑	0.9
*Pentecostals/Charismatics	644,260,000	8.3	↑	1.7
*Evangelicals	387,026,000	5.0	↑	1.6
Eastern Orthodox	220,266,000	2.8	–	0.1
Anglican	97,399,000	1.2	↑	1.0
Baptist	84,192,000	1.1	↑	0.8
United church or joint mission	77,792,000	1.0	↑	1.9
Oriental and other Orthodox	71,865,000	0.9	↑	1.9
Lutheran	69,894,000	0.9	↑	0.9
Reformed, Presbyterian	65,446,000	0.8	↑	0.8
Non-traditional, house, cell	58,092,000	0.7	↑	1.0
Methodist	31,873,000	0.4	↑	0.6
Nondenominational	29,059,000	0.4	↑	1.4
Adventist	29,011,000	0.4	↑	2.2
Jehovah's Witnesses	20,797,000	0.3	↑	2.1
Eastern-rite Catholic	20,305,000	0.3	–	0.5
Latter-day Saints (Mormons)	17,893,000	0.2	↑	2.2
Holiness	14,706,000	0.2	↑	1.8
Restorationist, Disciple	11,603,000	0.1	↑	1.2
Hidden believers in Christ	5,778,000	0.1	↑	2.3
Congregational	4,986,000	0.1	↑	2.0
Old Catholic Church	4,896,000	0.1	–	-0.4
Christian Brethren	3,959,000	0.1	↑	1.3

Many families of churches around the world are maintaining average annual growth rates similar to that of the global population; that is, they are technically growing but are not outpacing overall population growth. This is the case for Latin-rite Catholics (the largest global Christian family), Eastern Orthodox, Anglicans, Baptists, Lutherans, Reformed/Presbyterians, and Methodists. The fastest-growing Christian families are those that tend to fall outside of traditional Western Christianity, such as Pentecostal/Charismatics, non-traditional/house/cell networks, nondenominational churches, Jehovah's Witnesses, and the Church of Jesus Christ of Latter-day Saints (Mormons).

* These movements are found within Christian families
– no change

↑↑ extreme growth
↑ growth
↓↓ extreme decline
↓ decline

Christianity in Africa

Africa has experienced the most dramatic religious transformation of any continent over the last 120 years. In 1900 Africa was largely traditional religionist in the south and Muslim in the north, with 9.6 million Christians and 35 million Muslims. Christianity grew to more than 667 million (49%) by 2020, while Muslims grew to 562 million (42%). Ethnic religionists (practitioners of African Traditional Religion) dropped from 58% in 1900 to 8% by 2020. By 2050 it is expected that Christians and Muslims together will represent 93% of Africa's population. This has tremendous implications for how Christians get along with their Muslim neighbors, friends, and family members.

Christianity does not have a monolithic presence in Africa. Christianity has ancient origins in Africa, but many Africans were introduced to Christianity by European colonists who transplanted European Christianity and culture on the continent. Through the processes of translation of Christian texts and vernacularization, Africans created their own authentic understanding of Christianity. They also created their own churches, now known as African Independent Churches (AICs). These churches engage more seriously with African Traditional Religions and African culture. They also lead the way in insisting that Christianity is an African religion, dating to the 1st century. AICs tend to be more Pentecostal or Charismatic as well, with a deeper awareness of the spiritual dimensions of daily life. Today, Africans in these Independent churches and in Catholic, Orthodox, and Protestant churches are charting a truly African faith. Africa is also home to very large Catholic populations, such as those in the Democratic Republic of the Congo (43 million) and Nigeria (23 million).

Christianity in Africa is socially engaged and deeply political. Churches are often on the forefront of issues related to poverty, violence, and war. One striking example of this is the interfaith activism of Nobel Peace Laureate Leymah Gbowee, a Liberian Christian who led a nonviolent women's Christian/Muslim peace movement to help end the Second Liberian Civil War (1999–2003). African Christians are also increasingly participating in the global missions movement, both as migrants in the African diaspora and as missionaries sent across national boundaries.

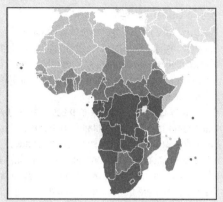

% Christian by country: 0 3 10 50 75 100

Religion in Africa

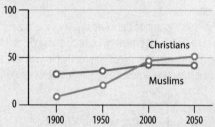

Christianity is the largest religion in Africa today, representing 49% of the population. Muslims are the second largest with 42%. Many countries have large populations of both religions, such as Nigeria (46% Christian, 46% Muslim), Benin (44% Christian, 28% Muslim), and Chad (35% Christian, 56% Muslim).

Indicators & Demographic Data

Population (2020)	1,352,622,000
% under 15 years	40%
Largest city (pop.)	Cairo, Egypt (20,901,000)
% urban dwellers	43% (3.65% p.a.)
Largest language	5% Egyptian Spoken Arabic
Largest people	5% Egyptian Arab
Development	54
Physicians	3.9
Gender gap	12%

Bible Translations		Churches		Missionaries		Gospel Access	
Languages	2,152	Denominations	18,600	Received	96,900	1900	Low
Full Bible	292	Congregations	1,021,000	Sent	39,400	2020	High

Facts to Consider

- Africa's population continues to grow at an astounding rate, over 2.5% per year. By 2050 there will likely be 2.5 billion people on the continent.
- There are more than 107 million followers of traditional religions in Africa, though many Christians and Muslims blend traditional beliefs and practices with their monotheistic faiths.
- Africa is home to the largest population of Christians but also the highest rates of HIV/AIDS, malaria, and infant mortality. Combined with lack of access to safe water, physicians, and education, these realities make for an arduous life.
- Though Christianity in Africa as a whole has shown remarkable growth, Northern Africa has seen a decrease in its Christian population due to emigration and persecution.
- The Circle of Concerned African Women Theologians has been working since 1989 to bring about equality between men and women in churches, particularly concerning leadership opportunities, ordination, theological education, and HIV/AIDS awareness.
- Despite the centrality of the Bible in African Christian life, 44% of Africans do not have a full translation of the Bible available in their mother tongue.

Christian Traditions in Africa

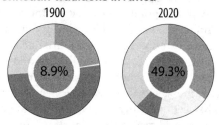

1900   2020

8.9%   49.3%

☐Independent ☐Protestant ■Catholic ■Orthodox ■Christian

All four major traditions are present in Africa, and thousands of unique denominations have grown from African soil. Some of the fastest Catholic growth rates in the early 21st century (2000–2020) were in Africa, such as in the Democratic Republic of the Congo, Nigeria, Uganda, and Angola. The largest Independent denomination in Africa is the Church of Jesus Christ on Earth by His Special Envoy Simon Kimbangu in the Democratic Republic of the Congo.

Christian Families in Africa

Family	Population 2020	%	Trend	Change
Latin-rite Catholic	235,803,000	17.4	↑	2.8
*Pentecostals/Charismatics	230,220,000	17.0	↑	2.7
*Evangelicals	161,716,000	12.0	↑	2.7
Anglican	63,556,000	4.7	↑	1.9
Oriental and other Orthodox	56,886,000	4.2	↑	2.4
Baptist	29,053,000	2.1	↑	2.5
Reformed, Presbyterian	23,911,000	1.8	↑	1.8
United church or joint mission	19,207,000	1.4	↑	3.0
Nondenominational	16,886,000	1.2	↑	1.4
Lutheran	16,403,000	1.2	↑	2.8
Adventist	12,826,000	0.9	↑	3.3
Methodist	12,229,000	0.9	↑	1.4
Jehovah's Witnesses	5,170,000	0.4	↑	3.7
Restorationist, Disciple	4,908,000	0.4	↑	2.3
Holiness	4,225,000	0.3	↑	3.3
Congregational	3,373,000	0.2	↑	2.5
Christian Brethren	1,555,000	0.1	↑	1.4
Friends (Quaker)	1,455,000	0.1	↑↑	7.8
Mennonite	1,413,000	0.1	↑	3.8
Salvationist	1,025,000	0.1	↑	1.1
Latter-day Saints (Mormons)	928,000	0.1	↑↑	10.6
Moravian	731,000	0.1	↑	2.2
Eastern Orthodox	572,000	<0.1	↑	0.9

Every Christian family grew faster in Africa than in other continents between 1970 and 2020. The largest Christian families in Africa are Catholic, Pentecostal/Charismatic, and Evangelical. Many churches averaged more than 4% growth each year between 1970 and 2020—a rapid pace—including several mission-founded Protestant churches, such as Anglicans, Baptists, Lutherans, and Mennonites. Pentecostals, Charismatics, and Evangelicals have experienced some of the fastest growth on the continent, though their churches look very different in Africa than they do in the West, as they operate within African worldviews and realities. The Church of Jesus Christ of Latter-day Saints (Mormons) reported the greatest increase due to missionary activity in Malawi, Uganda, and Ethiopia. Also notable are Orthodox Christian missions in Eastern Africa, particularly Kenya and Madagascar.

* These movements are found within Christian families
− no change

↑↑ extreme growth
↑ growth
↓↓ extreme decline
↓ decline

Christianity in Asia

Asia was a popular destination for missionaries from the United States and the United Kingdom in the 19th and 20th centuries, as many Western Christians believed in the superiority of Asian cultures, religions, and philosophies. Many missionaries thought Asians would readily accept the Christian message paired with Western science and education. This well-meaning but shortsighted approach failed to take into consideration the importance of family and tradition in Asian societies, Asia's geographical complexity, and the negative impacts of Western colonization. After centuries of missionary activity in Asia, the continent was 8% Christian in 2020. This represents modest growth from 2% in 1900, but that has been due to indigenous efforts and the substantial growth of Christianity in China and India, the continent's two largest countries. Despite the modest growth of Christianity in most of Asia, it has been in severe decline in Western Asia, also known as the Middle East. Western Asia was 23% Christian in 1900 but only 5% in 2020. Moreover, historic Catholic and Orthodox churches in Iraq and Syria have suffered tremendously in the 21st century due to violence, war, and persecution.

The diversity of Christianity in Asia is profound. Jesus was born a Middle Eastern infant in Bethlehem, and the religion spread east from Jerusalem. Early missionaries traveled along the Silk Road through central Asia (Kazakhstan, Uzbekistan) all the way to China. Christianity in India, for example, dates to the year 52 CE with the apostle Thomas in Kerala. Today, China's 106 million Christians worship in a variety of settings: state-sanctioned and clandestine Catholic churches, underground house churches, and the state-sanctioned Three-Self Patriotic Movement (Protestants). Throughout Asia one can find creative contextualization efforts between Christianity and cultures, where local Christians continue to discover what it means for Christianity to be an indigenous, not foreign, faith. As minorities, most Christians in Asia face a different set of challenges than do Christians in many other parts of the world. Living in tremendous religious diversity, they have deep insight into love and ministry across religious lines.

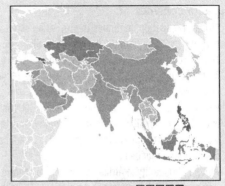

% Christian by country: 0 3 10 50 75 100

Religion in Asia

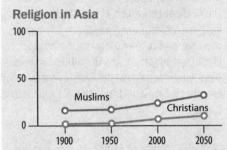

Asia is home to ten religions over 1% of the population, in order of size: Muslims, Hindus, Buddhists, agnostics, Chinese folk religionists, Christians, ethnic religionists, atheists, New Religionists, and Sikhs. Most of the world's religions first began in Asia, including Christianity. Islam is the largest religion in Asia, also home to seven of the top ten largest Muslim populations in the world.

Indicators & Demographic Data

Population (2020). 4,623,454,000
% under 15 years 24%
Largest city (pop.). . Tokyo, Japan (37,393,000)
% urban dwellers. . . . . 51% (2.00% p.a.)
Largest language. . . . . . 21% Mandarin Chinese
Largest people . . 20% Han Chinese (Mandarin)
Development. 70
Physicians. 18.1
Gender gap 10%

Bible Translations	Churches	Missionaries	Gospel Access
Languages. 2,150	Denominations 7,100	Received. 60,800	1900 . . . . Very low
Full Bible. 240	Congregations. . .1,412,000	Sent 91,100	2020 . . . . High

Facts to Consider

- Asia is home to some of the largest economies in the world: China, Japan, South Korea, and Taiwan. Yet it is also home to roughly 70 million people living in extreme poverty, living with income below US$1.90 a day.
- Many Christians in Asia suffer from a lack of political recognition, social inequality, and faith-based persecution. This is particularly the case in Muslim-majority nations such as Afghanistan, Morocco, and Saudi Arabia.
- Many Christian converts in traditionally caste-based societies (India, Pakistan) are from impoverished tribal and lower castes, which puts them in even more precarious standing in society.
- The USA's involvement in the Middle East has had catastrophic consequences for Christian minorities. This is particularly the case for Iraqi Christians, who were protected under President Saddam Hussein until the US-led military invasion of 2003.
- Asian churches are very active in Christian mission, including home missions within their countries. Important organizations include the YMCA, YWCA, and national Bible societies.
- Asian Christian women are caught between negotiating gendered expectations from their churches, from foreign missionaries, and from their indigenous cultures—all while trying to live out their own ministerial callings.

Christian Traditions in Asia

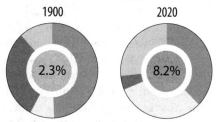

1900   2020

2.3%   8.2%

☐Independent ☐Protestant ■Catholic ■Orthodox ■Christian

Although Christianity in Asia is small compared with its general population, it is quite diverse. Due to Western colonization and mission, Catholics have been in the region for many centuries, and in 2020 Catholics were 38% of Christians in Asia. Independent Christianity experienced substantial growth over the period, growing from 8% of Christians to 31% of Christians, mostly due to an increase in house church movements. Orthodox declined from 31% to 5% due to ongoing political conflict in the Middle East.

Christian Families in Asia

Family	Population 2020	%	Trend	Change
Latin-rite Catholic	142,401,000	3.1	↑	1.2
*Pentecostals/Charismatics	125,395,000	2.7	↑	1.9
*Evangelicals	81,642,000	1.8	↑	1.1
Non-traditional, house, cell	56,373,000	1.2	↑	1.0
United church or joint mission	42,300,000	0.9	↑	2.7
Reformed, Presbyterian	23,733,000	0.5	↑	1.0
Lutheran	11,673,000	0.3	↑	3.0
Eastern Orthodox	9,712,000	0.2	–	-0.2
Oriental and other Orthodox	9,027,000	0.2	–	0.2
Nondenominational	8,789,000	0.2	↑	1.4
Baptist	8,609,000	0.2	↑	0.6
Eastern-rite Catholic	7,559,000	0.2	↑	1.1
Hidden believers in Christ	5,547,000	0.1	↑	2.3
Holiness	5,369,000	0.1	↑	1.4
Adventist	4,888,000	0.1	↑	1.5
Methodist	4,412,000	0.1	↑	0.8
Old Catholic Church	3,491,000	0.1	↓	-0.6
Restorationist, Disciple	2,525,000	0.1	↑	1.5
Media	1,605,000	<0.1	↑	1.4
Jehovah's Witnesses	1,578,000	<0.1	↑	1.8
Latter-day Saints (Mormons)	1,273,000	<0.1	↑	2.4
Anglican	1,230,000	<0.1	↑	1.0
Christian Brethren	843,000	<0.1	↑	1.8

The diversity of Christianity in Asia shines when viewed through the lens of Christian families. The Catholic Church is the largest Christian family in Asia due to very large populations in the Philippines (78 million), India (20 million), and Indonesia (8 million). Eastern Orthodox have a historic presence in Asia, particularly the Middle East, where ancient churches in Syria, Lebanon, Iran, and Iraq have been under intense pressure in the 21st century due to ongoing political conflict and violence. Mission-founded Protestant churches such as Baptists (particularly in Myanmar), Lutherans, and Methodists continue to experience modest growth. Some of the most significant gains over the 20th century were made by Evangelicals and Pentecostals/Charismatics. In 2020, 21% of all Evangelicals in the world lived in Asia, up from 2% in 1900.

* These movements are found within Christian families	↑↑ extreme growth
	↑ growth
	↓↓ extreme decline
– no change	↓ decline

Christianity in Europe

Christianity in Europe experienced a tremendous decline over the course of the 20th century, with the continent dropping from 95% Christian in 1900 to 76% Christian in 2020. Europe is often considered the "most secular" when it comes to religion, but the reality is much more complex.

Christianity's long history on the continent, dating to the time of the apostles, has made for a very different relationship between European and Christian identity. Looking at church membership alone, Europe is still one of the "most Christian" continents because of the entanglement of European identity with the Christian faith due to centuries of state-supported Catholicism, Anglicanism, and Eastern Orthodoxy. Although the majority of Europeans are connected to churches in some way via rituals such as infant baptism, weddings, and funerals, surveys consistently rank Europeans low on many religious beliefs and practices. Most countries report declining rates of church attendance, despite outliers such as Poland and Romania. For example, only 5% of self-identified French Catholics attend Mass once a month. Fewer than 50% of people surveyed in the United Kingdom, the Netherlands, Czechia, and Sweden, for example, professed belief in God, and rates are even lower for belief in life after death, hell, and heaven. A further divide exists between the older and younger generations, where youth are even more disconnected from communal faith and practice.

The increase of Muslims has challenged European Christian identity, particularly at the height of the refugee crisis in 2015. The number of Muslims in Europe grew from 9 million (2%) in 1900 to nearly 54 million in 2020 (7%), with the most growth between 2010 and 2016. An estimated 710,000 Syrians, 370,000 Moroccans, and 280,000 Pakistanis arrived during this time. The top destination countries for these migrants were the United Kingdom, Germany, France, Italy, and Sweden. Since 2016, Greece has been a top destination.

Some of the most vibrant expressions of Christianity in Europe are found among ethnic minorities. In the United Kingdom, for example, an estimated 40% of churchgoers in London are of Black or Asian ethnicity, with White British Christians in the minority. Considering these trends, the future of Christianity in Europe appears to be in the hands of immigrants and ethnic minorities.

% Christian by country:　0　3　10　50　75　100

Religion in Europe

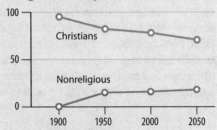

The nonreligious (atheists and agnostics) combined are now the second largest "religion" in Europe, with nearly 16% of the population. This is down from 21% in 1970, which marked the height of Communism in the Soviet Union and state-sponsored atheism.

Indicators & Demographic Data

Population (2020)	743,390,000
% under 15 years	16%
Largest city (pop.)	Moscow, Russia (12,538,000)
% urban dwellers	75% (0.27% p.a.)
Largest language	17% Russian
Largest people	17% Russian
Development	87
Physicians	36.0
Gender gap	1%

Bible Translations		Churches		Missionaries		Gospel Access	
Languages	352	Denominations	5,800	Received	103,100	1900	Very high
Full Bible	136	Congregations	423,000	Sent	80,900	2020	Very high

Facts to Consider

- The Christian population of Europe is expected to continue its decline, reaching perhaps 70% by 2050.
- The Muslim population of Europe has grown to 54 million (7%), providing opportunity for Christian hospitality, interreligious education, and outreach. Integration remains contentious, and some countries (Poland, Hungary, Czechia) have not accepted the mandatory quota of refugees.
- Surveys in Western Europe have closely linked religious identity with nationalism, where Christians hold more xenophobic attitudes than non-Christians, especially regarding immigration.
- Europeans have an eclectic approach to Christianity. Many of the beautiful large churches are empty on Sunday mornings, but Europeans maintain their own individualized spirituality, borrowing from other religious traditions.
- The population of Europe is aging rapidly, with consistently low birth rates and higher life expectancies. These dynamics exist within the churches as well, with younger people far less interested in religion than older generations.
- The decline of Christianity in Europe has made it a new destination for foreign missionaries, including many from sub-Saharan Africa.

Christian Traditions in Europe

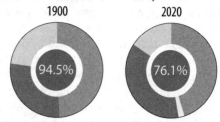

1900   2020

94.5%   76.1%

☐Independent ☐Protestant ■Catholic ■Orthodox ■Christian

Catholics and Orthodox together made up 82% of Christians in Europe in 2020, but Independents are the fastest-growing tradition. The share of Independents has increased substantially since 1900, with groups such as the Jehovah's Witnesses, New Apostolic Church, and the Universal Church of the Kingdom of God. Protestants' share of Christians in Europe dropped slightly over the period due to decline of older groups and modest increase of newer Independent Pentecostal/Charismatic churches.

Christian Families in Europe

Family	Population 2020	%	Trend	Change
Latin-rite Catholic	242,998,000	32.7	–	-0.3
Eastern Orthodox	201,284,000	27.1	–	0.0
Lutheran	32,307,000	4.3	–	-0.1
Anglican	24,400,000	3.3	↓	-0.7
*Pentecostals/Charismatics	21,116,000	2.8	–	0.5
*Evangelicals	15,907,000	2.1	–	0.3
United church or joint mission	12,464,000	1.7	–	-0.3
Reformed, Presbyterian	10,368,000	1.4	–	-0.2
Eastern-rite Catholic	5,380,000	0.7	↓	-0.6
Oriental and other Orthodox	3,802,000	0.5	↓	-0.7
Jehovah's Witnesses	3,087,000	0.4	–	0.2
Baptist	886,000	0.1	↓	-0.6
Methodist	551,000	0.1	↓	-2.3
Latter-day Saints (Mormons)	535,000	0.1	↑	1.1
Christian Brethren	494,000	0.1	–	-0.5
Adventist	421,000	0.1	↓	-0.8
Old Catholic Church	328,000	<0.1	–	-0.4
Nondenominational	290,000	<0.1	↑	0.5
Congregational	183,000	<0.1	–	-0.1
Mennonite	131,000	<0.1	↓	-0.7
Holiness	129,000	<0.1	↑	1.2
Exclusive Brethren	104,000	<0.1	–	-0.1
Salvationist	97,900	<0.1	↓	-1.9

Europe is home to many headquarters of global Christian traditions such as Catholics (Rome), Anglicans (England), Russian Orthodox (Moscow), and Lutherans (Geneva). But many of these traditions are on the decline. Europe has the lowest shares of Evangelicals and Pentecostals/Charismatics in the world (2% Evangelical and 3% Pentecostal/Charismatic). One of the fastest-growing movements in Pentecostal Christianity, however, is among Europe's 11 million Roma people who routinely experience displacement, discrimination, poverty, and unemployment. Revivals began in the 1990s, and there have been large-scale conversion movements of Roma to Pentecostal Christianity in Romania, France, and Spain. Evangelicalism has been growing largely through the efforts of immigrants and those of persecuted and marginalized people. Some of the largest churches are found among Nigerians in Ukraine, Arabs in Paris, and East Asians in Spain.

* These movements are found within Christian families
– no change

↑↑ extreme growth
↑ growth
↓↓ extreme decline
↓ decline

Christianity in Latin America

Although in the global South, Latin America has a much different Christian history and trajectory than Asia and Africa. The continent is marked by 500 years of Catholic dominance, beginning with brutal colonization and the decimation of indigenous populations by violence and disease. The initial indigenous encounters with Christianity in the context of conquest led to a diversity of practices as local people tried to reconcile traditional beliefs with those of European Catholicism. Latin America was 95% Christian in 1900, the vast majority of whom were Catholic (97%). Throughout the 20th century, the Catholic Church tried to adapt to new realities, especially regarding extreme poverty and rapid urbanization. Priests learned and performed Mass in indigenous languages. Many were also active in social justice concerns, like Óscar Romero, the archbishop of San Salvador, who spoke out against political and social injustice in a deeply polarized El Salvador and was martyred in 1980 while performing Mass.

One of the major stories of Christianity in Latin America in the 20th and 21st centuries is the introduction and growth of Protestantism (*evangélicos*). The arrival of Protestants in Latin America made Catholics either define themselves as more vigorously Catholic or convert. Protestant leadership quickly passed to local converts who were successful in growing these new kinds of churches. Protestantism (now 10% of Latin America's population, up from 3% in 1900) is popular among marginalized people who have felt passed over or oppressed by the Catholic majority. Most importantly, the arrival of Protestantism has created a religious marketplace in Latin America for perhaps the first time, where people now have more options for what kind of Christian they will be.

The Pentecostal/Charismatic movement in Latin America dates to the founding of the Methodist Pentecostal Church in Chile, which was sparked by revival in 1909. Pentecostal churches range from large denominations such as the Assemblies of God in Brazil (20 million) to many thousands of small rural congregations scattered throughout the continent. Latin America is also home to a large Catholic Charismatic movement that continues to grow in Brazil, Mexico, Colombia, Chile, and beyond.

% Christian by country: 0 3 10 50 75 100

Religion in Latin America

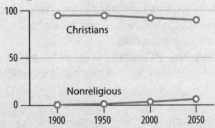

Latin America remains a majority Christian continent, though the percentage of Christians dropped from 95% in 1900 to 92% in 2020. Most of the gains were made by atheists and agnostics in urban areas, who together rose from less than 1% of the population in 1900 to 4% in 2020.

Indicators & Demographic Data

Population (2020)	664,474,000
% under 15 years	24%
Largest city (pop.)	São Paulo, Brazil (22,043,000)
% urban dwellers	81% (1.18% p.a.)
Largest language	55% Spanish
Largest people	28% Latin American Mestizo
Development	75
Physicians	20.5
Gender gap	2%

Bible Translations		Churches		Missionaries		Gospel Access	
Languages	793	Denominations	7,100	Received	102,000	1900	Very high
Full Bible	96	Congregations	655,000	Sent	65,300	2020	Very high

Facts to Consider

- Many Pentecostal pastors in Latin America lack theological education. Accessible leadership has been part of the movement's success but can cause problems related to theology and church management.
- The Protestant missionary movement from the United States and Europe has helped grow Latin American Protestantism. At the same time, the short-term mission movement to Latin America is often criticized for helping the missionaries themselves instead of local communities.
- Catholic churches have created movements to help both the rural and urban poor, encouraging laity to take more active roles in the churches and help transform neighborhoods.
- One of the most powerful theological trends of the 20th century was born in Latin America: liberation theology, pioneered by Peruvian Dominican priest Gustavo Gutiérrez and exported worldwide.
- Women in Latin America struggle against patriarchy, where men are the heads of the family and women lack decision-making power. Pentecostalism has provided new economic and social benefits, especially to poor women through churches that pool resources and give women support to resist *machismo* (aggressive masculinity).

Christian Traditions in Latin America

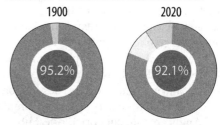

1900   2020

95.2%   92.1%

☐Independent ☐Protestant ■Catholic ■Orthodox ■Christian

Catholicism has been the largest Christian tradition in Latin America since its arrival in the 15th century. But the Catholic share of Christians dropped from 97% in 1900 to 80% in 2020. Gains were made by Protestants (3% in 1900 to 10% in 2020) and Independents (less than 1% to 9%). Both the largest Protestant and Independent denominations are in Brazil: the Assemblies of God (20 million) and the Universal Church of the Kingdom of God (7.5 million).

Christian Families in Latin America

Family	Population 2020	%	Trend	Change
Latin-rite Catholic	502,939,000	75.7	↑	0.7
*Pentecostals/Charismatics	195,222,000	29.4	↑	0.9
*Evangelicals	50,595,000	7.6	↑	0.7
Adventist	8,693,000	1.3	↑	1.7
Jehovah's Witnesses	7,607,000	1.1	↑	2.7
Latter-day Saints (Mormons)	7,074,000	1.1	↑	2.5
Baptist	5,532,000	0.8	↑	3.5
Eastern-rite Catholic	4,827,000	0.7	↑	0.8
Reformed, Presbyterian	3,284,000	0.5	↑	1.4
Holiness	2,167,000	0.3	↑	1.1
Nondenominational	1,716,000	0.3	↑	2.3
Non-traditional, house, cell	1,487,000	0.2	↑	1.6
Methodist	1,361,000	0.2	↑	1.4
Lutheran	1,270,000	0.2	↑	0.9
Eastern Orthodox	1,231,000	0.2	↑	1.6
Anglican	959,000	0.1	–	0.2
Christian Brethren	787,000	0.1	↑	2.1
Restorationist, Disciple	580,000	0.1	↑	3.7
Old Catholic Church	579,000	0.1	–	-0.5
Congregational	320,000	<0.1	↑	2.3
Moravian	234,000	<0.1	↑	1.0
Mennonite	223,000	<0.1	↑	2.0
United church or joint mission	141,000	<0.1	–	0.0

Latin American Christianity is considerably diverse despite the numerical dominance of Catholicism. It is becoming increasingly more diverse in the 21st century due to the continued growth of Protestant, Evangelical, and Pentecostal/Charismatic churches. Pentecostalism has a massive variety of churches ranging from classical Pentecostals such as the Assemblies of God to Independent Charismatic churches such as the Brazilian God is Love Pentecostal Church. The Church of Jesus Christ of Latter-day Saints has been growing rapidly (over 6% per year between 1970 and 2020), now with large populations in Mexico, Brazil, and Chile. Historic Protestant churches such as Baptists and Presbyterians continue to experience modest growth. The Orthodox community has experienced growth in Chile and has the third-fastest growth rate among churches in Latin America.

* These movements are found within Christian families
– no change

↑↑ extreme growth
↑ growth
↓↓ extreme decline
↓ decline

Christianity in North America

North America consists of the United States of America, Canada, Bermuda, Greenland, and Saint Pierre and Miquelon. Demographically, the United States (331 million people) and Canada (38 million people) dominate the region. Christianity arrived via both European colonization in the 15th century and migrants seeking a destination to build a specific kind of Christian society separate from European Catholic and Anglican state-supported rule. Subsequently, the region became majority Christian by the forced displacement and epidemic genocide of Native American and First Nations peoples. At the beginning of the 20th century, North America was one of the most religious continents in the world (99% religious), but this dropped to just under 80% by 2020. Christianity remains the largest religion (73% in 2020, down from 97% in 1900), with remarkable diversity.

One of the major trends in North American Christianity is the rise and decline of mainline Protestantism. The United States and Canada were majority Protestant nations for much of their histories, in which Christian families such as Congregationalists, Presbyterians, Baptists, Quakers, and Lutherans made their mark through revivals, church growth, and institutions of higher and theological education. Nevertheless, their ethos was shaped by the dominance of White mainline Protestant men producing church history and theology. Over time, the Christian demography of the continent shifted, largely through immigration and secularization. Catholics initially predated Protestants by roughly a generation, and they grew at least tenfold in the early 19th century. The 19th century also saw the founding of the Church of Jesus Christ of Latter-day Saints and other restorationist movements that have spread worldwide.

Most mainline Protestant families in North America today are experiencing either stagnancy or decline in their membership. Some Christians are leaving these churches for Pentecostal/Charismatic Christianity, which was virtually nonexistent in 1900 but grew to 18% of the continent's population in 2020. Others are leaving institutionalized Christianity entirely, choosing to express their spirituality independently and privately.

% Christian by country: 0 3 10 50 75 100

Religion in North America

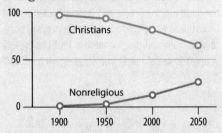

Religion in North America changed substantially over the 20th century. The drop in Christians (97% to 73%) was due largely to increased secularization, driving up the number of nonreligious, which grew from 1% in 1900 to nearly 21% in 2020. Immigration brought millions of Muslims, Hindus, and Buddhists to the region.

Indicators & Demographic Data

Population (2020)	369,159,000
% under 15 years	18%
Largest city (pop.)	New York, USA (18,804,000)
% urban dwellers	83% (0.96% p.a.)
Largest language	67% English
Largest people	34% USA White
Development	92
Physicians	25.7
Gender gap	1%

Bible Translations		Churches		Missionaries		Gospel Access	
Languages	333	Denominations	5,200	Received	46,200	1900	Very high
Full Bible	96	Congregations	488,000	Sent	143,000	2020	Very high

Facts to Consider

- Christianity continues to decline in North America and is estimated to drop to 66% by 2050. Surveys in Canada have reported that most Canadians believe religion does more harm than good in the world.
- North America is home to 11% of the world's Christians but 49% of global Christian wealth, raising questions about severe income inequality.
- Christianity in North America is deeply divided by race. In the USA, 86% of congregations have an ethnic makeup dominated by a single ethnicity.
- Women have long outnumbered men in North American pews but have never constituted the majority of leadership. Women form 13.5% of Protestant clergy in the USA, despite that 72% of people believe women should be allowed to preach and 56% believe women can be religious leaders.
- Christians from around the world have made North America their home, including Chinese Christians in Vancouver, Iraqi Christians in Detroit, and Nigerian Christians in Brooklyn.
- Theological education faces a crisis in North America, with the closing of many Bible colleges and seminaries as costs rise and interest wanes.
- Younger generations tend to be less religious than their parents. Compared to their parents, teens in the USA pray less often (27% vs. 48%) and believe in God with less certainty (40% vs. 63%).

Christian Traditions in North America

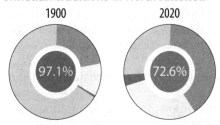

1900   2020

97.1%   72.6%

☐Independent ☐Protestant ∎Catholic ∎Orthodox ∎Christian

In 1900, Christians in North America were 67% Protestant and 22% Catholic. By 2020, Protestants had declined to 26% of Christians, and Catholics increased to 40%. Independent Christianity grew rapidly as well, representing 30% of Christians in 2020. Independents in North America include traditional Black churches in the United States, the Church of Jesus Christ of Latter-day Saints (Mormons), Jehovah's Witnesses, and many different varieties of Charismatic networks and congregations.

Christian Families in North America

Family	Population 2020	%	Trend	Change
Latin-rite Catholic	86,090,000	23.3	↑	0.5
*Evangelicals	71,102,000	19.3	↑	1.1
*Pentecostals/Charismatics	67,771,000	18.4	↑	0.7
Baptist	39,697,000	10.8	↓	-0.6
Methodist	12,724,000	3.4	–	-0.1
Latter-day Saints (Mormons)	7,456,000	2.0	↑	1.4
Lutheran	6,791,000	1.8	↓	-1.2
Eastern Orthodox	6,475,000	1.8	↑	0.8
Reformed, Presbyterian	3,566,000	1.0	↓	-2.6
Restorationist, Disciple	3,378,000	0.9	↓	-0.6
Jehovah's Witnesses	3,166,000	0.9	↑	0.7
Anglican	2,689,000	0.7	–	0.2
Holiness	2,670,000	0.7	↑	1.4
Eastern-rite Catholic	1,925,000	0.5	↑	0.6
Oriental and other Orthodox	1,895,000	0.5	↑	1.7
United church or joint mission	1,714,000	0.5	↓	-3.4
Adventist	1,567,000	0.4	↑	1.4
Nondenominational	991,000	0.3	↑	0.7
Congregational	757,000	0.2	↑	0.8
Mennonite	618,000	0.2	↑	1.0
Salvationist	461,000	0.1	↓	-0.5
Dunker	222,000	0.1	↓	-0.5
Christian Brethren	180,000	<0.1	–	0.5

Catholics have remained steady in their share of Christians on the continent (40%). The Catholic churches in the USA and Canada are the first and third largest denominations in the region, respectively. Baptists (11% of Christians) are represented by many different groups, such as the Southern Baptist Convention and Black Baptist groups such as the National Baptist Convention USA, the National Baptist Convention of America, and the Progressive National Baptist Convention. Pentecostal/Charismatics (18% of Christians) represent almost a dizzying array of traditions, ranging from large groups such as the United House of Prayer for All People to small nondenominational networks. Like Charismatics, Evangelicals (27% of Christians) are found within many different traditions, though the movement is mainly associated with White conservative churches.

* These movements are found within Christian families
– no change

↑↑ extreme growth
↑ growth
↓↓ extreme decline
↓ decline

Christianity in Oceania

The continent of Oceania consists of Australia and New Zealand and three regions with dozens of island nations: Melanesia, Micronesia, and Polynesia. The territory was first used as a penal colony for Britain, dispossessing indigenous people for criminals starting in 1788. As a result, there has been—and continues to be—distrust between Christian institutions and local Aboriginal and Maori populations. The religious demography of the region was much like that of the British Isles up until the 1950s; since then, Australia and New Zealand have become far more diverse with the arrival of migrants from all over Europe, then Asia, Africa, and the Pacific Islands. The fastest-growing religions are currently Sikhism, Hinduism, and Coptic Orthodoxy, with trends that reflect immigration patterns to the region. Australia and New Zealand have experienced a significant decline in their Christian population, from 97% Christian in 1900 to 54% in 2020.

Christianity in the islands has taken a much different trajectory than in Australia and New Zealand. Christianity arrived in most of these islands between the 15th and 19th centuries, and it grew substantially in the 20th century, mostly due to the efforts of indigenous Christians. Papua New Guinea, for example, grew from just 4% Christian in 1900 to 95% Christian in 2020. However, at the same time, violence against women in the country is endemic, and women are often accused of witchcraft. Many indigenous churches have embraced local styles of leadership and modes of theology, despite colonial officials who initially suppressed these expressions of faith. Indigenous missionary sending has always been a feature of Pacific Island Christianity, with many islands being introduced to Christianity by Christians from neighboring islands.

A major concern for Christians in Oceania is climate change. Many people have been forced to leave their homes because of rising sea levels, mostly because of dangerous environmental policies from large industrialized nations like the United States and China that have outsized impacts on smaller island nations. Islands just barely above sea level, such as in Kiribati (six feet above sea level), are especially affected. Many churches are advocating for the development of new ecotheologies to survive.

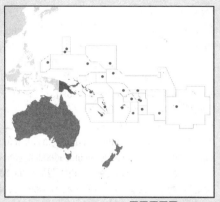

% Christian by country: 0 3 10 50 75 100

Religion in Oceania

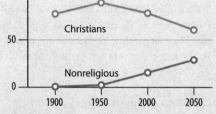

Oceania has grown more religiously diverse in the last 120 years. From 77% Christian in 1900 to 65% Christian in 2020, the region has seen the nonreligious (atheists and agnostics) grow from less than 1% to 25% over the same time period. Most of that change occurred in Australia and New Zealand.

Indicators & Demographic Data

Population (2020)	42,384,000
% under 15 years	23%
Largest city (pop.)	Melbourne, Australia (4,968,000)
% urban dwellers	68% (1.60% p.a.)
Largest language	58% English
Largest people	38% Anglo-Australian
Development	83
Physicians	24.9
Gender gap	6%

Bible Translations		Churches		Missionaries		Gospel Access	
Languages	1,278	Denominations	1,000	Received	15,900	1900	Very high
Full Bible	140	Congregations	59,700	Sent	5,200	2020	Very high

Facts to Consider

- Oceania is home to the world's only two countries where the Church of Jesus Christ of Latter-day Saints makes up the majority: Tonga (60% Latter-day Saint) and Samoa (40%).
- Although most of Australia's Aboriginal and New Zealand's Maori populations are Christian, the churches in each of these countries still grapple with issues related to historical forced assimilation, land issues, and lack of indigenous rights.
- Women in Fiji (a majority Christian country) experience one of the highest rates of violence in the world, with studies suggesting that roughly 74% of women have experienced physical, sexual, or emotional violence.
- Christians in Oceania are on the forefront of developing theologies that emphasize the sacredness of life, land, and creation, thus uniting spirit and nature.
- Most countries in Oceania have ecumenical councils that bring together Christians from different denominations to work in education, health care, and development work.
- Pacific Theological College in Suva, Fiji, was established in 1965 and was the first degree-granting institution of higher education, secular or religious, in the Pacific Islands.

Christian Traditions in Oceania

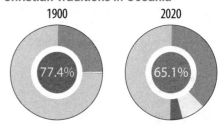

1900   2020

77.4%   65.1%

☐ Independent ☐ Protestant ■ Catholic ■ Orthodox ■ Christian

From a Protestant and Evangelical majority in 1900, Oceania has experienced a proportional decline in both kinds of Christianity. Catholics grew from 24% of Christians to 39%, largely due to arrival of Catholics to Australia from Italy, Malta, the Netherlands, Croatia, Poland, and elsewhere in Europe. The Protestant share of Christians declined from 75% in 1900 to 49%. Independents are growing and in 2020 represented 8% of Christians.

Christian Families in Oceania

Family	Population 2020	%	Trend	Change
Latin-rite Catholic	9,372,000	22.1	↑	0.9
*Evangelicals	6,063,000	14.3	↑	0.6
Anglican	4,565,000	10.8	–	-0.3
*Pentecostals/Charismatics	4,536,000	10.7	↑	1.4
United church or joint mission	1,966,000	4.6	–	-0.2
Lutheran	1,451,000	3.4	↑	1.0
Eastern Orthodox	993,000	2.3	↑	1.5
Latter-day Saints (Mormons)	628,000	1.5	↑	2.6
Adventist	616,000	1.5	–	0.5
Methodist	596,000	1.4	–	0.1
Reformed, Presbyterian	584,000	1.4	↓	-0.8
Baptist	414,000	1.0	↑	1.2
Nondenominational	387,000	0.9	↑	1.0
Eastern-rite Catholic	317,000	0.7	↑	1.9
Jehovah's Witnesses	188,000	0.4	↑	1.3
Congregational	160,000	0.4	–	0.0
Holiness	147,000	0.3	↑	1.6
Restorationist, Disciple	139,000	0.3	↑	0.6
Oriental and other Orthodox	122,000	0.3	↑	2.9
Christian Brethren	100,000	0.2	↑	0.9
Salvationist	76,100	0.2	↓	-1.3
Exclusive Brethren	11,800	<0.1	–	-0.4
Friends (Quaker)	2,600	<0.1	↑	0.5

The largest Christian families in Oceania in 2020 were Anglicans, Evangelicals, Catholics, and Pentecostals/Charismatics. Evangelicals, Anglicans, and Catholics have a historic presence in the region due to British colonization and European migration and settlement. Each of these families has experienced stagnancy or decline in their membership from 1970 to 2020. Pentecostal/Charismatic churches have been growing quite rapidly, such as the Assemblies of God, Australian Christian Churches, and the International Church of the Foursquare Gospel. Eastern and Oriental Orthodox have experienced some growth in the region due to immigration; Orthodox overall grew in the region from less than 1% in 1900 to 4% in 2020. The Pacific Islands were one of the first regions to be visited by missionaries from the Church of Jesus Christ of Latter-day Saints (Mormons), which continues to experience growth.

* These movements are found within Christian families	↑↑ extreme growth
	↑ growth
	↓↓ extreme decline
– no change	↓ decline

CHRISTIANITY BY TRADITION AND MOVEMENT

———

Catholics

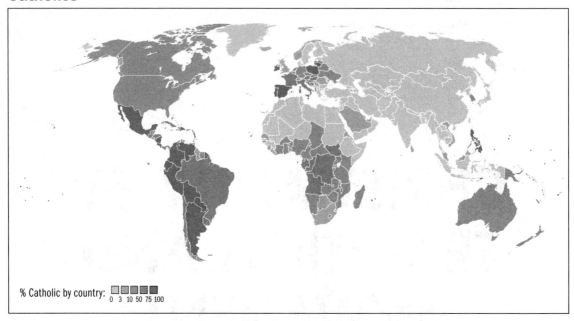

% Catholic by country: 0 3 10 50 75 100

Just under half of Christians in the world today are Catholics (1.2 billion). Because of European colonization coupled with missionary efforts, Catholicism became the majority religion of Latin America and one of the fastest-growing traditions in Africa. Catholicism is a majority global South faith today. In 2020, 73% of all Catholics lived in Asia, Africa, Latin America, and Oceania, while only 27% lived in Europe and North America.

The church's diverse makeup is increasingly apparent in the hierarchy of the church, which in 2013 elected its first pope born outside Europe since the 8th century. Pope Francis is also the first Jesuit pope, the first from the Americas, and the first from the Southern Hemisphere. Argentinian-born, Pope Francis has emphasized a variety of issues during his papacy. His first major work was about the importance of evangelization and the missionary task in the world. He has also been outspoken about environmental issues, climate change, and concern for the poor and disenfranchised. The church has more work to do to represent global Catholicism in the College of Cardinals, which consists of the most senior leaders of the church; of the 222 cardinals, 91 are from the global South.

The Catholic Church has a tremendous social outreach around the world. The number of Catholic-run elementary and secondary schools and orphanages has risen substantially in the last several decades. Religious brothers and sisters often staff these services, though these kinds of religious vocations have dropped substantially. Africa and Asia are the only two continents where religious vocations are growing; sisters in Africa represent 12% of all sisters worldwide. Religious sisters are incredibly active and outnumber priests and brothers combined on every continent. Roughly a quarter of the 41,000 women religious (nuns and sisters) in the United States, for example, are foreign-born, originating from 83 countries and are engaged in various kinds of ministry, formation, and formal study.

The revelation of sex scandals in the priesthood has been one of the most serious challenges to Catholicism in the 21st century. Accusations of priests abusing minors emerged in the 1980s with publicity increasing in the early 2000s throughout Europe, the United States, Australia, and Chile. In many cases, priests were moved to other parishes and abuse was covered up. The scandals implicated church leaders around the world and corroded public trust.

Facts to Consider

- Many Europeans are Catholics in name only, having been baptized in the church but rarely attend or participate in other rites. Even Poland, one of the most Catholic countries in Europe, experienced a 15% decline in Mass attendance from 2009 to 2014.
- The Catholic Church runs over 103,000 elementary and 49,500 secondary schools, in addition to over 5,100 hospitals and 9,200 orphanages worldwide. They are particularly active in places where governments lack the ability to provide these kinds of social services for their people.
- The Catholic Charismatic movement, concentrated in Latin America but found all over the world, is one of the largest Pentecostal/Charismatic movements today (195 million worldwide).

Catholics by Continent

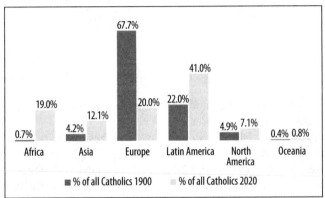

% of all Catholics 1900   % of all Catholics 2020

Europe is the historic home of Catholicism, where 68% of all Catholics resided in 1900. This changed dramatically over the 20th century, and now only 20% of all Catholics live there. Catholicism grew rapidly in Africa, which was less than 2% Catholic in 1900 and was 18% Catholic in 2020.

Countries with the Most Catholics

Country	Population 1900	Country	Population 2020
France	40,214,600	Brazil	150,000,000
Italy	32,903,000	Mexico	115,574,000
Spain	18,794,200	Philippines	83,000,000
Poland	18,716,500	United States	73,900,000
Brazil	17,200,000	DR Congo	49,200,000
Germany	15,050,000	Colombia	43,400,000
Mexico	12,380,200	Italy	43,100,000
United States	10,775,000	Spain	38,970,000
Czechia	6,984,000	France	37,540,000
Belgium	6,518,000	Argentina	35,500,000

Catholicism's shift to the global South is evident in the list of countries with the most Catholics in 1900 and 2020. In 1900, seven of the top ten countries were in the global North; in 2020, that number dropped to four.

Catholics Over Time

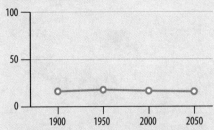

Catholicism experienced a tremendous growth of adherents over the 20th century, rising from 266 million in 1900 to over 1.2 billion by 2020. Despite this growth—especially in Africa—Catholics are slowly declining as a proportion of Christians. In 1900, Catholics were 51% of Christians but by 2020 had dropped to 49%. Individuals are leaving Catholic churches in Europe and Latin America, typically for agnosticism or Protestantism (respectively). The decline of Catholicism in Europe has happened concurrently with the shift of Catholicism—and Christianity over all—to the global South, with momentum continuing further southward. In 1900, 27% of all Catholics lived in Asia, Africa, and Latin America. That figure grew to 73% by 2020. The largest Catholic populations today are in Brazil, Mexico, and the Philippines.

Quick Facts

Population (2020)	1,240 million
Percent of population (2020)	15.9%
Percent of Christians (2020)	49.2%
Denominations (2020)	370
Congregations (2020)	303,000
Largest country (pop.)	Brazil
Highest percent	Holy See
Fastest growth	Norway
Largest decline	Italy
Largest tradition	Latin-rite

Independents

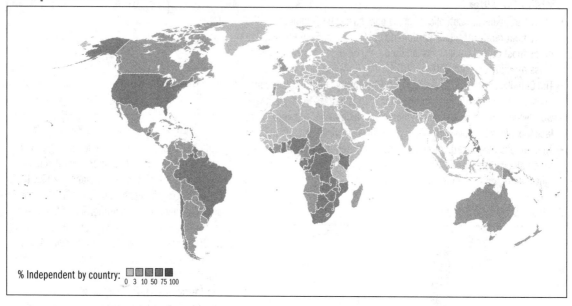

% Independent by country: 0 3 10 50 75 100

Independent Christians are those who do not self-identify with historic Protestant, Catholic, or Orthodox churches. They are independent of historic, organized, institutionalized, and denominational Christianity. The increasing prominence of Independent Christianity is a major feature of Christianity in the 20th and 21st centuries.

There are two main ways for a denomination to be Independent. The first is splitting from an existing denomination. One example is the Anglican Church of North America (ACNA), which split from the Episcopal Church USA in 2009, meaning the ACNA is no longer part of the Anglican Communion. The creation of Independent churches from Protestantism is common both in the past and present. The second kind of Independents is those that sprout up entirely on their own. These movements, which often begin with revivals or around charismatic leadership, typically grow into legitimate denominations in their own right. The Church of Jesus Christ of Latter-day Saints is an example, founded by Joseph Smith in the 1820s. Another example is the Universal Church of the Kingdom of God in Brazil, founded by Edir Macedo in 1977. Macedo founded the denomination after he was denied by the leaders of the mission-founded Pentecostal church of which he was part. Independent churches have been grow-

ing by leaps and bounds and represent a new era of World Christianity.

Many Independent churches are also Pentecostal/Charismatic in nature. The house church movement in China is the largest Independent movement in the world, with over 30 million members. Some of the largest Independent groups are African Independent Churches, house church movements in China, and informal Charismatic networks. Black churches in the United States are also considered Independent because most formed entirely independently of White Protestant churches beginning in the 19th century.

One important feature of Independent Christianity is its remarkable diversity. The category itself highlights the theological spectrum that exists in World Christianity, from Christians who "look like" mainline Protestants in belief and practice to newer groups that have a substantive emphasis on the power of the Holy Spirit in Christian life. Self-identification is also critical in considering Independent Christianity. For the purposes of this volume, and in accordance with the sociological study of religion, if a particular group calls themselves "Christian," then they are considered as such, even if their theology might deviate from what is considered "orthodox" or "traditional" by Catholic, Orthodox, or Protestant Christians.

Facts to Consider

- Of the roughly 5 million pastors and priests across World Christianity, only an estimated 5% have formal theological training, and 70% of those are in Independent congregations.
- Many Charismatic denominations are considered Independent, such as the Association of Vineyard Churches, who consider themselves "post-denominational."
- Much of the growth of Independent churches was in response to oppression from European colonialism. These newer churches strove to create culturally authentic expressions of Christianity amid discrimination against indigenous history and practices.
- Independent Christianity also grows within house networks in places where it is dangerous or illegal to be a Christian, such as in Algeria.

Independents by Continent

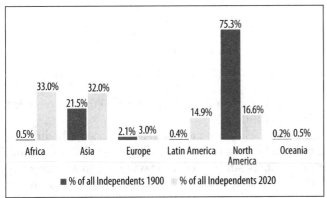

% of all Independents 1900   % of all Independents 2020

Independent Christianity changed substantially between 1900 and 2020. As the movement grew outside the Western world, large populations of Independent Christians sprang up, especially in Africa and Asia.

Countries with the Most Independents

Country	Population 1900	Country	Population 2020
United States	6,650,000	United States	63,800,000
Philippines	1,800,000	China	62,000,000
India	90,200	Nigeria	28,285,000
Romania	57,000	Brazil	26,000,000
Switzerland	41,000	South Africa	24,325,000
Belgium	28,000	DR Congo	23,930,000
Austria	20,000	Philippines	19,300,000
Jamaica	20,000	India	19,130,000
Canada	19,000	South Korea	11,330,000
Tonga	16,360	Kenya	9,000,000

The United States is the only country in the global North to make the list of top ten countries with the most Independents in 2020. Of the list, four are in Asia, four are in Africa, and one is in Latin America.

Independents Over Time

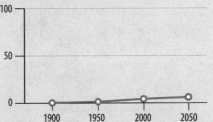

Independent Christians numbered 391 million in 2020 and represent a vast diversity of beliefs and practices. Like Christianity as a whole, Independent Christianity has shifted to the global South with the increase of Independent denominations in Asia and Africa, mostly since the 1950s, moving the center of gravity away from North America. In 1900, just 0.5% of the global population was Independent. By 2020, this had grown to 5%. In 2020, 33% of all Independents were Africans, mostly found in indigenous-founded churches such as Zion Christian Churches, the Church of the Lord (Aladura), and Apostolic churches. By 2050, 18% of Christians could be Independent, with 86% living in Asia, Africa, Latin America, and Oceania. Some Independent groups are non-Trinitarian but were originally founded as restorationist movements in their attempt to restore the original first century church, such as the Church of Jesus Christ of Latter-day Saints (Mormons) and Jehovah's Witnesses.

Quick Facts

Population (2020)	391 million
Percent of population (2020)	5.0%
Percent of Christians (2020)	15.5%
Denominations (2020)	31,900
Congregations (2020)	1,871,000
Largest country (pop.)	United States
Highest percent	Tonga
Fastest growth	Mozambique
Largest decline	Germany
Largest tradition	Baptistic-Penecostal

Orthodox

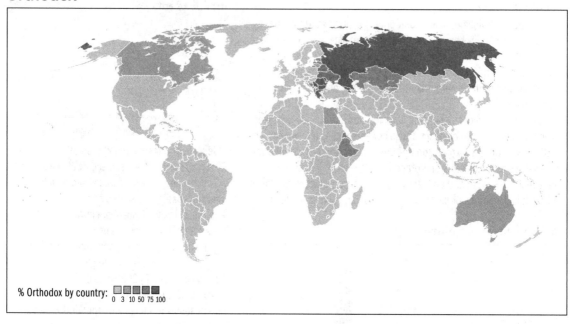

% Orthodox by country: 0 3 10 50 75 100

Orthodox Christianity traces its roots to Greek-speaking Christians in the Eastern Roman Empire, separate from Latin-speaking Christians in the West. The name "Byzantine" was given to the eastern half of the Roman Empire, largely today's Turkey and Greece; this empire lasted until 1453. The formal break between Eastern and Western Christianity occurred in 1054, the "Great Schism," when the popes of each tradition denounced each other. The rise of Islam in the Middle East beginning in the 9th century was a threat to the Eastern Orthodox churches; Muslims took over three of the four centers of Orthodox faith (Antioch, Alexandria, and Jerusalem), leaving only Constantinople (today's Istanbul, Turkey). Orthodoxy spread to today's Russia, Syria, and northern Iraq, the latter of which was lost to the Turkish empire in the early 1000s, marking the long, slow decline of the Byzantine Empire and the Orthodox Church. Orthodox churches became increasingly fragmented after this loss; rather than consolidating toward an empire, individual churches became more closely associated with specific countries and languages. As a result, Orthodox Christianity today is intricately tied with various ethnic and national identities. Today's largest Orthodox communities are Russian

(110 million), Ethiopian (39 million), and Romanian (17 million).

The Orthodox churches experienced a different set of trends over the 20th century than most other Christian traditions. Having begun as a majority global South faith in the 1st century, it gradually shifted more and more to the North, so that in 2020, 73% of Orthodox lived in the North (mostly Eastern Europe) and only 27% lived in the South. Orthodox Christians suffered tremendously, first with the Armenian Genocide (beginning in 1915) and then with the rise of Communism and state-imposed atheism in the Soviet Union. Albania was declared the first officially atheistic state in the world in 1967, dropping its share of Orthodox from 20% in 1900 to under 5% in 1970. Many Orthodox laity and clergy were imprisoned and killed for their faith. The fall of the Soviet Union in 1991 prompted a rebound of Orthodox life in Eastern Europe.

In the 21st century, ancient Orthodox populations in the Middle East have experienced deep persecution amid turmoil in Syria and Iraq. In Syria, Orthodox were 15% of the population in 1900 but only 2% in 2020. For Iraq, the population dropped from 4% to less than 1%.

Facts to Consider

- In 2013, two Syrian bishops, Mor Gregorios Yohanna Ibrahim (Syrian Orthodox) and Boulos Yaziji (Greek Orthodox), were kidnapped while negotiating the release of two priests who had been kidnapped months earlier. It is unclear if they are alive.
- In some places, the Orthodox church suffers from internal division in matters unrelated to theology but pertaining to history and national identity. Ukraine, for example, is home to 16 million Orthodox under the Kyiv Patriarchate and 13.5 million under the Moscow Patriarchate.
- Women are not allowed ordination to the priesthood but are seen as keepers of the Orthodox faith. Many women did so at great risk to their own lives under Communist rule.

Orthodox by Continent

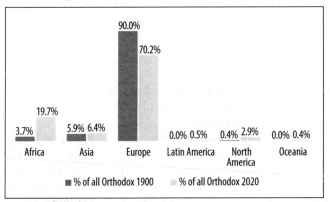

■ % of all Orthodox 1900   ■ % of all Orthodox 2020

Orthodoxy remains a majority European tradition, though their share dropped from 90% of European Christians in 1900 to 70% in 2020. Africa was home to 4% of all Orthodox in 1900 and 20% in 2020.

Countries with the Most Orthodox

Country	Population 1900	Country	Population 2020
Russia	56,709,700	Russia	113,900,000
Ukraine	20,781,000	Ethiopia	45,600,000
Romania	9,702,000	Ukraine	31,715,000
Belarus	3,936,500	Romania	17,100,000
Turkey	2,950,000	Greece	9,670,000
Bulgaria	2,848,050	Egypt	8,800,000
Ethiopia	2,751,600	United States	7,150,000
Greece	2,573,800	Belarus	5,675,000
Serbia	2,487,200	Bulgaria	5,620,000
Poland	2,020,000	Serbia	5,545,000

In both 1900 and 2020, eight of the ten largest Orthodox populations were in the global North. Ethiopia's Orthodox population grew from 3 million to 45 million, now the second largest Orthodox population in the world.

Orthodox Over Time

Although Orthodox Christianity has grown in terms of absolute numbers (116 million in 1900; 292 million in 2020), it has decreased as a percentage of the world's population from 7% in 1900 to less than 4% in 2020. The Orthodox suffered tremendously from genocide, war, and persecution in the 20th century, causing their communities to be driven underground. The trends in Eastern Europe depict the challenges of the century; the region was 90% Christian in 1900, 57% in 1970 (the height of Communism), and 84% in 2020. While Orthodox churches had a rich history of missionary sending in the 4th–6th and 9th–11th centuries, the tradition more recently has been focused on survival rather than multiplication. This, coupled with low birth rates and high death rates, has made it difficult for Orthodox churches to grow. Nevertheless, there has been renewed interest in Orthodoxy in the 21st century, evidenced by growth in East Africa. Kenya, for example, is now home to 370,000 Orthodox Christians.

Quick Facts

Population (2020)	292 million
Percent of population (2020)	3.7%
Percent of Christians (2020)	11.6%
Denominations (2020)	580
Congregations (2020)	142,000
Largest country (pop.)	Russia
Highest percent	Moldova
Fastest growth	Guatemala
Largest decline	Romania
Largest tradition	Russian Orthodox

Protestants

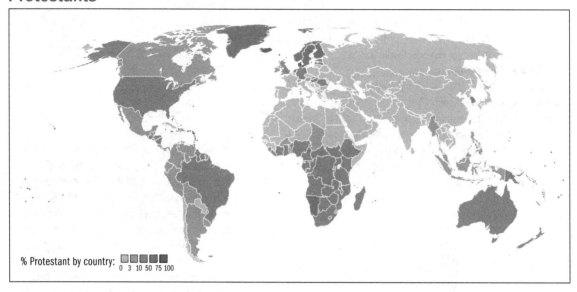

% Protestant by country: 0 3 10 50 75 100

Protestantism traces its roots to Martin Luther nailing his Ninety-Five Theses to the door of the All Saints' Church, Wittenberg (Germany) in October 1517. Undeterred from the ensuing religious wars in Europe was the growth of Protestantism, a new kind of Christianity that challenged the Catholic Church by emphasizing the priesthood of all believers, a high view of Scripture over tradition, and a theology of justification by faith, not works. Protestantism spread from Europe via Western colonial expansion, missionary activity, and migration, making it a truly global religion today. Because of Protestantism's emphasis on personal experience of Jesus and individual reading of Scripture, there are a multitude of expressions of Protestant faith, including those of Lutherans, Baptists, Brethren, Churches of Christ, Congregationalists, Mennonites, Methodists, and so on.

Protestant missionary outreach began 200 years after the start of Reformation with two German missionaries, Bartholomäus Ziegenbalg and Heinrich Plütschau, arriving in India in 1706. A flurry of missionary activity ensued from Europe and North America in the 19th century, often attempting to replicate Western churches and society in very different cultural contexts. Protestantism spread most effectively when coupled with cultural awareness by local converts, such as the many unnamed Bible women (indigenous evangelists) in Asia and sub-Saharan Africa who worked as local evangelists to spread the faith in their communities.

Protestantism experienced a profound transformation over the 20th century. In 1900, only 7% of Protestants lived in Asia, Africa, Latin America, and Oceania. By 2020, this number had surged to 75%. Many Protestant churches in the global South, now run by indigenous Christians, are flourishing and are involved in education, evangelism, development, and a variety of social services. In Africa, these churches have taken on political, moral, and social credibility. Protestantism has also become a part of the social fabric of many island nations in the South Pacific.

Since the mid-20th century, mainline Protestantism has been generally on the decline in Europe and North America, both in cultural influence and membership. Gradual secularization of society has made once-majority-Protestant nations lose interest in institutionalized Christianity. This is especially the case among younger generations who want to explore faith and spirituality on their own terms. As a result, Protestant churches in the West are seeking new ways of being the church and engaging society. In the United States (the country with the second largest population of Protestants, after Nigeria), Protestants declined from 49% of the country's population in 1900 to 16% in 2020.

Facts to Consider

- Latin America has become increasingly Protestant (*evangélico*), rising from 3% Protestant in 1900 to 10% today. Protestants have mainly drawn converts from the Catholic Church.
- Although mainline Protestants are active in unity efforts across Christian traditions, it is a very fragmented movement. For example, there are at least 200 Presbyterian denominations in South Korea alone.
- Many Protestant groups have been ordaining women for a long time, such as Quakers, Methodists, the Salvation Army, the Church of the Nazarene, and the Anglican Communion.
- Many Protestant churches are divided over the full inclusion of LGBTQ people in their churches. In 2019, for example, the United Methodist Church strengthened a ban on LGBTQ clergy and same-sex weddings.

Protestants by Continent

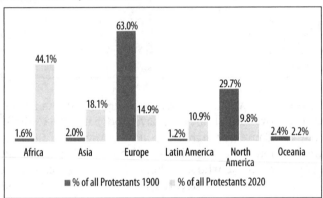

■ % of all Protestants 1900   % of all Protestants 2020

In 1900, most Protestants were White Europeans and North Americans, but today Protestants are as diverse as World Christianity itself. In 2020, 44% of all Protestants were African.

Countries with the Most Protestants

Country	Population 1900	Country	Population 2020
United States	37,042,000	Nigeria	62,059,000
United Kingdom	33,680,400	United States	54,035,000
Germany	25,735,000	China	34,000,000
Sweden	5,074,200	Brazil	32,140,000
Netherlands	3,113,700	United Kingdom	26,826,000
Canada	2,847,000	Kenya	26,000,000
Finland	2,635,600	Germany	24,931,300
Denmark	2,430,480	India	23,000,000
Australia	2,377,100	Indonesia	20,204,200
Norway	2,208,000	Uganda	19,300,000

In 1900, only one country in the global South was on the list of top ten largest Protestant populations: Australia. By 2020, seven of the top ten countries with the most Protestants were in the global South.

Protestants Over Time

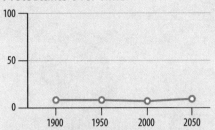

White Christians dominated Protestantism from the time of its inception in the 16th century until around the start of the 21st century. The tradition was defined historically, theologically, and demographically by trends in Europe and North America. The expansion of Protestantism via Western colonization and the worldwide missionary movement caused Protestantism to shift rapidly to the global South starting in the late 19th century and continuing to the present day. The Protestant share of Christians worldwide remained nearly the same from 1900 to 2020 (roughly 23%), but its internal composition has changed dramatically. The largest Protestant denominations today reflect Protestantism's global nature: the Three-Self Patriotic Movement in China (30 million), the Evangelical Lutheran Church in Germany (24 million), the Church of England in the United Kingdom (23 million), and the Anglican Church in Nigeria (22 million). Another large Protestant denominations worldwide is the Assemblies of God, a Pentecostal denomination established in over 100 countries.

Quick Facts

Population (2020)	586 million
Percent of population (2020)	7.5%
Percent of Christians (2020)	23.2%
Denominations (2020)	12,000
Congregations (2020)	1,743,000
Largest country (pop.)	Nigeria
Highest percent	Faeroe Islands
Fastest growth	Albania
Largest decline	United States
Largest tradition	Anglican

Evangelicals

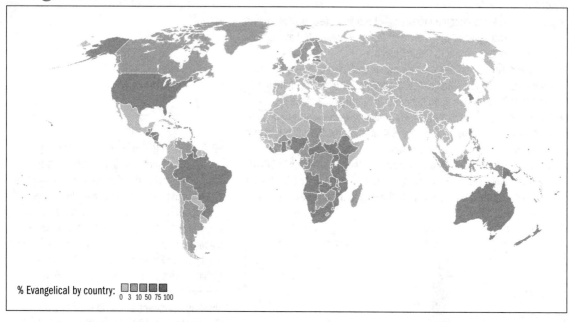

% Evangelical by country: 0 3 10 50 75 100

The historical origins of modern Evangelicalism lie in the first half of the 18th century in Europe. English-speaking Protestantism was renewed by a series of religious revivals, flamed by prominent evangelists like George Whitefield and John Wesley and supported by ordinary women and men. Many Evangelical churches in the West have their origins in the 16th-century Protestant Reformation. Initially, the term *Evangelical* was synonymous with "Protestant," especially in Germany. Over time, it came to describe the network of Protestant Christian movements in the 18th century in Britain and its colonies, the individuals who were associated with those movements, and a larger pattern of theological convictions and religious attitudes. One of the most popular descriptions of Evangelical Christians comes from historian David Bebbington, whose definition focuses on the centrality of Christ's death for salvation, the desire to share Christianity with others, dependence on the Bible to live a Christian life, and the importance of having a personal conversion experience. Nevertheless, these descriptors are interpreted in many ways across language, culture, and tradition, making Evangelicalism a wildly diverse movement across time and context.

Evangelicalism is a movement without a magisterium; it does not have a pope like the Catholic Church, an archbishop like the Anglican Communion, nor any kind of authoritative body to represent all those who call themselves Evangelicals. As a result, it is a deeply fractured segment of World Christianity where decisions regarding faith and practice are left up to individual Christians and congregations. Because of its lack of centralized hierarchy, Evangelicalism tends to be more of a grassroots effort within Protestant and Independent Christianity.

The number of Evangelicals in the world has increased from 81 million in 1900 to 387 million in 2020. Using a wider, theologically driven definition of Evangelicalism results in roughly 600 million Evangelicals worldwide. Evangelicalism is a non-White movement and becoming increasingly more so, with 78% of all Evangelicals living in the global South in 2020. This is up from only 8% in 1900. The denominations with the most Evangelicals include the Assemblies of God in Brazil, the Southern Baptist Convention in the United States, the Three-Self Patriotic Movement in China, and the Anglican Church of Nigeria.

Facts to Consider

- Evangelicalism is slowly declining in North America and Europe, which together were roughly 21% Evangelical in 2020 (down from 59% in 1900).
- In 2020, Africa was 12% Evangelical, up from less than 2% in 1900. The availability of culturally relevant theological education for pastors remains a concern.
- While many Evangelical Christians are involved in foreign mission, the countries with the most Christians—such as the United States, Russia, and Brazil—receive the most missionaries.
- Evangelical Christians have been active in education and health care around the world. In the Middle East, they pioneered women's education at the start of the 20th century, which resulted in many women gaining the right to vote and entering public service.

Evangelicals by Continent

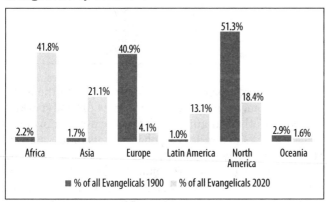

% of all Evangelicals 1900   % of all Evangelicals 2020

Like Christianity overall, Evangelicalism has shifted from a majority global North tradition to majority global South. In 2020, 78% of all Evangelicals lived in Asia, Africa, Latin America, and Oceania.

Countries with the Most Evangelicals

Country	Population 1900	Country	Population 2020
United States	40,020,000	United States	69,000,000
United Kingdom	19,158,000	Nigeria	45,500,000
Germany	3,932,000	China	35,000,000
Sweden	3,050,000	Brazil	29,000,000
Australia	1,736,000	Ethiopia	21,500,000
Netherlands	1,571,000	Kenya	16,500,000
Canada	1,504,000	South Korea	12,855,000
Norway	1,344,000	India	12,200,000
South Africa	1,082,000	Indonesia	9,414,000
Finland	557,000	Tanzania	9,400,000

Nine of the ten countries with the most Evangelicals in 2020 were in the global South. The United States is an outlier as the only country in the global North on the list and also the country with the most Evangelicals.

Evangelicals by Tradition

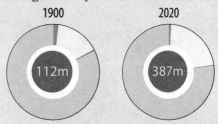

☐Independent ☐Protestant ▩Catholic ▩Orthodox ▩Christian

Most Evangelicals in the world are Protestants and Independents. Some large denominations in the world are considered 100% Evangelical by their affiliation with global Evangelical bodies such as the World Evangelical Alliance, regional groups such as the Association of Evangelicals of Africa, or national organizations such as the Christian Council of Korea.

Evangelicals Over Time

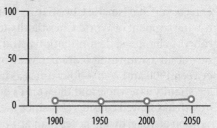

Evangelicals were 5% of the world's population in both 1900 and 2020. The movement has grown from 81 million to 387 million, with most of that growth occurring in the global South.

Quick Facts

Population (2020)	387 million
Percent of population (2020)	5.0%
Percent of Christians (2020)	15.4%
Denominations (2020)	8,100
Congregations (2020)	1,066,000
Largest country (pop.)	United States
Highest percent	Marshall Islands
Fastest growth	Belgium
Largest decline	Australia
Largest tradition	Baptist

Pentecostals/Charismatics

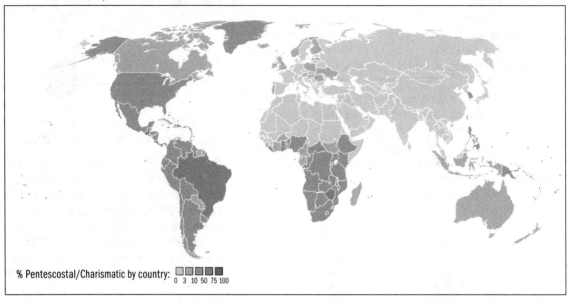

% Pentecostal/Charismatic by country: 0 3 10 50 75 100

Pentecostal/Charismatic Christianity is the fastest-growing segment of World Christianity today. This group of churches, denominations, and networks grew at an astounding 6.3% per year on average between 1900 and 2000—four times as fast as both Christianity as a whole and the world's population. Growth has slowed considerably since then, but this tradition is still growing faster than any other (from 2020–2050, it is expected to grow twice as fast as both). Less than 1% of Christians were Pentecostal/Charismatic in 1900; today that figure is 26%. Wherever Christianity reached during the 20th century, to a large extent the Pentecostal/Charismatic movement did as well.

Pentecostal/Charismatic Christians share a "family resemblance" with a shared emphasis on the baptism of the Holy Spirit, the gifts of the Spirit, and the experiential nature of Christian faith. Countries where large populations held to animistic traditions generally embraced Pentecostalism due to its emphasis on signs, wonders, and miracles—phenomena relatively compatible with those in their former traditional religions. The largest tradition within this movement is the Catholic Charismatic movement, concentrated in Latin America but found all over the world (195 million worldwide).

The origins of the Pentecostal/Charismatic movement date to the book of Acts when the Spirit was poured out on women and men in the upper room, accompanied by tongues of fire and speaking in other languages. The modern-day movement traces to a series of global revivals in the late 19th and early 20th centuries such as those in South India (1860s), Topeka, Kansas (1895), Wales (1904–1905), Northeast India (1905), Los Angeles, California (1906), Pyongyang, Korea (1907–1908), and Chile (1909). Many of today's Pentecostal/Charismatic traditions trace their roots directly to these revivals. Others are connected to revivals within mainline traditions throughout the 20th century, and yet even others have emerged only in the last 40 years. The historical revivals around the world are important because they indicate that the global expansion of Pentecostal/Charismatic Christianity in the 20th century was not solely the result of missionaries from North America and Europe, but instead the fruit of indigenous efforts to contextualize a Spirit-empowered Christianity in their own cultures. The early Pentecostal movement was marked by an evangelistic zeal to spread the power of the Holy Spirit to encourage revival among churches and reach those without any access to Christianity. The vast majority of newer churches planted in the global South in the 20th century are Pentecostal/Charismatic in faith, worship, and spirituality.

Facts to Consider

- Many Pentecostal churches are quite small and have bivocational (part-time) pastors with little to no theological training.
- Pentecostal churches tend to be more egalitarian, with men and women seemingly given equal access to leadership and ministerial opportunities. However, in reality, prominent women who help shape church leadership are often overlooked, with the credit for their labor given to men.
- One of the most common misconceptions about Pentecostalism is that it focuses too much on the spiritual life as opposed to the life on earth. To the contrary, Pentecostal churches are often on the forefront of all kinds of social issues such as emergency services, medical assistance, education, and economic development.

Pentecostals/Charismatics by Continent

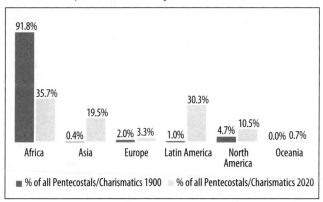

- % of all Pentecostals/Charismatics 1900 — % of all Pentecostals/Charismatics 2020

Africa is the continent with the most Pentecostal/Charismatic Christians, followed by Latin America and North America.

Countries with the Most Pentecostals/Charismatics

Country	Population 1900	Country	Population 2020
South Africa	805,000	Brazil	108,000,000
Nigeria	96,000	United States	65,000,000
United States	46,100	Nigeria	60,000,000
Germany	20,000	Philippines	38,000,000
Trinidad & Tobago	10,000	China	37,000,000
China	2,000	DR Congo	28,000,000
India	1,800	South Africa	27,700,000
South Korea	500	India	21,000,000
		Mexico	17,450,000
		Kenya	17,300,000

In 1900, the three largest populations were in South Africa, Nigeria, and the United States. In 2020, the countries with the most Pentecostal/Charismatic Christians were Brazil, the United States, and Nigeria.

Pentecostals/Charismatics by Tradition

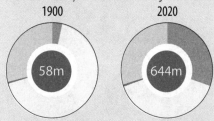

1900   2020

☐Independent ☐Protestant ■Catholic ■Orthodox ■Christian

Pentecostals/Charismatics are found in three types: (1) denominational Pentecostals such as the Assemblies of God; (2) Charismatics found within historic churches such as Catholics and Lutherans; and (3) Independent Charismatics in newer denominations and networks that either broke from established churches or began on their own.

Pentecostals/Charismatics Over Time

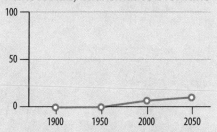

Between 1900 and 2020, many regions saw up to 15–17% annual growth rates where Christians embraced Pentecostal/Charismatic Christianity.

Quick Facts

Population (2020)	644 million
Percent of population (2020)	8.3%
Percent of Christians (2020)	25.6%
Denominations (2020)	19,300
Congregations (2020)	1,336,000
Largest country (pop.)	Brazil
Highest percent	Marshall Islands
Fastest growth	Kuwait
Largest decline	France
Largest tradition	Catholic Charasmatics

CHRISTIANITY BY COUNTRY

—

Christianity in Afghanistan

Christians lived in what is now Afghanistan as early as 200 CE and throughout the medieval era, but they have always existed as minority communities in this Muslim majority country. As of 2020, there were roughly 7,500 Christians in Afghanistan, mostly Muslim-background believers worshiping in secret. Christian missionaries are not legally allowed in the country, but many foreign Christians work with humanitarian groups, both secular and Christian. The largest Christian NGO, the International Assistance Mission, was established in 1966 by J. Christy Wilson Jr. and colleagues. Christians working with these organizations are often targeted by religious extremists and accused of illegal proselytism.

Facts to Consider

- Islam is the official religion of Afghanistan, and blasphemy is a crime punishable by beheading for men and life imprisonment for women.
- Many Catholic orders serve in Afghanistan, such as the Little Sisters of Jesus, the Sisters from the Missionaries of Charity, and Jesuit Relief Services.
- Afghans access information about Christianity primarily via the media. Organizations such as Afghan Christian Media provide television, radio, and news media both inside and outside the country via satellite TV.
- Christian converts face extreme pressure from their families and friends to return to Islam. Female converts in particular are at great risk for sexual violence, domestic control, and forced marriage.
- The Taliban takeover and subsequent American military withdrawal from Afghanistan in August 2021 left Christians—and Afghan women—in a precarious position, with uncertainties about their safety and future in the country.

Indicators & Demographic Data

Population (2020)	38,055,000
% under 15 years	41%
Capital city (pop.)	Kabul 4,222,000
% urban dwellers	26% (3.34% p.a.)
Official language	Dari, Pushto
Largest language	Pushto (37%)
Largest people	Southern Pathan (31%)
Largest culture	Afghani (37%)
Development	50
Physicians	3
Gender gap	37%

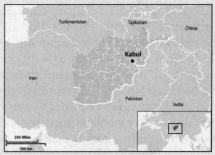

% Christian: 0 3 10 50 75 100

Christian Traditions in Afghanistan

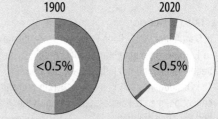

1900 — <0.5%
2020 — <0.5%

☐ Independent ☐ Protestant ■ Catholic ■ Orthodox ■ Christian

Most Afghan Christians choose to remain Muslims publicly and only identify as Christians secretly for their own safety. As a result, 58% of Christians in the country are Independents.

Religion in Afghanistan

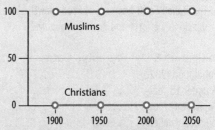

Islam is by far the majority religion (99.9%), and this is unlikely to change in the future. Christianity has grown only slightly since the start of the 20th century but remains significantly less than 1% of the population.

Bible Translations		Churches		Missionaries		Gospel Access	
Languages	62	Denominations	13	Received	200	1900	Very low
Full Bible	15	Congregations	100	Sent	0	2020	Very low

Christianity in Albania

Christianity has a long history in Albania, dating to the apostolic era. Albania was under the control of the Ottoman Empire (Turks) from 1479 to 1912, when the majority of the population became Muslim. Albania became the world's first officially atheist country in 1967. All organized religious life ceased to exist, all churches were closed, and many places of worship were destroyed. Albanian Christians continued to practice their faith in secret, even at the risk of death. Religious life rebounded after the fall of Communism in 1991, and today Albania is 60% Muslim and 37% Christian. Most Christians in Albania are Catholic or Orthodox (roughly half a million each).

Facts to Consider

- In September 2014, Pope Francis visited Albania as his first papal visit to Europe. He highlighted Albania's uniqueness as a country where people of all (and no) faiths peacefully coexist.
- The Orthodox Church is highly active in humanitarian work, including education, medical clinics, and interfaith friendship camps for Muslim and Christian children.
- Protestantism arrived in Albania in the early 19th century, but the number of Protestant churches is very small today, including the Assemblies of God, Baptists, and Word of Life Church (Charismatic).
- Many Evangelical Protestant missionaries entered the country after 1991, and today the country is home to roughly 12,500 Evangelicals.
- The Jehovah's Witnesses are the largest non-Orthodox/non-Catholic group in the country, with roughly 8,100 members.
- The Baha'i Faith has experienced growth since the year 2000 due to missionary efforts and now has roughly 16,000 adherents.

Indicators & Demographic Data

Population (2020)	2,942,000
% under 15 years	17%
Capital city (pop.)	Tirana 494,000
% urban dwellers	62% (1.29% p.a.)
Official language	Albanian
Largest language	Albanian (81%)
Largest people	Tosk Albanian (61%)
Largest culture	Albanian (80%)
Development	78
Physicians	13
Gender gap	3%

% Christian: 0 3 10 50 75 100

Christian Traditions in Albania

1900 — 31.3% 2020 — 36.8%

☐ Independent ☐ Protestant ▨ Catholic ▧ Orthodox ■ Christian

Most Christians in Albania have been Orthodox or Catholic for many centuries, though the Orthodox share of Christians declined from 71% in 1900 to 49% in 2020. The Catholic share increased from 29% to 47%.

Religion in Albania

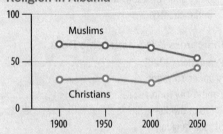

In 1900, Christians were 31% of the population, but this dropped to 8% by 1970 due to the Communist takeover. Both Christianity and Islam had rebounded by 2020, with Christians to 37% and Muslims to 60%.

Bible Translations		Churches		Missionaries		Gospel Access	
Languages	9	Denominations	65	Received	890	1900	Low
Full Bible	6	Congregations	1,600	Sent	60	2020	Very high

Christianity in Algeria

Algeria was home to some of Christianity's most important early theologians, such as Tertullian. The region came under Arab Muslim rule in the year 702 and has been majority Muslim ever since. Hundreds of thousands of European Christians settled in Algeria under French colonial rule from 1848 to 1962, but the number of Christians dropped substantially after their departure. Today, Algeria is less than 1% Christian, but it is difficult to know how many Christians might be worshiping in secret. Most indigenous Algerians who have become Christians in recent decades are from the Kabyle people group, though many immigrated to France due to persecution. Evangelical and Pentecostal/Charismatic churches are small but growing. There are also Christian expatriate workers from the Philippines and China.

Facts to Consider

- Islam is the state religion of Algeria, and it is illegal for non-Muslims to proselytize or "shake the faith" of Muslims.
- Religious groups must register with the government to operate, and Christians often experience difficulties with registration and obtaining visas.
- Although the indigenous Algerian church is small, they had already sent out 130 foreign missionaries by 2018, trained in a local mission school.
- Many Protestant communities have difficulty finding places to worship after changes in the law in 2006. In 2019, the government forcibly closed some Protestant churches. Some were allowed to reopen after a few months.
- Algerians who convert to Christianity are often exposed to the faith through dreams, visions, and Christian broadcasting. There are no Christian-run radio stations in the country, but programming is received from outside.

Indicators & Demographic Data

Population (2020)	43,333,000
% under 15 years	30%
Capital city (pop.)	Algiers 2,768,000
% urban dwellers	74% (1.99% p.a.)
Official language	Arabic, Amazigh
Largest language	Arabic (65%)
Largest people	Algerian Arab (58%)
Largest culture	Arab (Arabic) (73%)
Development	75
Physicians	12
Gender gap	14%

% Christian: 0 3 10 50 75 100

Christian Traditions in Algeria

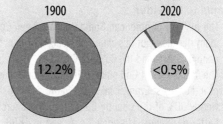

1900 — 12.2%   2020 — <0.5%

☐ Independent ☐ Protestant ■ Catholic ■ Orthodox ■ Christian

Most Christians were Catholic (98%) at the start of the 20th century due to the presence of foreigners. The share of Catholics had dropped substantially by 2020 (5%), and by 2020 most Christians were Independents (85%).

Religion in Algeria

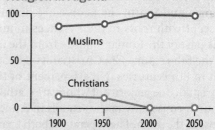

Islam remains the largest religion in Algeria and will likely remain so well into the future. Christianity continues to grow slowly and might represent 0.5% of the population by 2050.

Bible Translations		Churches		Missionaries		Gospel Access	
Languages	28	Denominations	29	Received	560	1900	Very low
Full Bible	9	Congregations	1,400	Sent	20	2020	Medium

Christianity in American Samoa

American Samoa has been an overseas territory of the United States since 1900. The country is 98% Christian, of which the largest denominations are the Congregational Church, Catholic Church, Church of Jesus Christ of Latter-day Saints, and the Assemblies of God. Christianity was introduced to the islands in 1830 first by Tahitian and then British missionaries. Initial interactions between islanders and Europeans were violent, but most islanders converted within a decade. Pentecostal Christianity arrived via Assemblies of God missionaries in 1928 and is still growing.

Facts to Consider

- The majority of American Samoans have been Congregationalists for many decades, but this church is losing members to newer Evangelical denominations and the Catholic Church.
- The Assemblies of God quickly shifted to indigenous leadership and is now the largest Evangelical group in the country.
- Nearly 30% of the country belongs to the Church of Jesus Christ of Latter-day Saints. Missionaries arrived in 1888, just a few decades after the founding of the church in the United States.
- The Women's Ecumenical Fellowship of American Samoa brings together women from five churches for prayer and for education.

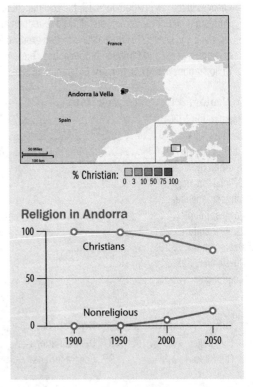

% Christian: 0 3 10 50 75 100

Religion in American Samoa

Christianity in Andorra

Andorra is one of the smallest countries in the world, with only 77,000 people in 180 square miles. It is bordered by France and Spain; the people are originally of Catalan descent with roots in the Pyrenees mountains. Andorra was part of the Roman Empire from the 2nd century BCE to the 5th century CE. Christianity spread there from the 5th to 8th centuries. Ninety percent of the population is Christian, the majority of whom are Catholic. The Catholic Church runs many of the schools in Andorra, particularly those in the south. They operate in both Spanish and Catalan.

Facts to Consider

- The constitution guarantees freedom of religion and prohibits discrimination based on religion. The country has a special relationship with the Catholic Church, in accordance with Andorran tradition.
- Andorra is home to around 1,300 Muslims, mainly from Morocco, Turkey, and Pakistan. There is no mosque, but an Islamic cultural center serves as a meeting place for the community.
- Tourism is a big industry for the country, with over 10 million visitors a year. But border closures related to the COVID-19 pandemic had serious economic consequences. Evangelical churches have joined with the Red Cross and the Catholic Caritas social organizations to provide relief.

% Christian: 0 3 10 50 75 100

Religion in Andorra

Christianity in Angola

Christianity arrived in modern-day Angola by way of Portuguese colonists in 1482. Angola was a Portuguese colony until it achieved independence in 1975. Under Portuguese rule, society was divided by race and class between "uncivilized natives" and "assimilated second-class Whites." Angola became an important part of the slave trade, which was abolished there in 1836. The Catholic Church stressed assimilation of Africans into a Portuguese way of life in order to become Christians. Protestant activities were discouraged during the colonial period, but Protestantism grew in the late 19th century. Independent churches had very little opportunity to develop at this time, even though indigenous African churches were blossoming in most neighboring countries. For decades, only churches linked to Catholicism or Western mission boards or churches grew in Angola. With the loosening of governmental restrictions on religion after 1988, African Independent Churches could develop out of a need for more culturally African expressions of Christianity. Many Africans became Christians despite a history of institutions advocating slavery, racist policies, and denial of citizenship under the banner of Christianity. The exodus of foreign missionaries during the Angolan Civil War (1975–2002) encouraged rapid Africanization of the churches. Angola is a majority Christian country (93%), most of whom are Catholic.

The historic Protestant denominations came to Angola between 1878 and 1960, including Baptists, Methodists, Congregationalists, Plymouth Brethren, Lutherans, Adventists, and other Evangelical groups. The first Protestants to arrive, from the Baptist Missionary Society (United Kingdom), opened a mission at São Salvador among the Kongo people of northern Angola in 1878. The Kikongo became the most Christianized people in Angola by 1960: 56% Catholic and 43% Protestant, with less than 2% remaining traditionalist. By 2015, the Kikongo in Angola were 95% Christian.

The second largest denomination today is the Assemblies of God, with over 2.5 million members. They trace their origins to American missionaries arriving in 1939, then Portuguese missionaries in the 1950s. By 2015, there were over 11,800 national Assemblies of God pastors, nearly 3,000 indigenous churches, and one Bible school.

% Christian: 0 3 10 50 75 100

Religion in Angola

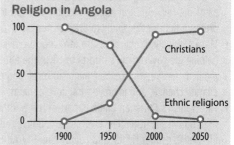

The dramatic growth of Christianity in Angola over the 20th century (less than 1% in 1900 to 93% in 2020) was due to conversions from traditional religions, which dropped from 99% of the population to just under 5%. A little more than 1% of the population is Muslim. Christianity grew from less than 1% of the population in 1900 to 93% in 2020.

Indicators & Demographic Data

Population (2020). 32,827,000
% under 15 years 46%
Capital city (pop.) . . . . Luanda 8,330,000
% urban dwellers. . . . . 67% (4.04% p.a.)
Official language. . . . . .Portuguese
Largest language. . . . . Umbundu (28%)
Largest people . . . Mbundu (Ovimbundu) (28%)
Largest culture . . . . Central Bantu (55%)
Development. 58
Physicians. 1.4
Gender gap. 15%

Bible Translations	Churches	Missionaries	Gospel Access
Languages. 58	Denominations 88	Received. 2,100	1900 . . . . Very low
Full Bible. 24	Congregations. 24,200	Sent 360	2020 . . . . Very high

Facts to Consider

- Women and youth account for most of the membership in Angolan churches. Between independence and the early 1990s, 21 new Catholic religious orders for women entered the country, and one new order was created in Angola, the Congregation of the Sisters of Saint Catherine.
- Both Catholic and Protestant churches have been major providers of social services throughout the country's history, particularly in education and health care.
- Many churches served as prophetic voices calling for peace during the civil war. The Evangelical Alliance of Angola, the Council of Christian Churches in Angola, the Catholic Church, and the Union of the Churches of the Holy Spirit in Angola together started a prayer and worship program that met regularly to pray for peace.
- Many Evangelical churches are involved in providing social services, helping the government's efforts to cover the entire country with good medical and health services, increase rural food production, adapt to climate change, and improve rural development.
- The Women's Christian Union is part of the worldwide Young Women's Christian Association and is involved in education (including teaching life skills), gender rights, and combatting HIV/AIDS.

Christian Traditions in Angola

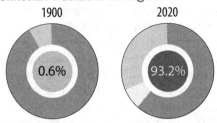

1900 2020

0.6% 93.2%

☐ Independent ☐ Protestant ■ Catholic ■ Orthodox ■ Christian

At the start of the 20th century, most Christians in Angola were Catholic (92%) due to the legacy of Portuguese rule. Over the course of the century, Protestant and Independent churches grew tremendously and together were 38% of Christians in 2020. Catholics declined to 62% of Christians. Many newer churches are also Pentecostal/Charismatic in theology and worship.

Christian Families in Angola

Family	Population (2020)	%	Trend	Change
Latin-rite Catholic	17,700,000	53.9	↑	3.5
*Pentecostals/Charismatics	8,200,000	25.0	↑	2.4
*Evangelicals	5,600,000	17.1	↑	2.3
Congregational	1,135,000	3.5	↑	2.9
Adventist	699,000	2.1	↑	0.6
Christian Brethren	557,000	1.7	↑	1.5
Baptist	537,000	1.6	↑	1.9
Reformed, Presbyterian	435,000	1.3	↑	3.5
Jehovah's Witnesses	342,000	1.0	↑↑	8.1
Methodist	243,000	0.7	↑	1.3
Nondenominational	118,000	0.4	↑	3.9
Lutheran	80,100	0.2	↑↑	5.3
Anglican	73,200	0.2	↑	4.3
Mennonite	71,000	0.2	↑↑	10.8
Restorationist, Disciple	17,500	0.1	↑	1.2
Holiness	11,100	<0.1	↑	1.5
Latter-day Saints (Mormons)	3,900	<0.1	↑↑	15.4

Catholics are 62% of Christians in Angola, with the remainder represented by an array of Protestant and Independent groups. Pentecostals/Charismatics and Evangelical groups have made considerable gains in the country in the last several decades. They represent a mixture of groups introduced by Western missionaries and groups established in Africa, by Africans. The largest non-Catholic groups include the Assemblies of God (2.5 million), the Evangelical Fraternity Church of Pentecost of Africa (1.5 million), the Evangelical Congregational Church of Angola (950,000), and the Seventh-day Adventist Church (608,000). The Jehovah's Witnesses are one of the country's fastest-growing groups; their missionaries entered the country in 1938 from South Africa, and the church received legal recognition in 1992. Angola is home to the largest population of Christian Brethren in the world (500,000).

* These movements are found within Christian families	↑↑ extreme growth
	↑ growth
	↓↓ extreme decline
− no change	↓ decline

Christianity in Anguilla

Anguilla is a small island in the Caribbean with only 18,000 inhabitants. In 1650, it was colonized by the British, who brought enslaved people from West and Central Africa to work primarily in the tobacco fields. Enslaved Africans and their descendants eventually outnumbered White settlers. With Anguilla still a British overseas territory, Christianity is its largest religion, with 89% of the population. The Anglican Church is the largest denomination in the territory, followed by Methodists, Seventh-day Adventists, and Baptists.

Facts to Consider
- Anguilla's constitution protects freedom of conscience, expression, assembly, and association.
- Ministers, defined as anyone who teaches or preaches in any congregation of any denomination, are prevented from nomination or election to membership positions in the House of Assembly.
- The Anglican Church ordained its first female Anguillan priest in 2013, Amonteen Ravenden Bryan-Doward.
- The territory has recently welcomed immigrant communities of Muslims and Hindus, mostly from Southeast Asia. There is also one group of followers of the Baha'i Faith.

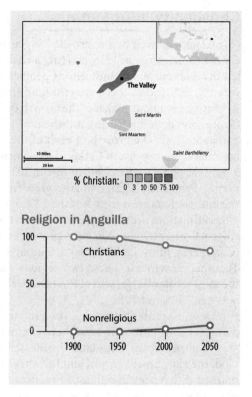

% Christian: 0 3 10 50 75 100

Religion in Anguilla

Christianity in Antigua and Barbuda

The country of Antigua and Barbuda consists of islands of those names plus many smaller islands in the West Indies. Most residents (97%) live on Antigua, especially after the near-complete destruction of Barbuda during Hurricane Irma (2017) when all the island's inhabitants were evacuated to Antigua. The British colonized Antigua in 1632 and, with Barbuda, it became a sovereign state in 1981 despite remaining a part of the British Commonwealth. As a result of British influence, Anglicanism has a long history and is the largest denomination today (26% of the country). The British introduced slavery to the islands and over time the descendants of enslaved people came to outnumber White settlers.

Facts to Consider
- The constitution provides for freedom of worship and the right to change and practice the religion of one's choosing; it also prohibits members of the clergy from running for elected office.
- The Seventh-day Adventist Church is the second largest denomination. After Hurricane Irma, the Adventist Development and Relief Agency dispatched relief teams throughout the Caribbean, and a local Seventh-day Adventist church in Antigua was essential in finding housing for Barbuda's evacuees.

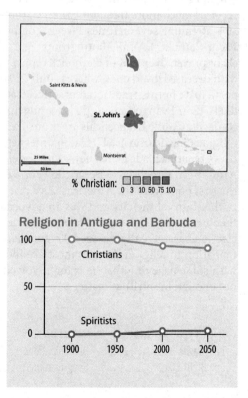

% Christian: 0 3 10 50 75 100

Religion in Antigua and Barbuda

Christianity in Argentina

Christianity arrived in modern-day Argentina via Spanish Catholic navigators in 1516, starting a chain of events that led to the expulsion of indigenous peoples from the territory in 1767. Today, there are two main trends related to Argentina's religious makeup: the growth of Evangelicalism (Protestantism; *evangélicos*) and the nonreligious (atheists and agnostics). The growth of each of these communities has been at the expense of Catholicism, which dropped from 97% of the population in 1900 to 78% in 2020. Over the same period, Pentecostals/Charismatics grew from zero to 20%; the nonreligious grew from less than 1% to nearly 8%. Religious affiliations are the highest in the northeast (Formosa, Chaco, Corrientes, and Misiones provinces) and northwest (Catamarca, Jujuy, La Rioja, Salta, Santiago del Estero, and Tucumán provinces). These two regions also experienced the most substantial growth of their Evangelical populations between 2008 and 2019.

Despite secularization and the growth of the nonreligious, Argentina remains a rather religious country. The vast majority of the population professes belief in Jesus, God, the Holy Spirit, angels, and life after death. There are marked differences in religious practices between Catholics and Evangelicals. Evangelicals tend to attend religious services much more frequently than Catholics, with nearly 30% attending several times a week (compared to less than 1% of Catholics). While both groups report very high levels of prayer, over half of Catholics report communicating with deceased loved ones, whereas only 23% of Evangelicals participate in this traditional practice. Catholics are more likely than Evangelicals to go on a pilgrimage and attend confession, while Evangelicals are more likely to engage with religious media (music, TV, radio, internet).

Argentina made global news with the election of Buenos Aires–born Jorge Mario Bergoglio (Pope Francis) in 2013, the first pope from the Americas. As a priest he ministered in the slums of the city and was an advocate for liberation theology, addressing structural sin in society. However, his election has not really changed Argentinian interest or participation in religion. In fact, most are indifferent to him, with some believing that he is too involved in politics and not enough in spiritual matters.

% Christian: 0 3 10 50 75 100

Religion in Argentina

Argentina remains a majority Christian country and will likely remain so for many decades to come. Most nonreligious people are young (18–44 years old), male, and college-educated. Regions with the highest nonreligious population are Greater Buenos Aires (26%) and Patagonia (24%).

Indicators & Demographic Data

Population (2020). 45,510,000
% under 15 years 24%
Capital city (pop.) . . . Buenos Aires 15,154,000
% urban dwellers. . . . . 92% (0.97% p.a.)
Official language. . . . . Spanish
Largest language. . . . . Spanish (81%)
Largest people . . . . . . Argentinian White (73%)
Largest culture . . . Latin-American White (75%)
Development. 82
Physicians. 39
Gender gap. 0%

Bible Translations		Churches		Missionaries		Gospel Access	
Languages.	55	Denominations	220	Received	10,000	1900	Very high
Full Bible.	38	Congregations	25,200	Sent	2,000	2020	Very high

Facts to Consider

- By law, the government sustains the Catholic Church, but it is not an official state religion. Most Argentinians reject state support of the Catholic Church.
- Divorce became legal in Argentina in 1987. While cultural forms of patriarchy in families are increasingly being challenged, Evangelical families are most likely to uphold traditional gender roles.
- Between 2008 and 2019, the proportion of the population who believe that abortion is the right of a woman doubled. Abortion became legal in 2021.
- Sunday attendance reveals a wide range in practice. Only about 7% of those eligible to attend Mass actually do in the 12 parishes of Greater Buenos Aires. In the smaller towns, between 8% and 20% attend.
- Argentinian Christians are increasingly involved in overseas mission and have begun sending missionaries among Muslims in the Middle East and North Africa.
- Anti-Semitism continues in Argentinian society, with reports of discrimination against Jews doubling between 2017 and 2018.
- The Muslim population of Argentina grew from just 4,000 to 970,000 between 1900 and 2020. The largest population of Muslims are Arabs from the Levant.

Christian Traditions in Argentina

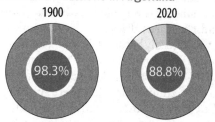

□ Independent □ Protestant ▨ Catholic ■ Orthodox ■ Christian

Catholicism remains the religion of the majority, although its proportion is gradually declining. In 1900, 99% of Christians were Catholic; this figure was 87% in 2020. Many Catholics have been converting to Protestantism; 55% of Protestants in Argentina claim to have been raised as Catholic. Most Catholics who have switched to Protestantism have done so in the most recent generation, and mostly before age 25. Independents and Protestants each represent 6% of Christians in the country.

Christian Families in Argentina

Family	Population (2020)	%	Trend	Change
Latin-rite Catholic	33,988,000	74.7	↑	0.6
*Pentecostals/Charismatics	9,300,000	20.4	↑	1.4
*Evangelicals	2,000,000	4.4	↑	1.5
Eastern-rite Catholic	1,512,000	3.3	↑	0.7
Latter-day Saints (Mormons)	483,000	1.1	↑	2.2
Jehovah's Witnesses	202,000	0.4	–	0.2
Baptist	185,000	0.4	↑	1.4
Nondenominational	179,000	0.4	↑	3.6
Non-traditional, house, cell	160,000	0.4	↑	0.8
Eastern Orthodox	158,000	0.3	↓	-0.9
Adventist	142,000	0.3	↑	0.6
Christian Brethren	140,000	0.3	–	0.4
Lutheran	78,700	0.2	↑	4.1
Holiness	39,300	0.1	↑	2.6
United church or joint mission	35,700	0.1	↓	-1.1
Reformed, Presbyterian	27,500	0.1	↑	1.0
Anglican	25,400	0.1	↑	1.0
Methodist	12,200	<0.1	–	0.2
Oriental and other Orthodox	11,800	<0.1	–	0.1
Congregational	9,300	<0.1	↓	-1.5
Mennonite	5,600	<0.1	↑	2.4
Dunker	3,100	<0.1	↑	0.9
Salvationist	2,000	<0.1	–	0.2

Independent denominations were the fastest growing in the 20th century and account for some of the largest churches in Argentina today. The largest Independent denomination is the Church of Jesus Christ of Latter-day Saints (Mormons). Latter-day Saints and Jehovah's Witnesses have been growing, particularly among younger populations, and now number 685,000 (though only 2% of the country's population). Historic Protestant groups such as Baptists, Adventists, and Brethren remain relatively small, though most of these groups date to the early 19th century. Pentecostal/Charismatic Christianity in Argentina has grown substantially since the mid-20th century, with revivals occurring throughout the 1990s. The Catholic Charismatic movement is growing but remains small compared with its presence in other Latin American countries.

*	These movements are found within Christian families	↑↑	extreme growth
		↑	growth
		↓↓	extreme decline
–	no change	↓	decline

Christianity in Armenia

Christianity is very old in Armenia, dating to Bartholomew and Thaddaeus, disciples of Jesus. Armenia was the first country to officially become Christian, in the year 301 CE (12 years before the Roman Empire). The Armenian Apostolic (Orthodox) Church is the national church of the country. From 1914 to 1923, ethnic Armenians were systematically murdered in the Ottoman Empire. Around 1.5 million Armenians died, while others were forced into hard labor and deportation. The Armenian diaspora around the world today is linked to this genocide. From 1922 to 1991, Armenia was part of the Soviet Union, where all religious communities suffered under Communism and state-sanctioned atheism. Decades after the fall of Soviet communism, Orthodox Christianity is now an integral part of Armenian life and national identity.

Facts to Consider

- Turkey denies the Armenian Genocide, while many diasporic Armenian communities continue to push for formal recognition of the tragedy from governments around the world.
- Protestant missionaries arrived in Armenia in the 19th century, but the Armenian Apostolic clergy largely opposed them, and they have had little impact in the country.
- It is common for women in Armenian Orthodox churches to serve as leading chanters and readers during liturgical services, unlike the practice of many other Orthodox traditions. The Armenian Orthodox Church has ordained women as deaconesses since the 5th century.
- The two largest Pentecostal/Charismatic groups are ethnic Russian Baptists and the Assemblies of God (arrived 1995).

Indicators & Demographic Data

Population (2020)................................2,939,000
% under 15 years 20%
Capital city (pop.)......................... Yerevan 1,086,000
% urban dwellers............................63% (0.23% p.a.)
Official language....................................Armenian
Largest language............................. Armenian (96%)
Largest people .... Armenian (Ermeni) (96%)
Largest culture .... Armenian (96%)
Development...76
Physicians..28
Gender gap..3%

% Christian: 0 3 10 50 75 100

Christian Traditions in Armenia

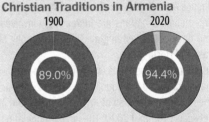

1900 — 89.0%   2020 — 94.4%

☐ Independent ☐ Protestant ■ Catholic ■ Orthodox ■ Christian

The Orthodox Church has been Armenia's largest Christian tradition from 1900 (99% of Christians) to 2020 (87% of Christians). In 2020, 9% of Christians were Catholic, and just under 5% Protestant and Independent together.

Religion in Armenia

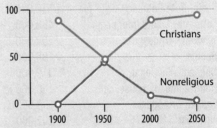

Christians

Nonreligious

Religious affiliation in Armenia dropped from nearly 100% in 1900 to only 39% at Communism's height in 1970. By 2020, Christianity had rebounded to 94%, and the nonreligious declined to just under 4%.

Bible Translations	Churches	Missionaries	Gospel Access
Languages...........24	Denominations 31	Received.............60	1900.......... Very high
Full Bible............19	Congregations......1,900	Sent 120	2020.......... Very high

Christianity in Aruba

Christians first arrived in Aruba, an island inhabited by the Arawak Caquetío Amerindians, via the voyages of Amerigo Vespucci (Italian) and Alonso de Ojeda (Spanish) in 1499. Aruba quickly became a Spanish colony, and the Dutch seized it in 1636. Today it is an autonomous state within the Kingdom of the Netherlands. Aruba is very small, with roughly 116,000 people. Catholicism, with a strong presence in Aruba due to a long history of European colonization, made up the majority of the population in 2020 (76%). The United Protestant Church of Aruba is the largest Protestant denomination, a merger of Lutheran and Dutch Reformed churches in 1984.

Facts to Consider

- The constitution prohibits religious discrimination and protects the freedom of religion and belief. In Aruba, it is a crime to engage in public speech inciting religious hatred.
- Aruba's economy is mainly driven by the tourist industry, representing 75% of its gross national product. Most tourists are from North America.
- The official languages of Aruba are Dutch and Papiamento, the latter of which is most widely spoken. It is a creole language that blends Portuguese, Dutch, Spanish, and various West African languages.
- Many newer churches in Aruba are Pentecostal or Charismatic in nature, such as the Assemblies of God, the Church of Christ in Aruba, and the Church of God of Prophecy.
- The second largest religion is Spiritism, which represents a blend of Afro-Brazilian, Afro-Cuban, and other African traditions mixed with Christianity.

Indicators & Demographic Data

Population (2020)	106,000
% under 15 years	17%
Capital city (pop.)	Oranjestad 29,000
% urban dwellers	44% (0.77% p.a.)
Official language	Dutch, Papiamento
Largest language	Papiamento (77%)
Largest people	Antillean Creole (77%)
Largest culture	Creole, Dutch-speaking (78%)
Development	68
Physicians	39
Gender gap	3%

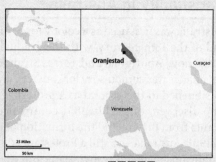

% Christian: 0 3 10 50 75 100

Christian Traditions in Aruba

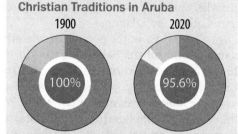

1900 — 100%
2020 — 95.6%

☐ Independent ☐ Protestant ■ Catholic ■ Orthodox ■ Christian

In both 1900 and 2020, most Christians in Aruba were Catholic (82% and 84%, respectively). Independent Christianity grew over this period, from none in 1900 to 5% of Christians by 2020.

Religion in Aruba

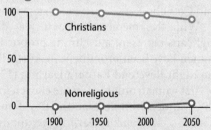

Christians

Nonreligious

Christianity has been and will likely remain the largest religion in Aruba for many decades to come (92% in 2050). Other religions grew over the 20th century, such as Spiritism, Islam, and Judaism, but these communities are very small.

Bible Translations		Churches		Missionaries		Gospel Access	
Languages	12	Denominations	37	Received	15	1900	Very high
Full Bible	9	Congregations	150	Sent	4	2020	Very high

Christianity in Australia

Australia was first used as a colony for British convicts at the end of the 18th century, with the gradual displacement of indigenous Aboriginal and Torres Strait Islanders. Church attendance was compulsory for convicts, and the first church was burned to the ground as a protest against that policy. The discovery of gold in 1851 commenced waves of emigrants from Britain and the formation of a commonwealth in 1901. Australia was still a Protestant country then, mostly Anglicans but also Presbyterians and Methodists. But the arrival of millions more migrants in the 20th century from elsewhere in Europe sparked a marked increase in the country's Catholic population.

In 2020, 54% of the population identified with Christianity, down substantially from 93% in 1970 and 97% in 1900. The largest Christian families in 2020 in Australia were Catholic (22% of the population) and Anglican (14%). Catholics were mostly Irish until after World War II and upon the arrival of Catholics from Italy, Malta, the Netherlands, Yugoslavia (Croatia), Poland, Austria, and other European countries. More recently, Catholic immigrants have come from many other countries around the world, including the Philippines, India, Vietnam, and various countries of Africa and South America. Although Catholics comprise the majority of Christians, most rarely, if ever, attend Mass, with only roughly 12% attending on a typical Sunday. Aboriginal and Torres Strait Islander Catholics make up less than 3% of all Catholics.

While their membership has increased in recent decades, Anglicans represent a declining proportion of Christians. Women have been prominent in Australian Anglicanism. The Right Reverend Barbara Darling (1947–2015) became the first woman ordained in the church in 1992, along with other women who became the first female priests in the Diocese of Melbourne. Darling eventually became the first female bishop for Melbourne in 2008.

Secularization has been a rapid process in Australia over the 20th century, with the nonreligious rising from 1% in 1900 to 35% in 2020. The highest proportions of nonreligious are in Tasmania, Australian Capital Territory, and South Australia.

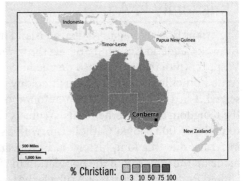

% Christian: 0 3 10 50 75 100

Religion in Australia

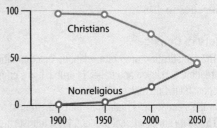

Australia became increasingly diverse in its religious population over the course of the 20th century. In 1900, 97% of the population was Christian; this has dropped to 54%. Gains were made by many religions, largely through immigration, such as Buddhists (3% in 2020), Muslims (3%), and Sikhs (1%). The country's nonreligious population also grew substantially, from 1% in 1900 to 35% in 2020.

Indicators & Demographic Data

Population (2020)	25,398,000
% under 15 years	19%
Capital city (pop.)	Canberra 457,000
% urban dwellers	86% (1.27% p.a.)
Official language	English
Largest language	English (80%)
Largest people	Anglo-Australian (62%)
Largest culture	Anglo-Australian (62%)
Development	94
Physicians	35
Gender gap	3%

Bible Translations		Churches		Missionaries		Gospel Access	
Languages	206	Denominations	270	Received	4,000	1900	Very high
Full Bible	98	Congregations	18,000	Sent	3,500	2020	Very high

Facts to Consider

- Surveys report that many Australians have no opinion about religion or God, or think religion is something they do not need to think about. A quarter of the population considers themselves spiritual but not religious.
- The proportion of Australians attending church at least once a month has declined from 36% in 1972 to around 15%.
- The majority of Aboriginal and Torres Strait Islander people consider themselves Christian, but the legacy of forced assimilation into European culture lives on. Their land having been stolen by European colonists, their population substantially declined by the end of the 19th century.
- Sikhs experienced one of the fastest growth rates over the 20th century, now with a population of 170,000 (more than Jews). Most are from Malaysia and have settled in Melbourne.
- The Muslim population in Australia grew quickly in the 1970s via immigration. Most Muslims are Sunni and come from many countries, including the Balkans, Lebanon, Indonesia, Malaysia, and Turkey.
- Hinduism arrived in Australia via indentured servants of the British. Today the community is growing via emigrants from India, Nepal, Sri Lanka, and Fiji.

Christian Traditions in Australia

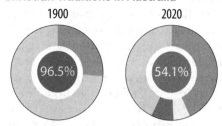

1900   2020

96.5%   54.1%

☐Independent ☐Protestant ■Catholic ■Orthodox ■Christian

Due to British colonization, Australia was majority Protestant (Anglican) for centuries. It was only in the 20th century that Catholics began to grow faster than Protestants, such that in 2020, there were more Catholics in the country than Protestants (6.6 million Catholics, 5.9 million Protestants). Independent Christianity grew from less than 1% of Christians to 6% in 2020.

Christian Families in Australia

Family	Population 2020	%	Trend	Change
Latin-rite Catholic	5,583,000	22.0	–	0.4
Anglican	3,491,000	13.7	↓	-0.5
*Evangelicals	2,553,000	10.1	↓	-0.9
*Pentecostals/Charismatics	1,550,000	6.1	–	-0.1
United church or joint mission	1,205,000	4.7	–	-0.4
Eastern Orthodox	978,000	3.9	↑	1.5
Eastern-rite Catholic	317,000	1.2	↑	1.9
Lutheran	288,000	1.1	↑	1.7
Latter-day Saints (Mormons)	195,000	0.8	↑	3.8
Baptist	168,000	0.7	↑	1.6
Oriental and other Orthodox	122,000	0.5	↑	2.9
Jehovah's Witnesses	115,000	0.5	↑	1.7
Adventist	76,900	0.3	↑	1.5
Restorationist, Disciple	74,400	0.3	–	0.1
Reformed, Presbyterian	67,600	0.3	–	0.5
Christian Brethren	58,500	0.2	↑	1.1
Salvationist	41,600	0.2	↓	-3.6
Nondenominational	36,500	0.1	↑	1.0
Methodist	31,500	0.1	↓	-1.9
Exclusive Brethren	11,800	<0.1	–	-0.4
Holiness	11,500	<0.1	↑	1.3
Congregational	3,000	<0.1	↓	-0.8
Friends (Quaker)	1,500	<0.1	–	0.5

The four largest denominations represent the diversity that exists in Christianity in Australia: Catholic, Anglican, Uniting Church in Australia (Protestant), and Greek Orthodox. Together they represent almost 70% of the country's Christians. The Uniting Church formed in 1977 with Congregationalists, Methodists, and Presbyterians. It is the country's largest nongovernmental provider of social services, including hospitals, schools, and emergency relief. Greek Orthodox arrived in the late 19th century, and immigration to the country accelerated until after World War II. Australia is home to one of the largest Greek communities in the world. Evangelicalism has deep roots in Australian culture but has been in gradual decline; on the contrary, Pentecostal/Charismatic Christianity is much more recent and is growing faster than any other religious tradition. The largest of these denominations is the Australian Christian Churches, founded by the Assemblies of God.

* These movements are found within Christian families	↑↑ extreme growth
	↑ growth
	↓↓ extreme decline
– no change	↓ decline

Christianity in Austria

Christianity has a long history in Austria, dating to Roman rule in the 1st century. But during the Middle Ages, the only centers of Christianity throughout most of the land were the monasteries of different religious orders. Protestants date to the early 16th century, around the start of the Protestant Reformation. Lutheranism became the major Protestant tradition and remains so today. Under the annexation by Nazi Germany from 1938 to 1945, Austrian Christians suffered persecution but also spiritual renewal. Although it is not the national church, the Catholic Church shares a close relationship with the Austrian government. Catholic holidays are official national holidays, and the government provides some financial support for Catholic ministry.

Christianity declined in Austria from 97% in 1900 to 72% in 2020. The majority of the population is Catholic (61%), followed by Protestants (4%). Despite unmistakable secularization trends in the country, 78% of people in Austria raised Christian still self-identify as Christian, a statistic that makes Austria a bit of an outlier from the rest of Western Europe. On average, 30% of Austrians attend religious services weekly or monthly, which is much higher than the rest of Western Europe. Nevertheless, prayer and tithing are the exception rather than the rule. Those who left Christianity did so over disagreements with particular positions on social issues or church-related scandals. Most notably, sex abuse scandals beginning in the mid-1990s devastated the Catholic Church in Austria. After multiple allegations of abuse, Cardinal Hans Hermann Groër was removed as archbishop of Vienna in 1998. The decline of Catholic Church membership has had a rippling effect, evident in the decline in priests, seminarians, and nuns. Protestants in Austria are mostly part of either the Augsburg Confession (Lutheran) or the Helvetic Confession (Reformed). Most Protestants are concentrated in Vienna.

Migration is an important feature of life in Vienna, the capital city, in which half the city's inhabitants have migrant backgrounds and the number of refugees and asylum seekers is increasing. In 2018, the largest origin countries were Syria, Afghanistan, and Iran.

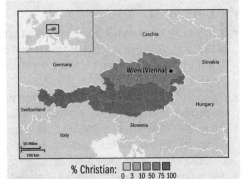

% Christian: 0 3 10 50 75 100

Religion in Austria

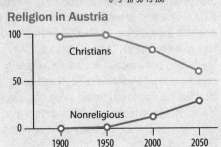

The Muslim community in Austria grew substantially from 1900 to 2020, from none to 7% (650,000). Most recent arrivals have been from Turkey, Bosnia, and Afghanistan. Muslim integration into Austrian society has proved a challenge, especially with a ban on full-face coverings in 2017. The nonreligious also grew over this period, from very few to 21%.

Indicators & Demographic Data

Population (2020)	8,782,000
% under 15 years	14%
Capital city (pop.)	Vienna 1,930,000
% urban dwellers	59% (0.68% p.a.)
Official language	German
Largest language	Bavarian (78%)
Largest people	Bavarian Austrian (78%)
Largest culture	Austrian (78%)
Development	91
Physicians	52
Gender gap	3%

Bible Translations		Churches		Missionaries		Gospel Access	
Languages	39	Denominations	90	Received	1,200	1900	Very high
Full Bible	32	Congregations	4,300	Sent	1,000	2020	Very high

Facts to Consider

- A destination for foreign Evangelical missionaries, Austria is a country that is less than 1% Evangelical. Most Evangelical churches in the country are less than 30 years old.
- Under the law, prisoners are entitled to pastoral care from religious societies. The Catholic Church is the only church with government funds for this kind of care.
- Islamophobia is a major challenge for Austrian society. Many Austrians support surveillance of Muslim communities and the banning of mosques.
- In a recent poll, 48% of Austrians reported that Islam is fundamentally incompatible with their country's culture and values; roughly a quarter thought Muslim women should not wear any religious clothing.
- In November 2020, Vienna experienced a terrorist attack that killed four people and wounded 22. The gunman, killed by police, had ties to the Islamic State in Syria.
- Austria's Jewish population was decimated under Nazi rule, dropping from 200,000 in 1938 to only 4,000 in 1945. A recent survey revealed that 28% of Austrian adults hold anti-Semitic opinions. Another survey of Austrians reported that 56% of respondents did not know that 6 million Jews died in the Holocaust.

Christian Traditions in Austria

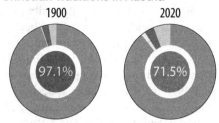

1900   2020

□Independent □Protestant ■Catholic ■Orthodox ■Christian

Austria has been a majority Catholic country for many centuries. In 1900, 95% of Christians were Catholic, though this dropped to 89% by 2020. Protestants increased their share of Christians from 3% in 1900 to 6% in 2020. The Orthodox represent a greater proportion of Christians, with modest growth of Serbian, Bulgarian, and Russian Orthodox churches. In 2020, Christians were 89% Catholic, 6% Protestant, 3% Orthodox, and 1% Independent.

Christian Families in Austria

Family	Population 2020	%	Trend	Change
Latin-rite Catholic	5,317,000	60.5	—	-0.5
Lutheran	284,000	3.2	↓	-0.9
*Pentecostals/Charismatics	270,000	3.1	—	0.4
Eastern Orthodox	187,000	2.1	—	0.5
*Evangelicals	54,400	0.6	↑	1.2
Jehovah's Witnesses	31,600	0.4	—	0.0
Reformed, Presbyterian	24,900	0.3	—	0.2
Oriental and other Orthodox	18,300	0.2	↑	2.9
Old Catholic Church	14,300	0.2	—	-0.2
Eastern-rite Catholic	10,000	0.1	↓	-2.3
Latter-day Saints (Mormons)	4,900	0.1	↑	1.4
Adventist	4,700	0.1	↑	0.7
Anglican	3,200	<0.1	—	-0.1
Baptist	2,800	<0.1	↑	5.0
Nondenominational	2,600	<0.1	↑	1.6
Methodist	1,400	<0.1	↓	-1.5
Holiness	840	<0.1	↑	1.1
Mennonite	370	<0.1	↓	-3.1

Catholics are the majority of Christians in Austria, although they have declined from 92% of the country's population in 1900 to 59% in 2020. There are smaller communities of mission-founded Protestant and Independent groups, though together, Protestants and Independents only represent 5% of Austria's population in 2020. The Free Pentecostal Church, founded by Swedish missionaries, became a publicly recognized church in 2013. Church of God (Cleveland) missionaries from the United States formed the Pentecostal Church of God in 1984. The Church of Jesus Christ of Latter-day Saints (Mormons) arrived via missionaries from Utah in 1922 and now numbers nearly 5,000 members. Orthodox make up 3% of Austria's Christians and include Serbians, Bulgarians, Russians, and Romanians.

* These movements are found within Christian families	↑↑ extreme growth
	↑ growth
	↓↓ extreme decline
— no change	↓ decline

Christianity in Azerbaijan

Although Christianity is a minority religion in Azerbaijan today, churches were there as far back as the 3rd century. Some claim that Muslim expansion missed an isolated indigenous group, the Udin, and that their descendants remain Christian today. Azerbaijan was part of the Soviet Union from 1920 until 1991, when it became independent. Most Christians in Azerbaijan are ethnic Russians and Armenian Orthodox and live in Baku and other urban areas. American Presbyterian missionaries arrived in 1834, and Russian Baptists have been active, but the Protestant community remains very small (just under 20,000 in 2020). Some small illegal Independent house churches operating in Baku have grown slightly in number since 2010.

Facts to Consider

- The law prohibits foreigners, but not citizens, from proselytizing. The law also states the government can dissolve a religious organization if they cause "racial, national, religious, or social animosity" or if they proselytize in a way that "degrades human dignity."
- Unregistered religious groups, both Muslim and non-Muslim, are sometimes harassed and subjected to fines for conducting religious services. Some Baptists and Jehovah's Witnesses have had trouble registering.
- Christianity is still widely perceived as a foreign religion to Azerbaijanis. Islam is seen as a symbol of national identity.
- Zoroastrianism was the traditional religion of Azerbaijan before the coming of Islam. The festival Nowruz on March 21 marks the start of the Zoroastrian new year and is a national holiday.

Indicators & Demographic Data

Population (2020)............................. 10,100,000
% under 15 years 23%
Capital city (pop.)............................Baku 2,341,000
% urban dwellers..........................56% (1.38% p.a.)
Official language...................................Azerbaijani
Largest language...........................Azerbaijani (89%)
Largest people ....Azerbaijani (Azeri Turk) (86%)
Largest culture ....Azerbaijani (89%)
Development...76
Physicians...34
Gender gap..5%

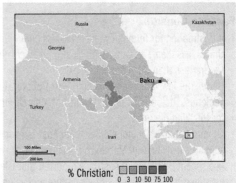

% Christian: 0 3 10 50 75 100

Christian Traditions in Azerbaijan

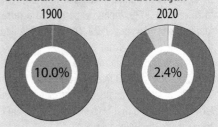

1900 — 10.0%   2020 — 2.4%

☐Independent ☐Protestant ▧Catholic ▨Orthodox ■Christian

The percentage of Orthodox declined from 99% of Christians in 1900 to 90% in 2020. Protestants and Independents were nonexistent in 1900 and in 2020 were 10% of Christians in the country.

Religion in Azerbaijan

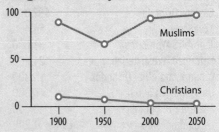

Islam is the largest religion and will likely remain to be in the future (97% in 2050). Christianity is the second largest religion. It is growing slowly but will likely be only 2.5% of the population by 2050.

Bible Translations		Churches		Missionaries		Gospel Access	
Languages	37	Denominations	19	Received	120	1900	Very low
Full Bible	20	Congregations	110	Sent	15	2020	Medium

Christianity in the Bahamas

Christianity arrived in the Bahamas in 1648 as British Anglican settlers encountered the Lucayan people. The territory subsequently became a critical source for the European slave trade; today 85% of the population of the Bahamas are descended from enslaved people. The slave trade was abolished in 1834, with the Bahamas becoming a haven for formerly enslaved people. Afro-Bahamians make up the vast majority of the population and are 95% Christian today. There are many kinds of Christianity for a relatively small country (population of 385,000). Baptists are the largest Christian family, representing 43% of the country; Reverend John James Kerr, a Bahamian, founded the Bahamas Baptist Union in 1892. Catholics are the next largest (13%), followed by Anglicans (11%).

Facts to Consider

- Christianity is an important part of Bahamian society. Official government events often include Christian prayers, and politicians regularly use religious imagery in speeches.
- Pentecostal/Charismatic Christianity has been growing, such as the Church of God of Prophecy, which arrived in 1911 and now has 5,500 members.
- The Bahamas Christian Council has broad denominational representation and is active in social, political, and economic issues, often in conjunction with the government.
- Haitian migrants, mostly Christians, in the Bahamas are denied citizenship and have been marginalized in mainstream society.
- Rastafarians have reported discrimination for their use of marijuana (which is illegal in the country) and their dreadlocks, despite constitutional freedom of religion.

Indicators & Demographic Data

Population (2020)................................... 407,000
% under 15 years 20%
Capital city (pop.)............................ Nassau 281,000
% urban dwellers............................83% (1.02% p.a.)
Official language.......................................English
Largest language.................. Bahamas Creole English (74%)
Largest people .... Black (67%)
Largest culture .... Black (African), English-speaking (68%)
Development...81
Physicians...23
Gender gap...3%

% Christian: 0 3 10 50 75 100

Christian Traditions in the Bahamas

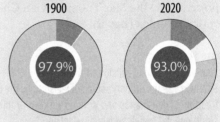

1900 — 97.9%   2020 — 93.0%

☐Independent ☐Protestant ■Catholic ■Orthodox ■Christian

Protestant and Independent groups such as Baptists and various Pentecostal/Charismatic churches have been growing in the Bahamas. The Protestant share of Christians declined from 90% in 1900 to 78% in 2020 with the growth of Independents (from 0.5% in 1900 to 8% in 2020).

Religion in the Bahamas

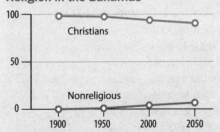

Small groups of Muslims, Hindus, Jews, and Baha'is exist, and about 4.5% of the population claims no religious allegiance. About 7,400 are Afro-American Spiritists. Baha'is arrived in the 1950s.

Bible Translations	Churches	Missionaries	Gospel Access
Languages............8	Denominations 43	Received............340	1900 .... Very high
Full Bible.............4	Congregations...... 1,200	Sent 20	2020 .... Very high

Christianity in Bahrain

Despite its presence since the 3rd century, Christianity is a minority tradition (12%) in Muslim-majority (82%) Bahrain. Most Christians in Bahrain are expatriates from India, the United Kingdom, or the United States, although some are Arab Christians from Jordan, Palestine, and Syria. Bahrain has around 500 indigenous Christians, with their own representative in Parliament. Half of Bahrain's 19 officially registered churches are in the capital, Manama. Catholics make up the largest Christian tradition due to Filipino workers, who represent 10% of the country's population and work largely in hotels, restaurants, and malls. The Orthodox are represented by the Mar Thoma Syrian Church (India) and Coptic Orthodox (Egypt).

Facts to Consider

- Islam is the official religion of Bahrain, and the constitution declares Sharia law as the primary source of legislation. The constitution provides freedom of conscience and worship yet also prohibits infringing on the "fundamental beliefs of Islamic doctrine."
- Islam is the religion of virtually all Bahraini citizens and immigrant Arabs. Muslims in urban areas are mostly Sunnis, while those in rural areas are Shia.
- Women in Bahrain are generally more publicly active and more educated than women in other Arab countries. Alice Samaan, a Christian woman, was appointed ambassador to the United Kingdom in 2011.
- There are no laws in Bahrain to protect women from domestic violence, despite widespread allegations of spousal abuse of women.

Indicators & Demographic Data

Population (2020)................................1,698,000
% under 15 years 18%
Capital city (pop.)......................... Manama 635,000
% urban dwellers...........................90% (1.99% p.a.)
Official language..................................... Arabic
Largest language............................... Arabic (61%)
Largest people ....Bahraini Arab (58%)
Largest culture .... Arab (Arabic) (61%)
Development...85
Physicians... 9.2
Gender gap...7%

% Christian: ▢▢▢▢▢ 0 3 10 50 75 100

Christian Traditions in Bahrain

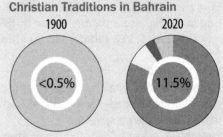

1900 — <0.5%

2020 — 11.5%

▢Independent ▢Protestant ▢Catholic ■Orthodox ■Christian

In 1900, 100% of Christians in Bahrain (only 200 people) were Protestant. By 2020, Christianity was more diverse: 83% Catholic, 7% Independent, 6% Protestant, and 3% Orthodox.

Religion in Bahrain

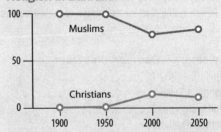

Since the Christian community is mostly expatriates, it is difficult to ascertain what Christianity's future will be in the country. Bahrain is likely to remain a Muslim-majority country far into the future (83% in 2050).

Bible Translations		Churches		Missionaries		Gospel Access	
Languages	13	Denominations	25	Received	60	1900	Very low
Full Bible	9	Congregations	130	Sent	5	2020	Medium

Christianity in Bangladesh

Christianity arrived in modern-day Bangladesh via Portuguese traders in the 16th century, though formal Catholic organization did not begin until 1886. Today, Catholicism is found mainly in urban areas, especially in Dhaka and among people of mixed Portuguese descent. The first Protestants were British Baptists who arrived in 1795. They made many converts in the Chittagong Hill Tracts, among tribes that are still concentrated in the area today. While Christianity is a minority religion in Bangladesh, fewer than 1 million and under 1% of the country's population, the country is home to the world's largest network of messianic mosques, where individuals gather and worship Jesus privately in homes. Known as *Jamaat* (Messianic Muslims), they retain many Bangladeshi cultural elements and do not identify with traditional Christian churches.

Facts to Consider

- Islam is the state religion. Although religious freedom is guaranteed by law, Christians face significant pressure by the government and society for "unlawful conversion."
- There have been several attacks on Christian communities since 2000, such as the bombings in 2001 (Baniarchar) and 2015 (Dinajpur).
- The *Jamaat* movement—with its adaptation of Islamic religious culture—is highly controversial, and some do not recognize it as authentic Christianity.
- Despite having a small Christian community, Bangladesh has a strong missionary-sending tradition to other people groups in the country.
- Most indigenous Christians are former lower-caste Hindu peasants and members of particular tribes, such as Garo, Santal, Khasi, Tripura, and Bawm.

Indicators & Demographic Data

Population (2020)	169,775,000
% under 15 years	27%
Capital city (pop.)	Dhaka 21,006,000
% urban dwellers	38% (2.88% p.a.)
Official language	Bengali (Bangla)
Largest language	Bengali (76%)
Largest people	Bengali (68%)
Largest culture	Bengali (97%)
Development	61
Physicians	4.7
Gender gap	12%

% Christian: ▫▫▫▪▪ 0 3 10 50 75 100

Christian Traditions in Bangladesh

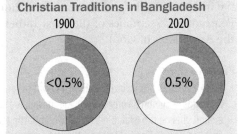

1900: <0.5% 2020: 0.5%

□ Independent □ Protestant ■ Catholic ■ Orthodox ■ Christian

In 1900, the small Christian population in Bangladesh was nearly evenly split between Catholics (49%) and Protestants (51%). By 2020, with the growth of hidden Muslim believers in Christ, who now number nearly 180,000, Independents nearly outnumbered Protestants.

Religion in Bangladesh

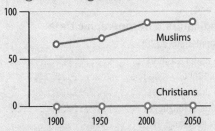

Muslims

Christians

In 1900, Bangladesh was 66% Muslim; by 2050 it is anticipated to be 90% Muslim. Hindus are the second largest religion, followed by Buddhists.

Bible Translations		Churches		Missionaries		Gospel Access	
Languages	60	Denominations	43	Received	1,000	1900	Very low
Full Bible	28	Congregations	9,700	Sent	30	2020	Medium

Christianity in Barbados

Christianity arrived in Barbados via Spanish and Portuguese explorers in the 15th and 16th centuries. The British colonized the island from 1625 to 1966 and sponsored the African slave trade, which was outlawed in 1807 but continued illegally until 1833. The largest people group today are descendants of enslaved Africans. Barbados has been majority Protestant (Anglican) due to the long British presence on the island, and a quarter of the population is Anglican. Pentecostal/Charismatic Christianity grew tremendously over the 20th century, from zero in 1900 to 22% of the country in 2020. The largest Pentecostal denomination is the Pentecostal Assemblies of the West Indies (affiliated with the Assemblies of God).

Facts to Consider

- Many churches are involved in the National Organization of Women in Barbados, an umbrella organization that advocates for the rights of women and girls on the island, particularly combatting domestic violence.
- The Anglican Church's Mothers' Union has over 2,000 members and focuses on families in need, with services that include hospital ministry, counseling, and education about HIV/AIDS.
- The second largest religion is the Baha'i Faith, with the first Local Spiritual Assembly established in 1965. They are involved in socioeconomic development on the island.
- The small Muslim community in Barbados (1%) are mostly descendants of immigrants from Gujarat, India. There are four mosques in the country.
- Rastafarians consistently report discrimination, particularly for their dreadlocks and marijuana use (which is illegal).

Indicators & Demographic Data

Population (2020)	288,000
% under 15 years	19%
Capital city (pop.)	Bridgetown 88,300
% urban dwellers	31% (0.46% p.a.)
Official language	English
Largest language	Bajan (87%)
Largest people	Barbadian Black (81%)
Largest culture	Black (African), English-speaking (81%)
Development	80
Physicians	18
Gender gap	-2%

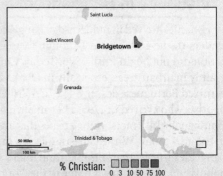

% Christian: 0 3 10 50 75 100

Christian Traditions in Barbados

1900: 100% 2020: 94.7%

☐ Independent ☐ Protestant ■ Catholic ■ Orthodox ■ Christian

Christians in Barbados were nearly entirely Protestant (Anglican) in 1900, but today there is a small but growing presence of Independents, namely, Jehovah's Witnesses, Churches of Christ, and various Pentecostal/Charismatic groups.

Religion in Barbados

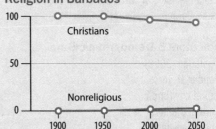

Barbados has always been a majority Christian country and is poised to remain so long into the future (93% in 2050). The nonreligious (atheists and agnostics together) were virtually nonexistent in 1900 and grew to 2% of the population by 2020.

Bible Translations		Churches		Missionaries		Gospel Access	
Languages	8	Denominations	58	Received	220	1900	Very high
Full Bible	5	Congregations	570	Sent	10	2020	Very high

Christianity in Belarus

Modern-day Belarus has been an Orthodox Christian country since the 10th century and came under the Russian Patriarchate of Moscow in the 13th century. Following the growth of Catholicism in the 15th century, the Belarus Byzantine Catholic (or Greek Catholic) Church formed in 1596 and represented a mixture of Catholicism and Orthodoxy: Catholic in doctrine and allegiance to the pope, Orthodox in ritual and liturgy, and Slavonic in language. What became Protestantism arrived early in Belarus via Hussites in 1413, and the Bible was translated into Old Church Slavonic (the language of modern-day Belarus) between 1517 and 1525, at the start of the Protestant Reformation. Coming under Nazi occupation in 1941, Belarus became part of the Soviet Union after World War II. Christianity suffered tremendously under Soviet rule. The Belarusian Greek Church, for example, was banned in 1946, and churches of all types were closed and forced underground. Freedom of religion came in 1989, and Belarus became an independent nation in 1991.

After the fall of the Soviet Union, the Orthodox Church rebounded and returned to its status as the majority church in the country (60% in 2020). Catholicism also grew, and today most Catholics are ethnic Poles. There are two Protestant unions in Belarus today, Pentecostals and Baptists. The Pentecostal Union (165,000 members) forms the largest Protestant group, though it faces pressure to avoid speaking in tongues (*glossolalia*), especially during periodic government crackdowns on non-Orthodox churches. The Union of Evangelical Christian Baptists (16,600 members) was joined with the Pentecostal Union for most of the 20th century but split over differences concerning church-state separation. As a result, many Baptist groups are not registered with the government and experience persecution.

Alexander Lukashenko has been the country's first and only president. His government is authoritarian, and he is often referred to as "Europe's last dictator." The country lacks free and fair elections, and the Committee for State Security (KGB) operates outside the control of the police and Ministry of Internal Affairs. There are serious human rights issues in Belarus, including arbitrary arrest, interference with privacy, human trafficking, and restrictions on the media and free expression.

% Christian: 0 3 10 50 75 100

Religion in Belarus

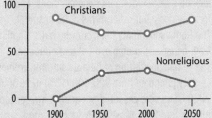

Christianity and atheists/agnostics have had mirroring trends over the course of the 20th century. The revival of Christianity after the fall of the Soviet Union meant a drop in the country's nonreligious population. The nonreligious peaked around 1970 with 40% of the population but declined to 21% by 2020.

Indicators & Demographic Data

Population (2020).	9,415,000
% under 15 years	17%
Capital city (pop.)	Minsk 2,028,000
% urban dwellers.	79% (0.28% p.a.)
Official language.	Belarusian, Russian
Largest language.	Belarusian (86%)
Largest people	Byelorussian (86%)
Largest culture	Byelorussian (86%)
Development.	81
Physicians.	41
Gender gap	-2%

Bible Translations		Churches		Missionaries		Gospel Access	
Languages.	26	Denominations	21	Received.	560	1900	Very high
Full Bible.	20	Congregations.	4,300	Sent	120	2020	Very high

Facts to Consider

- The constitution guarantees religious freedom but also recognizes the "determining role" of the Belarusian Orthodox Church in national identity and development. It is the only religion that receives state subsidies.
- All religious groups are required to register with the government, receive governmental approval to import and distribute religious literature, and organize religious activities in schools. A 2002 law made unregistered religious activity a criminal offense.
- In a general atmosphere of intimidation and fear of punishment, non-Orthodox groups are cautious about engaging in activities that could be deemed as proselytizing, such as distributing religious materials.
- The government engages in surveillance on minority religious groups, including many Protestant denominations. Leaders are often summoned for questioning or other forms of harassment.
- The Roma community (many of whom are Baptist) is socially marginalized, especially in employment and education.
- The Jewish population of Belarus suffered tremendously over the 20th century, dropping from 900,000 (13%) in 1900 to just 8,500 (0.1%) in 2020. Jews were executed under both Nazi occupation and early Soviet rule under Stalin. Most survivors emigrated.
- The roughly 25,000 Muslims in Belarus are descendants of historic Tatar populations from the 16th century or are newer immigrants from former Soviet states in central Asia.

Christian Traditions in Belarus

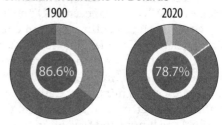

1900   2020

86.6%   78.7%

☐Independent ☐Protestant ■Catholic ■Orthodox ■Christian

Belarus has always been a majority Orthodox country, and 65% of Christians were Orthodox in 1900. In 2020, the Orthodox made up a greater share of Christians (81%) due to the shrinking share of Catholics (from 35% in 1900 to 14% in 2020). Belarus is home to a small Protestant community (250,000), most of whom are Pentecostals. The largest Pentecostal/Charismatic church is the Pentecostal Union, with 165,000 members. Grace Church in Minsk, one of the leading Pentecostal churches in the country, has the largest Protestant church building in Belarus, with seating for over 2,000 people.

Christian Families in Belarus

Family	Population 2020	%	Trend	Change
Eastern Orthodox	5,616,000	59.7	↑	0.6
Latin-rite Catholic	1,035,000	11.0	–	0.1
*Pentecostals/Charismatics	240,000	2.5	↑	3.6
*Evangelicals	80,000	0.8	↑	3.1
Oriental and other Orthodox	58,600	0.6	–	0.0
Baptist	17,100	0.2	–	0.4
Lutheran	13,400	0.1	↑	2.0
Adventist	7,700	0.1	↑	2.8
Restorationist, Disciple	6,400	0.1	↑	1.6
Jehovah's Witnesses	6,100	0.1	↓	-2.8

Over 95% of Christians in Belarus are Orthodox or Catholic. Compared to Orthodox and Catholics, considered the "traditional" faiths of the country, Protestant communities today are quite small after suffering under Bolshevik policies in the 20th century. Some Protestant churches have had trouble registering with the government because of their small size. Pentecostals are the largest Protestant group, followed by Baptists, Adventists, Lutherans, and Reformed. Jehovah's Witnesses number around 9,900 and have faced increased hostility after Russia banned the group in 2017, labeling them "religious extremists."

* These movements are found within Christian families
– no change

↑↑ extreme growth
↑ growth
↓↓ extreme decline
↓ decline

Christianity in Belgium

Christianity has a long history in modern-day Belgium, existing since the time of the Roman Empire. Roman Catholicism is intricately entwined with the history of the country, though Belgium had its own reformer in Guido de Brès at the time of the 16th-century Protestant Reformation. In 1648, the Peace of Westphalia, which ended the Thirty Years' War in Europe, divided Belgium into Calvinists in the North and Catholics in the South. Belgium became a unified independent nation in 1830, with freedom of religion enshrined in the constitution.

In 1900, nearly all Christians in Belgium were Catholic. Catholicism was part and parcel of Belgian identity, society, and culture and an integral part of the country's education and health systems. Over the 20th century, however, with increased secularization, Catholic influence waned with decreasing influence of the political Christian Democratic Party and a drop in priestly ordinations. Although most of the population are baptized Catholics, regular Mass attendance is only around 5%. Catholic education remains popular, with 59% of children in French- and German-speaking communities enrolled in Catholic elementary schools. Religious orders are also still quite active in Catholic education, such as the Jesuits, Salesians of Don Bosco, and Brothers and Sisters of the Christian Schools. Religious sisters make up 57% of all religious workers and outnumber religious brothers and priests combined.

While Protestants are a minority, they number higher in the French-speaking area than in the Flemish; roughly half of all Protestants are from Africa or Latin America. The United Protestant Church in Belgium, founded in 1839, has come to speak for Protestant churches in the country. It is the fourth largest denomination in the country, with about 41,700 members.

A 2018 study found that only 55% of baptized Christians in Belgium were currently still Christian, one of the lowest rates among Western European countries studied. The two most popular reasons for leaving the church were a gradual drifting away from religion and no longer believing in religious teachings. It is likely that by 2050, Christians will constitute 53% of the country's population.

% Christian: 0 3 10 50 75 100

Religion in Belgium

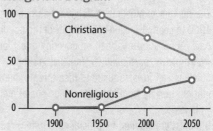

Christianity and the nonreligious (atheists and agnostics) had mirrored demographic trends over the 20th century. In 1900, Christians were 99% of the population and the nonreligious just under 1%. The gradual decline of Christianity has been somewhat matched by the rise of the nonreligious; in 2020, Christians were 65% and the nonreligious were 28%.

Indicators & Demographic Data

Population (2020). 11,620,000
% under 15 years 17%
Capital city (pop.) . . . . Brussels 2,081,000
% urban dwellers. . . . . 98% (0.38% p.a.)
Official language. . . . . . Dutch, French, German
Largest language. . . . . Dutch (32%)
Largest people .Fleming (Dutch, Flemish) (31%)
Largest culture . . . . Flemish (41%)
Development. 92
Physicians. 30
Gender gap. 3%

Bible Translations	Churches	Missionaries	Gospel Access
Languages. 36	Denominations 100	Received. 2,500	1900 . . . . Very high
Full Bible. 24	Congregations. 6,200	Sent 1,500	2020 . . . . Very high

Facts to Consider

- The majority of Belgians (68%) report that they seldom or never attend religious services. Only 11% reported weekly attendance. Sixty-four percent claimed that religion was simply not important to them.
- In 2019, half of Catholic priests in Belgium were over 75 years of age, raising questions about the future of the priesthood and the relevancy of the Catholic Church for younger generations.
- There is a shortage of Catholic priests in the country, which has caused an increase in the number of foreign priests assigned to Belgian parishes, especially in the French-speaking areas.
- Belgium has one of the lowest rates of belief in God in Western Europe (42%).
- The number of Muslims in Belgium has risen from practically zero in 1900 to nearly 1 million in 2020 (8% of the population). The "headscarf ban"—a constitutional ban on covering one's face in public—was met with protests, particularly by feminist groups.
- Muslims and Jews continue to face threats, harassment, and discrimination, ranging from hate speech on social media to outright acts of violence.
- Buddhist groups filed for official government recognition in 2008, and Hindus in 2013. As of 2020, neither had been granted despite tens of thousands of Buddhists and Hindus in the country.

Christian Traditions in Belgium

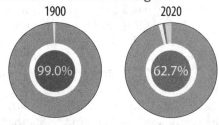

□Independent □Protestant ■Catholic ■Orthodox ■Christian

Despite its proportional decline, Christianity in Belgium has changed very little in its makeup over the last 120 years. In 1900, 99% of Christians were Catholic; by 2020, Catholics dropped only slightly to 95% of Christians. Protestants and Independents made some gains but together were only 4% of Christians. The largest Independent group—and the second largest denomination overall—is the Jehovah's Witnesses, with 51,000 members. The largest Protestant group is the Assemblies of God, with 43,000 members.

Christian Families in Belgium

Family	Population 2020	%	Trend	Change
Latin-rite Catholic	7,000,000	60.2	–	-0.4
*Pentecostals/Charismatics	300,000	2.6	↑	3.7
*Evangelicals	90,000	0.8	↑↑	8.3
Eastern Orthodox	65,500	0.6	–	0.3
Jehovah's Witnesses	48,100	0.4	–	-0.4
United church or joint mission	22,700	0.2	↓↓	-6.6
Latter-day Saints (Mormons)	7,100	0.1	↑	1.6
Anglican	5,200	<0.1	↓↓	-7.1
Nondenominational	4,100	<0.1	↓↓	-6.2
Christian Brethren	4,000	<0.1	↓↓	-5.2
Baptist	2,600	<0.1	–	0.4
Adventist	1,500	<0.1	↓	-4.2
Exclusive Brethren	800	<0.1	↓↓	-7.3
Lutheran	740	<0.1	↓↓	-5.2
Old Catholic Church	600	<0.1	↓	-1.6
Salvationist	520	<0.1	↓↓	-7.3
Restorationist, Disciple	350	<0.1	↓	-1.3

Catholicism is the largest Christian family in Belgium and is poised to remain so for quite some time. Meanwhile, Pentecostal/Charismatic Christianity has been growing. Pentecostals arrived in Belgium in 1909 and planted their first churches by 1930. The Assemblies of God is the oldest classical Pentecostal group, but the country is now home to many newer Independent Charismatic churches, many of which consist primarily of Latin and African immigrants. The largest Protestant church, the Church of God, is almost entirely French-speaking Africans. Evangelicalism grew particularly in the 1970s and 1980s after upheaval in the Catholic Church following the Second Vatican Council in the 1960s. Belgium is home to comparatively small communities of Holiness, Methodist, Adventist, and Baptist Christians.

* These movements are found within Christian families
– no change

↑↑ extreme growth
↑ growth
↓↓ extreme decline
↓ decline

Christianity in Belize

Spanish conquistadores and missionaries first visited Belize in the 16th century. Unlike most of Central America, the territory was colonized by the British as opposed to the Spanish or Portuguese. Belize became an official colony in 1862 after the displacement of the indigenous Mayan peoples. The slave import from other Central American British colonies left its mark on the country, as the largest people group in Belize today are descendants of those enslaved people. Despite the British presence, Catholicism became the primary form of Christianity in Belize due to the migration of peoples from Yucatán, Mexico. Catholic educational programs run by Jesuits and other religious orders brought many converts from Anglican and Methodist churches. In 1981, Belize achieved full independence.

Facts to Consider

- Because of insufficient government funds, churches run most public elementary and high schools. Christians also run many agricultural, medical, and social programs.
- Mennonites arrived in Belize in 1959 and have built up a substantial missionary staff for service and development programs. They live mostly in the western part of the country.
- The Belize Chaplain Services is an interfaith group that engages in several initiatives, including counseling services, prison ministry, and pastoral prayer.
- Most Hindus (7,600 in 2020) trace their lineage to the British colonial period from servants on sugarcane plantations.

Indicators & Demographic Data

Population (2020)	398,000
% under 15 years	30%
Capital city (pop.)	Belmopan 23,000
% urban dwellers	46% (2.30% p.a.)
Official language	English
Largest language	Belize Kriol English (44%)
Largest people	Belizean Black (36%)
Largest culture	Black (African), English-speaking (37%)
Development	71
Physicians	8.3
Gender gap	2%

% Christian: 0 3 10 50 75 100

Christian Traditions in Belize

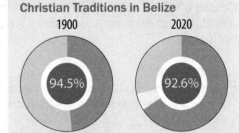

1900 — 94.5% 2020 — 92.6%

☐ Independent ☐ Protestant ▨ Catholic ▧ Orthodox ■ Christian

Christianity in Belize was nearly evenly split between Protestants (52%) and Catholics (48%) in 1900. By 2020, Catholics retained an even larger share of Christians (66%), while Protestants decreased (29%) and Independents increased (6%).

Religion in Belize

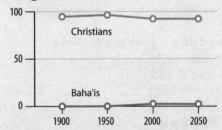

Belize is a majority Christian country and is likely to remain so well into the future (92% in 2050). The second largest religion is the Baha'i Faith, which arrived in 1965 and had 9,400 adherents (2%) in 2020.

Bible Translations		Churches		Missionaries		Gospel Access	
Languages	13	Denominations	44	Received	440	1900	Very high
Full Bible	8	Congregations	1,100	Sent	10	2020	Very high

Christianity in Benin

Portuguese traders brought Christianity to Benin in the late 17th century. By 1830, there were 2,000 Catholics in Dahomey. Mission work in the interior began in 1860, of which the Sisters of Our Lady of Apostles were key in the evangelization and social work in the country, particularly among women, children, and the marginalized. The first Protestants in the country were British Methodists, which is the third largest denomination today. Benin has received missionaries from neighboring Nigeria, including from the Church of the Cherubim and Seraphim. The Celestial Church of Christ was founded in Benin in 1947 and has spread throughout West Africa, with 4.1 million members in Nigeria.

Facts to Consider

- Christianity is concentrated mostly in the South and Islam in the North. Benin is 28% Muslim, of which include the Fulani, Dendi, and Bariba peoples.
- Islamic extremist groups from Mali via Burkina Faso are beginning to enter Benin, particularly near Pendjari National Park in the northwest.
- African Traditional Religion is popular in Benin, especially among women in rural areas.
- Benin is the birthplace of Vodun ("voodoo"), a spiritual practice and way of life based on deities and a divine essence that governs the world. It is pervasive throughout society.
- Catholic leadership in Benin has expressed concern over the mixing of Catholic beliefs and practices with traditional Vodun religion. This is a similar issue among Muslim communities.

Indicators & Demographic Data

Population (2020)	12,123,000
% under 15 years	42%
Capital city (pop.)	Cotonou 692,000; Porto-Novo 269,000
% urban dwellers	48% (3.74% p.a.)
Official language	French
Largest language	Fon (25%)
Largest people	Fon (Fo, Dahomean, Fogbe) (25%)
Largest culture	Fon (44%)
Development	51
Physicians	1.5
Gender gap	12%

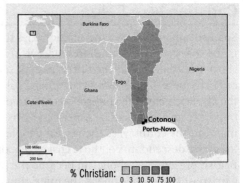

% Christian: 0 3 10 50 75 100

Christian Traditions in Benin

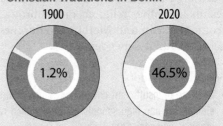

1900 — 1.2%
2020 — 46.5%

☐Independent ☐Protestant ▨Catholic ▤Orthodox ■Christian

Benin's small Christian community in 1900 was mostly Catholic (83%). Today, the country is home to much more Christian diversity, and Christians are 51% Catholic, 26% Independent, and 22% Protestant.

Religion in Benin

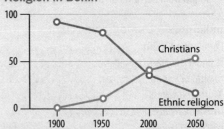

Over the last 120 years, Benin's population of ethnic religionists (African Traditional Religion) dropped substantially as the nation's Christian population increased. In 1900, ethnic religionists were 92% of the population; by 2020, they were 25%.

Bible Translations		Churches		Missionaries		Gospel Access	
Languages	63	Denominations	170	Received	660	1900	Very low
Full Bible	18	Congregations	8,200	Sent	55	2020	High

Christianity in Bermuda

Bermuda is a British Overseas Territory in the North Atlantic Ocean, with a population of roughly 71,000. Though the British encountered no indigenous population upon settling the island in 1609, they brought with them enslaved Africans and enslaved Native Americans from the American colonies. Today the country is 87% Christian, with a tremendous amount of Christian diversity for its size. The Anglican Church of Bermuda is the largest denomination (18% of the country), followed by Catholics (15%), the African Methodist Episcopal Church (12%), and the New Testament Church of God (11%).

Facts to Consider

- Anglicanism was disestablished as the state church in Bermuda in 1974. There is no government ministry or department dealing with churches or religious affairs.
- St. Paul's African Methodist Episcopal Church provided a place for Black Christians to worship during segregation. It helped establish the island's first Black high school in 1892.
- Bermuda is home to St. Peter's Church in St. George's Town, which is the oldest Anglican church in the New World (built in 1612).
- There were virtually zero nonreligious (atheists and agnostics) in 1900, but today they represent nearly 8% of the population.

Christianity in Bhutan

The Kingdom of Bhutan—a small landlocked nation bordered by China, Nepal, and India—is home to over 727,000 people. Christianity is a minority religion in this Buddhist-majority country, comprising only 2% of the population in 2020. Most Christians are of Nepali background and live in the south of the country. Changes in Bhutan's constitution in 2008 allowed Christians more religious freedom, though Christianity is often misunderstood and misrepresented as a religion offering financial gains for converts. Many Catholic and Protestant groups have attempted missionary work in Bhutan, with varying results.

Facts to Consider

- Christianity is technically an illegal religion in Bhutan since the government has not approved registration applications from Christian groups.
- Unregistered groups—including all Christian groups—may worship only in private and are not allowed to own property, import literature, or conduct public activities.
- Christians are consistently blocked from acquiring burial plots and various kinds of professional certifications.
- Converts to Christianity often face pressure to return to their former religion, especially by their own family members.

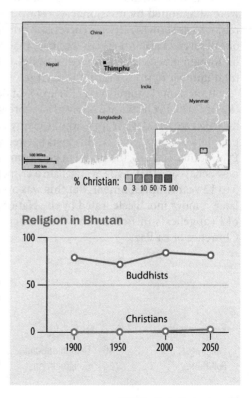

% Christian: 0 3 10 50 75 100

Religion in Bermuda

Religion in Bhutan

Christianity in Bolivia

Christianity first came to Bolivia via the 16th-century Spanish conquest of the Americas. Bolivia became part of the Catholic diocese of Cuzco (Peru) in 1537, when a Christian community was established among the Parias and Charcas. During the 16th and 17th centuries, Franciscans established 17 Indian missions; Jesuits established 31 *reductiones* (cooperative Indian villages) among the Moxos and Chiquitanos before the Society of Jesus was expelled from Spain and its colonies. Bolivia was one of the first Latin American colonies to revolt against Spain yet one of the last to achieve independence (1825). During the war for independence (1809–1825), Catholic bishops generally remained loyal to Spain, while some priests were involved in the rebellion and later elected to the new government. Protestantism arrived at the end of the 19th century.

While the constitution provides for religious freedom, the Catholic Church was recognized as the official church until 2009, and today more than 82% of the population identifies as Catholic. However, as in most other Latin American countries, popular Catholicism is widespread, representing a mixture of 16th-century Spanish Catholicism and the indigenous religions at the time of the Spanish conquest. Regions that remained outside the influence of Christianity or that were abandoned by missionaries retain much of the old religions as shown in their syncretistic practices. Bolivia is one of several Latin American countries that depends heavily on foreign priests. The proportion of Bolivians among the total number of priests is on the decline.

Protestants (*evangélicos*) made up 7% of Bolivia's population in 2020. Protestantism arrived as a foreign religion and faced severe backlash from Catholic clergy and the general population. Some tension still exists between Catholics and Protestants. In 2018, the Bolivian government authorized a new penal code that made evangelism a crime, punishable by 5 to 12 years imprisonment. But this was overturned a year later, a move much celebrated by the National Association of Evangelicals in Bolivia and the Association of United Churches of La Paz.

% Christian: 0 3 10 50 75 100

Religion in Bolivia

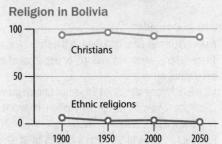

The second largest religion is ethnic religions, or traditional Indian religions. These religions are strongest among the Chiquitano, Guaraní, Guayaru, and Quechua, among whom (especially among the Quechua), however, are also baptized Catholics. Over the 20th century, ethnic religions decreased by half, from 6% in 1900 to just under 3% in 2020.

Indicators & Demographic Data

Population (2020)	11,544,000
% under 15 years	31%
Capital city (pop.)	La Paz 1,858,000; Sucre 272,000
% urban dwellers	70% (1.87% p.a.)
Official language	Spanish and 36 others
Largest language	Spanish (45%)
Largest people	Bolivian Mestizo (37%)
Largest culture	Mestizo (Spanish) (37%)
Development	69
Physicians	4.7
Gender gap	7%

Bible Translations		Churches		Missionaries		Gospel Access	
Languages	46	Denominations	150	Received	4,000	1900	Very high
Full Bible	14	Congregations	10,800	Sent	3,000	2020	Very high

Facts to Consider

- All religious organizations (except the Catholic Church) must register with the government's Ministry of Foreign Affairs. Some small Evangelical groups choose not to register to avoid giving the government access to internal information about their group.
- The Pentecostal/Charismatic movement has grown in Bolivia. A recent report stated that 83% of Protestants had spoken in tongues, prayed for miraculous healing, or engaged in prophesying.
- Many baptized Catholics also continue traditional religious practices and beliefs. Aymara religion, for example, is a mixture of ancient traditional beliefs with later Inca and Catholic additions.
- Although it is majority Christian, Bolivia receives many foreign Protestant missionaries, including from Cru, Scripture Union, Ethnos360, United World Mission, South American Mission, Compassion, Youth With A Mission, and Antioch Mission.
- Over 30 Protestant seminaries and Bible schools in the country are run by groups such as the World Gospel Church, the Langham Partnership, and other local organizations.
- The largest festival in Bolivia is the Carnaval de Oruro, which takes place the Saturday before Ash Wednesday. It was originally an indigenous festival for Andean gods.
- The Baha'i Faith has experienced tremendous growth since their arrival in 1956, now with 2% of the population.

Christian Traditions in Bolivia

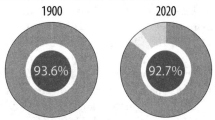

1900   2020

☐Independent ☐Protestant ▨Catholic ▩Orthodox ■Christian

The Catholic share of Bolivia's Christian population dropped from essentially 100% in 1900 to 85% in 2020, but Catholicism remains the largest Christian tradition and will likely remain so for quite some time. Protestants (*evangélicos*) grew dramatically over the same period, from practically zero in 1900 to nearly 10% of Christians in 2020. A recent study found that 88% of the population reported being raised Catholic, but only 77% claimed Catholic identity today. Similarly, 60% of Protestants in Bolivia today were raised Catholic.

Christian Families in Bolivia

Family	Population 2020	%	Trend	Change
Latin-rite Catholic	9,500,000	82.3	↑	1.2
*Pentecostals/Charismatics	1,620,000	14.0	↑	1.9
*Evangelicals	840,000	7.3	↑	3.0
Adventist	241,000	2.1	↑↑	9.1
Nondenominational	218,000	1.9	↑	4.2
Latter-day Saints (Mormons)	212,000	1.8	↑	2.1
Baptist	111,000	1.0	↑	2.7
Holiness	57,400	0.5	↑	2.2
Friends (Quaker)	54,600	0.5	↑	1.1
Jehovah's Witnesses	50,200	0.4	↑	4.2
Lutheran	36,400	0.3	↑	3.4
Christian Brethren	28,700	0.2	↑	1.5
Mennonite	26,100	0.2	↑	4.0
Non-traditional, house, cell	18,500	0.2	↑	2.1
Methodist	18,000	0.2	↑	1.8
Reformed, Presbyterian	8,100	0.1	↑	1.7
Salvationist	6,300	0.1	↑	0.9
Eastern Orthodox	2,700	<0.1	↑	0.8
Restorationist, Disciple	2,500	<0.1	↑↑	5.9
Anglican	1,600	<0.1	↑	0.5

Evangelical and Pentecostal/Charismatic Christianity have grown tremendously in Bolivia. After Catholics, the largest denominations are Assemblies of God (225,000), Church of Jesus Christ of Latter-day Saints (195,000), and Seventh-day Adventists (148,000). The first Pentecostal missionaries were Americans who arrived from Ecuador in 1913 and worked first among the Aymara people then the Quechua. There are now over 1.6 million Pentecostal/Charismatics in the country. Latter-day Saints are especially present in Cochabamba, where one of their largest temples in the world is located. There are five Mormon missions in the country. Adventists run a wide variety of ministries throughout the country, along with the Universidad Adventista de Bolivia, a university in Cochabamba that is one of ten such institutions in South America.

* These movements are found within Christian families
— no change

↑↑ extreme growth
↑ growth
↓↓ extreme decline
↓ decline

Christianity in Bosnia-Herzegovina

In the 4th century, Christianity arrived in modern-day Bosnia-Herzegovina, a region that was on the boundary between the Orthodox East and Catholic West. Nearly all Christians in the country are either Orthodox or Catholic. From the time of World War II until 1992, Bosnia-Herzegovina had been part of Yugoslavia, where people of all religions suffered: places of worship were destroyed and clergy were persecuted. Under Communist rule, the government strictly supervised all church activities. Though religious life was revived in the 1980s, the country subsequently experienced civil war among Orthodox Serbs, Catholic Croats, and Bosnian Muslims that ended with the dissolution of Yugoslavia in 1992. Today, nearly all the Serbs of Bosnia-Herzegovina are Orthodox, and vice versa. Likewise, nearly all the Croats of the country are Catholic, and nearly all the Catholics are Croat.

Facts to Consider

- During World War II, tens of thousands of Muslims were killed in a series of massacres. Islam experienced a revival in the 1950s and 1960s, linking Bosnian ethnic nationalism to Islam.
- Pope Francis promoted interfaith gatherings during his 2015 trip to Sarajevo and encouraged Catholics, Orthodox, and Muslims to leave behind the "deep wounds" of the past.
- The Roma people are often discriminated against in housing, employment, health care, and education.
- Most Jews were deported to concentration camps in World War II, and today the Jewish community is fewer than 400 people.

Indicators & Demographic Data

Population (2020)................................3,498,000
% under 15 years 14%
Capital city (pop.) .... Sarajevo 343,000
% urban dwellers............................. 49% (0.61% p.a.)
Official language..................... Bosnian, Croatian, Serbian
Largest language............................... Bosnian (41%)
Largest people .... Bosniak (Muslimani) (41%)
Largest culture .... Bosnian (41%)
Development...77
Physicians..19
Gender gap..8%

% Christian: 0 3 10 50 75 100

Christian Traditions in Bosnia-Herzegovina

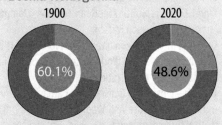

1900 — 60.1% 2020 — 48.6%

☐Independent ☐Protestant ▣Catholic ▪Orthodox ▪Christian

The Orthodox Church has been the majority Christian tradition since the 9th century, though Catholics are a substantial minority. Protestant and Independent Christianity remain quite small.

Religion in Bosnia-Herzegovina

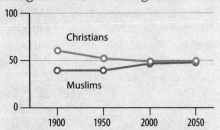

In 1900, Christians were 60% of the population, and Muslims 40%. By 2020, Christianity and Islam were each 48% of the population. Muslims in the country include Bosniaks, Albanians, Turks, and Croats.

Bible Translations		Churches		Missionaries		Gospel Access	
Languages	18	Denominations	26	Received	610	1900	High
Full Bible	12	Congregations	720	Sent	270	2020	High

Christianity in Botswana

The first Christians in Botswana were missionaries from the London Missionary Society in 1816, which founded the United Congregational Church of Southern Africa (2% of the population in 2020). Other Protestant churches include Seventh-day Adventists and Anglicans. However, the main story of Christianity in Botswana is the dramatic growth of African Independent Churches (AICs) in the 20th century, which were virtually nonexistent in 1900 but are now the main type of Christianity. Most of these churches were founded by Africans and for Africans, unlike the mission-founded Protestant churches established by White missionaries. Zion churches are particularly popular, such as the Zion Christian Church of South Africa.

Facts to Consider

- Most Christians are Pentecostal/Charismatic in worship and theology. The Assemblies of God is the largest Protestant Pentecostal denomination (1% of the population).
- AICs are involved in various kinds of social work, including poverty eradication and health care. Healing ministries are also prominent.
- Botswana has one of the highest HIV/AIDS rates in the world, with women and youth disproportionately affected. Many churches and Christian organizations have health care ministries to address this epidemic and other issues like malaria and tuberculosis.
- Independent churches give more freedoms to women than the historic Protestant churches. Pentecostalism's tremendous growth since 1980 has been accompanied by an increase in ordained women in classical Pentecostal churches as well as women breaking away to establish new churches.

Indicators & Demographic Data

Population (2020)................................. 2,416,000
% under 15 years 31%
Capital city (pop.)........................... Gaborone 253,000
% urban dwellers............................. 71% (2.47% p.a.)
Official language.......................................English
Largest language..............................Setswana (73%)
Largest people .... Ngwato Tswana (27%)
Largest culture ....Tswana (76%)
Development... 72
Physicians... 3.8
Gender gap...2%

% Christian: ▢▢▨▨▨ 0 3 10 50 75 100

Christian Traditions in Botswana

1900   2020

14.3%   71.6%

▢Independent ▢Protestant ▨Catholic ▨Orthodox ▨Christian

The very small Christian community in 1900 was largely Protestant (99% of Christians). By 2020, Independents became the majority Christian tradition, representing 66% of Botswana's Christian population.

Religion in Botswana

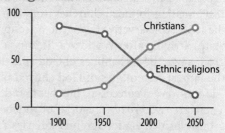

Christians and followers of African Traditional Religions had mirroring trends in the 20th century. In 1900, ethnic religions were 86% but by 2020 had dropped to 27%. Christianity grew from 14% to 72%.

Bible Translations	Churches	Missionaries	Gospel Access
Languages............40	Denominations 310	Received............440	1900 ....Very low
Full Bible.............17	Congregations......3,700	Sent 90	2020 ....Very high

Christianity in Brazil

The first Christians arrived in modern-day Brazil around 1500, after Pope Alexander VI gave Portugal authority over the land in 1493. The Portuguese tried to enslave indigenous people, but most of them fled inland or died. Brazil's indigenous population was initially over 3 million; today it is less than 200,000. Four million enslaved Africans were imported to Brazil from the mid-16th century to 1888, when slavery was abolished. Brazil was the destination for 40% of all enslaved people brought to the Americas. Today most Brazilians are of mixed-race ancestry that blend European ethnicities, descendants of enslaved Africans, and the indigenous peoples of the Americas.

Brazil is a remarkable country when it comes to its Christianity. It is home to the second largest Christian population in the world (194 million), the largest Catholic population (150 million), the most Pentecostals (24 million), and the most Charismatics (62 million). Catholicism in Brazil is not monolithic, but rather is found in three streams: the traditional/historical church, the Catholic Charismatic Renewal (CCR), and popular Catholicism. The traditional church represents the extensive network of seminaries, schools, and Brazilian religious congregations. The CCR arrived in Brazil in 1969, and in 2014, 58% of Brazilian Catholics identified as charismatics. Popular Catholicism includes a wide variety of beliefs and practices that are at most only loosely associated with the institutional Catholic Church. Protestants include immigrant communities that arrived in 1810, mission-founded churches from North America since the 1850s, conservative Evangelical groups from the United States arriving after World War II, missionary Pentecostal groups like the Assemblies of God (Brazil is now home to the largest Assemblies of God church in the world), and "second-wave" Pentecostal churches founded from the 1950s. There are two broad categories of Independents in Brazil: groups formed via foreign missionaries and those that are indigenous to Brazil. The Brazil-founded Universal Church of the Kingdom of God (UCKG) is the largest Independent denomination and the third largest denomination overall, after Catholics and the Assemblies of God. The UCKG has a significant missionary outreach and was present in 129 countries in 2019.

% Christian: 0 3 10 50 75 100

Religion in Brazil

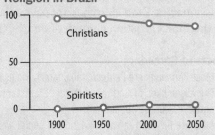

Brazil is the only country in the world where Spiritism is the second largest religion (5%). These traditions typically mix Catholicism with African and Amerindian religions; such as Candomblé, Umbanda, and Kardecism. Women have central roles as institutional and ritual leaders in many Afro-Brazilian religions, especially Candomblé, and make up half of practitioners of Umbanda and Candomblé.

Indicators & Demographic Data

Population (2020). 213,863,000
% under 15 years 21%
Capital city (pop.) . . . . Brasília 4,646,000
% urban dwellers. . . . . 87% (0.87% p.a.)
Official language. . . . . Portuguese
Largest language. . . . . Portuguese (98%)
Largest people . . . . Brazilian White (51%)
Largest culture . . . Latin-American White (51%)
Development. 76
Physicians. 19
Gender gap 1%

Bible Translations	Churches	Missionaries	Gospel Access
Languages. 197	Denominations 1,600	Received. 20,000	1900 . . . . Very high
Full Bible. 31	Congregations. . . . 300,000	Sent 40,000	2020 . . . . Very high

Facts to Consider

- Independent and Protestant Christianity are largely growing at the expense of Catholicism. One in five Brazilians are former Catholics. Many switched out of a desire to have a more personal connection with God.
- Pentecostal/Charismatic Christianity grew tremendously over the 20th century and now represents 50% of the population. In a recent survey, 72% of Protestants and 31% of Catholics reported to have witnessed a divine healing.
- Gender relations are generally conservative in Brazilian culture, and patriarchal hierarchies remain influential. Yet in popular Catholicism, women make up the majority of practitioners, and many rituals are led exclusively by women.
- Catholics, Protestants, and even the religiously unaffiliated report some beliefs associated with Afro-Caribbean, Afro-Brazilian, or indigenous religions, such as the evil eye.
- The UCKG is Evangelical-Pentecostal in theology and worship and holds traditional views of Spirit baptism, supernatural gifts, water baptism, and the Lord's Supper. The church has been accused of numerous illegal activities, including financial fraud and illegal adoption.
- Roughly 20,000 missionaries serving are from Brazil, with a growing number working among Muslims in North Africa.

Christian Traditions in Brazil

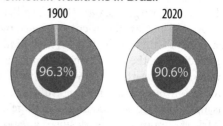

1900 — 96.3% 2020 — 90.6%

☐ Independent ☐ Protestant ▨ Catholic ■ Orthodox ■ Christian

Christianity in Brazil has become far more diverse since the start of the 20th century. In 1900, Brazil was 96% Christian and 99% were Catholic. By 2020, Catholics' share of all Christians had dropped to 72%. Protestants and Independents grew rapidly over this period, and together they represented 28% of Christians in 2020. However, Christianity as a whole has declined slightly, from 96% in 1900 to 91% in 2020.

Christian Families in Brazil

Family	Population 2020	%	Trend	Change
Latin-rite Catholic	146,905,000	68.7	–	0.1
*Pentecostals/Charismatics	108,000,000	50.5	↑	0.6
*Evangelicals	29,000,000	13.6	–	0.0
Eastern-rite Catholic	3,095,000	1.4	↑	0.8
Baptist	2,866,000	1.3	↑	4.3
Adventist	2,433,000	1.1	↑	4.5
Jehovah's Witnesses	2,112,000	1.0	↑	2.3
Latter-day Saints (Mormons)	1,513,000	0.7	↑	2.9
Lutheran	1,005,000	0.5	↑	0.6
Reformed, Presbyterian	612,000	0.3	–	-0.4
Methodist	566,000	0.3	↑	3.0
Old Catholic Church	528,000	0.2	↓	-0.6
Eastern Orthodox	229,000	0.1	↑	1.8
Congregational	205,000	0.1	↑	2.2
Holiness	170,000	0.1	↓	-0.9
Restorationist, Disciple	145,000	0.1	↑	3.5
Anglican	135,000	0.1	↑	2.1
Nondenominational	99,500	<0.1	↑	1.8
Christian Brethren	86,900	<0.1	↑	1.4
Oriental and other Orthodox	31,100	<0.1	↑	1.1
Mennonite	13,100	<0.1	–	0.5
Salvationist	3,900	<0.1	↓	-0.7

The main stories of Christianity in Brazil are its diverse Catholic majority and the explosive growth of Pentecostalism that has affected both Catholicism and Protestantism alike. Brazil is also home to large populations of Baptists; the Baptist Convention of Brazil alone has over 2 million members. Adventists are largely Seventh-day Adventists who arrived in 1902 and have 1.9 million members today. They have been particularly successful due to their use of radio and correspondence courses. The Church of Jesus Christ of Latter-day Saints (Mormons) began among German immigrants in the 1920s and have 1.3 million members. Numbers are declining for the historic Protestant denominations even though the membership of these churches is large compared with other Latin American countries. Their growth has not kept pace with the enormous increase in Pentecostalism.

* These movements are found within Christian families
– no change
↑↑ extreme growth
↑ growth
↓↓ extreme decline
↓ decline

Christianity in the British Virgin Islands

The British Virgin Islands (BVI) is a British Overseas Territory in the Caribbean consisting of over 50 islands, the largest of which is Tortola. With possibly no indigenous population on the islands when Europeans arrived, the Dutch were the first settlers in 1648, followed by the British, who took control soon after. As a result, most inhabitants of the islands today are descendants of the large numbers of enslaved Africans imported to work sugarcane plantations. The BVI is a majority Christian territory, with the Methodist Church its largest denomination, representing 19% of the country.

Facts to Consider

- There is no established church in the territory, and freedom of religion has been the norm.
- Primary and secondary education systems require religious instruction and daily worship in government-funded public and private schools.
- St. Phillip's Anglican Church, also known as the "African Church" in Kingstown, was built by formerly enslaved people in 1840.
- Hurricane Irma struck the islands in 2017, causing widespread damage and four deaths.
- There is a small population of the Baha'i Faith on the islands, but they have no formal organization.

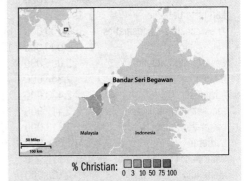

% Christian: 0 3 10 50 75 100

Religion in the British Virgin Islands

Christianity in Brunei

Brunei is a small country on the island of Borneo in Southeast Asia, completely surrounded by the Malaysian state of Sarawak. The country is majority Muslim (59%), followed by Christians (12%), then traditional religionists (10%) and Buddhists (9%). Brunei achieved independence in 1984 after being a British protectorate since 1888. Most Christians in the country are migrant workers from elsewhere in Southeast Asia. Besides migrant workers, Christians are also found among the Chinese population. Filipinos are the third largest people group in the country and are mostly Christian (Catholic).

Facts to Consider

- The adoption of Sharia law in 2014 put many restrictions on Christian activities, including a ban on the public celebration of Christmas. Christians are also forbidden to spread Christianity, import Bibles, and marry outside their religion.
- In 2018, the government implemented additional phases of Sharia law, including punishments such as stoning to death, amputation of hands or feet, and caning.
- Conversion from Islam is illegal. Christian converts face ostracism by their friends, family, and community, with pressure to recant. They might even be forced to divorce and lose custody of their children.

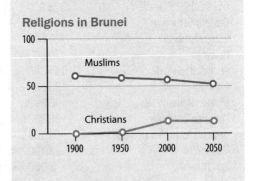

% Christian: 0 3 10 50 75 100

Religions in Brunei

Christianity in Bulgaria

Bulgaria has been an independent Christian nation with its own autocephalous Eastern Orthodox church since the year 927—that is, a church not subject to external leadership. Orthodoxy was the recognized and dominant religion in Bulgaria from 1879 to 1947, after which the Communist constitution was adopted, and under the occupation of the Soviet Union, the Bulgarian Orthodox Church ceased being the state religion. In 1989, the Communist Party allowed a multiparty election that led to Bulgaria's transition into a democracy and the reinstatement of the Bulgarian Orthodox Church. Since the fall of Communism in 1991, Orthodoxy has once again been equated with Bulgarian identity.

Catholics originate from missionaries sent to the Balkans from the 9th to 14th centuries. Today the majority of Bulgarian Catholics are descendants of Bogomils converted to Catholicism by Franciscans in the 17th century. In the early years of Communist rule, specifically 1946 to 1948, the church lost all its institutions and, apart from a few sanctuaries, all its possessions, buildings, schools, and orphanages. Foreign religious personnel and priests were expelled in 1948; most of the others were arrested and sentenced, and many died in prison. Nevertheless, the Catholic Church survived, despite further difficulties that included the material poverty and aging of priests and continual pressures to prevent church attendance and baptism of infants.

American Congregationalists, American Methodists, Russian Baptists, and Russian Seventh-day Adventists introduced Protestantism in the 19th century. As in many post-Soviet states, Western Evangelical and Pentecostal missionaries visited Bulgaria after the fall of the Soviet Union. Churches begun from these missions grew quickly in the 1990s, but growth has since leveled off. Orthodox are generally suspicious of non-Orthodox Christians. Russians established Pentecostal Christianity in the 1920s, and it grew to 2% of the population by 2020. Pentecostalism rapidly grew among the Roma population after 1989. Most Roma Christians belong to three main Pentecostal denominations: the Union of Evangelical Pentecostal Churches, the Bulgarian Church of God, and the United Church of God.

% Christian: 0 3 10 50 75 100

Religion in Bulgaria

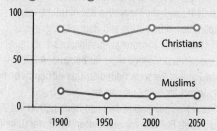

Islam is the second largest religion in Bulgaria, though the population dropped from 17% in 1900 to 14% in 2020. The Muslim population includes Turks, Roma, and ethnic Bulgarians known as Pomaks. Along with Christians, Muslims were suppressed under Communism and suffered severe attacks from atheist propaganda. Today, Turks are often looked at with suspicion.

Indicators & Demographic Data

Population (2020). 6,941,000
% under 15 years 15%
Capital city (pop.) . . . . Sofia 1,281,000
% urban dwellers. . . . . 76% (-0.28% p.a.)
Official language. . . . . Bulgarian
Largest language. . . . . Bulgarian (87%)
Largest people . . . . .Bulgar (81%)
Largest culture . . . . Bulgar (83%)
Development. 81
Physicians. 40
Gender gap. 1%

Bible Translations	Churches	Missionaries	Gospel Access
Languages. 26	Denominations 53	Received. 220	1900 . . . . Very high
Full Bible. 19	Congregations. 6,200	Sent 120	2020 . . . . Very high

Facts to Consider

- The constitution names Eastern Orthodoxy as the country's traditional religion and the Bulgarian Orthodox Church (BOC) as a legal entity, exempt from registration.
- All religious groups except the BOC must register with the government to receive funding and the right to own property, run schools and hospitals, and engage in other activities. Some Evangelical groups have reported not receiving appropriate funds despite being properly registered.
- Many municipalities have local ordinances banning door-to-door proselytizing and distribution of religious literature. These rules have particularly affected Jehovah's Witnesses.
- Nearly all Bulgarians are exposed to Protestant/Independent Christianity through the innovative use of tracts, magazines, the internet, and television in Bulgarian and Romani languages.
- It is not easy for foreign missionaries and religious leaders to obtain and renew residence visas for Bulgaria. A 2001 amendment to the Law on Foreign Persons added to this difficulty by not providing a clear category for religious workers.
- The Jewish population declined from 32,000 in 1900 to 3,500 in 2020; most left Bulgaria for Israel after World War II. In 2018, the first Jewish school in 20 years opened in Sofia. Nevertheless, anti-Semitic rhetoric continues online and in the mainstream press, while anti-Semitic graffiti continues to appear in public places.

Christian Traditions in Bulgaria

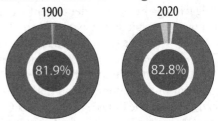

1900 — 81.9%
2020 — 82.8%

☐Independent ☐Protestant ◾Catholic ◾Orthodox ◾Christian

Bulgaria has been a majority Orthodox country for many centuries, even though the Orthodox share of Christians dropped from 99% in 1900 to 95% in 2020. Protestantism grew slowly over the same period, from hardly any in 1900 to 2% of Christians in 2020. Evangelical and Pentecostal/Charismatic Christianity continue to be minorities, but are experiencing some growth. From less than 1% of the country's population in 1900, Evangelicals grew to just under 2% in 2020, and 2.2% of all Christians. Pentecostal/Charismatics are 2.8% of all Christians.

Christian Families in Bulgaria

Family	Population 2020	%	Trend	Change
Eastern Orthodox	5,587,000	80.5	↓	-0.8
*Pentecostals/Charismatics	160,000	2.3	↑	1.5
*Evangelicals	125,000	1.8	↑	1.1
Latin-rite Catholic	63,000	0.9	—	0.0
Oriental and other Orthodox	33,300	0.5	↑	2.1
Eastern-rite Catholic	10,000	0.1	—	0.0
Christian Brethren	9,600	0.1	↑	1.2
Adventist	7,800	0.1	↓	-0.6
Congregational	6,300	0.1	—	0.1
Jehovah's Witnesses	6,100	0.1	↑↑	5.4
Baptist	5,500	0.1	↓	-0.6
Latter-day Saints (Mormons)	2,800	<0.1	↑	2.4
Methodist	2,300	<0.1	—	0.1
Holiness	530	<0.1	↑	0.5

Compared to other countries around the world, Christianity in Bulgaria is not very diverse given the country's long history with the Bulgarian Orthodox Church, which represents 81% of the population. Catholics make up 1% of the population, and there are many smaller Protestant and Independent denominations present, none of which are growing significantly. The largest Pentecostal/Charismatic groups are the Church of God (Cleveland), the Pentecostal Assemblies of Bulgaria (with links to the Assemblies of God in the United States), and the Church of God Union (indigenous to Bulgaria). Many Pentecostal groups are also 100% Evangelical. Other Orthodox groups in the country include Armenians, Romanians, Albanians, and Greeks.

* These movements are found within Christian families	↑↑	extreme growth
	↑	growth
	↓↓	extreme decline
— no change	↓	decline

Christianity in Burkina Faso

Burkina Faso is a Muslim-majority country (56%). French White Fathers (a Catholic religious order) arrived in Ouagadougou in 1901, and the White Sisters arrived in 1911. France's invasion and colonial conquest of modern-day Burkina Faso spanned from 1896 to 1904. The first indigenous Black Sisters formed in 1922, and the first indigenous priests were ordained in 1942. Catholics were active in education and have had a lasting influence as a result. The Pentecostal/Charismatic movement has grown to nearly 10% of the country's population, primarily due to the work of Assemblies of God (AoG) missionaries in 1921. The AoG achieved indigenous autonomy in 1955 and is active in primary and secondary education, missionary sending, and Bible schools.

Facts to Consider

- The country's armed forces appear unable to prevent terrorist attacks as they escalate against Protestants, Catholics, and even Muslims. In June 2021, jihadists attacked a village in Solhan and killed at least 138 people, causing thousands of people to flee.
- In April 2019, gunmen executed a pastor and several other worshipers in a Protestant church when they refused to renounce Jesus. In May 2019, six people, including a priest, were murdered during Mass at a Catholic church.
- Both Catholics and Protestants are highly active in education and health care, given a lack of these services provided by the government. Many schools have been forced to close because of violence, denying 330,000 children an education in 2018 alone.
- Traditional religions are prominent among the Lobi, Lele, Dagaaba, Kurumba, and Marka people groups.

Indicators & Demographic Data

Population (2020). 20,903,000
% under 15 years 44%
Capital city (pop.) . . . . Ouagadougou 2,780,000
% urban dwellers. . . . . 31% (4.75% p.a.)
Official language. . . . . .French
Largest language. . . . . Mòoré (37%)
Largest people . . . . Mossi (Moshi) (35%)
Largest culture . . . . Central Bantoid (Voltaic) (64%)
Development. 42
Physicians. 0.5
Gender gap. 13%

% Christian: 0 3 10 50 75 100

Christian Traditions in Burkina Faso

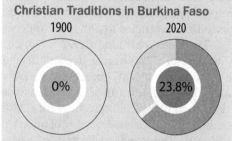

1900: 0% 2020: 23.8%

☐Independent ☐Protestant ▨Catholic ▦Orthodox ■Christian

Burkina Faso is one of the few places in the world that had no Christians in 1900. By 2020, 24% of the population was Christian. Most Christians are Catholic (64%) or Protestant (35%).

Religion in Burkina Faso

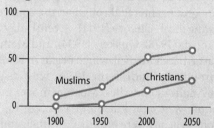

Burkina Faso is majority Muslim and, despite the modest growth of Christianity, is likely to remain so into the future. African Traditional Religions declined from 90% of the population in 1900 to 20% in 2020, making it the third largest religion.

Bible Translations	Churches	Missionaries	Gospel Access
Languages. 79	Denominations 69	Received. 1,000	1900 . . . . .Very low
Full Bible. 16	Congregations. 13,900	Sent 40	2020 . . . . .High

Christianity in Burundi

Modern-day Burundi was once German East Africa, colonized by the Germans after European nations carved up the African continent for land and trade at the Berlin Conference in 1884. Belgian troops from the Congo occupied the country in 1916, and German missions were forced to close after World War I. In 1923, Belgium received a League of Nations mandate to administer Ruanda-Urundi. But because Belgian Protestant missions were too few to meet the request to take over German missions, other Protestant groups were allowed to enter. There were hardly any Protestant Christians at the start of Belgian colonial rule (1916), but Catholicism spread during the interwar period and continued to grow after independence in 1962.

The Hutu rebellion in 1972–1973, known as the Ikiza ("catastrophe," "scourge"), deeply affected Christianity in Burundi, where 100,000 (some estimates are as high as 300,000) were killed, including 18 priests, seven male and female religious personnel, 2,100 catechists (of 4,580) and teachers in Catholic schools, a large number of nurses and Hutu medical assistants, thousands of Protestant pastors and teachers, and a major portion of the Hutu elite. This event sparked a mass exodus of mostly Hutus from the country to Rwanda, Tanzania, and Zaire (now the Democratic Republic of the Congo). Although it is debated, the Ikiza is sometimes referred to as the first documented genocide in postcolonial Africa.

Today the Catholic Church is the largest denomination in Burundi, with nearly 6.5 million members. Various Protestant groups entered throughout the 20th century, such as the Evangelical Alliance (1911), Seventh-day Adventists (1921), Baptists (1928), Quakers (1934), and Methodists (1935). The East African Revival, which began in Rwanda in 1927, swept through Burundi in the 1930s, with its greatest influence in Anglican churches. Most members were Tutsi, many of whom were later killed in tribal fighting. The first indigenous deacons were ordained in 1955, and the first Burundi bishop was consecrated in 1965.

The National Council of Churches of Burundi formed in 1989 with many members, including Anglicans, Methodists, and Kimbanguists. Inter-church cooperation has provided opportunities to speak out against human rights abuses, engage in humanitarian aid, and positively work with the national government.

% Christian: 0 3 10 50 75 100

Religion in Burundi

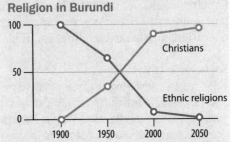

Christians and followers of African Traditional Religions had mirroring trends in the 20th century. In 1900, ethnic religionists were nearly 100% of the population but by 2020 had dropped to less than 4%. In contrast, while Christians in Burundi at the start of the 20th century numbered near zero, they now comprise the majority of its population (94%). The Twa pygmies are majority traditionalist.

Indicators & Demographic Data

Population (2020)	11,939,000
% under 15 years	45%
Capital city (pop.)	Bujumbura 1,013,000
% urban dwellers	14% (5.43% p.a.)
Official language	Rundi, French
Largest language	Rundi (96%)
Largest people	Hutu (81%)
Largest culture	Interlacustrine Bantu (97%)
Development	42
Physicians	0.3
Gender gap	0%

Bible Translations		Churches		Missionaries		Gospel Access	
Languages	12	Denominations	86	Received	1,200	1900	Very low
Full Bible	9	Congregations	12,900	Sent	170	2020	Very high

Facts to Consider

- Christian churches have been instrumental in building the educational system in Burundi. For example, Methodists established the largest private university in the country in 2000: Hope Africa University.
- Women make up 55% of Burundi's workforce, particularly in agriculture. Yet women and girls traditionally do not inherit land from their fathers, facing triple discrimination of tradition, law, and gender.
- HIV/AIDS is a leading cause of death in Burundi, but the country has made remarkable progress in controlling the disease, with new infections on the decline. Yet the Catholic Church and many Pentecostal churches were initially hesitant to address the HIV/AIDS crisis in the country, believing it to be a moral problem, not a health problem.
- Both the Hutu and Tutsi populations generally despise the Twa people. Many Christian organizations work among the Twa in education, health care, and economic opportunities.
- Burundi is 2% Muslim, most of whom live in urban areas, especially Bujumbura. Eid al-Fitr and Eid al-Adha are national holidays alongside Christian holidays.

Christian Traditions in Burundi

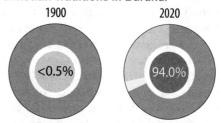

1900   2020

<0.5%   94.0%

☐Independent ☐Protestant ▨Catholic ■Orthodox ■Christian

The small handful of Christians present in modern-day Burundi were entirely Catholic in 1900. Today most Christians are Catholic (69%), followed by Protestants (27%). Protestantism is diverse, with large populations of Pentecostals (2 million), Anglicans (1.3 million), Adventists (180,000), and Baptists (151,000). Unlike in many other countries in sub-Saharan Africa, Independent Christianity remains comparatively small, with only 4% of Christians in 2020.

Christian Families in Burundi

Family	Population 2020	%	Trend	Change
Latin-rite Catholic	7,577,000	63.5	↑	3.1
*Evangelicals	2,120,000	17.8	↑	3.8
*Pentecostals/Charismatics	2,000,000	16.8	↑	3.5
Anglican	1,276,000	10.7	↑	4.1
Holiness	240,000	2.0	↑	4.5
Adventist	180,000	1.5	–	-0.5
Baptist	151,000	1.3	↑↑	9.0
Methodist	114,000	1.0	↑	2.9
Friends (Quaker)	49,600	0.4	↑	3.5
Christian Brethren	48,200	0.4	↑	3.0
Jehovah's Witnesses	18,000	0.2	↑	2.0
Eastern Orthodox	2,000	<0.1	↑	1.6

There were hardly any Protestant Christians at the start of Belgian colonial rule in 1923, but Catholicism spread during the interwar period and continued to grow after independence in 1962. Today the country is 94% Christian and majority Catholic (64% of the country's population). Despite the relatively recent arrival of Protestantism, the country is home to many different groups. The largest Protestant group in the country (besides Anglicans) is the Community of Pentecostal Churches in Burundi. Other Pentecostal groups include Kimbanguists, the Pentecostal Evangelical Fellowship of Africa (from East Africa), the United Church of the Holy Spirit, and the Assemblies of God (from the USA). However, most of the Charismatics in the country are Anglican or Catholic.

* These movements are found within Christian families	↑↑ extreme growth
	↑ growth
	↓↓ extreme decline
– no change	↓ decline

Christianity in Cabo Verde

Cabo Verde is an island nation off the coast of West Africa. Portuguese explorers arrived on the uninhabited island in the 15th century, followed soon after by Catholic clergy. The slave trade became an important part of Cabo Verde's economy due to its strategic location in the Atlantic Ocean. The islands achieved independence from Portugal in 1975. The government and the Vatican signed an agreement in 2011 that allowed the formal establishment of Catholic schools and gave the church greater influence in society. Bishop Arlindo Gomes Furtado became the first cardinal from Cabo Verde in 2015. Protestant groups include Seventh-day Adventists, Church of the Nazarene, and Assemblies of God.

Facts to Consider

- Portuguese is the major language of Cabo Verde, making it a destination for Brazilian missionaries. Two Brazilian-founded denominations are the God is Love Church and the Universal Church of the Kingdom of God.
- All religious and secular associations must register with the Ministry of Justice to operate. Religious groups must have notarized signatures of 500 members to legally begin public activities. Baptists and some Brazilian groups have had trouble meeting this threshold to purchase land, establish schools, and import supplies.
- The Church of Jesus Christ of Latter-day Saints (Mormons) is the second largest denomination in the country, with 2% of the population.
- Traditional African religions have some adherents among the Balanta and the Mandyak people groups.

Indicators & Demographic Data

Population (2020) 567,000
% under 15 years 29%
Capital city (pop.) . . . . Praia 158,000
% urban dwellers. . . . . 69% (1.57% p.a.)
Official language. . . . . Portuguese
Largest language. . . . . .Kabuverdianu (69%)
Largest people . . . . Caboverdian Mestico (45%)
Largest culture . . . . Eurafrican (69%)
Development. 61
Physicians. 3
Gender gap. 14%

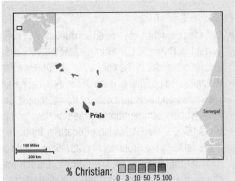

% Christian: 0 3 10 50 75 100

Christian Traditions in Cabo Verde

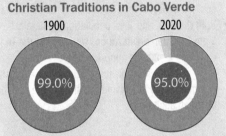

1900 — 99.0%
2020 — 95.0%

☐Independent ☐Protestant ◼Catholic ◼Orthodox ◼Christian

Cabo Verde has always been a Catholic-majority country, representing 100% of Christians in 1900. The Catholic share of Christians dropped to 89% in 2020 with the increase of Independents and Protestants (together 11% in 2020).

Religion in Cabo Verde

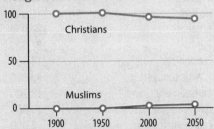

Christianity remains the largest religion in Cabo Verde and is likely to remain so in the future (93% Christian in 2050). Islam is the second largest religion; Muslims were less than 3% of the population in 2020.

Bible Translations	Churches	Missionaries	Gospel Access
Languages. 6	Denominations 12	Received. 120	1900 . . . . Very high
Full Bible. 1	Congregations. 370	Sent 90	2020 . . . . Very high

Christianity in Cambodia

Catholics were the first Christians to enter modern-day Cambodia, with Jesuits and Dominicans arriving in 1555. However, today, most Christians in Cambodia are Protestants or Independents due to missionary work throughout the 20th century. Protestants arrived after World War I. The violence and genocide of Pol Pot and the Khmer Rouge (1975–1979) at the end of the Cambodian Civil War mark Cambodia's history and therefore its churches. During the Khmer Rouge, upward of one-third of the population (2 million people) died from starvation, disease, forced labor, or executions. Virtually all Christians were killed during this period, yet by 1997, churches were again growing, and by 2020, Cambodia was 3% Christian.

Facts to Consider

- Buddhism (Theravada) is the largest religion in the country, with 85% of the population.
- The largest Christian denomination in the country is the International Church of the Foursquare Gospel, which entered Cambodia in 1995 via an orphanage care ministry. Care for orphans and victims of sex trafficking are prominent ministries among Christians.
- Two-thirds of Catholics in the country are Vietnamese, and many church services are held in both Cambodian and Vietnamese languages. The church is still reliant on foreign members of religious orders while indigenous leaders are trained.
- Cambodia is home to hundreds of Christian NGOs working in education, medical care, and rural development. Approximately 60% of churches in Cambodia have a partnership with a Christian NGO.

Indicators & Demographic Data

Population (2020). 16,716,000
% under 15 years 31%
Capital city (pop.) . . . . Phnom Penh 2,078,000
% urban dwellers. . . . . .24% (3.06% p.a.)
Official language. . . . . Khmer
Largest language. . . . . Khmer (90%)
Largest people . . . . Central Khmer (Cambodian) (89%)
Largest culture . . . . Khmer (89%)
Development. 58
Physicians. 1.4
Gender gap. 9%

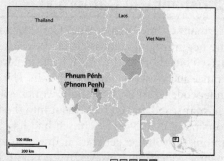

% Christian: 0 3 10 50 75 100

Christian Traditions in Cambodia

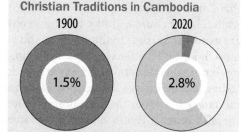

1900 — 1.5%
2020 — 2.8%

☐ Independent ☐ Protestant ☐ Catholic ◼ Orthodox ◼ Christian

The small Christian community in 1900 was entirely Catholic. In 2020, Catholics were only 5% of Christians, with Protestants at 58% and Independents at 37%.

Religion in Cambodia

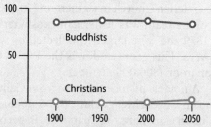

Cambodia's Buddhist population has remained relatively stable from 1900 to today and is expected to remain so into the future (84% in 2050). Christianity has grown as a proportion of the population, but only slightly, from 1.5% in 1900 to just under 3% in 2020.

Bible Translations	Churches	Missionaries	Gospel Access
Languages. 34	Denominations 240	Received. 340	1900 . . . . Very low
Full Bible. 13	Congregations. 7,400	Sent 10	2020 . . . . Medium

Christianity in Cameroon

Germany claimed modern-day Cameroon in 1884, marking the beginning of colonial rule. After the Germans were driven out after World War I, East Cameroon was given to France and West Cameroon to Britain. The country achieved independence in 1960. Catholic work began in 1890 via the Germans, and a mass movement into the Catholic Church took place in 1934. The church had its greatest influence among the younger generation, due to its extensive involvement in education. However, it was not until Pope John Paul II's visits to the country in August 1985 and September 1995 that Cameroonian bishops emphasized the need for Africanization of the church. Today, fewer and fewer missionaries are expected to come to the country, and local priests staff most dioceses. The church is also decreasingly dependent on foreign financial support. Efforts are made to incorporate indigenous languages and traditions, as well as to address human rights issues in the region. Former Archbishop of Douala Christian Tumi was widely considered a national icon for his outspoken criticisms of the government. In March 2016, at 86 years old, he called for President Paul Biya to step down. Biya has been serving as president since 1982 and continues being "re-elected," though many international observers suspect fraud and voting irregularities.

Presbyterians in Cameroon have two historical sources. The first was British Baptist missions that were turned over to the Germans in 1884, from which has descended the Presbyterian Church in Cameroon (700,000 members). The second stream was American Presbyterians who arrived in 1879 and were largely unaffected by warring European powers. This group today is the Presbyterian Church of Cameroon (800,000 members).

A notable historical figure from Cameroonian Protestantism is Lydia Mengwelune (1886–1966), one of the first 80 Bamoun Christians to be baptized. In becoming a Christian, she lost both her position of influence in the king's court and her husband. Together, she and Swiss missionary Anna Wuhrmann counseled women, evangelized, and encouraged dialogue among Christians, Muslims, and adherents of traditional religions. Generations of Christians have multiplied because of Mengwelune's ministry.

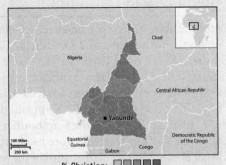

% Christian: 0 3 10 50 75 100

Religion in Cameroon

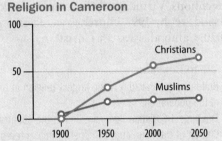

Cameroon is a very religious country, and 95% of the population followed traditional religions in 1900. But with the rapid growth of Christianity and Islam in the 20th century, by 2020, the country was 61% Christian and 21% Muslim. It is likely both will continue to grow into the future with the continued decline of traditional religions.

Indicators & Demographic Data

Population (2020)	25,958,000
% under 15 years	42%
Capital city (pop.)	Yaoundé 3,992,000
% urban dwellers	58% (3.43% p.a.)
Official language	French, English
Largest language	Cameroon Pidgin (14%)
Largest people	Cameroonian Creole (14%)
Largest culture	Highland Bantu (26%)
Development	56
Physicians	0.8
Gender gap	13%

Bible Translations		Churches		Missionaries		Gospel Access	
Languages	289	Denominations	390	Received	3,500	1900	Very low
Full Bible	29	Congregations	30,000	Sent	440	2020	Very high

Facts to Consider

- President Paul Biya is the second-longest running president in Africa and the oldest head of state in Africa at 89 years old. He is strongly opposed by the English-speaking population, and his administration has clear authoritarian characteristics.
- French and English are the official languages of Cameroon, but ethno-linguistic tensions exist within its churches and its society in general.
- The Catholic Church in Cameroon runs the country's largest network of schools and hospitals and is remarkably active. Weekly attendance at Sunday Mass is extraordinarily high, at least 70%.
- Africanization of the churches in Cameroon was slower than in neighboring countries, partly due to the large-scale absence of African Independent Churches.
- Pentecostal Christianity grew rapidly in the 1990s with the democratization of the country, providing the first real pushback against historic Catholic and Protestant churches. Pentecostal and Evangelical groups are often antagonistic toward the historic churches and traditional religions.
- Beginning in 2013, around 100 Pentecostal churches have been shut down, having been cited as "threats to social peace."
- The Islamic terrorist group Boko Haram is increasingly active in northern Cameroon, which is majority Muslim and is served by many missionaries and priests. Schools are routinely closed along its Nigerian border to protect children and teachers from attacks.

Christian Traditions in Cameroon

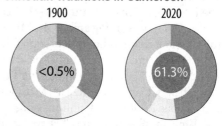

☐Independent ☐Protestant ▨Catholic ■Orthodox ■Christian

The small Christian population in Cameroon in 1900 was a mix of Protestant (52%) and Catholic (35%) Western missionaries who arrived in the mid-to-late 19th century. As indigenous churches grew, the Catholic Church became the majority tradition in the country, representing 48% of Christians in 2020. Protestants (41% of Christians) are mostly Reformed/Presbyterian, Lutherans, Baptists, and Adventists. Independent Christianity is growing and was 11% of Christians in 2020.

Christian Families in Cameroon

Family	Population 2020	%	Trend	Change
Latin-rite Catholic	7,055,000	27.2	↑	3.5
Reformed, Presbyterian	3,576,000	13.8	↑	1.8
*Pentecostals/Charismatics	2,400,000	9.2	↑	3.7
*Evangelicals	2,100,000	8.1	↑	3.4
Lutheran	945,000	3.6	↑↑	9.3
Baptist	361,000	1.4	↑	1.8
Adventist	113,000	0.4	↓	-3.3
Jehovah's Witnesses	82,300	0.3	↑	1.3
Nondenominational	82,000	0.3	↑	0.9
Restorationist, Disciple	50,200	0.2	↑	3.5
Anglican	10,700	<0.1	↑	1.7
Latter-day Saints (Mormons)	2,600	<0.1	↑↑	10.1
Eastern Orthodox	1,400	<0.1	↑	0.7

Christianity is concentrated in the western and southern parts of Cameroon. The central and northern parts of the country are largely Muslim. Catholics are the largest Christian family in the country, representing 27% of the population in 2020. The largest Protestant family is Reformed/Presbyterians (3.6 million), with the largest churches being the Evangelical Church of Cameroon, Presbyterian Church of Cameroon, and Presbyterian Church in Cameroon. Presbyterians have extensive educational programs, an increasing evangelistic outreach, and large numbers of national workers. Other Protestants include Lutherans (945,000), Baptists (361,000), and Adventists (113,000). Independent traditions are largely schisms from existing Protestant groups and some Pentecostal groups like the Apostolic Church. Pentecostal/Charismatic Christians made up 15% of Christians in 2020.

* These movements are found within Christian families	↑↑	extreme growth
	↑	growth
	↓↓	extreme decline
— no change	↓	decline

Christianity in Canada

The first Christians in Canada were French Catholic missionaries in 1608 working among the Mi'kmaq people. Jesuits and missionaries of other orders soon followed. Protestants from France and British Anglicans arrived afterward but found French Canada hostile to the Protestant message. Nevertheless, Congregationalists, Methodists, Presbyterians, and various Protestant denominations continued to arrive over time. In some ways the Christian landscape reflects the early settlements from the 18th century with the arrival of different French- and English-speaking groups. French and English are the two official languages of Canada today, and about 1% of the population speaks a variety of indigenous (First Nations) languages. Canada has been a majority Christian country for many centuries, but Christian influence and affiliation is slowly declining. The country was 98% Christian in 1900 and 63% in 2020; it is likely to continue dropping to 53% by 2050.

The Catholic Church is the largest Christian tradition. The impact of the nation's Catholic heritage is easily seen in everyday life, but Mass attendance has dropped sharply, and few Catholics are regular attenders. Many Canadian Catholics wish to see a greater progressivism in the church, especially concerning women's rights and sexuality. The United Church of Canada is the second largest denomination, founded in 1925, and is a union of Methodist, Congregational, and 70% of the Presbyterian churches. Several other denominations have joined over time as well. The churches came together to coordinate overseas mission efforts and ministry in the Canadian northwest. Anglicans are the next largest group due to the historic British presence.

Many of the churches in Canada have been advocating for women's rights for some time. In 1975, the General Synod of the Anglican Church voted for women to be ordained, and the following year four women were ordained in the dioceses of Cariboo, Huron, New Westminster, and Niagara. Notable Baptist women include Elizabeth Williams Shadd Shreve (1826–1890), who braved difficult journeys in southern Ontario to preach, minister, and advocate for women in leadership, and Jennie Johnson (1868–1967), a former enslaved woman from Maryland who became an ordained minister and founding member of the Union Baptist Church in Ontario.

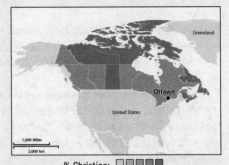

% Christian: 0 3 10 50 75 100

Religion in Canada

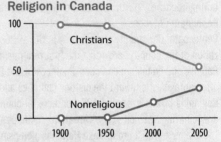

Canada is a religiously diverse country, with the following religions over 1% of the population: Christianity, Islam, Chinese folk religions, Buddhism, Sikhism, Hinduism, and Judaism. The second largest tradition is the nonreligious (atheists and agnostics), which grew from just 0.2% of the population in 1900 to 25% in 2020; it will likely increase to over 31% by 2050.

Indicators & Demographic Data

Population (2020)	37,603,000
% under 15 years	16%
Capital city (pop.)	Ottawa-Gatineau 1,393,000
% urban dwellers	82% (0.95% p.a.)
Official language	English, French
Largest language	English (49%)
Largest people	Anglo-Canadian (40%)
Largest culture	Anglo-Canadian (40%)
Development	93
Physicians	25
Gender gap	1%

Bible Translations		Churches		Missionaries		Gospel Access	
Languages	157	Denominations	420	Received	8,000	1900	Very high
Full Bible	71	Congregations	28,100	Sent	8,000	2020	Very high

Facts to Consider

- In 2021, mass graves were unearthed with remains of over 960 First Nations children housed in Catholic residential schools from the mid-19th to late-20th centuries. The Truth and Reconciliation Commission of Canada has called these schools a form of "cultural genocide" against indigenous peoples.
- Despite the growth of adherents of other religions, Canadian society is rapidly secularizing. Surveys consistently report that people believe religion does more harm than good.
- Missionary-sending from Canadian churches has decreased dramatically, although newer, Independent Charismatic churches now send many missionaries around the world.
- Islam has been growing in Canada mostly through the arrival of immigrants from Pakistan, India, Guyana, Uganda, and some Arab countries.
- Canada has the third largest Sikh population in the world (after India and the United Kingdom). Sikhs are prominent in society. In the 2015 election, for example, 20 Sikh members of parliament were elected, and four of these became part of the Cabinet of Canada (more than in India).

Christian Traditions in Canada

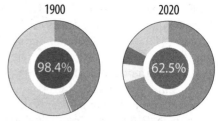

□ Independent □ Protestant ■ Catholic ■ Orthodox ■ Christian

Christianity in Canada has changed dramatically since the start of the 20th century, when 98% of the population was Christian. Protestants made up 56% of Christians, and Catholics 44%. The rapid decline of Protestantism (17% of Christians in 2020) happened concurrently with a rise in the Catholic share (70%). Because of immigration, the Orthodox have increased from less than 1% in 1900 to 6% of Christians in 2020.

Christian Families in Canada

Family	Population 2020	%	Trend	Change
Latin-rite Catholic	13,881,000	36.9	–	0.3
*Pentecostals/Charismatics	2,750,000	7.3	↑	1.0
*Evangelicals	2,085,000	5.5	–	0.2
Eastern Orthodox	1,015,000	2.7	↑	0.6
United church or joint mission	969,000	2.6	↓	-3.1
Anglican	636,000	1.7	–	0.0
Baptist	461,000	1.2	↑	2.3
Reformed, Presbyterian	256,000	0.7	↓	-1.0
Jehovah's Witnesses	231,000	0.6	–	0.2
Eastern-rite Catholic	219,000	0.6	↓	-0.8
Latter-day Saints (Mormons)	216,000	0.6	↑	1.3
Oriental and other Orthodox	205,000	0.5	↑	1.9
Holiness	202,000	0.5	↑	1.5
Lutheran	170,000	0.5	↓	-2.1
Mennonite	130,000	0.3	↑	0.9
Adventist	88,700	0.2	↑	2.2
Nondenominational	64,700	0.2	–	0.0
Salvationist	62,000	0.2	↓	-0.9
Christian Brethren	57,300	0.2	–	-0.1
Restorationist, Disciple	35,100	0.1	↑	3.3
Congregational	25,500	0.1	↑	1.8
Methodist	9,800	<0.1	↑	1.4
Old Catholic Church	3,600	<0.1	↓	-2.1

Although denominational Christianity has been declining in Canada, the country is home to a diverse array of Christian families. It remains a Catholic-majority country with over 14 million members. The absent "family" from the table at left, however, is unaffiliated Christians. Unaffiliated Christians are people who self-identify as Christian but are not formally attached to a particular denomination or network. They typically are not members of churches, but they show up in surveys and polls as Christians. In 2020, unaffiliated Christians were 11% of Canada's population (4 million) and growing. The Orthodox are represented by many ethnic traditions, the largest of which are Greek, Serbian, Syrian, Ukrainian, and Coptic. The Native American Church of Canada combines Christianity with indigenous beliefs. They are known for their practice of using peyote, which is considered a holy sacrament and is used to communicate with the Great Spirit (monotheistic God).

* These movements are found within Christian families
– no change

↑↑ extreme growth
↑ growth
↓↓ extreme decline
↓ decline

Christianity in the Caribbean Netherlands

The Caribbean Netherlands consist of three municipalities of the Netherlands: the islands of Bonaire, St. Eustatius, and Saba. Their combined population is roughly 26,200 people, with Papiamentu as the major spoken language. The Caribbean Netherlands has been a majority Christian country since the arrival of Europeans, though the country has a complex past, having been shifted 22 times between the Spanish, Dutch, and British during the colonial period. The largest denomination today is the Catholic Church, representing 69% of the country.

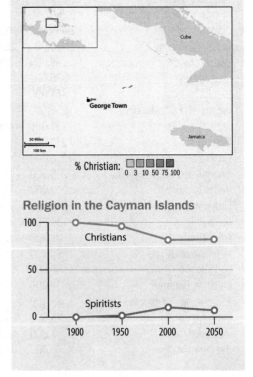

% Christian: 0 3 10 50 75 100

Facts to Consider

- Thirty percent of religious people attend weekly services. Over 40% of men and 25% of women never attend religious services.
- Methodism was established first on St. Eustatius by an enslaved African, Black Harry, in the 18th century. Enslaved people were beaten and imprisoned for practicing Methodism. Today there are over 200 Methodists descended from this period.
- St. Eustatius was home to one of the first Jewish settlements in the Western Hemisphere, and they built a synagogue in Oranjestad in 1739. There are only a few Jews there today, and they travel to Curaçao to worship in a synagogue.

Religion in the Caribbean Netherlands

(Chart showing Christians near 100% declining slightly over time; Nonreligious near 0% rising slightly, across years 1900, 1950, 2000, 2050)

Christianity in the Cayman Islands

The Cayman Islands is an autonomous British Overseas Territory in the Caribbean, consisting of the islands Grand Cayman, Cayman Brac, and Little Cayman. The islands were uninhabited when Christopher Columbus encountered them in 1503. Britain took control of the islands in 1670, and many enslaved people were brought from Africa. As a result, the majority of inhabitants today are descendants of enslaved people. In 2020, the largest Christian denominations were Catholic (13% of the country) and Seventh-day Adventist (12%).

% Christian: 0 3 10 50 75 100

Facts to Consider

- The Cayman Islands is a deeply religious country, with ports closed on Sundays and Christian holidays.
- There is only one Catholic parish on Grand Cayman, the largest island, served by one Jesuit priest who occasionally visits Little Cayman and Cayman Brac.
- The Seventh-day Adventist Church operates Cayman Adventist Television and Three Angels Broadcasting Network 24 hours a day.
- The United Church in Jamaica and the Cayman Islands has a robust women's ministry that dates to 1920. Now in union with the Disciples of Christ, it has seven branches throughout the islands and engages in evangelism, children's education, and theological education.

Religion in the Cayman Islands

(Chart showing Christians near 100% declining slightly over time; Spiritists near 0% rising slightly, across years 1900, 1950, 2000, 2050)

Christianity in the Central African Republic

Christianity grew significantly in the Central African Republic after independence in 1960. By 2020, Christians were 75% of the population. The Central African Republic Civil War, fought between Muslims and Christians, has been ongoing since at least 2012. The ousting of President François Bozizé in 2013 ushered in political crises that pitted Muslim Séléka rebels against Christian anti-balaka militias created by former president François Bozizé. A peace accord was signed in Brazzaville in 2014, but the government has had little control of the country since then. Over 1 million people have been internally displaced or fled the country, mainly to Cameroon, the Democratic Republic of the Congo, and Chad.

Facts to Consider

- Catholic Relief Services has been tremendously active in the country since 1999, attempting to secure peace and offering humanitarian aid. Many people have sought refuge in Catholic churches during times of conflict.
- The ongoing conflicts in the country have left children particularly vulnerable and lacking education, health care, and safety. There are roughly 643,000 internally displaced people and 574,000 refugees in the country.
- Women have roughly half the literacy rates as men (24% versus 50%), and twice as many girls are unschooled as boys. Furthermore, a recent report claimed that 68% of married women were married before the age of 18.
- Pentecostal/Charismatic Christianity has grown significantly in the country, from 5% in 1970 to nearly 19% of the population by 2020.
- Traditional ethnic religions are professed by a small minority of each of the main tribes, as well as by 99% of the Binga Pygmies.

Indicators & Demographic Data

Population (2020)	4,921,000
% under 15 years	42%
Capital city (pop.)	Bangui 889,000
% urban dwellers	42% (3.32% p.a.)
Official language	Sango, French
Largest language	Gbaya (20%)
Largest people	Sango (8%)
Largest culture	other Sudanic (31%)
Development	37
Physicians	0.5
Gender gap	22%

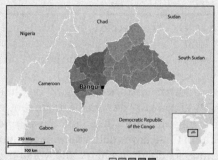

% Christian: 0 3 10 50 75 100

Christian Traditions in the Central African Republic

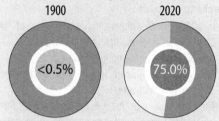

1900 — <0.5% 2020 — 75.0%

☐ Independent ☐ Protestant ■ Catholic ■ Orthodox ■ Christian

The small community of Christians in 1900 was entirely Catholic religious brothers. By 2020, with the growth of Independents and Protestants (each about a quarter of Christians), Catholics had dropped to about half of Christians.

Religion in the Central African Republic

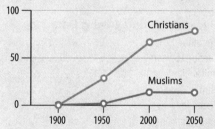

Nearly the entire population (99%) followed African Traditional Religions in 1900. By 2020, the population was mostly Christian (75%), with a large Muslim minority (13%).

Bible Translations		Churches		Missionaries		Gospel Access	
Languages	91	Denominations	91	Received	1,200	1900	Very low
Full Bible	12	Congregations	7,600	Sent	90	2020	Very high

Christianity in Chad

Chad was a French colony from 1900 until its independence in 1960. The country has experienced a series of civil wars between Arab Muslims in the north and Christians in the south, the most recent ending in 2010. Relatively robust in the southern territories, the Catholic Church is more sparse in Muslim areas, except in the urban centers where Catholics have migrated from the south. Most Protestant denominations in Chad have youth and women's movements, Sunday schools for children, choirs, and worship groups. Many also send Chadian missionaries to other areas of the country for evangelistic ministry.

Facts to Consider

- In 2015, the government imposed a state of emergency in the Lake Chad region after multiple attacks by Boko Haram. In the same year, bombings also occurred in N'Djamena.
- Faith-based health care, largely in the south, represents about 20% of national health coverage.
- The missionary movement is deployed mainly through home missions, which also promote water resource development, civil peace, maternal and infant health, and children's education.
- Denominations and local churches operate schools at the primary and secondary levels due to weaknesses in the public school system.
- The Shalom Faculty of Evangelical Theology outside of N'Djamena is the only degree-granting Bible school and seminary in Chad.
- Radio broadcasting is an effective form of communication due to the country's illiteracy and poverty rates; the large number of radio receivers makes broadcasting an important ministry for many churches.

Indicators & Demographic Data

Population (2020)	16,285,000
% under 15 years	46%
Capital city (pop.)	N'Djaména 1,423,000
% urban dwellers	24% (4.10% p.a.)
Official language	Arabic, French
Largest language	Arabic (12%)
Largest people	Sara Gambai (11%)
Largest culture	other Sudanic (43%)
Development	40
Physicians	0.4
Gender gap	22%

% Christian: 0 3 10 50 75 100

Christian Traditions in Chad

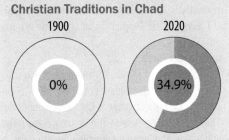

1900 — 0%   2020 — 34.9%

☐ Independent ☐ Protestant ▨ Catholic ■ Orthodox ■ Christian

Chad's Christians are mostly Catholic (57%) but with a large Protestant minority (29%). Following Catholics, the largest denominations are the Evangelical Church, Assemblies of God, and Baptists.

Religion in Chad

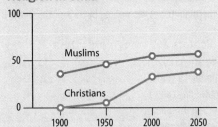

In 2020, Chad was 58% Muslim and 35% Christian. African Traditional Religions are significant among the sub-Saharan populations. Many Chadians practice a mixture of traditional religion and either Christianity or Islam.

Bible Translations		Churches		Missionaries		Gospel Access	
Languages	132	Denominations	150	Received	830	1900	Very low
Full Bible	17	Congregations	5,400	Sent	30	2020	Medium

Christianity in the Channel Islands

The Channel Islands are an archipelago in the English Channel off the coast of France. The largest islands are Jersey and Guernsey. Most citizens are of British descent, followed by French. Christianity came to the islands in the 6th century via missionaries; Presbyterianism arrived in the 16th century, followed by Methodism in the 18th and 19th. Catholicism is concentrated in Jersey, and Mass is held regularly in Portuguese and Polish and occasionally in French. The Church of England is the largest Christian tradition today, its members comprising around 46% of the population.

Facts to Consider

- Two local church councils are active, the Guernsey Council of Churches and the Jersey Council of Churches. Both are associate members of the British Council of Churches.
- The Catholic Church (14% of the population) has had difficulty recruiting priests and has had to sell off some of their buildings.
- In 2021, more than 100 Kenyans arrived in the Channel Islands to work in the hospitality industry as chefs, housekeepers, and wait staff.
- Several Asian families of Muslim, Buddhist, and Hindu background live on Jersey.
- A few Jewish families live on Jersey and have one synagogue in the countryside.
- The nonreligious increased from less than 1% of the population in 1900 to 14% in 2020. There is a small but active community of Humanists that gather via social media.

Indicators & Demographic Data

Population (2020)................................. 168,000
% under 15 years 14%
Capital city (pop.)............................St. Helier 34,200
% urban dwellers..............................31% (0.68% p.a.)
Official language................................English, French
Largest language................................English (97%)
Largest people .... British (97%)
Largest culture .... English (British) (97%)
Development..92
Physicians..32
Gender gap..3%

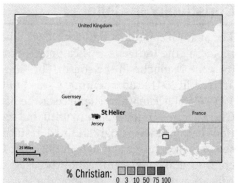

% Christian: 0 3 10 50 75 100

Christian Traditions in the Channel Islands

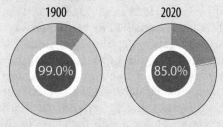

1900 — 99.0% 2020 — 85.0%

□ Independent □ Protestant ■ Catholic ■ Orthodox ■ Christian

Protestants have been the largest Christian denomination due to the long presence of British Anglicans. Catholics have increased slightly with Anglicans leaving the church. Most Catholics are on Jersey.

Religion in the Channel Islands

The Channel Islands have been majority Christian for many centuries, though the Christian share of the population dropped from 99% in 1900 to 85% in 2020. The nonreligious grew to 14% in 2020, up from less than 1% in 1900.

Bible Translations		Churches		Missionaries		Gospel Access	
Languages	4	Denominations	19	Received	10	1900	Very high
Full Bible	3	Congregations	110	Sent	15	2020	Very high

Christianity in Chile

The Spanish conquest of modern-day Chile began in 1540, replacing the indigenous Inca people but unable to take over the Mapuche in the south. The first Catholic priest arrived in 1541, and a seminary was built in Santiago in 1584. Catholicism was recognized as the state religion when Chile became independent in 1810, but church-state relations became increasingly strained, resulting in the formal separation of church and state in 1925. The Catholic Church continued to enjoy significant privileges, such as Catholic education in public schools, though the constitution maintains the separation of religion and the state.

Chile suffered from two military coup d'états in the 20th century (1924 and 1973), followed by the brutal regime of General Augusto Pinochet, which was marked by severe human rights violations. The Catholic Church provided support for victims of governmental repression and made an explicit policy to excommunicate anyone who participated in the Pinochet regime's practice of torture. Despite this forward-thinking activism, the Catholic Church was unprepared to deal with the abuse of children by priests within the church, with allegations beginning in 1984 and finally simmering over in 2010 with the trial and removal of Fr. Fernando Karadima. The crisis is ongoing, with a wide-ranging investigation launched in 2018. This scandal has severely damaged the Catholic Church's reputation among the Chilean people.

Although Protestantism arrived in Chile in 1821 (via the British and Foreign Bible Society), it is the Pentecostal/Charismatic movement that has offered the deepest challenge to the country's Catholic majority. The movement dates to 1909, with American Methodist missionaries praying for revival that led to widespread baptisms in the Holy Spirit. This led to the founding of the Methodist Pentecostal Church and eventually the breakoff groups Evangelical Pentecostal Church and the Pentecostal Church of Chile. The latter is notable for their affirmation of women's ordination and commitment to ecumenism, having joined the World Council of Churches. An estimated 95% of all Pentecostal/Charismatic churches today trace their roots to the founding of the Methodist Pentecostal Church in the early 20th century.

% Christian: 0 3 10 50 75 100

Religion in Chile

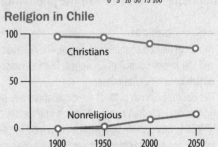

Chile has been a majority Christian country for many centuries and is anticipated to remain so for quite some time, even though the Christian share of the population dropped from 97% in 1900 to 88% in 2020. The nonreligious (atheists and agnostics together) have made considerable gains, from representing well under 1% in 1900 to comprising 11% in 2020.

Indicators & Demographic Data

Population (2020). 18,473,000
% under 15 years 20%
Capital city (pop.) . . . . Santiago 6,767,000
% urban dwellers. . . . . 88% (0.78% p.a.)
Official language. . . . . Spanish
Largest language. . . . . Spanish (95%)
Largest people . . . . Chilean Mestizo (67%)
Largest culture . . . . . . Mestizo (Spanish) (67%)
Development. 84
Physicians. 10
Gender gap 4%

Bible Translations		Churches		Missionaries		Gospel Access	
Languages. 23		Denominations 320		Received. 8,500		1900 . . . . Very high	
Full Bible. 13		Congregations. 23,300		Sent 2,000		2020 . . . . Very high	

Facts to Consider

- Chileans report comparatively lower rates of the importance of religion in their lives compared with other Latin American countries. Roughly 51% of Protestants and 14% of Catholics report that they attend religious services at least once a week.
- Both Catholics and Protestants have been involved in missions, with most missionaries sent out to neighboring countries. Increasingly, Chilean missionaries are being sent to North Africa and Asia as a result of Redemptoris Missio by Catholics and COMIBAM (Cooperación Misionera Iberoamericana) by Protestants.
- Protestantism in Chile has suffered tremendously from division. There are at least 50 Pentecostal/Charismatic denominations in the country, plus numerous nondenominational or cell-like groups.
- Recently, several foreign Pentecostal missions have entered Chile, often preaching a prosperity theology at odds with the teaching and preaching of traditional Chilean Pentecostalism.
- The Mapuche are the largest indigenous people group in Chile, and many are polytheists with a belief in a supreme being, Nenechen. They experience discrimination from the wider population and are often considered second-class citizens.
- The Jewish population of Chile is only around 20,000 (0.1%), but there has been a rise in anti-Semitism, including vandalism of cemeteries and Jewish-run businesses and chants by groups during protests.

Christian Traditions in Chile

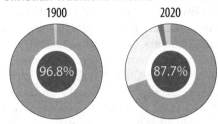

□Independent □Protestant ■Catholic ■Orthodox ■Christian

Catholics were 99% of Christians in 1900, but their monopoly on religion was challenged in the 20th century with the rise of Protestant, Independent, and Pentecostal/Charismatic Christianity starting in the early 1900s. By 2020, the Catholic share of Christians had dropped to 70%, with Protestants and Independents together representing nearly 28% of Christians. The Church of Jesus Christ of Latter-day Saints (Mormons) are the fourth largest denomination in the country, growing from 20,000 members in 1970 to just over 600,000 by 2020.

Christian Families in Chile

Family	Population 2020	%	Trend	Change
Latin-rite Catholic	12,900,000	69.8	↑	0.6
*Pentecostals/Charismatics	6,500,000	35.2	↑	1.0
Latter-day Saints (Mormons)	609,000	3.3	↑	0.8
*Evangelicals	520,000	2.8	↑	2.7
Eastern Orthodox	399,000	2.2	↑	2.0
Non-traditional, house, cell	218,000	1.2	–	0.4
Jehovah's Witnesses	176,000	1.0	↑	1.0
Adventist	141,000	0.8	–	-0.3
Baptist	133,000	0.7	↑↑	5.5
Holiness	71,200	0.4	↑	2.7
Restorationist, Disciple	37,800	0.2	↑↑	9.8
Anglican	23,300	0.1	↑	2.6
Reformed, Presbyterian	17,100	0.1	↑	0.9
Salvationist	16,100	0.1	↑	2.3
Lutheran	13,100	0.1	–	-0.3
Methodist	12,400	0.1	↓	-1.2
Nondenominational	10,900	0.1	↑	2.0
Christian Brethren	3,200	<0.1	↓	-0.7
Oriental and other Orthodox	1,100	<0.1	↑	1.0

Still the largest Christian family in Chile, Catholics are growing modestly with the general population. However, Pentecostals/Charismatics and Evangelicals are growing at a faster pace as people leave Catholicism for what is perceived as more personal and spiritual forms of Christianity. The Pentecostal movement, which started in 1909, already had nearly 1.5 million adherents (16% of the country) by 1970 and was 35% of the country in 2020. The largest Pentecostal movement is the Methodist Pentecostal Church of Chile, which exists in three denominations that together number over 1.8 million members. Evangelicals also experienced significant growth, but in 2020 numbered only around half a million Christians.

* These movements are found within Christian families	↑↑	extreme growth
	↑	growth
	↓↓	extreme decline
– no change	↓	decline

Christianity in China

Christianity has been present in China since missionaries from the Church of the East traveled along the Silk Road in the 7th century. Despite Christianity's ancient roots in China, the country consistently ranks as one of the most difficult places to be a Christian due to governmental oppression and social hostilities. With the Cultural Revolution in 1966, spontaneous attacks led by Red Guard youth groups were directed against all visible forms of religion as part of their assault on the "Four Olds" (old habits, old customs, old ideas, old culture). Public religion of all kinds was driven underground.

In 1982, China established a new religious policy that represented a clear break from policies of the 1950s and 1960s. The constitution bans the state, public organizations, and individuals from compelling citizens to believe in, or not believe in, any religion. After registering with the government, only religious groups belonging to one of the five state-sanctioned "patriotic religious associations" (Buddhism, Daoism, Islam, Catholicism, and Protestantism) are permitted to legally hold worship services and engage in religious activities. Chinese Communist Party members are required to be atheists and are forbidden from engaging in religious practices.

Nevertheless, China has the fifth largest Christian population in the world at 106 million (7%). Christians in China are divided between government-sanctioned (or registered) groups and those that operate without governmental approval. Catholics (10 million) are in both churches under the Chinese Patriotic Catholic Association and underground churches, causing tensions between Beijing and the Vatican. Protestants and Independents (96 million) are found among different underground church networks (urban, rural, and ethnic churches) and the state-sponsored Three-Self Patriotic Movement (TSPM).

House churches have experienced the majority of Christianity's explosive growth in China. In the early decades after the Cultural Revolution, the house churches primarily grew in the countryside among women. Beginning in the 1990s, however, and at least partially because of significant foreign missionary activity on China's university campuses, the house church movement has grown tremendously in the urban areas among both men and women.

% Christian: 0 3 10 50 75 100

Religion in China

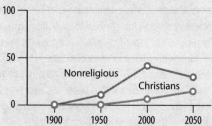

In 1900, China was 100% religious, mostly a mixture of traditional Chinese religionists, Buddhists, and Confucianists (with a sizable Muslim population of 24 million). By 1970, the country was majority nonreligious (60%), with traditional religions driven underground. Since then, religion has rebounded slightly so that in 2020, China was 39% nonreligious, 31% Chinese folk religionist, and 17% Buddhist.

Indicators & Demographic Data

Population (2020)	1,424,548,000
% under 15 years	17%
Capital city (pop.)	Beijing 20,463,000
% urban dwellers	61% (1.78% p.a.)
Official language	Chinese (Mandarin)
Largest language	Chinese (93%)
Largest people	Han Chinese (Mandarin) (63%)
Largest culture	Han Chinese (91%)
Development	75
Physicians	36
Gender gap	4%

Bible Translations		Churches		Missionaries		Gospel Access	
Languages	265	Denominations	310	Received	4,000	1900	Very low
Full Bible	58	Congregations	614,000	Sent	15,000	2020	High

Facts to Consider

- Restrictions on the internet and social media are strictly applied and seriously limit personal freedoms. The government monitors and closes many churches, which are a perceived threat if they become too large.
- There is great potential for division among house church leaders as the movement shifts from rural to urban contexts. Current issues include Sunday school, Christian education, and homeschooling, since proselytization of children under 18 years old is illegal.
- Theological education and pastoral training are in high demand among house churches in China, especially as congregations grow larger. Many Chinese now spend time overseas receiving theological education in the United States.
- Chinese Christians consider theologically how to remain authentically Chinese and authentically Christian at the same time; as a result, they are developing new contextual theologies that make sense for the Chinese context.
- Many Chinese Christians serve as missionaries abroad, such as in the Back to Jerusalem movement, which aims to send missionaries to all countries between China and Jerusalem.
- Women have played a critical role in the growth of Christianity in China, including Bible women (indigenous evangelists) who introduced other women and children to Christianity. Pastors' wives are seen as coworkers with their husbands and carry significant leadership and authority in house churches.

Christian Traditions in China

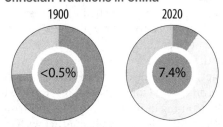

□Independent □Protestant ■Catholic ■Orthodox ■Christian

China's Christian community in 1900 was mostly Catholic (74%); there were 3.3 million Catholics in 1949 when Mao Zedong came to power, and 1.3 million Protestants. All public Christian activity ceased, and foreign missionaries were expelled. Partly as a result, Independent Christianity grew abundantly, along with Chinese house churches that numbered around 55 million in 2020 (59% of Christians). Although many house churches are nondenominational, some are taking on denominational identities, for example, adopting Presbyterian or Baptist ecclesiologies.

Christian Families in China

Family	Population 2020	%	Trend	Change
Non-traditional, house, cell	55,720,000	3.9	↑	1.0
*Pentecostals/Charismatics	37,000,000	2.6	↑	1.7
*Evangelicals	35,000,000	2.5	↑	0.5
United church or joint mission	33,446,000	2.3	↑	3.3
Latin-rite Catholic	10,000,000	0.7	↓	-1.0
Nondenominational	1,903,000	0.1	↑	2.4
Media	481,000	<0.1	–	-0.4
Adventist	481,000	<0.1	↑	0.6
Old Catholic Church	107,000	<0.1	↑	2.8
Baptist	53,500	<0.1	↑	2.8
Eastern Orthodox	10,000	<0.1	–	0.0

China is one of the few places in the world where nontraditional, cell-group-like Christianity is the largest expression of the faith. Numbering over 55 million in 2020, Chinese house churches vary in size, worship styles, and church organization. The house church movement is organized under several broad headings, including Han traditional house churches (20 million), rural Han house churches known as the "big five" (19.5 million), and urban Han emerging house church networks (15 million). The latter is seeing growth in Shanghai, Beijing, Chongqing, Guangzhou/Guangdong, Tianjin, Shenzhen, and Wuhan. Other Independent Christians include ethnic churches among minority peoples such as the Lisu, Yi, and Miao. Many members of house churches also practice Pentecostal/Charismatic Christianity, which accounts for 35% of Christians.

* These movements are found within Christian families	↑↑ extreme growth
	↑ growth
	↓↓ extreme decline
– no change	↓ decline

Christianity in Colombia

Spanish explorers touched northwestern South America in 1499, and it became known as New Granada, with headquarters at Bogotá. In 1610, Spanish Jesuit Peter Claver arrived at the slave trade capital, Cartagena, and over four decades baptized 300,000 enslaved Africans. The Spanish established *encomiendas* (commissions) responsible for organizing and overcoming indigenous populations. However, missionaries often found themselves in conflict with the *encomienda* system because of the abuse of indigenous people. A declaration of independence in 1819 was followed by a severe decline in the number of Catholic clergy that rebounded only somewhat in the 21st century (9,975 priests in 2019). The Catholic Church in Colombia has traditionally been considered more conservative than Catholic churches in other Latin American countries. A recent report found that 78% identified religion as important in their lives, 37% of Catholics prayed every day, and weekly service attendance was at 49%.

The first Protestant missionary, with the British and Foreign Bible Society, arrived in 1825. Many groups followed, such as Presbyterians, Evangelical Alliance Mission, Christian and Missionary Alliance, Adventists, and the Salvation Army all arriving before 1930. In 2014, 89% of Protestants indicated that religion was very important in their lives, 62% prayed daily, and 73% attended services weekly. Today, Protestants continue to grow with the social and governmental loosening of religious restrictions. Small churches are multiplying, especially in urban shanty towns. Pentecostal/Charismatic Christianity represents 32% of the population, most of which is the Catholic Charismatic movement (roughly 25% of Catholics identify as Charismatic).

Colombia today cannot be understood apart from recent efforts to secure peace among the government, leftist groups, and paramilitary groups. Many identify the roots of the ongoing conflicts in La Violencia (the undeclared civil war from 1948 to 1958). Both Catholic and Protestant churches have played a role in peace efforts since both have experienced violence at the hands of guerrilla groups. In 2012, an ecumenical organization for peace was established, Mesa Ecuménica por la Paz (Ecumenical Table for Peace), by representatives of Catholic, Presbyterian, Lutheran, Orthodox, Mennonite, and other Protestant groups.

% Christian: 0 3 10 50 75 100

Religion in Colombia

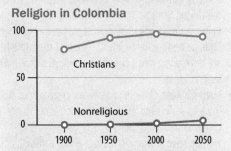

Colombia has been a majority Christian country for many centuries and is poised to remain so into the future. The Christian share of the population grew from 80% in 1900 to 95% in 2020, one of the few Latin American countries to increase its Christian percentage over that period. At the same time, the nonreligious continue to grow and now represent 3% of the population.

Indicators & Demographic Data

Population (2020)	50,220,000
% under 15 years	22%
Capital city (pop.)	Bogotá 10,978,000
% urban dwellers	81% (1.01% p.a.)
Official language	Spanish
Largest language	Spanish (98%)
Largest people	Colombian Mestizo (47%)
Largest culture	Mestizo (Spanish) (47%)
Development	75
Physicians	18
Gender gap	0%

Bible Translations		Churches		Missionaries		Gospel Access	
Languages	90	Denominations	290	Received	7,500	1900	Very high
Full Bible	5	Congregations	26,600	Sent	4,500	2020	Very high

Facts to Consider

- In June 2016, a long-negotiated peace agreement was signed between the Colombian government and the FARC–EP (Revolutionary Armed Forces of Colombia–People's Army), the result of joint efforts among church, government, and other organizations.
- Protestants have been given more freedoms and rights in Colombia, but there are still indications that the Catholic Church retains favored status. Even though non-Catholic groups can offer chaplaincy and religious education in public schools, the permission to do so has been reportedly difficult to obtain.
- Many Colombian Catholics have served in missions outside the country, but few Protestants have embraced this kind of ministry. However, roughly 60% of Protestants and 40% of Catholics report involvement with their church to help the poor in their community.
- A number of lowland and jungle peoples in the interior practice Amerindian ethnic religions, including the Arhuaco, Coreguaje, Cuna, Guajiro, Macu, Barasano, and Tatuyo.
- Afro-Colombians who reside on the Pacific coast practice a mixture of Catholicism with elements of African Traditional Religions.
- The Jewish population in Colombia is small, only 5,000 in 2020 and 70% living in Bogotá, but anti-Semitism continues to be a problem on social media and by way of an anti-Israel protest movement using anti-Semitic slogans.

Christian Traditions in Colombia

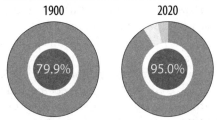

□Independent ▨Protestant ▧Catholic ▩Orthodox ■Christian

In both 1900 and 2020, Colombia's Christians were majority Catholic and are likely to remain so into the future. The Catholic share of Christians dropped only slightly from 1900 to 2020, from nearly 100% to 91%. Protestants and Independents grew from virtually zero to 9% of Christians in 2020. Begun in 1967, the Catholic Charismatic Renewal has gained many members, evidenced by large gatherings and high attendance in local prayer groups.

Christian Families in Colombia

Family	Population 2020	%	Trend	Change
Latin-rite Catholic	43,400,000	86.4	↑	0.7
*Pentecostals/Charismatics	16,250,000	32.4	↑	1.2
*Evangelicals	1,300,000	2.6	↑	3.9
Jehovah's Witnesses	429,000	0.9	↑	1.8
Adventist	221,000	0.4	↓	-4.8
Latter-day Saints (Mormons)	211,000	0.4	↑	2.0
Holiness	155,000	0.3	–	-0.3
Nondenominational	124,000	0.2	–	0.3
Non-traditional, house, cell	81,400	0.2	↑	0.9
Anglican	24,300	<0.1	↑	1.0
Baptist	21,300	<0.1	↓	-0.8
Reformed, Presbyterian	18,900	<0.1	↓	-1.5
Eastern Orthodox	10,700	<0.1	↑	1.5
Exclusive Brethren	7,700	<0.1	–	-0.4
Lutheran	6,600	<0.1	–	-0.5
Christian Brethren	6,400	<0.1	↑	1.0
Old Catholic Church	4,600	<0.1	↑	1.5
Mennonite	4,400	<0.1	–	-0.3
Restorationist, Disciple	2,500	<0.1	–	0.2
Methodist	1,200	<0.1	–	-0.4

The Catholic Church is the largest Christian family in the country, with 43 million members. Yet there is quite a lot of diversity in Colombian Christianity, with many Protestant, Pentecostal/Charismatic, and Evangelical churches having taken root in the late 19th and early 20th centuries. Several Independent, mostly Pentecostal, churches have been formed in Colombia since World War II, but all remain comparatively small. One exception stems from the massive schism in 1970 of Colombian Pentecostals rejecting centralized control from the USA headquarters of the United Pentecostal Church. This resulted in the founding of the Pentecostal Union of Colombia, which is the largest non-Catholic denomination in the country, with 1.2 million members in 2020.

* These movements are found within Christian families

– no change

↑↑ extreme growth
↑ growth
↓↓ extreme decline
↓ decline

Christianity in Comoros

Comoros is an island nation in the Indian Ocean off the coast of Mozambique to the west and Madagascar to the east. The islands adopted Islam as early as the 7th century and participated in Islamic trade routes. Portuguese explorers encountered the archipelago in 1503. France colonized Comoros in 1841, and it became independent in 1975. Catholicism thus has a long history on the islands, but it still represents less than 1% of the population today. Comoros is the only Muslim-majority country in southern Africa. There are a small number of Malagasy Protestants, some of whom are seasonal workers, on the islands. The country has three official languages: Comorian, French, and Arabic.

Facts to Consider

- According to the constitution, Sunni Islam is the state religion and proselytism for any religion except Sunni Islam is illegal. Foreigners who proselytize can be deported.
- Any religious group other than Sunni Muslims typically self-censor and keep their beliefs and practices private.
- In October 2018, President Azali Assoumani stated that Shia Muslims cannot be Comorians and required Shias to renounce their faith or leave the country.
- The Evangelical Church was formed in the 1970s as a house church of mostly Malagasy from Madagascar. There is also an underground movement of secret Christians.
- Economic stress, including lack of jobs, has led to an increase of extremist Muslim groups recruiting young people for their cause. There have been at least 20 coup d'états in the country since 1975.

Indicators & Demographic Data

Population (2020)	870,000
% under 15 years	39%
Capital city (pop.)	Moroni 60,400
% urban dwellers	29% (2.97% p.a.)
Official language	Comorian (Shikomor), Arabic, French
Largest language	Ngazidja Comorian (49%)
Largest people	Comorian (Ngazija) (49%)
Largest culture	Northeast Coastal Bantu (97%)
Development	50
Physicians	1.5
Gender gap	12%

% Christian: 0 3 10 50 75 100

Christian Traditions in Comoros

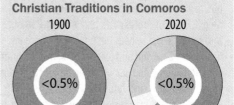

1900   2020

<0.5%   <0.5%

☐ Independent ☐ Protestant ▨ Catholic ■ Orthodox ■ Christian

In 2020, the small Christian community was 62% Catholic, 31% Protestant, and 7% Independent. There are small populations of Protestants and Independents.

Religion in Comoros

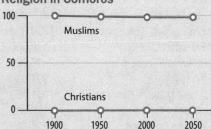

Comoros is a majority Muslim country and is likely to remain so well into the future (98% in 2050). The country was nearly 100% Muslim in 1900 and 98% in 2020. There were virtually no Christians in the country in 1900, but by 2020 there was a very small population of about 4,200.

Bible Translations		Churches		Missionaries		Gospel Access	
Languages	11	Denominations	5	Received	40	1900	Very low
Full Bible	4	Congregations	76	Sent	2	2020	Low

Christianity in the Republic of the Congo

The first Christians in the modern-day Republic of the Congo were Portuguese explorers in 1482. The French colonized Congo in 1903, and it gained independence in 1960. At the beginning of the 20th century, Congo was 2.5% Christian, but this figure rose dramatically to 90% by 2020. Although the country is majority Catholic (60%), the Congo is home to many large Pentecostal/Charismatic Independent traditions, such as the Church of Jesus Christ on Earth by his Special Envoy Simon Kimbangu and the Assemblies of God of Pentecost. Catholic growth has been steady partly due to the indigenous nature of the church. In 1957, Bishop Barthélemy Batanta of Brazzaville was the first to integrate music, rhythm, and dance into the Mass to give a Congolese face to the Catholic Church.

Facts to Consider

- Kimbanguism has a large following in the Congo. It started as a perse-cuted underground church in 1921 and is now found throughout Africa.
- Protestant groups in the country include the Evangelical Church of the Congo, begun by Swedish missionaries in 1909. It has a strong focus on humanitarian work, such as teacher training, deaf ministries, and medical work.
- Although the Congo is majority Christian, many mix traditional beliefs and practices with Christianity. There is widespread ancestor worship and belief in witchcraft, or *ndoki*.
- Muslims are 1% of the country and are mostly immigrants from West Africa, North Africa, or Lebanon and live in urban areas.

Indicators & Demographic Data

Population (2020)	5,687,000
% under 15 years	42%
Capital city (pop.)	Brazzaville 2,388,000
% urban dwellers	68% (3.19% p.a.)
Official language	French
Largest language	Kongo (20%)
Largest people	Kongo (Congo) (17%)
Largest culture	Central Bantu (52%)
Development	61
Physicians	1
Gender gap	7%

% Christian: 0 3 10 50 75 100

Christian Traditions in the Republic of the Congo

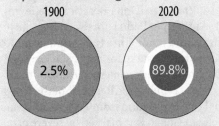

1900 — 2.5%   2020 — 89.8%

☐ Independent ☐ Protestant ▨ Catholic ■ Orthodox ■ Christian

Christians in 1900 were mostly Catholic (60%), but over the 20th century, many Protestant groups entered the country, and Independent groups sprang up, such as the Kimbanguist Church.

Religion in the Republic of the Congo

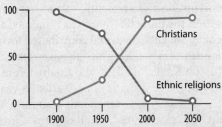

In 1900, the country was majority ethnic religions (98%), but this dropped to 5% in 2020. Reverse-ly, Christians were only 2.5% of the population in 1900 but grew to 90% by 2020.

Bible Translations		Churches		Missionaries		Gospel Access	
Languages	79	Denominations	130	Received	890	1900	Very low
Full Bible	19	Congregations	6,100	Sent	140	2020	Very high

Christianity in the Democratic Republic of the Congo

Christianity reached Congo in 1482 with the arrival of a Portuguese explorer. However, the first missionary party in 1491 consisted of Franciscans, Dominicans, and other Catholic religious orders. Before long, they had baptized the king and built a large stone church at the royal capital in present-day northern Angola. Between 1506 and 1543, one of the most remarkable Christians of African history, Afonso I, ruled the Kongo Kingdom. The growth of the Portuguese slave trade became an increasingly negative factor, sapping the vitality of the Christian movement. Several messianic prophets arose in the second half of the 17th century, especially Kimpa Vita (also known as Dona Beatrice). Believing that the spirit of St. Anthony of Padua possessed her, she preached that Jesus, Mary, and other Christian saints were Kongolese. She was burned at the stake for heresy by Catholic missionaries, but the Antonian movement she began outlasted her.

The Democratic Republic of the Congo was under colonial rule by Belgium from 1908 to independence in 1960. The Belgian Congo was marked by severe economic exploitation of people and resources for the benefit of the colonial power, coupled with the European "civilizing mission" aimed at converting indigenous peoples to both Christianity and Western culture. The Catholic Church enjoyed a privileged status during the colonial period. The church was slow to serve as a prophetic voice under the military dictatorship of Mobutu Sese Seko (1965–1997) and was long silent against corruption and economic mismanagement. But since the 1990s, the Catholic Church has emerged as a voice for social change in DR Congo and contributed toward the movement for democracy, taking an outspoken stance against President Joseph Kabila in 2015, who finally left office with the help of Congolese bishops in 2019 after 18 years in power.

The largest Independent church in DR Congo, and in all of Africa, is the Church of Jesus Christ on Earth by his Special Envoy Simon Kimbangu (EJCSK), founded in 1921. It was the first African Indigenous Church to receive full membership into the World Council of Churches, though their membership was revoked in 2021 over theological issues. The church generally avoids politics and rejects violence, polygamy, magic, witchcraft, alcohol, tobacco, and dancing.

% Christian: 0 3 10 50 75 100

Religion in the DR Congo

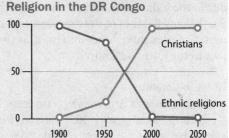

Christianity and African Traditional Religions headed in opposite directions over the 20th century. In 1900, the country was majority ethnic religions (98%) but dropped to 2.5% by 2020. Conversely, Christians were only 1% of the population in 1900 but grew to 95% by 2020. The growth of Christianity in the DR Congo is one of the most dramatic in all of World Christianity.

Indicators & Demographic Data

Population (2020). 89,505,000
% under 15 years 46%
Capital city (pop.) . . . . . . Kinshasa 14,342,000
% urban dwellers. . . . . 46% (4.33% p.a.)
Official language. . . . . French
Largest language. . . . . . . .Mongo-Nkundu (7%)
Largest people .Kongo Creole (Tuba, Leta) (6%)
Largest culture . . . . Central Bantu (25%)
Development. 46
Physicians. 0.9
Gender gap 15%

Bible Translations		Churches		Missionaries		Gospel Access	
Languages. 237		Denominations 1,000		Received. 15,000		1900 . . . . Very low	
Full Bible. 47		Congregations. 95,300		Sent 1,200		2020 . . . . Very high	

Facts to Consider

- While DR Congo's constitution provides for freedom of speech and press, these rights are highly restricted in practice.
- The Catholic Church's influence in the DR Congo cannot be overemphasized, having made tremendous contributions to education, medicine, agriculture, and philanthropic and social services.
- The EJCSK has extensive educational, medical, and social service programs, including an agricultural demonstration farm near Kinshasa.
- Violence began in the spillover of the 1994 Rwandan genocide when armed groups arose; the government was unable to control them. Approximately 5.4 million excess deaths occurred there between 1998 and 2007. Most victims die from indirect causes of violence, such as disease and starvation. The vast majority killed were Christians.
- Women lack equality with men. Maternal mortality rates are high, and health care is limited. Rape and sexual slavery are used as tools of warfare. The DR Congo was described as the "rape capital of the world" in 2010.
- Christian women—most of whom are survivors of sexual abuse—have advocated for peace-building efforts through groups such as the National Federation of Protestant Women in DR Congo and the World March of Women.

Christian Traditions in the DR Congo

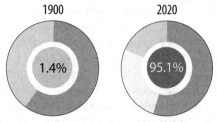

1900 · 1.4% 2020 · 95.1%

☐ Independent ☐ Protestant ▨ Catholic ▧ Orthodox ■ Christian

The small Christian community in 1900 was mostly Catholic (60%) and Protestant (40%) due to the historic missionary presence in the area. In 2020, Christianity in the DR Congo was 55% Catholic, 27% Independent, and 19% Protestant. The Pentecostal/Charismatic movement has impacted all Christian traditions, and most are increasingly adopting Pentecostal/Charismatic characteristics and an emphasis on the work of the Holy Spirit.

Christian Families in DR Congo

Family	Population 2020	%	Trend	Change
Latin-rite Catholic	49,200,000	55.0	↑	2.9
*Pentecostals/Charismatics	28,000,000	31.3	↑	3.3
*Evangelicals	6,023,000	6.7	↑	2.3
Baptist	3,791,000	4.2	↑	2.8
Restorationist, Disciple	2,319,000	2.6	↑	2.0
Reformed, Presbyterian	2,120,000	2.4	↑	2.2
Methodist	1,610,000	1.8	↑	1.2
Nondenominational	1,603,000	1.8	↑	1.8
Jehovah's Witnesses	886,000	1.0	↑	4.5
Adventist	857,000	1.0	↑	0.7
Congregational	776,000	0.9	↑	3.1
Anglican	557,000	0.6	↑	2.4
Mennonite	465,000	0.5	↑	1.6
Holiness	429,000	0.5	↑	1.7
United church or joint mission	207,000	0.2	–	0.3
Lutheran	192,000	0.2	↑	1.5
Christian Brethren	177,000	0.2	↑	1.2
Latter-day Saints (Mormons)	127,000	0.1	↑↑	16.7
Salvationist	79,700	0.1	↑	1.7
Exclusive Brethren	31,500	<0.1	↑	1.2
Eastern Orthodox	31,500	<0.1	↑	2.2
Moravian	17,400	<0.1	↑	1.8

Though the Catholic Church remains the largest Christian family in the DR Congo, with over 49 million members (representing 60% of the country's population), there is significant Christian diversity. Independent groups are quite visible, especially the Kimbanguists, who make up over 15% of the population with 12 million members. Other Independent denominations include those founded by foreign actors (New Apostolic Church, from Switzerland) and by Africans in Africa (African Apostolic Church of John Maranke, from Zimbabwe). Many Protestant groups have large followings in the country, such as Baptists (3.8 million), the Disciples of Christ and other Restorationist groups (2.3 million), and Reformed/Presbyterian groups (2.1 million). The vast majority of these denominations were established in the country under colonial rule, before independence in 1960.

* These movements are found within Christian families
– no change

↑↑ extreme growth
↑ growth
↓↓ extreme decline
↓ decline

Christianity in the Cook Islands

The Cook Islands consist of 15 islands in the South Pacific Ocean, with a total land area of 93 square miles and a population of 17,500. Most inhabitants live on the island of Rarotonga, though a larger population of Cook Islanders lives in New Zealand (over 60,000). Christianity grew quickly after British missionaries visited the Cook Islands in 1821, with all 15 islands becoming majority Christian by 1860. The largest denomination is the Cook Islands Christian Church (CICC), which originated with the London Missionary Society. Mission activity was important from the beginning for the CICC, which sent workers to evangelize Papua from 1872 to 1896. The CICC has a theological training institute at Takamoa, Rarotonga.

Facts to Consider

- Over half the country's population belongs to the CICC. The next two largest denominations are the Catholic Church (29%) and the Church of Jesus Christ of Latter-day Saints (11%).
- The Assemblies of God arrived in the 1960s and established a church by 1975. There are now eight congregations, and Pentecostal/Charismatics make up 17% of the country's population.
- Catholics arrived in 1894, and the Diocese of Rarotonga was established in 1966. They run St. Joseph's School and Nukutere College.
- Some new churches have been founded since 2000, including the Holy Spirit Revival Church, Cornerstone Church, and Celebration on the Rock Church.
- For such a small Christian population, the Cook Islands have comparatively sent out a tremendous number of missionaries to other islands in the Pacific as well as to south-central Asia.

Indicators & Demographic Data

Population (2020)	17,500
% under 15 years	36%
Capital city (pop.)	Rarotonga 12,800
% urban dwellers	75% (0.52% p.a.)
Official language	English, Cook Islands Maori
Largest language	Cook Islands Maori (56%)
Largest people	Cook Islands Maori (Kuki) (56%)
Largest culture	Rarotongan (73%)
Development	72
Physicians	4.4
Gender gap	5%

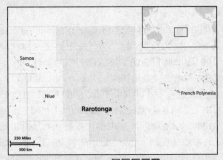

% Christian: 0 3 10 50 75 100

Christian Traditions in the Cook Islands

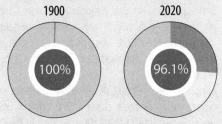

1900 — 100%
2020 — 96.1%

☐ Independent ☐ Protestant ◼ Catholic ◼ Orthodox ◼ Christian

Christianity in the Cook Islands was mostly Protestant in 1900 (99%) due to historical patterns of missionary receiving. By 2020, there was slightly more diversity among Christians: 58% Protestant, 26% Catholic, and 16% Independent.

Religion in the Cook Islands

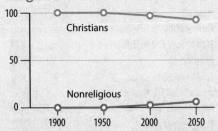

The Cook Islands have been majority Christian since the 19th century and were 100% Christian by 1900. The Christian share of the population dropped only slightly to 96% in 2020 with a small increase in the nonreligious population (3% in 2020).

Bible Translations		Churches		Missionaries		Gospel Access	
Languages	7	Denominations	35	Received	80	1900	Very high
Full Bible	3	Congregations	130	Sent	10	2020	Very high

Christianity in Costa Rica

The Spanish colonized Costa Rica in the 16th century, and the first Catholic missionaries arrived in 1514. It became independent in 1821, with the Catholic Church as the only recognized religious body. Expatriate businessmen arrived in the mid-19th century to help with the banana and coffee trades and also started the first Protestant services, in private homes. Religious practice among Catholics is largely confined to Sunday observance. Today religion is more individualistic, centered on the veneration of saints and often mixed with traditional beliefs. A recent study reported that 49% of Catholics attended weekly services.

Facts to Consider

- Pope John Paul II was the only pope to visit Costa Rica (1983). In February 2022, he was granted honorary citizenship.
- Evangélico (Protestant) Christianity has made a mark on Costa Rican Christianity with its emphasis on living a life set apart from the surrounding culture.
- A recent survey found that 40% of Protestants in Costa Rica were raised Catholic. Protestants also had some of the highest rates in Latin America of having witnessed speaking in tongues and miraculous healing.
- The Bible Society of Costa Rica is working on a translation for the Ngäbe people, the only indigenous group in the country without a complete Bible in its own language.
- Costa Rica is a popular destination for short-term missionaries from the United States due to its geographic proximity and political stability. However, while well-intentioned, some of these groups have been critiqued for not working closely with local populations.

Indicators & Demographic Data

Population (2020)................................5,044,000
% under 15 years 21%
Capital city (pop.)..........................San José 1,400,000
% urban dwellers............................81% (1.50% p.a.)
Official language.......................................Spanish
Largest language.............................. Spanish (97%)
Largest people ....Costarican White (78%)
Largest culture ....Latin-American White (78%)
Development...79
Physicians...12
Gender gap...3%

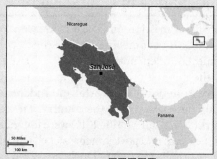

% Christian: 0 3 10 50 75 100

Christian Traditions in Costa Rica

1900   2020

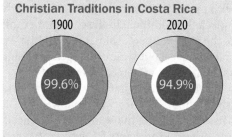

99.6%   94.9%

☐Independent ☐Protestant ■Catholic ■Orthodox ■Christian

Catholicism has been the major Christian tradition in Costa Rica since the Spanish Conquest, representing 99% of Christians in 1900. By 2020, the Catholic share had dropped to 81% with the rise of Protestant and Independents (together nearly 20% of Christians).

Religion in Costa Rica

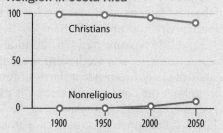

Costa Rica was 99% Christian in 1900 but dropped to 95% by 2020 with a slight increase in the nonreligious (just under 4% in 2020).

Bible Translations		Churches		Missionaries		Gospel Access	
Languages	16	Denominations	140	Received	1,500	1900	Very high
Full Bible	9	Congregations	5,300	Sent	800	2020	Very high

Christianity in Côte d'Ivoire

The first Christians in Côte d'Ivoire were Portuguese traders in 1482. It became an official French colony in 1893 and achieved independence in 1960. Christians make up 34% of the population today and are mostly Catholic, though large Protestant Pentecostal and Independent Charismatic churches are active in the country. The country's two civil wars (2002–2007; 2010–2011) were fought between Muslims in the north and government-backed Christians in the south. The Catholic mission in Duékoué served as the largest camp for displaced people during the Second Ivorian Civil War, with up to 28,000 people staying there daily. Catholicism is especially prominent in the cities; for example, around 29% of the population of Abidjan is Catholic. French is the official language, but various indigenous languages are widely spoken, such as Baoulé, Mòoré, and Jula.

Protestantism first arrived after World War I via British Methodists. They were followed by the Christian and Mission Alliance, the Worldwide Evangelisation Crusade, and others. Protestants follow comity agreements through which different denominations work among various people groups. Methodists, for example, work among the Alagya, Attie, Ari, Avikam, and Dida in the southeast. The Union of Evangelical Churches works among the Dan, Bete, Wobe, and Ngere of the southwest. However, the second largest denomination, Assemblies of God, does not participate in these agreements. Many leaders of Evangelical and Pentecostal churches do not have biblical or theological training.

Côte d'Ivoire experienced the revival ministry of one of the most famous African evangelists of the 20th century: Liberian Grebo prophet William Wadé Harris. Between 1913 and 1915 he converted 120,000 adults, many of whom became Catholics and Methodists. This also led to the formation of a large Independent Harris Church. With branches throughout the country, the church is particularly active in rural areas and it is a member of the World Council of Churches. But numerous groups have broken away from the Harris Church. The Pentecostal/Charismatic movement is prominent among both Catholic and Protestant churches, continuing a "pentecostalization" of Christianity in the country since the 1980s.

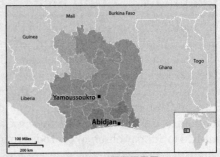

% Christian: 0 3 10 50 75 100

Religion in Côte d'Ivoire

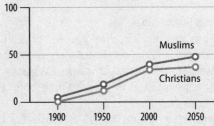

The two largest religions in Côte d'Ivoire are Christianity and Islam, with Christians comprising 34% of the population and Muslims 44% in 2020. Traditional religionists comprised 95% of the population in 1900 and 22% in 2020. Christianity and Islam likely will continue to grow as traditional religions decline.

Indicators & Demographic Data

Population (2020). 26,172,000
% under 15 years 42%
Capital city (pop.) . . . . Abidjan 5,203,000;
Yamoussoukro 222,000
% urban dwellers. . . . . 52% (3.38% p.a.)
Official language. . . . . French
Largest language. . . . . Baoulé (13%)
Largest people . . . . Baule (Bawule) (13%)
Largest culture . . . . .Akan (25%)
Development. 49
Physicians. 1.4
Gender gap 16%

Bible Translations		Churches		Missionaries		Gospel Access	
Languages. 101		Denominations 79		Received. 1,900		1900 . . . . Very low	
Full Bible. 18		Congregations. 17,900		Sent 340		2020 . . . . .High	

Facts to Consider

- Missionaries have been sent out from Côte d'Ivoire for the last several decades, primarily to surrounding Francophone countries. Some have been trained specifically to reach Muslims.
- The Association Feminine des Eglises Protestantes Evangéliques de Côte d'Ivoire formed in 1900 to gather women from different denominations for unity, prayer, and evangelization. Their conferences have focused on issues such as HIV/AIDS and movements for peace.
- Nearly 22% of the country adheres to African Traditional Religions. Several people groups are over 90% ethnic religionist, such as the Banda, Bondoukou Kulango, Bouna Kulango, Gagu, Kulele, Lobi, Neyo, Tenbo, and Western Krahn.
- Islam has been growing in Côte d'Ivoire largely due to immigrants from Mali, Niger, and Burkina Faso. It is concentrated in the northwest of the country. The capital, Abidjan, is about 39% Muslim.
- The government supervises and organizes Hajj pilgrimages for Muslims and funds pilgrimages to Israel, Portugal, Spain, and France for Christians. The government also funds local pilgrimages for members of African Independent Churches.
- Interfaith cooperation is strong in the country, with many people regularly celebrating each other's religious holidays and attending neighborhood gatherings regardless of differences in faith.

Christian Traditions in Côte d'Ivoire

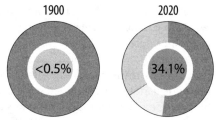

1900   2020

☐Independent ☐Protestant ▦Catholic ▪Orthodox ▪Christian

There were hardly any Christians in Côte d'Ivoire in 1900, just a small community of Catholics from French colonial rule. In 2020, Christianity exhibited considerable diversity, with Catholics comprising 52% of Christians, followed by Protestants (34%) and Independents (14%). Most Protestants and Independents are also part of the Pentecostal/Charismatic movement, which includes the Assemblies of God (Protestant) and the Harris Church (Independent).

Christian Families in Côte d'Ivoire

Family	Population 2020	%	Trend	Change
Latin-rite Catholic	4,800,000	18.3	↑	2.5
*Pentecostals/Charismatics	2,550,000	9.7	↑	2.7
*Evangelicals	2,250,000	8.6	↑	2.5
Methodist	1,246,000	4.8	↑	1.8
Holiness	630,000	2.4	↑	3.8
Nondenominational	273,000	1.0	↑	1.8
Baptist	151,000	0.6	↑	1.7
Non-traditional, house, cell	90,700	0.3	↑	1.9
Latter-day Saints (Mormons)	62,700	0.2	↑↑	14.9
Jehovah's Witnesses	26,300	0.1	↑	4.0
Eastern Orthodox	24,000	0.1	↑	0.9
Restorationist, Disciple	9,200	<0.1	↑	4.4
Lutheran	6,200	<0.1	↑	2.2
Adventist	5,800	<0.1	↓↓	-10.7
Anglican	1,900	<0.1	↓	-0.6

Catholics make up 18% of the country, and the first indigenous priests were ordained as early as 1934 (the first bishops in 1960). The largest Protestant denomination is the Assemblies of God (1 million). The Methodist family includes the Harris Church, the Protestant Methodist Church (from the United Kingdom), the Free Protestant Church, and the Church of the Twelve Apostles (from Ghana). There are two main Holiness groups in the country. The largest (nearly half a million members) is the Evangelical Protestant Church (founded by the American Christian and Missionary Alliance), followed by the Church of the Nazarene. Many of the Independent churches in Côte d'Ivoire were founded as breakaway movements from either Protestantism or Catholicism. The Church of Ashes of Purification was a schism from the Catholic Church by a self-proclaimed female pope, Marie Dawono Lalou, in 1923.

* These movements are found within Christian families
– no change

↑↑ extreme growth
↑ growth
↓↓ extreme decline
↓ decline

Christianity in Croatia

As early as the 1st century, Christians, along with converted Jews of the diaspora, were present in what is now known as Croatia and were eventually defined by the presence of both the Eastern (Orthodox) and Western (Catholic) churches. Adolf Hitler's invasion of Yugoslavia in 1941 created the Independent State of Croatia, led by a fascist regime responsible for the deaths of hundreds of thousands of Serbs, Jews, Roma, and political dissidents. As the Orthodox population has always almost entirely been ethnic Serbs, during the war all Orthodox schools were closed, and many were forced to convert to Catholicism. Even today, Catholic and national identity are closely connected—to be Croatian is to be Catholic. Since the turn of the 21st century, however, Protestant, Evangelical, and Pentecostal/Charismatic Christianity has been growing.

Facts to Consider

- Western missionary efforts have resulted in new groups of Evangelical churches. Protestant women's groups are active in ministry empowerment, children's work, Sunday school training, and family retreats.
- Since 2000, different kinds of Pentecostal/Charismatic churches have formed, such as Word of Life, Full Gospel Church, and Christian Bethsaida Church. The Healing Evangelism Movement, the Latter Rain Movement, and the Faith Movement have influenced these churches.
- The Catholic Charismatic movement dates to the 1980s, emphasizing soul care, healing, and small prayer groups for lay people.
- Muslims in Croatia are mostly Bosnian immigrants and number around 2% of the population.

Indicators & Demographic Data

Population (2020)	4,116,000
% under 15 years	15%
Capital city (pop.)	Zagreb 685,000
% urban dwellers	58% (0.05% p.a.)
Official language	Croatian
Largest language	Croatian (87%)
Largest people	Croat (87%)
Largest culture	Croatian (87%)
Development	83
Physicians	31
Gender gap	1%

% Christian: 0 3 10 50 75 100

Christian Traditions in Croatia

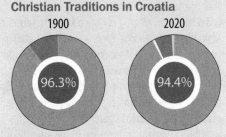

1900 — 96.3% 2020 — 94.4%

☐ Independent ☐ Protestant ■ Catholic ■ Orthodox ■ Christian

Catholicism was the majority Christian tradition in both 1900 and 2020, and the Catholic share of Christians increased to 92% in 2020 despite an increase in the Protestant and Independent populations. The Orthodox are the second largest tradition, with 6% of Christians.

Religion in Croatia

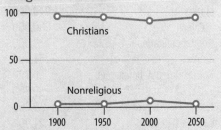

Croatia was 96% Christian in 1900 and 94% in 2020, offset only by a slight increase in the nonreligious population (just under 4% in 2020).

Bible Translations		Churches		Missionaries		Gospel Access	
Languages	29	Denominations	33	Received	1,500	1900	Very high
Full Bible	20	Congregations	2,300	Sent	340	2020	Very high

Christianity in Cuba

Christopher Columbus landed in Cuba in 1492 and claimed the island for Spain. The first settlement formed in 1511, subjecting the indigenous Taíno population to forced labor in the *encomienda* system. Within a century, the harsh colonial rule and the spread of foreign diseases like smallpox wiped out the indigenous population. Upon Cuba's independence from Spain in 1898, Protestantism entered the country and challenged the Catholic Church's 400-year monopoly on the island. Many of these late-19th-century Protestants were Cubans and supporters of Cuba's independence from Spain. Many Catholics became Protestants at the beginning of the 20th century.

Christians of all kinds faced persecution and repression after the Communist takeover in 1959 under Fidel Castro. The Catholic Church clashed with the state; all seminarians left the country in 1961, and the number of priests, sisters, and brothers quickly declined. By 1974, 650,000 Cubans had fled to the United States.

Since the 1990s, Christianity has continued to grow because amendments to the constitution in 1992 outlawed religious discrimination and removed atheism as the official ideology of the state. This growth is especially notable in Pentecostal/Charismatic churches. Meanwhile, though 73% of the population in 1957 was Catholic, with about 27% attending Mass every Sunday, these figures today have dropped to 54% and 4%, respectively. Protestantism had been active in the country since the early 18th century and grew to include Anglicans, Methodists, Baptists, Presbyterians, and others. Pentecostalism (the Assemblies of God) came from the United States in 1920. Moreover, the 2015 restoration of diplomatic relations between Cuba and the United States encouraged the growth of USA-style denominationalism and megachurches.

The Cuban Council of Churches has over 50 participating groups, including historic Protestant churches and Pentecostal, Orthodox, and Charismatic groups. They have a good working relationship with the government and help the registration process for unregistered Christian groups. The Alliance of Cuban Evangelical Churches formed in 2019 with seven churches. Although religious restrictions have loosened over the decades, the Cuban Communist Party, through its Office of Religious Affairs and the Ministry of Justice, continues to control most aspects of religious life.

% Christian: 0 3 10 50 75 100

Religion in Cuba

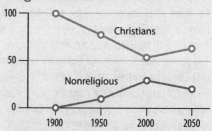

Christianity has had a tumultuous experience in Cuba over the course of the century. In 1900, Cuba was 99% Christian, but this figure dropped to 46% by 1970 before rebounding to 62% in 2020. Meanwhile, the nonreligious population, which was virtually nonexistent in 1900, represented 21% of the population in 2020. Cuba has a large following of Spiritists (17%).

Indicators & Demographic Data

Population (2020)	11,495,000
% under 15 years	16%
Capital city (pop.)	Havana 2,140,000
% urban dwellers	77% (0.19% p.a.)
Official language	Spanish
Largest language	Spanish (99%)
Largest people	Cuban White (72%)
Largest culture	Latin-American White (72%)
Development	78
Physicians	75
Gender gap	6%

Bible Translations		Churches		Missionaries		Gospel Access	
Languages	9	Denominations	85	Received	270	1900	Very high
Full Bible	8	Congregations	7,400	Sent	20	2020	Very high

Facts to Consider

- Governmental pressure on religious groups has increased, with escalating violence, detentions, and threats. Authorities have continued surveillance and detained leaders of some religious groups, without charges.
- A coalition of Evangelical Protestant churches, Apostolic churches, and the Catholic Church has been pressing for constitutional amendments to ease registration demands on religious groups, ownership of church property, and new church construction.
- Jehovah's Witnesses arrived in 1910, were banned in 1974, and were reinstated in 1994. They are not approved by the government but have become the second largest denomination in 2020, representing 1% of the population. They meet privately in homes.
- For many years under Communism, Cuban Christians were prohibited from participating in foreign outreach. A small number of Evangelicals have recently traveled overseas as missionaries.
- The Evangelical Theological Seminary was formed in 1946 by Presbyterians and Methodists, and joined by Episcopalians in 1951. The Methodists split to form their own seminary in 2006. It offers bachelor's and master's degrees in theology and Christian education.
- Afro-Cuban religions are syncretistic movements that borrow from Catholicism (mainly the veneration of saints) and conduct services during Catholic feasts. Santería, which blends Yoruba religion from West Africa with Catholicism, developed during the Atlantic slave trade.

Christian Traditions in Cuba

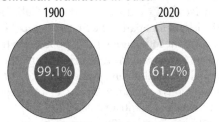

□Independent □Protestant ■Catholic ■Orthodox ■Christian

Like much of Christianity throughout the Caribbean, Christianity in Cuba has been majority Catholic for many centuries. In 1900, nearly 100% of Christians were Catholic. This dropped to 89% by 2020 with the growth of Pentecostal/Charismatic, Evangelical, Protestant, and Independent Christianity. Protestants and Independents together now account for 10% of Christians. The first Pentecostal group was the Assemblies of God in 1920, and the denomination it founded, the Evangelical Pentecostal Church of Cuba, is the third largest denomination today.

Christian Families in Cuba

Family	Population 2020	%	Trend	Change
Latin-rite Catholic	6,150,000	53.5	–	0.5
*Pentecostals/Charismatics	960,000	8.4	↑	0.7
*Evangelicals	185,000	1.6	↑	1.4
Jehovah's Witnesses	161,000	1.4	–	-0.4
Baptist	85,600	0.7	↑	1.6
Methodist	49,500	0.4	–	-0.3
Eastern Orthodox	45,000	0.4	↑	1.7
Adventist	36,800	0.3	–	0.3
Media	27,300	0.2	↓	-0.9
Nondenominational	23,800	0.2	↑	1.1
Reformed, Presbyterian	22,000	0.2	↑	1.0
Holiness	16,800	0.1	↑	2.6
Mennonite	13,700	0.1	↑↑	10.6
Anglican	10,700	0.1	–	-0.4
Lutheran	1,500	<0.1	↑	2.5
Christian Brethren	960	<0.1	–	-0.4
Friends (Quaker)	960	<0.1	–	-0.4
Salvationist	880	<0.1	↓	-2.2

There is quite a lot of Christian diversity in Cuba despite decades of governmental suppression of religion. Evangelicals grew from being virtually nonexistent in 1900 to representing 2% of the population in 2020; the same can be said for Pentecostals/Charismatics, who are now 8% of the population. Baptist groups include the Baptist Convention of Western Cuba (from the Southern Baptist Convention of the USA), the Fraternity of Baptist Churches of Cuba (a schism from the Baptist Convention), and the Free Baptist Convention of Cuba (established by Free Will Baptists from the USA). Numerous Pentecostal churches range in size from 2,000 to over 10,000 members, including the Evangelical Pentecostal Church (from the Assemblies of God), the Christian Pentecostal Church, and Open Bible Standard Churches—all of which are from the United States.

* These movements are found within Christian families
– no change
↑↑ extreme growth
↑ growth
↓↓ extreme decline
↓ decline

Christianity in Curaçao

Curaçao is a country in the Caribbean, just north of Venezuela. Reformed Protestants arrived with Dutch colonial rule, and the slave trade became the primary economic driver until it was abolished in 1863. The main languages of Curaçao are Papiamentu (spoken most widely), Dutch, English, and Spanish, reflecting the colonial history of the island. Catholicism became prominent with the immigration of the Portuguese in the early 19th century and Catholic missionaries working among the Black population. Today, Catholic churches worship in both English and Papiamentu and are known for high attendance, popular clergy, and lavish services. The largest Protestant denominations are Seventh-day Adventists, Baptists, and the United Protestant Church.

Facts to Consider

- The Charismatic renewal began in the Catholic Church in the 1970s. There are also many rapidly growing Protestant Pentecostal churches and several other Christian groups known for indigenous leadership and contextual preaching and worship.
- The Seventh-day Adventists are active in various ministries that range from serving women and children to advocating education, health, evangelism, publishing, youth, and religious liberty.
- Curaçao is home to the oldest active Jewish community in the Western Hemisphere, dating to 1651 with Sephardic Jews arriving from Amsterdam. There are two synagogues on the island and around 500 Jews.
- Muslims in Curaçao are largely immigrants from Syria, Lebanon, and Suriname. There is one mosque in the capital, Willemstad.

Indicators & Demographic Data

Population (2020)................................. 163,000
% under 15 years 18%
Capital city (pop.) .... Willemstad 146,000
% urban dwellers.............................89% (0.57% p.a.)
Official language...................... Dutch, Papiamentu, English
Largest language............................. Papiamentu (68%)
Largest people .... Antillean Creole (72%)
Largest culture .... Creole, Dutch-speaking (73%)
Development..68
Physicians...39
Gender gap...3%

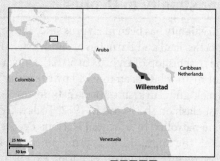

% Christian: 0 3 10 50 75 100

Christian Traditions in Curaçao

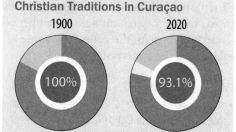

1900   2020

100%   93.1%

☐Independent ☐Protestant ▨Catholic ■Orthodox ▣Christian

Christianity in Curaçao was majority Catholic in 1900 (82%) and 2020 (79%), with a notable Protestant minority (17% both years). Independent Christianity has grown over that same period (4% in 2020).

Religion in Curaçao

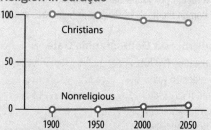

The Christian share of the population declined from 1900 to 2020, from 100% to 93%. This has given way to a slight increase of the nonreligious, which was 4% of the population in 2020.

Bible Translations	Churches	Missionaries	Gospel Access
Languages............13	Denominations 37	Received............460	1900.......... Very high
Full Bible.............8	Congregations.......180	Sent 10	2020.......... Very high

Christianity in Cyprus

Christianity has been in Cyprus since the first missions of the apostles Paul and Barnabas around 45 CE. Barnabas became the first bishop of Cyprus in 50 CE. However, modern Cypriot history has been marked by the bitter tension between Greek and Turkish nationalists in the country since the first clash on the island in 1912. Today, Cyprus is a divided state patrolled by a United Nations Peacekeeping Force. In 2004, the Republic of Cyprus joined the European Union (EU) de jure, but no other nation except Turkey recognizes the Turkish Republic of Northern Cyprus. Nevertheless, Christianity maintains a considerable presence, with two-thirds of the population being members of the Orthodox Church of Cyprus; the country is home to around a dozen major Orthodox monasteries.

Facts to Consider

- Only a small percentage of people attend regular liturgical services, but Orthodox life in Cyprus is centered in the home, each household equipped with its own honored icon.
- Cyprus is home to one of the oldest monasteries in the world: Stavrovouni Monastery. It was founded by the mother of Constantine and reportedly contains a piece of the cross on which Christ was crucified.
- Anglicans are the largest Protestant group, with 11,000 adherents, mostly citizens of the United Kingdom.
- The Turkish-Cypriot population is concentrated in the north and is mostly Sunni Muslim. There are eight mosques in the country.
- A recent poll found that 48% of respondents believed that discrimination on the basis of religion or belief was widespread in the country.

Indicators & Demographic Data

Population (2020)	1,207,000
% under 15 years	17%
Capital city (pop.)	Nicosia 273,000
% urban dwellers	67% (0.76% p.a.)
Official language	Turkish, Greek
Largest language	Greek (70%)
Largest people	Greek Cypriot (69%)
Largest culture	Greek (69%)
Development	87
Physicians	25
Gender gap	2%

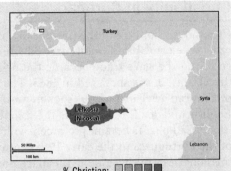

% Christian: ☐☐☐☐☐ 0 3 10 50 75 100

Christian Traditions in Cyprus

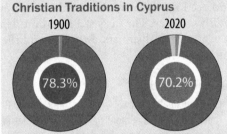

1900 — 78.3%   2020 — 70.2%

☐ Independent ☐ Protestant ☐ Catholic ■ Orthodox ■ Christian

Christians in Cyprus have historically been, and indeed remain, majority Orthodox. Orthodox were 99% of Christians in 1900 and 96% in 2020. Catholics, Protestants, and Independents have grown steadily since 1900.

Religion in Cyprus

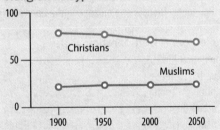

Christianity and Islam are the two largest religions in Cyprus. Christians declined from 78% in 1900 to 70% in 2020, while Muslims grew slightly from 22% to 23% over the same period.

Bible Translations		Churches		Missionaries		Gospel Access	
Languages	14	Denominations	51	Received	260	1900	High
Full Bible	11	Congregations	1,000	Sent	60	2020	Very high

Christianity in Czechia

Historically, both Eastern (Orthodox) and Western (Catholic) Christianity influenced Czechia. Famous missionaries Cyril and Methodius contributed to the growth of Christianity in Moravia (modern-day eastern Czechia), while the Kingdom of Bohemia became Catholic in the 10th century. Protestants were present from the time of the Reformation. Christianity declined with the rise of Communism in Czechoslovakia after World War II. The Czech Republic (now Czechia) was established with the fall of the Soviet Union in 1991, and unlike in many former Soviet Union states, Christianity has not reclaimed its former status in the country.

Facts to Consider

- Under the Act on Church Reconciliation in January 2012, the Czech government agreed to compensate the churches $2.7 billion over 30 years for property seized during the totalitarian regime (1948-1990).
- The second largest denomination is the Czechoslovak Hussite Church, which was formed after World War I by those who exited the Catholic Church after Rome's refusal to use vernacular in the liturgy, allow for married priests, and encourage greater participation of the laity. The Czechoslovak Hussite Church considers itself Reformed Catholic, and roughly half of all Hussite priests are women.
- Jehovah's Witnesses from Germany entered Bohemia and Moravia in 1907, and they were persecuted under Communism for refusing military service. Today they number around 29,500 and are the fourth largest denomination in the country.

Indicators & Demographic Data

Population (2020)................................10,633,000
% under 15 years 16%
Capital city (pop.)........................... Prague 1,306,000
% urban dwellers............................. 74% (0.20% p.a.)
Official language..................................... Czech
Largest language.................................Czech (94%)
Largest people .... Czech (Bohemian) (92%)
Largest culture .... Czech (92%)
Development...89
Physicians..37
Gender gap..1%

% Christian: ▢▢▢▣▣ 0 3 10 50 75 100

Christian Traditions in Czechia

1900 — 96.9%   2020 — 34.7%

☐Independent ☐Protestant ▣Catholic ▣Orthodox ▣Christian

Christianity in Czechia has historically been majority Catholic (89% in 1900 and 2020). Protestants and Independents grew over the 20th century and together represented 11% of Christians in 2020.

Religion in Czechia

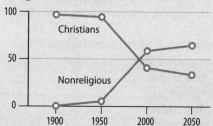

The Christian population of Czechia declined dramatically over the 20th century, from 97% in 1900 to 35% in 2020. Meanwhile, the nonreligious realized the largest gains, growing from less than 1% to 65% during the same period.

Bible Translations	Churches	Missionaries	Gospel Access
Languages............30	Denominations 64	Received.......... 1,700	1900.......... Very high
Full Bible............22	Congregations...... 4,100	Sent 270	2020.......... Very high

Christianity in Denmark

Christianity in Denmark dates to the 9th century. By 1536, one of its monarchs, King Christian III, adopted Lutheranism. Despite the presence of Catholics and other forms of Protestantism, such groups made little numeric gains. Today the Evangelical Lutheran People's Church of Denmark (ELC, the country's national church) represents over 75% of the country's population, a decline in membership since the early 2000s when it comprised 86%. The ELC has about 2,400 ordained pastors, nearly 56% of whom are women. New ordinations have steadily fallen in recent years. Despite high membership figures, regular church attendance is only around 2%. Denmark has been a destination for migrants and refugees, which has resulted in churches for immigrants from Nigeria, Uganda, Burundi, and Iran.

Facts to Consider

- Most Catholics in Denmark live in or near Copenhagen and are increasingly served by Catholics from Poland, Croatia, and the Philippines.
- The Charismatic renewal spread across Denmark starting in the 1990s and grew both within the Lutheran church and in new churches. Many ethnic minorities identify as Charismatic.
- Islam in Denmark grew from zero in 1900 to 6% of the population in 2020 (320,000). Most Muslims are from Turkey, Iraq, Lebanon, Syria, Pakistan, the Balkans, Somalia, and Iran. The largest Muslim communities are in Copenhagen, Odense, and Aarhus.
- Jews in Denmark date to the 17th century and represent less than 1% of the population. Yet, since 2018, anti-Semitic incidents have escalated with assaults, physical harassment, threats, and vandalism.

Indicators & Demographic Data

Population (2020)	5,797,000
% under 15 years	16%
Capital city (pop.)	Copenhagen 1,346,000
% urban dwellers	88% (0.54% p.a.)
Official language	Danish
Largest language	Danish (89%)
Largest people	Danish (Dane) (89%)
Largest culture	Danish (89%)
Development	93
Physicians	37
Gender gap	2%

% Christian: 0 3 10 50 75 100

Christian Traditions in Denmark

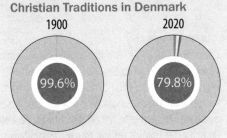

1900 — 99.6%
2020 — 79.8%

☐ Independent ☐ Protestant ■ Catholic ■ Orthodox ■ Christian

Christians in Denmark have historically been predominantly Protestant, as was the case in both 1900 (100%) and 2020 (97%). This changed very little over the 20th century, with only slight growth of Independents (1%) and Catholics (1%).

Religion in Denmark

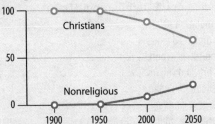

Denmark was nearly 100% Christian in 1900 but dropped to 80% by 2020. This trend is expected to continue, with Christians further declining to 69% by 2050. The nonreligious grew from virtually zero to 14% by 2020.

Bible Translations		Churches		Missionaries		Gospel Access	
Languages	44	Denominations	110	Received	1,000	1900	Very high
Full Bible	38	Congregations	2,900	Sent	600	2020	Very high

Christianity in Djibouti

Djibouti, in the Horn of Africa, is bordered by Somalia and Ethiopia and Eritrea. It was a French colony from 1883 to 1977. The country is 98% Muslim today, with only a small population of Christians (1%), most of whom are Catholic (72%). The slight increase of Christians in recent years is mostly due to the presence of Ethiopian migrants. Most Christians in the country are of Ethiopian or European ancestry; half of all Catholics live in the capital and are poor. Formed in 1978, Caritas Djibouti offers humanitarian aid to help with food shortages and the resettlement of refugees. Nearly all Protestants in the country are Europeans (French, Germans).

Facts to Consider

- Islam is the state religion, and conversions to other religions are highly discouraged. Public proselytizing is illegal.
- Converts are often ostracized, and there are very few indigenous Christians in Djibouti. Once converted, they often keep their faith a secret.
- The Family Code prohibits Muslim women from marrying non-Muslim men. In addition to its civil courts, the country also has a court under Islamic law that can see cases related to marriage, divorce, and inheritance.
- Djibouti is home to about 30,000 refugees, mostly from Somalia, Ethiopia, Yemen, and Eritrea.

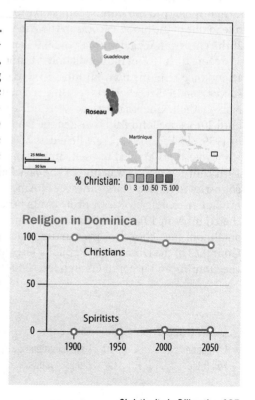

% Christian: 0 3 10 50 75 100

Religion in Djibouti

Christianity in Dominica

Dominica is an island nation in the Caribbean near Guadeloupe and Martinique. It has a population of roughly 75,000, most of whom are Christian (94%). The French began settling Dominica in 1720 and required all enslaved Africans to be baptized, though enslaved people were not considered legitimate Catholics until 1829. The island was an important stop on the Atlantic slave trade until abolition in 1833. It became an independent republic in 1978. The Catholic Church is the largest tradition on the island, followed by the Pentecostal Assemblies of the West Indies.

Facts to Consider

- The Pentecostal/Charismatic renewal came to Dominica first in the 1960s, then again in the 1980s. Nearly every village in Dominica today has a Pentecostal or Catholic Charismatic church.
- Rastafarians have experienced harassment for their use of marijuana for religious purposes. The government is debating decriminalization of less than one ounce of marijuana. Dreadlocks are prohibited in government-funded schools and prisons.
- No laws prohibit discrimination on the basis of sexual orientation or gender identity, and same-sex activity (known as "buggery") is illegal. The Dominica Christian Council has been outspoken in their support of antigay laws.

% Christian: 0 3 10 50 75 100

Religion in Dominica

Christianity in the Dominican Republic

The Dominican Republic consists of the eastern portion of the Caribbean island of Hispaniola, which it shares with Haiti. Christopher Columbus claimed the island for Spain in 1492, displacing the indigenous Taíno peoples and their civilization. Under Spanish rule, indigenous peoples worked in the gold mines and were placed in the *encomienda* system of forced labor. Disease wiped out the local population in one generation. Enslaved Africans arrived starting in 1503 to work sugarcane fields. Significant mixing occurred among Europeans, Blacks, and Taíno, and today the majority of the country is *mestizo* (mixed race). With the continued conquest of the Americas, the economy of the Dominican Republic declined, resulting in widespread poverty. Independence from Spain was achieved in 1821.

The history of the Dominican Republic is intertwined with that of the Catholic Church. Santo Domingo was both the first European settlement and the first Catholic diocese in the Americas. With the country under the dictatorship of Rafael Trujillo from 1930 to 1961, the Catholic Church and the regime initially benefited from mutual support. But in 1960, the Church became outspoken against Trujillo and advocated for democracy in the country. Trujillo was assassinated in 1961. In 2011, the Catholic Church offered a formal apology to the Dominican people for their complicit role in one of the bloodiest eras in the Americas during the 20th century, in which more than 50,000 people died.

More than 79% of the population is Catholic today. Mass attendance remains high (around 53% of Catholics), and surveys report that religion is very important in people's lives. Non–Catholic Church marriages were not legally recognized until 2013. Pope John Paul II visited the Dominican Republic in 1979, 1984 and 1992; Pope Benedict XVI visited in 2011.

Protestants arrived in the Dominican Republic in the 19th century, and it was one of the last Latin American countries to receive a large number of American Protestant missionaries. Puerto Rican Protestants began missions in the country in 1911. The Protestant community remains small, but new churches are starting, such as the Baptist Churches of the Dominican Republic (est. 2002–2003) and the Dominican Lutheran Church (est. 2004).

% Christian: 0 3 10 50 75 100

Religion in the Dominican Republic

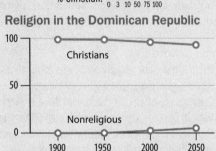

The Dominican Republic has been majority Christian for many centuries and is poised to remain so, despite a slow decline in the Christian share of the population from 98% in 1900 to 95% in 2020. It is projected to drop to 93% in 2050. The nonreligious are growing slightly, rising from virtually zero in 1900 to 3% in 2020. Spiritists have held steady at 2% of the population.

Indicators & Demographic Data

Population (2020)	11,108,000
% under 15 years	28%
Capital city (pop.)	Santo Domingo 3,318,000
% urban dwellers	83% (1.64% p.a.)
Official language	Spanish
Largest language	Spanish (96%)
Largest people	Dominican Mulatto (70%)
Largest culture	Mulatto, Spanish-speaking (70%)
Development	74
Physicians	15
Gender gap	1%

Bible Translations		Churches		Missionaries		Gospel Access	
Languages	10	Denominations	100	Received	2,000	1900	Very high
Full Bible	7	Congregations	7,300	Sent	150	2020	Very high

Facts to Consider

- Catholicism is the official state religion, and it enjoys privileges not offered to other religious groups, such as governmental funding and visa exceptions. Some religious minorities have complained of a lack of constitutional protection.
- The second largest non-Catholic group in the Dominican Republic is the Church of Jesus Christ of Latter-day Saints (Mormons). The first Dominicans converted in the United States and returned home in 1978; American missionaries followed soon after. The Santo Domingo Dominican Republic Temple, dedicated in 2000, was the first Latter-day Saint temple in the Caribbean.
- The Pentecostal/Charismatic movement has swept through the country, with 90% of Protestants and 77% of Catholics witnessing to speaking in tongues, prayers for miracles, or experiencing prophecy in church.
- Pentecostalism has been growing among former gang members escaping violence and seeking a haven for social and personal transformation. For many young men the choice is to join a gang or join a Pentecostal church.
- Many immigrants from Haiti as well as numerous Dominicans follow voodoo (Haitian Vodoun; Dominican Vudú), a mixture of Catholic and traditional African practices.
- Haiti and the Dominican Republic have been in conflict since colonial times. Haiti is poorer, and many Haitians travel to the DR for work, and though economically beneficial to both countries, this arrangement prolongs cross-cultural tensions.

Christian Traditions in the Dominican Republic

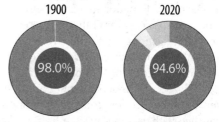

1900 — 98.0% 2020 — 94.6%

☐ Independent ☐ Protestant ▨ Catholic ■ Orthodox ■ Christian

Catholicism is the historic Christian tradition of the country; nearly 100% of Christians were Catholic in 1900 and 86% in 2020. Protestant and Independent groups have made some gains. In 1900, there were only small populations of non-Catholic groups. In 2020, Protestants and Independents together accounted for 14% of Christians. The Pentecostal/Charismatic movement has also made gains, again from virtually zero in 1900 to 14% of the country's population. Evangelicals grew from less than 1% of the population in 1900 to 5% in 2020.

Christian Families in Dominican Republic

Family	Population 2020	%	Trend	Change
Latin-rite Catholic	8,798,000	79.2	↑	0.9
*Pentecostals/Charismatics	1,500,000	13.5	—	-0.2
*Evangelicals	550,000	5.0	↑	1.1
Adventist	457,000	4.1	↑	2.5
Latter-day Saints (Mormons)	150,000	1.4	↑	2.4
Jehovah's Witnesses	104,000	0.9	↑	2.7
Holiness	84,700	0.8	↑	2.5
Nondenominational	34,400	0.3	↑	2.1
Reformed, Presbyterian	22,300	0.2	↑	2.8
Christian Brethren	16,700	0.2	↑	1.8
United church or joint mission	16,300	0.1	↑	1.2
Salvationist	14,800	0.1	↑	2.2
Non-traditional, house, cell	11,100	0.1	↑	1.2
Baptist	10,300	0.1	↑	2.3
Anglican	9,400	0.1	↑	4.0
Restorationist, Disciple	5,100	<0.1	↑	3.9
Methodist	4,300	<0.1	↑	1.8
Mennonite	3,600	<0.1	↑	1.8

Despite a long history of a Catholic majority, the Dominican Republic is now marked by Christian diversity. Pentecostal/Charismatics make up the second largest family of Christians. This includes groups founded outside the country, such as the Assemblies of God, the Church of God, and the Church of God of Prophecy, as well as groups that are indigenous to the region, such as the Assemblies of Christian Churches, the Ark of Salvation, and the Defenders of the Faith. Seventh-day Adventists are the largest non-Catholic denomination, arriving in 1907. The Church of Jesus Christ of Latter-day Saints (Mormons) are the second largest non-Catholic group. Holiness churches include the Church of the Nazarene, the Christian and Missionary Alliance, and the Free Methodists.

* These movements are found within Christian families
— no change

↑↑ extreme growth
↑ growth
↓↓ extreme decline
↓ decline

Christianity in Ecuador

Spanish *conquistadores* and Catholic friars arrived in modern-day Ecuador in 1526, home to the sophisticated Quechua-speaking Inca Empire. Subsequently, massive numbers of indigenous people died from new infectious diseases, and those that survived were subjugated to the *encomienda* system of forced labor. Catholicism was the state religion when Ecuador became independent of Spain in 1830. In the 19th century, Ecuador lost tremendous amounts of territory in conflicts with neighboring countries. In the 1970s, the country experienced a series of civilian and military coups; in 1979, Ecuador transitioned to democracy under a new constitution.

About 84% of the country is Catholic. In the mountain areas, Catholicism is closely linked to traditional religious beliefs in a kind of "folk," or "popular," Catholicism. In the coastal areas, Catholic observance is more formal, and many participate in Catholic education.

Protestant groups arrived in Ecuador in the late 19th and early 20th centuries, the first being the British and Foreign Bible Society. Eventually its work led to the largest Protestant church in the country, the Evangelical Missionary Union Church (280,000 members). In 1956, a Peruvian evangelist introduced the Assemblies of God, which now numbers 224,000. Other larger Protestant groups include the International Church of the Foursquare Gospel, the Christian and Missionary Alliance, and Seventh-day Adventists. Protestant missionaries have been particularly effective in indigenous areas where poorer communities have felt disenfranchised by the Catholic Church. An estimated 62% of Protestants in Ecuador were raised Catholic.

The Pentecostal/Charismatic movement has grown in Ecuador, with 80% of Protestants and 50% of Catholics having witnessed speaking in tongues, prayers for miraculous healing, and prophecies. This kind of Christianity is more popular among indigenous peoples in the highland provinces. One of the most famous martyrdoms in Evangelical Christianity took place in Ecuador: the murder of five American missionaries by the Waodani Amerindians, as told in the popular movie *End of the Spear*. Most Waodani have now become Christians partly due to the work of Elisabeth Elliot and Rachel Saint, the widow and sister of two of the slain missionaries. The first Waodani convert was a woman named Dayuma.

% Christian: 0 3 10 50 75 100

Religion in Ecuador

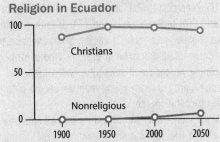

Ecuador has been majority Christian for many centuries and is poised to remain so despite a slow decline in the Christian share of the population, dropping from 98% in 1970, to 95% in 2020, and an estimated 94% by 2050. The nonreligious grew slightly, from virtually zero in 1900 to nearly 4% in 2020.

Indicators & Demographic Data

Population (2020)	17,336,000
% under 15 years	28%
Capital city (pop.)	Quito 1,874,000
% urban dwellers	64% (1.62% p.a.)
Official language	Spanish
Largest language	Spanish (87%)
Largest people	Mestizo (46%)
Largest culture	Mestizo (Spanish) (46%)
Development	75
Physicians	17
Gender gap	2%

Bible Translations		Churches		Missionaries		Gospel Access	
Languages	27	Denominations	240	Received	3,500	1900	Very high
Full Bible	9	Congregations	10,200	Sent	440	2020	Very high

Facts to Consider

- The 1937 concordat between the Holy See and Ecuador continues, with the Catholic Church receiving certain financial privileges. All other religious groups must register with the government, and some have reported that the process is confusing and difficult for smaller groups.
- Same-sex marriage was legalized in July 2019 even though surveys and polls consistently show a lack of public support for it (74% against same-sex marriage). Churches are particularly outspoken against LGBTQ rights, and the country's machismo culture frowns upon same-sex relations. Yet Ecuador is one of the few countries in the world that bans conversion therapy.
- The first Christian radio station in the world was founded in Ecuador in 1931, The Voice of the Andes. Today, known as Heralding Christ Jesus' Blessings (HCJB), the station focuses on ministry via satellite, AM/FM radio, and online.
- Several jungle and lowland indigenous tribes in the eastern headwaters of the Amazon practice traditional ethnic religions, including the Araguro, Auca, Cayapa, Cofán, Tsáchilas, Jivaro, Salasaca, and Secoyas.
- Ecuador is home to small Buddhist (17,700) and Muslim (2,400) populations, mostly concentrated in large urban areas such as Quito, Guayaquil, and Cuenca.

Christian Traditions in Ecuador

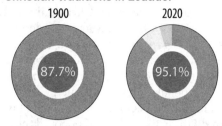

□Independent ▨Protestant ▨Catholic ▨Orthodox ▨Christian

Catholicism is the historic Christian tradition of the country; Christians were 100% Catholic in 1900 and 88% in 2020. In 1900, there were virtually no Christian groups outside of Catholicism. But Protestant and Independent groups have made some gains. In 2020, Protestants and Independents together accounted for 11% of Christians. The Pentecostal/Charismatic movement has also made gains, from virtually zero in 1900 to 13% of the country's population in 2020.

Christian Families in Ecuador

Family	Population 2020	%	Trend	Change
Latin-rite Catholic	14,555,000	84.0	↑	1.3
*Pentecostals/Charismatics	2,150,000	12.4	↑	1.1
*Evangelicals	850,000	4.9	↑	1.8
Holiness	438,000	2.5	↑	3.5
Jehovah's Witnesses	366,000	2.1	↑↑	5.2
Latter-day Saints (Mormons)	306,000	1.8	↑	4.6
Adventist	107,000	0.6	↑↑	7.3
Baptist	45,800	0.3	↑	2.7
Anglican	27,100	0.2	↑↑	8.6
Congregational	17,400	0.1	↑	3.3
Christian Brethren	5,800	<0.1	↑	3.0
Nondenominational	3,200	<0.1	↑	1.3
Eastern Orthodox	2,200	<0.1	↑	1.0
United church or joint mission	2,200	<0.1	↑	0.9
Lutheran	2,100	<0.1	↓	-1.0
Restorationist, Disciple	1,500	<0.1	—	0.4
Mennonite	1,100	<0.1	—	-0.1

Despite a long history of a Catholic majority, Ecuador is now home to considerable Christian diversity. Pentecostal/Charismatics make up the second largest family of Christians. This includes groups founded outside the country, such as the Assemblies of God, the Church of God, and the United Pentecostal Church, as well as groups that are indigenous to the region, such as the Church of the Holy Spirit and the Universal Independent Church of Christ. Jehovah's Witnesses (with high concentrations in coastal areas) and the Church of Jesus Christ of Latter-day Saints together have more than 600,000 members. Holiness churches include the Evangelical Missionary Union Church, the Church of the Nazarene, and the Christian and Missionary Alliance.

* These movements are found within Christian families
— no change

↑↑ extreme growth
↑ growth
↓↓ extreme decline
↓ decline

Christianity in Egypt

According to tradition, Christianity in Egypt dates to the 1st century when St. Mark founded the church of Alexandria. Egypt is the location of many important early Christian movements, including monasticism and the Arian-Athanasian controversy in the 4th century. The majority of the population was affiliated with the Coptic Orthodox Church at the beginning of the Arab Muslim conquest in the mid-7th century. Muslims opposed the use of human forms in art and destroyed many Coptic Christian paintings and icons of Jesus. Christians lost their majority status in the 11th century and suffered persecution under various Muslim regimes up to contemporary times. Despite their minority status, Christians in Egypt form the largest Christian groups in the Middle East–North Africa region.

The Coptic Orthodox Church makes up roughly 9% of the country (figures are difficult to ascertain; estimates range from 6% to 15%). The pope of Alexandria is the head of the Coptic Church, based in Cairo. Christians began to emigrate in the 1950s, and some minority Christian groups such as Greek Orthodox, Armenian Catholics, Chaldeans, and Syrians are rapidly disappearing.

The 2011 Arab Spring had severe ramifications for the Christian community. Many Coptic Orthodox left in the face of growing sectarian pressures. There was an increase of targeted killings of Christians and church bombings after the overthrow of President Mohamed Morsi in 2013. Vicious attacks by the Islamic State (ISIS) also targeted Christians. At the same time, the Arab Spring brought Muslim and Christian communities closer together. Protecting each other during prayer in Tahrir Square, they also came together to demonstrate against Morsi. In addition, President Abdel Fattah al-Sisi was the first Egyptian president to visit the Coptic Orthodox Cathedral during a religious service, which he did on Christmas in 2015.

Protestants arrived in Egypt in the 19th century. The largest Protestant group is the Coptic Evangelical Church, formed by American and Scottish Presbyterians in 1854. Coptic leaders have complained about Protestant "sheep stealing" with the arrival and evangelistic efforts of newer churches. However, Christians have come together in times of strife, and the Coptic pope symbolizes leadership for all Christians in Egypt.

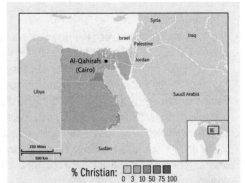

% Christian: 0 3 10 50 75 100

Religion in Egypt

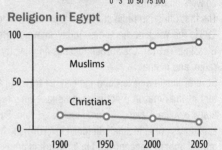

Egypt has been majority Muslim for many centuries in the future. The country was 85% Muslim in 1900, 90% in 2020, and is anticipated to be 92% by 2050. Christianity dropped from 15% in 1900 to 9% in 2020. Jews also declined from 30,000 in 1900 to fewer than 100 in 2020.

Indicators & Demographic Data

Population (2020)	102,941,000
% under 15 years	33%
Capital city (pop.)	Cairo 20,901,000
% urban dwellers	43% (1.90% p.a.)
Official language	Arabic
Largest language	Arabic (98%)
Largest people	Egyptian Arab (61%)
Largest culture	Arab (Arabic) (93%)
Development	70
Physicians	8.1
Gender gap	13%

Bible Translations		Churches		Missionaries		Gospel Access	
Languages	31	Denominations	91	Received	1,500	1900	Low
Full Bible	14	Congregations	4,200	Sent	340	2020	High

Facts to Consider

- Egypt is a major world center for Islam, home to Al-Azhar University (founded around 975), which is the main authority for theology and Islamic affairs and is responsible for spreading Islam in Egypt and around the world.
- Converting from Islam is not illegal, but the government recognizes only conversions to Islam, not from it. Christians face consistent discrimination; Christian women have been particularly targeted for abduction and forced conversion.
- There has been an uptick of violence against Christians in Egypt, such as the New Year's Eve attack in 2011, the beheading of Coptic Christians on a beach in Libya in 2015, the cathedral bombing in 2016, and the bus attack in 2018.
- Evangelical Christians were among the early supporters of the Egyptian Revolution in 2011. The Kasr el-Dobara Evangelical Church, situated just off Tahrir Square, served as a field hospital and a place of refuge during violence.
- Coptic Orthodox have served as missionaries in sub-Saharan Africa, founding several churches. Orthodox monks are increasingly sent abroad to serve as priests in the Coptic diaspora.
- The government bans public religious gatherings of Baha'i, the Church of Jesus Christ of Latter-day Saints, Jehovah's Witnesses, and Shia Muslims.

Christian Traditions in Egypt

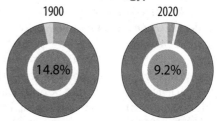

1900   2020

14.8%   9.2%

☐ Independent ☐ Protestant ■ Catholic ■ Orthodox ■ Christian

Orthodoxy is the historic Christian tradition of the country; Christians were 90% Orthodox in 1900 and 91% Orthodox in 2020. In 1900, there were small populations of Catholics and Protestants that made some gains in the 20th century. In 2020, non-Orthodox groups together accounted for 9% of Christians, but their growth is largely due to natural reasons or switching from Orthodox churches, rather than conversion of Muslims. The Pentecostal/Charismatic and Evangelical movements have grown slowly but steadily.

Christian Families in Egypt

Family	Population 2020	%	Trend	Change
Oriental and other Orthodox	8,798,000	8.5	↑	1.0
*Pentecostals/Charismatics	680,000	0.7	↑	1.5
*Evangelicals	420,000	0.4	↑	1.0
Reformed, Presbyterian	288,000	0.3	↑	0.6
Eastern-rite Catholic	205,000	0.2	↑	1.4
Latin-rite Catholic	75,300	0.1	↑↑	10.1
Holiness	53,300	0.1	↑	1.4
Hidden believers in Christ	26,400	<0.1	↑	1.0
Exclusive Brethren	25,400	<0.1	–	0.1
Baptist	4,600	<0.1	↑	1.6
Eastern Orthodox	2,300	<0.1	↓	-3.4
Jehovah's Witnesses	2,300	<0.1	↑↑	5.2
Anglican	2,000	<0.1	–	-0.1
Christian Brethren	2,000	<0.1	–	-0.1
Adventist	850	<0.1	↓	-1.0
Congregational	590	<0.1	–	-0.1
Latter-day Saints (Mormons)	50	<0.1	↓	-3.2

Egypt is home to only meager Christian diversity after many centuries of Coptic Orthodox influence. Pentecostal/Charismatics make up the second largest family of Christians, mostly consisting of groups imported into the country, like the Assemblies of God and United Pentecostal Church. Catholics in Egypt are in seven communities, each with its own rite for worship and serving its own ethnic group: Coptic, Greek, Maronite, Syrian, Armenian, Chaldeans, and Latin-rite (mostly Italians). The Association of Evangelicals in Egypt was founded in 1981 by the General Evangelical Council and is a member of the World Evangelical Alliance. Egypt is home to around 26,400 hidden Muslim-background believers who choose to keep their faith in Christ private for security reasons. Discrimination and persecution against Christians are widespread in the country, but worse for converts from Islam.

* These movements are found within Christian families

– no change

↑↑ extreme growth
↑ growth
↓↓ extreme decline
↓ decline

Christianity in El Salvador

Spain colonized El Salvador beginning in 1525. A smallpox epidemic in the region had already reduced the indigenous population of Nahua-speaking Pipil peoples, as well as Lenca and Mayans. Because the territory of modern-day El Salvador lacked precious metals, unlike elsewhere in the Americas, it experienced a slower rate of both Christianization and colonization. After El Salvador gained independence from Spain in 1821, successive governments alternated in their acceptance or rejection of Catholicism as the official religion. The constitution of 1886 established freedom of religion and secular education. However, the country experienced a series of governmental overthrows in the 20th century, by groups that included Marxist-Leninist influences, in addition to a civil war from 1979 to 1992. The Catholic Church became known as the "church of the martyrs" during this time, as priests and lay leaders risked their lives to challenge the poverty and oppression that the majority of Salvadorans experienced. The Salvadoran military retaliated in the form of death squads, including the famous murder of Archbishop Óscar Romero in 1980, the day after he called upon soldiers to cease their suppression of the Salvadoran people. An estimated 75,000 people were killed or "disappeared" during the war. Pope Francis canonized Romero in 2018.

Protestants arrived in El Salvador in 1896. While traditional Protestant groups have grown modestly, the largest growth has been among the Assemblies of God and the Seventh-day Adventists. Most Evangelicals in the country are members of the Assemblies of God. The Pentecostal/Charismatic movement has also grown rapidly since the 1970s. Many, especially those who live in slums, have found Pentecostalism to be more accessible than Catholicism and have embraced the movement's emphasis on personal transformation. A survey found that 38% of Protestants were raised Catholic, with the most common reason for switching being a desire for a more personal connection with God. The Pentecostal/Charismatic movement has also influenced Catholicism. Both Protestants and Catholics often report witnessing speaking in tongues, miraculous healing, and prophecy in church services.

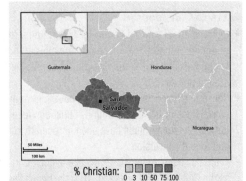

% Christian: 0 3 10 50 75 100

Religion in El Salvador

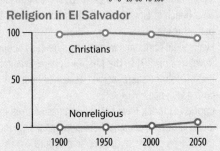

El Salvador has been majority Christian for many centuries and is poised to remain so despite a slow decline in the Christian share of the population from 98% in 1900 to 96% in 2020 and an estimated 94% by 2050. The nonreligious are growing slightly, from virtually zero in 1900 to nearly 3% of the population in 2020.

Indicators & Demographic Data

Population (2020). 6,479,000
% under 15 years 27%
Capital city (pop.) . . . .San Salvador 1,106,000
% urban dwellers. . . . . 73% (1.33% p.a.)
Official language. . . . . Spanish
Largest language. . . . . Spanish (99%)
Largest people . . . . Mestizo (88%)
Largest culture . . . . . .Mestizo (Spanish) (88%)
Development. 67
Physicians. 16
Gender gap. 3%

Bible Translations		Churches		Missionaries		Gospel Access	
Languages.	11	Denominations	110	Received.	1,600	1900	Very high
Full Bible.	6	Congregations.	12,500	Sent	220	2020	Very high

Facts to Consider

- El Salvador is consistently ranked as one of the most violent and deadly countries in the world. Young men in El Salvador have found hope in Evangelical Christianity in the face of violent gangs such as Barrio 18 and MS-13. Joining an Evangelical church is often the only safe alternative to joining, or leaving, a gang.
- Gang members who join Evangelical Protestant churches are often monitored by former gang members to ensure they are routinely attending church and participating in the Evangelical community.
- Prison ministries are particularly effective in spreading Evangelical Christianity, especially among former gang members who seek safety in churches upon their release.
- Some clergy and faith-based NGO workers have reported the government's suspicion of their ministry among active and former gang members. Their work can be perceived as sympathetic to gangs. Some religious workers avoid this kind of ministry out of fear of prosecution.
- The Church of Jesus Christ of Latter-day Saints (Mormons) arrived in the 1950s and now have more than 134,000 members and one temple in San Salvador, dedicated in 2011.
- The majority of the population is baptized Catholic, but traditional indigenous religious practices exist among the indigenous Pipil and Lenca peoples.

Christian Traditions in El Salvador

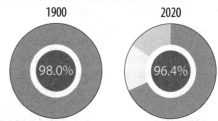

1900 — 98.0% 2020 — 96.4%

☐Independent ☐Protestant ■Catholic ■Orthodox ■Christian

Catholicism is the historic Christian tradition of the country; Christians were virtually 100% Catholic in 1900 and 68% Catholic in 2020. In 1900, there were very few Christian groups outside of Catholicism, but Protestant and Independent groups made significant gains in the 20th century. In 2020, Protestants and Independents together accounted for 32% of Christians. The Pentecostal/Charismatic movement has also made tremendous gains, from being virtually absent in 1900 to representing 26% of the country's population in 2020.

Christian Families in El Salvador

Family	Population 2020	%	Trend	Change
Latin-rite Catholic	4,600,000	71.0	–	-0.3
*Pentecostals/Charismatics	1,700,000	26.2	↑	2.0
*Evangelicals	780,000	12.0	↑	2.5
Non-traditional, house, cell	215,000	3.3	↑	3.0
Adventist	209,000	3.2	↓	-2.5
Latter-day Saints (Mormons)	134,000	2.1	↑	2.1
Jehovah's Witnesses	95,400	1.5	↑	1.1
Restorationist, Disciple	49,200	0.8	↑↑	7.4
Nondenominational	38,200	0.6	–	0.0
Lutheran	33,600	0.5	–	0.5
Holiness	24,500	0.4	–	0.2
Baptist	8,300	0.1	–	0.2
Reformed, Presbyterian	8,200	0.1	↑	4.1
Christian Brethren	1,700	<0.1	–	-0.5
Friends (Quaker)	1,500	<0.1	↓	-0.7
Mennonite	820	<0.1	↑	3.2
Anglican	680	<0.1	↑	1.5

Despite a long history of a Catholic majority, El Salvador is now home to a high level of Christian diversity. Pentecostal/Charismatics make up the second largest family of Christians. This includes groups founded outside the country, such as the Assemblies of God (the largest) and the United Pentecostal Church, but also groups indigenous to the region, such as the Church of the Prince of Peace and the Apostolic Church of the Apostles and Prophets. The country is also home to many nontraditional or cell-like movements, such as networks connected to the Elim Christian Mission and other Independent groups like the Spring of Eternal Life Church of God. Seventh-day Adventists experienced significant growth since their arrival in 1915, now with over 200,000 members.

* These movements are found within Christian families
– no change

↑↑ extreme growth
↑ growth
↓↓ extreme decline
↓ decline

Christianity in Equatorial Guinea

The first Christians in Equatorial Guinea were Portuguese explorers on the island of Bioko in 1472. The area became a Spanish colony in 1778 and gained independence in 1968. Various Protestant missionaries came to the country in the 19th century but never made much headway. The country is 71% Catholic today, partly due to the long European presence there and partly due to the Fang people group who became Catholic starting in the late 1920s. The proportion of baptized Catholics in Equatorial Guinea is higher than in any other African country. The Basilica of the Immaculate Conception in Mongomo is the second largest Catholic Church in Africa.

Facts to Consider

- There is no national religion in Equatorial Guinea, but the Catholic Church and the Reformed Church are the only churches that do not need to register with the government to operate.
- Small Protestant denominations in the country include the Evangelical Church of Equatorial Guinea, the Assemblies of God, the Church of God, and Seventh-day Adventists.
- The Pentecostal/Charismatic renewal arrived in the mid-1990s. Most villages and neighborhoods have several small Pentecostal churches among them, even in areas that are majority Catholic. Some suggest that attendance in Pentecostal churches is higher than in Catholic churches.
- Equatorial Guinea has one of the highest rates of HIV in the world, at 6% of the population. Few Christian organizations are addressing the epidemic.
- African Traditional Religions count 1% of the population as adherents, mostly among the Okak and Ntumu peoples.

Indicators & Demographic Data

Population (2020). 1,406,000
% under 15 years 37%
Capital city (pop.) . . . . Malabo 298,000
% urban dwellers. . . . . .73% (3.62% p.a.)
Official language. . . . . Spanish, French
Largest language. . . . . Fang (62%)
Largest people . . . . Fang (Ntumu, Okak, Pahouin) (62%)
Largest culture . . . . Equatorial Bantu (62%)
Development. 59
Physicians. 3
Gender gap. 15%

% Christian: 0 3 10 50 75 100

Christian Traditions in Equatorial Guinea

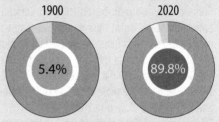

1900 — 5.4% 2020 — 89.8%

☐Independent ☐Protestant ▧Catholic ▨Orthodox ■Christian

The small Christian population in 1900 was mostly Catholic (92%) from the colonial period. By 2020, Catholics were still the majority of Christians (94%), and Protestants and Independents together represented 6% of Christians.

Religion in Equatorial Guinea

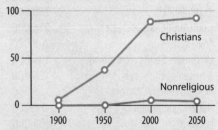

Christians grew from 5% of the population in 1900 to 90% in 2020, mostly at the expense of traditional religionists, who declined from 95% to 1% over the same period. In 2020, the country was also 5% nonreligious and 4% Muslim.

Bible Translations		Churches		Missionaries		Gospel Access	
Languages.	23	Denominations	33	Received.	340	1900	Very low
Full Bible.	10	Congregations. . . .	820	Sent	60	2020	Very high

Christianity in Eritrea

Christianity first arrived in what is now Eritrea in the 4th century. Ethiopian Orthodox immigrants and Catholic missionaries arrived at the beginning of the 19th century, after which Catholics increased during the period of Italian colonization from 1882 to 1936. Eritrea achieved independence from Ethiopia in 1991, which also made the Eritrean Orthodox (Tewahedo) Church independent. Today the country is 41% Orthodox and 51% Muslim. The Eritrean Orthodox Church is the youngest church in the Oriental Orthodox Church family even though its traditions are many centuries old. The largest people group in Eritrea are Tigrai, with Tigrinya the most widely spoken language in the country. Eritrea's government is a dictatorship under President Isaias Afwerki, and there has not been a presidential election since the first one in 1993.

Facts to Consider

- There are four legally recognized religions: Sunni Islam, the Eritrean Orthodox Church, Catholicism, and Evangelical Lutheran churches. All others are subject to surveillance, raids, and imprisonment. Other kinds of Christianity are associated with the West and are considered a threat to the state.
- The government deposed the patriarch of the Eritrean Orthodox Church, Abune Antonios, in 2006 and has controlled the church ever since. Antonios is still under house arrest.
- Eritrea has a terrible record concerning human rights. Eritreans are indefinitely assigned military or civil service for low pay and often in abusive conditions.
- There has been no independent media in Eritrea since 2001. It is one of the most censored countries in the world and routinely puts journalists in jail.

Indicators & Demographic Data

Population (2020)................................5,432,000
% under 15 years 41%
Capital city (pop.) ....Asmara 963,000
% urban dwellers...........................41% (3.67% p.a.)
Official language...................................... none
Largest language..............................Tigrigna (45%)
Largest people ....Tigrai (45%)
Largest culture ....Tigrai (45%)
Development...44
Physicians...0.5
Gender gap..10%

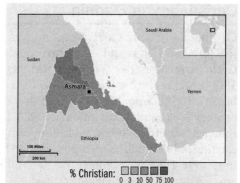

% Christian: ☐☐▨▨▨ 0 3 10 50 75 100

Christian Traditions in Eritrea

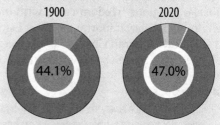

1900 — 44.1%   2020 — 47.0%

☐Independent ☐Protestant ▨Catholic ▨Orthodox ▨Christian

Orthodox Christianity is the historic Christian tradition in Eritrea. Orthodox made up 89% of Christians in 1900 and 85% in 2020. Catholics remained the same at 10%, while both Protestants and Independents grew.

Religion in Eritrea

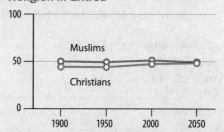

Eritrea is one of a few countries in the world that is nearly equally split between Christians and Muslims. Christianity grew slightly faster than Islam in the 20th century; by 2020 the country was 51% Muslim and 47% Christian.

Bible Translations	Churches	Missionaries	Gospel Access
Languages............15	Denominations 46	Received............220	1900 .... Low
Full Bible.............7	Congregations......1,800	Sent 140	2020 ....High

Christianity in Estonia

Orthodox Christians arrived in modern-day Estonia in the 10th and 11th centuries via missionaries from Russia. Catholic missionaries (Teutonic Knights) arrived in the 13th century. The Estonian Evangelical Lutheran Church became the majority Christian tradition during the 16th-century Protestant Reformation. By 1920, Estonia achieved independence from Russia but fell under authoritarian rule starting in 1934 and was incorporated into the Soviet Union until 1991. The Soviet Union persecuted all religious people and encouraged anti-religious attitudes. Church property was confiscated, and some theologians were deported to Siberia. Religious freedom came with independence, but religion is not very important to most Estonians today. The Evangelical Lutheran Church is the largest denomination, followed by Russian Orthodox and Estonian Orthodox.

Facts to Consider

- Religious observance is very low in Estonia. Polls have suggested that 5% of people attend worship services weekly, 9% pray daily, and 13% believe in God with certainty. It ranks as one of the least religious countries in Europe.
- Interest in neopaganism (traditional nature spirituality) has been on the rise since the turn of the 21st century. These groups claim to represent the pre-Christian religion of Estonia's past.
- The Evangelical Lutheran Church has ordained women since 1967. The church officially opposes same-sex marriage, but church membership is split over the issue.
- Estonia's small Jewish population continues to deal with anti-Semitism, including Holocaust denial and anti-Semitic vandalism.

Indicators & Demographic Data

Population (2020)	1,301,000
% under 15 years	17%
Capital city (pop.)	Tallinn 445,000
% urban dwellers	69% (-0.03% p.a.)
Official language	Estonian
Largest language	Estonian (68%)
Largest people	Northern Estonian (53%)
Largest culture	Estonian (69%)
Development	87
Physicians	34
Gender gap	-2%

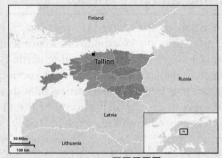

% Christian: 0 3 10 50 75 100

Christian Traditions in Estonia

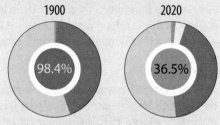

1900 — 98.4%
2020 — 36.5%

☐ Independent ☐ Protestant ▨ Catholic ▨ Orthodox ▨ Christian

In 1900, Christians in Estonia were 56% Protestant and 44% Orthodox. By 2020, Protestants dropped to 52% and Orthodox dropped to 43%.

Religion in Estonia

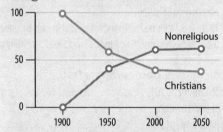

Nonreligious

Christians

Christianity was the historic religion in Estonia until the mid-20th century, when state-sponsored atheism was instituted under the Soviet Union. Christianity has been in decline ever since, with 37% of the population in 2020. The nonreligious were 63% in 2020.

Bible Translations	Churches	Missionaries	Gospel Access
Languages...........23	Denominations 28	Received............170	1900 .... Very high
Full Bible............19	Congregations........590	Sent 40	2020 .... Very high

Christianity in Eswatini

Eswatini (known as Swaziland from 1903–2018) is a small country but has a significant amount of Christian diversity. Different Protestant groups arrived in the region in the 19th century, such as Methodists (1880), Anglicans (1881), and German Lutherans (1887). The African Methodist Episcopal Church, the region's first African-founded church, was formed in 1904 and later received missionary support from the United States. Today most Christians are members of various kinds of African Independent Churches (AICs), including Zionist churches. These churches emphasize Pentecostal-like gifts of the Spirit and charismatic worship as well as many aspects of traditional African culture. These churches are typically more appealing than Western missionary-founded denominations. Catholics make up 5% of the country.

Facts to Consider

- Despite being a monarchy under the rule of King Mswati III since 1986, Eswatini also has an elected parliament with a prime minister. Prime Minister Ambrose Mandvulo Dlamini died in 2020 from COVID-19 after only two years of service.
- The country has many health issues, especially HIV/AIDS. Roughly a quarter of the population is HIV positive. Eswatini also has one of the lowest life expectancies in the world: 58 years.
- Malla Moe and Laura Strand, both of whom were single female missionaries, founded, respectively, The Swazi Evangelical Church and the Free Evangelical Assemblies. Churches in Eswatini are generally majority female.
- The first female Anglican bishop in Africa was Swazi: Bishop Ellinah Ntombi Wamukoya was consecrated in 2012.

Indicators & Demographic Data

Population (2020) 1,439,000
% under 15 years 37%
Capital city (pop.) . . . . Mbabane 64,900
% urban dwellers. . . . . 24% (2.42% p.a.)
Official language . . . . Swati, English
Largest language. . . . . Swati (83%)
Largest people . . . . Swazi (Tekeza) (83%)
Largest culture . . . . Nguni (93%)
Development. 59
Physicians. 1.5
Gender gap 6%

% Christian: 0 3 10 50 75 100

Christian Traditions in Eswatini

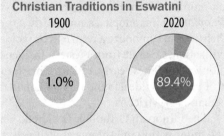

1900 — 1.0%
2020 — 89.4%

☐ Independent ☐ Protestant ▨ Catholic ▧ Orthodox ■ Christian

The very small population of Christians in 1900 (less than 1,000) were mostly Protestants (85%). In 2020, Independents made up the largest Christian tradition (73%), followed by Protestants (20%). The country is 51% Pentecostal/Charismatic.

Religion in Eswatini

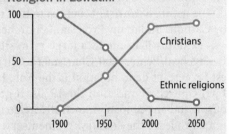

Christianity and African Traditional Religions had contrasting trends over the 20th century. In 1900, the country was 99% traditional religions and 1% Christian. But by 2020, it was 89% Christian and 8% traditionalist.

Bible Translations	Churches	Missionaries	Gospel Access
Languages. 10	Denominations 140	Received. 890	1900 . . . . Very low
Full Bible. 8	Congregations. 2,500	Sent 120	2020 . . . . Very high

Christianity in Ethiopia

Christianity arrived in modern-day Ethiopia in the early 4th century. It was the official religion of the Kingdom of Aksum and the successive Ethiopian Empire until 1974. Ethiopia is one of only two countries in Africa (the other is Liberia) to have largely avoided European colonization in the 19th and 20th centuries (though Italy briefly occupied it from 1936 to 1947). Ethiopia has tremendous symbolic importance for African Christians. Psalm 68:31 speaks of Ethiopia (Cush) stretching out her hands unto God, and some believe that the Queen of Sheba (who visited King Solomon) was from Ethiopia. In the 19th century, the term *Ethiopianism* was adopted among early African Independent Christians to symbolize a return to the golden age of African civilization, separate from Western influence, missions, and colonization. These early African Christians looked toward Ethiopia to provide a foundation of Christianity that was in the hands of Africans.

The Ethiopian Orthodox Tewahedo Church is the largest denomination in Ethiopia as well as the largest Oriental Orthodox Church in the world. It also lays claim to being one of very few precolonial churches in sub-Saharan Africa. Ethiopian Christianity has taken on many unique practices, such as ritual circumcision, Saturday and Sunday sabbath, and dietary laws from the Hebrew Bible. Ge'ez is the liturgical language of the church, though sermons are usually delivered in the local language. *Tewahedo* is Ge'ez for "united as one," in reference to their belief in the unified human and divine nature of Christ in contrast to the "two natures" held by Catholic and many Protestant churches.

Ethiopia is home to a large minority of Protestant/Evangelical/Pentecostal/Charismatic Christians. The largest Protestant denomination is the Kale Heywet (Word of Life) Church, founded in the 1920s. It grew substantially during Italian occupation when all foreign missionaries were forced to leave the country. Women served as evangelists, even at great risk to their lives. The Pentecostal/Charismatic movement arrived in the 1950s and grew substantially in the following decade. Today it is a dominant current in Ethiopian Protestant and Independent Christianity.

% Christian: 0 3 10 50 75 100

Religion in Ethiopia

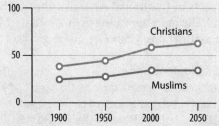

Christianity was the largest religion in Ethiopia in 1900 (38%), followed by traditional religionists (37%) and Muslims (25%). These were still the largest religions in the country 120 years later, though Christianity has grown more rapidly. In 2020, Ethiopia was 60% Christian, 34% Muslim, and less than 6% traditional religionist.

Indicators & Demographic Data

Population (2020)	112,759,000
% under 15 years	39%
Capital city (pop.)	Addis Ababa 4,794,000
% urban dwellers	22% (4.40% p.a.)
Official language	none
Largest language	Oromo (34%)
Largest people	Amhara (26%)
Largest culture	Oromo (34%)
Development	46
Physicians	0.2
Gender gap	15%

Bible Translations		Churches		Missionaries		Gospel Access	
Languages	108	Denominations	82	Received	2,500	1900	Medium
Full Bible	26	Congregations	61,400	Sent	270	2020	Very high

Facts to Consider

- In November 2020, Ethiopia was on the brink of civil war in the Tigray region. The war was between the Tigray Regional Government, led by the Tigray People's Liberation Front, and Prime Minister Abiy Ahmed's military forces, with support from Eritrean forces. This has caused a humanitarian conflict where millions of people, especially children, have been cut off from aid such as food, medicine, and water.
- The Ethiopian Orthodox Tewahedo Church is a founding member of the World Council of Churches and the All Africa Council of Churches and continues to be active in ecumenical activities and relationships.
- The Inter-Religious Council of Ethiopia includes Orthodox, Catholics, Protestants, and Muslims and helps promote interreligious harmony in the country.
- Women generally outnumber men in Ethiopian churches, especially in youth movements and Sunday schools, teaching children, and serving on committees.
- Islam has had a long presence in Ethiopia, and Muslims make up 34% of the country. Muslims are concentrated in the east and southwest of the country. Ethiopia is becoming increasingly vulnerable to radical Islamists who claim that Ethiopia was historically a "land of Islam."
- Over 60% of the Darasa, Ometo, and Oromo peoples practice traditional ethnic religions. Many smaller people groups, such as the Anuak, Bako, and Gimira, are over 90% traditionalist.

Christian Traditions in Ethiopia

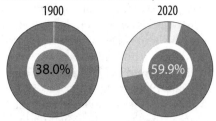

□Independent □Protestant ■Catholic ■Orthodox ■Christian

Orthodox Christianity is the historic Christian tradition of Ethiopia, representing 99% of Christians in 1900. This dropped over the 20th century, with Orthodox representing 67% in 2020. Protestants and Independents made significant gains over this period, together growing from virtually zero in 1900 to 32% of Christians (over 21 million). Many of these newer churches are in the Pentecostal/Charismatic and Evangelical traditions. Evangelicals, for example, made up 19% of the country's population in 2020.

Christian Families in Ethiopia

Family	Population 2020	%	Trend	Change
Oriental and other Orthodox	45,599,000	40.4	↑	2.7
*Evangelicals	21,500,000	19.1	↑	3.5
*Pentecostals/Charismatics	14,000,000	12.4	↑	3.9
United church or joint mission	9,259,000	8.2	↑↑	5.2
Baptist	8,222,000	7.3	↑	0.6
Latin-rite Catholic	841,000	0.7	↑	3.4
Mennonite	530,000	0.5	↑↑	5.9
Adventist	183,000	0.2	↓	-3.8
Restorationist, Disciple	73,000	0.1	↑	2.0
Holiness	61,400	0.1	↑	2.4
Eastern-rite Catholic	58,500	0.1	—	0.3
Christian Brethren	22,200	<0.1	↑	4.0
Jehovah's Witnesses	20,300	<0.1	↑	2.9
Lutheran	20,100	<0.1	—	0.0
Latter-day Saints (Mormons)	3,300	<0.1	↑↑	11.4
Anglican	580	<0.1	↓	-1.9
Eastern Orthodox	520	<0.1	—	0.4

Orthodox Christianity is the largest Christian family, with 40% of the population. Evangelicals are the second largest family, largely due to the Kale Heywet (Word of Life Church) with 8.5 million members. The Evangelical Church of Mekane Yesus is a Lutheran denomination most prominent in the western part of the country and is growing quickly in the south. It is the largest member church of the Lutheran World Federation. Pentecostals/Charismatics are represented by denominations throughout the country, such as Assemblies of God, Place of Paradise Church, International Church of the Foursquare Gospel, and Light of Life Church. There are also small Charismatic groups in Orthodox and Catholic churches. Catholicism is present in two streams: a Catholic Church of the Ethiopian rite and a Western Latin-rite Catholic Church.

*	These movements are found within Christian families	↑↑	extreme growth
		↑	growth
		↓↓	extreme decline
—	no change	↓	decline

Christianity in the Faeroe Islands

The Faeroe Islands is an archipelago north of Scotland, halfway between Norway and Iceland. The autonomous territory of the Kingdom of Denmark is comprised of roughly 50,000 inhabitants within 540 square miles. The main language is Faroese, followed by Danish. Most Faeroese are Protestant Christians (98% in 2020), and as in Denmark, the largest denomination is the Evangelical Lutheran Church (also known as the Danish National Church). Most priests are native Faeroese and trained in Danish universities. The small community of Catholics is served by one priest and six women religious.

Facts to Consider

- There is a small missionary-sending movement among the Faeroese, initially in Greenland and Iceland and now expanding to other countries.
- Traveling among the islands is difficult, so priests can hold only one service per district on Sundays; in his absence, lay parish-clerks conduct worship services.
- There are some Pentecostal movements in the country, such as the Friends of Jesus.
- The Baha'i Faith is the only other religion in the Faeroe Islands. The first Baha'i arrived from Sweden in 1953.

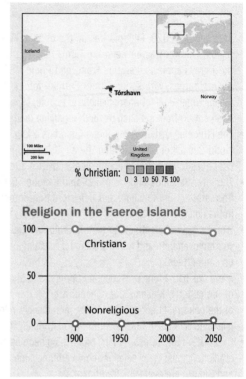

% Christian: 0 3 10 50 75 100

Religion in the Faeroe Islands

Christianity in the Falkland Islands

The Falkland Islands comprise an archipelago in the South Atlantic Ocean off the coast of Argentina. The islands have been fought over by the French, British, Spanish, and Argentinians. Today it is a British overseas territory, although its sovereignty is disputed between the United Kingdom and Argentina. Only roughly 3,000 people inhabit the country, and most are native-born Falkland Islanders who are English speakers of British descent. The islands are majority Christian, mostly Protestants (46%) and Catholics (25%). The Church of England is the largest denomination, first established in the mid-19th century.

Facts to Consider

- The constitution provides fundamental rights and freedoms without distinction of religion or political or other opinions. Freedom of thought and religion, as well as the freedom to change one's religion, are guaranteed.
- Catholics make up 25% of the island, but that is only around 700 people. There are two priests in the country, but no religious brothers or sisters. Most Catholics are expatriates.
- The first Baha'i in the Falkland Islands arrived in 1954. A congregation was established in 1973 and is still active today.

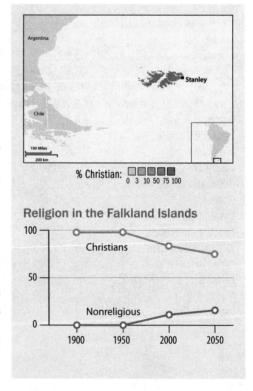

% Christian: 0 3 10 50 75 100

Religion in the Falkland Islands

Christianity in Fiji

The first Christians in Fiji were escaped convicts from Australia in 1804. By 1830, Tahitian missionaries from the London Missionary Society arrived, followed by Wesleyans from Tonga and Britain (1835), French Catholics (1844), Adventists (1890), and Assemblies of God (1926). The churches all grew quickly in the 19th century, mostly due to the conversion of chiefs. However, indigenous Christian leadership did not develop until the mid-20th century. Today, Fiji is 31% Methodist, and Wesleyan Christianity is prominent in the culture. Methodists comprise two-thirds of the indigenous Fijian population and are involved in education, especially in villages. Fiji is a very religious country, with upward of 80% of people in urban areas attending religious services at least once a week.

Facts to Consider

- The Methodist Church has a plan that currently emphasizes personal evangelism, theological education, nurture of the laity, urban mission, and ecumenical and interfaith dialogue. Methodists are also on the forefront of environmental advocacy, especially combating climate change.
- Catholics are the second largest denomination in the country, with the first Fijian priest ordained in 1955. Most Catholics are indigenous Fijians and Indo-Fijians. The Catholic Church is a major provider of emergency relief.
- The Christian Mission Fellowship International was founded in Fiji by a Pentecostal minister and evangelist, Suliasi Kurulo. The church is heavily involved in mission, evangelism, theological education, and media outreach.
- Women in Fiji experience one of the highest rates of violence in the world. An estimated 74% of women have experienced physical, sexual, and/or emotional abuse.

Indicators & Demographic Data

Population (2020)	925,000
% under 15 years	28%
Capital city (pop.)	Suva 166,000
% urban dwellers	57% (1.37% p.a.)
Official language	none
Largest language	Fijian (44%)
Largest people	Fijian (Bauan, Mbau) (30%)
Largest culture	Fijian (55%)
Development	74
Physicians	8.4
Gender gap	5%

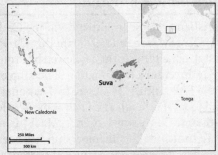

% Christian: 0 3 10 50 75 100

Christian Traditions in Fiji

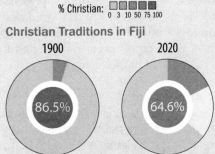

1900 — 86.5% 2020 — 64.6%

☐ Independent ☐ Protestant ■ Catholic ■ Orthodox ■ Christian

Christianity in Fiji is historically majority Protestant (95% in 1900), but over the 20th century, the Protestant share declined with the increase of other groups. Independents were virtually non-existent in 1900, but in 2020 Independents and Catholics were each 17% of Christians.

Religion in Fiji

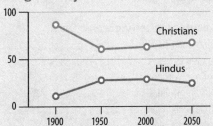

Fiji is a religiously diverse country. In 2020, Christianity was the largest religion (65%), followed by Hindus (27%), Muslims (6%), and smaller communities of Sikhs, Baha'i, and Jains.

Bible Translations		Churches		Missionaries		Gospel Access	
Languages	25	Denominations	47	Received	660	1900	Very high
Full Bible	16	Congregations	4,100	Sent	120	2020	Very high

Christianity in Finland

Christianity came to Finland via the Catholic crusade by Eric IX of Sweden in 1155. Orthodox Christianity came via Russia in the 12th century, followed by Protestants soon after the 16th-century Reformation. The king became Lutheran in the 17th century. There are two national churches in Finland today, Lutheran and Orthodox. While the Evangelical Lutheran Church of Finland (ELCF) is much larger and more influential, its membership has been declining over time despite its strong historical presence and integration into Finnish culture. Regular Sunday attendance is low, around 4% attending weekly and 10% monthly. Around 18% of Finns report praying daily, and 10% say religion is very important in their lives.

Facts to Consider

- The Pentecostal Church of Finland is the second largest denomination. Pentecostalism grew rapidly in the 1990s through the Vineyard movement, the Toronto Blessing, and the Faith Movement.
- The Lighthouse Christian Centre is an English-speaking, primarily African Pentecostal congregation in Helsinki. Roughly 54,000 people in Finland have African backgrounds.
- The ELCF has around 300 missionaries abroad, about 70% of whom are women.
- The ELCF struggles with the ongoing debate over same-sex marriage. National parliament approved it in 2014 with the support of the ELCF archbishop. Though the 2016 synod did not authorize a rite for same-sex marriage, it did grant pastors permission to pray with couples in same-sex unions.

Indicators & Demographic Data

Population (2020)	5,580,000
% under 15 years	17%
Capital city (pop.)	Helsinki 1,305,000
% urban dwellers	86% (0.42% p.a.)
Official language	none
Largest language	Finnish (89%)
Largest people	Finnish (Finn) (89%)
Largest culture	Finnish (89%)
Development	92
Physicians	32
Gender gap	0%

% Christian: 0 3 10 50 75 100

Christian Traditions in Finland

1900 — 100%
2020 — 77.1%

☐ Independent ☐ Protestant ■ Catholic ■ Orthodox ■ Christian

Protestantism is the historic Christian tradition of Finland, representing 98% of Christians in 1900. By 2020, Orthodox, Catholics, and Independents had each grown only slightly, with Protestants still 97% of Christians.

Religion in Finland

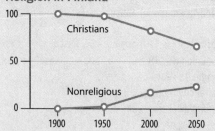

Finland is historically a majority Christian country, but the Christian share of the population dropped from 100% in 1900 to 77% by 2020. The nonreligious grew from virtually zero in 1900 to nearly 20% in 2020.

Bible Translations		Churches		Missionaries		Gospel Access	
Languages	31	Denominations	77	Received	560	1900	Very high
Full Bible	23	Congregations	1,700	Sent	1,000	2020	Very high

Christianity in France

The first Christians believed to have set foot in France were female followers of Jesus around 49 CE. Christianity quickly became the major religion of France and has played an integral part in its history, cultural development, and society. France owes its importance in Western church history to its monastic movements (Beguines), Christian scholarship (Anselm of Canterbury, Thomas Aquinas), and missionary sending (Jesuits and others), among other contributions. French Protestants (Huguenots), with a strong passion for missionary expansion, challenged the Catholic majority of the 16th century and suffered severe persecution and then exodus in the 17th century. The French Revolution of 1789 was detrimental to Christianity and encouraged the growth of secular rational thinking. Secularizing trends continued in the early 20th century with the separation of church and state in 1905 and the closure of many religious schools; many religious orders left the country as well.

Although Catholic affiliation remains somewhat high (57%), Catholic beliefs and practices are on the decline. Currently 5% of French attend Mass monthly, and 2% attend weekly. Most practicing Catholics are in urban centers. The number of priests has also fallen rapidly, as have the number of religious brothers and sisters. While many dioceses are facing closures or mergers, foreign priests are arriving to help from sub-Saharan Africa and Southeast Asia.

French Protestants, including Evangelicals and Pentecostals, have increased since the 1960s. The Evangelical Gypsy (Roma) Mission has had tremendous growth, and in 2015 the largely Roma group Vie et Lumière had 150,000 members. There are also immigrant Protestant groups from Francophone Africa, the Caribbean, Asia, and central Europe. The largest Protestant group is the United Protestant Church of France, consisting of Lutherans and the Reformed Church. One-third of their pastors are women.

France is widely considered a secular country. In the last few decades, many have criticized France's particular brand of militant secularism, *la laïcité*, as a veiled fundamentalist form of Islamophobia. The government prohibition against the wearing of symbols of religious belief—the hijab, in particular—has led to arrests, school expulsions, and protests.

% Christian: 0 3 10 50 75 100

Religion in France

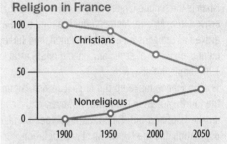

France's Christian population has been in decline, dropping from 99% in 1900 to 63% in 2020. The country is becoming more religiously diverse with the increase of Muslims, increasing from 0.1% (50,000) in 1900 to over 9% in 2020 (6.2 million); France now has the largest Muslim population in Western Europe. The nonreligious (atheists and agnostics) are 25% of the population.

Indicators & Demographic Data

Population (2020)	65,721,000
% under 15 years	18%
Capital city (pop.)	Paris 11,017,000
% urban dwellers	81% (0.67% p.a.)
Official language	French
Largest language	French (65%)
Largest people	French (42%)
Largest culture	French (42%)
Development	90
Physicians	32
Gender gap	1%

Bible Translations		Churches		Missionaries		Gospel Access	
Languages	79	Denominations	370	Received	10,000	1900	Very high
Full Bible	44	Congregations	23,700	Sent	10,000	2020	Very high

Facts to Consider

- An October 2021 report estimated that around 3,000 priests had sexually abused 330,000 children in France in the last 70 years, all of which was systematically covered up by the church's hierarchy.
- The Charismatic renewal began in the French Catholic Church with prayer groups in 1971. Many of these groups grew into larger Charismatic communities. Pentecostalism has been introduced largely through immigrant groups.
- France has historically been a missionary-sending country and still sends out many thousands of missionaries, though many have reconceptualized mission as development work around the world.
- Islam is the second largest religion in France. In 2016, many immigrants arrived from Algeria, Morocco, Tunisia, and sub-Saharan Africa. Others arrived as refugees from Syria, Lebanon, and Turkey. Anti-Muslim sentiment is on the rise, especially since the ISIS attacks in 2015 that killed 130 people in Paris.
- Jews in France make up the largest Jewish community in Europe and the fourth largest in the world. However, anti-Semitic attacks are also on the rise, and anti-Semitic stereotypes persist among the French population and the French Muslim population.

Christian Traditions in France

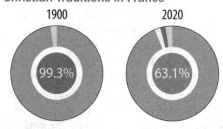

1900   2020

☐Independent ☐Protestant ☐Catholic ■Orthodox ■Christian

Catholics were 98% of Christians in 1900 but dropped to 94% by 2020. Protestants and Independents, who together were 2% of Christians in 1900, doubled to 4% by 2020. Pentecostals/Charismatics now number around 1 million and are 2% of Christians. The Jehovah's Witnesses are the largest Independent Christian group, with 267,000 members. The Church of Jesus Christ of Latter-day Saints built their first temple in France in 2017.

Christian Families in France

Family	Population 2020	%	Trend	Change
Latin-rite Catholic	37,396,000	56.9	–	0.0
*Pentecostals/Charismatics	1,000,000	1.5	↓	-1.1
Reformed, Presbyterian	417,000	0.6	–	0.2
Eastern Orthodox	412,000	0.6	↑	0.8
Oriental and other Orthodox	358,000	0.5	–	-0.1
*Evangelicals	300,000	0.5	↓	-4.1
Lutheran	279,000	0.4	↑	0.8
Jehovah's Witnesses	267,000	0.4	↑	0.8
Eastern-rite Catholic	144,000	0.2	↑	4.0
Old Catholic Church	66,200	0.1	–	0.2
Nondenominational	66,100	0.1	↑	0.7
Latter-day Saints (Mormons)	42,000	0.1	↑	1.6
Exclusive Brethren	24,900	<0.1	–	0.3
Adventist	19,000	<0.1	↑	2.7
Anglican	15,300	<0.1	–	0.2
Baptist	14,500	<0.1	↑	1.5
Christian Brethren	5,900	<0.1	↓	-0.8
Mennonite	3,800	<0.1	–	-0.3
Hidden believers in Christ	3,100	<0.1	–	0.5
Restorationist, Disciple	2,700	<0.1	↑	2.2
Holiness	1,700	<0.1	↑	1.5
Methodist	1,700	<0.1	↑	0.8
Salvationist	930	<0.1	↓	-1.7

Catholics are by far the largest Christian family in France. Pentecostals/Charismatics make up the second largest family, consisting of large groups such as the Assemblies of God and Vie et Lumière as well as smaller networks such as the New Apostolic Church, the Open Door, and the Evangelical Revival Church. Catholic Charismatics also number among them. While Reformed/Presbyterians mostly include the large Protestant Union Church, they also include smaller denominations that declined the 1938 merger of Lutherans and Reformed churches. Orthodox in France are from many ethnic groups, including Greeks, Armenians, and Russians. France is also home to several Old Catholic churches, some of which are Celtic-rite (as opposed to Latin-rite). There are at least five denominations of Jehovah's Witnesses, the most of any country in the world.

* These movements are found within Christian families
– no change

↑↑ extreme growth
↑ growth
↓↓ extreme decline
↓ decline

Christianity in French Guiana

French settlers arrived in modern-day French Guiana in the 16th century. It was a slave colony until the time of the French Revolution (1789–1799) and then used as a penal colony for prisoners. Today, French Guiana is a French overseas department and is ethnically diverse, with a large population of Hmong from Vietnam and Laos who arrived in the 1970s with the help of Catholic missionaries. The largest spoken languages are Guianese Creole French, French, Haitian Creole, and Aukan. Catholicism is the largest religion, and most Catholics are either people born in Guiana (Whites, mixed race, and indigenous people) or immigrant laborers from France, the Antilles, and Brazil, mainly working at the Guiana Space Center. There are small communities of Protestants, including Adventists, Assemblies of God, and Christian Brethren.

Facts to Consider

- The Jehovah's Witnesses are the second largest denomination in the country, first arriving from Guadeloupe. In 1993, a large complex was built featuring an Assembly Hall, five Kingdom Halls, three apartments, and three missionary homes.
- Muslims in French Guiana are mostly Sunnis from Lebanon and Afghanistan. There is one Islamic center and one Islamic school in Cayenne.
- Hindus in French Guiana are largely descendants of indentured servants brought from India during the colonial period.
- The Chinese population (roughly 15,000) is primarily from Zhejiang Province and Guangdong Province in mainland China.

Indicators & Demographic Data

Population (2020)	304,000
% under 15 years	32%
Capital city (pop.)	Cayenne 58,600
% urban dwellers	86% (2.55% p.a.)
Official language	French
Largest language	Guianese Creole French (43%)
Largest people	Guianese Mulatto (36%)
Largest culture	Creole, French-speaking (40%)
Development	76
Physicians	19
Gender gap	1%

% Christian: 0 3 10 50 75 100

Christian Traditions in French Guiana

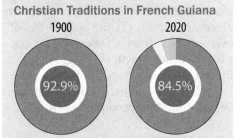

1900 — 92.9%

2020 — 84.5%

☐Independent ☐Protestant ▨Catholic ▨Orthodox ▮Christian

In 1900, all Christians in French Guiana were Catholic. By 2020, Protestants and Independents made some gains so that the Catholic share dropped to 91%.

Religion in French Guiana

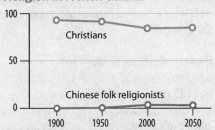

Christians

Chinese folk religionists

French Guiana has been majority Christian for many centuries (85% in 2020). The second largest religion is Chinese folk religionists (nearly 4%), who are followers of indigenous religions of China that include elements of Daoism, Confucianism, and/or Buddhism.

Bible Translations		Churches		Missionaries		Gospel Access	
Languages	20	Denominations	13	Received	220	1900	Very high
Full Bible	5	Congregations	180	Sent	20	2020	Very high

Christianity in French Polynesia

Explorers from Spain and Britain were the first Europeans to sight the islands. The two countries alternated control during the 17th and 18th centuries, with the territory finally coming under French rule in the 19th century. Protestant and Catholic influence shifted accordingly with colonial powers. French Polynesia stretches over 1,200 miles in the South Pacific Ocean and consists of 118 islands and atolls. Tahiti is the most populated island, with 69% of the population, and home to the capital, Papeete. The 118 islands have been an overseas collectivity of France since 1946, when residents also gained French citizenship. The Archdiocese of Papeete (Tahiti) is the center of Catholic life and oversees the suffragan Diocese of Taiohae o Tefenuaentata, which depends heavily on foreign missionaries. The Maohi Protestant Church traces its origins to the London Mission, Basel Mission, and Paris Mission as early as 1797. It is the largest Protestant denomination today.

Facts to Consider

- French Polynesia has many indigenous Christian movements, including a group that is entirely Hakka Chinese (Alleluia Church) and the Church of Jesus Christ of Latter-day Saints, which is the third largest denomination.
- Traditional Chinese religion is practiced among the Hakka Chinese mostly in Papeete, but many have become Christians, especially the youth.
- There is no formal Christian council in French Polynesia, but Catholics and Protestants come together to participate in the Week of Prayer for Christian Unity.

Indicators & Demographic Data

Population (2020)	291,000
% under 15 years	22%
Capital city (pop.)	Papeete 136,000
% urban dwellers	62% (0.65% p.a.)
Official language	French
Largest language	Tahitian (72%)
Largest people	Tahitian (62%)
Largest culture	Tahitian (63%)
Development	72
Physicians	4.4
Gender gap	5%

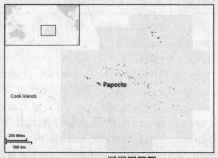

% Christian: 0 3 10 50 75 100

Christian Traditions in French Polynesia

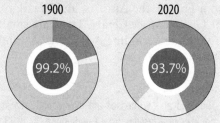

1900 — 99.2%
2020 — 93.7%

☐ Independent ☐ Protestant ▨ Catholic ■ Orthodox ■ Christian

French Polynesia has historically been majority Protestant (77% in 1900) but became more diverse in its Christian presence over the 20th century. In 2020, Christians were 44% Catholic, 38% Protestant, and 19% Independent.

Religion in French Polynesia

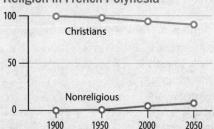

French Polynesia has been a majority Christian country for many centuries and saw its Christian population drop only slightly from 99% in 1900 to 94% in 2020. The nonreligious have increased to 5% of the population.

Bible Translations		Churches		Missionaries		Gospel Access	
Languages	13	Denominations	13	Received	440	1900	Very high
Full Bible	4	Congregations	600	Sent	30	2020	Very high

Christianity in Gabon

Italian Catholic missionaries established a mission in Gabon in 1673. The area was under French colonial rule from 1910 until independence in 1960. Today, Gabon is majority Catholic (49%) but is also home to a large nondenominational strand of Christianity. The second largest denomination in the country is the Church of the Initiates, also known as the Religion of d'Iboga, or the Bwiti movement, which arose at the end of the 19th century. It is most popular among the Fang people and represents a mixture of Christian and traditional religious beliefs. It practices an *iboga* initiation instead of baptism. The movement is explicitly Christian, however, in its belief in Jesus as divine Savior.

Facts to Consider

- The largest Protestant church is the Evangelical Church of Gabon, which was founded in 1842 and represents 7% of the country's population.
- The Catholic Charismatic movement actively works to attract people to the Catholic Church against the growing Evangelical Protestant churches.
- The number of Muslims in Gabon has grown from virtually zero in 1900 to more than 205,000 in 2020. Most Muslims are foreigners from elsewhere in West Africa.
- Although most of the population is Christian or Muslim, many people practice faiths that combine elements of these monotheistic religions with traditional beliefs.
- Muslim, Protestant, and Catholic leaders meet regularly and attend each other's religious festivals to promote religious tolerance in the country.
- The number one cause of death in Gabon is HIV/AIDS; roughly 51,000 adults and children live with the disease.

Indicators & Demographic Data

Population (2020)	2,151,000
% under 15 years	36%
Capital city (pop.)	Libreville 834,000
% urban dwellers	90% (2.27% p.a.)
Official language	French
Largest language	Fang (31%)
Largest people	Fang (Ogowe) (24%)
Largest culture	Northwestern Bantu (46%)
Development	70
Physicians	4.1
Gender gap	9%

% Christian: 0 3 10 50 75 100

Christian Traditions in Gabon

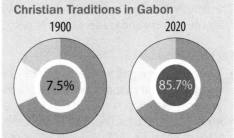

1900 — 7.5% 2020 — 85.7%

☐ Independent ☐ Protestant ▦ Catholic ▨ Orthodox ■ Christian

The small Christian community in Gabon in 1900 was mostly Catholic (69%) with some Protestants (16%) and Independents (15%). These percentages were nearly the same in 2020.

Religion in Gabon

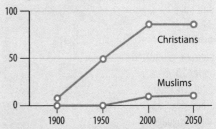

Gabon was mostly traditional religionists at the start of the 20th century (93%). By 2020, nearly the entire population had become Christian (86%) or Muslim (9.5%). Just under 3% of the population exclusively practices traditional religions.

Bible Translations		Churches		Missionaries		Gospel Access	
Languages	50	Denominations	29	Received	440	1900	Low
Full Bible	9	Congregations	3,800	Sent	20	2020	Very high

Christianity in The Gambia

The Portuguese arrived in the Muslim-majority Gambia in the 15th century and participated in the lucrative slave trade, in which an estimated 3 million people were enslaved. The first permanent Catholic mission was established in 1849. The country is 5% Christian today, mostly Catholic and mostly in urban areas among the Aku Creoles, descendants of freed enslaved people. Among the indigenous peoples, some Mandingo and larger numbers of Wolof have become Christians as well. The New Apostolic Church is the second largest denomination, arriving in the 1970s from Germany. The country also has many Yoruba churches, consisting of migrant workers and traders from Nigeria.

Facts to Consider

- The Catholic relief organization Caritas began work in 2011 and engages in various kinds of work, including HIV/AIDS support, sanitation, and emergency response.
- Worldwide Evangelisation Crusade (WEC International) has been at work in the country since 1966. They have 20 national staffers alongside various ministries that operate a health clinic, nursery and primary school, and a boys' hostel.
- The Gambia is 89% Muslim, with Islam concentrated among the Mandingo, Fula, Wolof, and Sarakole peoples. Most are Sunni of the Maliki school, though there are also influential Sufi brotherhoods.
- Intermarriage between Muslims and Christians is common, and their religious differences are generally respected among family members and neighbors.

Indicators & Demographic Data

Population (2020). 2,293,000
% under 15 years 44%
Capital city (pop.) . . . . Banjul 451,000
% urban dwellers. . . . . .63% (3.75% p.a.)
Official language. . . . . .English
Largest language. . . . . .Mandingo (41%)
Largest people . . . . Mandinka (Sose) (37%)
Largest culture . . . . Western Bantoid (Atlantic) (46%)
Development. 46
Physicians. 1.1
Gender gap. 11%

% Christian: 0 3 10 50 75 100

Christian Traditions in The Gambia

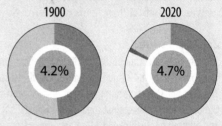

1900 — 4.2%
2020 — 4.7%

☐ Independent ☐ Protestant ▣ Catholic ▪ Orthodox ▪ Christian

The small Christian population in 1900 was nearly evenly split between Protestants (51%) and Catholics (49%). In 2020, Christians were 66% Catholic and 16% each Protestant and Independent.

Religion in The Gambia

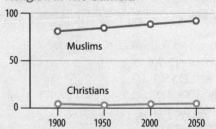

The Gambia is a majority Muslim country, and the Muslim share increased from 81% in 1900 to 89% in 2020. Traditional religions are the second largest, followed by Christians, each just under 5% in 2020.

Bible Translations	Churches	Missionaries	Gospel Access
Languages. 30	Denominations 44	Received. 190	1900 . . . . Very low
Full Bible. 11	Congregations. 350	Sent 4	2020 . . . . Medium

Christianity in Georgia

The Georgian Orthodox Church is one of the oldest churches in the world, born from missionary activity as early as the time of the apostles. The conversion of Georgia is attributed to a young female slave, Nino of Cappadocia, in the 4th century. Muslims ruled the region at various times throughout history, but few Georgians converted. Georgia was under Soviet rule from 1921 to 1991, causing a drastic drop in the number of Christians. However, the Georgian Orthodox Church was a major force in preserving Georgian identity and culture, with many returning to their ancient tradition after the fall of the Soviet Union. The Armenian Orthodox Church is the second largest denomination, nearly all ethnic Armenians.

Facts to Consider

- The Jehovah's Witnesses are the largest non-Orthodox and non-Catholic group. The first convert learned of the faith in a Soviet prison camp in Siberia and returned to Georgia in 1964. They spread through small meetings and today have 37,000 members.
- The Georgia regions of Abkhazia and South Ossetia are outside the control of the government and occupied by Russia. These regions have banned the Jehovah's Witnesses.
- Baptists are the largest Protestant group and have experienced hostility from the Orthodox establishment.
- Muslims in Georgia make up 11% of the population and have faced roadblocks in building new mosques from both the government and local communities.

Indicators & Demographic Data

Population (2020)	3,899,000
% under 15 years	20%
Capital city (pop.)	Tbilisi 1,078,000
% urban dwellers	59% (0.35% p.a.)
Official language	Georgian
Largest language	Georgian (66%)
Largest people	Georgian (Gruzin, Adzhar) (66%)
Largest culture	Georgian (76%)
Development	78
Physicians	48
Gender gap	2%

% Christian: 0 3 10 50 75 100

Christian Traditions in Georgia

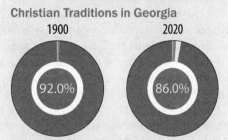

1900 — 92.0%   2020 — 86.0%

☐ Independent ☐ Protestant ▨ Catholic ▣ Orthodox ▣ Christian

Nearly all Christians in Georgia are Orthodox, which was the case in 1900 (99%) and 2020 (97%). Other communities have had slight growth, with Catholics at 1% of Christians in 2020.

Religion in Georgia

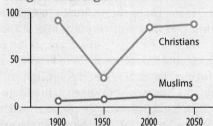

Christians

Muslims

Georgia was majority Christian for most of the 20th century except for a dip in 1970 while the country was part of the Soviet Union. Christians were 86% of the population in 2020, followed by Muslims (11%) and the nonreligious (nearly 3%).

Bible Translations		Churches		Missionaries		Gospel Access	
Languages	33	Denominations	29	Received	120	1900	Very high
Full Bible	20	Congregations	2,700	Sent	70	2020	Very high

Christianity in Germany

Christianity became the prominent religion of Germany in the 4th century under the influence of Clotilde, who persuaded her husband, Clovis I, to abandon paganism for the Christian faith. Clotilde is credited with spreading Christianity throughout the Frankish peoples of Western Europe and is venerated as a saint in both the Eastern Orthodox and Roman Catholic churches. The Protestant Reformation began in Wittenberg in 1517 with Martin Luther issuing his Ninety-Five Theses against the Catholic Church, which sparked religious wars throughout Europe. The Thirty Years' War (1618–1648) between Catholics and Protestants devastated Germany, reducing its population and destroying its economy. While the Peace of Westphalia (1648) allowed princes to determine the religion of their subjects, the region retained the Reformed Protestant traditions of John Calvin and Ulrich Zwingli. The monarchy fell after World War I; Germany split after World War II, and most of its large Protestant tradition was suddenly in Communist East Germany. Protestant churches played a role in the collapse of East Germany by welcoming protesters and revolution. German reunification came in 1990 with the fall of the Berlin Wall. Ironically, there are today more houses of worship in the former East Germany, though church membership is lower there.

Today, Protestants are the majority in northern, eastern, and middle Germany. The largest Protestant "denomination" is the Evangelical Church in Germany, formed after World War II to unify Protestantism. Today it is more like a federation of autonomous churches rather than as a single church, and it consists of United Protestant, Lutheran, and Reformed churches. The Federation of Evangelical Free Churches brings together Baptist, Brethren, and Elim congregations. Catholics are more concentrated in the south of the country. Catholic Church membership has rapidly decreased; in 2015, for example, the church lost over 181,000 members. Weekly Mass attendance is low (10%), Catholic marriages are in decline, and the number of baptisms is dropping. Nevertheless, as the home of eight popes, Germany has an important place in Catholic history. The largest Independent denomination is the New Apostolic Church, founded in 1863 and now found in over 180 countries.

% Christian: 0 3 10 50 75 100

Religion in Germany

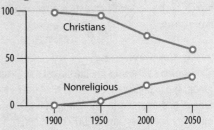

Germany has been a majority Christian country for many centuries and still is today. However, the Christian share of the population declined substantially from 99% in 1900 to 66% in 2020. The nonreligious (atheists and agnostics) grew from less than 1% to 27% over that same period. The country has also had a substantial increase in its Muslim population, now over 6% (5.4 million).

Indicators & Demographic Data

Population (2020)	82,540,000
% under 15 years	13%
Capital city (pop.)	Berlin 3,562,000
% urban dwellers	77% (0.13% p.a.)
Official language	German
Largest language	Standard German (60%)
Largest people	German (High German) (59%)
Largest culture	German (78%)
Development	94
Physicians	42
Gender gap	3%

Bible Translations		Churches		Missionaries		Gospel Access	
Languages	75	Denominations	350	Received	10,000	1900	Very high
Full Bible	56	Congregations	37,000	Sent	10,000	2020	Very high

Facts to Consider

- Although religious affiliation is high in Germany, only 11% of the population report that religion is very important in their lives, 9% pray daily, and 10% believe in God with absolute certainty.
- During the 2015 migrant crisis, Germany received upward of 1 million asylum seekers, mostly from Syria, Afghanistan, Iraq, Eritrea, and Iran. The arrival of so many migrants caused a rift in German society. Integration has been an issue; for example, migrants are still much less likely to have a job than the average German.
- Muslims in Germany have increased to over 6% of the population. Offenbach has the highest percentage of Muslims of any German city at 14%; Berlin is 9% Muslim.
- In 1925, the Jewish population of Germany was 564,400. Between 1933 and 1939, nearly 300,000 Jews emigrated. By the end of World War II, 8,000 Jews returned from exile to join the 19,000 who had survived the Holocaust. There are 127,000 Jews today, mostly because of migration from former Soviet Union states.
- Anti-Semitic and anti-Muslim incidents are common, including assaults, harassment, threats, and discrimination.

Christian Traditions in Germany

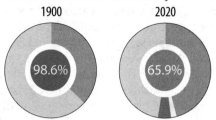

1900   2020

98.6%   65.9%

☐ Independent ☐ Protestant ■ Catholic ■ Orthodox ■ Christian

Germany has always been home to large Catholic and Protestant communities. In 1900, Protestants made up 63% of Christians, and Catholics 37%. The gap between them narrowed significantly over the 20th century; in 2020, Protestants were 47% of Christians and Catholics were 46%. There are now large communities of Orthodox (5% of Christians) and Independents (2%). The Evangelical movement has its roots in late 17th-century German Pietism, but today Evangelicals are less than 2% of the country's population.

Christian Families in Germany

Family	Population 2020	%	Trend	Change
Latin-rite Catholic	23,958,000	29.0	—	-0.5
Lutheran	12,029,000	14.6	—	-0.3
United church or joint mission	11,868,000	14.4	—	-0.3
Eastern Orthodox	2,346,000	2.8	↑	3.5
*Evangelicals	1,282,000	1.6	—	-0.2
*Pentecostals/Charismatics	1,250,000	1.5	—	0.0
Reformed, Presbyterian	372,000	0.5	—	-0.3
Jehovah's Witnesses	291,000	0.4	—	-0.1
Baptist	94,800	0.1	—	-0.3
Oriental and other Orthodox	93,800	0.1	↓	-1.6
Nondenominational	68,400	0.1	—	0.4
Mennonite	67,800	0.1	↑	0.8
Methodist	50,300	0.1	↓	-0.7
Congregational	47,200	0.1	—	-0.1
Christian Brethren	44,200	0.1	↓	-1.2
Eastern-rite Catholic	42,300	0.1	↓	-0.5
Latter-day Saints (Mormons)	41,900	0.1	↑	0.9
Adventist	38,000	<0.1	—	-0.3
Moravian	32,100	<0.1	↑	1.4
Anglican	31,000	<0.1	↑	0.7
Old Catholic Church	14,500	<0.1	↓	-1.6
Restorationist, Disciple	6,800	<0.1	↓	-0.8
Holiness	5,100	<0.1	↓	-4.0

Christianity in Germany is diverse, made up of a large Catholic presence (24 million) and many varieties of Protestant and Independent churches. Orthodox churches have grown in recent years due to immigration. Eastern Orthodox churches include Serbs, Romanians, Russians, Bulgarians, and Georgians; Oriental Orthodox include Armenians, Copts, Ethiopians, Eritreans, and Syrians. Jehovah's Witnesses arrived at the end of the 19th century and have grown substantially. Two breakaway groups from the Witnesses are the Kingdom of God Church and the Free Bible Congregation. Witnesses were outspoken in their condemnation of the Nazi regime and were persecuted for their refusal to perform military service and pledge allegiance to Adolf Hitler. Many were killed in concentration camps and forced to wear a purple triangle on their clothing. They received legal church standing in 2006.

* These movements are found within Christian families
— no change

↑↑ extreme growth
↑ growth
↓↓ extreme decline
↓ decline

Christianity in Ghana

Portuguese traders first arrived in the Gold Coast region in the 15th century, followed by the Dutch, Swedes, and Danes. The Portuguese, Dutch, English, and French also participated in the Atlantic slave trade in this area. Great Britain took control in 1874. By the time the country achieved independence in 1957, it was roughly one-third Christian. Today, Ghana is a majority Christian country (73%) with large populations of Protestant, Catholic, and African indigenous churches. Since the 1980s, Pentecostal/Charismatic Christianity has come to characterize Ghanaian Christianity both in Ghana and in the diaspora.

Catholics in Ghana are 13% of the population and are particularly active in community development projects and peace building. The first Ghanaian bishop, John Kodwo Amissah, was consecrated in 1957 and became archbishop in 1959. Ghanaian Catholicism is inculturated into society, using traditional drumming, dancing, and cloths.

The four largest Protestant denominations are Methodists, Presbyterians, Seventh-day Adventists, and Anglicans, with all except Anglicans tracing their roots to the 19th century. The first Independent church in the Gold Coast was the short-lived Methodist Society in 1862. The African Methodist Episcopal Zion Church formed in 1896 and was later supported by African American missionaries. The Church of the Twelve Apostles formed just before World War I and was the first of many indigenous spiritual churches established through the preaching of John Nackabah, a disciple of the famous prophet William Wadé Harris. Other spiritualist churches include the Army of the Cross of Christ Church and the Apostles Revelation Society. The Church of Pentecost is the second largest denomination in the country, following the Catholic Church. It has an international conference center that can hold 3,000 people, accommodating many national and international Christian conferences. The Assemblies of God is the third largest denomination in the country, begun in 1931. Many older Protestant churches have adopted Pentecostal/Charismatic practices, including healing and deliverance ministries and all-night prayer vigils. Many Pentecostal megachurches are involved in community development, health care, prison ministry, and various kinds of media ministries.

% Christian: 0 3 10 50 75 100

Religion in Ghana

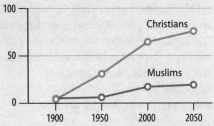

In 1900, 90% of Ghana's population followed African traditional religions. This declined to just under 9% in 2020 with the dramatic growth of both Christianity and Islam. Christianity grew from just under 5% in 1900 to 73% in 2020; Islam grew from 5% to 18%. Exclusive followers of traditional religions were 10% of the population in 2020.

Indicators & Demographic Data

Population (2020). 30,734,000
% under 15 years 38%
Capital city (pop.) . . . . .Accra 2,514,000
% urban dwellers. . . . . 57% (3.06% p.a.)
Official language. . . . . .English
Largest language. . . . . .Akan (33%)
Largest people . . . . . Ashanti (Akan, Twi) (13%)
Largest culture . . . . .Akan (46%)
Development. 59
Physicians. 1
Gender gap. 9%

Bible Translations	Churches	Missionaries	Gospel Access
Languages. 96	Denominations 710	Received. 2,200	1900 . . . . Low
Full Bible. 30	Congregations. 66,500	Sent 1,000	2020 . . . . Very high

Facts to Consider

- Ghanaian Christians are very involved as missionaries in the north of the country, as well as in other African countries. Since the 1980s, Pentecostal/Charismatic churches have sent out missionaries for church planting, particularly to countries in the West.
- The Christian Council of Ghana has 31 member churches and provides opportunities for united ministry, service, and outreach ranging from family planning clinics to religious education. The Ghana Pentecostal and Charismatic Council has over 200 member churches as well.
- Islam has grown in the country and is 18% of the population today. A higher concentration of Muslims is found in the north and in urban areas such as Accra, Kumasi, and Sekondi-Takoradi. Outside the north, Islam is found among Zongo communities.
- Traditional religions have declined sharply with the growth of Christianity and Islam. Followers of these traditions are mostly in rural areas, but many people who identify as Christian and Muslim practice some aspects of indigenous religion.
- The government has been trying to decide what to do about "self-styled" pastors and prophets who often preach prosperity theology to the detriment of their followers. Sometimes these "one man" churches result in financial fraud and extortion. This is a tricky issue since the constitution protects freedom of religion.

Christian Traditions in Ghana

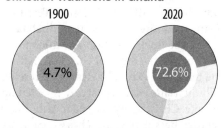

1900 — 4.7%   2020 — 72.6%

☐Independent ☐Protestant ■Catholic ■Orthodox ■Christian

The Christian population in 1900 was mostly Protestant (90%) due to British colonization and Evangelical missionaries. Throughout the 19th century, many Protestant missionaries arrived, and in the 20th century, indigenous forms of Christianity began to blossom. By 2020, 47% of Christians were Protestant, 32% were Independent, and 23% were Catholic. The Pentecostal/Charismatic movement is also tremendously influential in the country; over half of Christians were Pentecostal/Charismatic in 2020.

Christian Families in Ghana

Family	Population 2020	%	Trend	Change
*Pentecostals/Charismatics	11,500,000	37.4	↑	1.9
*Evangelicals	7,250,000	23.6	↑	1.7
Latin-rite Catholic	4,100,000	13.3	↑	3.0
Methodist	1,370,000	4.5	↑	3.2
Reformed, Presbyterian	1,212,000	3.9	↑	2.7
Restorationist, Disciple	829,000	2.7	↑	1.7
Anglican	652,000	2.1	↑	4.0
Jehovah's Witnesses	578,000	1.9	↑↑	5.3
Baptist	480,000	1.6	↑↑	8.8
Adventist	334,000	1.1	↓	-4.2
Latter-day Saints (Mormons)	134,000	0.4	↑↑	11.5
Lutheran	48,000	0.2	↑	3.2
Salvationist	38,800	0.1	↑	2.6
Nondenominational	35,200	0.1	↑	3.1
Holiness	20,200	0.1	↑↑	11.0
Congregational	15,000	<0.1	↑↑	6.5
Non-traditional, house, cell	14,900	<0.1	–	-0.1
Mennonite	9,400	<0.1	↑	1.7
Eastern Orthodox	5,200	<0.1	↑	2.7

Pentecostal/Charismatic Christianity is the largest Christian family in Ghana. A wide diversity of churches are included in this group, including those founded by foreign missionaries such as the Assemblies of God (1.3 million) and the New Apostolic Church (427,000). There are also numerous indigenous groups such as the Church of Pentecostal (2.9 million), the Christ Apostolic Church (700,000), and the Church of the Twelve Apostles (320,000). Pentecostal/Charismatic Christianity also includes Charismatics found within the older Protestant churches such as Methodists and Presbyterians. All these groups have significant overlap with Evangelicalism, emphasizing deliverance, evangelism, discipleship, and church growth. There are numerous Methodist groups in the country, including the African Methodist Episcopal Zion Church and the Savior Church of Ghana.

* These movements are found within Christian families
– no change

↑↑ extreme growth
↑ growth
↓↓ extreme decline
↓ decline

Christianity in Gibraltar

Gibraltar is a British Overseas Territory located between Spain and Morocco. Its 35,000 inhabitants live mostly at the foot of the Rock of Gibraltar, which forms a peninsula that juts out into the Strait of Gibraltar. Although Britain claims the territory, Spain also asserts sovereignty over it, though Gibraltarians have repeatedly rejected Spanish sovereignty by vote. Christianity arrived in Gibraltar as early as the 2nd century, but the first churches were not organized until 1309. The country is majority Catholic today (83%), with Anglicans as the largest Protestant tradition (6%). The largest ethnic groups are of Italian, Maltese, Portuguese, British, and Spanish descent, with Spanish as the mother tongue of most of the population, although English is the official language.

Facts to Consider

- Many Gibraltarians also speak Llanito, which is unique to Gibraltar and is a mixture of Andalusian Spanish, British English, and other European Romance languages.
- The Our Lady of Europe statue resides in the original chapel of the Cathedral of St. Mary the Crowned. It receives hundreds of pilgrims every year.
- Islam has grown in the country, first via the arrival of immigrant Moroccan Arabs in the 1960s. The Ibrahim-al-Ibrahim Mosque was a gift from Saudi Arabian King Fahd in 1997.
- The Jewish community in Gibraltar dates to the early 14th century, but most Jews were expelled in 1492. Jews returned in the mid-18th century, but many evacuated during World War II and never came back. There are a few hundred Jews there today.

Indicators & Demographic Data

Population (2020)	35,000
% under 15 years	18%
Capital city (pop.)	Gibraltar 35,000
% urban dwellers	100% (0.28% p.a.)
Official language	English
Largest language	Spanish (77%)
Largest people	Gibraltarian (75%)
Largest culture	other Latin (75%)
Development	87
Physicians	39
Gender gap	3%

% Christian: 0 3 10 50 75 100

Christian Traditions in Gibraltar

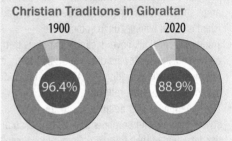

1900 — 96.4%   2020 — 88.9%

☐Independent ☐Protestant ■Catholic ■Orthodox ■Christian

Christianity in Gibraltar has always been majority Catholic. Christianity was 94% Catholic in 1900, dropping only to 91% by 2020. Protestants increased to 8% of Christians by 2020.

Religion in Gibraltar

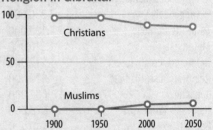

Gibraltar has been, and is poised to remain, a majority Christian country. Its Christian population declined from 96% in 1900 to 89% in 2020; during the same time, its Muslim population (nearly 5% in 2020) and nonreligious population (2%) slightly increased.

Bible Translations		Churches		Missionaries		Gospel Access	
Languages	5	Denominations	16	Received	40	1900	Very high
Full Bible	4	Congregations	18	Sent	10	2020	Very high

Christianity in Greece

Christianity arrived in Greece in the 1st century by way of the apostle Paul. Constantine, after his conversion to Christianity in 312 CE, built a new capital at Byzantium and renamed it Constantinople. After his death, the Roman Empire was divided, with the western capital in Rome and the eastern in Constantinople. The crowning of Charlemagne as emperor of the Holy Roman Empire in 800 was considered an act of schism by the Byzantine emperor, foreshadowing the Great Schism of 1054 between the Roman west (Catholic) and Byzantine east (Orthodox). Even today tensions exist between these two church bodies. Orthodoxy became the religion of Greece, and this has remained unchanged. The Greek Orthodox Church has enjoyed unique privileges from the state throughout Greek history. The church maintains a position of prominence and is named the "prevailing religion" of the country. Other Orthodox groups in the country include Oriental (Armenian, Apostolic, Coptic, Ethiopian), Bulgarian, and Russian.

Latin-rite Catholics (the largest non-Orthodox denomination) have been present in Greece since the time of the Crusades. Jehovah's Witnesses (the largest Independent denomination) grew substantially since it entered the country in 1900. However, some were imprisoned or executed during the Greek Civil War (1943–1949) for refusing military service. The Greek Evangelical Church, the largest Protestant body, was formed in 1858 and is Presbyterian in structure. Greece is one of the more religious countries in Europe, with 55% of the population identifying religion as very important in their lives, 38% attending worship services at least monthly, 29% reporting daily prayer, and 59% believing in God with absolute certainty.

The Greek debt crisis (2010–2018), triggered by the Great Recession of 2007–2009, caused a huge spike in homelessness, unemployment, and social and emotional strain on individuals and families. Amid this was the refugee crisis of 2015, in which hundreds of thousands of people fleeing conflict in the Middle East attempted to enter Greece—long considered a gateway to Europe for refugees—many via the island of Lesbos. Churches of many denominations rallied together to provide food and other provisions to assist refugees.

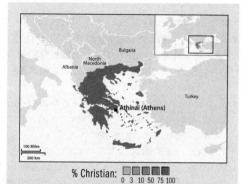

% Christian: 0 3 10 50 75 100

Religion in Greece

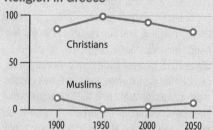

Christianity has been the major religion of Greece for many centuries. The country's Christian population rose from 85% in 1900 to 89% in 2020, largely because of a proportional decline in the Muslim population due to shifting geopolitical boundaries in the early 20th century. Muslims declined from 13% in 1900 to 2% in 1970 but surged again with immigration to 6% by 2020.

Indicators & Demographic Data

Population (2020)	11,103,000
% under 15 years	14%
Capital city (pop.)	Athens 3,153,000
% urban dwellers	80% (0.11% p.a.)
Official language	Greek
Largest language	Greek (81%)
Largest people	Greek (Hellenic, Dimotiki) (80%)
Largest culture	Greek (84%)
Development	87
Physicians	63
Gender gap	4%

Bible Translations		**Churches**		**Missionaries**		**Gospel Access**	
Languages	43	Denominations	90	Received	560	1900	Very high
Full Bible	28	Congregations	36,200	Sent	440	2020	Very high

Facts to Consider

- Refugees in urban settings are often unable to find work to support their families as the country continues to feel the ramifications of the debt crisis. In 2020, 15% of Greeks were unemployed, though this number was down from 27% in 2013.
- The Greek Orthodox Church is active in evangelistic work, with organizations for men, women, and youth as well as catechetical work in youth camps, choirs, and prison ministries.
- The Greek lay theologian Anastasios Yannoulatos, now the archbishop of Tirana, Dürres, and all Albania, revived Greek Orthodox mission outreach. Many Orthodox communities have been established in Africa, Southeast Asia, and Korea.
- Greek Muslims largely reside in Thrace, in the boundary region between Greek, Bulgaria, and Turkey. Greece is 6% Muslim, with newer immigrants from Afghanistan, Algeria, Bangladesh, Indonesia, Iran, and Iraq.
- Since 2017, interest has grown in neopaganism, which focuses on ancient Hellenic mythology and the Greek pantheon of gods. One of the most active organizations is the Supreme Council of the Ethnic Hellenes.
- The Jewish community of Greece is historic but small, around 5,000 people. Anti-Semitic attacks of Holocaust memorials, Jewish cemeteries, and synagogues are common. National polling reflects high rates of unfavorable opinions of both Muslims and Jews.

Christian Traditions in Greece

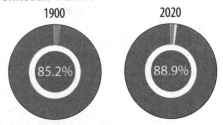

☐Independent ☐Protestant ■Catholic ■Orthodox ■Christian

The Greek Orthodox Church dominates Christianity in Greece. In 1900, 98% of Christians in Greece were Orthodox, and this remained largely the same in 2020 (97%). Protestants, Independents, and Catholics were around 2% of Christians in both 1900 and 2020, and this is unlikely to change much in the future. The Pentecostal/Charismatic movement has grown slightly, and is found among roughly 1% of Christians in the country.

Christian Families in Greece

Family	Population 2020	%	Trend	Change
Eastern Orthodox	9,416,000	84.8	↓	-0.6
Oriental and other Orthodox	254,000	2.3	—	0.2
Latin-rite Catholic	132,000	1.2	—	-0.1
*Pentecostals/Charismatics	132,000	1.2	—	0.0
Jehovah's Witnesses	55,800	0.5	—	-0.4
*Evangelicals	17,500	0.2	—	0.1
Reformed, Presbyterian	6,300	0.1	↑	0.5
Eastern-rite Catholic	6,200	0.1	↑↑	8.3
Christian Brethren	4,100	<0.1	↓	-2.1
Anglican	3,700	<0.1	↑	0.5
Congregational	1,100	<0.1	↑	0.5
Latter-day Saints (Mormons)	770	<0.1	↑	0.5
Baptist	600	<0.1	↑	2.7
Restorationist, Disciple	520	<0.1	—	0.3
Adventist	420	<0.1	↓	-3.5
United church or joint mission	380	<0.1	↓	-1.7

Eastern Orthodox are by far the largest Christian family in Greece, with 9 million members. Groups in this family include Greek, Bulgarian, and Armenians. Oriental and other Orthodox include Armenians and Old Calendarists. Pentecostal/Charismatics in Greece are mostly found among the country's Roma population (the Gypsy Evangelical Movement) but also among mission-founded churches such as the International Church of the Foursquare Gospel, the Assemblies of God, and the Church of God of Pentecost. Greece's Protestant community is small but represents a range of denominations, including Brethren, Congregationalist, Baptists, Anglicans, Holiness, and Reformed/Presbyterians.

* These movements are found within Christian families   — no change

↑↑ extreme growth
↑ growth
↓↓ extreme decline
↓ decline

Christianity in Greenland

Greenland is the world's largest island, situated between the Arctic and Atlantic Oceans and northeast of Canada. Politically and culturally, the country is part of Europe. With roughly 56,000 inhabitants spread across 840,000 square miles of land, Greenland is sparsely populated. Most of the peoples are Greenlandic-speaking Inuit. Though the first Christians in Greenland came with the Norse leader Leif Eriksson around the year 1000, the Norse population of around 5,000 people died out in the late 15th century. Moravian missionaries were active in Greenland between 1721 and 1900, but Lutheranism became the majority Christian tradition under Danish colonization. Greenland became an official territory (not a colony) of Denmark in 1953. Today, Greenland is 96% Christian, mostly members of the Lutheran Church of Greenland.

Facts to Consider

- The Bible was first translated into Greenlandic in the mid-19th century. The Lutheran Church of Greenland is in full communion with the Lutheran churches in the Nordic and Baltic states as well as with the Anglican Church in the British Isles.
- The Pentecostal Church is the second largest denomination, having begun with a Pentecostal missionary, a Swede, arriving in the 1950s. His son continues the work today.
- The New Life Church is the fastest-growing church, part of the Pentecostal/Charismatic movement. It is active in at least 15 towns.
- Greenland retains some influence of traditional Inuit religion, although most of the population is Christian.

Indicators & Demographic Data

Population (2020)...................................56,800
% under 15 years 16%
Capital city (pop.)...........................Nuuk 18,000
% urban dwellers..........................87% (0.41% p.a.)
Official language................................Greenlandic
Largest language..........................Greenlandic (79%)
Largest people ....Kalaallisut Eskimo (60%)
Largest culture ....Eskimo (79%)
Development..92
Physicians...26
Gender gap...1%

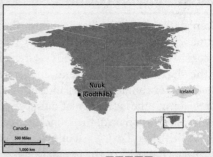

% Christian: 0 3 10 50 75 100

Christian Traditions in Greenland

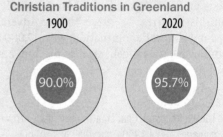

1900 — 90.0%   2020 — 95.7%

☐ Independent ☐ Protestant ■ Catholic ■ Orthodox ■ Christian

Greenland's Christian population has historically been majority Protestant. In 1900, Christians were 100% Protestant, and in 2020, 97% Protestant. Independent Christianity has grown (3% in 2020).

Religion in Greenland

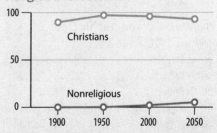

Greenland's Christian population increased slightly from 90% in 1900 to 96% in 2020. The proportion of nonreligious (atheists and agnostics) has also increased, from virtually zero in 1900 to nearly 3% in 2020.

Bible Translations	Churches	Missionaries	Gospel Access
Languages.............4	Denominations 22	Received.............70	1900 .... Very high
Full Bible.............3	Congregations........100	Sent 2	2020 .... Very high

Christianity in Grenada

Grenada is in the Caribbean Sea at the end of the Grenadines chain of islands, northwest of Trinidad and Tobago. It consists of three main islands—Grenada, Carriacou, and Petite Martinique—plus several smaller islands. Christopher Columbus encountered the islands in 1498 and claimed them for Spain, but the local population successfully resisted European colonization until the French arrived in 1650, followed by the British in 1763. The country gained independence in 1974. The majority of the population is Catholic, mostly on the main island of Grenada, yet with one parish on Carriacou and a station in Petite Martinique. It depends heavily on missionaries. The Seventh-day Adventist church is the second largest denomination, with 17,000 members and an emphasis on evangelism, discipleship, and children's and family ministries.

Facts to Consider

- The Pentecostal/Charismatic movement arrived via Canadian missionaries in the 1950s, and their original plant is home to the largest Pentecostal church in the country today. The largest Pentecostal denominations are the Pentecostal Assemblies of the West Indies and the New Testament Church of God.
- The Conference of Churches Grenada consists of Catholics, Anglicans, Methodists, Baptists, and Presbyterians. It works to promote mutual understanding and tolerance among Christian groups.
- Afro-American Spiritism is widespread in the country, including Shango (Yoruba syncretism), in which women have significant leadership roles.

Indicators & Demographic Data

Population (2020)................................. 109,000
% under 15 years 26%
Capital city (pop.) ....St. George's 38,100
% urban dwellers............................37% (0.86% p.a.)
Official language.....................................English
Largest language...................Grenadian Creole English (90%)
Largest people ....Black (47%)
Largest culture .... Black (African), English-speaking (50%)
Development...77
Physicians..6.6
Gender gap..3%

% Christian: 0 3 10 50 75 100

Christian Traditions in Grenada

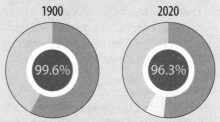

1900   2020

99.6%   96.3%

☐Independent ☐Protestant ▣Catholic ■Orthodox ■Christian

Christianity in Grenada has substantial Catholic and Protestant influences. In 1900, Christians were 58% Catholic and 42% Protestant. By 2020, this had shifted only slightly to 52% Catholic and 42% Protestant, plus 7% Independent.

Religion in Grenada

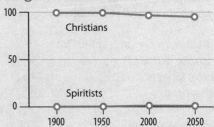

Christianity is the largest religion in Grenada and declined only slightly from nearly 100% in 1900 to 96% in 2020. The second largest religion is Spiritism, which represented 1% of the population in 2020.

Bible Translations	Churches	Missionaries	Gospel Access
Languages............7	Denominations 34	Received...........140	1900.......... Very high
Full Bible............4	Congregations.......280	Sent 10	2020.......... Very high

Christianity in Guadeloupe

Located in the Caribbean, south of Antigua and Barbuda, Guadeloupe consists of six inhabited islands plus many other uninhabited islands. Christopher Columbus came across Guadeloupe in 1493, but the French claimed it in 1635. Subsequent to the encounter, many indigenous peoples died from conflict and disease; Caribs killed the first Catholic missionaries in 1523. The first enslaved Africans arrived in 1650, resulting in immediate revolts. While Huguenot refugees became the first Protestants, Catholic missionaries sought to convert enslaved people. Slavery was outlawed in 1848. As French Protestants arrived in the early 20th century, Guadeloupe became an overseas department of France in 1946. The country is 89% Catholic today, served by 63 priests and 165 women religious.

Facts to Consider

- The official language of Guadeloupe is French, but most people also speak Guadeloupean Creole.
- Most of the population is Afro-Caribbean or mixed Creole; there is also a large population of Haitians.
- The Jehovah's Witnesses are the second largest denomination in the country, arriving in 1935 and drawing converts mostly from the Catholic Church.
- The country has a small Hindu population (2,500), which descended from enslaved people and indentured servants brought from South India in the 19th century. It is home to one of the largest South Indian populations in the Caribbean.
- Muslims number around 2,000. The Association of Muslims in Guadeloupe formed in 2005 to unite Muslims in a mosque-building project.

Indicators & Demographic Data

Population (2020)	448,000
% under 15 years	17%
Capital city (pop.)	Basse-Terre 58,200
% urban dwellers	98% (-0.04% p.a.)
Official language	French
Largest language	Saint Barthélemy Creole French (94%)
Largest people	French Creole (Mulatto) (74%)
Largest culture	Creole, French-speaking (84%)
Development	68
Physicians	39
Gender gap	3%

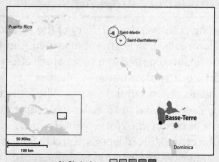

% Christian: 0 3 10 50 75 100

Christian Traditions in Guadeloupe

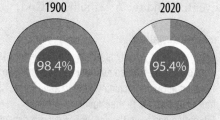

1900 — 98.4% 2020 — 95.4%

☐Independent ☐Protestant ▨Catholic ▪Orthodox ▪Christian

Historically, Christianity in Grenada has been majority Catholic. In 1900, Christians were 100% Catholic, dropping to 89%. In 2020, Protestants made up 7% of Christians and Independents 4%.

Religion in Guadeloupe

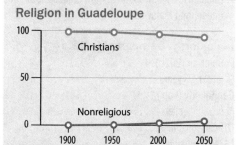

Christianity is the largest religion in Guadeloupe and declined only slightly from 98% in 1900 to 95% in 2020. The nonreligious represented just under 3% of the population in 2020.

Bible Translations		Churches		Missionaries		Gospel Access	
Languages	6	Denominations	16	Received	440	1900	Very high
Full Bible	3	Congregations	320	Sent	160	2020	Very high

Christianity in Guam

Guam is an overseas territory of the United States located in Micronesia. The Portuguese visited it in the 16th century, and Spain colonized it in 1668, which affected the indigenous Chamorros people whose population was reduced by warfare, disease, and natural disasters. The United States captured the Pacific island in 1898. Japan occupied the island for over two years during World War II, under which people were subjected to forced labor, incarceration, and torture. Guam is majority Christian today (94%), mostly Catholic, but also home to many denominations with roots in the United States. The largest Protestant denominations are the Seventh-day Adventists and the Assemblies of God.

Facts to Consider

- Koreans began arriving in Guam in 1971, and it is now home to a network of mission-planted Korean Presbyterian churches. There are 5,000 Koreans in Guam, including Korean Americans. Koreans also make up half of all tourists to the island.
- Education has been the center of Seventh-day Adventist work; women taught Christian education at the first SDA location in Dededo.
- Traditional ethnic religions have essentially disappeared among the Guamanian indigenous population. Some Korean migrants have brought East Asian forms of shamanism to the country.
- The island has small numbers of Baha'i, Buddhists, and Chinese folk religionists. Most Buddhists are Chinese, but some are Filipinos, Japanese, and Malaysians.

Indicators & Demographic Data

Population (2020). 169,000
% under 15 years 24%
Capital city (pop.) . . . . Hagåtña 148,000
% urban dwellers. . . . . 95% (0.84% p.a.)
Official language. . . . . Chamorro, English
Largest language. . . . . Chamorro (53%)
Largest people . . . . Guamanian (53%)
Largest culture . . . . Chamorro (53%)
Development. 65
Physicians. 3.5
Gender gap. 13%

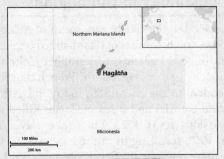

% Christian: 0 3 10 50 75 100

Christian Traditions in Guam

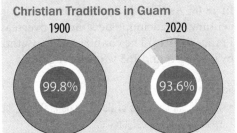

1900 — 99.8%
2020 — 93.6%

☐Independent ☐Protestant ▨Catholic ■Orthodox ■Christian

Historically, Christianity in Guam has been majority Catholic. In 1900, Christians were 100% Catholic. In 2020, Christians were 85% Catholic, 9% Protestant, and 5% Independent.

Religion in Guam

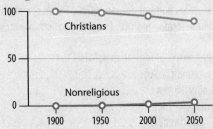

Christianity is the largest religion in Guam and declined only slightly from 99% in 1900 to 94% in 2020. The nonreligious represented 2% of the population in 2020. Baha'i, Buddhists, and Chinese folk religionists were each 1%.

Bible Translations	Churches	Missionaries	Gospel Access
Languages. 14	Denominations 42	Received. 510	1900 . . . . Very high
Full Bible. 10	Congregations. 160	Sent 25	2020 . . . . Very high

Christianity in Guatemala

Guatemala was impacted by the 16th century Spanish Conquest of the Americas, which resulted in the spread of foreign disease that wiped out a huge portion of the indigenous Quiché-speaking Maya population. Traditional worship included the recognition of a supreme being named Qabovil, with Tikal in the north as the great cultural center of the civilization. None of this survived Spanish colonization. Mayas were displaced into reservations to make Christianizing and taxation easier for colonizers. Indigenous peoples were forced to learn Catholic beliefs and practices that they incorporated into their own traditional religious worldviews. This resulted in the creation of "popular" or "folk" Catholicism that outwardly accepts the dogmas and rites of the Catholic Church but in reality assigns them a secondary role to traditional religious beliefs and practices. In some areas, indigenous and Spanish cultural elements exist side by side without blending at all. Guatemala achieved independence from Spain in 1821, which also resulted in the separation of church and state. During the civil war (1960–1996), many Catholic priests and catechists were assassinated for their stance in solidarity with the indigenous Maya people. Today the country is 97% Christian, mostly Catholic, with a rapidly growing Evangelical and Pentecostal/Charismatic community.

The Catholic Church in Guatemala, like much of Latin America, has always suffered from a shortage of priests. This is one reason why many Catholics have become Protestants, but it has also encouraged a high degree of lay participation in the Catholic Church. Many priests and bishops in the country are foreigners. Despite declining Catholic membership, Guatemalan Catholics report high levels of religiosity, such as devotion to the Virgin Mary and Mass attendance.

Protestants first arrived in 1882 but have grown steadily —almost entirely at the expense of Catholicism—since the mid-20th century. Nearly a quarter of all Protestants were raised Catholic, and most converted to seek a more personal relationship with God. Protestantism is popular among indigenous peoples; for example, 90% of Protestants in Huehuetenango are indigenous. The largest Protestant denomination is the Full Gospel Church of God (720,000 members).

% Christian: 0 3 10 50 75 100

Religion in Guatemala

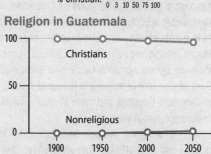

Guatemala has been majority Christian for many centuries, and the Christian share of the population decreased only slightly from 99% in 1900 to 97% in 2020. Just about 1% of the country adheres exclusively to traditional ethnic religions, and there are less than 1% of Spiritists, Baha'i, and other religions. The nonreligious make up 1.5%.

Indicators & Demographic Data

Population (2020)............. 17,911,000
% under 15 years 33%
Capital city (pop.) .. Guatemala City 2,935,000
% urban dwellers.......... 52% (2.59% p.a.)
Official language................. Spanish
Largest language........... Spanish (54%)
Largest people ....Ladino (Mestizo) (53%)
Largest culture ......Mestizo (Spanish) (53%)
Development........................ 65
Physicians......................... 9
Gender gap......................... 5%

Bible Translations	Churches	Missionaries	Gospel Access
Languages............30	Denominations 890	Received..........3,600	1900 .... Very high
Full Bible............10	Congregations.....35,000	Sent 500	2020 .... Very high

Facts to Consider

- Both Protestants and Catholics are heavily involved in education, such as running secondary schools to universities.
- "Third wave" Pentecostal groups emerged in the 1980s; the largest is the Church of the Prince of Peace (320,000 members), which split from the Assemblies of God in 1955 over their refusal to accept foreign funds or missionaries.
- The Catholic Charismatic movement is prominent in the country, its growth partly a reaction against Catholics becoming Protestant. Speaking in tongues, prophecy, and divine healings are common.
- Although almost all Guatemalans are Christians, many Mayas (especially the Quiché) accommodate traditional ethnic religious rites and beliefs to those of Catholicism. These practices represent a mixture of ancient Mayan religion and veneration of Catholic saints.
- Violence against women in Guatemala is endemic. The country has the third highest rate of femicide in the world, female human rights activists are regularly targeted, and many women—especially adolescent girls—experience sexual violence.
- Indigenous women in particular experience high levels of violence by the military and state officials; they are even less likely than nonindigenous women to obtain justice for crimes enacted against them.
- Guatemala suffers from widespread poverty and serious political corruption, which has caused massive immigration—documented or undocumented—to neighboring countries and the United States.

Christian Traditions in Guatemala

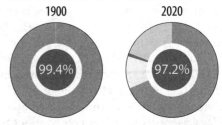

1900   2020

☐Independent ☐Protestant ◻Catholic ◼Orthodox ◼Christian

In 1900, Christianity was nearly 100% Catholic. This changed rather dramatically over the 20th century so that by 2020, only 69% of Christians were Catholic. Protestants and Independents both grew from virtually zero in 1900 to 19% and 11% of Christians, respectively. Orthodox Christianity also arrived in the 21st century, now 1% of Christians. Nondenominational Christianity is also popular, such as the large Evangelical Gethsemane Church founded in 1961.

Christian Families in Guatemala

Family	Population 2020	%	Trend	Change
Latin-rite Catholic	12,150,000	67.8	↑	1.3
*Pentecostals/Charismatics	8,980,000	50.1	↑	2.5
*Evangelicals	2,580,000	14.4	↑	2.2
Nondenominational	412,000	2.3	↑	2.3
Adventist	359,000	2.0	↑	1.3
Latter-day Saints (Mormons)	316,000	1.8	↑	3.4
Holiness	225,000	1.3	↑	1.1
Reformed, Presbyterian	171,000	1.0	↑	1.9
Christian Brethren	160,000	0.9	↑	2.9
Eastern Orthodox	159,000	0.9	↑	4.8
Non-traditional, house, cell	145,000	0.8	↑	1.1
Jehovah's Witnesses	104,000	0.6	↑↑	5.7
Restorationist, Disciple	98,200	0.5	↑↑	6.0
Baptist	97,000	0.5	↑	2.6
Oriental and other Orthodox	40,700	0.2	↑↑	129.6
Friends (Quaker)	30,200	0.2	↓	-0.9
Mennonite	18,000	0.1	↑	2.1
Lutheran	6,300	<0.1	↑	2.3
Anglican	2,300	<0.1	↑	1.5

Guatemala is home to a significant amount of Christian diversity. Although Catholics are the largest Christian family (12 million), the Pentecostal/Charismatic movement is not far behind (9 million). Guatemala is home to a number of Pentecostal groups, including (in order of size): Full Gospel Church of God, Assemblies of God, Church of the Prince of Peace, Elim Christian Mission, and Calvary Christian Ministries. There are also many house or cell-like groups in the country. Reformed/Presbyterians pioneered a new method of theological education, Theological Education by Extension, which quickly became a worldwide movement. It allows men and women to study in their homes plus in regional centers, with weekly visits from seminary teachers.

* These movements are found within Christian families	↑↑ extreme growth
	↑ growth
	↓↓ extreme decline
− no change	↓ decline

Christianity in Guinea

Guinea is a Muslim-majority country in West Africa. In the 18th century, the Fulani people introduced Islam via a jihad; the Dialonke, Sarakole, and Susu peoples are majority Muslim. Portuguese passed by Guinea in 1462 in their explorations of the African coast, but Christianity never became widespread in the country. The area, declared a French protectorate in 1849 and a colony in 1891, first received Catholic missionaries in 1877 and Protestants in 1918. Christianity remains a minority religion, at 3% of the population. Most Christians are Catholics (69%), and the first Guinean priest was ordained in 1940. The largest non-Catholic groups are the New Apostolic Church and the Evangelical Protestant Church.

Facts to Consider

- The Secretariat General of Religious Affairs issues guidance on themes for discussion in Muslim Friday sermons and Christian Sunday services. Not every sermon is monitored, but inspectors are present around the country to ensure consistency with the guidelines.
- Four churches were burned down and a number of Christians were killed in March 2020. Conversion from Islam is highly discouraged.
- Several African Independent Churches have arrived in Guinea from surrounding countries, such as the Shekina Church (from Liberia), Deeper Life (from Nigeria), and Church of Pentecostal (from Ghana).
- Radio is important in Guinea, as it is the only communications method that can reach the entire country. But by law, religious groups cannot own radio or television stations.
- Traditional ethnic religions are followed by 8% of the population, especially among peoples in the Forest Region.

Indicators & Demographic Data

Population (2020). 13,751,000
% under 15 years 42%
Capital city (pop.) . . . . Conakry 1,938,000
% urban dwellers. . . . . .37% (3.64% p.a.)
Official language . . . . French
Largest language. . . . . Fulah (41%)
Largest people . . . . Fula Jalon (Futa Dyalon) (41%)
Largest culture . . . . Western Bantoid (Atlantic) (48%)
Development. 46
Physicians. 0.8
Gender gap 19%

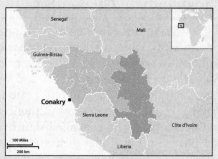

% Christian: 0 3 10 50 75 100

Christian Traditions in Guinea

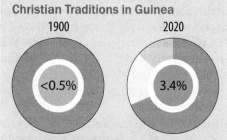

1900 — <0.5%
2020 — 3.4%

☐Independent ☐Protestant ■Catholic ■Orthodox ■Christian

The small Christian community in 1900 (1,800) was entirely Catholic. By 2020, Christianity had grown to 3% of the population, with slightly more diversity, but it is still majority Catholic (69%), with smaller Protestant (13%) and Independent (18%) communities.

Religion in Guinea

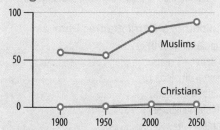

Islam is the largest religion in Guinea and grew from 58% of the population in 1900 to 88% in 2020. Traditional religions constituted the second largest religion, 8% of the population in 2020.

Bible Translations	Churches	Missionaries	Gospel Access
Languages. 54	Denominations 87	Received. 120	1900 . . . . Very low
Full Bible. 11	Congregations. 1,800	Sent 2	2020 . . . . Low

Christianity in Guinea-Bissau

Guinea-Bissau was a Portuguese trading center starting in the mid-15th century. Catholic missionaries arrived in 1462. Catholicism grew during Portuguese rule, which ended in 1973. However, Catholicism was found mostly in the upper classes and along the coast, as Europeans were banned from moving inland. Islam predated Catholicism (pre-12th century) via traders and expanded significantly in the 18th and 19th centuries. Today the country is 46% Muslim and nearly 13% Christian. Catholics make up the majority of Christians, with two dioceses, Bissau and Bafatá, while Protestants and Independents make up a third of Christians. The largest non-Catholic group is the New Apostolic Church. The Worldwide Evangelisation Crusade (WEC International) arrived in 1939 and was the only Protestant mission group permitted until 1990.

Facts to Consider

- Guinea-Bissau is a linguistically diverse country. While Portuguese is the official language, it is spoken by few in comparison to the local languages of Balanta-Kentohe, Fulah, Mandingo, and Mandjak. Most speak Creole.
- The Catholic relief agency Caritas arrived in the country in 1982 and runs various health care projects and facilities in the country.
- The largest Protestant church is the Evangelical Church of Guinea, a result of WEC International work. It is found mostly among the Balanta, Papel, Mankanha, Bijago, Felupe, and Bayote peoples.
- Traditional religions are prominent among the northern and western tribes. Tribes that are majority animist include the Balanta, Banyum, Bayot, Ganja (Bandal), Kasanga (Haal), Kobiana and Mandyak (Manjaco, Caio).

Indicators & Demographic Data

Population (2020). 2,001,000
% under 15 years 41%
Capital city (pop.) . . . . Bissau 600,000
% urban dwellers. . . . . 44% (3.22% p.a.)
Official language. . . . . Portuguese
Largest language. . . . . Balanta-Kentohe (25%)
Largest people . . . . Fulakunda (Fula Cunda) (19%)
Largest culture . . . . Western Bantoid (Atlantic) (79%)
Development. 46
Physicians. 0.5
Gender gap. 14%

% Christian: 0 3 10 50 75 100

Christian Traditions in Guinea-Bissau

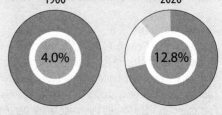

1900 — 4.0% | 2020 — 12.8%

☐ Independent ☐ Protestant ■ Catholic ■ Orthodox ■ Christian

The small Christian community in 1900 was entirely Catholic. In 2020, Catholics were 72% of Christians, followed by Independents (17%) and Protestants (11%).

Religion in Guinea-Bissau

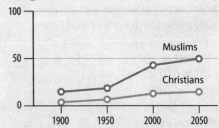

Muslims

Christians

Guinea-Bissau was 81% traditional religionist and 15% Muslim in 1900. The country is still home to one of the largest proportions of traditional religionists in the world at 40%. Muslims grew to 46%, and Christians were nearly 13%.

Bible Translations		Churches		Missionaries		Gospel Access	
Languages.	33	Denominations	12	Received.	210	1900	Very low
Full Bible.	6	Congregations.	480	Sent	10	2020	Medium

Christianity in Guyana

The first Christians in modern-day Guyana were Portuguese Catholics in 1548. The Dutch subsequently colonized the region from 1620 to 1796, followed by the British until independence in 1966. The country was 50% Christian at independence, and today the country is roughly 54% Christian. Christians include a majority of the Black and mixed-race populations and are more frequently found in urban areas. A considerable number are also East Indians. Some early Protestant mission groups in the country included Moravians (1738), Dutch Lutherans (1743), Scottish Presbyterians (1766), Methodists from Nevis (1802), and Baptists (1860). The Seventh-day Adventists are the largest denomination at 10% of the country's population. Several indigenous churches have emerged, such as the Hallelujah Church, which mixes traditional religion with Christianity.

Facts to Consider

- The Guyana Council of Churches includes 15 member churches, both Protestant and Catholic. Its makeup reflects the ethnic diversity of the country: five have a mixed population, seven are majority Black, and two are majority East Indian.
- Guyana is home to a small Rastafarian movement, comprised of less than 1% of the population and mostly of African descent. They claim discrimination due to laws that criminalize possession of 15 grams or more of marijuana, which they use for religious purposes.
- Interfaith engagement among Christians, Muslims, and Hindus is generally positive. Eid al-Adha, Easter, and Diwali are national holidays.

Indicators & Demographic Data

Population (2020)	791,000
% under 15 years	28%
Capital city (pop.)	Georgetown 107,000
% urban dwellers	27% (1.01% p.a.)
Official language	English
Largest language	Guyanese Creole English (87%)
Largest people	Hindi (Hindustani) (38%)
Largest culture	Hindi (42%)
Development	65
Physicians	2.1
Gender gap	5%

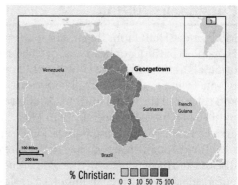

% Christian: 0 3 10 50 75 100

Christian Traditions in Guyana

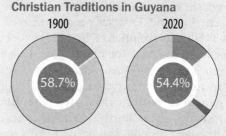

1900 — 58.7%
2020 — 54.4%

Independent   Protestant   Catholic   Orthodox   Christian

Christians in 1900 were mostly Protestants (84%) due to its history of British and Dutch colonization and missionary efforts. This was still true in 2020, where 63% of Christians were Protestant, followed by smaller communities of Independents (21%) and Catholics (14%).

Religion in Guyana

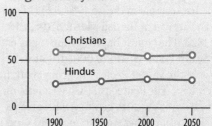

In 1900, Guyana was 59% Christian, 25% Hindu, and 6% Muslim. In 2020, the country was 54% Christian, 30% Hindu, and 8% Muslim.

Bible Translations		Churches		Missionaries		Gospel Access	
Languages	19	Denominations	69	Received	340	1900	High
Full Bible	6	Congregations	1,700	Sent	10	2020	Very high

Christianity in Haiti

Modern-day Haiti forms the western portion of the island of Hispaniola in the Caribbean, east of Cuba and Jamaica. The original inhabitants of the land were the indigenous Taíno people from South America. The Spanish arrived in 1492 and colonized the island until 1625, followed by the French until Haiti achieved independence in 1804. Catholic missions arrived in 1493. The Taíno population disappeared within a century of Spanish arrival due to the spread of infectious diseases and the harshness of the colonial *encomienda* system of forced labor. The French imported enslaved Africans to work the sugarcane fields, making the colony one of the richest in the world. Enslaved people and freed Blacks launched the Haitian Revolution (1791–1804) under the leadership of formerly-enslaved Toussaint Louverture and defeated the French to achieve independence—the first country in Latin America to defeat a colonial power and abolish slavery. Protestant missionaries arrived a few years after independence.

Haiti is a majority Catholic country today (67%). Although Catholics had been in Haiti since the 15th century, the first indigenous clergy were not ordained until the opening of the Seminary of Haiti (1872) and the St. James Seminary (1894). Pope John Paul II visited Haiti in 1983 and sparked a Catholic movement to advocate for improved human rights and to fight poverty. The first democratically elected president in Haiti was Catholic priest Jean-Bertrand Aristide (1991), a proponent of liberation theology. The first Catholic cardinal from Haiti was named in 2014, Bishop Chibly Langlois.

Protestants make up 19% of Haiti's population and date to the arrival of British Methodists in 1807. Baptists arrived in 1823. The largest Baptist group today is the Baptist Mission of South Haiti, with 120,000 affiliates. Seventh-day Adventists are the largest Protestant group, with nearly half a million members. The Pentecostal/Charismatic movement has grown rapidly over the 20th century, with groups such as the Church of God of Prophecy and Church of God (Cleveland). Haiti is also home to many majority Black denominations from the United States, such as the African Methodist Episcopal Church. Without outside aid, Haitians have founded over 25 churches.

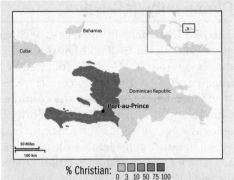

% Christian: 0 3 10 50 75 100

Religion in Haiti

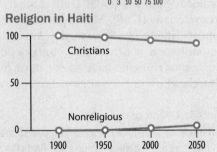

Haiti has been majority Christian for many centuries, and the Christian share of the population decreased only slightly from virtually 100% of the population in 1900 to 94% in 2020. Just about 3% of the country are Spiritists. The nonreligious (atheists and agnostics) made up 3% in 2020, up from essentially zero in 1900.

Indicators & Demographic Data

Population (2020) 11,371,000
% under 15 years 32%
Capital city (pop.) . . . Port-au-Prince 2,774,000
% urban dwellers . . . . 57% (2.47% p.a.)
Official language . . . . . . Haitian Creole, French
Largest language . . . . Haitian Creole (99%)
Largest people . . . . Haitian Black (94%)
Largest culture . . Black, French-speaking (94%)
Development 50
Physicians 39
Gender gap 3%

Bible Translations		Churches		Missionaries		Gospel Access	
Languages 7		Denominations 360		Received 1,700		1900 . . . . Very high	
Full Bible 5		Congregations 10,200		Sent 30		2020 . . . . Very high	

Facts to Consider

- Haiti is one of the poorest countries in the Americas, ranking very low in education, literacy, internet availability, and on other development indexes. Income per capita is $1,700/year, compared with $14,600/year in neighboring Dominican Republic.
- Haiti was struck by a magnitude 7.0 earthquake in 2010, causing massive devastation in an already economically challenged country. At least 100,000 people died, and 3 million people were affected.
- Haiti relies heavily on foreign aid, the largest donors being the United States, Canada, and the European Union. The 2010 earthquake led to a spike in the number of short-term missionaries, mostly from the United States, working in relief, medical care, and evangelism.
- Most Protestant pastors in Haiti are Haitians, but levels of theological education are low, causing reliance on foreign missionaries rather than national church organizations. Many rely heavily on financial resources from North America.
- Vodoun is a mixture of African rites (particularly from Benin) with Catholic practices, resulting in a form of Spiritism. Often, African spirits are identified with Catholic saints, and many Haitian Catholics also practice Vodoun. The government recognizes Vodoun as a distinctive element of Haitian life and culture.

Christian Traditions in Haiti

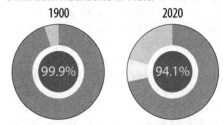

□Independent □Protestant ▨Catholic ▨Orthodox ■Christian

In 1900, 95% of Christians were Catholic. The Catholic share of Christians dropped over the 20th century so that by 2020, 72% of Christians were Catholic. Protestants and Independents made significant gains, growing to 21% and 8% of Christians, respectively. The Pentecostal/Charismatic movement also experienced tremendous growth over this period, now 19% of Christians (2 million).

Christian Families in Haiti

Family	Population 2020	%	Trend	Change
Latin-rite Catholic	7,600,000	66.8	↑	1.0
*Pentecostals/Charismatics	2,000,000	17.6	↑	1.5
*Evangelicals	1,367,000	12.0	↑	1.4
Adventist	673,000	5.9	↑	3.3
Baptist	397,000	3.5	↑	1.9
Holiness	279,000	2.5	↓	-0.6
Anglican	133,000	1.2	↑	0.9
Methodist	76,000	0.7	↑	0.7
Jehovah's Witnesses	53,900	0.5	↑	4.2
Latter-day Saints (Mormons)	28,000	0.2	↑	3.9
Lutheran	16,000	0.1	↑	1.3
Restorationist, Disciple	15,600	0.1	↑	1.1
Mennonite	10,000	0.1	↑	3.7
Salvationist	3,600	<0.1	↑	1.8
Reformed, Presbyterian	2,000	<0.1	↑	2.2

Haiti is home to a significant amount of Christian diversity. Catholics are the largest Christian family (7.6 million), and the Pentecostal/Charismatic movement is the second largest (2 million). Haiti is home to a number of Pentecostal groups, including (in order of size): Church of God, Church of God in Christ, Church of God of Prophecy, Assemblies of God, and United Pentecostal Church. Evangelicals (over 1.3 million) are found throughout all kinds of Protestant and Independent denominations, especially Baptists. Baptist groups include Independent Baptists, Ebenezer Mission, and Conservative Baptists. Seventh-day Adventists are the fourth largest family and make up 5% of the country's population.

* These movements are found within Christian families	↑↑ extreme growth
	↑ growth
	↓↓ extreme decline
− no change	↓ decline

Christianity in the Holy See

The Holy See is the supreme authority of the Roman Catholic Church in addition to an internationally recognized legal entity. It has full ownership of Vatican City and is technically an absolute monarchy as the home of the bishop of Rome (the pope), who oversees the worldwide Catholic Church. The State of Vatican City is the smallest country in the world by both land and population. It includes St. Peter's Square, St. Peter's Basilica, the Apostolic Palace, and the Vatican Gardens. Only two groups of people live there: Catholic clergy who work for the Holy See, and the Swiss Guard, who serve as the army of Vatican City. Most of the 2,400 Vatican lay workers live outside the Vatican and are citizens of other nations, primarily Italy.

The College of Cardinals is in charge of selecting a new pope. In May 2021, the number of cardinals (electors and nonelectors) for each continent was Africa (28), North America (26), Central America (9), South America (24), Asia (26), Europe (105), and Oceania (5). Countries with the largest number of cardinals were Italy (47), the United States (15), Spain (14), Brazil (8), Germany (8), Mexico (7), France (6), and Portugal (5).

Facts to Consider

- The position of the pope (also known as the bishop of Rome, sovereign pontiff, Holy Father, and head of the universal church) is considered of divine origin dating to the time of the apostle Peter, whom Jesus appointed as the head of the apostles.
- The Holy See is the focal point for Catholic missionaries. Every Catholic order has a representative in the Vatican. In 2019, there were 630,099 religious sisters and 50,295 religious brothers worldwide. Both figures were down significantly compared with 1970: 1,004,304 million religious sisters and 79,408 religious brothers.
- The Catholic Church is deeply involved in charitable work worldwide in schools, hospitals, orphanages, and other social services. It runs over 103,000 Catholic elementary and 49,500 Catholic secondary schools, plus over 5,100 hospitals and 9,200 orphanages.
- In March 2022, Pope Francis's new constitution of the Roman Curia expanded the potential role of laypeople to serve in management positions, opening the possibility for more women in Vatican leadership. There are eight women in positions of leadership at the Holy See.

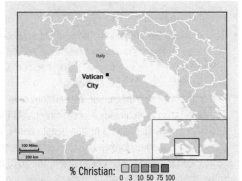

% Christian: 0 3 10 50 75 100

Christian Traditions in the Holy See

1900 — 100%
2020 — 100%

Independent ☐ Protestant ☐ Catholic ■ Orthodox ■ Christian

The Holy See is very unique compared to other countries. It is designed to be a Catholic state and indeed has been so, with Catholics comprising 100% of Christians in both 1900 and 2020, and likely into the future.

Religion in the Holy See

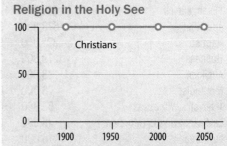

Christianity remains the largest and only religion in the Holy See and it is designed to remain that way far into the future.

Christianity in Honduras

Honduras was the major center of ancient Mayan culture before the 10th century. In 1501, Christopher Columbus sighted modern-day Honduras (specifically, the Bay Islands), and in 1524, Hernán Cortés and other *conquistadores* arrived in search of gold. The territory became part of Spanish-controlled Guatemala in 1538 for the next three centuries, with Spanish Franciscans arriving around 1550. By 1807 there were 145 Catholic churches. Honduras achieved independence from Spain in 1821 and has held independent elections since 1838. The country was 97% Christian by 1900.

Honduras remains majority Catholic at 68% of the population in 2020. Catholic concern and activity in the areas of society, laity, and evangelization increased in the 1960s. Today the church continues to suffer from its troubled track record of a lack of leadership, clergy, and resources. Honduran priests, both expatriate and indigenous, carry an enormous amount of responsibility and often care for several congregations simultaneously. Around half of Catholic priests in Honduras are foreign-born.

Protestants (Central American Mission) first arrived in Honduras in 1896. Next came groups such as Friends (Quakers), Evangelical and Reformed Church, and Moravians. The largest Protestant group is the Church of the Foursquare Gospel, followed by Seventh-day Adventists (concentrated in the Bay Islands). The Church of Jesus Christ of Latter-day Saints (Mormons) arrived in the 1950s and is the fourth largest denomination today, with a temple in Tegucigalpa, dedicated in 2013. The Pentecostal/Charismatic movement stems from the arrival of the Assemblies of God in 1937 from El Salvador. The movement has been popular in Honduras, partly because of the lack of Catholic priests but also because Pentecostals are particularly active in helping youth escape street violence and gang culture.

The growth of Protestantism has been at the expense of Catholics; roughly 26% of Protestants in Honduras were raised Catholic. One survey reported "wanting a personal relationship with God" as the main reason for switching from Catholicism to Protestantism. Nevertheless, the Catholic Charismatic movement is present in the country, with many Catholics witnessing divine healings, speaking in tongues, and prophesying in church.

% Christian: 0 3 10 50 75 100

Religion in Honduras

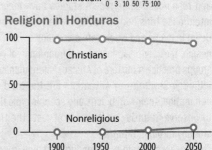

Honduras has been majority Christian for many centuries, and the Christian share of the population decreased only slightly from 97% of the population in 1900 to 96% in 2020. Spiritists make up just under 1% of the country, while Baha'i and followers of traditional religions are at 0.5% each. The nonreligious made up 2% in 2020, up from virtually zero in 1900.

Indicators & Demographic Data

Population (2020)	9,719,000
% under 15 years	30%
Capital city (pop.)	Tegucigalpa 1,444,000
% urban dwellers	58% (2.48% p.a.)
Official language	Spanish
Largest language	Spanish (96%)
Largest people	Mestizo (82%)
Largest culture	Mestizo (Spanish) (85%)
Development	62
Physicians	3.7
Gender gap	2%

Bible Translations		Churches		Missionaries		Gospel Access	
Languages	18	Denominations	180	Received	890	1900	Very high
Full Bible	8	Congregations	11,600	Sent	220	2020	Very high

Facts to Consider

- Gang violence is a major problem. Catholic Cardinal Óscar Rodríguez Maradiaga has been an outspoken critic of the drug trade in Honduras and as a result has received many death threats.
- Evangelical pastors with churches and ministries in areas known for narcotics trafficking have become targets of gang threats. Some Evangelical pastors have been kidnapped and killed in these areas, which have minimal state presence.
- Honduras is a major destination for short-term mission trips from the United States, with foreigners spending large sums of money on travel and resources. Some recent studies have indicated that these well-intentioned trips end up having limited impact on local communities.
- Belief in magic and witchcraft is common in both rural and urban areas despite the near disappearance of traditional religions. Some indigenous groups practice a mixture of African, Amerindian, and Christian religions.
- Although Seventh-day Adventists are the third largest Christian denomination, their workplaces and schools typically do not permit them to observe Saturday as their day of rest. The Honduran workweek is Monday through Saturday.
- The Muslim community of Honduras is small, roughly 13,000, but Muslims have reported intolerance from Evangelical Protestants who show up at their places of worship to intimidate them.

Christian Traditions in Honduras

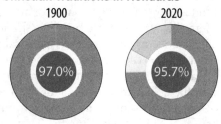

1900   2020

☐Independent ☐Protestant ■Catholic ■Orthodox ■Christian

Virtually all Christians were Catholic in 1900. The Catholic share of Christians dropped over the 20th century, such that by 2020, only 76% of Christians were Catholic. Protestants and Independents made significant gains, growing to 17% and 8% of Christians, respectively. The Pentecostal/Charismatic movement also experienced tremendous growth over this period, now representing 18% of Christians (1.7 million).

Christian Families in Honduras

Family	Population 2020	%	Trend	Change
Latin-rite Catholic	6,620,000	68.1	↑	1.2
*Pentecostals/Charismatics	1,700,000	17.5	↑	1.7
*Evangelicals	1,135,000	11.7	↑	2.2
Latter-day Saints (Mormons)	222,000	2.3	↑	4.5
Adventist	181,000	1.9	↓↓	-5.8
Christian Brethren	159,000	1.6	↑	4.2
Baptist	127,000	1.3	↑	1.5
Holiness	91,100	0.9	↑	3.2
Jehovah's Witnesses	60,500	0.6	↑	4.3
Nondenominational	39,200	0.4	↑	2.1
Non-traditional, house, cell	32,900	0.3	↑	1.6
Moravian	26,200	0.3	↑	2.8
Mennonite	16,100	0.2	↑	2.2
Reformed, Presbyterian	10,400	0.1	↑	1.3
Restorationist, Disciple	9,200	0.1	↑	4.4
Anglican	8,100	0.1	↓↓	-16.6
Eastern Orthodox	5,300	0.1	↓	-0.6
Oriental and other Orthodox	4,200	<0.1	↑↑	7.8
Friends (Quaker)	4,100	<0.1	↑	1.2
Methodist	3,000	<0.1	↑	1.4
Lutheran	2,200	<0.1	↑	4.8

Honduras is home to a significant amount of Christian diversity. Catholics are the largest Christian family (6.6 million), and the Pentecostal/Charismatic movement is the second largest (1.7 million). Honduras is home to a number of Pentecostal groups, including (in order of size): International Church of the Foursquare Gospel, Church of God in Honduras, Assemblies of God, and Prince of Peace Church. Evangelicals (over 1.1 million) are found throughout all kinds of Protestant and Independent denominations, especially Baptists and Pentecostals. Baptist groups include the National Baptist Convention of Honduras and the Bay Islands Baptist Association. The Church of Jesus Christ of Latter-day Saints (Mormons) make up 2% of the population. Seventh-day Adventists are the third largest family and make up about 3% of the country's population.

* These movements are found within Christian families	↑↑ extreme growth
	↑ growth
	↓↓ extreme decline
– no change	↓ decline

Christianity in Hong Kong

Hong Kong is a special administrative region of China. It is one of the most densely populated places in the world, with a population of over 7.5 million people living in 410 square miles. Christians have been present in Hong Kong since the arrival of Catholics in 1840, followed by the arrival of American Baptists, Anglicans, and the Basel Mission. Hong Kong has historically been a player in East Asian political turmoil, such as the overthrowing of the Chinese dynasty (1911), Japanese imperialism (1941–1945), the Communist takeover (1949), and the handing over of Hong Kong from the British to China (1997). Both Protestants and Catholics were involved in the Umbrella Revolution, the pro-democracy protests of 2014, in which they marched on streets with crosses, read the Bible, and sang hymns during protests.

Facts to Consider

- Most Catholics in Hong Kong are Chinese, but there are also large populations of Filipinos, Koreans, Japanese, and Indians. Services are in Cantonese, English, and sometimes Tagalog.
- The Catholic Church runs hundreds of schools that serve over 100,000 students, as well as numerous hospitals and other social services.
- Over 30 new American mission groups entered the British colony of Hong Kong between 1949 and 1970.
- Evangelical Christians in Hong Kong have been speaking out against the Chinese government's 2020 decision to end the "one country, two systems" policy, in place since 1997. They released a statement of repentance for not living out the fullness of the gospel and not standing up against authoritarianism in the region.

Indicators & Demographic Data

Population (2020) 7,548,000
% under 15 years 13%
Capital city (pop.) . . . . Hong Kong 7,548,000
% urban dwellers. . . . . 100% (0.58% p.a.)
Official language. . . . . Chinese, English
Largest language. . . . . Chinese (95%)
Largest people . . . . Han Chinese (Cantonese) (77%)
Largest culture . . . . Han Chinese (94%)
Development. 93
Physicians. 35
Gender gap 3%

% Christian: 0 3 10 50 75 100

Christian Traditions in Hong Kong

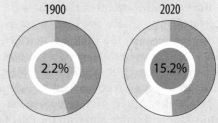

1900 — 2.2%
2020 — 15.2%

☐ Independent ☐ Protestant ▨ Catholic ▨ Orthodox ■ Christian

In 1900, Hong Kong had large populations of both Protestants (54% of Christians) and Catholics (45%). This was still true in 2020; 49% of Christians were Catholic, 37% Protestant, and 14% Independent.

Religion in Hong Kong

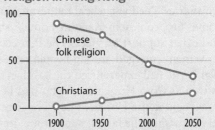

Chinese folk religion

Christians

1900   1950   2000   2050

In 1900, Hong Kong was 90% Chinese folk religionist, 8% Buddhist, and 2% Christian. In 2020, the country was 42% Chinese folk religionist, 16% Buddhist, and 15% Christian.

Bible Translations	Churches	Missionaries	Gospel Access
Languages. 24	Denominations 220	Received. 950	1900 . . . . Very low
Full Bible. 21	Congregations 1,900	Sent 450	2020 . . . . Very high

Christianity in Hungary

Christianity arrived in modern-day Hungary in the 3rd century while the territory was under Roman control. It had both Eastern (Byzantine) and Western (German; Roman) influences, but Latin-rite Catholicism prevailed in the 10th century with the support of princes. Hungary resisted the invasion of the Ottoman Empire for 100 years but was finally defeated in 1526 and was under Ottoman control until 1699. Lutheranism arrived in 1518, resulting in the creation of the Reformed Church. By the end of the 16th century, most Hungarians were Reformed Protestants. Their numbers were reduced to one-third of the population by the end of the 18th century with the arrival of Catholic settlers in regions left desolate by Ottoman wars. The Austro-Hungarian Empire came into being in 1867 and was defeated in World War I. The atheist, Communist dictatorship (a satellite state of the Soviet Union) from 1949 to 1989 affected all churches, but especially the Catholic Church. Outspoken critics were imprisoned, tortured, and exiled. Hungary transitioned to democracy and capitalism with the fall of the Soviet Union in 1991.

Today, Hungary is majority Christian (87%), with large populations of Catholics and Protestants. Catholics are found throughout the country except in the northeast around Debrecen ("the Calvinist Rome") and Nyíregyháza (where Greek Catholics live). The largest Protestant denomination is the Reformed Church in Hungary. It offers a range of health care and educational services, including four theological seminaries. The Evangelical Lutheran Church also operates homes for people experiencing homelessness, elder homes, and other support services. The Pentecostal/Charismatic movement emerged among people returning from World War I who had experienced the baptism of the Holy Spirit, as well as from Hungarians who had become part of the movement in the United States. The Evangelical Pentecostal Fellowship, the largest such group, formed in 1962 with the merger of the Evangelical Pentecostal Church and the Evangelical Christian Churches. The Catholic Charismatic renewal arrived in Hungary in the 1970s. In 2020, more than 2,000 people attended the Hungarian Catholic Charismatic Conference, which included 120 participants at a leadership training day for Catholic Charismatics.

% Christian: 0 3 10 50 75 100

Religion in Hungary

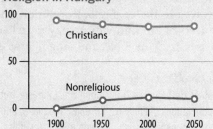

Hungary has been majority Christian for many centuries, and Christians' share of the population decreased from 94% of the population in 1900 to 87% in 2020. Less than 1% of the country each are Jewish or Muslim. The nonreligious made up nearly 12% in 2020, up from 0.5% in 1900.

Indicators & Demographic Data

Population (2020). 9,621,000
% under 15 years 14%
Capital city (pop.) . . . . . . Budapest 1,768,000
% urban dwellers. . . . . 72% (0.05% p.a.)
Official language. . . . . .Hungarian
Largest language. . . . . .Hungarian (92%)
Largest people . . . . Hungarian (Magyar) (87%)
Largest culture . . . . Magyar (87%)
Development. 84
Physicians. 31
Gender gap 1%

Bible Translations	Churches	Missionaries	Gospel Access
Languages. 24	Denominations 89	Received. 1,400	1900 . . . . Very high
Full Bible. 17	Congregations. 5,800	Sent 270	2020 . . . . Very high

Facts to Consider

- Hungary has been under the influence of the Christian-conservative neo-nationalism of Prime Minister Viktor Orbán (1998–2002; 2010–present), who has attracted international attention and accusations of authoritarianism for centralizing legislative and executive power and restricting freedom of speech.
- Hungary's constitution recognizes the role of Christianity in "preserving the nation," and significant percentages of society hold anti-Semitic and anti-Muslim views.
- During the height of the European refugee crisis in 2015, Hungary made asylum rules stricter and reduced the number of refugees in the country. Migrants, especially Muslims, are portrayed as dangerous and are treated as scapegoats for societal problems.
- The Romani population of around 300,000 people live mainly in the northern part of the country. Pentecostalism has been particularly attractive among the Romani.
- Different strands of Christianity are tied to different sides of the political spectrum. In general, Pentecostal churches are more connected to the political left, while historical Christian churches are loyal to the Christian-conservative right wing. Catholics have been loyal to the latter as well.
- Before World War II, Jews numbered more than 800,000, but 600,000 died in the Nazi Holocaust. Hungary's Jews have expressed concern over government officials praising the country's World War II–era leaders and Adolf Hitler allies, fearing increases in anti-Semitic attacks and vandalism.

Christian Traditions in Hungary

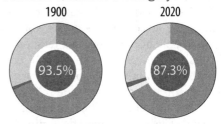

1900   2020

93.5%   87.3%

☐Independent ☐Protestant ▨Catholic ▧Orthodox ■Christian

Hungary has always had large populations of both Catholics and Protestants. The Catholic share of Christians dropped from 68% in 1900 to 67% in 2020; the Protestant share also decreased slightly from 31% to 29% over the same period. Independents made slight gains to nearly 2%, and Orthodox to just over 2% by 2020. The Evangelical and Pentecostal/Charismatic movements also experienced some growth over this period. Evangelicals were just over 4% of Hungary's population in 2020 and Pentecostal/Charismatics were just under 4%.

Christian Families in Hungary

Family	Population 2020	%	Trend	Change
Latin-rite Catholic	5,552,000	57.7	–	-0.3
Reformed, Presbyterian	2,180,000	22.7	–	0.3
*Evangelicals	410,000	4.3	–	0.1
*Pentecostals/Charismatics	350,000	3.6	↓	-2.7
Lutheran	304,000	3.2	–	0.1
Eastern-rite Catholic	248,000	2.6	↓	-1.6
Eastern Orthodox	149,000	1.5	–	0.0
Jehovah's Witnesses	38,700	0.4	↓	-1.0
Baptist	14,100	0.1	–	0.0
Methodist	10,200	0.1	↑	1.3
Adventist	10,200	0.1	–	0.4
Latter-day Saints (Mormons)	5,800	0.1	↑	2.1
Holiness	3,500	<0.1	↓	-1.9
Christian Brethren	3,400	<0.1	–	0.2

Hungary is home to a modicum of Christian diversity. Catholics are the largest Christian family (5.6 million), and Reformed/Presbyterians make up the second largest (2.2 million) due to the Reformed Church of Hungary. Evangelicals are the third largest family (410,000), found across many denominations, such as the Baptist Union and the Fellowship of Evangelical Pentecostals. Evangelicals are found among the older Reformed and Lutheran churches as well. Besides the Fellowship of Evangelical Pentecostals, the largest Pentecostal/Charismatics denominations include Faith Church, formed underground in 1979 and popular among Roma people in urban areas. Orthodox churches in the country include Romanians, Russians, Hungarians, and Serbs.

* These movements are found within Christian families	↑↑ extreme growth
	↑ growth
	↓↓ extreme decline
– no change	↓ decline

Christianity in Iceland

The first Christians in Iceland were missionaries from Ireland in the 8th century. Soon after Norwegians arrived in 874, Christianity became the state religion. The creation of the Danish-Norwegian state in 1381 shifted cultural influence to Denmark. With the majority of the population adherents, Lutheranism became the state religion in 1550. Today the majority of Icelanders belong to the National Church of Iceland. The second largest denomination is the Evangelical Lutheran Free Churches. The Charismatic renewal arrived in the mid-1980s, and today there are many Charismatic churches throughout the country. Iceland is the most sparsely populated country in Europe, with a population of around 343,000 living in 40,000 square miles.

Facts to Consider

- Agnes M. Sigurðardóttir became the National Church of Iceland's first female bishop in 2012; one-third of the church's pastors are women.
- Many Catholics in Iceland are from Eastern Europe or the Philippines; most priests and sisters are also foreigners.
- The nonreligious Icelandic Ethical Humanist Association has around 2,000 members and aims to teach people how to lead ethical lives outside of a religious context.
- Norse pagan religion (Ásatrúarfélagið) was reintroduced in Iceland in the 1960s. The Ásatrú Fellowship is officially recognized by the government and one-third of its members are women.
- Muslims in Iceland are mostly immigrants, and the Muslim Foundation of Iceland offers translation assistance to asylum seekers and other social supports.

Indicators & Demographic Data

Population (2020). 343,000
% under 15 years 20%
Capital city (pop.) . . . . Reykjavík 219,000
% urban dwellers. . . . . 94% (0.74% p.a.)
Official language. . . . . Icelandic
Largest language. . . . . Icelandic (93%)
Largest people . . . . Icelander (93%)
Largest culture . . . . Icelander (95%)
Development. 93
Physicians. 38
Gender gap. 3%

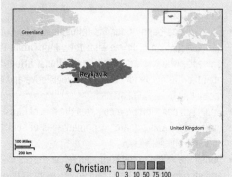

% Christian: 0 3 10 50 75 100

Christian Traditions in Iceland

1900 — 99.9%   2020 — 92.2%

☐ Independent ☐ Protestant ■ Catholic ■ Orthodox ■ Christian

In 1900, Christians in Iceland were 100% Protestant. Protestants were still the majority in 2020 (88%), with smaller populations of Independents (7%) and Catholics (4%).

Religion in Iceland

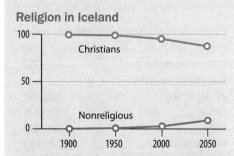

In 1900, virtually the entire population of Iceland was Christian. The Christian share of the population declined to 92% in 2020 with the rise of atheists and agnostics, who represented nearly 6% in 2020.

Bible Translations	Churches	Missionaries	Gospel Access
Languages. 11	Denominations 23	Received. 40	1900 . . . . Very high
Full Bible. 10	Congregations. 390	Sent 40	2020 . . . . Very high

Christianity in India

According to some accounts, Christianity has been in India since the 1st century with the arrival of the apostle Thomas in Kerala in 52 CE. St. Thomas Christians (also known as Syrian Christians) in India today trace their roots to his arrival, and there are several denominations in this tradition: Orthodox Syrian Church, the Chaldean Church of the East, the Mar Thoma Church, and the Syro-Malankara Catholic rite. Portuguese explorers and missionaries brought Catholicism to India beginning in the 16th century. Catholicism in the country has been Indianized since the mid-20th century, with increased participation from the laity, more concern for inter-Christian cooperation, and the use of rituals reminiscent of Indian culture. Pentecostals/Chrasmatics are the largest Christian tradition, with 21 million members.

The first Protestant missionaries in India were Pietist Lutherans, Bartholomäus Ziegenbalg and Heinrich Plütschau in Tranquebar in 1706. English Baptist missionary William Carey arrived in Serampore in 1800 and continued the Protestant tradition of translation into local languages. Mass movements of people into Christianity began in the 19th century, mostly the result of indigenous initiatives. The second largest denomination today is the United Church of South India, which represents an ecumenical merger of Reformed, Congregational, Anglican, and Methodist denominations. The Church of North India is similar, bringing together Presbyterian, Congregational, Anglican, Baptist, Brethren, Disciple, and Methodist churches.

The northeastern states of Meghalaya, Mizoram, and Nagaland are nearly entirely Christian, while most states in the north, such as Rajasthan, Himachal Pradesh, and Jammu and Kashmir, have much smaller proportions of Christians. Much of Indian Christianity is Pentecostal/Charismatic in nature, which also serves as a powerful social and theological movement that crosses ethnic, regional, class, and caste lines. India experienced many large-scale revivals, such as that led by Pandita Ramabai at her Mukti Mission in 1905. Christianity is also heavily Indianized, and there are many attempts to create Hindu-Christian churches and movements to fully contextualize Christianity to Indian society. One example of this is Christian ashrams that serve as centers of prayer, silence, and meditation to experience God.

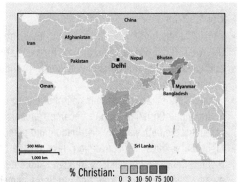

% Christian: 0 3 10 50 75 100

Religion in India

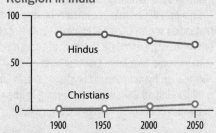

India has always been a Hindu majority country. In 1900, the country was 80% Hindu, but this dropped to 73% by 2020. India is home to a substantial Muslim minority, which grew slightly from 13.7% to 14.5% over the same period. Other large religious minorities in 2020 included traditional religionists (4%), Sikhs (2%), and Buddhists (1%).

Indicators & Demographic Data

Population (2020)	1,383,198,000
% under 15 years	27%
Capital city (pop.)	Delhi 30,291,000
% urban dwellers	35% (2.33% p.a.)
Official language	Hindi, English
Largest language	Hindi (12%)
Largest people	Bengali (8%)
Largest culture	Hindi (21%)
Development	64
Physicians	7.6
Gender gap	16%

Bible Translations		Churches		Missionaries		Gospel Access	
Languages	424	Denominations	1,800	Received	9,500	1900	Very low
Full Bible	92	Congregations	348,000	Sent	10,000	2020	Medium

Facts to Consider

- A major hurdle for Christianity in India is its negative association with the West. Hundreds of years of British colonization has resulted in anti-Western and anti-Christian backlash, particularly among more fundamentalist Hindus.
- Women have made tremendous contributions to Christianity in India. Many Indian Christian women became teachers and Bible women, spreading the faith via Bible distribution and personal evangelism.
- Eight states have "anticonversion" laws on the books that serve to regulate religious conversions through "allurement" or "fraudulent" means. Penalties range from fines to imprisonment. These laws are routinely used to harass Christians.
- The majority of Christians come from Dalit or tribal backgrounds, those that Indian society deemed "outcasts" or "untouchables." In converting to Christianity, Dalits lose government-sponsored affirmative action.
- India is home to a large cross-cultural mission movement within its borders led by indigenous Christians. Within this movement, nearly a million Indian Christians are working in their own country among thousands of peoples, languages, and castes.

Christian Traditions in India

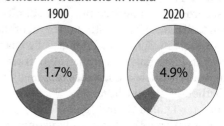

□Independent □Protestant ▨Catholic ■Orthodox ■Christian

Christianity in India has always been diverse. In 1900, half of Christians were Catholic, followed by Protestants at 31% and smaller proportions of Orthodox and Independents. By 2020, this had changed with the tremendous growth of Independent Christianity, typically in the form of hypercontextualized Christian communities. In 2020, Protestants made up 34%, Catholics 31%, Independents 27%, and Orthodox 8%.

Christian Families in India

Family	Population 2020	%	Trend	Change
*Pentecostals/Charismatics	21,000,000	1.5	↑	2.3
Latin-rite Catholic	15,915,000	1.2	↑	1.2
*Evangelicals	12,200,000	0.9	↑	1.7
United church or joint mission	6,062,000	0.4	↑	1.1
Oriental and other Orthodox	5,345,000	0.4	↑	1.2
Eastern-rite Catholic	5,185,000	0.4	↑	1.3
Lutheran	5,169,000	0.4	↑↑	5.6
Hidden believers in Christ	4,409,000	0.3	↑	2.2
Baptist	4,072,000	0.3	↑	0.9
Restorationist, Disciple	2,013,000	0.1	↑	1.6
Adventist	1,927,000	0.1	–	-0.3
Reformed, Presbyterian	1,597,000	0.1	↑	2.6
Holiness	1,258,000	0.1	↑	2.3
Nondenominational	1,243,000	0.1	↑	1.0
Media	912,000	0.1	↑	2.7
Methodist	906,000	0.1	–	-0.3
Christian Brethren	603,000	<0.1	↑	1.9
Salvationist	405,000	<0.1	↑	0.8
Anglican	271,000	<0.1	–	0.3
Non-traditional, house, cell	270,000	<0.1	↑	1.6
Mennonite	199,000	<0.1	–	0.3
Jehovah's Witnesses	136,000	<0.1	↑↑	5.1
Congregational	51,500	<0.1	↑	1.1

The largest Christian family is the Pentecostal/ Charismatic movement, which accounts for 2% of the country's population (21 million). There is a seemingly endless array of Charismatic, Holiness, and Pentecostal groups in the country. The largest group of Charismatic Christians are hidden Hindu believers in Christ, which is an umbrella term for many kinds of movements as well as individuals and families who remain within Hinduism but secretly profess belief in Jesus Christ. There are many Charismatic Christians within the traditional Protestant bodies as well, such as the United churches (North and South), Lutherans, and Baptists. India is also home to large Pentecostal churches, such as the Indian Pentecostal Church of God and the Assemblies of God. Likewise, Evangelicals are found throughout most Protestant and Independent denominations. The largest Oriental Orthodox groups are the Orthodox Syrian Church of the East and the Mar Thoma Syrian Church of Malabar.

*	These movements are found within Christian families	↑↑ extreme growth
		↑ growth
		↓↓ extreme decline
–	no change	↓ decline

Christianity in Indonesia

Indonesia is a geographically unique country consisting of more than 17,000 islands nestled between the Indian and Pacific Oceans. The largest island is Java, home to more than half the country's population. Indonesia's geography has shaped the arrival and history of Christianity. Catholics were on the island of Sumatra as early as the 7th century, then Java and Borneo. Portuguese colonization extended to the Moluccas and the Celebes in 1522, then Timor in 1530. The Netherlands defeated Portugal in 1605, and all Catholic missionaries were expelled, beginning 300 years of Dutch colonization and influence of the Dutch Reformed Church. Britain began exerting influence in the region in 1811, with German Lutherans arriving in Sumatra soon after, and Catholics returned in the 19th century. In the 20th century, numerous new Protestant missionary groups arrived, and tens of thousands of people became Christians, particularly in the following areas and in order of magnitude: central Java, east Java, north Sumatra, Alor, eastern Timor, Lampung, Sulawesi (among the Torajas), and the interiors of Kalimantan and West Irian.

Today, Christianity is Indonesia's second largest religion (after Islam) and is the second largest Christian population in Southeast Asia (after the Philippines). Christians are concentrated in particular areas: the majority of Papua, West Papua, East Nusa Tenggara, and North Sulawesi. Many Chinese Indonesians have become Christians as well. Nearly 60% of Indonesia's Christians are Protestants and are concentrated in Papua, West Papua, Maluku, and parts of East Nusa Tenggara. North Sulawesi and Papua have Protestant majorities. The largest Protestant denomination is the Batak Christian Protestant Church, which was founded by German Lutheran missionaries in 1861. Protestants are heavily involved in education, medical, and social services. Catholics are a local majority in Flores, Timor and Sumba, Papua, and Moluccas. The archdiocese of Semarang on Java is home to the most Catholics in the country, over half a million. Pentecostalism has been growing rapidly since its arrival in the late 1920s. The spiritual worldview of Indonesians aligns well with Pentecostalism's emphasis on the spiritual realm.

% Christian: 0 3 10 50 75 100

Religion in Indonesia

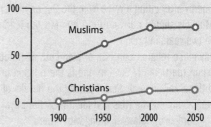

The religious makeup of Indonesia changed dramatically over the 20th century. In 1900, 45% of the population were primarily adherents of traditional religions, with another 40% Muslim. In 2020, Indonesia was the country with the largest population of Muslims in the world (80%). Christians make up 12%, followed by traditional religionists (2%) and Hindus (2%).

Indicators & Demographic Data

Population (2020)	272,223,000
% under 15 years	26%
Capital city (pop.)	Jakarta 10,770,000
% urban dwellers	57% (1.99% p.a.)
Official language	Indonesian
Largest language	Javanese (24%)
Largest people	Javanese (Orang Jawa) (32%)
Largest culture	Javanese (32%)
Development	69
Physicians	2
Gender gap	7%

Bible Translations		Churches		Missionaries		Gospel Access	
Languages	680	Denominations	330	Received	6,000	1900	Low
Full Bible	44	Congregations	63,300	Sent	900	2020	High

Facts to Consider

- The officially recognized religions of Indonesia are Islam, Catholicism, Protestantism, Buddhism, Hinduism, Confucianism, and indigenous religions. The law requires religious instruction in public schools, but teachers are not always available to lead all the courses for those religions.
- Indonesia is home to around 600 distinct ethnic and linguistic groups. The Javanese are the largest, followed by the Sundanese.
- Christians in Indonesia face persecution as a religious minority in the world's largest Muslim country (216 million Muslims). Extremist groups are more influential in certain areas such as West Java and Aceh (the latter of which is the only province governed by Sharia law).
- In 2016, the former Christian governor of Jakarta was convicted of blasphemy after citing a verse from the Qur'an in a speech that suggested Muslims should not vote for a non-Muslim leader. He was sentenced to two years in prison.
- Javanese religion consists of elements of Hinduism, Buddhism, and Islam (particularly Sufism) and is the religion of many Javanese. Traditional religions also exist among the Bataks of northern Sumatra as well as among the Nias and Mentawai, the Dayaks of Kalimantan, and the Torajas of Sulawesi, along with others.
- Hinduism is the main religion among the Balinese, who blend it with pre-Hindu and Hindu-Javanese elements.

Christian Traditions in Indonesia

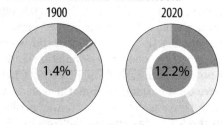

1900   2020

1.4%   12.2%

□ Independent □ Protestant ■ Catholic ■ Orthodox ■ Christian

The Christian population in 1900 (around half a million) was mostly Protestant (85%) due to Dutch colonization and other missionary efforts. By 2020, this had dramatically changed. Protestants made up 58% of Christians, followed by Catholics (23%) and Independents (18%), the last of which experienced tremendous growth over the period, with increased contextualization efforts by both missionaries and indigenous Christians. The Pentecostal/Charismatic movement (which was nonexistent at the start of the century) represented 33% of Christians in 2020; Evangelicals were 28%.

Christian Families in Indonesia

Family	Population 2020	%	Trend	Change
*Pentecostals/Charismatics	11,000,000	4.0	↑	2.5
*Evangelicals	9,414,000	3.5	↑	2.4
Reformed, Presbyterian	8,496,000	3.1	↑	1.0
Latin-rite Catholic	8,100,000	3.0	↑	1.4
Lutheran	6,260,000	2.3	↑	1.4
Nondenominational	870,000	0.3	↑	1.5
Holiness	747,000	0.3	↑	0.8
Adventist	246,000	0.1	↓	-1.2
Methodist	170,000	0.1	↑	1.6
Baptist	169,000	0.1	↓	-0.6
Hidden believers in Christ	130,000	<0.1	↑	1.7
Mennonite	127,000	<0.1	–	0.5
Jehovah's Witnesses	92,800	<0.1	↑	4.1
Salvationist	70,900	<0.1	↑	0.6
Restorationist, Disciple	32,800	<0.1	↑	1.7
Latter-day Saints (Mormons)	8,100	<0.1	↑	1.9
Anglican	4,000	<0.1	↑	0.5
Eastern Orthodox	3,000	<0.1	↑	2.7

Christianity in Indonesia is quite diverse and varies regionally. The largest Christian family is the Pentecostal/Charismatic movement, which accounts for 4% of the country's population (11 million). There is a wide array of Charismatic, Holiness, and Pentecostal groups in the country. The largest group of Pentecostal/Charismatic Christians is the Bethel Church in Indonesia, with over 4 million members. Other large groups include the Pentecostal Church of Indonesia, the Evangelical Christian Church of Indonesia, and the Assemblies of God. Like Charismatics, Evangelical Christians are found within numerous Protestant and Independent congregations. Reformed/Presbyterian Christians are the third largest family, with denominations such as the Protestant Church in Jakarta (Bethel), Evangelical Christian Church in West Papua, and the Toraja Christian Church. There are at least ten nondenominational networks.

* These movements are found within Christian families

– no change

↑↑ extreme growth
↑ growth
↓↓ extreme decline
↓ decline

Christianity in Iran

Iran is a Muslim majority country in West Asia, though Christianity has been present in the region since the 1st century. The Armenian Apostolic Church is the largest church in the country today (103,000) and traces its roots to Thaddaeus and Bartholomew, disciples of Jesus. There are three kinds of Catholics: Chaldean Catholics, Latin-rite Catholics, and Armenian Catholics. Protestants have been in the country since 1832, but missionaries experienced tension with the existing Orthodox churches and have largely grown through Christians switching from Orthodoxy to Protestantism, not from Islam. Iran is home to a large and difficult to enumerate "underground" (illegal) community of Christians from Muslim backgrounds. Estimates range from 100,000 of these underground Christians to upward of 1 million.

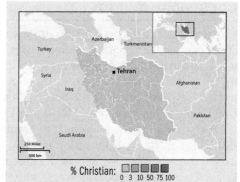

% Christian: 0 3 10 50 75 100

Facts to Consider

- Converting from Islam to Christianity is illegal, and those that do are often arrested, interrogated, and detained. Security agents regularly raid house churches. Christians are typically encouraged to emigrate.
- Perhaps tens of thousands of Iranians have converted to Christianity in the 21st century, mostly young people.
- Many people have attributed the recent growth of Christianity in Iran to the work of women, who are highly engaged in teaching, evangelizing, and introducing other women to Christianity.
- Iran (historical Persia) is the historic home of the Baha'i Faith, dating to Sayyid Ali Muhammad (Bab al-Din) in 1844. Baha'i are highly persecuted by Muslims, even more than Christians, and are twice as likely to end up in prison or fined for their religious beliefs and activities.

Christian Traditions in Iran

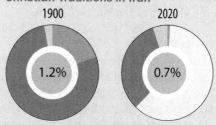

1900 — 1.2%
2020 — 0.7%

☐Independent ☐Protestant ▨Catholic ▨Orthodox ▨Christian

Iran is home to historic Orthodox and Catholic churches, which together made up 97% of Christians in 1900. Christianity was more diverse in 2020 with an increase of Independents (61% of Christians) and Protestants (6%).

Religion in Iran

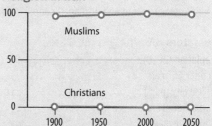

In 1900, 96% of Iran's population was Muslim, followed by small communities of Baha'i (2%) and Christians (1%). The Muslim share of the population increased to 99% in 2020 with the numeric and proportional decline of both Christians and Baha'i.

Indicators & Demographic Data

Population (2020)	83,587,000
% under 15 years	23%
Capital city (pop.)	Tehran 9,135,000
% urban dwellers	76% (1.32% p.a.)
Official language	Persian (Farsi)
Largest language	Persian (34%)
Largest people	Persian (Irani) (34%)
Largest culture	Persian (34%)
Development	80
Physicians	15
Gender gap	13%

Bible Translations		Churches		Missionaries		Gospel Access	
Languages	73	Denominations	37	Received	220	1900	Very low
Full Bible	20	Congregations	3,000	Sent	20	2020	Low

Christianity in Iraq

Christianity has been present in Iraq since the year 104 CE. Islam became the majority religion in the 7th century and is the largest today (98%). The largest Christian denomination is the Catholic Church in Iraq (185,000), followed by the Assyrian Church of the East (70,000), and a sizable community of "underground" Muslim-background believers (50,000). Life for Christians in Iraq became increasingly difficult after the US-led invasion in 2003. Christians were driven from their homes, harassed, kidnapped, raped, and killed. Circumstances became worse with the rise of ISIS in 2014, especially for Christians in the north, in Mosul, and in the villages of the Nineveh Plain.

Facts to Consider

- Islam is the official religion of the country, and the constitution technically guarantees the freedom of religious belief and practice for Christians, Yazidis, and Mandaeans. In practice, Islamic extremists still discriminate against, attack, and frequently kidnap Christians.
- Christians who fled Iraq during the rule of ISIS have settled in the Kurdistan Regional Government–administered region of northern Iraq or, if possible, to the West. They had been in Iraq peacefully for centuries prior.
- Protestants arrived in the 19th century but sought to make converts from historic Orthodox and Catholic communities, not Muslims. These tensions still exist today.
- Catholic and Orthodox churches are active in efforts toward peacebuilding, food distribution, health care, and service of displaced peoples.
- Iraqi Christians in Need funds various medical and educational projects for Christians in Iraq and displaced people in Syria and Jordan.

Indicators & Demographic Data

Population (2020)	41,503,000
% under 15 years	40%
Capital city (pop.)	Baghdad 7,144,000
% urban dwellers	71% (2.91% p.a.)
Official language	Arabic, Kurdish
Largest language	Arabic (72%)
Largest people	Iraqi Arab (46%)
Largest culture	Arab (Arabic) (72%)
Development	69
Physicians	8.5
Gender gap	18%

% Christian: 0 3 10 50 75 100

Christian Traditions in Iraq

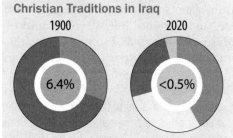

1900 — 6.4%
2020 — <0.5%

☐ Independent ☐ Protestant ▨ Catholic ■ Orthodox ▨ Christian

Iraq is home to historic Orthodox and Catholic churches, dating to the second century. Christians have declined proportionally, but they are now more diverse, with tens of thousands of Protestants and Independents.

Religion in Iraq

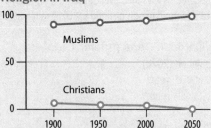

Muslims

Christians

100

50

0

1900   1950   2000   2050

In 1900, 89% of Iraq's population was Muslim. The Muslim share of the population increased to 98% in 2020 with the numeric and proportional decline of Jews, nearly all of which have emigrated, and the decline of Christianity.

Bible Translations		Churches		Missionaries		Gospel Access	
Languages	34	Denominations	27	Received	500	1900	Low
Full Bible	13	Congregations	1,100	Sent	40	2020	Medium

Christianity in Ireland

After missionaries arrived in the early 5th century, Ireland quickly became a center for the spread of Christianity to other countries. Irish identity became tied to Catholicism, especially in the face of British rule for over 600 years (until 1829). Catholicism is the majority religion in Ireland today, though their share of the population is declining. Beginning in the 1990s, a series of allegations of sexual abuse by Catholic priests came to light. A governmental investigation revealed systemic cover-up of such scandals for decades, with hundreds of priests abusing thousands of children. This scandal has caused severe distrust in the church. The Church of Ireland (Anglican) is the second largest denomination.

Facts to Consider

- Ireland has experienced an increase of Pentecostal/Charismatic Christianity. Many of these churches are a result of immigration (Nigerian, Indian, Chinese), though some are indigenous Irish and multiethnic.
- In 2015, Ireland was the first country in the world to legalize same-sex marriage through a national referendum, despite opposition from both Catholic and Protestant churches. Abortion was legalized in 2018.
- Limitations on women's roles in the Catholic Church is one of the most negative factors affecting public attitudes toward the church. Women's organizations accuse the church of misogyny because only men can be ordained, and the most prominent positions in the church require ordination.
- Islam is one of the fastest-growing religions in Ireland, from just 25,000 in 2000 to 80,000 by 2020. Most are immigrants, representing over 40 nationalities. Most live in Dublin.

Indicators & Demographic Data

Population (2020)	4,888,000
% under 15 years	21%
Capital city (pop.)	Dublin 1,228,000
% urban dwellers	64% (1.15% p.a.)
Official language	Irish, English
Largest language	English (91%)
Largest people	Irish (60%)
Largest culture	Irish (90%)
Development	94
Physicians	30
Gender gap	2%

% Christian: 0 3 10 50 75 100

Christian Traditions in Ireland

1900 — 99.9% 2020 — 90.7%

☐ Independent ☐ Protestant ■ Catholic ■ Orthodox ■ Christian

Ireland is historically Catholic, entailing 90% of Christians in 1900. This had changed only somewhat by 2020, when Catholics made up 94% of Christians. Protestants declined from 10% of Christians in 1900 to 4% by 2020.

Religion in Ireland

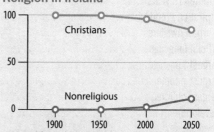

Ireland has been a majority Christian country for many centuries. In 1900, virtually the entire population was Christian. By 2020, Christianity had dropped to 91% of the population with an increase in atheists and agnostics (7%).

Bible Translations		Churches		Missionaries		Gospel Access	
Languages	36	Denominations	57	Received	560	1900	Very high
Full Bible	31	Congregations	3,100	Sent	5,000	2020	Very high

Christianity in the Isle of Man

The Isle of Man is a self-governing country of the United Kingdom that is located in the Irish Sea between Great Britain and Ireland. It received missionaries from Scotland in the 6th century, but the church was not officially organized until the 12th century. The Church of England (Anglican) is the largest denomination, followed by Catholics and Methodists. Most Catholics are Irish or of Irish descent.

Facts to Consider

- The Isle of Man is quite small, home to only 85,000 people. The majority are English-speaking and of British or Irish descent.
- Unlike neighboring Britain, the Isle of Man has not experienced significant immigration of people of other religions. However, there are now around 200 Muslims (with one mosque) and 200 Hindus in the country, primarily immigrants from Africa and Asia.
- Churches Alive in Man is an ecumenical group that brings together Catholic, Anglican, United Reformed, Salvation Army, Elim Pentecostal, Methodist, and other churches. In 2010, Churches Alive in Man signed a Covenant for Mission, which was a statement of unity to work together in witness on the island.
- In 2022, it was discovered that the Isle of Man was dumping over 766,000 gallons of wastewater, including raw sewage, into the Irish Sea, causing serious ecological and health concerns.

Indicators & Demographic Data

Population (2020)	85,900
% under 15 years	18%
Capital city (pop.)	Douglas 26,600
% urban dwellers	53% (0.97% p.a.)
Official language	English
Largest language	English (98%)
Largest people	British (88%)
Largest culture	English (British) (88%)
Development	92
Physicians	32
Gender gap	3%

% Christian: 0 3 10 50 75 100

Christian Traditions in the Isle of Man

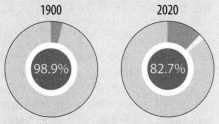

1900 — 98.9%   2020 — 82.7%

☐ Independent ☐ Protestant ▨ Catholic ▧ Orthodox ▨ Christian

The Isle of Man is traditionally a Protestant country, and within that, a large proportion Evangelical. Protestants were 93% of Christians in 1900; this dropped to 86% in 2020 with an increase of Catholics (12%) and Independents (2%).

Religion in the Isle of Man

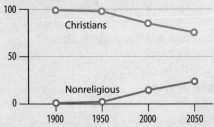

The Isle of Man was 99% Christian in 1900, with only a small population of nonreligious. This slowly changed over the 20th century so that by 2020, Christians were 83% and the nonreligious were 17%.

Bible Translations		Churches		Missionaries		Gospel Access	
Languages	3	Denominations	30	Received	4	1900	Very high
Full Bible	2	Congregations	130	Sent	20	2020	Very high

Christianity in Israel

The Romans put down a Jewish rebellion in Palestine from 67 to 73 CE and again from 132 to 135 CE. Both of these resulted in the dispersal of the Jews, and of Jewish Christians, throughout the Mediterranean world and the Near East. Subsequently, Palestine came under the rule of Byzantines (324 CE), Arabs (636), Crusaders (1099), Mamluks (1291), Ottoman Turks (1517), and the British (1917) before the founding of the State of Israel in 1948. There are four main populations of Christians in Israel: Palestinian Arab citizens of the State of Israel; expatriate Catholic male and female religious, clergy, and other personnel; Hebrew-speaking Christian citizens of the State of Israel; and migrant workers and asylum seekers.

Facts to Consider

- There are at least 72 female Catholic religious orders and 30 male orders working in different kinds of charitable and humanitarian organizations, orphanages, and homes for the elderly.
- Orthodox Christianity has been declining due to a shortage of priests, inadequate finances, members switching to other Christian denominations, and emigration.
- The number of Messianic Jews has increased since 2000. Many congregations consist of both Jews and gentiles and are Charismatic in worship. Messianic Judaism is extremely controversial, and members are often subject to harassment.
- More than 20% of the population is Muslim, and the number of mosques has increased by 500% since 1988. Seventy percent of Muslims live in Galilee and Haifa in the north.

Indicators & Demographic Data

Population (2020)	8,714,000
% under 15 years	28%
Capital city (pop.)	Jerusalem 932,000
% urban dwellers	93% (1.51% p.a.)
Official language	Hebrew, Arabic
Largest language	Arabic (26%)
Largest people	Palestinian Arab (19%)
Largest culture	Jewish (74%)
Development	90
Physicians	36
Gender gap	3%

% Christian: 0 3 10 50 75 100

Christian Traditions in Israel

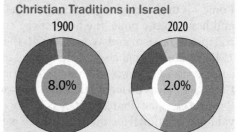

1900 — 8.0% 2020 — 2.0%

☐ Independent ☐ Protestant ☐ Catholic ■ Orthodox ■ Christian

In 1900, most Christians in the area that became Israel were historic Orthodox (67% of Christians) and Catholic (30%). By 2020, modern-day Israel was home to a wide diversity of churches: Catholics (57% of Christians), Orthodox (21%), Independents (17%), and Protestants (6%).

Religion in Israel

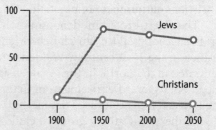

Israel has been a majority Jewish state since its founding in 1948. In 1970, the country was 85% Jewish. This declined to 71% by 2020, followed by 21% Muslim and 2% Christian.

Bible Translations		Churches		Missionaries		Gospel Access	
Languages	49	Denominations	100	Received	1,200	1900	Low
Full Bible	25	Congregations	750	Sent	60	2020	Medium

Christianity in Italy

Christianity has been present in modern-day Italy since the ministry of Jesus's disciples Peter and Paul in the 1st century. Rome has a prominent place in Christian history as the Church of Rome morphed into Roman Catholicism, the world's largest Christian tradition today. The separation of Eastern and Western Christianity, formalized in 1054, confirmed Rome's place at the center of Western Christianity. The modern Italian nation state began in 1861 with a population that was entirely Roman Catholic, a majority that still exists today. Vatican City—a city-state surrounded by Rome—is the headquarters of the Roman Catholic Church and home to the pope, the head of the church. After the collapse of fascism and World War II, the constitution of 1947 declared Catholicism the religion of the state. In 1984, a new concordat between Italy and the Vatican declared that Catholicism was no longer the state religion.

The Catholic Church in Italy is an important symbol of values and national identity, but there is a great diversity of attitudes toward official belief and practice. Many Italians belong to the church but do not necessarily believe in its tenets. People practice less frequently than they used to, and church membership is on the decline. Around 25% of self-identified Catholics are practicing; only 5% attend Mass every week, and 15% attend once or twice a month. More attend church for major holidays (31%), and 21% of them attend for baptisms, communions, confirmations, funerals, and other similar rites of passage. Despite this, Italy is the only country in Western Europe where church-attending Christians outnumber nonpracticing Christians.

The oldest Protestant denomination in the country is the Evangelical Waldensian Church, originating in southern France in the 12th century. Waldensians today are concentrated in the north, in the "Waldensian Valleys" of the Piedmont region, after fleeing from Catholic persecution in the 18th and 19th centuries. They merged with Methodists in 1975. Other non-Catholic groups include Romanian Orthodox, Jehovah's Witnesses, Greek Orthodox, and Assemblies of God. Over the last 30 years, Italy has become a destination for immigrants from Nigeria and Ghana, who have planted Pentecostal churches throughout the country (around 500 congregations, mostly in the north).

% Christian: 0 3 10 50 75 100

Religion in Italy

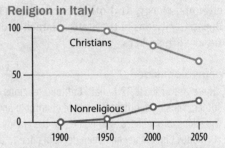

In 1900, essentially the entire population was Catholic (99%), with small populations of Jews (35,000) and nonreligious (60,000). Over the next 120 years, Catholicism declined to 73% with an increase of both Muslim (6%) and nonreligious (17%) populations. There are also communities of Chinese folk religionists, Hindus, Buddhists, and Sikhs due to 20th-century immigration.

Indicators & Demographic Data

Population (2020)	59,132,000
% under 15 years	13%
Capital city (pop.)	Rome 4,257,000
% urban dwellers	71% (0.27% p.a.)
Official language	Italian
Largest language	Italian (29%)
Largest people	Italian (28%)
Largest culture	Italian (84%)
Development	88
Physicians	40
Gender gap	3%

Bible Translations		Churches		Missionaries		Gospel Access	
Languages	55	Denominations	470	Received	10,000	1900	Very high
Full Bible	30	Congregations	36,400	Sent	10,000	2020	Very high

Facts to Consider

- Interfaith work is important in Italy, especially Jewish-Catholic relations. Pope Francis has prioritized intercultural and interfaith dialogue in his papal mission. There are 13 interfaith organizations in Rome alone.
- The number of Muslims in Italy, rising from just 1,000 in 1900 to 3.5 million in 2020, includes 400,000 Italian citizens. Muslims lack full legal rights, which affects their participation in public schools, dietary needs, and religious dress. The Grand Mosque of Rome is Europe's largest mosque.
- Italy's Jewish population decreased substantially during the fascist period of the 1930s. Around 10,000 Jews were deported to concentration and death camps; 7,700 died in the Holocaust. Today most Jews live in the north.
- Buddhism has grown to nearly 100,000 affiliates, most belonging to the Italian Buddhist Union or Soka Gakkai. The former's leadership largely consists of converted White Italians. There is a significant Chinese Buddhist population in Rome.
- There are frequent reports of anti-Semitic and anti-Muslim incidents, including harassment, discrimination, hate speech, and vandalism. Muslims face difficulties acquiring permission to build mosques.

Christian Traditions in Italy

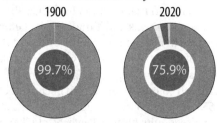

1900   2020

99.7%   75.9%

☐Independent ☐Protestant ■Catholic ■Orthodox ■Christian

Virtually the entire Christian population in 1900 (nearly 34 million) was Catholic, as has been the case in Italy for many centuries. By 2020, this had changed only slightly. Catholics made up 95% of Christians, but there are now larger communities of Orthodox (3%), Independents (2%), and Protestants (1%). The Pentecostal/Charismatic movement grew gradually over this period as well, and in 2020 represented 2% of the country's population and 3% of Christians.

Christian Families in Italy

Family	Population 2020	%	Trend	Change
Latin-rite Catholic	43,045,000	72.8	↓	-0.6
Eastern Orthodox	1,231,000	2.1	↑	2.3
*Pentecostals/Charismatics	1,220,000	2.1	↑	0.7
Jehovah's Witnesses	463,000	0.8	↑	1.1
*Evangelicals	280,000	0.5	↑	1.3
Anglican	95,200	0.2	↑	0.6
Eastern-rite Catholic	54,600	0.1	↓	-1.1
Latter-day Saints (Mormons)	30,600	0.1	↑	2.5
Christian Brethren	20,100	<0.1	↓	-1.4
Nondenominational	14,700	<0.1	↑	0.9
Baptist	10,500	<0.1	↑	1.1
Adventist	9,300	<0.1	↓	-1.0
Lutheran	6,000	<0.1	↓	-1.5
Restorationist, Disciple	3,600	<0.1	↑	1.3
Oriental and other Orthodox	1,800	<0.1	↑	1.1
Reformed, Presbyterian	1,300	<0.1	—	-0.1

After Latin-rite Catholics, the largest Christian family in Italy is Eastern Orthodox, the largest of which is the Romanian Orthodox Church, with 900,000 members. Pentecostal/Charismatics are the next largest family, representing a variety of groups such as the Assemblies of God, Independent networks of Pentecostal churches, Elim churches, and Pentecostal/Charismatic churches begun by immigrants from sub-Saharan Africa (in particular, Nigeria and Ghana) and elsewhere. Italian Pentecostalism has its origins in 1908 in Rome and La Spezia. Jehovah's Witnesses have been active in Italy since at least 1891 and have 463,000 members. They have had legal status in the country since 1976 but have always been opposed by the Catholic Church. Evangelicals make up 0.5% of the country's population and are represented by the Federation of Evangelical Churches in Italy, which formed in 1967 and includes Methodists, Waldensians, Baptists, Lutherans, and other smaller churches (around 140,000 members).

* These movements are found within Christian families	↑↑ extreme growth
	↑ growth
	↓↓ extreme decline
— no change	↓ decline

Christianity in Jamaica

Jamaica is an island nation in the Caribbean Sea, originally settled by Arawak and Taíno peoples before the arrival of the Spanish in the late 15th century. Most of the local population died of foreign diseases and were then replaced with enslaved Africans. Having replaced Catholicism after the island became a British colony, Anglicanism became the official religion in 1655 until Jamaica's independence in 1962. Christianity in Jamaica is quite diverse. Pentecostal/Charismatic Christianity has grown and represented nearly 16% of the island's population in 2020. The largest denominations are the Seventh-day Adventist Church, the New Testament Church of God, the Anglican Church, and the Catholic Church.

Facts to Consider

- Jamaica is home to around 60 Independent churches, most of which are Pentecostal in worship style. Even older Protestant churches are becoming "pentecostalized."
- Jamaican Baptist churches historically made major contributions to missions in West Africa; in the 20th century, missionaries worked among expatriate Jamaican populations in the United States and United Kingdom.
- Women outnumber men overall in Jamaican society, but especially in the churches and lately in the pulpits. Women have become key leaders in various denominations. The first female president of the Jamaica Baptist Union was elected in 2018, the same year the first woman became a bishop in the Methodist Church.
- Afro-Caribbean religions are found all over Jamaica and represent a mixture of Spiritism, Christianity, and African Traditional Religion. The Rastafari movement has 25,000 affiliates.

Indicators & Demographic Data

Population (2020)................................2,913,000
% under 15 years 22%
Capital city (pop.) .... Kingston 591,000
% urban dwellers............................56% (0.79% p.a.)
Official language.......................................English
Largest language...................Jamaican Creole English (95%)
Largest people .... Jamaican Black (78%)
Largest culture .... Black (African), English-speaking (78%)
Development..73
Physicians...4.7
Gender gap...1%

% Christian: 0 3 10 50 75 100

Christian Traditions in Jamaica

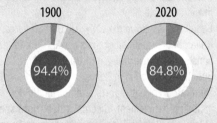

1900 — 94.4%   2020 — 84.8%

☐ Independent ☐ Protestant ▨ Catholic ▨ Orthodox ▨ Christian

In 1900, Jamaica was largely Protestant (94% of Christians), with small communities of Independents (4%) and Catholics (2%). By 2020, Protestants were still the majority (72%), but Independents grew dramatically to 22% of Christians.

Religion in Jamaica

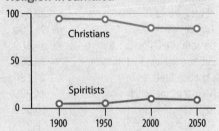

Jamaica is a majority Christian country, though Christianity has been in a slight decline since the early 20th century. In 1900, the country was 94% Christian and 5% Spiritist; in 2020, it was 85% Christian and 10% Spiritist.

Bible Translations		Churches		Missionaries		Gospel Access	
Languages	9	Denominations	190	Received	780	1900	Very high
Full Bible	6	Congregations	5,500	Sent	50	2020	Very high

Christianity in Japan

Christianity is a minority religion in Japan today (2% of the population), though it has a long history in the country. The first Christian mission was by famous Catholic missionary Francis Xavier in 1549; there were 300,000 baptized Catholics by 1593. However, missionaries were expelled in 1587, and the ruling Daimyo class persecuted Christians until the mid-19th century; Christianity could be practiced only in secret. Foreign missionaries were allowed to return in 1859, but they struggled because of their association with Western powers in the face of Japanese nationalism. Catholics in Nagasaki today (formerly known as the "Rome of Japan") trace their roots to those who survived the persecutions in the 16th and 17th centuries. The largest Protestant denomination is the United Church of Christ in Japan. The country suffers from a shortage of Japanese priests and nuns, with priests from Vietnam and the Philippines filling the gap.

Facts to Consider

- On the islands in southern Japan lives a group of descendants of 40,000 former Catholics who survived the earlier persecutions but today refuse to join the Catholic Church. Known as "hidden" or "separated" Christians, they incorporate Buddhist and Shinto elements into their religious ceremonies.
- Christians in Hiroshima and Nagasaki—areas devastated by American nuclear bombs at the end of World War II—have taken a stance against nuclear power. Many churches have called for nuclear abolishment, especially after the Fukushima Daiichi Nuclear Power Plant disaster in 2011.
- Jehovah's Witnesses are the second largest denomination. Upward of 70% of members are women.

Indicators & Demographic Data

Population (2020) 126,496,000
% under 15 years 13%
Capital city (pop.) . . . . Tokyo 37,393,000
% urban dwellers. . . . . 92% (-0.25% p.a.)
Official language. . . . . none
Largest language. . . . . Japanese (98%)
Largest people . . . . Japanese (98%)
Largest culture . . . . Japanese (98%)
Development. 91
Physicians. 24
Gender gap. 2%

% Christian: 0 3 10 50 75 100

Christian Traditions in Japan

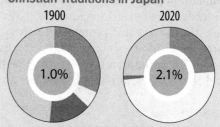

1900 — 1.0% 2020 — 2.1%

☐ Independent ☐ Protestant ■ Catholic ■ Orthodox ■ Christian

The historic Christian population of Japan was primarily Catholic, though in 1900 Protestants had the largest share of Christians (49%). In 2020, Protestants and Catholics were nearly equal in size (each around a quarter of Christians), but Independents were the largest (49%).

Religion in Japan

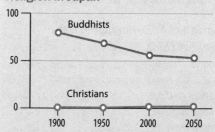

In 1900, Japan was 80% Buddhist, 15% Shintoist, and 5% New Religionist. By 2020, these figures had shifted to 56% Buddhist, 26% New Religionist, and 2% Shintoist. Christianity increased from 1% to 2%.

Bible Translations	Churches	Missionaries	Gospel Access
Languages. 28	Denominations 250	Received. 8,000	1900 . . . . Very low
Full Bible. 14	Congregations. 17,600	Sent 900	2020 . . . . .High

Christianity in Jordan

Jesus visited what is now Jordan in the 1st century; the region became home to many kinds of Christian churches from both Eastern and Western traditions. Today's Christians are descendants of the ancient Palestinian and Transjordanian peoples of the apostolic era. However, the arrival of Islam eclipsed Christianity, and today the country is 96% Muslim and 1% Christian. Most Christians are Orthodox (Greek, Coptic, Armenian, Syriac), and the faith has been particularly well preserved among farmers in villages. Christians are found throughout Jordanian society, except among the nomadic population. The largest problem facing churches in Jordan has been the economic crises caused by three Palestinian wars that prompted Christians to emigrate in large numbers. Many Christians fleeing Iraq and Syria have stopped in Jordan on their way to new homes in Europe and North America, but most refugees are Sunni Muslims.

Facts to Consider

- Jordan is home to important Christian pilgrimage sites such as the baptismal site of Jesus on the Jordan River, the mosaic map of the Holy Land in Madaba, and the traditional burial site of Moses near Mount Nebo.
- Some of the most respected schools in the country are run by Christians.
- Most Muslims in Jordan are Sunnis. Nomadic Bedouins also practice pre-Islamic tribal law alongside orthodox Islam.
- Druze are found mostly on the Jordanian border with Syria and practice a schism from Isma'ilism, a branch of Shia Islam.
- Jordan is home to over 800,000 migrant workers. Most are from Egypt, South and East Asia, and sub-Saharan Africa.

Indicators & Demographic Data

Population (2020)	10,209,000
% under 15 years	34%
Capital city (pop.)	Amman 2,148,000
% urban dwellers	91% (0.98% p.a.)
Official language	Arabic
Largest language	Arabic (97%)
Largest people	Palestinian Arab (49%)
Largest culture	Arab (Arabic) (96%)
Development	74
Physicians	34
Gender gap	14%

% Christian: 0 3 10 50 75 100

Christian Traditions in Jordan

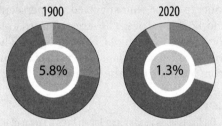

1900 — 5.8%   2020 — 1.3%

☐ Independent ☐ Protestant ☐ Catholic ◼ Orthodox ◼ Christian

In 1900, Jordan's 15,000 Christians were majority Orthodox (69%), followed by Catholics (28%). In 2020, Orthodox were 64% of Christians and Catholics were 21%. Protestants/Independents grew from virtually zero in 1900 to 16% of Christians in 2020.

Religion in Jordan

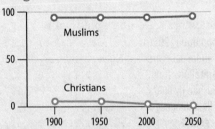

Jordan has been a majority Muslim country: 94% Muslim in 1900 and 96% in 2020. Christians represent a large but declining minority, dropping from 6% Christian in 1900 to 1% in 2020.

Bible Translations		Churches		Missionaries		Gospel Access	
Languages	18	Denominations	45	Received	220	1900	Very low
Full Bible	6	Congregations	350	Sent	15	2020	Medium

Christianity in Kazakhstan

The Church of the East reached what is today Kazakhstan as early as the 6th century. Christianity grew until the 15th century when the plague and the reign of Tamerlane wiped out most of the Christian population. In 1860, the region fell under Russian control, causing Orthodox to migrate to the area. Around the time of World War II, tens of thousands of Ukrainians and other Orthodox, as well as Catholics and German Lutherans, were deported to Kazakhstan from the Soviet Union. Despite the emigration of nonethnic Kazakhs after independence in 1991, Orthodox Christianity began to revive after decades of atheistic Soviet influence. The Russian Orthodox Church is the largest denomination today.

Facts to Consider

- Soviet authorities were the most severe against Catholics in Kazakhstan, destroying every associated building. In 1981, only 15 priests were in the country, all of them elderly and survivors of prisons or labor camps. Catholicism has grown since then, and the first Kazakh priests were ordained in 2006.
- Evangelical Protestants began ministering in the country in 1990, both in humanitarian efforts and by offering support to struggling churches. Many churches formed in the 1990s via Korean, American, European, Australian, Ukrainian, and Chinese missionaries. The number of Kazakh Evangelicals is between 10,000 and 15,000.
- Many in Kazakhstan consider Jesus the "Russian god" and Christianity a threat to the Kazakh nation. Although Protestant Evangelical churches are found in all major cities and many rural areas, some choose to meet in house churches and "underground" fellowships.

Indicators & Demographic Data

Population (2020)	18,777,000
% under 15 years	29%
Capital city (pop.)	Astana 1,166,000
% urban dwellers	58% (1.19% p.a.)
Official language	Kazakh, Russian
Largest language	Kazakh (62%)
Largest people	Kazakh (63%)
Largest culture	Kazakh (63%)
Development	80
Physicians	33
Gender gap	-1%

% Christian: 0 3 10 50 75 100

Christian Traditions in Kazakhstan

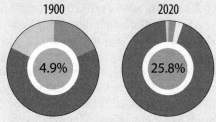

1900 — 4.9%
2020 — 25.8%

☐ Independent ☐ Protestant ■ Catholic ■ Orthodox ■ Christian

The Christian population in 1900 was majority Orthodox (64% of Christians), followed by equal numbers of Protestants and Catholics (18% each). By 2020, the number of Orthodox had swelled and represented 94% of Christians.

Religion in Kazakhstan

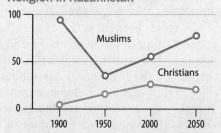

Kazakhstan has been a majority Muslim country, with 94% Muslim in 1900 and 71% in 2020. Christians represent a growing minority, increasing from 5% in 1900 to 26% in 2020. There are small communities of traditional religionists and Buddhists.

Bible Translations		Churches		Missionaries		Gospel Access	
Languages	48	Denominations	100	Received	220	1900	Very low
Full Bible	31	Congregations	1,400	Sent	30	2020	High

Christianity in Kenya

The first Christian interaction with what is today Kenya was in 1498 with the arrival of Portuguese explorers. Early Catholic missions initially collapsed and were not revived until 1889. Anglican missionaries arrived in 1844, followed by Scottish Presbyterians (1891) and the African Inland Mission (1895). Response to Christianity in Kenya was swift; the number of converts doubled or even tripled every year in the first decade of the 20th century. By 1916, mass movements to Catholic, Anglican, and other kinds of Protestant churches had started, and 30% of the population was Christian by 1948. This figure kept rising such that by 2020, Kenya was 82% Christian, with over 120 denominations in the country. Around 90 of such denominations are Independent indigenous churches, numbering particularly in western Kenya among the Luo and Kikuyu peoples. The first of these formed in 1914, with the Nomiya Luo Mission (now Nomiya Church). For Christians in Kenya, denominational and ethnic identity are closely connected. Even a "national" church like the Anglican Church has ethnic dioceses, with bishops of the same ethnicity.

The Catholic Church is the largest denomination and has been growing since 2000. Over half of all clergy are African, and many Kenyan women and girls have become sisters. Anglicans are the second largest denomination, partly due to missions but largely because of British colonization from 1895 to 1963. Anglicans are found throughout the country but are concentrated among the Kikuyu, Luo, and Luhya communities. The preponderance of institutes of theological education throughout the country has contributed to a rise in African clergy members. Pentecostal/Charismatic Christianity is popular, of which the two most prominent churches are the Pentecostal Assemblies of God and the Pentecostal Evangelistic Fellowship of Africa. Many Evangelical churches established daughter churches, with regional churches to implement local missionary efforts. Many Independent churches in Kenya trace their roots to the early 20th century Roho (Holy Spirit) movement in Nyanza Province. Christianity in Kenya is generally outward facing, with most churches engaged in both community and national outreach and serving in ministries dealing with a wide range of issues that include HIV/AIDS, orphan care, and children at risk.

% Christian: 0 3 10 50 75 100

Religion in Kenya

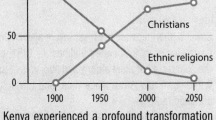

Kenya experienced a profound transformation in its religious population over the 20th century. Historically, the country has been, and remains, very religious. In 1900, nearly the entire populace followed traditional religions (96%), with only 3% Muslim. By 2020, Christianity had grown to 82% of the population, followed by 8% traditional religionists and just under 8% Muslim.

Indicators & Demographic Data

Population (2020)	53,492,000
% under 15 years	39%
Capital city (pop.)	Nairobi 4,735,000
% urban dwellers	28% (4.09% p.a.)
Official language	Swahili, English
Largest language	Luyia (16%)
Largest people	Kikuyu (15%)
Largest culture	Kenya Highland Bantu (36%)
Development	59
Physicians	2
Gender gap	7%

Bible Translations		Churches		Missionaries		Gospel Access	
Languages	89	Denominations	1,300	Received	6,000	1900	Very low
Full Bible	41	Congregations	89,100	Sent	1,000	2020	Very high

Facts to Consider

- Human rights groups have stated that government antiterrorism efforts disproportionately target Muslim groups, especially among ethnic Somalis along the border with Somalia. Such efforts include extrajudicial killings, torture, and forced interrogations. The government denies these actions.
- Kenyan Christian faith-based organizations are active in addressing issues such as poverty, illiteracy, child mortality, drug addiction, agriculture, and climate change. They work in both urban and rural areas.
- Women and children are the majority of church attendees in Kenya. Women's ordination is controversial, with some denominations in support and some against. Women are highly involved in churches, ranging from ordained ministry to wives' forums and mothers' unions.
- Kenya is home to a significant number of megachurches, with many branches throughout the country, including Nairobi Chapel (nondenominational), Mavuno Church (many youth), and All Saints Cathedral (Anglican).
- While the majority of Kenyans are Christian, traditional religious practices and beliefs continue. For example, at least 10% of Christians believe that traditional shrines and objects could keep one safe from harm.
- Muslims in Kenya number over 4 million (nearly 8%) and have their largest presence at the coast and in the northeast among the Somali, Digo, Boran, Pokomo, and Duruma peoples.

Christian Traditions in Kenya

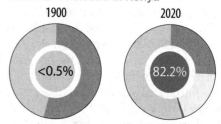

1900   2020

<0.5%   82.2%

□ Independent □ Protestant ■ Catholic ■ Orthodox ■ Christian

The small Christian population in 1900 (5,000) was mostly Catholic (54% of Christians) and Protestant (46%). By 2020, Kenyan Christianity was extremely diverse. Protestants made up 55% of Christians, followed by Catholics (26%), Independents (19%), and Orthodox (1%). Cutting through most of these traditions is the Pentecostal/Charismatic movement, representing nearly 40% of Christians. Most of the growth of Christianity has been due to conversion from traditional religions. Missionaries from many traditions are also active in the country.

Christian Families in Kenya

Family	Population 2020	%	Trend	Change
*Pentecostals/Charismatics	17,300,000	32.3	↑	2.7
*Evangelicals	16,500,000	30.8	↑	2.0
Latin-rite Catholic	12,100,000	22.6	↑	2.9
Anglican	8,288,000	15.5	↑	3.3
Reformed, Presbyterian	6,165,000	11.5	↑	1.0
Nondenominational	4,330,000	8.1	↑	1.0
Adventist	1,538,000	2.9	↑	4.5
Friends (Quaker)	1,359,000	2.5	↑↑	8.2
Baptist	1,152,000	2.2	–	-0.3
Holiness	820,000	1.5	↑	3.4
Methodist	511,000	1.0	↓	-2.5
Salvationist	397,000	0.7	↑	0.9
Eastern Orthodox	370,000	0.7	↑	1.1
Old Catholic Church	307,000	0.6	↑	4.4
Restorationist, Disciple	244,000	0.5	↑	3.7
Lutheran	146,000	0.3	–	0.4
Jehovah's Witnesses	80,100	0.1	↑	2.7
Mennonite	50,400	0.1	↑↑	6.4
Latter-day Saints (Mormons)	17,700	<0.1	↑↑	5.6
United church or joint mission	2,200	<0.1	↑	0.8

The largest Christian family in Kenya is the Pentecostal/Charismatic group of churches (over 17 million). This group represents a wide variety of denominations, including groups founded within Africa and those established through the efforts of foreign missionaries. Some of the largest Pentecostal/Charismatic denominations include the New Apostolic Church, Assemblies of God, and Full Gospel churches. There are also many Charismatics within the traditional Protestant churches, such as Anglicans and Baptists. Large African Independent Churches founded in Kenya include Maria Legio of Africa, African Israel Nineveh Church, and the Nomiya Luo Church. Each of these were breakaway groups from existing denominations such as the Catholic Church, Pentecostal Assemblies of Canada, and Church Missionary Society. Like Charismatics, Evangelicals are found throughout most denominations.

* These movements are found within Christian families

– no change

↑↑ extreme growth
↑ growth
↓↓ extreme decline
↓ decline

Christianity in Kiribati

Kiribati is an island nation in the Pacific Ocean, consisting of 32 atolls and one raised coral island. Half of the country's roughly 120,000 people live on the Tarawa atoll. The first missionary, a Samoan from the London Missionary Society, arrived in 1870, followed by Catholics in 1888. Catholicism was introduced by two native Gilbertese who became Catholic while working in Tahiti and brought their new faith home. Kiribati was a British colony from 1892 to 1976. Today the country is 97% Christian, the largest denominations being Catholicism, the Uniting Church, and the Church of Jesus Christ of Latter-day Saints. The Uniting Church represents a merger of Congregationalists, Anglicans, Evangelicals, and Presbyterians and is found mostly in Batio and Bonriki.

Facts to Consider

- Kiribati lies only six feet above sea level, and islanders are extremely concerned about rising sea levels and climate change. Some church buildings and meeting houses are surrounded by water at high tide, unable to be used.
- Many Christians have trouble reconciling the biblical promise that God will not again destroy the earth in a flood and the evidence of climate change.
- Women were granted permission to attend Tangintebu Theological College in the 1970s. The Kiribati Uniting Church began ordaining women in 1984, with special reference to a female rite of passage ceremony called te Katekateka—affirming that women are just as capable as men to lead congregations.
- The Church of Jesus Christ of Latter-day Saints began working in Kiribati in 1975 and is the third largest denomination, with nearly 20,000 members.

Indicators & Demographic Data

Population (2020)................................. 122,000
% under 15 years 36%
Capital city (pop.)............................Tarawa 57,800
% urban dwellers...........................56% (2.77% p.a.)
Official language.....................................English
Largest language................................ Kiribati (98%)
Largest people .... Kiribertese (Gilbertese) (97%)
Largest culture .... Gilbertese (97%)
Development...61
Physicians...2
Gender gap..13%

% Christian: 0 3 10 50 75 100

Christian Traditions in Kiribati

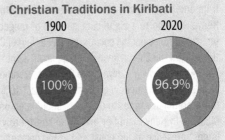

1900 — 100%
2020 — 96.9%

☐Independent ☐Protestant ■Catholic ■Orthodox ■Christian

In 1900, 55% of Christians were Protestant and 45% were Catholic. Independent Christianity has grown tremendously (16% of Christians in 2020). Catholics are found mostly in the northern islands, while Protestants are the majority in the southern islands.

Religion in Kiribati

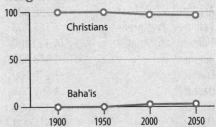

Kiribati remains a majority Christian country: 100% Christian in 1900 and still 97% in 2020. There is a small population of followers of the Baha'i Faith (2%).

Bible Translations		Churches		Missionaries		Gospel Access	
Languages.............5		Denominations 13		Received.............60		1900......... Very high	
Full Bible.............4		Congregations........270		Sent 10		2020.......... Very high	

Christianity in Kosovo

Kosovo, in the Balkan region of south-central Europe, is a partially recognized state in the international community. Historically, it changed hands among Romans, Slavs, Bulgarians, Byzantines, Ottomans, and Serbs. The country was majority Slavic and Orthodox from the 8th to the mid-19th century. After World War I, Serbia (of which Kosovo was a part) and Montenegro joined Yugoslavia. Tensions between Albanian and Serb communities boiled over in the Kosovo War (1998–1999). Hundreds of thousands of refugees fled genocidal violence in Kosovo for Albania, Macedonia, and Montenegro. Kosovo declared independence from Serbia in 2008 and is 6% Christian today. Catholics are the largest tradition, followed by Serbian Orthodox and the Kosovo Protestant Evangelical Church.

Facts to Consider

- Mother Teresa was born in the Vilayet of Kosovo in the Ottoman Empire in 1910 (Skopje, now the capital of North Macedonia); today the Mother Teresa Catholic Cathedral stands in the center of Kosovo's capital, Priština.
- In the early 2010s, members of the new Kosovar Albanian Protestant churches were mostly teenagers or men, since women were more often prohibited from attending Christian meetings.
- Catholics in Kosovo are known for extensive education and compassion work, including orphan care. Foreign Evangelicals are also heavily involved in humanitarian work, education, and health care.
- Interreligious and interethnic conflict has been a significant part of Kosovo's troubled history. The country still suffers from religiously and ethnically motivated incidents of harassment, violence, threats, and general intolerance.

Indicators & Demographic Data

Population (2020) 2,096,000
% under 15 years 16%
Capital city (pop.) . . . . Pristina 204,000
% urban dwellers. . . . . .56% (0.04% p.a.)
Official language. . . . . .Albanian, Serbian
Largest language. . . . . Albanian (90%)
Largest people . . . . .Kosovar (Gheg Albanian) (90%)
Largest culture . . . . Albanian (90%)
Development. 87
Physicians. 39
Gender gap 3%

% Christian: 0 3 10 50 75 100

Christian Traditions in Kosovo

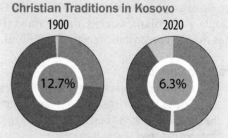

1900 — 12.7%   2020 — 6.3%

☐ Independent ☐ Protestant ■ Catholic ■ Orthodox ■ Christian

In 1900, Kosovo's Christian population was mostly Orthodox (73%), with a sizable Catholic minority (26%). By 2020, Catholics and Orthodox were still the largest Christian traditions, but Protestants and Independents together grew to 12% of Christians.

Religion in Kosovo

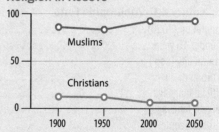

Kosovo's Muslim population grew from 86% in 1900 to 93% in 2020. Christianity declined over the same period from 13% to 6%.

Bible Translations		Churches		Missionaries		Gospel Access	
Languages. 7		Denominations 28		Received. 110		1900 . . . . Low	
Full Bible. 6		Congregations. 280		Sent 30		2020 . . . . Medium	

Christianity in Kuwait

Kuwait is located on the northern edge of the Arabian Peninsula and home to 10% of the world's crude oil reserves. Upward of 70% of the country's population of 4.3 million are expatriates working in the oil industry. The country is 83% Muslim, with large minorities of Christians and Hindus. Christians come from a variety of denominational backgrounds, and only around 300 of the country's 500,000 Christians are Kuwaiti. Catholicism is the largest Christian tradition, with members of many Eastern-rite churches: Melkites, Maronites, Chaldeans, and others. The largest group of expatriate Catholics are Filipinos. Orthodox include Copts, Armenians, Greeks, and Syrians (Indians). Kuwait has many Pentecostals, mostly from Kerala, south India.

Facts to Consider

- The constitution declares Islam the religion of the state and Sharia law as the main source of legislation. The law prohibits the defamation of the three Abrahamic religions: Islam, Christianity, and Judaism (though there are no known Jews in the country).
- The government provides a full basic text for weekly sermons to be preached at Sunni mosques. Guidelines and laws are in place to avoid stoking sectarianism, and all religious content must be in line with the Ministry of Awqaf and Islamic Affairs.
- The Gulf Churches Fellowship formed in 2013 with leaders from Catholic, Eastern Orthodox, Oriental Orthodox, Anglican, and other Protestant churches. The Bible Society in the Gulf has two centers in Kuwait to provide Bible resources in the country.

Indicators & Demographic Data

Population (2020)	4,303,000
% under 15 years	21%
Capital city (pop.)	Kuwait City 3,115,000
% urban dwellers	100% (1.35% p.a.)
Official language	Arabic
Largest language	Arabic (73%)
Largest people	Kuwaiti Arab (31%)
Largest culture	Arab (Arabic) (70%)
Development	80
Physicians	26
Gender gap	1%

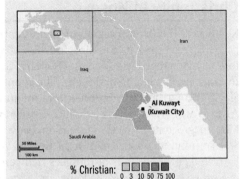

% Christian: 0 3 10 50 75 100

Christian Traditions in Kuwait

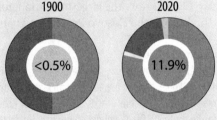

1900 — <0.5%   2020 — 11.9%

☐ Independent ☐ Protestant ☐ Catholic ■ Orthodox ■ Christian

In 2020, Kuwait's Christian community was largely Catholic (79%), followed by Orthodox (18%), Protestants (3%), and Independents (1%). There is also a large number of Pentecostals/Charismatics, 21% of Christians.

Religion in Kuwait

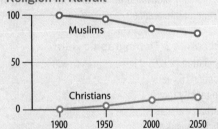

Kuwait has historically been a Muslim majority country. In 1900, the country was 99% Muslim. In 2020, the Muslim share had dropped to 83% with a rise in Christianity (12%), mostly a result of migrant workers.

Bible Translations		Churches		Missionaries		Gospel Access	
Languages	23	Denominations	25	Received	120	1900	Very low
Full Bible	12	Congregations	170	Sent	10	2020	Medium

Christianity in Kyrgyzstan

Christianity reached what is now Kyrgyzstan in the 6th or 7th century via missionaries of the Church of the East. Russians began colonizing the area that is now Kyrgyzstan in the mid-19th century, causing an influx also of Slavs and other Europeans into the area, most of them Orthodox and some Protestant. In the 20th century, the Christian population of Kyrgyzstan changed with shifting borders and movement of people. Christians suffered under atheist Soviet rule from 1919 to 1991, but Orthodox Christianity rebounded upon national independence in 1991. The country now has 40 Russian Orthodox congregations. Pentecostal and Evangelical churches have also grown since the 1990s, and in the capital, Bishkek, these churches outnumber Orthodox churches.

Facts to Consider

- Most ethnic Kyrgyz are Muslim (Hanafi Sunnis with Sufi influence). Kyrgyz who become Christians do so while challenging their ethnic religious identity since Christianity is typically associated with Russia.
- There are roughly 50,000 followers of Tengrism, an indigenous religion. Shamanism is active in the mountains, helping the living speak with the dead, conduct funerals, wrestle against evil spirits, and serve as healers.
- Korean Methodists have been helping in national development and teaching in Bible schools. There are roughly 16,000 Koreans in the country.
- The State Commission on Religious Affairs holds interfaith dialogues in all seven oblasts in the country, with Muslim, Russian Orthodox, Catholic, Protestant, and Baha'i participants. The purpose is to promote tolerance among religious groups as well as understanding between religious communities and the state.

Indicators & Demographic Data

Population (2020)	6,302,000
% under 15 years	32%
Capital city (pop.)	Bishkek 1,038,000
% urban dwellers	37% (2.05% p.a.)
Official language	Kyrgyz, Russian
Largest language	Kyrgyz (71%)
Largest people	Kirghiz (71%)
Largest culture	Kirgiz (71%)
Development	67
Physicians	19
Gender gap	4%

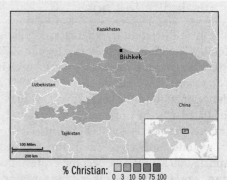

% Christian: 0 3 10 50 75 100

Christian Traditions in Kyrgyzstan

1900 — 3.0%   2020 — 4.4%

☐ Independent ☐ Protestant ■ Catholic ■ Orthodox ■ Christian

The small Christian population in 1900 (only 17,000 people) was largely Orthodox (63% of Christians) and Catholic (31%). In 2020, Orthodox had a much greater share (84%), but Protestant and Independents together made up 16% of Christians.

Religion in Kyrgyzstan

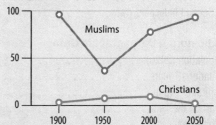

In 1900, Kyrgyzstan was 96% Muslim and 3% Christian. Under Soviet rule, religion declined, but has since rebounded. By 2020, the country was 87% Muslim, 4% Christian, and 7% nonreligious.

Bible Translations		Churches		Missionaries		Gospel Access	
Languages	40	Denominations	34	Received	60	1900	Very low
Full Bible	28	Congregations	490	Sent	30	2020	Medium

Christianity in Laos

The first Christian in what is today Laos was a Jesuit in 1642. Vietnamese Catholics arrived in 1771, and American Presbyterians in 1782. The Gospel Church in Laos—now the Lao Evangelical Church—formed in 1957 and is the largest denomination in the country, with 120,000 members. It is affiliated with the Christian and Missionary Alliance. Christianity grew in the 1990s but continues to face opposition from state-supported Buddhism. Around 35,000 Hmong and 25,000 Khmu have become Protestants, and significant numbers of Khmu and other ethnic minorities are Catholics. The majority of Lao people are Buddhist and have been largely resistant to Christianity.

Facts to Consider

- Theravada Buddhism is the main religion of the ethnic, or "lowland," Lao, who make up over half the country's population. Buddhists often mix Hindu, traditional religionist, and Buddhist practices and beliefs. Traditional religions are important for all ethnic groups, an important aspect of which is belief in nature spirits, gods, goddesses, and the veneration of ancestors.
- The only two churches registered by the government are the Lao Evangelical Church and the Seventh-day Adventist Church. The authorities monitor Christian activities, especially in rural areas where house churches meet in secret as illegal gatherings of unregistered churches. Some authorities are deeply suspicious of Christians.
- In 2016, the government surprisingly permitted the Catholic Church in the capital, Vientiane, to celebrate the beatification of 17 Laotian Catholic martyrs killed between 1954 and 1970 during the First and Second Indochina Wars.

Indicators & Demographic Data

Population (2020)	7,165,000
% under 15 years	32%
Capital city (pop.)	Vientiane 683,000
% urban dwellers	36% (2.99% p.a.)
Official language	Lao
Largest language	Lao (39%)
Largest people	Lao (Laotian Tai, Lao-Lu) (39%)
Largest culture	Lao (40%)
Development	60
Physicians	4.9
Gender gap	7%

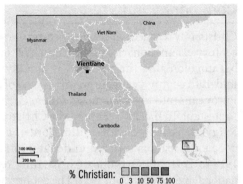

% Christian: 0 3 10 50 75 100

Christian Traditions in Laos

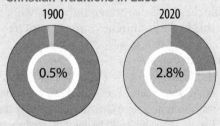

1900 — 0.5%   2020 — 2.8%

☐ Independent ☐ Protestant ■ Catholic ■ Orthodox ■ Christian

The small Christian population in 1900 (only 8,200 people) was almost entirely Catholic (98%) due to historic mission activity. By 2020, Protestantism had grown and represented 76% of Christians, a large portion of whom are Evangelical.

Religion in Laos

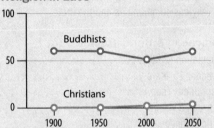

Laos has been and continues to be a majority Buddhist country. In 2020, Laos was 53% Buddhist, 42% ethnic religionist, and just under 3% Christian.

Bible Translations		Churches		Missionaries		Gospel Access	
Languages	99	Denominations	24	Received	90	1900	Very low
Full Bible	15	Congregations	1,500	Sent	5	2020	Medium

Christianity in Latvia

In 1180, the first missionary, a German monk, arrived in what is today Latvia. Christianity grew slowly until soldier-missionaries of the Livonian Order conquered the region in the early 13th century. Through at least the 18th century, people mixed Christianity with beliefs and practices from local traditional religions. Today, Latvia is 82% Christian, with mostly Protestants in the west and central region and Catholics in the east. All churches, including the largest denomination, Evangelical Lutheran Church (700,000 members), suffered under Nazi and, subsequently, Soviet occupation from 1940 to 1991. Much of the churches' leadership was killed, emigrated, or sent to Siberia. The religious climate of Latvia changed in the post-Soviet era, with increased church membership, reconstruction of church buildings, and Christian instruction in schools.

Facts to Consider

- The Evangelical Lutheran Church allowed female ordination beginning in 1975 but stopped in 1994. In 2016, the church officially ruled that women could not be pastors. Women continue to serve as evangelists.
- The Catholic Church is the second largest denomination. The church grew after 1991, but by 2015, baptisms had declined by half.
- The nonreligious (atheists and agnostics) are the largest non-Christian group in the country. At the height of Communism in 1970, 60% of the country was nonreligious. This figure dropped to 17% in 2020.
- The 100,000-member Jewish community was nearly annihilated during the Nazi occupation (1941–1945). Only 8,000 people of Jewish heritage lived in Latvia in 2020.

Indicators & Demographic Data

Population (2020)...............................1,893,000
% under 15 years 16%
Capital city (pop.) ....Riga 631,000
% urban dwellers...........................68% (-0.68% p.a.)
Official language................................... Latvian
Largest language...................... Standard Latvian (39%)
Largest people ....Latvian (Lett, Lettish) (37%)
Largest culture .... Latvian (59%)
Development..85
Physicians...32
Gender gap..-3%

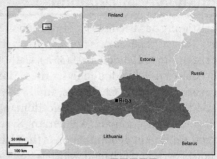

% Christian: 0 3 10 50 75 100

Christian Traditions in Latvia

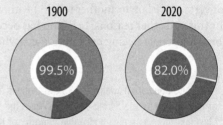

1900 — 99.5%   2020 — 82.0%

☐Independent ☐Protestant ◪Catholic ■Orthodox ■Christian

In 1900, Latvia was home to large populations of Protestants (49% of Christians), Catholics (36%), and Orthodox (16%). By 2020, the Orthodox population of the country had grown to 27% of Christians, and Protestants remained about the same at 46%.

Religion in Latvia

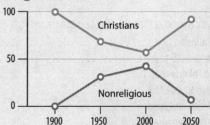

Over the 20th century, the Christian share of the population changed dramatically, dropping from virtually 100% in 1900 to 39% in 1970 and then back up to 82% in 2020 in the post-Soviet era.

Bible Translations		Churches		Missionaries		Gospel Access	
Languages	34	Denominations	74	Received	440	1900	Very high
Full Bible	24	Congregations	1,300	Sent	70	2020	Very high

Christianity in Lebanon

Christianity has been present in Lebanon since the 1st century. Today the country is home to the largest proportion of Christians in the Middle East (35%). Catholics, as the largest Christian family, are found in six rites: Maronites, Melkites, Armenians, Syrians, Chaldeans, and Latin. Orthodox are the second largest family, both Chalcedonian (Greek, Russian) and non-Chalcedonian (Armenian, Syrian, Coptic). The largest Protestant denomination is the National Evangelical Synod of Syria and Lebanon, which is Reformed/Presbyterian. Lebanon is unique in the Middle East in that it grants true freedom of religion and conscience, including the freedom to convert from Islam to another religion without recrimination. For this and other reasons, Lebanon has become a temporary home for people fleeing persecution elsewhere in the region.

Facts to Consider

- Lebanon's population swelled by 35% starting in 2011 with the arrival of people fleeing the Syrian civil war. While the majority were Sunni Muslims, there was also a sizeable minority of Kurds. Lebanon also received more than 50,000 Iraqi immigrants, including Shiites, Sunnis, Yazidis, and Christians of all kinds.
- The Maronite Church (Eastern Catholic) enjoys special privileges. The president of the republic and commander-in-chief of the army, as well as other political positions, are reserved for Maronites.
- The Middle East Council of Churches is important in Lebanon and includes Protestants, Oriental Orthodox, and Greek Orthodox churches to engage in interfaith dialogue, youth and women's work, and various social justice ministries.

Indicators & Demographic Data

Population (2020)	6,020,000
% under 15 years	22%
Capital city (pop.)	Beirut 2,424,000
% urban dwellers	89% (-1.23% p.a.)
Official language	Arabic
Largest language	Arabic (87%)
Largest people	Lebanese Arab (65%)
Largest culture	Arab (Arabic) (87%)
Development	76
Physicians	24
Gender gap	11%

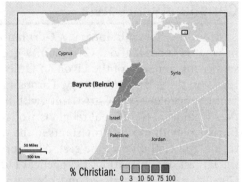

% Christian: 0 3 10 50 75 100

Christian Traditions in Lebanon

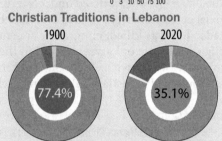

1900 — 77.4%   2020 — 35.1%

☐Independent ☐Protestant ■Catholic ■Orthodox ■Christian

Lebanon was home to a significant Catholic majority in 1900 (95% of Christians). By 2020, Christians were 82% Catholic, 16% Orthodox, and 1% each Protestant and Independent.

Religion in Lebanon

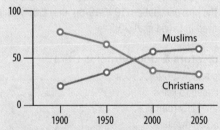

Muslims

Christians

Lebanon's religious makeup changed significantly from 1900 to 2020. In 1900, the country was 77% Christian and 21% Muslim. By 2020, Christians had dropped to 35%; Muslims had grown to 59%.

Bible Translations		Churches		Missionaries		Gospel Access	
Languages	20	Denominations	88	Received	660	1900	Very high
Full Bible	14	Congregations	2,000	Sent	220	2020	Very high

Christianity in Lesotho

The first Christian missionaries in Lesotho were Protestants from the Paris Evangelical Mission Society in 1833, which became the Lesotho Evangelical Church, the third largest denomination today. Over half of Christians in Lesotho are Catholics, owing to the first arrival of missionary priests in 1862. The first Mosotho priest was ordained in 1930 and the first indigenous bishop concentrated in 1853. The country is home to many kinds of Independent Christian groups, starting with groups such as the "Secret Prayer" movement, founded by women in the late 19th century. Lesotho has over 200 indigenous denominations, most of which are breakaway groups from the missions-founded churches. Many have been introduced from South Africa, such as the Zion Christian Church.

Facts to Consider

- All churches are involved in education, including primary and secondary schools, vocational training centers, seminaries, and even the National University of Lesotho (founded by the Catholic Church in 1945).
- Most churches are also involved in health care, including running hospitals and clinics. HIV/AIDS rapidly spread in the 1990s and continues to be an issue addressed across the denominational spectrum.
- Christians have been heavily involved in politics, from the founding of political parties to working together for political peace and reconciliation.
- Churches have raised concerns over the increase of prosperity-type preaching and theology that is becoming more popular in Lesotho, stressing the need for more formal theological education.
- African Traditional Religions are practiced by 6% of the population, and many practice traditional rituals alongside Christianity.

Indicators & Demographic Data

Population (2020)	2,322,000
% under 15 years	35%
Capital city (pop.)	Maseru 178,000
% urban dwellers	29% (2.77% p.a.)
Official language	Southern Sotho, English
Largest language	Southern Sotho (82%)
Largest people	Southern Sotho (Sutu) (80%)
Largest culture	Sotho (84%)
Development	52
Physicians	0.5
Gender gap	0%

% Christian: 0 3 10 50 75 100

Christian Traditions in Lesotho

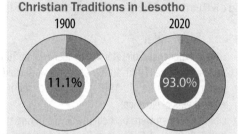

1900 — 11.1%

2020 — 93.0%

☐ Independent ☐ Protestant ▨ Catholic ■ Orthodox ■ Christian

Christians in 1900 were majority Protestant (82%) due to the historic missionary presence. In 2020, Christianity was much more diverse, with 54% of Christians being Catholics, followed by Protestants (35%), then Independents (11%).

Religion in Lesotho

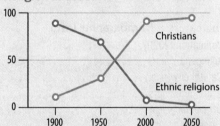

Lesotho's religious makeup changed significantly from 1900 to 2020. In 1900, the country was 89% traditional religionist and 11% Christian. By 2020, Christians had swelled to 93%, while traditional religions had dropped to 6%.

Bible Translations		Churches		Missionaries		Gospel Access	
Languages	10	Denominations	350	Received	730	1900	Low
Full Bible	8	Congregations	2,000	Sent	60	2020	Very high

Christianity in Liberia

The first Christians in Liberia were formerly enslaved African Baptist and Methodist Christians from the United States in 1822 who were part of the African Mission Society that formed in 1815. Many Western Christians thought Liberia could become a launching point for the evangelization of Africa by former enslaved people. William Wadé Harris is the most famous indigenous evangelist from Liberia, taking a missionary journey from Liberia to Ghana in 1913 and baptizing 100,000 new Christians in 18 months. The Catholic Church is the largest denomination today, with significant growth among the Kru, Grebo, Bassa, and Mano people.

Facts to Consider

- Liberia experienced dictatorships under William Tubman (1944-1971) and Samuel Doe (1980-1990). Churches were used as shelters during the first civil war (1989-1997) as many priests, brothers, and sisters were targets of violence.
- Liberian women were particularly active during the second civil war (1999-2003). Lead by Leymah Gbowee, Christian and Muslim women's protests captured international attention and hastened the end of the war and the founding of the Women in Peacebuilding Network.
- Liberia experienced an Ebola outbreak in 2014-2015. There were only 50 doctors at the start of the outbreak, in a country of 4.3 million. Church response to the outbreak was slow and came only after many deaths.
- Pentecostal/Charismatic churches are entirely indigenous, and response from indigenous peoples has been notable, with entire villages burning their traditional charms.

Indicators & Demographic Data

Population (2020)	5,104,000
% under 15 years	41%
Capital city (pop.)	Monrovia 1,517,000
% urban dwellers	52% (3.39% p.a.)
Official language	English
Largest language	Kpelle (19%)
Largest people	Kpelle (19%)
Largest culture	Kru (37%)
Development	44
Physicians	0.2
Gender gap	15%

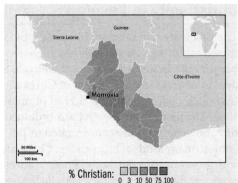

% Christian: 0 3 10 50 75 100

Christian Traditions in Liberia

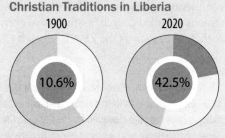

1900 — 10.6% 2020 — 42.5%

☐ Independent ☐ Protestant ■ Catholic ■ Orthodox ■ Christian

Christians in 1900 were mostly Protestant (61%) and Independent (39%) due to the historic missionary presence. In 2020, Christianity was much more diverse: Protestants were 46% of Christians, followed by Independents (32%) and Catholics (22%).

Religion in Liberia

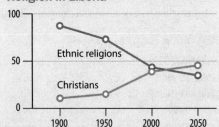

Liberia's religious makeup changed significantly from 1900 to 2020. In 1900, the country was 88% traditional religionist and 11% Christian. By 2020, Christianity had increased to 43%, and traditional religions had dropped to 39%. Muslims were 16%.

Bible Translations		Churches		Missionaries		Gospel Access	
Languages	36	Denominations	420	Received	560	1900	Low
Full Bible	10	Congregations	5,900	Sent	80	2020	High

Christianity in Libya

Libya is a majority Muslim country (99%) in Northern Africa. Christianity has a historic presence there and was home to some of the early church's most distinguished theologians. However, Christianity diminished during the 7th-century Muslim conquest, and today there are few indigenous Christians in the country. Most Christians are Catholics and Orthodox from Greece and Egypt, but some are Protestants from Europe and North America. Christians suffered at the outbreak of the civil war in 2011 between forces loyal to Muammar Gaddafi and those who sought to oust him.

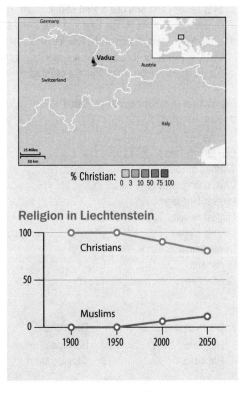

% Christian: 0 3 10 50 75 100

Religion in Libya

Facts to Consider

- Islam is the state religion of Libya, and Sharia law is the principal source of legislation. While the interim constitution allows for freedom of religion, the law prohibits "instigating division" and insulting Islam or the Prophet Muhammad, with a maximum sentence of death.
- Christians have a longer history in the country than Muslims, but the largest Christian community today is made up of expatriates from Egypt (Coptic Orthodox).
- In 2015, ISIS executed a group of 20 Coptic (plus one Ghanaian) Christian construction workers on a beach in the middle of the night; other groups of Christians were killed in December 2014 and January 2015.

Christianity in Liechtenstein

Liechtenstein is a small country bordered by Switzerland to the west and south and Austria to the east and north. It has a population of just under 40,000 people, most of whom speak German. Christianity arrived during the Roman occupation in the first few centuries CE and was fully established as the major religion by the year 450. Christianity is still the largest religion today (88%), with most adherents Catholic (86%). There is a close connection between the church and the state. The largest Protestant group is the interdenominational Evangelical Church, with 2,600 members.

% Christian: 0 3 10 50 75 100

Religion in Liechtenstein

Facts to Consider

- The constitution declares that everyone is free to choose their own faith, but Muslims are unable to obtain permission from local authorities to establish their own cemetery or build a mosque.
- Public schools must teach either Catholic or Reformed Protestant education, though parents can request exemptions for an "ethics and religions" course instead.
- The law prohibits slaughtering animals without anesthetization, which means kosher and halal slaughter is illegal. Meat slaughtered in this way must be imported into the country.

Christianity in Lithuania

In the 13th century, Lithuania became the last country in Europe to adopt Christianity, after the threat of invasion from the German Teutonic Knights. Subsequently, Lithuania vacillated between Eastern (Orthodox) and Western (Catholic) Christianity for many decades, eventually becoming a Catholic country in the 14th century. Lithuania is still a Catholic country today (77%). Germany and then the Soviet Union occupied Lithuania from 1940 to 1990, during which thousands were deported to Siberia or killed. The Catholic Church resisted Soviet dominance, though it suffered under state-sponsored atheism. Although most of the population still claims to be Christian, surveys report low church attendance, belief in God, and importance of religion.

Facts to Consider

- Protestant churches in Lithuania are generally small and have continued to struggle even decades after the fall of the Soviet Union.
- The largest charity organization in Lithuania is Caritas (Catholic), active since the early 1990s.
- The 2011 census reported 5,100 people who identified as followers of Romuva, the pre-Christian religion of Lithuania. It is a polytheistic religion that practices ancestor worship.
- Most of Lithuania's Muslims trace their ancestry to Tatars from the 14th century and practice a kind of folk Islam. There are also recent immigrants from the Middle East and Africa who are Sunni Muslim.
- Lithuania is home to one of the few Jewish Karaite populations in the world, a branch of Judaism that only accepts as binding the Tanakh, not the oral tradition of the Midrash or Talmud.

Indicators & Demographic Data

Population (2020)	2,852,000
% under 15 years	15%
Capital city (pop.)	Vilnius 539,000
% urban dwellers	68% (-0.12% p.a.)
Official language	Lithuanian
Largest language	Lithuanian (85%)
Largest people	Lithuanian (81%)
Largest culture	Lithuanian (85%)
Development	86
Physicians	44
Gender gap	-3%

% Christian: 0 3 10 50 75 100

Christian Traditions in Lithuania

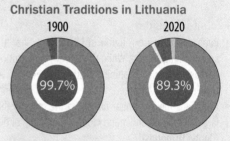

1900   2020

99.7%   89.3%

☐Independent ☐Protestant ◼Catholic ◼Orthodox ◼Christian

Catholicism has been, and remains, the largest Christian tradition in Lithuania. In 1900, Catholics were 96% of Christians, dropping only slightly to 91% in 2020. Orthodox make up 6% of Christians.

Religion in Lithuania

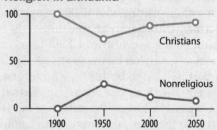

Christians

Nonreligious

Lithuania has been majority Christian for many centuries. In 1900, the country was 99% Christian, with a small population of Jews. By 2020, Christianity had declined to 89%, and the nonreligious had grown to 10.5%.

Bible Translations		Churches		Missionaries		Gospel Access	
Languages	22	Denominations	56	Received	440	1900	Very high
Full Bible	18	Congregations	1,100	Sent	240	2020	Very high

Christianity in Luxembourg

Luxembourg is one of the smallest countries in the world (1,000 sq. mi.), a landlocked nation in Western Europe between Belgium, Germany, and France. It has three official languages: French, German, and Luxembourgish. Christianity has been in modern-day Luxembourg since the time of the Romans, and the country is 74% Catholic today, though this is down from 97% in 1900. Catholic practices, such as Mass attendance, have been in decline. Protestants are a small minority, comprised mostly of noncitizens or foreigners living in Luxembourg City and in the mining basin. The fastest-growing denominations are the Assemblies of God, Church of Jesus Christ of Latter-day Saints, and Seventh-day Adventists.

Facts to Consider

- Islam became a legal religion in Luxembourg in 2015. The number of Muslims began to increase substantially with the arrival of Bosniak asylum-seekers from the former Yugoslavia. The Muslim community estimates between 18,000 and 20,000 Muslims in the country.
- A 2018 survey reported that 38% of Muslim women who wear a hijab, turban, or niqab experienced discrimination. The law prohibits wearing face coverings in certain public spaces such as government buildings, hospitals, and schools.
- Nazi occupation during World War II decimated the Jewish community, dwindling from 2,000 in 1940 to 800 in 2020. Anti-Semitism appears to be on the rise, in the form of graffiti and in-person and virtual harassment.
- Formed in 2010, the Alliance of Humanists, Atheists and Agnostics ran a pro-nonreligious bus campaign the following year. They work to promote secularism and advance the rights of nonreligious people.

Indicators & Demographic Data

Population (2020)	604,000
% under 15 years	17%
Capital city (pop.)	Luxembourg 120,000
% urban dwellers	91% (1.43% p.a.)
Official language	none
Largest language	Luxembourgish (59%)
Largest people	Luxemburger (59%)
Largest culture	Luxemburger (59%)
Development	90
Physicians	29
Gender gap	3%

% Christian: 0 3 10 50 75 100

Christian Traditions in Luxembourg

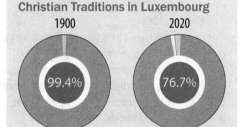

1900 — 99.4% 2020 — 76.7%

☐Independent ☐Protestant ▨Catholic ◼Orthodox ◼Christian

Catholicism has been, and remains, the largest Christian tradition in Luxembourg, dropping from 99% of Christians in 1900 to 97% in 2020. Protestants and Independents together made up 3% of Christians in 2020.

Religion in Luxembourg

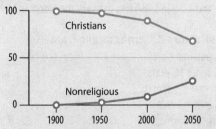

Luxembourg has been majority Christian for many centuries. In 1900, the country was 99% Christian, with a small population of Jews (1,200). By 2020, Christianity had declined to 77%, and the nonreligious had grown to 20%.

Bible Translations		Churches		Missionaries		Gospel Access	
Languages	14	Denominations	42	Received	40	1900	Very high
Full Bible	8	Congregations	380	Sent	120	2020	Very high

Christianity in Macao

Macao is a city and a special administrative region of the People's Republic of China. It is one of the most densely populated places in the world, with over 650,000 people in 11 square miles. Macao was a Portuguese colony from the mid-16th century until 1999, when it was the last remaining European colony in Asia. Under China's "one country, two systems" rule, Macao has its own government and legal and economic systems. The Catholic Church is the largest denomination, followed by the Chinese Evangelical Church and the Church of Jesus Christ of Latter-day Saints.

Facts to Consider

- Macao is widely known as a top destination for gambling, with an industry seven times larger than Las Vegas, Nevada. Casinos are growing more quickly than churches, spurring an economic boom. However, Hong Kong closed its borders to foreigners during the height of the COVID-19 pandemic, severely impacting the casino industry and causing unemployment to skyrocket.
- Sex trafficking is a problem in Macao, where both local and foreign women and girls are forced into prostitution.
- Chinese folk religion and Buddhism are the largest religions, representing a mixture of East Asian religions and local practices. Most people seamlessly practice elements from each.
- Mazu, the Chinese sea goddess, is particularly popular in Macao and other coastal regions. Many worshipers see her as the queen of heaven, and she is often combined with similar figures such as the bodhisattva Guanyin and the Christian Virgin Mary. The A-Ma Temple in São Lourenço was built in 1488 and is one of the oldest in Macao.

Indicators & Demographic Data

Population (2020)	652,000
% under 15 years	15%
Capital city (pop.)	Macao 652,000
% urban dwellers	100% (1.46% p.a.)
Official language	Chinese (Cantonese), Portuguese
Largest language	Chinese (92%)
Largest people	Han Chinese (Cantonese) (90%)
Largest culture	Han Chinese (94%)
Development	77
Physicians	35
Gender gap	4%

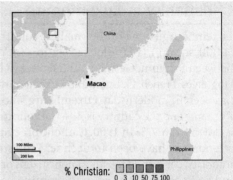

% Christian: 0 3 10 50 75 100

Christian Traditions in Macao

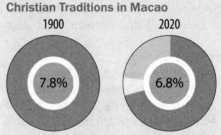

1900 — 7.8% 2020 — 6.8%

☐ Independent ☐ Protestant ■ Catholic ■ Orthodox ■ Christian

The small Christian population in Macao (5,000) in 1900 was entirely Catholic. In 2020, Christianity was more diverse, though still mostly Catholic (71%), followed by Protestants (23%) and Independents (6%).

Religion in Macao

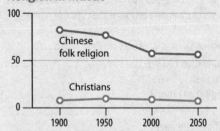

In 1900, Macao was 82% Chinese folk religionist, 10% Buddhist, and 8% Christian. Over the 20th century, the number of atheists and agnostics rose dramatically, to 16%. Meanwhile, Chinese folk religion, Buddhism, and Christianity all declined.

Bible Translations		Churches		Missionaries		Gospel Access	
Languages	9	Denominations	27	Received	50	1900	Low
Full Bible	7	Congregations	130	Sent	50	2020	High

Christianity in Madagascar

The first notable Christian contact with Madagascar came with the Europeans, welcomed by King Radama I in the beginning of the 19th century. Catholic Missionaries opened schools and churches and developed a written form of the Malagasy language. The Bible translation from 1836 is still in use today. Though Queen Ranavalona I initially persecuted, expelled, and executed Christians, their numbers grew during her reign, and Christianity became the primary religion of the country under Queen Ranavalona II (1868–1883). The growth of Christianity halted with French colonization of Madagascar from 1896 to 1960. Many churches were destroyed and Christians killed due to France's forceful anti-religious stance. Christianity grew once again in the late 20th century because of indigenous initiatives of local Christians, particularly Charismatic revival movements. Today most Christians are found in the highlands among the Merina and Betsileo. Catholics historically outnumbered Protestants, but that has now reversed.

After many failed attempts, costing the lives of several missionaries, Catholics (Jesuits) finally established work in Madagascar in 1961. In the 20th century, many Malagasy priests and bishops were consecrated, and today the majority of priests, brothers, and sisters are indigenous. More than 5,200 women religious serve in the country, twice the number of priests and religious men combined.

Revivals in Africa typically result in the founding of new churches, but the Fifohazana ("awakening" in Malagasy) revival is unique in that it brings converts into the Malagasy Lutheran Church, the largest Protestant denomination in the country. The Fifohazana began in 1894 and continues today as one of the longest-running revival movements in the world. An estimated 80% of shepherds (leaders) in the revival are women—despite the exclusion of women from formal leadership in traditional church and society. With around 4 million members, the Malagasy Lutheran Church is followed in size by the Church of Jesus Christ in Madagascar (3 million), which was founded by a merger of Protestant missionary efforts in 1968. Anglicans have grown since 1965 and number around 350,000.

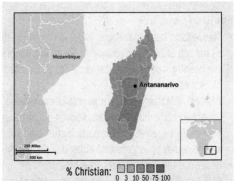

% Christian: 0 3 10 50 75 100

Religion in Madagascar

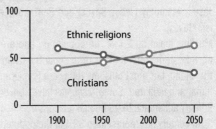

Madagascar has historically been, and remains, a religious country. In 1900, the country was 60% traditional religionist and 39% Christian. By 2020, Christianity had grown to 59% of the population, with a drop in traditional religion to 39%. Islam also grew from under 1% to just over 2%.

Indicators & Demographic Data

Population (2020). 27,691,000
% under 15 years 40%
Capital city (pop.) . . . .Antananarivo 3,369,000
% urban dwellers. . . . . 39% (4.26% p.a.)
Official language. . . . . Malagasy, French
Largest language. . . . . Malagasy (92%)
Largest people . . Merina (Hova, Imerina) (13%)
Largest culture . . . . Malagasy (96%)
Development. 52
Physicians. 1.4
Gender gap. 4%

Bible Translations		Churches		Missionaries		Gospel Access	
Languages. 27		Denominations 67		Received. 2,000		1900 . . . . Medium	
Full Bible. 9		Congregations. 27,500		Sent 340		2020 . . . . Very high	

Facts to Consider

- Madagascar has experienced extreme drought in the south since 2014. By the end of 2020, an estimated 1.3 million people were food insecure. The country is particularly vulnerable to climate shocks, such as periods of heavy rain that destroy crops.
- Women in Madagascar are generally considered secondary to men, especially in the public sphere. Various organizations in the country are working to increase female participation and representation, fighting against gender pay gaps and hiring discrimination.
- State-run television offers free broadcasting to Catholic, Lutheran, Anglican, Presbyterian, and Seventh-day Adventist groups on weekends.
- Indigenous Pentecostal movements appeared in the 1990s, such as Jesosy Mamonjy (Jesus Saves) and Pentecotiste Afaka (Pentecostalism Saves).
- Muslims make up 2% of the population and are found mostly on the northwestern coastal areas of the country. Islam has a long history on the island, but most Muslims today are immigrants from the Comoros, India, and Pakistan. Some Malagasy have converted.
- Primary adherence to traditional religions declined substantially over the 20th century but represented 39% of the population in 2020. Malagasy mythology is rooted in oral history and transmitted through storytelling. Many people incorporate elements of traditional religion into their practice of Christianity and Islam.

Christian Traditions in Madagascar

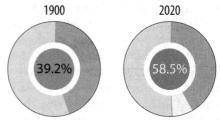

1900   39.2%   2020   58.5%

☐Independent ☐Protestant ◪Catholic ■Orthodox ■Christian

Madagascar's Christian population of roughly a million in 1900 was nearly evenly split between Catholics and Protestants due to massive numbers of conversions at the end of the 19th century. By 2020, Christianity was much more diverse, and Protestants outnumbered Catholics by over 1.5 million: 51% Protestant, 42% Catholic, 7% Independent. Around 11% of Christians are Pentecostal/Charismatic, and 14% are Evangelical. The largest Pentecostal denominations are the United Pentecostal Church and the Assemblies of God, both with around 200,000 members.

Christian Families in Madagascar

Family	Population 2020	%	Trend	Change
Latin-rite Catholic	7,000,000	25.3	↑	3.1
Lutheran	4,396,000	15.9	↑	2.6
United church or joint mission	3,340,000	12.1	↑	1.8
*Evangelicals	2,200,000	7.9	↑	2.9
*Pentecostals/Charismatics	1,750,000	6.3	↑	3.3
Anglican	435,000	1.6	↑	2.1
Congregational	356,000	1.3	↑	2.6
Adventist	238,000	0.9	↑	2.9
Jehovah's Witnesses	96,700	0.3	↑↑	7.4
Nondenominational	38,800	0.1	↑	1.3
Reformed, Presbyterian	34,700	0.1	↑	1.5
Eastern Orthodox	30,000	0.1	↑	3.2
Latter-day Saints (Mormons)	21,400	0.1	↑↑	12.2
Baptist	19,800	0.1	↑↑	5.2

After Latin-rite Catholics, the largest Christian family in Madagascar is Lutherans. This is different from many other countries in Africa where Pentecostals/Charismatics typically make up one of the top two or three largest families; in Madagascar, Pentecostals/Charismatics are the fifth largest family. The country has two main Lutheran denominations, consisting of over 4.3 million members together: the Malagasy Lutheran Church and the Lutheran Gospel Church. The next largest family is united churches, which are the Church of Jesus Christ in Madagascar, the Paris Evangelical Missionary Society, the Friends Foreign Missionary Association, and a consolidation of work from the London Missionary Society.

* These movements are found within Christian families	↑↑ extreme growth
	↑ growth
	↓↓ extreme decline
– no change	↓ decline

Christianity in Malawi

Various Catholic and Protestant missions entered modern-day Malawi between 1861 and 1900. Malawi became a British protectorate in 1891, touching off a series of human rights abuses. Though missionaries largely fought in defense of indigenous interests, they often came into conflict with colonial authorities. Malawi achieved independence from the British in 1964. While Presbyterians and Catholics were active in the independence movements and Anglicans remained closer to the government, all churches helped during the political transition to a multiparty democracy (1992–1994). All missions engaged in offering education as part of their evangelizing efforts, and after World War II, indigenous churches took over these efforts. Catholics number over 6 million and are the largest denomination. They are very involved in education and a variety of social services, including hospitals and health centers throughout the country.

Famous missionary-explorer David Livingstone explored the Zambezi and Shire rivers from 1858 to 1864, which encouraged more missionaries to arrive from the Church of Scotland (Presbyterian) and Church of England (Anglican). Other groups eventually arrived, including Dutch Reformed, Seventh-day Adventists, Baptists, and Disciples. Like Catholics, Protestants are involved in education, medical, and social services. The Christian Council of Malawi, which is mostly Protestant, operates hospitals, clinics, schools for the blind, teacher training colleges, and many other services. Malawi also has over 90 African Independent Churches (AICs). The first was the Providence Industrial Mission, formed in 1898. Other groups include the Chewa Church (1920), the African Covenant Church (1923), and the Last Church of God and His Christ (1924).

Pentecostal Christianity dates to the 1930s with the arrival of the Apostolic Faith Mission started by returning Malawian migrants from Zimbabwe and South Africa. The Assemblies of God began in 1947. Both churches, along with many other Pentecostal groups, grew rapidly in the second half of the 20th century. Today half the country's Protestant population is Pentecostal/Charismatic.

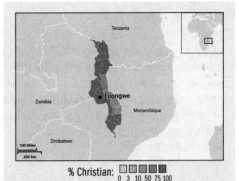

% Christian: 0 3 10 50 75 100

Religion in Malawi

Malawi experienced a profound change in its religious makeup in the 20th century. In 1900, the country was 95% followers of traditional religions. But by 2020, Christianity had surged from just under 2% of the population to 81%. Islam also grew over this period, from 3% to nearly 14%. Traditional religions were 5% of the population in 2020.

Indicators & Demographic Data

Population (2020) 20,284,000
% under 15 years 43%
Capital city (pop.) . . . . Lilongwe 1,122,000
% urban dwellers . . . . 17% (4.41% p.a.)
Official language . . . . none
Largest language . . . . Chichewa (51%)
Largest people . . Chewa (Western Nyanja) (38%)
Largest culture . . . . Central Bantu (83%)
Development 48
Physicians 0.2
Gender gap 6%

Bible Translations	Churches	Missionaries	Gospel Access
Languages 31	Denominations 510	Received 1,500	1900 . . . . Very low
Full Bible 18	Congregations 29,600	Sent 440	2020 . . . . Very high

Facts to Consider

- Malawi is one of the least developed countries in the world, with 82% of the population living in rural areas. Thirty-seven percent of children suffer from malnutrition and just over half of students complete primary school. The rural areas in the south suffer the most from poverty.
- Childhood marriage and pregnancy often end educational opportunities for girls and young women. Women generally lack access to productive economic resources, a major impediment to gender equality and women's empowerment.
- Women and girls in Malawi are highly susceptible to violence and threats, including rape, economic dependence on men, and HIV/AIDS. Religious organizations are on the forefront of raising awareness of these issues and often provide the only reliable resources to reach rural areas. Yet many faith-based organizations emphasize abstinence, faithfulness as a female (not male) virtue, and restricted condom use—all of which further impact women.
- There is a growing missionary movement from Malawi, mostly to surrounding countries like South Sudan. Malawian churches in the United States and United Kingdom serve the spiritual needs of Malawians abroad.
- Muslims in Malawi are 14% of the population, and there are two Muslim majority districts: Mangochi (73% Muslim) and Machinga (67%) among the Yao people at the southern end of Lake Malawi.

Christian Traditions in Malawi

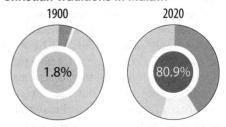

1900   2020

1.8%   80.9%

☐Independent ☐Protestant ■Catholic ■Orthodox ■Christian

The small Christian population in 1900 (around 13,500 people) was mostly Evangelical Protestant due to missionary work in the region. By 2020, Christianity in Malawi had become very large and quite diverse: 46% Protestant, 41% Catholic, and 13% Independent, many of whom are Evangelical and Pentecostal/Charismatic. In 2020, Malawi's Christians were 24% Evangelical and 22% Pentecostal/Charismatic.

Christian Families in Malawi

Family	Population 2020	%	Trend	Change
Latin-rite Catholic	6,350,000	31.3	↑	3.1
*Evangelicals	3,600,000	17.7	↑	2.4
*Pentecostals/Charismatics	3,300,000	16.3	↑	2.2
Reformed, Presbyterian	2,896,000	14.3	↑↑	5.2
Baptist	1,048,000	5.2	↑	3.7
Anglican	1,042,000	5.1	↑	1.5
Adventist	909,000	4.5	↑↑	5.5
Nondenominational	335,000	1.6	↑	0.5
Jehovah's Witnesses	265,000	1.3	↑	3.8
Restorationist, Disciple	252,000	1.2	↑	3.4
Lutheran	122,000	0.6	↑	4.3
Holiness	57,700	0.3	↓	-3.3
Christian Brethren	28,100	0.1	–	-0.4
Methodist	18,800	0.1	–	0.4
Mennonite	11,300	0.1	↑	1.5
Latter-day Saints (Mormons)	8,400	<0.1	↑↑	24.8
Moravian	7,800	<0.1	↑↑	10.0
Eastern Orthodox	3,500	<0.1	–	0.0

After Latin-rite Catholics, the largest Christian family in Malawi is Evangelicals, then Pentecostals/Charismatics. Evangelicals are found throughout most of the Protestant churches (Presbyterians, Anglicans, Assemblies of God) and number 3.6 million. There are dozens of Pentecostal/Charismatic churches, and some of the largest are the Assemblies of God, New Apostolic Church, Church of God of Prophecy, and Apostolic Faith Mission. Reformed/Presbyterian Christianity is the fourth largest family, mostly because of the size and scope of the Church of Central Africa Presbyterian, with 2.2 million members. There are many Baptist groups, ranging in size from the Baptist Convention of Malawi (over half a million) to Seventh-day Baptists (tens of thousands). The largest nondenominational group is the Zambezi Evangelical Church, founded via independent Baptist missionaries.

*   These movements are found within Christian families
    – no change

↑↑ extreme growth
↑ growth
↓↓ extreme decline
↓ decline

Christianity in Malaysia

Malaysia has a complex geography split into two regions. Peninsular Malaysia shares a border with Thailand, and East Malaysia borders Brunei and Indonesia. Christianity arrived in waves and at different geographic points. Some historical records suggest that Christianity was present in Malaysia as the Church of the East as early as the 7th century. In 1511, the Portuguese colonized Malacca and in 1641 were replaced by the Dutch, who introduced Catholicism and the Dutch Reformed Church. The British colonized Penang in 1786. Most Christians today live in Sabah (which is 26% Christian) and Sarawak (42% Christian); Labuan is 12% Christian. West Malaysia has lower concentrations of Christians, from Terengganu (0.2%) to Kuala Lumpur (7%).

Facts to Consider

- The main religion of Malaysia is Sunni Islam. Shia Islam, Sufism, and Ahmadiyya Islam are banned by the government.
- Christianity is more commonly found among indigenous peoples, with Bahasa Malaysia the primary language used in churches. Services are also held in English, Tamil, Malayalam, Mandarin Chinese, and other Chinese dialects and indigenous languages.
- Christians historically used the word *Allah* for the translation of *God* in the Malay Bible. This came under scrutiny in 2015 when courts restricted the use of *Allah* to Muslims only. In March 2021, however, the country's high court ruled that Christians could use *Allah* for *God*.
- Malaysian society is becoming increasingly intolerant of religious diversity. Converts from Islam face severe stigmatization and often have to keep their new religion quiet.

Indicators & Demographic Data

Population (2020)	32,869,000
% under 15 years	24%
Capital city (pop.)	Kuala Lumpur 7,997,000
% urban dwellers	77% (1.87% p.a.)
Official language	Malay
Largest language	Malay (29%)
Largest people	Malay (Melaju, Melayu) (28%)
Largest culture	Malay (48%)
Development	80
Physicians	15
Gender gap	2%

% Christian: 0 3 10 50 75 100

Christian Traditions in Malaysia

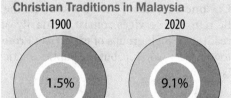

1900 — 1.5%   2020 — 9.1%

□ Independent □ Protestant ■ Catholic ■ Orthodox ■ Christian

Christianity in Malaysia has always been a mixture of Catholicism and Protestantism. In 1900, Christians were 63% Catholic and 38% Protestant. The number of Independent Christian groups has grown since then, with Independents 8% of Christians in 2020.

Religion in Malaysia

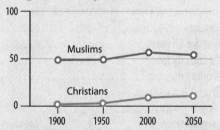

In 1900, Malaysia was 49% Muslim, 25% Chinese folk religionist, and 2% Christian. By 2020 the country was 56% Muslim and 18% Chinese folk religionist; Christianity grew to 9%.

Bible Translations		Churches		Missionaries		Gospel Access	
Languages	154	Denominations	70	Received	1,000	1900	Very low
Full Bible	35	Congregations	6,800	Sent	100	2020	Medium

Christianity in the Maldives

The Maldives is an archipelago of nearly 1,200 islands in the Indian Ocean, southwest of Sri Lanka and India. The country has historical links with the Catholic Church in Sri Lanka. But the Maldives has been a Muslim state since the 12th century, with Islam the religion of the entire indigenous population. Despite the country's transition to democracy in 2008, Islam in the country has become increasingly conservative and extremist. The country has supplied more jihadists per capita to Iraq and Syria than any other country in the region. In 2020, 800 Catholics, mostly Filipinos and Ceylonese teachers, were working on the islands. Catholic religious services consist primarily of informal Bible readings. Small groups of expatriate Protestants also meet together for worship, but the public practice of Christianity is illegal.

Facts to Consider

- Islam is the state religion, and no law can be contrary to any tenet of Islam. The constitution states that every citizen has the responsibility to "preserve and protect the State religion of Islam, culture, language and heritage of the country."
- Every citizen is expected to be Muslim, and freedom of religion is nonexistent. Punishments for crimes include death by stoning and flogging.
- Non-Muslim forms of public religious worship and practice, including proselytism, are prohibited. The Law on the Protection of the Religious Unity promotes national unity around Islam and the country's civil law based on Sharia law.

Indicators & Demographic Data

Population (2020)	459,000
% under 15 years	23%
Capital city (pop.)	Male 164,000
% urban dwellers	41% (2.34% p.a.)
Official language	Maldivian (Divehi)
Largest language	Maldivian (97%)
Largest people	Maldivian (Malki, Mahl) (97%)
Largest culture	Sinhalese (98%)
Development	72
Physicians	36
Gender gap	8%

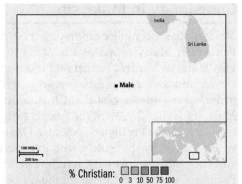

% Christian: 0 3 10 50 75 100

Christian Traditions in the Maldives

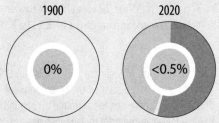

1900 — 0%
2020 — <0.5%

Independent Protestant Catholic Orthodox Christian

Most of the small Christian community in the Maldives is Catholic. The two Protestant groups are the Church of South India and the Evangelical Mennonite Church. There is a small community of Independents (Muslim-background believers).

Religion in the Maldives

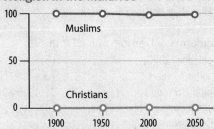

The Maldives is historically and currently nearly entirely Muslim. The population was 100% Muslim in 1900, which changed very little over the 20th century. There were roughly 2,700 Buddhists and 1,600 Christians in the country in 2020.

Bible Translations	Churches	Missionaries	Gospel Access
Languages 13	Denominations 7	Received 10	1900 Very low
Full Bible 9	Congregations 11	Sent 0	2020 Low

Christianity in Mali

The Mali Empire (1235–1670) was the largest empire of West Africa. During the European Scramble for Africa in the late 19th century, the French colonized Mali until independence in 1960. Catholics arrived in 1888 and Protestants in 1919. Mali is a Muslim-majority country today, but Christians have a voice in the public square and in education, partly due to the work of foreign missionary organizations. Most Christians are Catholics (275,000 members), and the first Malian bishop was consecrated in 1962. Protestant and Catholic churches have regular times to broadcast shows on the radio. More recently, churches from Nigeria and other surrounding countries are being planted in Mali.

Facts to Consider

- Bible translation is underway in Mali. Nine languages have complete Bibles, and another 20 translations are in progress. Because Mali is an oral society, Scripture recordings are popular.
- Radio programs of the lives of the prophets are popular in Mali, as are radio theaters based on social issues brought to light with biblical insight.
- Missionaries have been arriving from Cameroon and Nigeria and are engaged in holistic work melding education, health care, and evangelization.
- Mali is 89% Muslim, and many people practice elements of traditional religion alongside Islam. Evangelical Protestants and Charismatic Catholics ask converts to burn their fetishes, but sometimes Evangelicals also encourage people to reject all elements of traditional culture.
- African Traditional Religions are especially prominent among the Dogon, Bobo, Kagoro, Minyanka, and Senufo peoples.

Indicators & Demographic Data

Population (2020)................................20,284,000
% under 15 years 47%
Capital city (pop.) .... Bamako 2,618,000
% urban dwellers.............................44% (4.57% p.a.)
Official language.......................................French
Largest language........................... Bamanankan (22%)
Largest people ....Bambara (Bamanakan) (22%)
Largest culture .... Bambara (22%)
Development...43
Physicians..0.9
Gender gap..19%

% Christian: 0 3 10 50 75 100

Christian Traditions in Mali

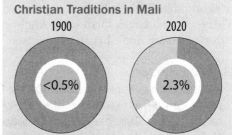

1900 — <0.5%   2020 — 2.3%

☐Independent ☐Protestant ▨Catholic ▤Orthodox ▨Christian

The very small Christian population in 1900 (just under 700 people) was entirely Catholic. By 2020, Christianity had grown to nearly half a million adherents, mostly Catholic (61% of Christians) but also many Protestants (34%).

Religion in Mali

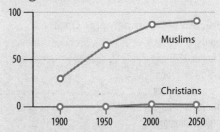

In 1900, Mali was 70% traditional religionist and 30% Muslim. Over the 20th century, traditional religions declined, replaced mostly by Islam. In 2020, the country was 89% Muslim, 9% traditional religionist, and 2% Christian.

Bible Translations		Churches		Missionaries		Gospel Access	
Languages	55	Denominations	49	Received	500	1900	Very low
Full Bible	9	Congregations	1,400	Sent	10	2020	Low

Christianity in Malta

Malta, off the coast of Italy, is a small nation of around half a million people. According to the book of Acts, the apostle Paul was shipwrecked in Malta and remained there three months on his way to Rome. Christianity has a long history there, and the country changed hands among many foreign entities, including the British, who colonized Malta from 1813 until the nation's independence in 1964. The official and national language is Maltese, though most people are also conversant in English and Italian. The majority of the population is baptized Catholic, with the Catholic Church wielding significant influence and power in the country. There are also Greek Orthodox, Anglicans, Methodists, Salvation Army, and Christian Scientists.

Facts to Consider

- The constitution establishes the Roman Catholic Church as the state religion but allows for freedom of worship and prohibits discrimination based on religion. Catholic education is compulsory in public schools.
- Malta has one of the longest histories of missionary sending of any country in the world. Throughout most of Christian history, the country has had an unusually high per capita ratio of missionary sending.
- Estimates for the country's Muslim population vary from 2% to 7%. Most Muslims are foreigners and are Sunni.
- In February 2018, members of Jewish, Christian, Muslim, and other faith communities signed a declaration of interreligious friendship and solidarity, reaffirming their commitment to support and dialogue with one another across religious groups.

Indicators & Demographic Data

Population (2020) 434,000
% under 15 years 15%
Capital city (pop.) . . . . Valletta 212,000
% urban dwellers. . . . . .95% (0.28% p.a.)
Official language. . . . . .Maltese, English
Largest language. . . . . Maltese (94%)
Largest people . . . . Maltese (94%)
Largest culture . . . . Maltese (92%)
Development. 88
Physicians. 39
Gender gap. 4%

% Christian: 0 3 10 50 75 100

Christian Traditions in Malta

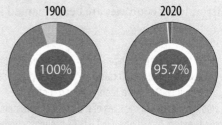

1900 — 100%
2020 — 95.7%

☐Independent ☐Protestant ■Catholic ■Orthodox ■Christian

The vast majority of Christians in Malta in 1900 were Catholic (94%). This was still true in 2020 (98% Catholic), but there are now small populations of Protestants, Orthodox, Independents, and a growing Catholic Charismatic movement.

Religion in Malta

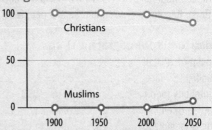

Malta has historically been a Christian country. Virtually the entire population was Christian in 1900, and this dropped to only 96% in 2020. There were 10,000 Muslims (2%) and 8,500 non-religious (2%) in 2020.

Bible Translations		Churches		Missionaries		Gospel Access	
Languages.	8	Denominations	27	Received.	30	1900	Very high
Full Bible.	6	Congregations.	120	Sent	700	2020	Very high

Christianity in the Marshall Islands

The Marshall Islands is an island nation in the Pacific Ocean, near the equator. The nation consists of 29 coral atolls and over 1,000 islands, and its population of roughly 50,000 people lives on only 70 square miles of land. Micronesians settled the islands in the 2nd millennium BC. In 1529, Christian explorers visited the islands, which were claimed by Spain. Eventually, Spain sold some of the islands to Germany in 1885. Japan occupied the Marshall Islands during World War I, after which the United States took control during World War II, conducting nuclear tests there from 1946 to 1958, including tests for the world's first hydrogen bomb. The Marshall Islands achieved independence from the United States in 1979. The country is mostly Protestant today, with the largest denomination the Assemblies of God.

Facts to Consider

- The United States contaminated the islands with nuclear bomb tests in the 1940s and 1950s, causing thousands of Marshallese to leave for the USA (most went to Arkansas).
- The islands are in grave danger from rising sea levels due to climate change, with rising waters eroding seaside cemeteries. Many islands are projected to be uninhabitable by the mid-21st century.
- Most of the nongovernmental schools are run by the major Christian denominations. Churches have also implemented educational programs on health challenges such as alcoholism, substance abuse, and HIV/AIDS.
- The Church of Jesus Christ of Latter-day Saints arrived in 1977 and grew to over 7,000 members and is the third largest denomination.

Indicators & Demographic Data

Population (2020)....................................53,300
% under 15 years 24%
Capital city (pop.).............................Majuro 29,300
% urban dwellers.............................78% (0.61% p.a.)
Official language.................................Marshallese
Largest language............................Marshallese (89%)
Largest people ....Marshallese (89%)
Largest culture ....Marshallese (88%)
Development...71
Physicians..4.6
Gender gap..5%

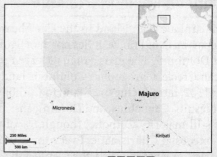

% Christian: 0 3 10 50 75 100

Christian Traditions in the Marshall Islands

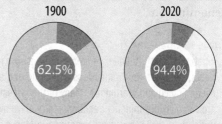

1900 — 62.5%   2020 — 94.4%

☐Independent ☐Protestant ◨Catholic ■Orthodox ■Christian

In 1900, nearly all Christians in the Marshall Islands were Protestant due to historic missionary efforts. By 2020, Christianity was slightly more diverse, still comprised of mostly Protestants but also with more Independents and Catholics. Many are also Pentecostal/Charismatic and Evangelical.

Religion in the Marshall Islands

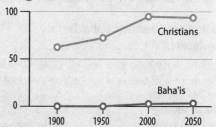

In 1900, the Marshall Islands were 63% Christian and 38% followers of traditional religions. By 2020, the country was 94% Christian and the Baha'i Faith was the second largest religion (3%).

Bible Translations	Churches	Missionaries	Gospel Access
Languages.............3	Denominations 16	Received.............90	1900...............High
Full Bible.............2	Congregations........280	Sent 10	2020......... Very high

Christianity in Martinique

Martinique is an island in the Caribbean and an overseas department of France. It lies north of Saint Lucia and south of Dominica. The main languages are French and Martinican Creole. Christopher Columbus landed in Martinique in 1502, introducing the island to Catholicism via the work of Jesuits, Capuchins, and Dominicans. Today, Martinique is still majority Catholic, though 5% of the population is Pentecostal/Charismatic. Every town in Martinique has a parish in what is called the "centerville" section of town. The largest Protestant denomination is the Seventh-day Adventist church; Jehovah's Witnesses is the third largest denomination.

Facts to Consider

- Inhabitants of Martinique are French citizens with full legal and political rights, but there are tremendous economic and social disparities between France and Martinique. Many of the largest banana plantations are run by White-minority descendants of slave owners.
- In February 2021, seven organizations in Martinique and Guadeloupe filed a complaint against the French government citing "reckless endangerment" for use of a toxic insecticide on the islands. Over 90% of the adult population suffers from chlordecone poisoning, which is linked to prostate, stomach, and pancreatic cancer.
- Charismatic Christianity is growing quickly on the island and is often a combination of African Spiritism and North American prosperity teaching. There is also a large Catholic Charismatic movement.
- Maldivian Spiritism, a mixture of Hinduism and Catholicism, is practiced among East Indians. There are many temples in the north of the island.

Indicators & Demographic Data

Population (2020)................................... 385,000
% under 15 years 17%
Capital city (pop.) ....Fort-de-France 79,000
% urban dwellers.............................89% (0.03% p.a.)
Official language.......................................French
Largest language................. Martiniquan Creole French (96%)
Largest people .... Mulatto (93%)
Largest culture ....Creole, French-speaking (93%)
Development..68
Physicians...39
Gender gap..3%

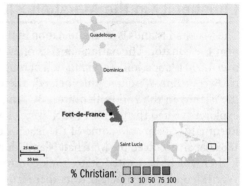

% Christian: 0 3 10 50 75 100

Christian Traditions in Martinique

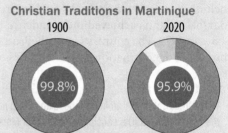

1900 — 99.8%
2020 — 95.9%

□ Independent □ Protestant ■ Catholic ■ Orthodox ■ Christian

In 1900, nearly all Christians in Martinique were Catholic. Catholics were still the largest tradition in 2020 (88%), but there has been growth in Protestant/Independent Christianity, as well as in Evangelicals and Pentecostals/Charismatics.

Religion in Martinique

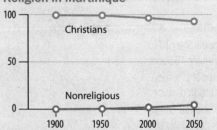

Martinique has been a majority Christian country for many centuries, dropping only from 99% Christian in 1900 to 96% in 2020. There are small communities of Baha'i, Hindus, Muslims, and Spiritists.

Bible Translations		Churches		Missionaries		Gospel Access	
Languages	7	Denominations	24	Received	220	1900	Very high
Full Bible	4	Congregations	380	Sent	90	2020	Very high

Christianity in Mauritania

Modern-day Mauritania traces its history to the Berber kingdom of Mauretania from the 3rd century BCE to the 7th century CE. Berbers inhabited it until the Arab conquest of the 8th century and became a French colony from the late 19th century to its independence in 1960. Nearly all Mauritanians are Muslims, but the government has been tolerant of Christian activity, including that of Christian NGOs, as long as they do not proselytize. Catholics are both the largest and the only formally organized Christian group in the country. Roughly 80% of active Catholics (service attenders) and the majority of clergy are African, in particular, Senegalese. Both French and Wolof are used in services.

Facts to Consider

- Mauritania is an Islamic republic, and only Muslims can be citizens. Anyone who converts from Islam loses citizenship. Blasphemy is a capital offense and subject to the death penalty.
- Nearly all Muslims are Sunnis of the Maliki rite, though many follow some pre-Islamic customs. There are also some Shias. Citizens are not allowed to attend non-Islamic religious services, as they are exclusively for foreigners.
- There are very few Protestants in the country, most of whom are expatriates. The last Protestant group to work in Mauritania was WEC International, who left in 1965. The first and only Protestant church building was consecrated in Nouakchott in December 2018.
- Women in Mauritania face many challenges, including polygamy, less access to education, female genital mutilation, and forced child marriage; 37% of girls are married before age 18.

Indicators & Demographic Data

Population (2020)	4,784,000
% under 15 years	39%
Capital city (pop.)	Nouakchott 1,315,000
% urban dwellers	55% (3.84% p.a.)
Official language	Arabic
Largest language	Hassaniyya (76%)
Largest people	Black Moor (Maure) (24%)
Largest culture	Moor (44%)
Development	52
Physicians	0.7
Gender gap	16%

% Christian: 0 3 10 50 75 100

Christian Traditions in Mauritania

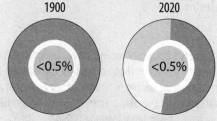

1900   2020

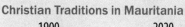

□ Independent □ Protestant ■ Catholic ■ Orthodox ■ Christian

There were virtually no Christians in Mauritania at the start of the 20th century. By 2020, a small community of around 10,000 had developed, half Catholic and half Protestant/Independent.

Religion in Mauritania

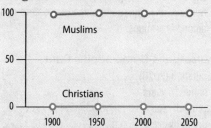

Mauritania historically being a Muslim country, Islam increased between 1900 and 2020, from 98% to 99%. Traditional religions and Christians were each less than 1% of the population in 2020.

Bible Translations		Churches		Missionaries		Gospel Access	
Languages	15	Denominations	25	Received	60	1900	Very low
Full Bible	6	Congregations	90	Sent	0	2020	Low

Christianity in Mauritius

Mauritius consists of several islands off the eastern coast of Madagascar. Most of the population lives on the largest island, also called Mauritius. Uninhabited when the Portuguese first visited in the early 16th century, the islands became a Dutch colony from 1638 to 1710, a French colony from 1715 to 1810, and then a British possession from 1810 until independence in 1968. The country is 32% Christian, mostly Catholic, but Pentecostal/Charismatic groups have been growing in recent years. The population of Rodrigues Island is 98% Catholic. The Assemblies of God is the second largest denomination, first established by French missionaries in 1967.

Facts to Consider

- There is a strong connection between religion and ethnicity in Mauritius. Indians are either Hindu or Muslim; Chinese are Buddhists, Anglicans, or Catholics; people of African and/or European descent are Catholic.
- Mauritius is the only country in Africa where Hindus are the largest religious group (45% Hindu in 2020).
- Most Muslims in Mauritius are Sunnis, with Urdu as a common language. There are also Ahmadiyya and Shias. There are low-level tensions between Muslims and Hindus in the country.
- The Ecumenical Working Group consists of members from the Catholic, Anglican, Presbyterian, Assemblies of God, and Protestant Community Evangelical churches. They meet regularly for discussion and prayer.
- The Council on Religion consists of representatives from over a dozen religious and Christian groups to promote understanding and peace among Mauritians.

Indicators & Demographic Data

Population (2020)	1,274,000
% under 15 years	17%
Capital city (pop.)	Port Louis 150,000
% urban dwellers	41% (0.28% p.a.)
Official language	English
Largest language	Morisyen (43%)
Largest people	Indo-Mauritian (Hindi) (31%)
Largest culture	Hindi (52%)
Development	79
Physicians	20
Gender gap	3%

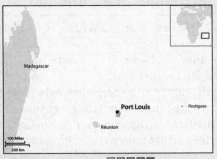

% Christian: 0 3 10 50 75 100

Christian Traditions in Mauritius

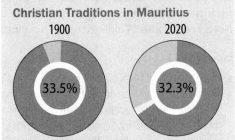

1900 — 33.5%　　2020 — 32.3%

☐Independent ☐Protestant ■Catholic ■Orthodox ■Christian

In 1900, most Christians in Mauritius were Catholic (94%), followed by a small Protestant community. By 2020, Catholics and Protestants had both grown and were joined by many Independent Pentecostal/Charismatic groups.

Religion in Mauritius

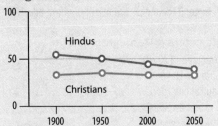

The religious makeup of Mauritius changed little over the 20th century. In 1900, the country was 55% Hindu, 34% Christian, and 11% Muslim. This changed only slightly to 45%, 32%, and 17%, respectively.

Bible Translations		Churches		Missionaries		Gospel Access	
Languages	20	Denominations	30	Received	340	1900	Medium
Full Bible	16	Congregations	540	Sent	40	2020	High

Christianity in Mayotte

Mayotte is an overseas territory of France consisting of a main island (Grande-Terre), a smaller island (Petite-Terre), and many islets. The islands are located off the east coast of Africa between Mozambique and Madagascar in the Indian Ocean. Islam arrived via East Africa in the late 14th to early 15th centuries. The islands were taken over by Madagascar in 1832 and purchased by France in 1841. The local population voted against national independence in 1976, and it became an overseas department of France in 2011. While most Catholics in Mayotte are French, Réunionese, or Malagasy, most Protestants are Malagasy migrant workers, with some French expatriates. Jehovah's Witnesses began working in 1980 and have around 300 affiliates.

Facts to Consider

- The 2017 census reported that 35.8% of people living in Mayotte were immigrants born in other countries. Most people on the islands are culturally Comorians.
- The most widely spoken language in Mayotte is Shimaore, related to languages found in the neighboring Comoros Islands, followed by Kibushi of the Malagasy language family. French is the official language in schools and public media.
- Muslims are Sunnis of the Shafi'i school. Polygamy and child marriage became prohibited after Mayotte voted to become an overseas department of France in 2011. French civil code is expected to gradually replace Islamic law.
- Most members of the Protestant International Church of Mayotte are Malagasy.

Indicators & Demographic Data

Population (2020)................................. 273,000
% under 15 years 39%
Capital city (pop.)...........................Mamoudzou 6,700
% urban dwellers............................46% (2.19% p.a.)
Official language.......................................French
Largest language....................... Maore Comorian (55%)
Largest people ....Comorian (Mauri, Mahorais) (55%)
Largest culture .... Northeast Coastal Bantu (59%)
Development...50
Physicians... 0.8
Gender gap...10%

% Christian: 0 3 10 50 75 100

Christian Traditions in Mayotte

1900 <0.5% 2020 0.5%

□Independent □Protestant ■Catholic ■Orthodox ■Christian

There were hardly any Christians in Mayotte in 1900. The very small population in 2020 was 46% Independent, 40% Catholic, and 14% Protestant.

Religion in Mayotte

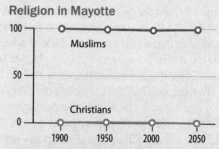

Muslims

Christians

1900   1950   2000   2050

Mayotte was, and continues to be, a majority Muslim country. Christians are the second largest religion, but there are very few in the country, with only 1,400 in 2020 (0.5% of the population).

Bible Translations	Churches	Missionaries	Gospel Access
Languages............9	Denominations 6	Received.............30	1900 .... Very low
Full Bible.............3	Congregations.........18	Sent 0	2020 .... Low

Christianity in Mexico

Christianity—in particular, Catholicism—has been a major driver of Mexican society, culture, and politics for nearly 500 years. The first Spanish settlers arrived in 1518, soon followed by Catholic missionary orders (Franciscans, Dominicans, Augustinians, and Jesuits). Although Catholicism is experiencing a slow decline, Catholics still make up 90% of the country's population, and an estimated 40% attend Mass once a week or more. The majority of clergy are Mexican, not foreigners. While the religious attitudes and customs of Mexican Catholics differ from region to region, most are still overall theologically conservative. In 2015, 31% favored the ordination of women and marriage for priests. However, 28% believed artificial birth control was wrong, and 32% were against divorce. The Catholic Church is split on how to respond to the violent drug cartels in the country. Some parishes, for example, profit from drug money via donations from cartels.

One of the major features of Mexican Christianity has been the acceptance of Protestantism, though Mexico remains one of the most Catholic countries in Latin America. Protestants (known as *evangélicos* in Spanish) first arrived in 1824 via the American Bible Society, followed by Anglicans in 1857, Southern Baptists in 1880, and Seventh-day Adventists in 1893. Protestant missions were quickly indigenized and turned over to local leadership, which has encouraged continued Protestant growth in the country. A survey reported that 44% of Protestants in Mexico were raised Catholic. In a country that has chronically lacked adequate numbers of priests, urban areas were typically better served than rural areas. Protestants sent missionaries and pastors to these areas to fill the gap. The Mexican state of Chiapas is an estimated 35% Evangelical, the highest percentage of any state. This is partially because of its proximity to the American border and American cultural and religious influences. Chiapas is also home to the largest indigenous populations in the country. Bible translation has also been a major player in the acceptance of Evangelicalism, with work by SIL International particularly impactful. Most Protestants and half of Catholics report that they witnessed speaking in tongues, praying for miraculous healing, and prophesying in church.

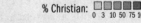

% Christian: 0 3 10 50 75 100

Religion in Mexico

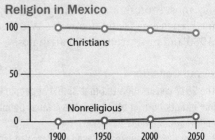

On the surface, Mexico appears to have changed very little in its religious makeup over the 20th century. In 1900, the country was 99% Christian and just under 1% followers primarily of traditional religions. By 2020, Christians were still 96% of the population, though Christianity had changed dramatically in its internal composition. Mexico was also 3% nonreligious and 1% traditional religionists.

Indicators & Demographic Data

Population (2020). 133,870,000
% under 15 years 25%
Capital city (pop.) . . . . Mexico City 21,782,000
% urban dwellers. . . . . 81% (1.40% p.a.)
Official language. . . . . Spanish
Largest language. . . . . Spanish (91%)
Largest people . . . . . . .Mexican Mestizo (55%)
Largest culture . . . . . .Mestizo (Spanish) (55%)
Development. 77
Physicians. 22
Gender gap 5%

Bible Translations	Churches	Missionaries	Gospel Access
Languages. 283	Denominations 480	Received. 8,000	1900 . . . . Very high
Full Bible. 27	Congregations. 72,300	Sent 6,000	2020 . . . . Very high

Facts to Consider

- One of the major human rights challenges in Mexico is "enforced disappearances" related to drug trafficking and organized crime with support from state forces. Since 2006, 275,000 people have been killed and over 70,000 have disappeared.
- The largest Protestant denomination is the National Presbyterian Church of Mexico, with 1.8 million members. They are found particularly in Chiapas, Tabasco, Campeche, and Yucatan. It ended its 139-year relationship with the Presbyterian Church (USA) in 2011 over the PCUSA's decision to ordain LGBTQ clergy.
- The Catholic Church has been deeply affected by clergy sex abuse scandals, such as the controversy surrounding Marcial Maciel, who abused seminarians and fathered several children with different women.
- Women in Mexico were historically excluded from public life but have always had a central role in church life, ranging from joining Catholic religious orders to participating in lay organizations. Mexico is home to one of the most widely known examples of indigenous Christianity in the Americas: the veneration of the Virgin of Guadalupe. At least 20 million pilgrims annually visit the Basilica of Our Lady of Guadalupe.

Christian Traditions in Mexico

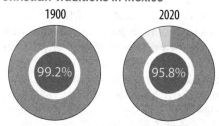

□Independent □Protestant ▨Catholic ■Orthodox ■Christian

In 1900, Mexican Christianity was nearly entirely Catholic (99%). By 2020, this had changed dramatically. Catholics are still the majority (89%), but Evangelicals and Pentecostals/Charismatics are growing rapidly. The 2020 Mexican census reported that for the first time in the country's history, Protestants surpassed 10% of the population. Even historic Protestantism—Baptists, Presbyterians, Methodists—are becoming "pentecostalized."

Christian Families in Mexico

Family	Population 2020	%	Trend	Change
Latin-rite Catholic	115,404,000	86.2	↑	1.0
*Pentecostals/Charismatics	17,450,000	13.0	↑	1.3
*Evangelicals	2,800,000	2.1	↑	2.0
Jehovah's Witnesses	2,484,000	1.9	↑	3.4
Reformed, Presbyterian	2,015,000	1.5	↑	2.1
Latter-day Saints (Mormons)	1,505,000	1.1	↑	2.0
Adventist	870,000	0.7	–	-0.2
Baptist	553,000	0.4	↑↑	5.2
Methodist	339,000	0.3	–	0.3
Eastern-rite Catholic	170,000	0.1	↑	0.8
Eastern Orthodox	122,000	0.1	↑	1.0
Holiness	92,300	0.1	–	-0.1
Non-traditional, house, cell	85,900	0.1	↑	1.6
Restorationist, Disciple	60,600	<0.1	↑	1.1
Nondenominational	43,700	<0.1	↑	0.9
Old Catholic Church	40,200	<0.1	↑	0.6
Anglican	31,800	<0.1	↑	1.5
Mennonite	29,600	<0.1	–	-0.1
Christian Brethren	15,700	<0.1	↑	1.1
Salvationist	13,100	<0.1	↑	1.3
Congregational	12,700	<0.1	↑	1.7
Lutheran	5,300	<0.1	↓	-0.6

There are many Christian families present in Mexico. After Latin-rite Catholics, the largest Christian family is Pentecostals/Charismatics, which numbered well over 17 million in 2020. There are dozens of Pentecostal groups, ranging in size from a few thousand to over a million. Some of the largest denominations in this family are the Light of the World Church (1.5 million members), Assemblies of God (1 million), and the Union of Evangelical Independent Churches (750,000). Evangelicalism is diverse and found throughout numerous historic Protestant churches such as Baptists and Methodists. The fourth largest family is Jehovah's Witnesses, which grew from 100,000 members in 1970 to over 2.5 million by 2020. The largest Reformed/Presbyterian denomination is the National Presbyterian Church in Mexico (1.8 million members).

* These movements are found within Christian families   ↑↑ extreme growth
↑ growth
↓↓ extreme decline
– no change   ↓ decline

Christianity in Micronesia

The Federated States of Micronesia is an island nation in Oceania with four states—Yap, Chuuk, Pohnpei, and Kosrae—spread across the Pacific Ocean, just north of the equator. While the islands themselves are small, the country has over 1 million square miles of ocean. Christianity first arrived via six Jesuits in 1668, who were followed by Hawaiian missionaries with the American Board of Commissioners for Foreign Mission in 1852. The country is 95% Christian today. Kosrae is mostly Protestant, Pohnpei is divided between Catholics and Protestants, and Chuuk and Yap are both mostly Catholic.

Facts to Consider

- The constitution forbids establishing a state religion, but some Christians have advocated amending the constitution to prohibit the presence of non-Christian groups in the country.
- Formal education in Micronesia began with Christian missionaries and the first mission-operated school opened in 1669. Local people were taught to read, and missionaries translated materials into local languages.
- The foreign worker population is mostly Filipino and Fijian, groups that are both primarily Christian.
- Operation Christmas Drop has been operating in Micronesia since 1951, annually dropping between 400 and 600 pounds of food, toys, and other goods to residents on the islands.
- Most in the country have accepted Christianity, but some traditional ethnic religious practices continue. There are very small communities of Ahmadi Muslims, Baha'i, Buddhists, Hindus, and Jews.

Indicators & Demographic Data

Population (2020)	108,000
% under 15 years	32%
Capital city (pop.)	Palikir 6,700
% urban dwellers	23% (1.52% p.a.)
Official language	English
Largest language	Chuukese (28%)
Largest people	Trukese (28%)
Largest culture	Trukese (32%)
Development	63
Physicians	1.8
Gender gap	13%

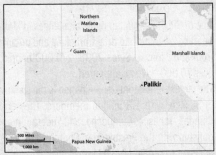

% Christian: 0 3 10 50 75 100

Christian Traditions in Micronesia

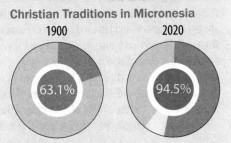

1900 — 63.1%
2020 — 94.5%

☐ Independent ☐ Protestant ◼ Catholic ◼ Orthodox ◼ Christian

Christians in 1900 were mostly Protestants (some Evangelicals), with a small Catholic community. By 2020, Catholics were the largest tradition (53%), followed by Protestants (40%), then Independents (7%).

Religion in Micronesia

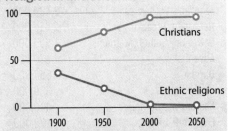

Micronesia's Christian population grew substantially over the 20th century. In 1900, the country was 63% Christian and 37% followers of traditional religions. By 2020, traditional religions had declined to just under 3%, and the country was 95% Christian.

Bible Translations		Churches		Missionaries		Gospel Access	
Languages	23	Denominations	14	Received	540	1900	Very high
Full Bible	7	Congregations	350	Sent	60	2020	Very high

Christianity in Moldova

Moldova is a landlocked country in Eastern Europe, bordering Romania and Ukraine. Christianity arrived in the region in the 3rd century and has retained a significant presence. Moldovans consider themselves ethnic Romanians and are largely Orthodox Christians. For much of the 20th century, Moldova was part of the Soviet Union and thus subject to the suppression of public religion; most Orthodox churches and monasteries were demolished or converted for other purposes. Christianity was restored after the fall of the Soviet Union in 1991, and there are two jurisdictions of Moldavian Orthodoxy, split only on political lines: the Moldovan Orthodox Church Metropolis of Chisinau and All Moldova, and the Metropolitan Church of Bessarabia.

Facts to Consider

- Moldova is one of the most Orthodox countries in Eastern Europe (by percentage). At least 95% profess belief in God and 48% pray daily, but only 13% of Orthodox attend church weekly.
- Baptists arrived in Moldova at the end of the 19th century and are the largest Protestant tradition. They frequently send missionaries to Russian-speaking peoples abroad.
- The largest non-Orthodox church in Moldova is the Jehovah's Witnesses, with nearly 40,000 members. They are regularly denied governmental recognition as a religious group.
- Islam has been slowly growing and there are nearly 15,000 Muslims in the country. Muslims, especially Muslim women, experience harassment, discrimination, and bias throughout Moldovan society.

Indicators & Demographic Data

Population (2020)	4,018,000
% under 15 years	16%
Capital city (pop.)	Chişinău 499,000
% urban dwellers	43% (0.09% p.a.)
Official language	Romanian
Largest language	Romanian (77%)
Largest people	Moldavian (74%)
Largest culture	Moldavian (74%)
Development	70
Physicians	32
Gender gap	0%

% Christian: 0 3 10 50 75 100

Christian Traditions in Moldova

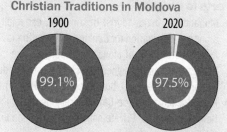

1900 — 99.1% 2020 — 97.5%

☐ Independent ☐ Protestant ■ Catholic ■ Orthodox ■ Christian

Christians in 1900 were mostly Orthodox (97%), with smaller Protestant and Catholic communities. In 2020, Christianity in Moldova was still mostly Orthodox (97%) but now includes newer Independent groups (1%).

Religion in Moldova

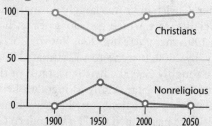

Moldova is historically a majority Christian country, dropping only from 99% to 98% between 1900 and 2020 but experienced a dip midcentury due to official Soviet atheistic policies. The nonreligious followed the opposite pattern and were 2% in 2020.

Bible Translations		Churches		Missionaries		Gospel Access	
Languages	30	Denominations	29	Received	560	1900	Very high
Full Bible	24	Congregations	2,900	Sent	120	2020	Very high

Christianity in Monaco

Monaco is a small city-state bordered by France and the Mediterranean Sea. It is one of the wealthiest countries in the world, with a high cost of living. Christians have been present in the region since the 1st century. Catholicism is the state religion, and the majority of the population is Catholic, with the first parish formed in 1247. Protestants make up just under 3% of the population and include Reformed/Presbyterians and Anglicans. Christian groups often share buildings for events and services.

Facts to Consider

- Monaco is a major tourist destination, especially for gambling, and a popular destination for banking and wealth management services.
- An estimated 30% of Monaco's population are millionaires, and it is home to the world's highest Gross Domestic Product (GDP) and Gross National Income (GNI), both over $180,000 per person.
- Public schools provide Catholic religious instruction with authorization from parents. Private schools may provide instruction from other religions.
- The Jewish community is small (less than 1,000). In 2015, Prince Albert II apologized for Monaco's deportation of Jews to Nazi concentration camps during World War II.

% Christian: 0 3 10 50 75 100

Religion in Monaco

Christians

Nonreligious

1900   1950   2000   2050

Christianity in Mongolia

Christianity arrived in Mongolia in 650 CE via missionaries from the Church of the East but disappeared 300 years later. Christianity was largely dormant until the fall of the socialist state, which had close ties with the Soviet Union. In 1991, there were only four known Christians in the country; by 2000, there were an estimated 30,000. Today, there are roughly 62,000 Christians, most of them in the capital city, Ulaanbaatar. Many Mongolian Protestants are first-generation Christians, or what the Mongolian Evangelical Alliance has termed the "First Modern Christians."

Facts to Consider

- Mongolia is a popular destination for Korean missionaries who are engaged in church planting, evangelism, and discipleship.
- Mongolian society is patriarchal, yet most churches are majority female, though run by men. Local church pastors are roughly 80% male.
- Shamanism is Mongolia's traditional religion, and many Buddhists hold shamanistic beliefs and practices. After Mongolia's 70 years under socialist rule, Tibetan Buddhism quickly returned as the majority religion in the country; 58% of the population now identifies as Buddhist.
- Muslims are 5% of the population and are mostly Kazakhs in the west. There are over 40 mosques and several Islamic student centers.

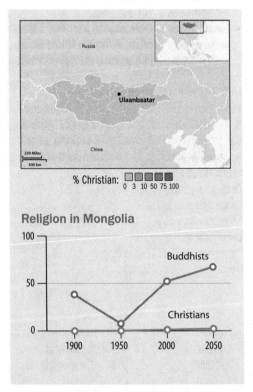

% Christian: 0 3 10 50 75 100

Religion in Mongolia

Buddhists

Christians

1900   1950   2000   2050

Christianity in Montenegro

Montenegro is a country in the Balkans bordered by Bosnia and Herzegovina, Serbia, Kosovo, and Albania. It declared independence from Serbia in 2006. Christianity arrived in this region in the 1st century, and the first converts were likely Jews of the diaspora. Orthodox Christianity, reestablished in the 1990s after decades of Communist rule, has been the largest tradition since the turn of the 13th century. However, there has been tension between the Montenegrin and Serbian Orthodox churches over which should be the national church of the Montenegrin people. Catholics are the second largest tradition, and Montenegro is home to one of the oldest archdioceses in the Balkans, dating from 1089.

Facts to Consider

- The country's first religious freedom law passed in 2020, but many fear that the rules target the Serbian Orthodox in favor of the Montenegrin Orthodox. Much of the debate lies in the historical identity of the people and property rights.
- The government has banned some public religious celebrations, fearing clashes between the Montenegrin and Serbian Orthodox churches, such as the 10-year ban from celebrating the Transfiguration of Christ at the Church of Christ's Transfiguration at Ivanova Korita.
- Introduced in the 15th century, Islam is represented by 17% of the population. After 1912, discrimination against Muslims intensified, and many were forcibly converted to Orthodoxy or killed. Most Muslims are ethnic Albanians or Bosniaks.
- The country has several hundred Jews, and their first synagogue opened in 2013 in Podgorica.

Indicators & Demographic Data

Population (2020)	629,000
% under 15 years	18%
Capital city (pop.)	Podgorica 169,000
% urban dwellers	67% (0.45% p.a.)
Official language	Montenegrin
Largest language	Montenegrin (78%)
Largest people	Montenegrin (46%)
Largest culture	Montenegrin (46%)
Development	81
Physicians	23
Gender gap	4%

% Christian: 0 3 10 50 75 100

Christian Traditions in Montenegro

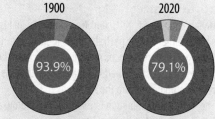

1900 — 93.9%   2020 — 79.1%

☐ Independent ☐ Protestant ▨ Catholic ■ Orthodox ■ Christian

Christians in 1900 were mostly Orthodox (94%), with a small Catholic minority. In 2020, Christianity in Montenegro was still mostly Orthodox (90%), but now with newer Protestant and Independent groups (2%).

Religion in Montenegro

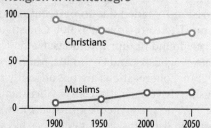

Montenegro has historically been a majority Christian country, but the Christian share of the population dropped from 94% in 1900 to 79% in 2020. Gains were mostly by Muslims (17% in 2020) and the nonreligious (3%).

Bible Translations		Churches		Missionaries		Gospel Access	
Languages	22	Denominations	15	Received	110	1900	Very high
Full Bible	16	Congregations	910	Sent	30	2020	Very high

Christianity in Montserrat

Montserrat is a British Overseas Territory in the Caribbean with a population of around 5,000 people. The vast majority of the population is of mixed African-Irish ancestry from the legacies of enslaved Africans and indentured Irish servants. The island is often called "The Emerald Isle of the Caribbean" for both its climate and people. In July 1995, volcanic eruptions destroyed the capital city, Plymouth, and forced two-thirds of the population to flee, mostly to the United Kingdom. To this day, an exclusion zone extends across the southern part of the island. Montserrat is 90% Christian.

Facts to Consider

- Unlike Antigua, St. Kitts and Nevis, and Anguilla, Montserrat has not sought either full or partial independence from the United Kingdom. Such political differences have little effect on church-state relations. There are no established churches, and there is equal status for all religious bodies before the law.
- The largest denomination is the Anglican Church, part of the Church of the Province of the West Indies.
- Other denominations on the island include Seventh-day Adventists, the Church of God of Prophecy, Catholics, Methodists, and other Pentecostals.

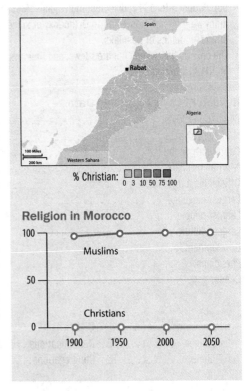

% Christian: 0 3 10 50 75 100

Religion in Montserrat

Christianity in Morocco

Morocco is a Muslim-majority (99%) country in northwestern Africa. Though present since the second century, Christianity faded due to persecution and the arrival of Islam. There are around 31,000 Christians in the country, largely found in four traditions: Catholics, French Protestants, Anglicans, and Orthodox. Many house churches and migrant congregations are not officially recognized. Some Muslims have been attracted to Christianity via radio, satellite TV, and social media ministries, as well as via personal visions and dreams of Jesus. Morocco has an estimated 3,500 Muslim-background believers.

Facts to Consider

- Islam is the state religion of Morocco. Although the constitution guarantees freedom of religion, religious minorities often experience harassment and violence from religious extremists.
- In 2010, 120 to 150 expatriate Christian workers were expelled from the country with only 48 hours' notice. This crackdown significantly reduced the number of Christian workers in the country.
- The Evangelical Church of Morocco consists mostly of sub-Saharan African students and migrants highly engaged in church activities.

% Christian: 0 3 10 50 75 100

Religion in Morocco

Christianity in Mozambique

The region of modern-day Mozambique has always been strategic for global trade, with visitors from Somalia, Ethiopia, Egypt, the Arabian Peninsula, Persia, and India. In the 15th century, the region was inhabited by Bantu-speaking peoples that led to the development of a distinct East African Swahili culture. In 1498, Portuguese explorer Vasco de Gama arrived, marking the beginning of nearly 500 years of Portuguese colonial rule over the territory and the introduction of Catholicism. Mozambique achieved independence from Portugal in 1975, but then experienced a series of civil wars from 1977 to 1992. Democratic elections in 1994 resulted in a relatively stable modern republic. Churches, in particular the Catholic Church, served as peace brokers during the transition. Mozambique's indigenous population carries with it a unique legacy challenged by colonization and trade. Many rejected colonial rule and the Christianity associated with it, instead opting for Islam introduced by Arab traders. In the 20th century, African Independent Churches, notably Zionist churches, arrived from nearby Malawi. Today, Mozambique is 54% Christian, 28% traditional religionist, and 17% Muslim.

The Catholic Church is the largest Christian tradition in the country. After the country's independence in 1975, the Catholic Church became a target of anti-colonial backlash. Today, Catholics are active in orphanage work, technical centers, and education. Caritas, the Catholic Church's global social services arm, arrived in the country in 1977. They are currently involved in emergency relief, rural development, health care, education, housing, and a host of other services.

Over the 19th and 20th centuries, many Protestant groups arrived in the region and worked among different people groups. Even today different denominations are home to different ethnic groups (for example, Presbyterianism among the Tsonga and Shangaan peoples northwest of Lourenço Marques, Baptists north of Maputo and Inhambane, Adventists among the Lomwe and Chuabo peoples north of the Zambezi River). One newer feature of Mozambiquan Christianity is the arrival of Brazilian churches, such as the Universal Church of the Kingdom of God (arrived in 1992). Brazilian-founded churches and evangelization efforts will likely increase in the country due to their shared language.

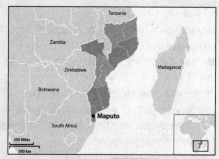

% Christian: 0 3 10 50 75 100

Religion in Mozambique

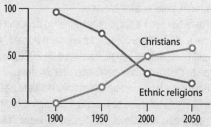

The religious makeup of Mozambique changed dramatically over the 20th century. In 1900, the country was made up nearly entirely of followers of traditional religions (96%), followed by Muslims (3%). By 2020, traditional religions had declined to 28%, while Christianity surged, growing to 54% of the population. Islam also grew to 17% by 2020.

Indicators & Demographic Data

Population (2020)	32,309,000
% under 15 years	44%
Capital city (pop.)	Maputo 1,110,000
% urban dwellers	37% (4.24% p.a.)
Official language	Portuguese
Largest language	Makhuwa (17%)
Largest people	Makuana (17%)
Largest culture	Central Bantu (63%)
Development	44
Physicians	0.6
Gender gap	10%

Bible Translations		Churches		Missionaries		Gospel Access	
Languages	57	Denominations	680	Received	3,500	1900	Very low
Full Bible	26	Congregations	32,700	Sent	170	2020	Very high

Facts to Consider

- Mozambique is one of the world's poorest countries and relies heavily on international aid. Corruption and bribery are rampant.
- Mozambique is particularly susceptible to changes in weather patterns due to its long coastline and sprawling delta region; natural disasters are becoming more frequent and more severe. In March 2019, Cyclone Idai devasted parts of Mozambique, Zimbabwe, and Malawi, killing over 1,300 people and affecting over 3 million people during its five-day onslaught across the region.
- Cyclone Kenneth (April 2019) was the strongest recorded cyclone to make landfall in Africa and primarily affected the Cabo Delgado province. Methodists, Lutherans, Anglicans, Catholics, and others offered various kinds of assistance.
- There has been a surge of extremist violence in northern Mozambique since 2017, where churches have been burned, young girls kidnapped, and thousands of people displaced. In 2020, rebels captured two Brazilian Catholic missionary sisters for 24 days.
- Customary laws in some regions discriminate against women, where the only rights afforded to them are through a brother or maternal uncle. Young girls are sometimes forced to leave school and marry young, especially in rural areas. Restrictions exist that limit women's access to land, economic benefits, and certain types of work.

Christian Traditions in Mozambique

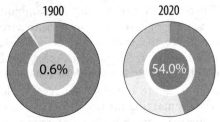

The small Christian population in 1900 (16,700 people) was mostly Catholic (90%) due to historical missions and Portuguese colonization. In 2020, Catholicism was still prominent (44% of Christians), but Protestants and Independents together outnumbered Catholics, with over 4.5 million followers each (together 56% of Christians). The Pentecostal/Charismatic movement is also quite prominent and represented over 19% of the population in 2020.

Christian Families in Mozambique

Family	Population 2020	%	Trend	Change
Latin-rite Catholic	7,300,000	22.6	↑	3.3
*Pentecostals/Charismatics	6,000,000	18.6	↑	3.3
*Evangelicals	4,200,000	13.0	↑	1.9
Baptist	675,000	2.1	↑	4.0
Adventist	674,000	2.1	↑↑	5.4
Reformed, Presbyterian	428,000	1.3	↑	1.8
Holiness	284,000	0.9	↑	0.7
Methodist	266,000	0.8	↑	4.0
Jehovah's Witnesses	190,000	0.6	↑	2.5
Anglican	142,000	0.4	↑	1.7
Lutheran	25,800	0.1	↑↑	7.4
United church or joint mission	18,100	0.1	−	0.0
Congregational	17,200	0.1	↑	1.4
Latter-day Saints (Mormons)	14,200	<0.1	↑↑	10.2
Restorationist, Disciple	13,100	<0.1	↑	1.8
Salvationist	9,000	<0.1	↑	0.5
Eastern Orthodox	5,000	<0.1	−	0.0
Mennonite	3,100	<0.1	↑	2.2

Many Christian families are present in Mozambique. After Latin-rite Catholics, the largest Christian family is Pentecostals/Charismatics, which numbered 6 million in 2020. There are dozens of Pentecostal groups, ranging in size from a few thousand to over a million. Some of the largest denominations in this family are the Assemblies of God (1.5 million, from the United States), the Pentecostal Assemblies of God (320,000, from Canada), and the African Assemblies of God (100,000, from Zimbabwe). Evangelicalism, the next largest family, is diverse and is found throughout numerous historic Protestant churches such as Baptists and Nazarenes. The fourth largest family is Baptists, including the United Baptist Church of Mozambique (400,000, from Sweden) and the Baptist Convention of Mozambique (137,000, from Brazil).

* These movements are found within Christian families
− no change
↑↑ extreme growth
↑ growth
↓↓ extreme decline
↓ decline

Christianity in Myanmar

Christianity has a long history in Myanmar, with the presence of the Church of the East in modern-day Bago (10th century), Catholics (1554), and Protestants (1807). While very few ethnic Burmese people have adopted Christianity, other ethnic groups—in particular the Karen, Chin, and Kachin—have embraced it. Christians are largely found in the Irrawaddy Delta region and ethnic minority regions, and the largest denominations are the Myanmar Baptist Convention, Catholics, and Assemblies of God. Baptists owe their origins to American missionaries Ann and Adoniram Judson, who learned the Pali and Burmese languages, beliefs, and customs. Their translation of the Bible is still in use today. Responsibility for the Myanmar Baptist Convention's work transferred from American to indigenous leadership in 1945.

Facts to Consider

- In February 2021, Myanmar's military seized control of the democratically elected government. Ann Roza Nu Tawng, a Catholic sister who stood before police to plea for protestors' lives, became a symbol of the movement. At least 1,500 people died in the first year of the protests.
- Cyclone Nargis (2008) and the massive flooding of the Irrawaddy Delta (2015) brought increased awareness to climate change, where flooding, cyclones, and droughts are more frequent and intense.
- Formed by Baptists in 1872, the first college in Myanmar is now the University of Rangoon. Education is still an important missional activity, with more than 100 Bible colleges and seminaries in the country.
- Theravada Buddhism has been the main religion of Myanmar since the 9th century and has greatly influenced Burmese culture.

Indicators & Demographic Data

Population (2020).................................54,808,000
% under 15 years 25%
Capital city (pop.) ....Naypyidaw 594,000
% urban dwellers............................31% (1.85% p.a.)
Official language................................... Burmese
Largest language............................. Burmese (53%)
Largest people .... Burmese (Myen, Bhama) (53%)
Largest culture .... Burmese (63%)
Development...58
Physicians..5.7
Gender gap...4%

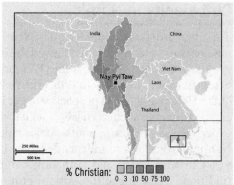

% Christian: 0 3 10 50 75 100

Christian Traditions in Myanmar

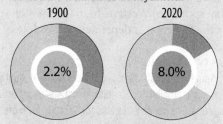

1900 — 2.2% 2020 — 8.0%

☐Independent ☐Protestant ■Catholic ■Orthodox ■Christian

Christians in 1900 were mostly Protestants (70% of Christians), followed by Catholics (30%). In 2020, Christianity was more diverse with the introduction of Independent Christianity (17% of Christians).

Religion in Myanmar

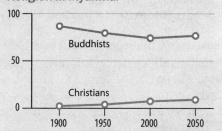

Myanmar is historically a majority Buddhist country, but the Buddhist share of the population dropped from 87% in 1900 to 76% in 2020. Gains were mostly by Christians (from 2% in 1900 to 8% in 2020).

Bible Translations		Churches		Missionaries		Gospel Access	
Languages	126	Denominations	200	Received	220	1900	Very low
Full Bible	53	Congregations	20,100	Sent	270	2020	Medium

Christianity in Namibia

The first Christians in modern-day Namibia were British missionaries in 1801, who encountered the indigenous Bantu peoples, the largest of which is the Ovambo. Germany colonized the region from 1884 to 1915, under which the majority of the Herero and Nama peoples were put in concentration camps and subject to forced labor, sexual violence, medical experiments, and death. South Africa ruled what became Namibia from 1915 to independence in 1990. Namibia is 91% Christian today, and Lutherans comprise the largest tradition largely due to the work of Finnish missionaries. There are numerous Independent churches in the country that split from Western-founded missionary churches, such as the Ovambo Independent Church (est. 1970).

Facts to Consider

- Namibia's constitution guarantees women equal protection under the law and prohibits gender discrimination—a rare provision in sub-Saharan Africa. The country has also taken steps for more female participation in government.
- HIV/AIDS, which has been the leading cause of death since 1996, has heavily affected Namibia. In 2019, 12% of adults ages 15 to 49 were living with HIV/AIDS. Some Christian organizations have HIV/AIDS ministries.
- Namibia Evangelical Theological Seminary was formed in 1991 as the nation's only Evangelical college. It has graduated over 300 students from both Namibia and abroad.
- African Traditional Religion is followed among a small minority of Ambo and Herero and over 90% of the Heikum and Kung Khoisan peoples. Some combine elements of traditional religions with Christianity.

Indicators & Demographic Data

Population (2020)	2,697,000
% under 15 years	36%
Capital city (pop.)	Windhoek 431,000
% urban dwellers	52% (3.64% p.a.)
Official language	English
Largest language	Ndonga (30%)
Largest people	Ndonga (Ambo, Ovambo) (30%)
Largest culture	Southwestern Bantu (59%)
Development	65
Physicians	3.7
Gender gap	-1%

% Christian: 0 3 10 50 75 100

Christian Traditions in Namibia

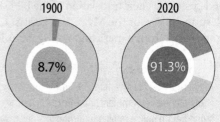

1900 — 8.7%
2020 — 91.3%

☐ Independent ☐ Protestant ◼ Catholic ◼ Orthodox ◼ Christian

The small Christian population in 1900 was mostly Protestant (98%). This was still the case in 2020 (70% Protestant), but Catholics and Independents grew to 19% and 11% of Christians, respectively.

Religion in Namibia

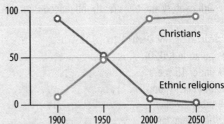

Christians

Ethnic religions

1900 1950 2000 2050

Christianity in Namibia grew tremendously in the 20th century, from just under 9% of the population in 1900 to 91% in 2020. Most converts were from traditional religions, which declined from 91% to 5% in 2020.

Bible Translations		Churches		Missionaries		Gospel Access	
Languages	30	Denominations	140	Received	1,400	1900	Very low
Full Bible	12	Congregations	3,200	Sent	60	2020	Very high

Christianity in Nauru

An island in the Pacific Ocean, Nauru is one of the smallest countries in the world by both land mass (8 square miles) and population (11,000 people). People from Micronesia and Polynesia settled there around the year 100 BCE, and it was a German colony (1888–1914), an Australian territory (1914–1919), Japanese-occupied (1942–1945), and a United Nations trust territory from 1947 until independence in 1968. The first missionary was from modern-day Kiribati in the 19th century, but not having learned the local Nauru language, he made little impact. Additional missionaries arrived from Hawaii and translated the Bible into the vernacular with local Nauruan converts. The country is 74% Christian today, mostly Congregationalists and Catholics.

Facts to Consider

- The constitution provides for the freedom of conscience, expression, assembly, and freedom to change one's religious beliefs. Religious groups must register with the government.
- To be registered, groups must have at least 750 enrolled members, a building in the country, and a Nauruan member of the clergy living in the country. All of these measures are difficult for newer groups, and there are only five officially registered churches.
- The Nauru Congregational Church includes members of Presbyterian, Lutheran, Methodist, and Baptist backgrounds. The church ordained its first female ministers in 2015.
- Unemployment in Nauru is around 23%. The government employs 95% of all working people on the island. There are few natural resources.

Indicators & Demographic Data

Population (2020). 11,200
% under 15 years 24%
Capital city (pop.) . . . . .Yaren 11,200
% urban dwellers. . . . . .100% (0.18% p.a.)
Official language . . . . none
Largest language. . . . . .Nauruan (44%)
Largest people . . . . .Nauruan (48%)
Largest culture . . . . .Nauruan (48%)
Development. 65
Physicians. 14
Gender gap 13%

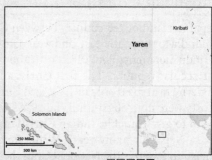

% Christian: 0 3 10 50 75 100

Christian Traditions in Nauru

1900   2020

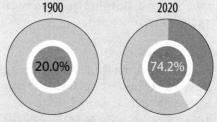

20.0%   74.2%

☐Independent ☐Protestant ▨Catholic ▨Orthodox ■Christian

The small Christian population in 1900 (only 300 Christians) was 100% Protestant. Protestants were still the largest Christian group in 2020 (58%), but Catholics and Independents grew to 33% and 8% of Christians, respectively.

Religion in Nauru

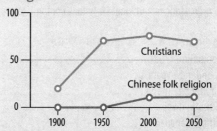

Christianity in Nauru grew tremendously in the 20th century, from 20% of the population in 1900 to 74% in 2020. Chinese folk religion is the second largest religion, with 11% of the population.

Bible Translations	Churches	Missionaries	Gospel Access
Languages. 9	Denominations 13	Received. 20	1900 . . . . Medium
Full Bible. 8	Congregations. 44	Sent 2	2020 . . . . Very high

Christianity in Nepal

Nepal is a landlocked country between China to the north and India to the south, east, and west. Until 2008, Nepal was a Hindu monarchy. The 2015 constitution established Nepal as a secular republic. The first Christians in Nepal in the modern era arrived only in 1951, and Christian missionary efforts were not robust until the 1990s, when Christianity began to grow quickly. Indian Christians have been working in Nepal for many years. While the largest organized Christian group is the National Churches Fellowship, with 120,000 members, most Christians in Nepal are found in Independent Charismatic churches and house churches. The spread of Christianity in Nepal can be largely attributed to the conversion of women.

Facts to Consider

- Hinduism is no longer the official state religion, but its influence is everywhere in Nepal. The caste system is technically illegal, but it is still widely accepted.
- Hindu practices are closely related to Nepali culture such that a conversion to Christianity is understood as a rejection of traditional religion, culture, and family. Converts are often ostracized from their families.
- Women are of low social status and lack education, health care, and political opportunities, especially in rural areas. Among other things, Christianity has provided women a form of protection, an education, and a social outlet.
- The magnitude 7.8 earthquake in 2015 demolished more than 600,000 structures and killed over 8,000 people in the region. Landslides added to the damage in Kathmandu and surrounding villages. Christian organizations and local Christians continue to provide emergency relief.

Indicators & Demographic Data

Population (2020)	30,260,000
% under 15 years	29%
Capital city (pop.)	Kathmandu 1,424,000
% urban dwellers	21% (3.09% p.a.)
Official language	Nepali
Largest language	Nepali (46%)
Largest people	Nepalese (Eastern Pahari) (40%)
Largest culture	Nepalese (50%)
Development	57
Physicians	6
Gender gap	8%

% Christian: 0 3 10 50 75 100

Christian Traditions in Nepal

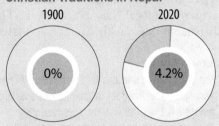

1900 — 0%

2020 — 4.2%

☐ Independent ☐ Protestant ■ Catholic ■ Orthodox ■ Christian

There were no Christians in Nepal at the start of the 20th century. By 2020, there were over 1.2 million. The vast majority are Hindu-background believers in Christ or other kinds of Independents (77% of Christians).

Religion in Nepal

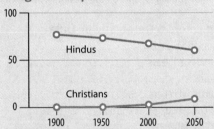

Nepal is historically a Hindu majority country, though the Hindu share dropped from 77% in 1900 to 66% in 2020. Traditional religions grew from 2% to 13%, and Buddhism dropped from 20% to 12%.

Bible Translations	Churches	Missionaries	Gospel Access
Languages......121	Denominations 340	Received.........1,000	1900 ....Very low
Full Bible............17	Congregations.....10,700	Sent 120	2020 ....Medium

Christianity in the Netherlands

Christianity reached modern-day Netherlands in the 7th century, with the first church established in Utrecht. English missionaries Willibrord and Boniface arrived in the 8th century. However it was during and after the 16th century Protestant Reformation that the Netherlands became a haven for the followers of Martin Luther, Ulrich Zwingli, and John Calvin, with Protestantism becoming intertwined with Dutch identity and the struggle for freedom from the Hapsburg Empire (1566–1648). The Dutch Reformed Church became the official religion in 1651 and spread around the world via missionary work to the East Indies, Formosa (Taiwan), New York, India, Brazil, and South Africa. In the 19th century, Catholics were concentrated in the south and Protestants in the north. The Protestant Church of the Netherlands is the result of a denominational merger that began in 1961 and ended in 2004. The church of the Dutch royal family, the second largest denomination after the Catholic Church, includes merged Protestant denominations, Dutch Reformed, Reformed (formerly the Reformed Churches of the Netherlands), and Lutherans.

The 20th century was the beginning of Christianity's decline in the Netherlands, beginning in the Protestant rural town Groningen and province of Friesland, expanding to the large cities in the west (Amsterdam and Rotterdam), and then in the south among Catholics. The exception is in the "Bible belt" that stretches from Zeeland to the northern parts of Overijssel, where the Bible continues to play an important role in society and residents largely resist the progressive stances on social issues such as sexuality, marriage, LGBTQ rights, and abortion. For the rest of the country, religion is a private, not public, matter and should not have an important role in national affairs.

The Netherlands is broadly considered to be culturally open and tolerant of religious pluralism, but these stances have been challenged by waves of immigration that have helped increase the Muslim population to 7% of the country. The most recent wave was the migration crisis sparked by the Syrian Civil War beginning in 2011. In 2018, a bill was approved banning face-covering veils in public places other than streets, known as the "burqa ban." In 2021, parliament decided to continue monitoring mosques and Muslim organizations for "foreign influence."

% Christian: 0 3 10 50 75 100

Religion in the Netherlands

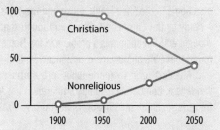

The religious makeup of the Netherlands changed substantially over the 20th century. In 1900, the country was nearly entirely Christian (97%), followed by Jews (2%). By 2020, Christianity had declined to 55% with a surge of the nonreligious, growing from 1% of the population to 35%. Islam also grew from nearly zero in 1900 to over 1.2 million (7%) in 2020.

Indicators & Demographic Data

Population (2020)	17,181,000
% under 15 years	16%
Capital city (pop.)	Amsterdam 1,149,000
% urban dwellers	92% (0.59% p.a.)
Official language	Dutch
Largest language	Dutch (69%)
Largest people	Dutch (68%)
Largest culture	Dutch (76%)
Development	93
Physicians	35
Gender gap	3%

Bible Translations		Churches		Missionaries		Gospel Access	
Languages	45	Denominations	430	Received	2,000	1900	Very high
Full Bible	29	Congregations	8,100	Sent	3,000	2020	Very high

Facts to Consider

- Prostitution is legal and regulated in the Netherlands. The Amsterdam Red Light District is a major destination for sex tourism but is also associated with trafficking, drugs, and other criminal activity. In 2008–2010, steps were taken to reduce the size of the district and curb illegal activity.
- A 2015 report from Statistics Netherlands claimed the country was 50% unaffiliated from religion and that only one in six Dutch regularly attended religious services. There are two Dutch Humanist movements, Humanitas and Humanistisch Verbond.
- The Dutch Jewish population was decimated during World War II and the Holocaust, dropping from 140,000 to around 30,000 today. Most live in the major cities in the west, and 44% of all Jews lives in Amsterdam, also home to the Anne Frank House and the Jewish Historical Museum.
- A study by the European Commission found that 65% of respondents thought anti-Semitism was a problem in the Netherlands. Another survey found that 95% of Muslims experienced an anti-Muslim incident. Jews and Muslims report experiencing verbal abuse, discrimination, and vandalism. Combating religious intolerance has become a major issue for governmental and nongovernmental organizations.

Christian Traditions in the Netherlands

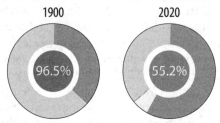

1900   2020

96.5%   55.2%

☐Independent ☐Protestant ■Catholic ■Orthodox ■Christian

Christianity in the Netherlands has historically been majority Protestant (63% of Christians), largely in the form of the Protestant Church of the Netherlands. There was also a substantial population of Catholics (37%). By 2020, these patterns had somewhat reversed. There are now almost twice as many Catholics as Protestants (4.4 million versus 2.8 million; 58% of Christians versus 37%). Evangelicalism declined from 30% of the country's population in 1900 to 3% in 2020.

Christian Families in Netherlands

Family	Population 2020	%	Trend	Change
Latin-rite Catholic	4,415,000	25.7	—	-0.5
Reformed, Presbyterian	2,548,000	14.8	↓	-0.7
*Evangelicals	580,000	3.4	—	0.5
*Pentecostals/Charismatics	425,000	2.5	—	0.3
Jehovah's Witnesses	43,800	0.3	—	-0.4
Anglican	35,200	0.2	—	0.3
Moravian	20,700	0.1	—	0.3
Baptist	17,000	0.1	—	-0.3
Congregational	13,000	0.1	↓	-1.7
Eastern Orthodox	12,000	0.1	—	0.1
Holiness	11,900	0.1	↑	2.5
Lutheran	10,500	0.1	↓	-1.4
United church or joint mission	10,300	0.1	—	0.3
Mennonite	10,000	0.1	↓	-1.4
Latter-day Saints (Mormons)	9,300	0.1	—	0.3
Exclusive Brethren	9,300	0.1	—	0.3
Adventist	7,700	<0.1	↑	3.0
Salvationist	4,600	<0.1	↓↓	-5.5
Old Catholic Church	4,500	<0.1	↓	-1.5
Christian Brethren	3,500	<0.1	↓	-0.8

Many Christian families are present in the Netherlands. After Latin-rite Catholics, the largest Christian family is Reformed/Presbyterian, which numbers over 2.5 million. The largest denomination is the Protestant Church of the Netherlands, with over 2 million members, but it is declining. There are many other Reformed/Presbyterian churches, many of which broke from the main group: Reformed Churches (Liberated), Christian Reformed Churches in the Netherlands, and Netherland Reformed Churches. Pentecostals/Charismatics numbered 425,000 in 2020, and the largest denomination is the United Pentecostal and Evangelical Churches, formed in 2002 with the merger of the Brotherhood of Pentecostal Churches and the Full Gospel Churches of the Netherlands. The United Pentecostal and Evangelical Churches (UPEC) is the Dutch branch of the Assemblies of God and has just under 40,000 members. The country has 50 other Independent Pentecostal/Charismatic churches, including various immigrant churches.

* These movements are found within Christian families	↑↑	extreme growth
	↑	growth
	↓↓	extreme decline
— no change	↓	decline

Christianity in New Caledonia

New Caledonia is in the southwest Pacific Ocean, south of Vanuatu. Christianity first came to the islands by a native Tongan in 1834. Subsequently, the London Missionary Society sent two Samoans, and the first Western missionaries arrived in the 1850s. The islands became a French territory in 1843, and today it remains an overseas special collectivity of France. Since 1999, citizens have had both French and New Caledonian citizenship. The population is 85% Christian, and the indigenous population tends to be more devout than those with European ancestry. The Catholic Church is the largest denomination, with half the population, followed by the Evangelical Churches in New Caledonia, the Free Evangelical Church, and the Assemblies of God.

Facts to Consider

- The Nouméa Accord (1998) mandated a series of national referendums to vote on attaining full sovereignty from France. Voters overwhelming rejected independence in each (2018, 2020, and 2021). The indigenous Kanak people favor independence, but many did not participate in the 2021 vote because of the COVID-19 pandemic.
- Church-state relations are the same in New Caledonia as they are in France. Large Catholic and Protestant school programs receive funding from the government.
- The country has 8,000 Muslims, mostly Javanese immigrants from Indonesia and some Arabs. There are two Islamic centers, in Nouméa and Bourail.

Indicators & Demographic Data

Population (2020)	287,000
% under 15 years	22%
Capital city (pop.)	Nouméa 191,000
% urban dwellers	72% (1.72% p.a.)
Official language	none
Largest language	French (47%)
Largest people	French (32%)
Largest culture	French (32%)
Development	56
Physicians	1.4
Gender gap	13%

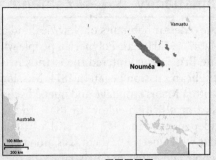

% Christian: 0 3 10 50 75 100

Christian Traditions in New Caledonia

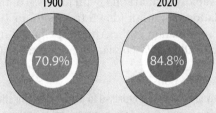

1900 — 70.9% 2020 — 84.8%

☐Independent ☐Protestant ■Catholic ■Orthodox ■Christian

Christians in 1900 were majority Catholic (89%), with a small population of Evangelical Protestants (11%). In 2020, Christianity was much more diverse: still majority Catholic (68%), but with larger populations of Protestants (20%) and Independents (12%).

Religion in New Caledonia

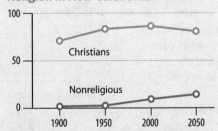

In 1900, New Caledonia was 71% Christian and 27% followers of traditional religions. There are virtually no exclusive followers of traditional religions today.

Bible Translations		Churches		Missionaries		Gospel Access	
Languages	46	Denominations	13	Received	340	1900	High
Full Bible	12	Congregations	490	Sent	30	2020	Very high

Christianity in New Zealand

The oldest inhabitants of New Zealand are the indigenous Maori, a Malaysian-Polynesian people who arrived by 1350. The British encountered the islands in 1768, and the first Anglican mission began in 1814. Missionaries developed a written Maori language and opened schools. New Zealand became a British colony in 1841, and though it achieved independence in 1947, it is still a British Commonwealth state with Queen Elizabeth II as monarch. Most of the Maori people converted to Christianity in the 19th century, but their population declined to about 40% of its prior size before European contact, mostly through disease. New Zealand is rapidly secularizing, with just 54% of the country's population Christian (down from 98% in 1900). The largest denomination is the Anglican Church in Aotearoa, New Zealand and Polynesia, with around 600,000 members.

Facts to Consider

- Women were first ordained to the Anglican priesthood in 1977, and the first female diocesan bishop in the entire Anglican Communion was Rev. Dr. Penny Jamieson, ordained bishop of Dunedin in 1990.
- The country has served as a strategic sending base for missionaries to the South Pacific since the 19th century.
- New Zealand is becoming more religiously diverse with the arrival of Hindus, Buddhists, and Muslims from Polynesia, China, and elsewhere.
- Men are more likely than women to be nonreligious, and youth are more likely than the elderly. The country elected its first agnostic prime minister, Helen Clark, who held office from 1999 to 2008.

Indicators & Demographic Data

Population (2020)	4,834,000
% under 15 years	20%
Capital city (pop.)	Wellington 415,000
% urban dwellers	87% (0.92% p.a.)
Official language	English, Maori, New Zealand Sign Language
Largest language	English (80%)
Largest people	Anglo-New Zealander (59%)
Largest culture	Anglo-New Zealander (59%)
Development	92
Physicians	31
Gender gap	3%

% Christian: 0 3 10 50 75 100

Christian Traditions in New Zealand

1900 — 98.3%
2020 — 54.2%

☐ Independent ☐ Protestant ■ Catholic ■ Orthodox ■ Christian

Christians in 1900 were majority Protestant (85% of Christians), with a smaller population of Catholics (15%). In 2020, Christianity was much more diverse: still majority Protestant (59%), but with larger populations of Catholics (25%) and Independents (15%).

Religion in New Zealand

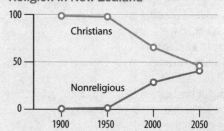

The Christian share of the population dropped from 98% in 1900 to 54% by 2020. The nonreligious (atheists and agnostics together) were 36% in 2020.

Bible Translations		Churches		Missionaries		Gospel Access	
Languages	76	Denominations	180	Received	3,000	1900	Very high
Full Bible	64	Congregations	5,600	Sent	800	2020	Very high

Christianity in Nicaragua

In the 15th century, modern-day Nicaragua was inhabited by the Toltec and Maya, indigenous peoples of ancient Mesoamerican civilizations. Christopher Columbus was the first European to reach the area in 1502, beginning what would become 300 years of Spanish colonization. Many indigenous people died from new infectious diseases, while other peoples were captured and forced into slavery by the Spanish. Spanish took wives from the local peoples, beginning the multiethnic mix of peoples known as "Mestizo" that make up the majority of the population today (63%). Though Catholic missionaries arrived in 1526, Christianity did not reach the Pacific coast until 1689. Nicaragua achieved independence from Spain in 1821, was occupied by the United States from 1909 to 1933, and experienced a series of corrupt dictatorships of the US-backed Somoza family from 1927 to 1979, before the Nicaraguan Revolution (1962–1990).

The Catholic Church supported the Somoza family and it struggled during the Revolution between supporters of liberation theology on one hand and conservatives on the other. The church eventually withdrew support for the Somoza family in 1969. Catholicism declined in the 20th century. Today the upper and middle classes are more likely to be practicing Catholics, while lower classes are less sacramental.

German Moravians were the first Protestants who worked among Afro-Caribbean and other people groups on the Caribbean coast. The first Nicaraguan pastor was ordained in 1899. The 20th century was a time of Protestant expansion, with the arrival of many denominations, including Seventh-day Adventists (1904), Assemblies of God (1911), and Baptists (1917). Pentecostal/Charismatic Christianity has been growing rapidly since the 1970s, and now 23% of Christians in the country are a part of this movement. Evangelical churches are also growing; a recent survey reported that half of Evangelicals in the country were raised Catholic. Most Evangelical churches are small and found in both rural and urban areas. The Church of Jesus Christ of Latter-day Saints (Mormons) are the fifth largest denomination, and in 2018, a temple was announced for the capital city, Managua.

% Christian: 0 3 10 50 75 100

Religion in Nicaragua

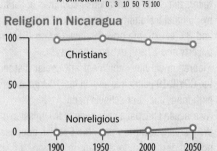

Nicaragua is historically a majority Christian country, and the Christian share of the population declined only slightly from 98% in 1900 to 95% in 2020. The nonreligious (atheists and agnostics) made up 3% of the population in 2020, followed by Spiritists at 1.5%. There are small populations of Baha'is, Buddhists, and Muslims.

Indicators & Demographic Data

Population (2020). 6,417,000
% under 15 years 28%
Capital city (pop.) . . . . Managua 1,064,000
% urban dwellers. . . . . 59% (1.45% p.a.)
Official language. . . . . Spanish
Largest language. . . . . Spanish (79%)
Largest people . . . . Mestizo (Ladino) (63%)
Largest culture . . . . . . Mestizo (Spanish) (63%)
Development. 66
Physicians. 9.1
Gender gap 3%

Bible Translations	Churches	Missionaries	Gospel Access
Languages. 16	Denominations 110	Received. 2,000	1900 . . . . Very high
Full Bible. 6	Congregations. 9,100	Sent 270	2020 . . . . Very high

Facts to Consider

- Daniel Ortega has been president of Nicaragua since 2007 and has been accused of attempting to dismantle democracy. The 2018 unrest related to social security and taxes marked the beginning of the country's current sociopolitical crisis.
- The Catholic Church has spoken out against violence perpetrated by the government and progovernment groups, calling for respect for human rights and the release of political prisoners. The government has responded by cutting funding and support to both Catholic and Protestant education and programming.
- Nicaragua is one of the poorest countries in Latin America, exacerbated by political instability. Thirty percent of the population live in poverty and 8% in extreme poverty; however, in the rural areas, 50% live in poverty and 12% in extreme poverty.
- Nicaragua did not implement any social distancing measures during the COVID-19 pandemic and, in fact, the government encouraged social gatherings and kept schools open.
- Nicaraguan Christians have been active missionaries in surrounding Latin American countries since the Spanish conquest. Nicaragua is also a popular destination for short-term mission trips from the United States, which are often more for the benefit of Americans than Nicaraguans.

Christian Traditions in Nicaragua

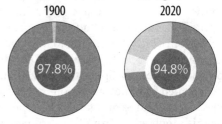

1900   2020

97.8%   94.8%

☐Independent ☐Protestant ■Catholic ■Orthodox ■Christian

Christianity in Nicaragua has historically been majority Catholic. In 1900, 99% of Christians were Catholic. This dropped to 73% in 2020 with the tremendous growth of Protestant, Evangelical, and Pentecostal/Charismatic Christianity. Protestants and Independents together made up 27% of Christians in 2020. Evangelicals grew from less than 1% of the population in 1900 to 17% in 2020; Pentecostal/Charismatics also grew to 21% over the same period.

Christian Families in Nicaragua

Family	Population 2020	%	Trend	Change
Latin-rite Catholic	5,150,000	80.3	↑	0.6
*Pentecostals/Charismatics	1,400,000	21.8	↑	1.5
*Evangelicals	1,100,000	17.1	↑	1.7
Adventist	190,000	3.0	↑	2.2
Baptist	138,000	2.1	↑	3.3
Latter-day Saints (Mormons)	115,000	1.8	↑	4.8
Moravian	101,000	1.6	↑	1.4
Jehovah's Witnesses	69,700	1.1	↑	4.3
Mennonite	24,700	0.4	↑	1.7
Restorationist, Disciple	23,300	0.4	↑	1.5
Christian Brethren	20,700	0.3	↑	1.0
Holiness	17,400	0.3	−	0.1
Nondenominational	17,200	0.3	↑	0.7
Lutheran	15,100	0.2	↑↑	5.3
Anglican	11,400	0.2	↑	1.3

After Catholicism, the Pentecostal/Charismatic movement is the second largest Christian family, representing nearly 20% of the country's population. The largest of these denominations is by far the Assemblies of God, with 680,000 members, introduced by missionaries from the United States in 1911. Other groups include the Church of God, the Church of God of Prophecy, plus dozens of other independent and indigenous Pentecostal churches. Baptists include the National Baptist Convention (70,000) and the Good Samaritan Baptist Church (50,000). Moravians arrived in 1847 and worked primarily with ethnic groups on the Caribbean coast; today, 96% of Moravian membership is still in this area.

* These movements are found within Christian families

− no change

↑↑ extreme growth
↑ growth
↓↓ extreme decline
↓ decline

Christianity in Niger

Niger is a landlocked Muslim-majority country in West Africa. Berber Christians lived there in the 7th century but were driven out by Muslims. Christianity did not return to Niger until the 20th century. Niger was a French colony from 1900 until its independence in 1960. Catholicism arrived from Benin in 1931, and the first indigenous priest was ordained in 1972. Pope Francis appointed the first indigenous archbishop in 2014. The largest Protestant denomination is the Assemblies of God, which arrived in 1990 via missionaries from France, Burkina Faso, and the United States; an Assemblies of God church with indigenous leadership began in 2006. Immigrants from Nigeria introduced the Cherubim and Seraphim Church, and immigrants from Benin brought the Heavenly Christian Church, each with over 2,000 members.

Facts to Consider

- Poverty is widespread in Niger, and the country is one of the least developed in the world. Over 40% of the population lives on less than $1 a day. This has been compounded by the arrival of over 200,000 refugees from Nigeria and Mali.
- Food insecurity is a major issue in Niger, with an estimated 5.4 million people being food insecure; children are particularly vulnerable.
- Christians and Muslims generally live peacefully, but there have been interreligious clashes. In 2015, 96 churches were burned over two days after the depiction of the Prophet Muhammad in a French magazine.
- Some border regions are under control of Islamic extremists, and Boko Haram has kidnapped and threatened Christians in the south.

Indicators & Demographic Data

Population (2020)................................24,075,000
% under 15 years 50%
Capital city (pop.)..........................Niamey 1,292,000
% urban dwellers............................ 17% (4.72% p.a.)
Official language......................................French
Largest language............................... Hausa (48%)
Largest people .... Tazarawa (30%)
Largest culture .... Hausa (48%)
Development...35
Physicians.. 0.2
Gender gap...19%

% Christian: 0 3 10 50 75 100

Christian Traditions in Niger

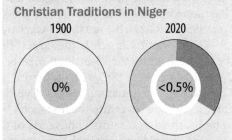

1900 — 0% 2020 — <0.5%

☐ Independent ☐ Protestant ▨ Catholic ▨ Orthodox ▨ Christian

There were no Christians in Niger in 1900. The small population in 2020 (around 63,000) was nearly an even mix of Catholics, Protestants, and Independents.

Religion in Niger

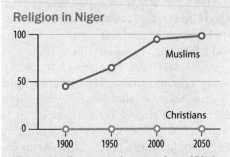

Niger's Muslim population grew from 45% in 1900 to nearly 97% in 2020, mostly at the expense of traditional religions, which declined from 55% to 3%. Christianity grew slightly but was less than 1% in 2020.

Bible Translations		Churches		Missionaries		Gospel Access	
Languages	30	Denominations	86	Received	500	1900	Very low
Full Bible	8	Congregations	500	Sent	10	2020	Low

Christianity in Nigeria

The indigenous peoples of Nigeria had contact with various European traders beginning in the 15th century. In the 17th century, the Atlantic slave trade began, in which 3.5 million people were taken from Nigeria until the practice was outlawed in 1807 (though some illegal trade occurred after that). Nigeria became a British protectorate in 1900 and a colony in 1914 until independence in 1960. The country experienced coups in 1966 and 1975–1976, a civil war (1967–1970), and another series of coups from 1983 to 1999 before establishing the Fourth Nigerian Republic in 1999. Nigeria is a very religious country and is nearly equally split between Muslims in the north and Christians in the south.

The Catholic Church is the largest denomination in the country, with over 23 million members. Modern-day Catholicism dates to 1865 with the arrival of French priests. The first Nigerian Catholic priest was Cyprian Michael Iwene Tansi in 1937, who was also the first monk from West Africa to be beatified as a saint. Thousands of Catholic priests, brothers, and sisters work in the country across a variety of evangelization and social service ministries.

One of the largest Anglican churches in the world, the Anglican Church of Nigeria, is only slightly smaller than the Catholic Church (22 million members). The first Anglicans in Nigeria were formerly enslaved people from Sierra Leone, and the Church Missionary Society arrived in 1842. Samuel Ajayi Crowther was consecrated as the first African bishop, but his appointment was controversial because of his race, and a European replaced him in 1891.

Nigeria is known for being home to a plethora of Independent denominations. The first in a long line of such groups was the Native Baptist Church, which split from Southern Baptist work among Yoruba peoples in 1888. There were many schisms from historic denominations, such as from Anglicans (African Church; Christ Army Church) and Methodists (United African Methodist Church). More common are charismatic groups that began on their own, such as the Cherubim and Seraphim, the Church of the Lord (Aladura), and the Christ Apostolic Church. Because historic churches did not allow African Christians to contextualize Christianity to their own cultural surroundings, these African Independent Churches formed separately from their oversight.

% Christian: 0 3 10 50 75 100

Religion in Nigeria

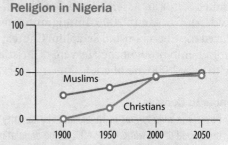

Nigeria experienced a massive transformation of its religious makeup over the 20th century. In 1900, 73% of the country primarily followed traditional religions, while 26% were Muslim, and just 1% Christian. This changed dramatically by 2020, when the country was nearly split between Christianity and Islam (46% each), followed by around 7% traditional religionist.

Indicators & Demographic Data

Population (2020). 206,153,000
% under 15 years 43%
Capital city (pop.) . . . . Abuja 3,278,000
% urban dwellers. . . . . 52% (3.92% p.a.)
Official language. . . . . English
Largest language. . . . . Hausa (22%)
Largest people . . . . . . Hausa (Hausawa) (17%)
Largest culture . . . . Yoruba (21%)
Development. 53
Physicians. 4
Gender gap. 13%

Bible Translations	Churches	Missionaries	Gospel Access
Languages. 494	Denominations 3,100	Received. 6,000	1900 . . . . Very low
Full Bible. 41	Congregations. . . . 180,000	Sent 20,000	2020 . . . . High

Facts to Consider

- Muslims are 46% of the country's population and mostly found in the northern states and in southwestern Nigeria among the Hausa, Fulani, Kanuri, Nupe, and among many Yoruba. Twelve states have introduced Sharia law. Northeastern Nigeria is home to the terrorist organization Boko Haram.
- Northern Nigeria is particularly insecure, with attacks from Boko Haram and ethno-religious conflicts. Children are particularly vulnerable to kidnapping, murder, and being sold as sex slaves. Boko Haram specifically targets schools, hospitals, and centers for internally displaced people.
- Nigerian Christians are committed to missions outside of Nigeria and are found all over West Africa and around the world. Tens of thousands of Nigerian churches have been planted worldwide.
- Women are active in Nigerian Independent churches as founders and leaders of all kinds. As in traditional African cultures, parallel leadership structures exist for men and women where Christians can hold spiritual power regardless of gender.
- There are numerous megachurches in Nigeria, and many of them preach a form of the prosperity gospel where God rewards Christians for faithful financial giving. This puts strain on Christians that already live in extreme poverty. Pentecostalism has become synonymous with prosperity teaching.

Christian Traditions in Nigeria

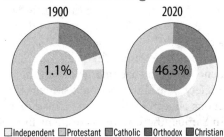

☐Independent ☐Protestant ☐Catholic ■Orthodox ■Christian

The Christian community in Nigeria in 1900 (around 176,000 Christians) was majority Protestant (76%), followed by Catholic (19%) and Independent (5%) minorities. Many of those Protestants were Evangelicals and/or Pentecostals/Charismatics. In 2020, Nigerian Christianity was much more diverse: still majority Protestant (54%) but now with a larger population of Independent Christian groups (24%), many of which are indigenous to Nigeria. Catholicism also grew to more than 25 million members (22% of Christians).

Christian Families in Nigeria

Family	Population 2020	%	Trend	Change
*Pentecostals/Charismatics	60,000,000	29.1	↑	3.2
*Evangelicals	45,500,000	22.1	↑	3.4
Latin-rite Catholic	25,536,000	12.4	↑	1.8
Anglican	21,604,000	10.5	↑	0.6
Baptist	8,427,000	4.1	↑	4.8
Nondenominational	7,278,000	3.5	↑	1.3
United church or joint mission	3,827,000	1.9	↑	1.3
Methodist	3,504,000	1.7	↑	1.6
Jehovah's Witnesses	1,077,000	0.5	↑	2.2
Reformed, Presbyterian	696,000	0.3	↑	1.1
Restorationist, Disciple	361,000	0.2	↑	3.5
Latter-day Saints (Mormons)	235,000	0.1	↑↑	8.5
Adventist	229,000	0.1	↓↓	-5.9
Christian Brethren	197,000	0.1	↑	0.9
Lutheran	154,000	0.1	–	0.4
Holiness	95,800	<0.1	–	0.2
Mennonite	34,500	<0.1	–	0.3
Salvationist	31,300	<0.1	↓	-1.1
Eastern Orthodox	3,000	<0.1	–	0.3

Christianity in Nigeria is extremely diverse. The Pentecostal/Charismatic movement is the largest Christian family in the country at 29% of the country's population (and 63% of Christians). Some Pentecostal denominations were imported to Nigeria, such as the Assemblies of God (5.9 million, from the United States) and the Apostolic Church of Nigeria (5.3 million, from the United Kingdom). Others are indigenous to the region, such as the Celestial Church of Christ (4.1 million, from Benin), the Church of the Lord (Prayer Fellowship) (4 million), and Christ Apostolic Church (2.6 million). Evangelicalism is also a large movement in the country, with groups such as the Evangelical Churches Winning All (6.8 million) and the Fellowship of Churches of Christ in Nigeria (3.8 million), both 100% Evangelical. There are also large populations of Evangelicals in the historic churches, such as the Methodist Church.

* These movements are found within Christian families
– no change

↑↑ extreme growth
↑ growth
↓↓ extreme decline
↓ decline

Christianity in Niue

Niue, an island nation in the South Pacific Ocean, is in a triangle between Tonga, Samoa, and the Cook Islands. It is a majority Christian country (97%), and its largest denomination is the Niue Christian Church, a Congregational denomination that emerged from the London Missionary Society. The church's establishment is traced to an indigenous Niuean in 1846 who trained in a missionary school in Samoa; there were no resident European missionaries on the island for the next 20 years. There is a branch of the Niue Christian Church in New Zealand to minister to the large community of Niueans there. The Federation of Christian Women plays an active role in the church and includes women from many denominations.

Facts to Consider

- One of the biggest challenges facing the country is emigration, primarily to New Zealand, for employment. The Niue Christian Church has tried to work with the government to discourage emigration as they see churches decline. It is often stated that Niue's largest export is its people.
- Introduced in 1952, the Church of Jesus Christ of Latter-day Saints is the second largest denomination on the island.

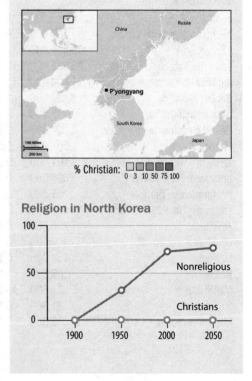

% Christian: 0 3 10 50 75 100

Religion in Niue

Christianity in North Korea

Christianity has a long history in North Korea, from Catholic missionaries in the 1840s to the Pyongyang and Wonsan revivals in 1907. But the establishment of the Communist government in 1948 led to the confiscation of church buildings, imprisonment of Christian leaders, and massacres of Christians. There is very little information on Christianity's current state in the "Hermit Kingdom." There is believed to be a growing number of new Christians resulting from work by North Koreans who have become Christians in China and returned to share the faith. Gathering in groups is extremely dangerous.

Facts to Consider

- The Communist government formed the Chosun (Korean) Christian Federation in 1946, and it has 10,000 members. It is under government supervision and oversees the two official Protestant churches: Bongsu Church and Chilgol Church in Pyongyang.
- Most Christians gather in homes for worship; there could be over 500 house churches in the country.
- The vast majority (upwards of 85%) of defectors who escape North Korea for South Korea are women. Many escaped women end up as trafficked sex workers or in arranged marriages in China.

% Christian: 0 3 10 50 75 100

Religion in North Korea

Christianity in North Macedonia

Located in southeast Europe, North Macedonia is a land-locked country bordering Kosovo, Serbia, Bulgaria, Greece, and Albania. It was part of Yugoslavia until its breakup in 1991. Christianity has been present in this region since the journeys of the apostle Paul in the 1st century. In the New Testament, Lydia of Thyatira was the first Macedonian to become a Christian. Eastern Orthodoxy spread throughout the region, and most of the population is still Orthodox today (63%). The Macedonian Orthodox Church was under the authority of the Serbian Orthodox Church until 1943, after which it became independent. The Macedonian Orthodox Church has roughly 2,000 churches, monasteries, chapels, and other religious facilities in the country.

Facts to Consider

- The government favors the Macedonian Orthodox Church, while smaller religious groups face discrimination and intimidation.
- One of the most popular tourist destinations is the Church of St. John at Kaneo, overlooking Lake Ohrid. It is dedicated to John of Patmos, the author of the book of Revelation.
- After Orthodox and Catholics, the largest denomination is the Jehovah's Witnesses, with 3,300 members. It gained legal recognition from the government in 2014.
- Ethnic and religious tensions exist between ethnic Macedonians and ethnic Albanians, ranging from physical attacks to the burning of churches.
- Only around 200 Jews are left in North Macedonia after nearly the entire population was killed in the Holocaust. Over 7,000 were deported to the Treblinka death camp in Poland.

Indicators & Demographic Data

Population (2020)	2,088,000
% under 15 years	16%
Capital city (pop.)	Skopje 595,000
% urban dwellers	58% (0.61% p.a.)
Official language	Macedonian
Largest language	Macedonian (56%)
Largest people	Macedonian (56%)
Largest culture	Macedonian (56%)
Development	76
Physicians	29
Gender gap	5%

% Christian: ☐☐☐▨▨▨ 0 3 10 50 75 100

Christian Traditions in North Macedonia

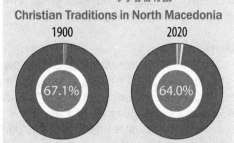

1900 — 67.1%   2020 — 64.0%

☐Independent ☐Protestant ▨Catholic ▨Orthodox ▨Christian

Christians in 1900 were majority Orthodox (99% of Christians), with a very small population of Catholics (1%). This was largely the same in 2020, though there has been an increase of Protestants and Independents (together 2% of Christians).

Religion in North Macedonia

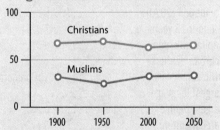

Historically a majority Christian country, North Macedonia has had a large Muslim minority (67% Christian and 32% Muslim in 1900). In 2020, the country was 64% Christian and 33% Muslim.

Bible Translations		Churches		Missionaries		Gospel Access	
Languages	20	Denominations	65	Received	170	1900	Very high
Full Bible	14	Congregations	1,500	Sent	60	2020	Very high

Christianity in the Northern Mariana Islands

The Northern Mariana Islands is a commonwealth of the United States consisting of 14 islands in the northwestern Pacific Ocean. The Chamorro people emigrated from Malaysia, the Philippines, and other Pacific Islands before the islands came under Spanish rule in the 14th century. They were ruled by Germany, Japan, and then the United States during World War II. The islands are majority Christian, mostly Catholic. There are large ethnic churches of Filipino Baptists (2,500 members) and Korean Presbyterians (1,500 members). The largest Protestant group is the United Church of Christ, with 2,200 members.

Facts to Consider

- Citizens of the Northern Mariana Islands also have citizenship in the United States, including birthright citizenship for people born in the islands. However, citizens do not vote in US presidential elections.
- The islands are ethnically and linguistically diverse. The largest languages are Tagalog (due to the large Filipino presence), Chinese, Chamorro, Carolinian, and Tanapag.
- Historic Japanese occupation (1919–1945) and the large Chinese migrant worker population has meant a large Buddhist presence in the islands, 13% in 2020. Around 800,000 Japanese tourists visit the islands every year.
- During the COVID-19 pandemic, the number of foreign workers fell 73% due to travel restrictions and business closures. Foreigners account for roughly half of all workers in the commonwealth.

Indicators & Demographic Data

Population (2020)	55,300
% under 15 years	24%
Capital city (pop.)	Saipan 50,200
% urban dwellers	92% (0.36% p.a.)
Official language	Chamorro, Carolinian, English
Largest language	Tagalog (28%)
Largest people	Filipino (28%)
Largest culture	Tagalog (28%)
Development	65
Physicians	3.5
Gender gap	13%

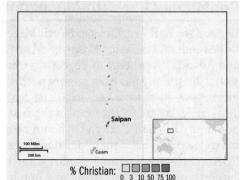

% Christian: 0 3 10 50 75 100

Christian Traditions in the Northern Mariana Islands

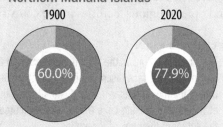

1900 — 60.0% 2020 — 77.9%

☐ Independent ☐ Protestant ■ Catholic ■ Orthodox ■ Christian

Christianity in 1900 was mostly Catholic (83% of Christians). In 2020, Christianity was much more diverse; still majority Catholic, the islands are now home to many more Protestants and Independents.

Religion in the Northern Mariana Islands

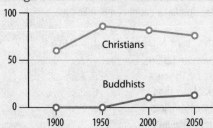

The Northern Mariana Islands were 60% Christian and 40% traditional religionist in 1900. By 2020, most of the population was Christian (78%), followed by Buddhists (13%) and Chinese folk religionists (6%).

Bible Translations		Churches		Missionaries		Gospel Access	
Languages	12	Denominations	26	Received	140	1900	High
Full Bible	7	Congregations	74	Sent	5	2020	Very high

Christianity in Norway

Norway became Christian during the Scandinavian Viking Age from the 8th to 11th centuries. Norwegian Vikings encountered Christianity through their raids, trade, and attempted colonization of Ireland and the British Isles. Norwegian kings became Christian and so did their subjects, often by force. Lutheranism was the state church from 1536 to its disestablishment in 2012. The Norwegian constitution was amended to separate the government from the Church of Norway, which is still the largest denomination, with 3.7 million members. Despite most of the population being members of the church, Norway is a secular society, and many do not practice Christianity or hold to its core beliefs.

Facts to Consider

- The Norwegian Christian Student and School Association is the largest organization working in secondary schools, high schools, and universities, with around 4,000 members.
- Nearly 15% of Norway's population is foreign-born, from over 200 countries. The largest groups are workers from Eastern Europe and the European Union; most of the non-Europeans are from Pakistan.
- The Council for Religious and Life Stance Communities was established in 1996 and has engaged in Christian-Humanist dialogues and works toward equality among religious and life stance groups.
- The Norwegian Humanist Association reports 94,000 members, making it the largest life stance organization in the country. It is an organization for people who base their ethics on human, not religious, values.
- Anti-Semitism and anti-Muslim rhetoric are prevalent among far-right and far-left groups, especially in online chat rooms and social media sites.

Indicators & Demographic Data

Population (2020). 5,450,000
% under 15 years 18%
Capital city (pop.) . . . . Oslo 1,041,000
% urban dwellers. . . . . .83% (1.32% p.a.)
Official language. . . . . Norwegian, Saami
Largest language. . . . . Norwegian (89%)
Largest people . . . . Norwegian (Dano-Norwegian) (64%)
Largest culture . . . . Norwegian (88%)
Development. 95
Physicians. 44
Gender gap. 1%

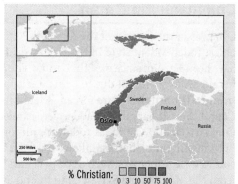

% Christian: 0 3 10 50 75 100

Christian Traditions in Norway

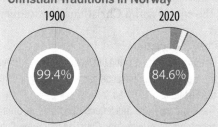

1900 — 99.4%
2020 — 84.6%

☐Independent ☐Protestant ▨Catholic ■Orthodox ■Christian

Nearly the entire population was Protestant in 1900. Christianity was slightly more diverse in 2020, with proportional growth of Catholic (4% of Christians), Independent (2%), and Orthodox (<1%) churches.

Religion in Norway

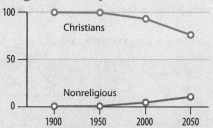

Norway has historically been a Christian country, though the Christian share of the population declined from 99% in 1900 to 85% in 2020. The nonreligious grew from less than 1% in 1900 to 8% in 2020, though is likely much higher.

Bible Translations		Churches		Missionaries		Gospel Access	
Languages.	44	Denominations	110	Received.	800	1900	Very high
Full Bible.	35	Congregations	3,100	Sent	1,000	2020	Very high

Christianity in Oman

Oman is in the far east of the Arabian Peninsula and is the oldest independent state in the Arab world. Its inhabitants have been Muslim since the 7th century. The Portuguese lived in and around Muscat due to its strategic location for trade from 1507 until they were forced to leave in 1650. The first Catholic missionary in the modern era came to Aden in 1841. Oman's 120,000 Catholics today are all foreigners, mostly Filipino migrant laborers. Likewise, all the Orthodox in the country are foreigners, such as Copts from Egypt and those from the Mar Thoma Syrian Church and Syrian Church of the East from South India. Christianity has little influence in the country, and Christians face many restrictions.

Facts to Consider

- Islam is the state religion of Oman, and it is assumed all Omani citizens are Muslim. The penal code has a maximum prison sentence of 10 years for "insulting the Qur'an."
- There are very few indigenous Christians in Oman, and it is illegal to openly preach or distribute Christian literature. Converts face significant pressure to return to Islam, especially in rural areas. Nonregistered groups are allowed to worship freely, though privately, in their homes.
- The Protestant Church in Oman is a partnership between the Reformed Church of America and the Anglican Church. They meet on two campuses in Muscat and in a church in Sohar. There are English, Arabic, Filipino, and Korean-speaking congregations.
- The Pentecostal Assembly in Muscat is the largest Malayali (from India) Pentecostal group in the Middle East, with over 1,000 affiliates. Services are held in English, Hindi, Tamil, and Malayalam.

Indicators & Demographic Data

Population (2020). 5,150,000
% under 15 years 21%
Capital city (pop.) . . . . Muscat 1,550,000
% urban dwellers. . . . . .86% (2.32% p.a.)
Official language. . . . . Arabic
Largest language. . . . . Arabic (64%)
Largest people . . . . Omani Arab (46%)
Largest culture . . . . Arab (Arabic) (59%)
Development. 82
Physicians. 19
Gender gap. 6%

% Christian: 0 3 10 50 75 100

Christian Traditions in Oman

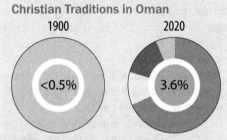

1900   2020

<0.5%   3.6%

☐ Independent ☐ Protestant ■ Catholic ■ Orthodox ■ Christian

There were very few Christians in Oman in 1900. The small community in 2020 was mostly Catholic (68%), though with Orthodox (14%) and Independent (11%) minorities. Some Protestants are Evangelical or Pentecostal/Charismatic.

Religion in Oman

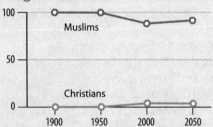

Oman is historically a Muslim country, though the Muslim share of the population declined from 100% in 1900 to 90% in 2020. In 2020, Hindus were 5% and Christians were 4% of the population.

Bible Translations		Churches		Missionaries		Gospel Access	
Languages.	27	Denominations . . .	37	Received.	40	1900	Very low
Full Bible.	13	Congregations. . . .	390	Sent	2	2020	Medium

Christianity in Pakistan

The region of Pakistan was part of numerous empires throughout history, most recently as part of the British India Empire until its partition from India and independence in 1947. Pakistan was formed as a homeland for Muslims of British India and today is one of the largest Muslim-majority countries in the world, with over 200 million Muslim citizens. Many Pakistani Christians believe the apostle Thomas introduced Christianity to the Indian subcontinent in the 1st century. Churches work primarily among the Punjabis and 83% of Christians are from this ethnic group, having converted from low-caste Hinduism. The largest denomination is the Church of Pakistan (1.4 million members), which is a 1970 merger of Anglicans, Methodists, Lutherans, and Sialkot Presbyterians.

Facts to Consider

- Islam has been the state religion in Pakistan (meaning "land of the pure") since 1956. The constitution technically provides the right to religious freedom, but neither the government nor society practice this freedom. Punishments include the death sentence for "defiling the Prophet Muhammad," life imprisonment for "defiling, damaging, or desecrating the Qur'an," and 10 years imprisonment for "insulting one another's religious feelings."
- Life is dangerous for Christians, who are considered second-class citizens. Christians are often accused of blasphemy as a threat to settle family disputes. There is minimal Christian representation in the government.
- Many Protestant churches have Pakistani leadership. Catholics have made significant contributions to national education, health services, and religious peace building.

Indicators & Demographic Data

Population (2020)	208,362,000
% under 15 years	34%
Capital city (pop.)	Islamabad 1,129,000
% urban dwellers	37% (2.51% p.a.)
Official language	English, Urdu
Largest language	Lahnda (54%)
Largest people	Western Punjabi (Lahnda) (40%)
Largest culture	Punjabi (54%)
Development	56
Physicians	9.8
Gender gap	25%

% Christian: 0 3 10 50 75 100

Christian Traditions in Pakistan

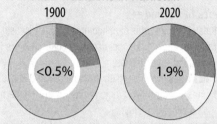

1900   2020

<0.5%   1.9%

☐Independent ☐Protestant ◼Catholic ◼Orthodox ◼Christian

In 1900, most Christians in Pakistan were Protestant (78% of Christians), followed by a sizable Catholic minority (22%). In 2020, Christians were still majority Protestant (58%), followed by Catholics (27%) and Independents (15%).

Religion in Pakistan

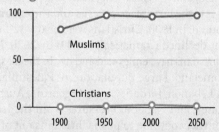

Pakistan is historically a Muslim country, and the Muslim share of the population has increased from 82% in 1900 to 96% in 2020. The second largest religion in 2020 was Hinduism, at 1% of the population.

Bible Translations		Churches		Missionaries		Gospel Access	
Languages	87	Denominations	90	Received	1,200	1900	Very low
Full Bible	17	Congregations	13,900	Sent	60	2020	Medium

Christianity in Palau

Palau is a nation comprised of around 340 islands in the Pacific Ocean. The islands were under control of Spain, Germany, the Philippines, Japan, and the United States before independence in 1981. The first map of Palau, drawn by a Czech Jesuit priest in 1696, sparked several failed Jesuit expeditions to the islands where locals killed and cannibalized some Jesuits. The first Protestants arrived in 1921. Christianity grew rapidly in the 20th century. Today the country is 92% Christian. The Catholic Church is the largest denomination, followed by the nondenominational Koror Evangelical Church.

Facts to Consider

- Palau has high rates of noncommunicable diseases, attributable to high rates of drug and alcohol use. Many churches are involved in ministries to combat these issues.
- Palau's sea level has risen dramatically in the last 30 years. With some homes flooding every day, residents are concerned about continued global climate change.
- The Modekngei movement began in 1921 as a syncretistic religion of Christianity and traditional Palauan beliefs. The United States government banned it in 1945, but it later took on more explicit Christian symbolism and was accepted as a mainstream Christian faith.

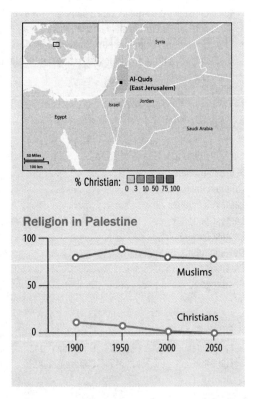

% Christian: 0 3 10 50 75 100

Religion in Palau

Christianity in Palestine

Palestine, defined here as the West Bank (including East Jerusalem) and the Gaza Strip, has a long history with Christianity, as it is the birthplace of Jesus and the expansion of the early church. In 1900, Christians were nearly 12% of the population but declined dramatically to 1% by 2020. Most Palestinian Christians have emigrated and live in the diaspora outside their homeland. Large populations of Palestinian Christians live in Lebanon, Jordan, Chile, Argentina, Australia, the United States, and Canada. Pressures from the Israeli-Palestinian conflict continue to push Christians out of the territory.

Facts to Consider

- Basic Law states that Islam is the official religion, makes Sharia law the main source of legislation, and criminalizes anything that insults the "religious feelings" of others.
- Palestinian Christians often see themselves first as Arab Palestinians and second as Christian. Christians are increasingly marginalized in society despite their shared identity with Arab Muslims.
- About 81% of Palestinians are Sunni Muslims, and the Gaza Strip is almost entirely Muslim.
- Though an estimated 427,000 Jewish Israelis live in the Israeli settlements in the West Bank, they are in violation of international law.

% Christian: 0 3 10 50 75 100

Religion in Palestine

Christianity in Panama

The indigenous inhabitants of Panama at the time of Spanish arrival in the 16th century were Cuevas and Coclé tribes. They were wiped out by foreign diseases. The region came under Spanish rule in 1538. Catholicism became the official religion when Panama joined Colombia in 1832, but Panama achieved independence from Colombia in 1904 and disestablished the Catholic Church. Still, Catholicism has had a tremendous impact on Panamanian culture. West Indian Protestants (Methodists) arrived in 1815 and Protestantism increased via immigration from the Caribbean. Many American denominations arrived after independence. Seventh-day Adventists, the largest Protestant denomination due to evangelism and institution building, is largely indigenous. Panama was 90% Christian in 2020.

Facts to Consider

- Though Catholicism is not the state religion, the constitution states that it is the religion of most citizens. Public schools are required to provide instruction on Catholic teachings, though parents can exempt their children.
- Panama has one of the highest rates of teen pregnancy in the world. Girls with only a primary education or no education at all are four times as likely to get pregnant at a young age.
- Pentecostalism grew rapidly in the 20th century, with groups like the Assemblies of God and the International Church of the Foursquare Gospel.
- Islam grew in Panama with the arrival of immigrants from Lebanon, Palestine, India, and Pakistan. Some locals have converted, and a Panamanian mosque was built in 2016. Muslims make up 1% of the population and they live primarily in Panama City, Colón, and Penonomé.

Indicators & Demographic Data

Population (2020)	4,289,000
% under 15 years	27%
Capital city (pop.)	Panama City 1,860,000
% urban dwellers	68% (1.92% p.a.)
Official language	Spanish
Largest language	Spanish (68%)
Largest people	Panamanian Mestizo (59%)
Largest culture	Mestizo (Spanish) (59%)
Development	79
Physicians	16
Gender gap	1%

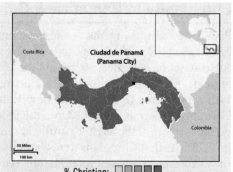

% Christian: 0 3 10 50 75 100

Christian Traditions in Panama

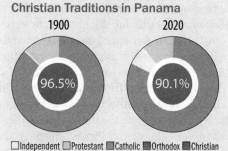

1900 — 96.5% 2020 — 90.1%

☐ Independent ☐ Protestant ☐ Catholic ▨ Orthodox ■ Christian

In 1900, most Christians in Panama were Catholic (87% of Christians), followed by Protestants (13%). In 2020, Christians were still majority Catholic (82%), but with many more Independents and Protestants (together 18%).

Religion in Panama

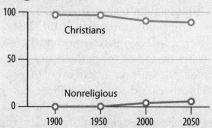

Panama is historically a Christian country, though the Christian share of the population decreased from 97% in 1900 to 90% in 2020. The second largest religion in 2020 were the nonreligious, with 4.5% of the population.

Bible Translations		Churches		Missionaries		Gospel Access	
Languages	23	Denominations	120	Received	2,000	1900	Very high
Full Bible	12	Congregations	4,400	Sent	700	2020	Very high

Christianity in Papua New Guinea

Papua New Guinea is one of the most culturally diverse countries in the world. Indigenous peoples from Africa and Australasia have settled the region for tens of thousands of years. Virtually undisturbed by Europeans until the 19th century, the country has a complicated history, with Germany, Australia, and the United Kingdom colonizing various sectors of the territory until national independence in 1975. The first Christians were Catholic in 1847, and the first Protestants arrived in 1871. The region was known for head-hunting and ritual cannibalism, which existed in some isolated communities until as recently as the 1970s. Missionary deaths due to cannibalism were common. Papua New Guinea experienced one of the most dramatic changes in its religious affiliation in the 20th century, growing from 4% Christian in 1900 to 95% in 2020. Catholics and Protestants differed over the church's relationship to traditional religion. While Catholics were generally more willing to keep traditional rituals and translate them into Christian ceremonies, the stricter Protestants purged anything related to traditional worship or practices. Today several indigenous churches in the country embrace the development of indigenous theology.

The Catholic Church is the largest denomination in the country, with 2.1 million members. It initially grew slowly but was strengthened with the development of base Christian communities that encouraged laity's participation in church life. The first Papuan priest, ordained in 1937, became the first Papuan bishop in 1970. The country received its first indigenous cardinal in 2016. Most church services are delivered in Tok Pisin. However, there is a huge shortage of Catholic personnel in the country to serve the population despite the presence of over 500 priests and more than 170 brothers and 800 sisters. Protestant missionaries from the United Kingdom, Australia, the Cook Islands, and New Zealand helped establish different streams of Protestantism in Papua New Guinea. Some of the largest denominations today are Lutherans, Assemblies of God, and Seventh-day Adventists. Both Catholics and Protestants operate numerous schools and colleges throughout the country. Many denominations also send missionaries abroad.

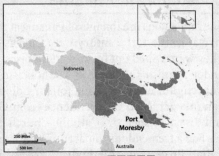

% Christian: 0 3 10 50 75 100

Religion in Papua New Guinea

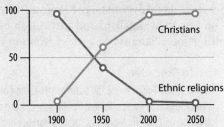

Papua New Guinea experienced a massive transformation of its religious makeup over the 20th century, perhaps more than any other country in the world. In 1900, the country was 96% followers of traditional religions and just 4% Christian. This essentially reversed by 2020. Papua New Guinea was 95% Christian and 3% traditional religionist in 2020.

Indicators & Demographic Data

Population (2020). 8,756,000
% under 15 years 35%
Capital city (pop.) . . . . . Port Moresby 383,000
% urban dwellers. . . . . 13% (2.91% p.a.)
Official language. . English, Hiru Motu, Tok Pisin
Largest language. . . . . .Tok Pisin (13%)
Largest people . . . . Detribalized (10%)
Largest culture . . . . New Guinea Papuan (63%)
Development. 54
Physicians. 0.6
Gender gap 16%

Bible Translations	Churches	Missionaries	Gospel Access
Languages. 825	Denominations 130	Received. 3,600	1900 . . . . Very low
Full Bible. 22	Congregations. 23,200	Sent 130	2020 . . . . Very high

Facts to Consider

- Even though most of the population is now Christian, witchcraft is still a major problem for churches in Papua New Guinea. Witch hunts are common, and women are accused of witchcraft far more frequently than men, sometimes suffering violence or death as a result.
- Violence against women is endemic, and the majority of women have experienced gender-based violence at some point in their lives. NGOs and some missionaries are working to protect women and educate others on the consequences of violence. Though grassroots activism is bringing attention to this issue, there is a need for more women's medical clinics.
- Climate change is a pressing issue for Papua New Guinea. With rising sea levels, the Carteret Islands were deemed uninhabitable in 2015, and its inhabitants became the first environmental refugees in the world. Church leaders try to educate people on the importance of conservation efforts.
- In 2020, the National Executive Council approved a proposal to amend the country's constitution to formally make Papua New Guinea a Christian country. Consultations on the issue are on hold, and there has been pushback against the notion of unifying church and state.
- Traditional ethnic religions are followed exclusively by a small portion of the population, but their influence continues among Christians.

Christian Traditions in Papua New Guinea

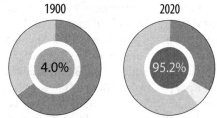

□ Independent □ Protestant ■ Catholic ■ Orthodox ■ Christian

The Christian community in Papua New Guinea in 1900 (around 47,000 Christians) was majority Catholic (65% of Christians), followed by Protestants (35%). Most of those Protestants were Evangelicals due to missionaries in the region. In 2020, Christianity in Papua New Guinea was much more diverse, with almost twice as many Protestants (61% of Christians) as Catholics (33%) and with a large population of Independent Christians (6%), many of which are indigenous to the country. Evangelicals and Pentecostals have also grown rapidly.

Christian Families in Papua New Guinea

Family	Population 2020	%	Trend	Change
*Evangelicals	2,300,000	26.3	↑	2.5
Latin-rite Catholic	2,300,000	26.3	↑	2.2
*Pentecostals/Charismatics	1,950,000	22.3	↑	3.0
Lutheran	1,162,000	13.3	↑	0.8
United church or joint mission	628,000	7.2	–	0.1
Adventist	331,000	3.8	↓	-0.7
Anglican	221,000	2.5	↑	1.2
Nondenominational	202,000	2.3	↑	1.0
Baptist	200,000	2.3	↑	1.0
Holiness	127,000	1.4	↑	1.5
Restorationist, Disciple	43,900	0.5	↑	2.2
Latter-day Saints (Mormons)	33,900	0.4	↑↑	6.3
Christian Brethren	22,400	0.3	↑	1.5
Salvationist	22,300	0.3	↑	4.1
Jehovah's Witnesses	13,900	0.2	↓	-1.6
Eastern Orthodox	400	<0.1	↑	1.1

Christianity in Papua New Guinea is diverse. There are roughly the same number of Evangelicals in the country as there are Catholics, both with 25% of the population. Evangelicals are found throughout a wide variety of denominations, ranging from historic groups such as Evangelical Lutherans (nearly 1 million members) to Pentecostal groups like the Assemblies of God (560,000) and the International Church of the Foursquare Gospel (280,000). The third largest family, Pentecostals/Charismatics, include, in order of size, the Assemblies of God, Foursquare Gospel, Christian Revival Crusade, New Apostolic Church, and United Pentecostal Church, all of which were introduced to the country in the 20th century via missionaries, mostly from Australia. Lutheran churches grew with missionary assistance from Europe, Australia, and the United States.

* These movements are found within Christian families	↑↑ extreme growth
	↑ growth
	↓↓ extreme decline
– no change	↓ decline

Christianity in Paraguay

The indigenous tribes of Paraguay included the agricultural Guaraní people to the east of the Paraguay River and nomadic peoples to the west. The Spanish arrived in 1516 and established Asunción in 1537; colonization continued until official independence in 1842. Paraguay lost terribly in the War of the Triple Alliance (1864–1870) against Argentina, Brazil, and Uruguay, where half the country's population died, mostly young men. In a visit from Pope Francis in 2015, he praised Paraguayan women for rebuilding the country after the war. Paraguay had more than 30 presidents in the 20th century, a civil war in 1947, and a 35-year-long dictatorship under Alfredo Stroessner until 1989. Democracy was established in 1992. With Catholicism the state religion of Paraguay until 1992, there was significant tension between the church and these unstable governments in the 19th and 20th centuries. After 1992, Protestant churches have experienced some growth, albeit slowly.

Jesuits were extremely active in bringing Catholicism, education, and written language to the Guaraní people starting in the mid-16th century. Even today, 93% percent of the population are members of the Catholic Church, and more people are mother tongue speakers of Guaraní than Spanish. According to surveys, Mass attendance is around 29% and daily prayer among Catholics at 82%. Popular Catholicism, traditionally a blend of Catholicism and pre-Columbian religions, is present among lower-class and lower-educated people.

The American Bible Society was the first Protestant organization in Paraguay (1856). Protestantism struggled to grow under Stroessner's rule, but today there are small communities of Baptists, Mennonites, Anglicans, and Pentecostals. The People of God (El Pueblo de Dios) movement began in 1963 as a communitarian, agrarian group of Christians who experienced the baptism of the Holy Spirit in 1940 and is the third largest denomination today. Though Pentecostalism was slow to grow in Paraguay—facing competition from Catholics, Latter-day Saints, and Jehovah's Witnesses—many historic churches have adopted charismatic worship styles. Initially unpopular, the Catholic Charismatic movement is the smallest in Latin America, which the Catholic hierarchy tolerates for its helping reduce the number of converts to Protestantism.

% Christian: ▢▢▢▢▢ 0 3 10 50 75 100

Religion in Paraguay

Paraguay's religious makeup changed very little in the 20th century. In 1900, the country was 97% Christian and 3% followers of traditional religions. By 2020, Christians had dropped only slightly to 95% and traditional religions to 2%. The nonreligious grew from virtually zero to 2% of the population. There are also small communities of Buddhists, Baha'is, and Muslims.

Indicators & Demographic Data

Population (2020)	7,066,000
% under 15 years	29%
Capital city (pop.)	Asunción 3,337,000
% urban dwellers	62% (1.64% p.a.)
Official language	Spanish, Guarani
Largest language	Guarani (86%)
Largest people	Paraguayan Mestizo (83%)
Largest culture	Lowland Amerindian (85%)
Development	70
Physicians	13
Gender gap	3%

Bible Translations		Churches		Missionaries		Gospel Access	
Languages	35	Denominations	120	Received	1,400	1900	Very high
Full Bible	21	Congregations	3,300	Sent	500	2020	Very high

Facts to Consider

- Exclusive adherence to traditional ethnic religions is rare in Paraguay, but a report found that 26% of Catholics and 21% of Protestants also engaged with some indigenous beliefs and practices, including witchcraft, sorcery, communicating with spirits, and consulting traditional healers.
- Jehovah's Witnesses number around 11,000. Their view that it is against God's will to receive blood transfusions has resulted in lawsuits against the government for refusing their "right to bodily self-determination." These cases mostly involved parents refusing transfusions for their children, who were given blood against their will.
- The Vice Ministry of Worship has recorded around 350 officially registered missionaries in the country, most of them members of the Church of Jesus Christ of Latter-day Saints. Nonregistered missionaries may enter the country on tourist visas.
- There could be upward of 10,000 Muslims in Paraguay, mostly concentrated in Ciudad del Este. There are Lebanese Muslims in Alto Parana and around the tri-border point between Brazil, Paraguay, and Argentina, where a mosque was built in 1983.

Christian Traditions in Paraguay

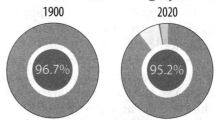

□Independent □Protestant ■Catholic ■Orthodox ■Christian

The Christian community in Paraguay in 1900 (nearly the entire population) was Catholic. This gradually shifted in the 20th century with the introduction of different Protestant groups from abroad. In 2020, Christianity in Paraguay was slightly more diverse. Catholics were still the majority (89% of Christians), but Protestants grew to 200,000, and Independents surged to over half a million (together, 10% of Christians).

Christian Families in Paraguay

Family	Population 2020	%	Trend	Change
Latin-rite Catholic	6,237,000	88.3	↑	1.1
*Pentecostals/Charismatics	560,000	7.9	↑	0.6
Non-traditional, house, cell	255,000	3.6	↑	2.2
*Evangelicals	185,000	2.6	↓	-1.3
Latter-day Saints (Mormons)	104,000	1.5	↑	2.5
Baptist	49,700	0.7	↑↑	5.6
Mennonite	35,700	0.5	↑	1.6
Eastern Orthodox	32,600	0.5	↑	2.1
Anglican	24,300	0.3	↑	3.1
Jehovah's Witnesses	21,300	0.3	↑	2.1
United church or joint mission	14,600	0.2	↑	1.2
Adventist	13,700	0.2	↓	-2.3
Lutheran	7,200	0.1	↑	0.9
Christian Brethren	6,500	0.1	↑	1.6
Reformed, Presbyterian	5,000	0.1	↑	2.3
Restorationist, Disciple	4,800	0.1	↑	3.0
Congregational	4,500	0.1	↑	4.1
Holiness	3,600	0.1	↑	2.7
Methodist	2,800	<0.1	—	-0.1
Nondenominational	1,300	<0.1	↓	-1.9

The Catholic Church in Paraguay is by far the largest Christian family, representing 88% of the country's population and 93% of Christians. Other Christian families exist but are much smaller. Pentecostals/Charismatics are the second largest family, with almost 8% of the population. Nevertheless, Paraguay has one of the lowest percentages of Pentecostal/Charismatics of Christians in all of Latin America (8% of Christians are Pentecostal/Charismatic, compared with, for example, neighboring Brazil at 55%). The largest of these churches are the Pentecostal Church of Chile and the Evangelical Missionary Assemblies of God Church. Paraguay is unique compared with other Latin American countries in its large population of Christians who form house churches in the Pentecostal People of God (El Pueblo de Dios) movement. The Church of Jesus Christ of Latter-day Saints is the third largest denomination, and the Temple in Asunción was completed in 2002.

* These movements are found within Christian families	↑↑ extreme growth
	↑ growth
	↓↓ extreme decline
— no change	↓ decline

Christianity in Peru

With its capital in Cusco, the Inca Empire was the largest empire in pre-Columbian America. The empire was weakened by a war of succession as well as by infectious diseases spreading from Central America at the time of the Spanish arrival in 1532. The Spanish conquered the last Inca stronghold and forced the indigenous population to accept Christianity. This initial conversion was superficial, and traditional religious practices continued, cloaked by Catholic symbols. Peru declared independence in 1821 under the leadership of Simón Bolívar, and Catholicism was named the state religion in 1845. In the 20th century, a series of unstable presidents and dictators led the country, resulting in widespread human rights violations, terrorist campaigns, and economic troubles. Since 2000, Peru has been fighting political corruption and instability.

In 2020, 86% of the population was Catholic, and the Catholic Church has had significant influence in society. It receives preferential treatment in education in public schools where Catholicism is the only religion taught, and Catholic symbols are found throughout society, including in governmental buildings. The Catholic Charismatic Movement also swept through the country in the 1960s.

The first Protestants in Peru were Bible translators in 1822. Various missions entered in the 19th and 20th centuries. Arriving in 1898, Seventh-day Adventists made many converts among the Aymara people and today make up the largest Protestant church in the country. Adventists are extremely active in education and run the second largest Adventist university in the world, Peruvian Union University (established in 1919). Pentecostalism grew rapidly in the 20th century after the arrival of Assemblies of God missionaries from the United States in 1919. Roughly 70% of all Pentecostal churches in Peru trace their origins to the original American missionaries and the groups that separated from them. There is a great diversity of Pentecostal/Charismatic churches, from Classical Pentecostals to a neo-Pentecostal movement that is much closer to Catholicism in practice. The growth of these churches has been at the expense of Catholicism.

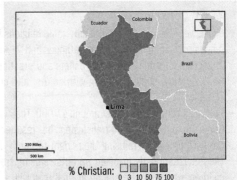

% Christian: 0 3 10 50 75 100

Religion in Peru

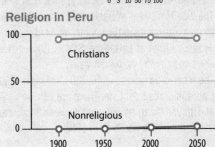

Peru's religious makeup changed very little in the 20th century. In 1900, the country was 95% Christian and 5% followers of traditional religions. By 2020, Christians had grown slightly to 97% and traditional religions declined to 1%. The nonreligious grew from virtually zero to 2% of the population. There are also small communities of Buddhists and Baha'is.

Indicators & Demographic Data

Population (2020)	33,312,000
% under 15 years	27%
Capital city (pop.)	Lima 10,719,000
% urban dwellers	78% (1.33% p.a.)
Official language	Spanish, Quechua, Aymara
Largest language	Spanish (75%)
Largest people	Peruvian Mestizo (30%)
Largest culture	Quechua (50%)
Development	75
Physicians	11
Gender gap	5%

Bible Translations		Churches		Missionaries		Gospel Access	
Languages	97	Denominations	150	Received	7,000	1900	Very high
Full Bible	13	Congregations	26,400	Sent	1,000	2020	Very high

Facts to Consider

- Peru has become a major destination for displaced Venezuelans—over 1 million, with 80% settling in Lima. This has stressed Peru's health care, housing, and labor systems, especially with the loss of jobs during the COVID-19 pandemic. Xenophobic attitudes have increased.
- Women suffer many disadvantages in Peruvian society, including higher rates of illiteracy (especially in rural areas), disproportionate poverty, and higher rates of unemployment. Much of this is due to traditional views about women's roles.
- Violence against women is a longstanding problem, with an average of five women reported missing every day. Female disappearances rose significantly during the COVID-19 pandemic, and the number of calls to a national hotline for victims of domestic and sexual violence also skyrocketed.
- Many people in rural areas have converted to Christianity through Christian radio programming such as Radio Pacífico, Abba Christian Radio, and Radio Fiel y Verdadero (Faithful and True).
- Some indigenous peoples, including the Chayahuita, practice traditional ethnic religions, usually in combination with Catholic practices.
- The Jewish and Muslim populations in Peru are small, but these communities report discrimination, such as the spread of anti-Semitic conspiracy theories and employers' refusal of vacation leave to observe religious holidays.

Christian Traditions in Peru

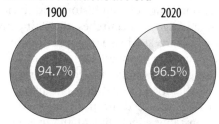

1900   2020

94.7%   96.5%

□Independent □Protestant ■Catholic ■Orthodox ■Christian

The Christian community in Peru in 1900 (nearly the entire population) was majority Catholic. This gradually shifted in the 20th century with the introduction of different Protestant groups from abroad. In 2020, Christianity in Peru was slightly more diverse, with Catholics by far still the majority (87% of Christians), but with Protestants growing to 1.8 million and Independents surging to 2.2 million (together, 13% of Christians).

Christian Families in Peru

Family	Population 2020	%	Trend	Change
Latin-rite Catholic	28,200,000	84.7	↑	1.0
*Pentecostals/Charismatics	4,300,000	12.9	↑	1.2
*Evangelicals	1,350,000	4.1	↑	1.0
Adventist	899,000	2.7	–	0.3
Latter-day Saints (Mormons)	680,000	2.0	↑	3.3
Jehovah's Witnesses	332,000	1.0	↑	1.7
Reformed, Presbyterian	259,000	0.8	↑	0.6
Non-traditional, house, cell	212,000	0.6	↑	1.7
Holiness	187,000	0.6	–	-0.4
Baptist	104,000	0.3	↑	2.5
Christian Brethren	57,000	0.2	↑↑	5.0
Nondenominational	43,400	0.1	↑	3.1
Methodist	38,800	0.1	↑	2.6
Congregational	30,700	0.1	↑	3.6
Restorationist, Disciple	17,700	0.1	↑	2.7
Eastern Orthodox	7,600	<0.1	↑	2.4
Friends (Quaker)	6,800	<0.1	↑	3.2
Mennonite	6,800	<0.1	↑	3.2
Lutheran	4,200	<0.1	↑	1.9
Salvationist	3,800	<0.1	↑	1.9
Anglican	2,300	<0.1	↑	1.3

The Catholic Church in Peru is by far the largest Christian family, representing 85% of the country's population. While other Christian families exist, they are comparatively much smaller. Pentecostals/Charismatics are the second largest family, with almost 13% of the population. The largest of these churches are the Assemblies of God (357,000) and the Evangelical American Indigenous Churches (120,000). Evangelicals are also found throughout many historic Protestant churches such as Seventh-day Adventists and the Peruvian Evangelical Church. There are two large Adventist denominations in Peru: Seventh-day Adventists and a breakaway group, Evangelical Israelite Church of the New Covenant established in the 1950s. The Church of Jesus Christ of Latter-day Saints is the second largest denomination, with over half a million members, and the Jehovah's Witnesses have over 300,000 members.

* These movements are found within Christian families
– no change

↑↑ extreme growth
↑ growth
↓↓ extreme decline
↓ decline

Christianity in the Philippines

With its long colonial history and the founding of several large indigenous churches, the Philippines is home to the second largest Christian population in Asia (after China). The Spanish conquest of the islands began in 1565. Later, numerous Catholic missionary orders arrived to spread Christianity. The sale of the Philippines to the United States in 1898 catalyzed the arrival of many Protestant mission organizations, including Methodists, Presbyterians, Episcopalians, and Baptists. During World War II, Japan invaded the Philippines, which became independent in 1946. The Philippines has experienced several corrupt presidencies (embezzlement, fraudulent elections) and political turmoil (coup attempts, national debt) despite economic growth later in the 20th century. The Philippines is 5% Muslim. Not all Muslims are violent, but ISIS affiliates and other militant groups engage in killings, bombings, and kidnappings.

The Philippines is home to the third largest Catholic population in the world, after Brazil and Mexico. The majority of church members are women, and there are nearly 12,000 women religious in the country. A decline in Mass attendance has been occurring along generational lines, where younger people are showing less interest in the church. The Catholic Church is generally conservative in its opposition to divorce, same-sex relations, and abortion. Catholicism's vigor is reinforced through the celebration of colorful and extravagant feast days, such as the Feast of the Black Nazarene, where 10 million people take to the streets for a procession of a life-sized statue of the suffering Jesus.

The Philippines is home to hundreds of indigenous churches, some of which date to the mid-19th and late 20th centuries. The largest is the Philippine Independent Church, which was originally formed by Catholic influence but is now in full communion with the Anglican Communion and the Mar Thoma Syrian Church (Orthodox). This church has 3.5 million members and is the second largest denomination in the country. Indigenous churches are diverse, and most were founded by charismatic leaders seeking to establish more contextual forms of the faith. Filipino Independent churches have also spread to other countries through missionary work. Numerous megachurches in the country are influential in society, including in politics.

% Christian: 0 3 10 50 75 100

Religion in the Philippines

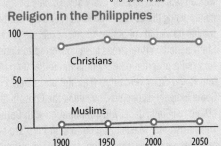

In 1900, the country was 86% Christian, 10% followers of traditional religions, and 4% Muslim. By 2020, Christians had grown to 91%, Muslims to 5%, and traditional religions declined to 2%. The nonreligious grew from virtually zero to 1% of the population. There are also small communities of Baha'is, Chinese folk religionists, Hindus, and followers of other religions.

Indicators & Demographic Data

Population (2020)	109,703,000
% under 15 years	31%
Capital city (pop.)	Manila 13,923,000
% urban dwellers	47% (2.04% p.a.)
Official language	Filipino, English
Largest language	Tagalog (32%)
Largest people	Tagalog (Pilipino) (28%)
Largest culture	Visayan (33%)
Development	70
Physicians	12
Gender gap	0%

Bible Translations		Churches		Missionaries		Gospel Access	
Languages	183	Denominations	830	Received	8,000	1900	Very high
Full Bible	25	Congregations	145,000	Sent	25,000	2020	Very high

Facts to Consider

- President Rodrigo Duterte has been criticized, including by Catholic clergy, for his policy of extrajudicial killings in his "war on drugs" that has taken the lives of at least 12,000 people since taking office in 2016; many deaths have been attributed to the Philippine National Police. Duterte has been highly critical of the Catholic Church, calling it the "most hypocritical institution" after the Catholic Bishops' Conference called some of his positions "morally reprehensible."
- Pope Paul VI visited the Philippines in 1970, Pope John Paul II in 1981 and 1995, and Pope Francis in 2015. Francis' open-air Mass at Rizal Park drew between 6 and 7 million attendees—the largest in papal history.
- Most Muslims in the Philippines live in Mindanao, Palawan, and the Sulu Archipelago. The Autonomous Region consists of the majority Muslim provinces of Basilan, Lanao del Sur, Maguindanao, Sulu, and Tawi-Tawi. The region's local governance is integrated into the national government by way of its representatives in congress.
- Although relations among Catholics, Protestants, and Muslims are generally positive, there are tensions among ethnic groups, especially in the rural areas in the south.

Christian Traditions in the Philippines

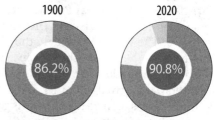

1900 2020

☐Independent ☐Protestant ☐Catholic ■Orthodox ■Christian

The Christian community in the Philippines in 1900 (6.5 million people) was majority Catholic (77% of Christians), with a substantial minority of Independents (23%). This changed over the 20th century with the introduction of different Protestant groups from abroad. In 2020, Christianity in the Philippines was substantially more diverse. Catholics were still by far the majority (76%), but Independents surged to 19.3 million and Protestants grew to 6.4 million (together, 24% of Christians).

Christian Families in Philippines

Family	Population 2020	%	Trend	Change
Latin-rite Catholic	83,000,000	75.7	↑	1.4
*Pentecostals/Charismatics	38,000,000	34.6	↑	2.0
*Evangelicals	3,863,000	3.5	↑	1.9
Nondenominational	3,623,000	3.3	↑	0.8
Old Catholic Church	3,381,000	3.1	↓	-0.7
Adventist	1,670,000	1.5	↑↑	5.3
Baptist	917,000	0.8	↑	0.7
United church or joint mission	907,000	0.8	–	-0.5
Methodist	860,000	0.8	↑	0.7
Latter-day Saints (Mormons)	843,000	0.8	↑	2.7
Jehovah's Witnesses	599,000	0.5	↑	2.6
Holiness	596,000	0.5	↑	1.3
Restorationist, Disciple	342,000	0.3	↑	0.5
Anglican	156,000	0.1	↑	0.7
Reformed, Presbyterian	50,800	<0.1	↑	2.4
Lutheran	37,400	<0.1	↑	1.3
Christian Brethren	36,800	<0.1	↑	1.1
Exclusive Brethren	19,700	<0.1	–	0.5
Congregational	14,200	<0.1	↑	0.9
Salvationist	11,800	<0.1	↓	-1.0
Mennonite	8,000	<0.1	↑	4.8
Eastern Orthodox	4,000	<0.1	↑	1.9
Friends (Quaker)	2,200	<0.1	↑	1.2

The Catholic Church in the Philippines is by far the largest Christian family, with 76% of the country's population. Pentecostals/Charismatics are the second largest family, with 35% of the population (and 38% of Christians). The largest of these churches are the Kingdom of Jesus Christ (3.5 million), Jesus Miracle Crusade (1.6 million), and the Jesus is Lord Church (1.5 million). All of these, founded after 1970, are completely indigenous to the Philippines. The Catholic Charismatic movement is also prominent, with perhaps upward of 25 million Catholics. Evangelicals are the third largest Christian family, found across many Protestant groups: Presbyterians, Congregationalists, Disciples of Christ, and others. The Philippines is home to dozens of nondenominational churches, most of which are indigenous to the country. The largest is the Church of Christ, with 2.5 million members.

* These movements are found within Christian families
– no change

↑↑ extreme growth
↑ growth
↓↓ extreme decline
↓ decline

Christianity in Poland

Christianity in modern-day Poland dates to Duke Mieszko I's conversion to Catholicism in the year 966 via his wife, Dobrawa. The work of German and Czech missionaries heavily influenced Polish Christianity. Lutheranism arrived in 1518 and was adopted by the higher classes; Calvinism and Moravians arrived soon after, and Protestantism spread. Polish history is marked by numerous geographic changes, insurrections, and partitions that altered its population and affected Christianity, including the Polish-Lithuanian Commonwealth, one of the largest nations in 16th- and 17th-century Europe. By 1918, Poland was an independent nation but was invaded by Nazi Germany and the Soviet Union in 1939 and was split between the two. Catholics, severely persecuted during the initial years of Nazi rule, agreed to stay out of politics to operate more freely. Meanwhile, nearly 90% of the country's Jews were murdered in the Holocaust, with German concentration camps built in Treblinka, Sobibor, Belzec, and Auschwitz. With the fall of the Soviet Union and Communism in 1991, Poland once again became an independent state. Today, Poland is one of the most religious countries in Europe, with a close link between the national and religious identity of the Polish people. Until recently, the country resisted secularization trends evident across Western Europe, with surveys reporting that most Poles ascribe to a personal God, believe in heaven and hell, pray regularly, and attend religious services at least once a week. The 2020–2021 Women Strike consisted of anti-government protests against the tightening of anti-abortion laws in the country. The movement was particularly outspoken against the Catholic Church. It critiqued the church for being too influential in national public matters and called for Catholics to deregister from the church.

Poland is home to several breakaway groups from Catholicism. In 1906, a schism took place that produced the Old Catholic Mariavite Church, which was later accepted into the Old Catholic community. Most Protestants live in Upper Silesia, Lower Silesia, and Warmia-Masuria. Lutherans are the largest Protestant group. The Pentecostal Church of Poland is associated with the Assemblies of God and is the second largest Protestant denomination.

% Christian: 0 3 10 50 75 100

Religion in Poland

Poland's religious makeup changed little in the 20th century. In 1900, the country was 91% Christian and nearly 9% Jewish. In 2020, Christians were 96% of the population and the nonreligious 4%. The Jewish community stands at around only 3,000 Jews, down from 2.1 million at the start of the 20th century.

Indicators & Demographic Data

Population (2020)............. 37,942,000
% under 15 years 15%
Capital city (pop.)........ Warsaw 1,783,000
% urban dwellers......... 60% (-0.16% p.a.)
Official language....................Polish
Largest language..............Polish (95%)
Largest people ... Polish (Pole, Silesian) (95%)
Largest culture ....Polish (95%)
Development......................... 87
Physicians........................... 23
Gender gap...........................-1%

Bible Translations	Churches	Missionaries	Gospel Access
Languages...........24	Denominations 92	Received...........780	1900 .... Very high
Full Bible............15	Congregations..... 13,100	Sent 2,500	2020 .... Very high

Facts to Consider

- Despite Poland reporting some of the highest rates of religiosity in Europe, Christianity appears to be slowly declining. In 1920, an estimated 70% of people attended services at least weekly; this dropped to 54% by 2015.
- Atheism and agnosticism are growing, and the nonreligious are becoming more vocal in public life. Several groups exist such as the Polish Association of Freethinkers, the Secular Culture Society, and the Polish Association of Free Thought.
- Poland's Muslim population grew from virtually zero in 1900 to 40,000 in 2020. Despite a European Union agreement binding members to accept refugees via Greece and Italy, the Polish government denied refugees from the Middle East at the height of the migrant crisis in 2015. Around 10% of Muslims in Poland are ethnic Tartars who have been in the country for several hundred years.
- Despite taking many steps to eradicate anti-Semitism after World War II, Poland has seen anti-Semitic attitudes and actions returning to society. Poland is the only country in the European Union that has not legislated property restitution for Holocaust victims.
- The Polish Catholic Church has around 2,000 clergy working in 25 countries, most among the Polish diaspora (around 15 million Poles) but many also serving local parishes.

Christian Traditions in Poland

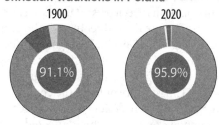

1900   2020

91.1%   95.9%

☐Independent ☐Protestant ■Catholic ■Orthodox ■Christian

The Christian community in Poland in 1900 (over 22 million people) was majority Catholic (87% of Christians), with substantial minorities of Orthodox (9%) and Protestants (3%). This barely changed throughout the 20th century. In 2020, Catholics in Poland had an even greater majority (97%). The Orthodox declined (largely due to shifting borders), while Protestants and Independents experienced some growth (yet together, just 1% of Christians).

Christian Families in Poland

Family	Population 2020	%	Trend	Change
Latin-rite Catholic	33,967,000	89.5	—	-0.1
*Pentecostals/Charismatics	1,800,000	4.7	—	0.1
Eastern Orthodox	579,000	1.5	—	0.1
Jehovah's Witnesses	190,000	0.5	↓	-0.6
Eastern-rite Catholic	153,000	0.4	—	-0.1
*Evangelicals	70,000	0.2	↑	2.9
Lutheran	49,800	0.1	↓	-3.4
Old Catholic Church	43,100	0.1	—	-0.3
Restorationist, Disciple	12,100	<0.1	↑	1.9
Adventist	6,100	<0.1	↓	-0.6
Baptist	6,000	<0.1	—	0.4
Nondenominational	5,900	<0.1	—	-0.1
Methodist	3,800	<0.1	↓	-1.8
Reformed, Presbyterian	3,000	<0.1	↓	-1.8
Christian Brethren	2,300	<0.1	↓	-1.7
Latter-day Saints (Mormons)	2,200	<0.1	↑	2.8
Oriental and other Orthodox	1,000	<0.1	—	0.1

After the Catholic Church (90% of the population), Pentecostals/Charismatics are the second largest family but are only just under 5% of the population. The largest Pentecostal churches are the Pentecostal Church of Poland (established by the Assemblies of God) and the New Apostolic Church (from Germany). Eastern Orthodox communities are largely of the Orthodox Church of Poland, which was 4 million strong before World War II and around half a million today. Jehovah's Witnesses are the third largest denomination, with 190,000 members. Eastern Catholics include the Old Catholic Mariavite Church of Poland (founded by Maria Franciszka Kozlowska in the 1890s to reform Polish Catholicism) and the Polish National Catholic Church (a schism from the Roman Catholic Church primarily found among people of Polish descent in the United States).

* These movements are found within Christian families	↑↑ extreme growth
	↑ growth
	↓↓ extreme decline
— no change	↓ decline

Christianity in Portugal

Christianity has been present in the western part of the Iberian Peninsula since the 2nd century; Catholicism was declared the state religion in 589 CE. Portugal was declared independent of Spain in 1143. In 1497, all Jews in Portugal—who had fled there escaping persecution in Spain—were either forced to accept Christianity or leave the country. This was followed by the Inquisition, designed to locate secretly practicing Jews known as *conversos*, which affected an estimated 40,000 Jews. Portugal's massive maritime expansion and colonization of other lands and people began in the 14th century, with the spread of the Portuguese Empire to Brazil, Cape Verde, Goa (India), and beyond. This empire was one of the most enduring in world history, lasting until the handover of Macao to China in 1999. Catholic missionaries usually accompanied Portuguese explorers, contributing to the spread of Christianity in Asia, Africa, and Latin America. Portugal's heavy involvement in the African slave trade, however, was a cancer on its Christian presence around the world.

Portugal remains a Catholic majority country, with nearly 85% of the population. Although no longer the state religion (as of 1974), Catholicism remains influential in society despite growing secularism. Religious beliefs and practices typically decline as people gain higher education and literacy and move to urban areas. Surveys report that around 19% to 25% of the population attends religious services weekly. Those who attend with some frequency are mostly women and children.

All non-Catholics were kept out of the country until the mid-19th century, when the first Protestants (British) arrived. A Catholic convert to Anglicanism opened the first Protestant chapel in 1839. The first Protestant missionaries arrived in 1867 (Brethren), followed by Methodists, Presbyterians, and Baptists. Today, Protestantism is still very small. The fastest-growing churches in the country are Independent denominations planted by Brazilian missionaries, such as the Universal Church of the Kingdom of God, which is the second largest denomination in the country, arriving in 1989. The church grew initially among immigrants (Brazilians and Black Africans), Roma people, and within low-income communities. There have been around 20 other Pentecostal churches imported from Brazil since 2005.

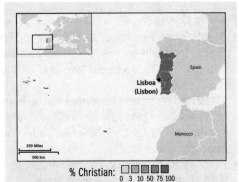

% Christian: 0 3 10 50 75 100

Religion in Portugal

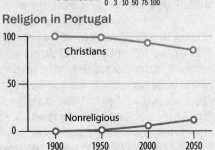

Portugal has been a majority Christian country for many centuries. In 1900, the country was 100% Christian. By 2020, Christianity had dropped to 89% of the population with the growth of atheism and agnosticism, which together were 9% of the population. Because of immigration, there are small communities of Buddhists, Muslims, and Hindus, each less than 1% of the country's population.

Indicators & Demographic Data

Population (2020)	10,218,000
% under 15 years	13%
Capital city (pop.)	Lisbon 2,957,000
% urban dwellers	66% (0.44% p.a.)
Official language	Portuguese
Largest language	Portuguese (95%)
Largest people	Portuguese (91%)
Largest culture	Portuguese (91%)
Development	85
Physicians	44
Gender gap	2%

Bible Translations		Churches		Missionaries		Gospel Access	
Languages	22	Denominations	110	Received	830	1900	Very high
Full Bible	15	Congregations	7,600	Sent	3,000	2020	Very high

Facts to Consider

- Portuguese society is becoming increasingly indifferent to religion. The nonreligious make up 9% of the population, but surveys have reported that this could be upward of 15%.
- Evangelicalism is declining in Portugal, despite the planting of 300 new Evangelical churches between 2000 and 2016. Many of these churches were formed among immigrant communities from former Portuguese colonies who returned home. Evangelicalism is largely seen as a foreign religion.
- Roma people, a minority ethnic group, number between 40,000 and 50,000 and often face discrimination and abuse because of their nomadic lifestyle and cultural differences. Their communities often lack basic infrastructure like access to drinking water, electricity, and waste disposal.
- Portugal received many asylum seekers at the height of the refugee crisis in 2015, but upward of 40% of all refugees left the country within 18 months. Half of the 115 organizations that shelter refugees are run by churches.
- Violence against women, including domestic violence, is an ongoing problem in Portugal. An estimated 24% of women have experienced physical or sexual violence since the age of 15. These incidents are chronically underreported.
- Portugal is home to roughly 52,000 Muslims, most of whom are from former Portuguese overseas colonies such as Guinea-Bissau and Mozambique. More recently, Muslim migrants have come from South Asia.

Christian Traditions in Portugal

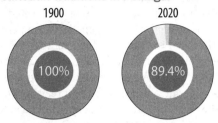

1900 · 100% 2020 · 89.4%

☐Independent ☐Protestant ▨Catholic ▰Orthodox ■Christian

The Christian community in Portugal in 1900—and thus, the entire country's population—was 100% Catholic. This shifted slightly throughout the 20th century. In 2020, Christianity in Portugal was still majority Catholic (94% of Christians), but Independents, Protestants, and Orthodox all experienced some growth. Protestants and Independents together made up over 6% of Christians (around half a million people) in 2020.

Christian Families in Portugal

Family	Population 2020	%	Trend	Change
Latin-rite Catholic	8,650,000	84.7	↓	-0.7
*Pentecostals/Charismatics	560,000	5.5	↑	0.6
*Evangelicals	130,000	1.3	↑	1.1
Jehovah's Witnesses	85,900	0.8	↓	-0.7
Non-traditional, house, cell	63,000	0.6	↑	1.4
Latter-day Saints (Mormons)	47,300	0.5	↑	1.9
Christian Brethren	12,600	0.1	–	0.0
Adventist	10,200	0.1	–	-0.4
Anglican	5,000	<0.1	–	0.0
Baptist	4,800	<0.1	–	-0.4
Holiness	2,000	<0.1	↑	1.3
Restorationist, Disciple	2,000	<0.1	↑	3.7
Nondenominational	1,900	<0.1	↑	1.9
Methodist	1,700	<0.1	↓	-1.1
Eastern Orthodox	1,200	<0.1	–	0.0
Reformed, Presbyterian	830	<0.1	↓	-3.6
Congregational	600	<0.1	↓	-1.5

The Catholic Church in Portugal is by far the largest Christian family, with nearly 90% of the country's population. Pentecostals/Charismatics are the second largest family, with 5% of the population. The largest Pentecostal churches are the Universal Church of the Kingdom of God (150,000; from Brazil), the Assemblies of God (95,000; from the United Kingdom), and the Christian Congregation in Portugal (35,000; from Brazil). Evangelicals are found throughout many church traditions, including Christian Brethren, Seventh-day Adventists, and Baptists. Jehovah's Witnesses have grown more quickly than most Protestant groups and number over 85,900 as the country's fourth largest denomination. The large number of "nontraditional" or "house churches" is due to the Manna Christian Church, a cell-based megachurch in Lisbon with around 60,000 affiliates.

* These movements are found within Christian families
– no change

↑↑ extreme growth
↑ growth
↓↓ extreme decline
↓ decline

Christianity in Puerto Rico

Puerto Rico is a territory of the United States. The islands were home to the indigenous Taíno people until they were displaced in the early 15th century by Spanish colonizers who also brought enslaved Africans. Slavery was abolished in 1873. The USA acquired Puerto Rico after the 1898 Spanish-American War, and a fraught relationship remains between the two. There are more people of Puerto Rican descent living in the United States than in Puerto Rico. The first Catholic diocese in the New World was in Puerto Rico (1511), and the country remains majority Catholic today (71%). The largest Protestant denominations are the Pentecostal Church of God and the Baptist Association.

Facts to Consider

- Though technically a part of the USA, Puerto Rico is distinct; though its people are conferred citizenship, they lack full political representation. In 2020, 52% of Puerto Ricans voted yes in a statehood referendum, but the US Congress is unwilling to admit it as a state.
- Puerto Rico suffers from a lack of economic sovereignty, a sustained recession, and remarkably high debt. Deficient infrastructure, compounded by deadly Category 5 Hurricane Irma and Hurricane Maria in 2017, has proved devasting to the island.
- Pentecostalism entered the island in 1916 with the return of Puerto Ricans who had joined the Assemblies of God while in Hawaii. It is now the largest denomination after the Catholic Church.
- Puerto Rico is home to a number of prominent Latina theologians both on the island and in the United States, such as Agustina Luvis-Núñez, Elizabeth Conde-Frazier, and Loida I. Martell-Otero.

Indicators & Demographic Data

Population (2020)	3,651,000
% under 15 years	17%
Capital city (pop.)	San Juan 2,448,000
% urban dwellers	94% (-0.12% p.a.)
Official language	Spanish, English
Largest language	Spanish (97%)
Largest people	Puerto Rican White (72%)
Largest culture	Latin-American White (72%)
Development	68
Physicians	39
Gender gap	3%

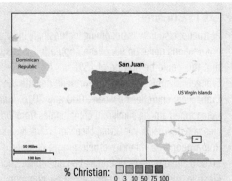

% Christian: 0 3 10 50 75 100

Christian Traditions in Puerto Rico

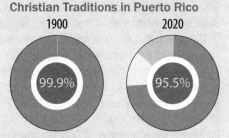

1900 — 99.9% 2020 — 95.5%

☐ Independent ☐ Protestant ▨ Catholic ■ Orthodox ■ Christian

In 1900, most Christians in Puerto Rico were Catholic (99%), followed by a Protestant minority. In 2020, Christians were still majority Catholic (73%) but with many more Protestants (14%) and Independents (13%), especially Pentecostals.

Religion in Puerto Rico

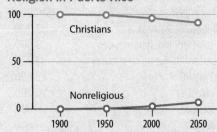

The Christian share of the population decreased only slightly from 99% in 1900 to 96% in 2020. The second largest "religion" in 2020 were the nonreligious, with 3% of the population.

Bible Translations		Churches		Missionaries		Gospel Access	
Languages	7	Denominations	150	Received	2,500	1900	Very high
Full Bible	5	Congregations	4,900	Sent	800	2020	Very high

Christianity in Qatar

Qatar is a small Muslim-majority country bordering Saudi Arabia and the Persian Gulf. Christianity arrived in the region in the 3rd century but was eclipsed by Islam in the 7th century. The Catholic Church is the largest denomination, comprised mostly of migrant workers, including Arabs and expatriate Catholics from the Philippines, India, South America, Lebanon, and Europe. The first church opened in Qatar in 2008, the Catholic Church of Our Lady of the Rosary in Doha. There are small numbers of indigenous Christians, but there is a large interdenominational expatriate Christian community of Westerners, Indians, and Arabs. Qatar also has a sizable Hindu population (3%), mostly from India and Nepal.

Facts to Consider

- Islam is the state religion, and Sharia law is a main source of legislation. The law punishes "offending" Islam and committing blasphemy against Islam, Christianity, and Judaism. Conversion to another religion from Islam is illegal.
- Human rights issues in Qatar include restrictions on free expression, peaceful assembly, migrant workers' freedom, and forced labor.
- Qatari converts to Christianity face discrimination, harassment, and police monitoring, as well as severe pressure from their Muslim families to reconvert. Conversion often jeopardizes personal status and property.
- The Anglican Centre in Doha provides space for over 80 Protestant, Pentecostal, and Evangelical congregations for worship and fellowship. Services are held in English, Tamil, Arabic, Tagalog, Hindi, and other languages.

Indicators & Demographic Data

Population (2020)	2,792,000
% under 15 years	14%
Capital city (pop.)	Doha 641,000
% urban dwellers	99% (1.66% p.a.)
Official language	Arabic
Largest language	Arabic (63%)
Largest people	Persian (Irani) (16%)
Largest culture	Arab (Arabic) (53%)
Development	86
Physicians	20
Gender gap	-3%

% Christian: 0 3 10 50 75 100

Christian Traditions in Qatar

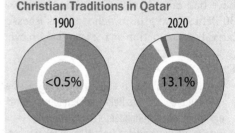

1900 — <0.5%

2020 — 13.1%

☐ Independent ☐ Protestant ■ Catholic ■ Orthodox ■ Christian

In 1900, the very small population of Christians in Qatar (less than 100 people) was 71% Catholic and 29% Protestant. In 2020, Christians in Qatar were majority Catholic (91%).

Religion in Qatar

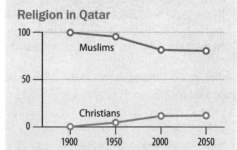

The Muslim share of the population decreased from nearly 100% of the population in 1900 to 80% in 2020. The second largest religion in 2020 was Christianity, with 13% of the population.

Bible Translations		Churches		Missionaries		Gospel Access	
Languages	18	Denominations	34	Received	10	1900	Very low
Full Bible	10	Congregations	210	Sent	4	2020	Medium

Christianity in Réunion

Réunion is an overseas department of France in the Indian Ocean, off the coast of Madagascar. The island was uninhabited when the Portuguese arrived in the early 16th century. France occupied the island in the early 17th century, and the first settlers arrived in 1665, with enslaved people imported from Africa, China, and India. Slavery was outlawed in 1848. Réunion is majority Christian today (87%), mostly Catholic. Protestants make up 1% of the population, and the largest denominations are the Evangelical Church of Réunion, Seventh-day Adventists, and Assemblies of God. Pentecostals have had many divisions among them, and there are over 30 Pentecostal groups. Jehovah's Witnesses are the second largest denomination on the island, with over 6,000 members.

Facts to Consider

- Réunion's population is ethnically diverse. Malbars are descendants of indentured laborers from southern India, Cafres are descendants of enslaved people and indentured servants from Africa and Madagascar, Zarabs are descendants from Muslim Indians, and Zoreys are people from mainland France. There are also Chinois, or Chinese.
- The number of French people living in Réunion increased from 37,000 in 1900 to over 97,000 by 2015. Native Réunionese have migrated to metropolitan France, and nearly 15% of the local population live outside Réunion.
- The official language of Réunion is French, though a majority of people speak primarily Réunion Creole.
- Réunion has around 200,000 people of Indian descent, some of which are Hindu and some Catholic. The most recent arrivals were Tamil Hindu refugees from Sri Lanka. Most large towns have a Hindu temple.

Indicators & Demographic Data

Population (2020)	897,000
% under 15 years	22%
Capital city (pop.)	Saint-Denis 149,000
% urban dwellers	100% (0.73% p.a.)
Official language	French
Largest language	Réunion Creole French (62%)
Largest people	Reunionese Creole (43%)
Largest culture	Eurafrican (43%)
Development	50
Physicians	0.8
Gender gap	10%

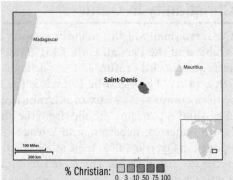

% Christian: 0 3 10 50 75 100

Christian Traditions in Réunion

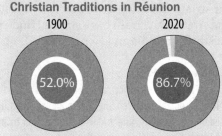

1900 — 52.0%   2020 — 86.7%

☐Independent ☐Protestant ■Catholic ■Orthodox ■Christian

In 1900, all Christians in Réunion were Catholic. Christianity in 2020 was still majority Catholic (97%), followed by smaller populations of Protestants (2%) and Independents (1%).

Religion in Réunion

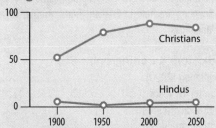

Réunion's religious makeup changed significantly over the 20th century. In 1900, the country was 52% Christian, 31% traditional religionists, and 12% Muslim. By 2020, Christianity had grown to 87%, and other religions dropped to 5% Hindu, 4% Muslim, and under 1% traditional religionists.

Bible Translations		Churches		Missionaries		Gospel Access	
Languages	12	Denominations	28	Received	260	1900	Medium
Full Bible	10	Congregations	270	Sent	10	2020	Very high

Christianity in Romania

Romania has had a turbulent geopolitical history since the 2nd century. Overrun by Goths, Huns, Avars, Slavs, Mongols, and Bulgars, Romania was caught between Slavic culture to the west and Mongols to the east. In the 17th century, the region was driven back and forth between the armies of the Hapsburg Empire, Austria, and Russia, resulting in Romania's varied religious history. Christianity arrived as early as the 3rd century. Latin was the original language of the church, but famous Orthodox missionaries Cyril and Methodius introduced Slavic liturgy. The Orthodox churches in areas under former Turkish rule came under pressure from Austria, Hungary, and Russia, making them Eastern Catholic churches under Rome in the 17th century. Lutheranism came first to Transylvania among Germans and then Hungarians. The Romanian Orthodox Church declared itself autocephalous (i.e., an independent Orthodox church not subject to the authority of a patriarch) in 1878.

From 1947 to 1989, Romania was under Soviet occupation, in which the Communist government under Nicolae Ceaușescu limited personal freedoms and suppressed political dissenters. Many resisters were deported, exiled, and forced into labor camps. Catholic churches were forcibly dissolved and required to rejoin the Orthodox Church. Several hundred priests and laity were imprisoned, and six bishops died in prison. Orthodox churches benefitted from the political situation despite the official atheism of the Communist government. Orthodoxy was used as a tool to help forge a national identity. In the post-Communist era, the Orthodox Church was both the most influential religious body in the country and criticized for its cooperation with the regime. Today there are over 10,000 priests and deacons and 400 monasteries staffed by thousands of monks and nuns.

Protestant denominations include the Reformed Church of Romania, Baptists, and Seventh-day Adventists. Pentecostalism arrived in 1922, and the community suffered imprisonments and murders as it grew under the Communist regime. In recent years, Pentecostalism has grown among the Roma, of which the largest group in Europe resides in Romania. A revival began among the Roma in the 1990s and peaked in 2003 in Toflea. There are several independent Roma congregations today.

% Christian: 0 3 10 50 75 100

Religion in Romania

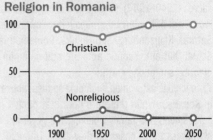

Romania has been a majority Christian country for many centuries. In 1900, the country was 94% Christian. Christianity suffered under Soviet rule and dropped to 83% in 1970 but rebounded to represent 99% of the population in 2020. The nonreligious (atheists and agnostics together) had mirroring patterns over the century, growing to 15% in 1970 but dropping below 1% in 2020.

Indicators & Demographic Data

Population (2020)	19,388,000
% under 15 years	15%
Capital city (pop.)	Bucharest 1,803,000
% urban dwellers	54% (-0.15% p.a.)
Official language	Romanian
Largest language	Romanian (90%)
Largest people	Romanian (88%)
Largest culture	Romanian (89%)
Development	81
Physicians	27
Gender gap	2%

Bible Translations		Churches		Missionaries		Gospel Access	
Languages	25	Denominations	51	Received	1,200	1900	Very high
Full Bible	19	Congregations	25,500	Sent	220	2020	Very high

Facts to Consider

- Pentecostals have been active in missionary sending through the Pentecostal Agency for Foreign Mission, which has sent 55 long-term missionaries to 21 countries, mostly Muslim-majority countries. It is fully funded by Romanian churches.
- Romania is home to tens of thousands of Muslims, mostly Turks and Tartars and a small community of Muslim Roma. Most (97%) live in Northern Dobruja (Constanța and Tulcea). The majority of Muslims are Sunnis of the Hanafi school.
- Before World War II, Jews numbered half a million. Their numbers began to decline in the 1930s and were drastically reduced by the Nazi massacres (1940–1944). Large-scale immigration to Israel occurred after World War II. The largest groups left today are three Hasidic dynasties: Satmar, Klausenburg, and Spinka. Romanian law forbids Holocaust denial, but anti-Semitic acts are still common, ranging from online messages to public graffiti.
- Violence against women, including spousal abuse, is a continuing issue in Romania. While there are laws that punish rape, sexual assault/harassment, and family violence, the government does not effectively address these cases as they arise. Domestic violence is common throughout the country. The government has also not established a mechanism to identify and treat child abuse or neglected children.

Christian Traditions in Romania

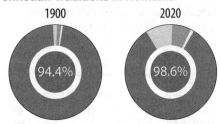

1900   2020

☐Independent ☐Protestant ■Catholic ■Orthodox ■Christian

Romanian Christianity has historically been majority Orthodox; 97% of Christians were Orthodox in 1900, with smaller populations of Protestants, Catholics, and Independents. In 2020, this was still largely true (83% of Christians were Orthodox), though Protestants grew rapidly to 10% of Christians, and Catholics to 7%. In 2020, Christians in Romania were 7% Evangelical and 6% Pentecostal/Charismatic.

Christian Families in Romania

Family	Population 2020	%	Trend	Change
Eastern Orthodox	16,971,000	87.5	↓	-0.7
*Evangelicals	1,370,000	7.1	↑	0.7
*Pentecostals/Charismatics	1,200,000	6.2	↑	0.6
Latin-rite Catholic	913,000	4.7	↓	-1.7
Reformed, Presbyterian	761,000	3.9	–	0.5
Eastern-rite Catholic	487,000	2.5	↓	-3.7
Baptist	132,000	0.7	–	0.4
Oriental and other Orthodox	129,000	0.7	–	0.4
Christian Brethren	76,100	0.4	↓	-0.6
Adventist	75,000	0.4	–	-0.1
Jehovah's Witnesses	63,800	0.3	↑	0.7
Lutheran	38,200	0.2	↓	-1.4
Non-traditional, house, cell	8,800	<0.1	↑	1.6
Holiness	5,400	<0.1	↑	1.2
Latter-day Saints (Mormons)	3,300	<0.1	↑	1.4

Eastern Orthodox churches in Romania are by far the largest Christian family, with 88% of the country's population. This family includes Romanian, Russian, Serbian, and Ukrainian Orthodox churches. Evangelicals are the next largest, with 7% of the population, followed by Pentecostal/Charismatics with 6%. There is a lot of overlap between Evangelicals and Pentecostals/Charismatics, such as the Pentecostal Union (770,000 members) and the Gypsy Evangelical Movement (52,000). The Pentecostal Union has close ties with the Church of God (Cleveland) and the Assemblies of God. There are also numerous independent Charismatic groups. Latin-rite Catholics are just under 5% of the population and the second largest denomination (and fourth largest family). The Reformed Church of Romania has 730,000 members. Baptists include the Baptist Union of Romania and the Hungarian Baptist Convention.

* These movements are found within Christian families	↑↑	extreme growth
	↑	growth
	↓↓	extreme decline
– no change	↓	decline

Christianity in Russia

Famous missionaries Cyril and Methodius from Macedonia translated parts of the Bible into Old Church Slavonic in the 9th century and helped pave the way for the Christianization of Slavic peoples in Eastern Europe. Russia adopted Christianity in the late 10th century, and the church grew extensively through monastic movements and its connection to Russian royalty. The Russian Orthodox Church in Moscow became known as the Third Rome (after Rome itself and then Constantinople) in the 16th century. During the October Revolution of 1917, church and state were separated, all church property was seized, and the church lost its legal entity until the fall of the Soviet Union in 1991. Christianity suffered terribly during the Soviet period. Antireligious propaganda abounded, and upward of 100,000 Orthodox priests were killed. Christians were frequently arrested and sent to labor camps. The first Russian concentration camp was established in a former Orthodox monastery in 1922. Christian intellectuals were purged from the country, and many died in prison camps. Christianity was driven underground, and many unregistered and illegal "underground" church movements numbered at least half a million Christians.

In 1990, Mikhail Gorbachev opened the doors for religious freedom in Russia, causing a massive growth of Christianity. Church life was revived after years of persecution, and many churches embarked on peacemaking activities and promoted moral values. Today the Russian Orthodox Church is the largest Orthodox Church in the world, with nearly 110 million members in Russia. Russia is also home to many Old Believers (or Old Ritualist) churches founded by Orthodox dissenters in the 17th century. Many survive today in isolated communities in Siberia and in diaspora in the United States and elsewhere.

Protestants and Independents together number over 3.4 million. The All-Union Council of Evangelical Christians-Baptists was formed in 1944 as a union of Baptists and several Evangelical groups; later, Mennonites and some Pentecostals joined as well. The Pentecostal movement began in the 1920s with roots in Finland when it was part of the Russian Empire. Pentecostalism has been attracting youth and typically engages in substantial social activism.

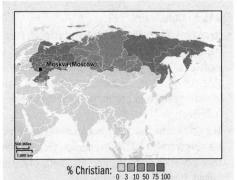

% Christian: 0 3 10 50 75 100

Religion in Russia

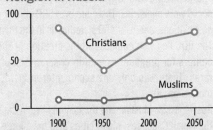

Russia has been a majority Christian country for many centuries. In 1900, the country was 85% Christian. Christianity suffered under Soviet rule and dropped to 38% in 1970 but rebounded to represent 82% of the population in 2020. Islam is the second largest religion (13%), followed by the nonreligious (4%).

Indicators & Demographic Data

Population (2020)............ 143,787,000
% under 15 years 18%
Capital city (pop.) ...... Moscow 12,538,000
% urban dwellers.......... 75% (0.11% p.a.)
Official language................. Russian
Largest language............ Russian (80%)
Largest people .... Russian (79%)
Largest culture .... Russian (79%)
Development........................ 82
Physicians........................... 40
Gender gap........................ -2%

Bible Translations		Churches		Missionaries		Gospel Access	
Languages	151	Denominations	600	Received	25,000	1900	Very high
Full Bible	54	Congregations	37,100	Sent	1,200	2020	Very high

Facts to Consider

- Russia has been under the control of Vladimir Putin since 1999. Human rights abuses are widespread, including extrajudicial killings of LGBTQ people in Chechnya, disappearances, arbitrary arrest, political and religious prisoners, violence against women, corruption at all levels of government, and politically motivated violence against dissenting individuals.
- The government cracked down on Jehovah's Witnesses (over 400,000 members) after a 2017 Supreme Court ruling banned and criminalized their activities as "extremist." Hundreds of members have been detained, imprisoned, and tortured.
- The Russian Orthodox Church (ROC) prioritizes the development of social work ministries. There are over 500 charity groups, 300 voluntary associations, and over 450 sisterhoods in the Russian Orthodox Church. The ROC has also emphasized the creation of shelters and assistance centers for pregnant women in crisis in aim of minimizing abortion rates. There was only one such center in 2011, and today there are more than 50.
- Russia is 13% Muslim, and the majority live in the Volga-Ural Region and the North Caucuses. Major cities also have large Muslim populations.

Christian Traditions in Russia

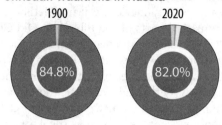

1900	2020
84.8%	82.0%

☐ Independent ☐ Protestant ■ Catholic ■ Orthodox ■ Christian

Russian Christianity has historically been majority Orthodox; 99% of Christians were Orthodox in 1900, but there were also half a million Protestants and a quarter of a million Catholics. In 2020, Orthodoxy was still the largest tradition (97% of Christians), though Independent Christianity and Protestantism each grew to represent 1% of Christians. Russian law recognizes the "special role" of Orthodox Christianity in the country's history and formation. It also criminalizes "offending the feelings of religious believers" and has unclear definitions of religious "anti-extremism" legislation.

Christian Families in Russia

Family	Population 2020	%	Trend	Change
Eastern Orthodox	111,650,000	77.6	–	0.2
*Pentecostals/Charismatics	3,400,000	2.4	↑	1.0
Oriental and other Orthodox	2,250,000	1.6	↓	-0.7
*Evangelicals	1,300,000	0.9	↑	2.1
Latin-rite Catholic	690,000	0.5	↓	-1.2
Jehovah's Witnesses	466,000	0.3	↑	1.4
United church or joint mission	212,000	0.1	↓	-1.6
Christian Brethren	163,000	0.1	–	-0.1
Baptist	76,500	0.1	↓	-1.9
Adventist	45,600	<0.1	↓	-4.7
Mennonite	43,900	<0.1	↓	-2.3
Lutheran	35,100	<0.1	–	0.0
Latter-day Saints (Mormons)	25,900	<0.1	↑	2.1
Hidden believers in Christ	22,000	<0.1	↑	1.7
Restorationist, Disciple	11,400	<0.1	↑	3.6
Eastern-rite Catholic	10,300	<0.1	–	0.3
Methodist	9,400	<0.1	–	0.5
Reformed, Presbyterian	4,200	<0.1	↓	-1.6
Anglican	3,400	<0.1	↓	-1.6
Salvationist	3,100	<0.1	–	-0.5
Holiness	3,000	<0.1	↓	-1.0
Nondenominational	1,000	<0.1	–	0.1

Eastern Orthodox churches in Russia are by far the largest Christian family, with 78% of the country's population. This family includes many ethnic churches, including Russian, Ukrainian, Georgian, Armenians, and Bulgarians. Pentecostals/Charismatics are the second largest family, with 2% of the population. The Pentecostal Union of United Churches is the largest Protestant Pentecostal church, with over 750,000 affiliates, and is also the largest Evangelical church body. The next largest is the Russian Association of Christians of the Evangelical Faith, with 700,000. Oriental and other Orthodox churches are the third largest family, with 2% of the population, and includes a wide array of groups such as Old Ritualist churches, the Assyrian Church of the East, and various Orthodox denominations that split from the Russian Orthodox Church.

* These movements are found within Christian families	↑↑ extreme growth
	↑ growth
	↓↓ extreme decline
– no change	↓ decline

Christianity in Rwanda

The early inhabitants of modern-day Rwanda were the hunter-gatherer Twa peoples, still in the country today. The Bantu migration beginning in 700 BCE made the primary people groups of the area the Hutu, Tutsi, and Twa. Differences between them concerned class, not race. Rifts relating to ruling power between the Hutu and Tutsi escalated in the 19th century. Meanwhile, the Berlin Conference of 1884 assigned the territory to Germany and ushered in the period of European colonization and conflict. Catholic White Fathers arrived in 1889, German Lutherans in 1907, and Anglicans in 1922. During World War I, Belgium took over the territory, Ruanda-Urundi. The East African Revival swept through the area beginning in 1933 among Anglicans and other historic Protestant churches. The revival was an indigenous African movement in partnership with Church Missionary Society personnel and African evangelists who emphasized personal conversion experiences.

Rwanda was 61% Christian by 1970. Both Germans and Belgians promoted Tutsi supremacy, believing them racially superior to Hutu. With national independence from Belgium in 1962 came the murder of roughly 150,000 Tutsis by Hutus, aided by Belgian military forces. Early missionaries aimed to convert Rwanda's ruling class by maintaining a collaborative relationship with them; but missionaries largely accepted the incorrect, racist interpretations of ethnic distinctions in the country. The country was roughly 90% Christian at the time of the 1994 Rwandan Genocide, which claimed the lives of 800,000 people in 100 days. Both Catholic and Protestant churches were complicit in the genocide and undercut their own potential to serve as prophetic voices.

Since the 1960s, Rwanda has transformed from a Francophone Catholic nation to an Anglophone Charismatic Protestant nation. Many Rwandans felt betrayed by the traditional churches that failed to prevent ethnic violence and protect their people. In the aftermath of the genocide, newer Charismatic churches emerged that advocated for reconciliation, prison ministries, and spiritual healing. In 2016, the Catholic Church of Rwanda officially apologized for its role in the genocide.

% Christian: 0 3 10 50 75 100

Religion in Rwanda

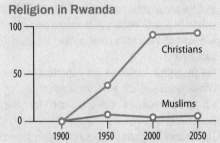

Rwanda experienced a massive transformation of its religious makeup in the 20th century. In 1900, the country was almost entirely followers of traditional ethnic religions. By 2020, this had changed dramatically: 91% Christian, 5% Muslim, and 3% traditional religionists. There are smaller communities of Baha'i and Hindus as well.

Indicators & Demographic Data

Population (2020)	13,087,000
% under 15 years	39%
Capital city (pop.)	Kigali 1,132,000
% urban dwellers	17% (3.07% p.a.)
Official language	Kinyarwanda, French, English
Largest language	Kinyarwanda (94%)
Largest people	Hutu (88%)
Largest culture	Interlacustrine Bantu (97%)
Development	52
Physicians	0.6
Gender gap	6%

Bible Translations		Churches		Missionaries		Gospel Access	
Languages	11	Denominations	120	Received	1,300	1900	Very low
Full Bible	9	Congregations	11,500	Sent	140	2020	Very high

Facts to Consider

- In 2017, voters elected President Paul Kagame to a third seven-year term, though international monitors reported flaws and irregularities in the process. Observers have identified several violations of humanitarian law, such as extrajudicial killings, promotion of division, and disappearances of political dissidents.
- Freedom of the press is limited, and journalists are pressured to avoid sensitive political and human rights issues. Pro-government views dominate much of the media.
- The 1994 genocide left many women as heads of households and gave women greater responsibilities in the public sector. Rwanda is unique in that the constitution requires that at least 30% of decision-making positions be held by women. At the same time, domestic violence against women and children is common and increased during the COVID-19 pandemic.
- Reconciliation ministries are important, as Rwandans still feel the consequences of the genocide. Corruption, regionalism, and ethnic hatred were exposed, urging the need for Christian forgiveness and justice ministries.
- The Rwanda Religious Leaders Forum includes representatives of Protestant, Catholic, Anglican, and Evangelical churches as well those of Islam to strengthen interfaith collaboration on education, to combat gender-based violence, and to promote socioeconomic development and reconciliation.
- Muslims comprise 5% of Rwanda's population and have long been present in Indo-Pakistani, Arab, and Swahili communities, mostly in Kigali and Butare.

Christian Traditions in Rwanda

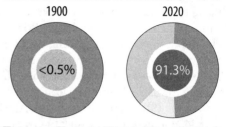

1900   2020

□Independent □Protestant ■Catholic ■Orthodox ■Christian

There were very few Christians in Rwanda in 1900. In 2020, Christianity was the largest religion and quite diverse. Catholics were the largest group (49% of Christians), followed by Protestants (38%, many Anglicans) and Independents (13%). The country is also home to large Evangelical and Pentecostal/Charismatic movements. Many Pentecostal/Charismatic churches formed after the genocide, such as the English-language Evangelical Revival Ministries (1996) and Christian Life Assembly (1998), the latter of which is the country's fastest-growing English-speaking church. However, the Kinyarwanda-language churches, especially those that teach prosperity theology, are growing much faster.

Christian Families in Rwanda

Family	Population 2020	%	Trend	Change
Latin-rite Catholic	5,410,000	41.3	↑	1.3
*Evangelicals	2,761,000	21.1	↑	2.6
*Pentecostals/Charismatics	2,420,000	18.5	↑	3.2
Anglican	1,557,000	11.9	↑	2.6
Adventist	1,254,000	9.6	↑↑	5.5
Baptist	541,000	4.1	↓	-0.5
Reformed, Presbyterian	297,000	2.3	↑	1.4
Holiness	114,000	0.9	↓	-1.4
Jehovah's Witnesses	106,000	0.8	↑↑	6.5
Lutheran	48,200	0.4	↑	1.9
Christian Brethren	12,900	0.1	↑	2.3
Friends (Quaker)	3,600	<0.1	↓	-1.5
Eastern Orthodox	1,500	<0.1	—	0.0

The largest Christian family is Catholicism, comprising 41% of the country's population. Evangelicals and Pentecostals/Charismatics are found throughout most denominations in the country and are the second and third largest families, respectively. Anglicans, for example, are the second largest denomination (12% of the country), with a large Evangelical, Charismatic Anglican movement. Other large Evangelical and Pentecostal/Charismatic groups include the Union of Baptist Churches, Association of Pentecostal Churches, and Free Methodists. Seventh-day Adventists represent 8% of the country and Baptists are 4%.

* These movements are found within Christian families		↑↑ extreme growth	
		↑ growth	
		↓↓ extreme decline	
— no change		↓ decline	

Christianity in Saint Helena

Saint Helena is an island nation in the South Atlantic Ocean far off the coast of southwestern Africa. It was uninhabited until the Portuguese arrived in 1502. They built a chapel in what is now Chapel Valley that was torn down by Dutch settlers who arrived in 1561. Saint Helena is a majority Christian (95%) overseas territory of the United Kingdom. Residents are mostly Anglicans, and there are three parishes with 12 churches. There are also Baptists, Salvation Army, and Seventh-day Adventists in Jamestown, the capital.

Facts to Consider

- As ships approach Jamestown, the first identifiable building on the island is the New Apostolic Hall of the New Apostolic Church, erected in 1994.
- With a congregation of around 250 members, Jehovah's Witnesses at Levelwood consider Half Tree Hollow their main place of worship.
- The Way International is a Pentecostal group that arrived in the 1980s and had 100 affiliates by 2015.
- Ecumenism has been an issue on the island, with disagreement over membership from Baptists, Seventh-day Adventists, and Anglicans.
- There is a small community of Baha'i (less than 100 people), with meetings held at the Baha'i Center in Gumwoods.

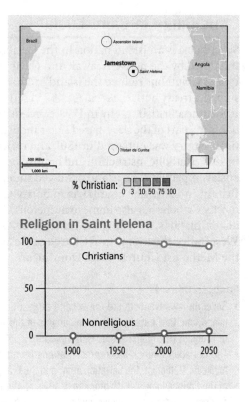

% Christian: 0 3 10 50 75 100

Religion in Saint Helena

Christianity in Saint Kitts and Nevis

Saint Kitts and Nevis is an island nation in the Caribbean and one of the smallest countries in the world by both land and population. The country's roughly 56,000 people are mostly Christian (94%), with smaller populations of Hindus and Spiritists, each roughly 1% of the population. French and English colonists looking to exploit the islands' natural resources displaced the indigenous population, Caribs. Saint Kitts was split between the English and French, and the English settled on Nevis. The Anglican Church is the original church of the islands and the largest denomination today.

Facts to Consider

- The constitution provides for religious freedom. Public schools offer Christian religious instruction, daily prayers, and religious assemblies.
- Several denominations indigenous to the islands were formed by Black Christians, of which the Spiritual Baptists are the best known.
- Rastafarians make up roughly 1% of the population and report social discrimination related to their use of cannabis for religious purposes, anti-vaccination positions, and dreadlocks.

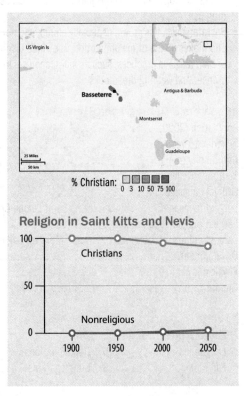

% Christian: 0 3 10 50 75 100

Religion in Saint Kitts and Nevis

Christianity in Saint Lucia

Saint Lucia is an island nation in the Caribbean originally inhabited by the native Arawak and Carib peoples. Christopher Columbus sighted the island in 1502, but the French signed a treaty with the local Caribs to settle there in 1660. It became a British colony in 1778. Subsequently, the island became a part of the slave-based sugar industry in the region until slavery was outlawed in 1807 and officially abolished in 1836. Catholic instruction and baptism were forced upon enslaved people. The island achieved independence from Britain in 1979. The country is majority Christian today, mostly Catholic but also home to numerous Caribbean-based denominations, including the Pentecostal Assemblies of the West Indies, the Evangelical Church of the West Indies, and the Methodist Church (from Dominica).

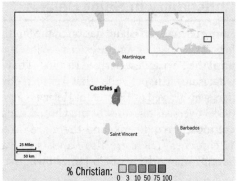

% Christian: 0 3 10 50 75 100

Christian Traditions in Saint Lucia

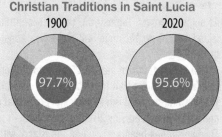

1900 — 97.7%   2020 — 95.6%

☐Independent ☐Protestant ◼Catholic ◼Orthodox ◼Christian

In 1900, most Christians in Saint Lucia were Catholic (84%), with a substantial Evangelical Protestant minority (16%). Christianity in 2020 was still majority Catholic (73%), but with larger populations of Protestants (24%) and Independents (3%).

Facts to Consider

- Seventh-day Adventists are the second largest denomination on the island, and they have an extension campus of the West Indies School of Theology (the main campus is in Trinidad).
- The Christian Council has representations from Catholic, Lutheran, Anglican, Methodist, the Salvation Army, and the Evangelical Association of the Caribbean. It aims to promote positive relations among churches and comes together for various joint services, such as combatting illegal drug use.
- Rastafarianism has grown, especially among unemployed young Blacks, and makes up 2% of the population. They face discrimination for some of their religious practices, such as marijuana use, their anti-vaccination stance, and wearing dreadlocks.

Indicators & Demographic Data

Population (2020). 181,000
% under 15 years 18%
Capital city (pop.) . . . . .Castries 21,400
% urban dwellers. . . . . .19% (0.98% p.a.)
Official language. . . . . .English
Largest language. . . . . .Saint Lucian Creole French (94%)
Largest people . . . . Black (45%)
Largest culture . . . . Mulatto, English-speaking (49%)
Development. 75
Physicians. 1
Gender gap. 1%

Religion in Saint Lucia

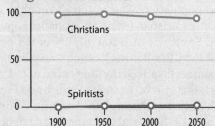

Saint Lucia's religious makeup changed little over the 20th century. In 1900, the country was 98% Christian and 2% Hindu. By 2020, Christianity had dropped slightly to 96%. Other religions include Spiritists (2%) and Hindus (1%).

Bible Translations	Churches	Missionaries	Gospel Access
Languages. 5	Denominations 30	Received. 170	1900 . . . . Very high
Full Bible. 3	Congregations. 220	Sent 4	2020 . . . . Very high

Christianity in Saint Pierre and Miquelon

Saint Pierre and Miquelon is a self-governing overseas collectivity of France in the northwest Atlantic Ocean, off the coast of Canada. It covers 93 square miles and has a population of 6,300 people, 95% of whom are Christian. There are small populations of nonreligious (4%). Though encountered by Portuguese explorers in 1520, the islands became French possessions in 1536. The islands were not permanently settled until the end of the 17th century. Catholic work began in 1689, and the Catholic Church is still the only major Christian tradition on the islands.

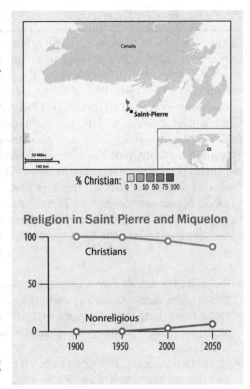

% Christian: 0 3 10 50 75 100

Religion in Saint Pierre and Miquelon

Facts to Consider

- Saint Pierre and Miquelon has been a French territorial collectivity since 1985. The separation of church and state and freedom of religion are guaranteed as in metropolitan France.
- Two priests and seven women religious serve two Catholic parishes on the islands.
- Jehovah's Witnesses have been active in Saint Pierre and Miquelon since the late 1970s, and there is one Kingdom Hall. A few Protestant denominations have arrived since the 1960s, but their numbers are extremely small.
- There is also a very small number of Baha'i on the islands, having arrived in the 1960s.

Christianity in Saint Vincent

Saint Vincent is an island nation in the Caribbean that consists of the main island of Saint Vincent, parts of the Grenadines islands, and 32 smaller islands. Some islands are inhabited, and others are not. The indigenous Garifuna people resisted European colonization and settlement, having defeated the English and Dutch but unable to hold off the French. The French settled the main island in 1719 and brought enslaved Africans to work on plantations. Saint Vincent turned over to British ownership until independence in 1979. The country is 89% Christian, and the largest denominations are the Seventh-day Adventist Church, the Anglican Church, and the Methodist Church.

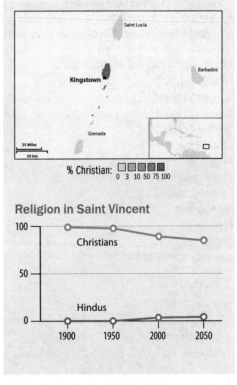

% Christian: 0 3 10 50 75 100

Religion in Saint Vincent

Facts to Consider

- The constitution provides for religious freedom. Public schools offer nondenominational Christian religious instruction.
- Spiritual Baptists are an Afro-American tradition that combines elements of traditional African religion with Christianity. The group was banned in 1913 and 1965.
- Hindus, agnostics, Spiritists, and Baha'is make up 2% each of the population; Muslims and New Religions each make up 1%. Hindus and Muslims are largely people of East Indian origin.

Christianity in Samoa

Samoa consists of two main islands (Savai'i and Upolu) and several smaller islands, some uninhabited. The indigenous Lapita people helped develop the Samoan culture ubiquitous in Polynesia. Samoa is one of the few countries in the world where the largest single Christian group is the Church of Jesus Christ of Latter-day Saints (38% of the country's population). Two Mormon missionaries arrived from Hawaii in 1863, but most church growth was by indigenous converts. The Congregational Christian Church in Samoa traces its origins to Tahitian teachers associated with the London Missionary Society in 1830. Samoans enthusiastically accepted Christianity and have been spreading it to neighboring islands in the Pacific ever since.

Facts to Consider

- The constitution describes the country as the following: "Samoa is a Christian nation founded on God the Father, the Son and the Holy Spirit."
- People report strong societal pressure, especially in the villages, to participate in church life and give large sums of money to Christian organizations.
- Christian instruction in public primary schools is mandated, and there are no opt-out provisions. Children of other religions typically attend private schools. It is not uncommon for Christians to have disparaging opinions of people of other religions.
- The Baha'i Faith grew rapidly in the 20th century, and in 1984 Samoa opened a Baha'i House of Worship, one of 10 such temples in the world.

Indicators & Demographic Data

Population (2020)	200,000
% under 15 years	36%
Capital city (pop.)	Apia 39,800
% urban dwellers	18% (-0.03% p.a.)
Official language	Samoan
Largest language	Samoan (88%)
Largest people	Samoan (88%)
Largest culture	Samoan (88%)
Development	71
Physicians	3.4
Gender gap	5%

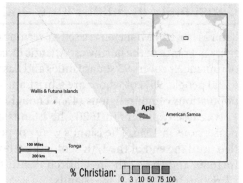

% Christian: 0 3 10 50 75 100

Christian Traditions in Samoa

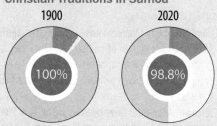

1900 — 100%
2020 — 98.8%

☐Independent ☐Protestant ◼Catholic ◼Orthodox ◼Christian

In 1900, most Christians in Samoa were Protestant (89%), with a substantial Catholic minority (9%). Christianity in 2020 was still majority Protestant (51%), but with larger populations of Independents (34%) and Catholics (15%).

Religion in Samoa

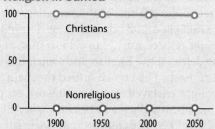

Samoa's religious makeup changed little over the 20th century. In 1900, the country was entirely Christian (100%). By 2020, Christianity had dropped only slightly to 99%. Other religions include Baha'i and the nonreligious (each less than 1%).

Bible Translations		Churches		Missionaries		Gospel Access	
Languages	5	Denominations	39	Received	800	1900	Very high
Full Bible	4	Congregations	1,000	Sent	300	2020	Very high

Christianity in San Marino

San Marino is a very small landlocked country (microstate) completely encompassed by Italy. Its 33,800 citizens inhabit 24 square miles and are mostly Catholic. The history of Christianity in San Marino goes back to Christians fleeing the Roman Empire during the Diocletianic Persecution (303 CE). With numerous Catholic organizations, the country is home to 81 parishes served by 22 priests and 20 women religious. Jehovah's Witnesses are the only other organized religious group in the country, with around 300 members.

Facts to Consider

- The constitution provides for freedom of religion. The law requires Catholic instruction in public schools, and ethics classes are offered for those who opt out.
- There are no private schools. Crucifixes are common in all governmental buildings and courtrooms.
- The government donates 0.3% of personal income taxes to registered religious organizations.
- In 2021, 77% of citizens voted to legalize abortion in the first 12 weeks of pregnancy, and beyond 12 weeks if the mother's health is at risk.
- Rape, spousal rape, and domestic violence are criminal offenses in San Marino. There are very few reported cases and all laws are effectively enforced to combat youth violence, intimate partner violence, sexual violence, elder abuse laws, and other laws protecting citizens.
- There are small populations of Baha'is and Muslims.

Indicators & Demographic Data

Population (2020)	33,800
% under 15 years	13%
Capital city (pop.)	San Marino 4,400
% urban dwellers	97% (0.41% p.a.)
Official language	Italian
Largest language	Italian (92%)
Largest people	Italian (91%)
Largest culture	Italian (100%)
Development	87
Physicians	64
Gender gap	3%

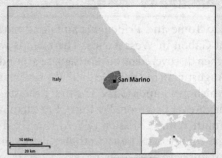

% Christian: 0 3 10 50 75 100

Christian Traditions in San Marino

1900 — 100%

2020 — 91.5%

☐ Independent ☐ Protestant ■ Catholic ■ Orthodox ■ Christian

In 1900, all Christians in San Marino were Catholic. Christianity in 2020 was still majority Catholic (99%), but with some Independents (1%).

Religion in San Marino

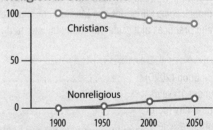

Christians

Nonreligious

San Marino's religious makeup changed little over the 20th century. In 1900, the country was entirely Christian (100%). By 2020, Christianity had dropped to 92%, mostly due to people leaving Christianity for atheism and agnosticism (together, 8% in 2020).

Bible Translations	Churches	Missionaries	Gospel Access
Languages............3	Denominations 2	Received.............20	1900 .... Very high
Full Bible.............1	Congregations........14	Sent 5	2020 .... Very high

Christianity in São Tomé and Príncipe

São Tomé and Príncipe is an island nation off the coast of Gabon in West Africa. The islands were uninhabited when discovered by the Portuguese around 1471. Soon after, Augustinian missionaries built the first church around 1504, which still stands today. The first Protestants were Seventh-day Adventists from Portugal. Brazilian missionaries with Youth With A Mission (YWAM) arrived in 1900. Despite the country's majority Catholic history, newer Evangelical groups have been growing. Pentecostal/Charismatic Christianity has also been growing, such as the New Apostolic Church and the Assemblies of God. São Tomé and Príncipe achieved independence in 1975.

Facts to Consider

- São Tomé and Príncipe is a secular state and provides for freedom of conscience, religion, and worship.
- The Universal Church of the Kingdom of God sent missionaries from Brazil to São Tomé and Príncipe; 2% of the population reported affiliation to the church in the latest census.
- Universal Church buildings were vandalized in 2019 after a São Toméan pastor was sentenced to prison in Côte d'Ivoire for denigrating an image related to the church.
- The number of Muslims in São Tomé and Príncipe has been growing because of migrants from Nigeria, Cameroon, and elsewhere in Africa.
- Traditional ethnic religions have nearly disappeared in the country, though some Christians and Muslims continue some traditional beliefs and practices alongside their monotheistic faith.

Indicators & Demographic Data

Population (2020)	218,000
% under 15 years	42%
Capital city (pop.)	São Tomé 75,600
% urban dwellers	74% (2.96% p.a.)
Official language	Portuguese
Largest language	Sãotomense (88%)
Largest people	Sãotomense Mestico (88%)
Largest culture	Eurafrican (94%)
Development	59
Physicians	4.9
Gender gap	11%

% Christian: 0 3 10 50 75 100

Christian Traditions in São Tomé and Príncipe

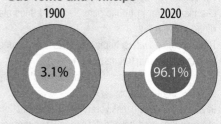

1900 — 3.1% 2020 — 96.1%

☐ Independent ☐ Protestant ☐ Catholic ■ Orthodox ■ Christian

The country's 1,300 Christians in 1900 were entirely Catholic. In 2020, Christians are still majority Catholic (75%), followed by Independents (17%) and Protestants (8%).

Religion in São Tomé and Príncipe

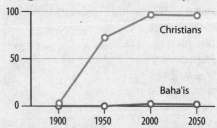

In 1900, the country was mostly followers of traditional religions (97%) and 3% Christian. By 2020, Christianity had grown to 96%, largely because of people converting from traditional religions, which dropped to less than 1%.

Bible Translations		Churches		Missionaries		Gospel Access	
Languages	8	Denominations	12	Received	120	1900	Very low
Full Bible	2	Congregations	400	Sent	20	2020	Very high

Christianity in Saudi Arabia

According to tradition, the apostle Bartholomew was the first missionary to Arabia. The Ancient Church of the East from Persia was at work in the region from the 5th to 7th centuries. Some tribal leaders converted on the coasts. Meanwhile, Greek Melkite Christian monks on the trade routes from Egypt to Syria helped introduce Christianity to nomadic Arabs. Christians were present at the time of Muhammad, and though these communities survived the rise of Islam, they gradually died out. Few Christians were left by the 10th century. Saudi Arabia is the geographic center of the Islamic faith, but there are at least 2 million Christians there today, mostly oil workers or domestic servants from the Philippines and South Korea.

Facts to Consider

- Islam is the official state religion of Saudi Arabia. Under Sharia law, there is no legal protection of religious freedom. Conversion from Islam is legally punishable by death. Blasphemy is a crime also punishable by death. All citizens must be Muslim.
- Mecca and Media are the two most important holy cities of Islam and are closed to non-Muslims. The annual pilgrimage to Mecca (*hajj*) attracts a large number of foreigners to the country.
- Women in Saudi Arabia have gained some rights in recent years, such as the ability to drive, study abroad without a male guardian, and serve as public prosecution investigators. But violence and discrimination against women are still widespread.
- Many Arabs have become Christians and must practice their Christianity in secret. There is an Arabic Bible and other Christian media to introduce people to Christianity, but Bibles are banned from public display.

Indicators & Demographic Data

Population (2020). 34,710,000
% under 15 years 24%
Capital city (pop.) . . . . Riyadh 7,231,000
% urban dwellers. . . . . .84% (1.69% p.a.)
Official language. . . . . Arabic
Largest language. . . . . Arabic (84%)
Largest people . . . . .Saudi Arab (37%)
Largest culture . . . . Arab (Arabic) (82%)
Development. 85
Physicians. 26
Gender gap. 12%

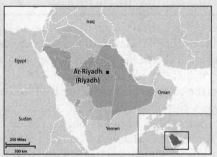

% Christian: 0 3 10 50 75 100

Christian Traditions in Saudi Arabia

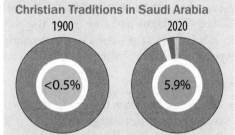

1900   2020
<0.5%   5.9%

☐Independent ☐Protestant ■Catholic ■Orthodox ■Christian

There were very few Christians in Saudi Arabia in 1900. In 2020, most Christians were Catholic (93%), though there are communities of Protestants (2%), Independents (3%), and Orthodox (3%).

Religion in Saudi Arabia

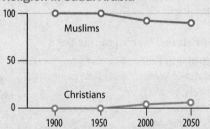

The religious makeup of Saudi Arabia changed little over the 20th century. In 1900, the country was entirely Muslim (100%). By 2020, Islam had dropped to 91% ,with the growth of Christianity (6%) and Hinduism (2%) due to migrant workers in the country.

Bible Translations	Churches	Missionaries	Gospel Access
Languages. 37	Denominations 45	Received. 120	1900 . . . . Very low
Full Bible. 20	Congregations. 1,400	Sent 10	2020 . . . . Medium

Christianity in Senegal

Senegal is a Muslim-majority country in West Africa, bordering Mauritania, Mali, Guinea, and Guinea-Bissau. The first encounter between the indigenous population and Christianity was via Portuguese traders in 1445. Its strategic location on the coast made it attractive for European powers, and it was a part of colonial French West Africa from 1895 until its independence in 1960. The Senegalese chief Behemoi was baptized Christian in 1486. The first Senegalese Catholic priests were ordained in 1840. In 1972, it was decided that all dioceses should have African, not foreign, priests. Protestants arrived in 1850 and began Scripture translation. Today, Christians make up 5% of the population and are mostly Catholic. The second largest denomination is the New Apostolic Church, mostly found in the Casamance region.

Facts to Consider

- Islam is concentrated in the north of the country among the Wolof people and in the east among the Fulani.
- The law requires young women to be at least 16 years old to marry, but this is not enforced in communities where arranged marriages are typical. One-third of women are married before age 18, and 12% before age 15.
- Child abuse is common, especially of boys in some Qur'anic schools (*daaras*). Instructors are known to exploit and physically abuse boys and force them to beg for food and money on the street.
- Dakar has an estimated 28,000 child street beggars, with 100,000 countrywide. The government has been trying unsuccessfully to combat the practice.

Indicators & Demographic Data

Population (2020). 17,200,000
% under 15 years 42%
Capital city (pop.) . . . . Dakar 3,140,000
% urban dwellers. . . . . .48% (3.59% p.a.)
Official language. . . . . French
Largest language. . . . . Wolof (36%)
Largest people . . . . Wolof (36%)
Largest culture . . . . Western Bantoid (Atlantic) (81%)
Development. 51
Physicians. 0.7
Gender gap. 9%

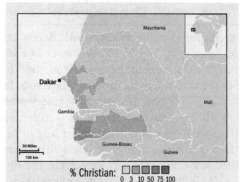

% Christian: 0 3 10 50 75 100

Christian Traditions in Senegal

1900 — 1.8%
2020 — 5.0%

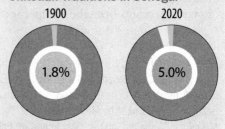

☐ Independent ☐ Protestant ▦ Catholic ▪ Orthodox ▪ Christian

The small Christian population in 1900 (just 18,400 people) was nearly entirely Catholic (98%). In 2020, Christianity was much larger (853,000) and more diverse, still majority Catholic (94%) but with smaller populations of Protestants (2%) and Independents (3%).

Religion in Senegal

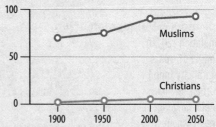

In 1900, Senegal was 70% Muslim, 28% traditional religionist, and just under 2% Christian. By 2020, Islam had grown to 91% and Christianity grew to 5%.

Bible Translations	Churches	Missionaries	Gospel Access
Languages. 52	Denominations 55	Received. 1,200	1900 . . . . Very low
Full Bible. 11	Congregations. 720	Sent 100	2020 . . . . Medium

Christianity in Serbia

Christianity has a long history in Serbia; the apostle Paul preached in Illyricum, the Roman province that included much of the country today. Slavic peoples migrated to the Balkans in the 6th to 8th centuries. While Western peoples (Croats and Slovenes) were more influenced by Rome's Latin-rite Catholicism, Eastern peoples (Serbs and Macedonians) were more influenced by Constantinople's Eastern Orthodox Christianity. In the mid-9th century, Christianity became the state religion. The Serbian Orthodox Church organized in the late 12th century under the leadership of St. Sava. It has remained the traditional church of the Serbs, though it was severely challenged during the massive geopolitical, ethnic, and religious conflicts of the 20th century. The aftermath of World War I gave rise to Yugoslavia, a merger of southern Slavic peoples (Slovenes, Croats, Serbs). However, the Ustaše movement murdered hundreds of thousands of Serbs, Jews, and Roma in Yugoslavia between 1929 and 1945. It became a Communist state in 1946. In 1989, Slobodan Milošević's rise to power led to ethnic tensions and bloody conflicts that eventually led to the breakup of Yugoslavia throughout the 1990s. Serbia and Montenegro remained federated until 2006, when Serbia became an independent state for the first time since 1918.

The Serbian Orthodox Church grew again in number and influence after the breakup of Yugoslavia. There continues to be a close nationalistic tie between the Serbian state and the church. The Church of St. Sava is located on the highest hill in Belgrade as a symbol of the nation as much as a place of worship. Catholics are the second largest denomination and are concentrated in or near Vojvodina province.

Lutheranism came to Serbia in the 16th century. Just as the Serbian Orthodox Church serves Serbian people by helping to preserve their ethnic identity, the Lutheran and Reformed churches serve the Slovak and Hungarian communities by preserving theirs. After the fall of Communism, Orthodox Christians found themselves in conflict with newer Pentecostal and Evangelical churches over members switching. Most Serbians have low opinions of Pentecostal/Charismatic and other newer Evangelical churches. They are perceived as dangerous proselytizers and threats to Serbian culture.

% Christian: 0 3 10 50 75 100

Religion in Serbia

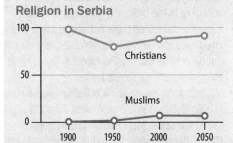

Serbia is historically a majority Christian country and remains so today. In 1900, Serbia was 98% Christian and 1% Jewish. By 2020, Christianity had dropped to 89% with an increase of Islam (7%) and the nonreligious (3%). Around 60,000 Jews—90% of the Jewish population—were killed during World War II. Only 3,000 Jews are left in the country, down from 32,000 in 1900.

Indicators & Demographic Data

Population (2020). 6,608,000
% under 15 years 16%
Capital city (pop.) . . . . Belgrade 1,398,000
% urban dwellers. . . . . 56% (0.04% p.a.)
Official language. . . . . Serbian
Largest language. . . . . Serbian (83%)
Largest people . . . . .Serb (82%)
Largest culture . . . . Serbian (82%)
Development. 79
Physicians. 25
Gender gap 2%

Bible Translations	Churches	Missionaries	Gospel Access
Languages. 28	Denominations 100	Received. 800	1900 . . . . Very high
Full Bible. 19	Congregations. 3,100	Sent 390	2020 . . . . Very high

Facts to Consider

- The government recognizes seven religious groups as "traditional": Serbian Orthodox, Roman Catholic, Slovak Evangelical, Reformed Christian, Evangelical Christian, Islamic, and Jewish communities. Another 25 groups are legally considered "nontraditional."
- Churches have been active in relief work, especially since the Yugoslav wars in the 1990s. Many humanitarian organizations and faith-based organizations have been involved in the migrant crisis of the 2010s, including Adventists, Catholics, and Serbian Orthodox.
- Most Pentecostal and Baptist churches worship in Serbian, but some use Hungarian, Slovak, or Romanian languages. They celebrate holidays according to the Orthodox, not Latin, calendar.
- A Pentecostal revival broke out among Roma people in Leskovac in the late 1980s and early 1990s, which led to a church planting movement throughout the country. Pentecostal/Charismatic Christians make up 1% of the country's population.
- Muslims, which comprise 7% of Serbia's population, are largely Bosniaks (Slavic Muslims) in the southwest Sandžak region, Albanians in the south, and some Roma throughout the country.
- The LGBTQ community in Serbia, around half a million people, experiences significant violence and discrimination, including hate crimes and sexual harassment. They seldom report because of a lack of institutional trust.

Christian Traditions in Serbia

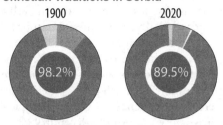

1900   98.2%

2020   89.5%

☐ Independent ☐ Protestant ◼ Catholic ◼ Orthodox ◼ Christian

Orthodox Christianity is the historic faith of Serbia. In 1900, Christians were 84% Orthodox, 11% Catholic, and 6% Protestant. In 2020, Orthodox had an even greater share than in 1900. Today, Christians in Serbia are 91% Orthodox, 7% Catholic, and 2% Protestant. The Evangelical and Pentecostal/Charismatic movements are quite small in Serbia. Evangelicals are around half a percent of the country's population, and Pentecostal/Charismatics are 1%.

Christian Families in Serbia

Family	Population 2020	%	Trend	Change
Eastern Orthodox	5,545,000	83.9	–	-0.4
Latin-rite Catholic	400,000	6.1	↓	-0.8
*Pentecostals/Charismatics	92,000	1.4	–	0.2
Lutheran	55,400	0.8	–	0.1
*Evangelicals	24,000	0.4	↑	0.7
Reformed, Presbyterian	14,700	0.2	↓	-0.5
Adventist	7,300	0.1	–	-0.4
Christian Brethren	6,900	0.1	↓	-1.2
Jehovah's Witnesses	5,800	0.1	–	-0.3
Baptist	2,300	<0.1	↓	-0.7
United church or joint mission	1,900	<0.1	–	0.1
Holiness	1,800	<0.1	–	0.1
Methodist	940	<0.1	↓	-3.2
Latter-day Saints (Mormons)	460	<0.1	↑	4.1
Anglican	300	<0.1	–	0.1

Eastern Orthodoxy is the largest Christian family in Serbia, with 84% of the population. Eastern Orthodox traditions include Serbian, Russian, Romanian, Bulgarian, and Albanian. Catholics make up 6% of the population and are the second largest family and denomination in the country. Pentecostals/Charismatics are the third largest family (1%) and are found throughout many Protestant and Independent groups, the largest of which is the Pentecostal Churches of Christ (10,000 members) and the Gypsy Evangelical Movement (8,000). Lutherans are found in two primary bodies, the Slovak Evangelical Christian Church (50,000) and a smaller Evangelical Church made up mostly of diaspora Hungarians (4,800).

* These movements are found within Christian families	↑↑ extreme growth
	↑ growth
	↓↓ extreme decline
– no change	↓ decline

Christianity in Seychelles

Seychelles, consisting of 115 islands, is an island nation in the Indian Ocean off the coast of East Africa. With a population of around 96,000, it is the smallest country in Africa by population. The French settled the uninhabited islands with planters and enslaved people beginning in 1768. Seychelles was a British colony from 1903 until independence in 1976. Catholicism is the largest Christian tradition and includes Creoles, Europeans, Blacks, Bantus, and Chinese. There are parishes with resident priests on Mahé, Praslin, and La Digue, while other islands receive only occasional pastoral visits. The largest Protestant group is the Anglican Church, found on Mahé and Praslin Islands.

Facts to Consider

- Most churches are involved in social action, including food distribution, agricultural development, education, and various kinds of relief work.
- Although rape and domestic abuse are criminal offenses, the government generally does not effectively enforce these laws. Many victims do not report these crimes because of social stigma or reluctance to begin lengthy court cases.
- Domestic violence against women is widespread; a recent report stated that 59% of women had been assaulted in their lifetime, mainly by their partners.
- The first shelter for victims of gender-based violence opened in 2018, but it is rarely used because of a no-children policy and a lack of admissions procedures.
- Other religions in Seychelles include small communities of Hindus, Muslim, Baha'i, Zoroastrians, and Jains.

Indicators & Demographic Data

Population (2020)................................... 96,100
% under 15 years 23%
Capital city (pop.)............................. Victoria 26,300
% urban dwellers.............................58% (0.99% p.a.)
Official language....................................... none
Largest language.................. Seychelles Creole French (92%)
Largest people ....Seychellese Creole (92%)
Largest culture .... Eurafrican (92%)
Development...80
Physicians.. 9.8
Gender gap...10%

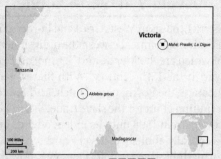

% Christian: □ ▦ ▦ ▦ ▦
0 3 10 50 75 100

Christian Traditions in Seychelles

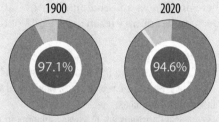

1900   2020

97.1%   94.6%

□ Independent □ Protestant ▦ Catholic ▦ Orthodox ▦ Christian

The Christian population of Seychelles is historically majority Catholic (92%) and remains so today. In 2020, Christians were 88% Catholic, 11% Protestant, and 1% Independent.

Religion in Seychelles

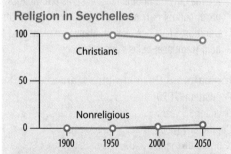

The religious makeup of Seychelles changed little over the 20th century. In 1900, the country was 97% Christian and 2% Hindu. By 2020, Christianity had dropped only slightly to 95%, Hinduism to 2%, while the nonreligious grew to just over 2%.

Bible Translations	Churches	Missionaries	Gospel Access
Languages............10	Denominations 12	Received............170	1900.......... Very high
Full Bible.............8	Congregations........51	Sent 15	2020.......... Very high

Christianity in Sierra Leone

Sierra Leone is in West Africa and borders Liberia and Guinea. The first encounter between the indigenous people (the largest of which are the Mende and Temne) and Portuguese traders was in the 15th century. With Sierra Leone as a strategic location, the Portuguese, Dutch, and French settled there as a trading point for the slave trade. Sierra Leone was a British colony from 1808 until its independence in 1961. The British eventually abolished slavery and founded a settlement for formerly enslaved people, Freetown, now the capital city. The Mende and Temne were partially responsive to Christianity, while few from other people groups have become Christians. There are almost an equal number of Catholics and Methodists in the country (each around 4% of the population).

Facts to Consider

- The Church of the Lord (Aladura), which spread to Sierra Leone from Nigeria and Ghana, is one of the most widespread and influential African Independent Churches.
- Evangelical Christians are a growing minority in the country, drawing members primarily from other Christian groups. Tensions are high between Evangelicals and Muslims, sometimes requiring police intervention.
- Intermarriage between Muslims and Christians is common. There are also many people who practice both Christianity and Islam together.
- Traditional ethnic religions are most prominent in the east. The Kono are majority traditional religionist, as are the Kissi and Koranko. In the north central part of the country, most of the Limba and Loko follow traditional religions as well. Many Christians and Muslims continue to hold traditional beliefs and practices.

Indicators & Demographic Data

Population (2020)	8,047,000
% under 15 years	41%
Capital city (pop.)	Freetown 1,202,000
% urban dwellers	43% (3.02% p.a.)
Official language	English
Largest language	Mende (26%)
Largest people	Mende (Boumpe, Kossa) (26%)
Largest culture	Western Bantoid (Atlantic) (43%)
Development	42
Physicians	0.2
Gender gap	13%

% Christian: 0 3 10 50 75 100

Christian Traditions in Sierra Leone

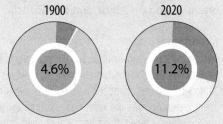

1900 — 4.6%   2020 — 11.2%

☐ Independent ☐ Protestant ▨ Catholic ■ Orthodox ■ Christian

The Christian population in 1900 (around 46,800 people) was majority Protestant (83%), followed by Catholic (7%). In 2020, Christianity was larger (over 900,000), still majority Protestant (49%) but with much larger Catholic (29%) and Independent (22%) populations.

Religion in Sierra Leone

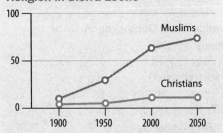

In 1900, Sierra Leone was 85% traditional religionist, 10% Muslim, and 5% Christian. By 2020, Islam had grown to 67% and Christianity to 11%.

Bible Translations		Churches		Missionaries		Gospel Access	
Languages	29	Denominations	100	Received	780	1900	Very low
Full Bible	13	Congregations	3,600	Sent	10	2020	High

Christianity in Singapore

Singapore is a small island city-state in Southeast Asia near Malaysia and Indonesia. The first Catholic priests arrived in Malacca after the Portuguese conquest in 1511. Protestantism began with the Dutch conquest of Malaysia in 1641 but was confined to Europeans until the first London Missionary Society personnel arrived in 1814. Singapore is a highly diverse country in language, ethnicity, religion, and culture. Christians were 20% of the population in 2020, but Chinese folk religionists, Muslims, Buddhists, Hindus, and the nonreligious were each also at least 5% of the population. Most churches are Chinese, but languages for worship include Mandarin, Hokkien, Cantonese, Teochew, English, Malay, Tamil, Malayalam, and numerous others.

Facts to Consider

- The Catholic Church is the largest denomination, and 70% of Catholics are Chinese. Most Masses are in English, but services are held in Mandarin, Tagalog, Tamil, Vietnamese, and other Asian languages.
- The Pentecostal/Charismatic movement is growing, and Singapore is home to many large churches such as City Harvest (1990), New Creation Church (1983), and Lighthouse Evangelism Church (1978).
- Singapore is a hub for international missions and serves as a launching point for missions throughout Southeast Asia. The Singapore Centre for Global Missions was founded in 1980 and is highly engaged in the missions movement, missiological thought, and global Evangelical gatherings.
- Buddhism and Chinese folk religion are the largest religions in Singapore, involving rituals and moral regulations common to Chinese culture.

Indicators & Demographic Data

Population (2020)..................................5,935,000
% under 15 years 14%
Capital city (pop.) ....Singapore 5,935,000
% urban dwellers............................ 100% (0.74% p.a.)
Official language...........Chinese (Mandarin), Malay, Tamil, English
Largest language................................ Chinese (50%)
Largest people ....Han Chinese (Min Nan) (19%)
Largest culture ....Han Chinese (70%)
Development..93
Physicians...23
Gender gap..2%

% Christian: 0 3 10 50 75 100

Christian Traditions in Singapore

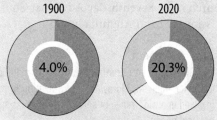

1900 — 4.0%   2020 — 20.3%

☐Independent ☐Protestant ◼Catholic ◼Orthodox ◼Christian

Christianity grew in Singapore from 10,000 Christians in 1900 to over 1.2 million in 2020. Today there are nearly equal shares of Catholics (38%) and Protestants (35%), followed by Independents (27%) and a small population of Orthodox.

Religion in Singapore

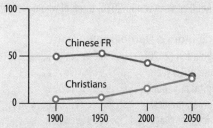

In 1900, Singapore was 50% Chinese folk religionist, 22% Muslim, 17% Buddhist, and 4% Christian. In 2020, the country was 37% Chinese folk religionist, 20% Christian, 15% Muslim, and 15% Buddhist.

Bible Translations		Churches		Missionaries		Gospel Access	
Languages	40	Denominations	81	Received	1,000	1900	Very low
Full Bible	29	Congregations	630	Sent	560	2020	High

Christianity in Sint Maarten

Sint Maarten is a constituent country of the Netherlands, consisting of the southern portion of the divided island of Saint Martin. The local Amerindian population declined dramatically after the arrival of Christopher Columbus in 1493, largely from new infectious diseases brought by the Europeans. France and the Netherlands divided the island in 1648 and imported massive numbers of enslaved people. Slavery ended in 1848. Sint Maarten is 89% Christian today, mostly Catholic. Churches formed in the 1970s and 1980s have grown, such as Baptists, Assemblies of God, and the New Testament Church of God. The largest Protestant church is the Seventh-day Adventist Church, founded by a missionary from Anguilla in 1950.

Facts to Consider

- The Sint Maarten Christian Council has members from Methodist, Catholic, Anglican, Moravian, and Salvation Army churches. They are involved in a wide range of services to address spiritual, physical, and political needs.
- Hurricane Irma landed in Sint Maarten in September 2017 and caused extensive damage across the island, with upward of 70% of infrastructure destroyed.
- Sint Maarten has received an influx of asylum seekers from Venezuela since 2014, causing competition for jobs with undocumented workers.
- Tourism is the largest sector of the economy, with over half a million tourists visiting annually.
- Sint Maarten has had seven prime ministers since the Netherlands Antilles dissolved in 2010, three of whom were women.

Indicators & Demographic Data

Population (2020)	41,400
% under 15 years	18%
Capital city (pop.)	Philipsburg 41,400
% urban dwellers	100% (1.16% p.a.)
Official language	Dutch, English
Largest language	Simaatn Creole English (36%)
Largest people	West Indian Black (42%)
Largest culture	Black (African), English-speaking (43%)
Development	68
Physicians	39
Gender gap	3%

% Christian: 0 3 10 50 75 100

Christian Traditions in Sint Maarten

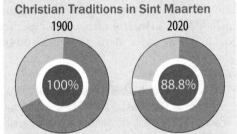

1900 — 100%
2020 — 88.8%

☐Independent ☐Protestant ▨Catholic ■Orthodox ■Christian

Christians in 1900 were roughly two-thirds Catholic and one-third Protestant. By 2020, the Catholic share had increased to 73%, while Protestants decreased to 23%. Independents were 4%.

Religion in Sint Maarten

The religious makeup of Sint Maarten changed little in the 20th century. In 1900, the country was 100% Christian. By 2020, Christianity had declined to 89% with an increase of Spiritists (7%) and the nonreligious (4%).

Bible Translations		Churches		Missionaries		Gospel Access	
Languages	9	Denominations	25	Received	130	1900	Very high
Full Bible	6	Congregations	57	Sent	4	2020	Very high

Christianity in Slovakia

The first missionaries to Slovakia were Franks in the 9th century. Christian culture spread quickly with the missionary work of Cyril and Methodius. Protestantism emerged in 1521 but was quickly persecuted by waves of anti-Reformation actions. Though the Edict of Tolerance (1782) encouraged the growth of Protestantism, the Catholic Church is the largest denomination today (72% of the country's population). Slovakia (then Czechoslovakia) became part of the Soviet-led Eastern bloc in 1948 and was under a Communist regime from 1969 to 1989. During this time, churches and the press were under government control, and thousands of people were sent to labor camps. The 1989 Velvet Revolution peacefully ended Communist rule and led to the creation of an independent state in 1993. The Catholic Church has grown in social and political influence, with a particular focus on combating abortion and same-sex marriage.

Facts to Consider

- The largest Protestant family is Lutheranism, with around 300,000 affiliates. Pentecostalism arrived in 1924 under the influence of American, Norwegian, and Swedish missionaries. The most stable Pentecostal movements are among the Roma people in the eastern part of the country.
- The Jewish population of Slovakia declined because of deportations in 1942, postwar pogroms in some cities, and emigration abroad (United States, Israel) after 1948. The population consists of just a few Jews today.
- Atheism and agnosticism waned after Communism collapsed in the former Czechoslovakia in 1989. Communist Party membership had already decreased from 20% of the population in 1948 to 8% in the 1970s.

Indicators & Demographic Data

Population (2020)................................5,451,000
% under 15 years 16%
Capital city (pop.)......................... Bratislava 435,000
% urban dwellers............................54% (0.17% p.a.)
Official language....................................... Slovak
Largest language................................ Slovak (86%)
Largest people .... Slovak (86%)
Largest culture .... Slovak (86%)
Development... 86
Physicians... 35
Gender gap... 1%

% Christian: ▭▭▭▭▪ 0 3 10 50 75 100

Christian Traditions in Slovakia

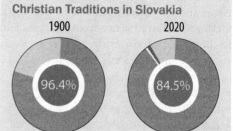

1900 — 96.4%
2020 — 84.5%

☐Independent ☐Protestant ▦Catholic ■Orthodox ▦Christian

Christianity in Slovakia is historically Catholic (79%), though there was a notable Protestant minority in 1900 (21%). By 2020, Christians were 89% Catholic and 9% Protestant. There is also a small Pentecostal/Charismatic movement (4% of the country's population).

Religion in Slovakia

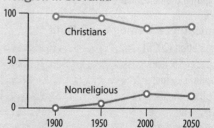

Christians

Nonreligious

1900   1950   2000   2050

Slovakia is historically a majority Christian country. In 1900, the country was 96% Christian and 3% Jewish. By 2020, Christianity had dropped to 85% with an increase in the nonreligious to 15%.

Bible Translations		Churches		Missionaries		Gospel Access	
Languages	17	Denominations	34	Received	1,200	1900	Very high
Full Bible	13	Congregations	2,400	Sent	80	2020	Very high

Christianity in Slovenia

After the Christianization of the Slovenes in the 6th century, the church was well established by the 10th century. Education was closely tied to the Catholic Church from the Middle Ages to the start of the 20th century, which began a turbulent period in Slovenia's history. A part of the first Yugoslavia in 1918, Slovenia was subsequently annexed into both Nazi Germany and fascist Italy during World War II, then absorbed into the second Yugoslavia in 1945, and then was a Communist republic until independence in 1991. Catholicism has been declining since the country's independence, and most Catholics are nonobservant. The Serbian Orthodox Church is the second largest Christian tradition in the country due to emigration from Bosnia-Herzegovina, Kosovo, and Macedonia in the 1960s and 1970s.

Facts to Consider

- Many Catholics disagree with the church's conservative stances on contraception, premarital sex, and abortion. Trust in the Catholic Church has declined because of its financial scandals.
- Pentecostalism was introduced in 1933 by a Hungarian missionary and Slovene missionary. Banned in the Communist era, it has been growing steadily since the 1990s.
- Muslims make up 4% of the population and are mostly Bosniaks and other Slavs who arrived in the 1960s and 1970s. After four decades of controversy, ground broke in Ljubljana in 2013 for the country's first mosque.
- Holocaust education is mandatory in public schools and focuses on the history of Jews, anti-Semitism in Europe, and the atrocities committed during the Holocaust.

Indicators & Demographic Data

Population (2020)	2,082,000
% under 15 years	15%
Capital city (pop.)	Ljubljana 271,000
% urban dwellers	55% (0.54% p.a.)
Official language	Slovene
Largest language	Slovene (88%)
Largest people	Slovene (88%)
Largest culture	Slovene (88%)
Development	90
Physicians	28
Gender gap	0%

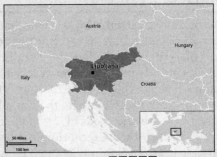

% Christian: 0 3 10 50 75 100

Christian Traditions in Slovenia

1900   2020

100%   82.3%

☐Independent ☐Protestant ◼Catholic ◼Orthodox ◼Christian

Christianity in Slovenia is historically Catholic (99%), with a very small Protestant minority in 1900. By 2020, Christians were 94% Catholic, 4% Orthodox, and 2% Protestant.

Religion in Slovenia

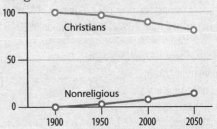

Slovenia is historically a majority Christian country. In 1900, the country was essentially 100% Christian. However, by 2020, Christianity had dropped to 83% with an increase in the nonreligious to 14%. Muslims are also now 4% of the population.

Bible Translations		Churches		Missionaries		Gospel Access	
Languages	17	Denominations	100	Received	890	1900	Very high
Full Bible	14	Congregations	1,400	Sent	170	2020	Very high

Christianity in Solomon Islands

Solomon Islands consist of six major islands and over 900 smaller islands located to the east of Papua New Guinea in Oceania. Early Catholic and Protestant missionaries were murdered by the indigenous people, who in turn died from foreign diseases. Missionaries arrived and survived in larger numbers in the 19th and early 20th centuries. Several islands were under the control of Germany and Britain until full independence in 1978. The Church of Melanesia (Anglican) is the largest denomination today and is found mostly in the eastern islands: Santa Isabel, Malaita, Guadalcanal, and San Cristobal. Catholics are the second largest denomination, with three dioceses in Honiara, Gizo, and Auki.

Facts to Consider

- In 2017, Parliament moved to amend the constitution to make Solomon Islands an officially Christian nation. Critics say the government should focus more on economic development and less on religion.
- The largest indigenous Christian movement is the Christian Fellowship Church, also known as "Etoism" after its founder-messiah, Silas Eto. It split from the Methodist church in 1960.
- The Solomon Islands Christian Association plays a leading role in public life, organizes joint religious activities, and encourages religious representation in national life. It is in regular conversation with government officials.
- The Christian Care Centre is the only place that serves women and girls who have been victims of violence. It is staffed by Anglican nuns.
- Traditional animistic religions are practiced among the Kwaio people group (about 20,000 people) on the island of Malaita.

Indicators & Demographic Data

Population (2020). 647,000
% under 15 years 38%
Capital city (pop.) . . . . Honiara 70,500
% urban dwellers. . . . . .25% (3.57% p.a.)
Official language. . . . . .English
Largest language. . . . . Kwara'ae (8%)
Largest people . . . . .Kwaraae (7%)
Largest culture . . . . .Solomoni Melanesian (72%)
Development. 55
Physicians. 1.9
Gender gap. 16%

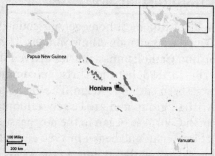

% Christian: 0 3 10 50 75 100

Christian Traditions in Solomon Islands

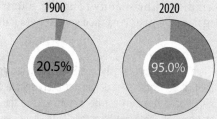

1900 — 20.5%   2020 — 95.0%

☐Independent ☐Protestant ■Catholic ■Orthodox ■Christian

The small Christian population in 1900 (15,400 Christians) were mostly foreign Protestants (97%). In 2020, Protestants had the largest share (71%), followed by Catholics (22%). About a quarter of the country is Evangelical.

Religion in Solomon Islands

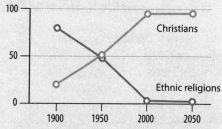

In 1900, Solomon Islands were 80% followers of traditional religions and 20% Christian. By 2020, Christianity had grown to 95% of the population and traditional religions had declined to 3%.

Bible Translations	Churches	Missionaries	Gospel Access
Languages. 75	Denominations 31	Received. 600	1900 . . . . Low
Full Bible. 10	Congregations. 3,100	Sent 45	2020 . . . . Very high

Christianity in Somalia

Somalia is the most homogenous country in Africa, with 75% of the population ethnic Somalis. The country is 99.9% Muslim. Catholic missionaries arrived in 1881 and Protestants in 1898, but the Christian community has almost always been entirely foreign. The Orthodox are the largest Christian group and are largely Ethiopian refugees. The Somali Civil War began in the northeast in 1979. The conflict in Somaliland began in 1982 and intensified in 1988. The collapse of the country in the 1990s led to the exodus of most Christians. A new government and constitution were adopted in 2012. In 2011, al-Shabaab jihadists swore to eradicate Christianity from the country. Proselytism is illegal, and Christians face severe persecution.

Facts to Consider

- Islam is the official religion, and Salafi Islam has grown in influence over the last 30 years. Islam dominates every sphere of life.
- Al-Shabaab regularly carries out attacks in the capital, Mogadishu, and controls large swaths of land in the south and central areas; they control upward of 20% of the country's territory. Their aim is to instate a strict version of Islamic law.
- Any efforts to spread Christianity in Somalia are carried out discreetly. Islamic extremists have murdered many Christians over the years. There are some Christian humanitarian organizations that serve needy populations.
- Christianity is generally not tolerated in society. For example, a woman in Burao, Somaliland, was beaten by her brothers, divorced by her husband, and separated from her children for having a Bible in her home.

Indicators & Demographic Data

Population (2020). 16,105,000
% under 15 years 46%
Capital city (pop.) . . . . Mogadishu 2,282,000
% urban dwellers. . . . . .46% (4.20% p.a.)
Official language. . . . . Somali, Arabic
Largest language. . . . . .Somali (86%)
Largest people . . . . .Somali (82%)
Largest culture . . . . .Somali (93%)
Development. 50
Physicians. 0.3
Gender gap 10%

% Christian: 0 3 10 50 75 100

Christian Traditions in Somalia

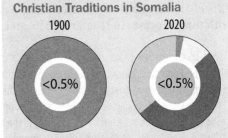

1900: <0.5% 2020: <0.5%

☐ Independent ☐ Protestant ■ Catholic ■ Orthodox ■ Christian

Somalia had only a few hundred Christians in 1900, all Catholics. By 2020, Christianity had grown to a few thousand, but declined proportionally to the country's population. Most Christians are foreign Orthodox (50%) or Protestants (35%).

Religion in Somalia

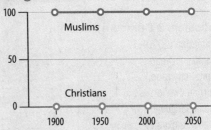

Somalia is one of the most Muslim countries in the world. Its religious makeup hardly changed between 1900 and 2020, during which Muslims were 99.9% of the population.

Bible Translations		Churches		Missionaries		Gospel Access	
Languages.	.23	Denominations	.9	Received.	.60	1900	Very low
Full Bible.	.10	Congregations	.56	Sent	.4	2020	Low

Christianity in South Africa

The main people groups in South Africa at the introduction of Christianity were Bantu speakers who migrated from elsewhere on the continent thousands of years prior, along with the Zulu and Xhosa peoples. Christianity has played a major role in South African race relations and politics since the establishment of a Dutch settlement in 1652. With economic opportunities in mining, the British occupation of Cape Colony in 1806 resulted in significant European immigration to the region. Conflicts between indigenous peoples and colonists occurred during the Anglo-Zulu War (1879), the First Boer War (1880–1881), and Second Boer War (1899–1902). Racial segregation had informally existed in the 19th century, but in 1948, segregation—known as apartheid—was made legal, giving the White minority control over the much larger Black majority. Apartheid was controversial, and churches had differing attitudes toward the policy. For example, Dutch Reformed churches supported it, but the South African Council of Churches and the Catholic Church openly opposed it. Desmond Tutu and other church leaders provided theological justification for resistance and protest. Apartheid ended in 1994 with the transition to majority governmental rule.

South Africa is a highly diverse society, home to 11 official languages, with Zulu and Xhosa spoken most commonly. The country's population (according to the latest census) is 79% Black African, 9% White, 9% mixed race, and 2.5% Indian or Asian. There is also a large refugee and asylum seeker population largely from Zimbabwe, the Democratic Republic of the Congo, and Somalia. The country is 82% Christian, and 22% of South Africans are Protestant, mostly Anglicans, Methodists, and the Apostolic Faith Mission.

South Africa has the most Independent churches of anywhere in the world, adherents of which comprise over 40% of the population. There are two major kinds of Independent churches, Ethiopian type (from the 19th century) and Zionist type (20th century). Ethiopian types campaigned for Christian leadership to be held by Africans. Zionist churches draw from African Traditional Religion, Pentecostalism, and Protestantism, all from an African worldview. Many Zionist prophets report the gift of healing and receive new revelations from God or angels.

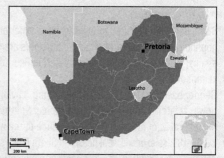

% Christian: 0 3 10 50 75 100

Religion in South Africa

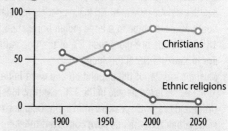

In 1900, South Africa was 57% traditional religionists and 41% Christian. By 2020, traditional religionists had declined to just under 7%, while Christianity increased to 82%. Hindus represent just over 2%, and Muslims just under 2% of the population.

Indicators & Demographic Data

Population (2020)	58,721,000
% under 15 years	28%
Capital city (pop.)	Cape Town 4,618,000; Pretoria 2,566,000
% urban dwellers	67% (1.72% p.a.)
Official language	Zulu and 10 others
Largest language	Zulu (21%)
Largest people	Zulu (21%)
Largest culture	Nguni (44%)
Development	70
Physicians	8.2
Gender gap	2%

Bible Translations		Churches		Missionaries		Gospel Access	
Languages	48	Denominations	6,400	Received	15,000	1900	Medium
Full Bible	33	Congregations	84,900	Sent	10,000	2020	Very high

Facts to Consider

- Some South Africans, as foreigners, have experienced widespread xenophobic harassment and attacks. Foreigners are openly discriminated against despite the recent National Action Plan to combat racism and xenophobia.
- Gender-based violence is also widespread, having spiked during lockdowns related to the COVID-19 pandemic. South Africa has one of the highest rates of intimate partner violence in the world.
- COVID-19 also exposed weaknesses in South Africa's social infrastructure, especially for children who lost access to education and food.
- HIV/AIDS stigma is prominent in society, and HIV-positive people experience discrimination in employment, housing, and access to education and health care. An estimated 7.5 million people in South Africa live with HIV.
- South Africa is home to a large Indian population, originating from the 1860s. Hindus are more than 2% of the population, and the majority live in KwaZulu-Natal Province.
- Muslims are 2% of the population and were initially brought to South Africa as enslaved people in the 17th century. Most are descendants of Urdu- and Gujarati-speakers from India. Because of missionary efforts, some urbanized Africans have converted to Islam.

Christian Traditions in South Africa

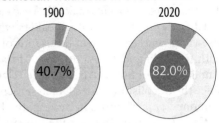

1900 — 40.7%   2020 — 82.0%

☐ Independent ☐ Protestant ▨ Catholic ■ Orthodox ■ Christian

There has always been great diversity of Christianity in South Africa. In 1900, most Christians by far were Protestant (95%), followed by much smaller communities of Catholics (4%) and Independents (1%). By 2020, Independent Christianity had grown to be the largest tradition, representing 59% of Christians. Protestants were 32%, and Catholics were 9%. Evangelicals are 10% of the country's population and Pentecostals/Charismatics are 47%.

Christian Families in South Africa

Family	Population 2020	%	Trend	Change
*Pentecostals/Charismatics	27,700,000	47.2	↑	1.2
*Evangelicals	6,100,000	10.4	↑	1.0
Latin-rite Catholic	3,850,000	6.6	↑	1.0
Anglican	3,502,000	6.0	↑	0.8
Reformed, Presbyterian	2,604,000	4.4	–	0.4
Methodist	1,857,000	3.2	↑	0.9
United church or joint mission	1,295,000	2.2	↑	0.6
Lutheran	648,000	1.1	–	0.1
Congregational	465,000	0.8	↑	0.5
Jehovah's Witnesses	249,000	0.4	↑	2.8
Adventist	227,000	0.4	↑↑	6.4
Nondenominational	205,000	0.3	↑	1.4
Baptist	145,000	0.2	–	-0.1
Moravian	120,000	0.2	↑	1.3
Holiness	113,000	0.2	–	0.2
Restorationist, Disciple	99,900	0.2	↑	1.7
Latter-day Saints (Mormons)	73,400	0.1	↑	2.9
Salvationist	61,400	0.1	↑	0.7
Eastern Orthodox	15,400	<0.1	↓	-1.0
Oriental and other Orthodox	14,600	<0.1	–	0.4
Old Catholic Church	5,100	<0.1	–	-0.2
Christian Brethren	3,500	<0.1	↓	-0.7

Christianity in South Africa is extremely diverse. It is one of the few countries in the world where unaffiliated Christians are one of the largest groups, that is, Christians who are not members or otherwise attached to a specific denomination. Largely because of the history of migratory labor, many Christians belong to more than one church, and many also practice a blend of Christianity and traditional beliefs. The largest Christian family is the Pentecostal/Charismatic movement, which dates to 1908 and has gained influence among all ethnic groups. The Zion Christian Church is the largest, with around 5 million members. Other groups include the International Pentecost Church and the Apostolic Faith Mission of South Africa. There is also substantial overlap between Evangelicals and Pentecostals/Charismatics. Anglicans are the fourth largest family. While the Church of the Province of Southern Africa is the largest (and part of the Anglican Communion), there are at least eight other breakaway Anglican groups.

* These movements are found within Christian families
− no change

↑↑ extreme growth
↑ growth
↓↓ extreme decline
↓ decline

Christianity in South Korea

The first encounter between Koreans and Christianity was in 1592 when a Catholic priest accompanied a Japanese invasion of Korea. Catholicism grew in Korea in the 16th century, with several martyred during the persecutions of 1791. Protestant missionaries arrived in 1832, with one martyred in 1865. Freedom of religion was not granted in Korea until the early 1880s. The first Presbyterian missionary arrived in 1884, followed by Methodists. Christianity became popular among Koreans at the turn of the 20th century because of Bible classes and a revival in 1907 in Pyongyang. Under Japanese colonization of Korea from 1910 to 1945, Christianity was perceived as a Western threat to the government, especially since many Korean Christians were educated in missionary schools. Because of relief work by missionaries, Christianity gained more respect during the Cold War (1945–1991) and the Korean War (1950–1953). The urban middle class particularly embraced Christianity in the 1960s and 1970s, and today the country is 34% Christian.

Various Protestant denominations were introduced to the country largely because of the efforts of Western missionaries. Protestants founded Korea's first modern schools and resisted Japanese occupation. Large Protestant families include Presbyterians, Methodists, Seventh-day Adventists, and Baptists. The Assemblies of God is the largest Protestant denomination, having begun in 1958 with the founding of Yoido Full Gospel Church by David Yonggi Cho. Catholicism grew substantially from the 1950s to 1970s, largely from immigration and relief work provided by the Catholic Church. Two million refugees fled the North for the South after the split of North and South Korea in 1952.

Many churches are indigenous to South Korea, most of which have been established in the last quarter of the 20th century. They include numerous schisms from the Presbyterian Church of Korea, plus Korean traditions that blend traditional religious beliefs and practices with Christianity. Some of these look more Christian than others. Korea has become one of the most prominent missionary-sending countries in the world, sending nearly 35,000 missionaries abroad annually. Women make up the majority of Korean churches today across all denominations.

% Christian: 0 3 10 50 75 100

Religion in South Korea

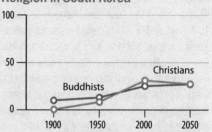

In 1900, South Korea was 81% traditional religionist, 10% Buddhist, 8% Confucianist, and 0.5% Christian. By 2020, traditional religionists had declined to just 15%, with Christianity increasing to 34%, Buddhism to 25%, and Confucianists to 11%. South Korea is now also home to over 250 New Religions, 14% of the population.

Indicators & Demographic Data

Population (2020). 51,507,000
% under 15 years 13%
Capital city (pop.) . . . . Seoul 9,963,000
% urban dwellers. . . . . 81% (0.31% p.a.)
Official language. . . . . .Korean
Largest language. . . . . .Korean (97%)
Largest people . . . . South Korean (97%)
Largest culture . . . . .Korean (97%)
Development. 90
Physicians. 23
Gender gap 7%

Bible Translations	Churches	Missionaries	Gospel Access
Languages. 9	Denominations 420	Received. 3,000	1900 . . . . Very low
Full Bible. 8	Congregations. 97,400	Sent 35,000	2020 . . . . Very high

Facts to Consider

- Korean Christianity is known for strong anti-ecumenical stances. Many churches have Evangelical alliances that oppose cooperation across denominational lines. In 2013, approximately 2,000 Korean Protestants protested the 10th assembly of the World Council of Churches, held in Busan.
- Several recent scandals related to finances, sexual abuse, and corruption have marred Korean Christianity, affecting communities in megachurches and in the Catholic Church. In 2020, Christians came under fire when the Shincheonji Church of Jesus was ground zero for the largest coronavirus outbreak in the country, where 5,000 members became infected. Its leader was also accused of embezzling nearly $5 million from the church. Many Evangelicals consider this church a cult.
- Shamanism is the traditional religion of Korea, dating to before the 10th century BCE. Many consider shamanism to be the core of not just Korean religion but also Korean culture and identity.
- The largest New Religion in South Korea is Ch'öndogyo (Religion of the Heavenly Way), a blend of shamanistic, Buddhist, Confucian, and Christian elements that arose in the 19th century in protest of Western influences.
- Muslims in South Korea could number upward of 200,000 but are difficult to track because many arrive without proper documentation. Many are migrant workers from Bangladesh, Indonesia, and Pakistan.

Christian Traditions in South Korea

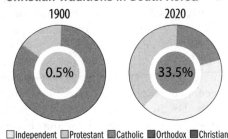

1900   2020
0.5%   33.5%

□Independent □Protestant ■Catholic ■Orthodox ■Christian

In 1900, most Christians in South Korea were Catholic (84%) due to historical missionary work and conversions, including many prominent Korean Catholic martyrs. In 2020, Christianity was quite diverse: 42% Independent, 38% Protestant, and 20% Catholic. There are also large Evangelical and Pentecostal/Charismatic communities. Evangelicals make up 25% of South Korea's population and Pentecostal/Charismatics are 24%.

Christian Families in South Korea

Family	Population 2020	%	Trend	Change
*Evangelicals	12,855,000	25.0	↑	0.7
Reformed, Presbyterian	12,334,000	23.9	↑	0.8
*Pentecostals/Charismatics	9,150,000	17.8	↑	1.0
Latin-rite Catholic	5,500,000	10.7	↑	0.7
Methodist	1,915,000	3.7	↑	1.3
Holiness	726,000	1.4	↓	-2.7
Baptist	688,000	1.3	↓	-2.7
Adventist	299,000	0.6	↑	1.8
Nondenominational	154,000	0.3	↑	1.0
Jehovah's Witnesses	145,000	0.3	–	-0.2
Restorationist, Disciple	115,000	0.2	↑	2.4
Latter-day Saints (Mormons)	87,100	0.2	–	0.3
Anglican	85,900	0.2	↑	1.4
Salvationist	52,700	0.1	↓	-4.1
Christian Brethren	13,600	<0.1	↑	0.8
Lutheran	5,900	<0.1	↑	1.6
Eastern Orthodox	2,300	<0.1	–	0.0

Christianity in South Korea is relatively diverse, but in unique ways compared with other countries. One of the largest Christian families is Reformed/Presbyterian (12.3 million in total), but there have been numerous schisms among these churches. South Korea is home to at least 200 Korean Presbyterian denominations and tens of thousands of registered Presbyterian churches. The largest two are the Presbyterian Church in Korea (Tonghap) and the Presbyterian Church in Korea (Hapdong), both with roughly 2.7 million members. Most divisions occurred after World War II over various theological issues. Many Korean Christians are Evangelicals, found throughout most Presbyterian, Methodist, Holiness, and Pentecostal churches. Evangelicals are 25% (12.8 million) of the country's population. Pentecostal/ Charismatic denominations include the Assemblies of God, Church of God (Cleveland), Church of Prophecy, and Assembly Hall Churches.

*	These movements are found within Christian families	↑↑	extreme growth
		↑	growth
		↓↓	extreme decline
–	no change	↓	decline

Christianity in South Sudan

Until 2011, Sudan and South Sudan were one country. The largest people groups are the Dinka, Nuer, and Zande. The region was ruled by Egypt from 1821, by the Islamic Madhiyya state in the 1880s, and then was rendered the Anglo-Egyptian Condominium from 1899 until Sudanese independence in 1956. The British conquest of Sudan rose from a desire to restrict access to the Nile River from the French in 1898. British attempts to modernize Sudan were greater in the Arab north than the Black African south, creating deep disparities in the country. The south was more remote, underdeveloped, and largely closed to outsiders. The slave trade, conducted by foreigners and northern Sudanese Muslims in the south, hindered Christian missionary efforts in the 19th century. Missionaries were banned from working in the north but encouraged in the south, especially in education, health care, and other social services. The south was 2% Christian at the time of Sudanese independence in 1956. Meanwhile, the north sought to impose Arab language, culture, and Islam on the south to foster national unity and in the name of the "superior" civilization. When the south resisted these efforts, civil war erupted from 1955 to 1972, followed by another civil war from 1983 to 2005. By 1970, the south was nearly 20% Christian.

Christianity continued to grow in the south, partly because southern Sudanese identity became intertwined with Christianity and in opposition to the Islam of the north. They favored English over Arabic and Christianity over Islam. Attending church was as much a political statement as an act of faith. South Sudan became a sovereign nation separate from Sudan after a referendum in 2011, with 98.8% of the population voting for independence. The country is 62% Christian today. The Catholic Church is the largest denomination (53% of the country's population), followed by Anglicans. An evangelistic festival was held after independence in 2011, attended by 100,000 Christians to celebrate the hope of a new Christian nation. Missionaries from the United States, South Korea, and elsewhere in Africa have introduced newer Evangelical groups. Pentecostal/Charismatic Christianity is also growing, with new churches cropping up, especially in the capital, Juba.

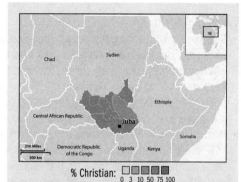

% Christian:

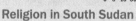

0 3 10 50 75 100

Religion in South Sudan

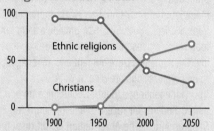

South Sudan experienced tremendous change in its religious makeup in the 20th century. In 1900, the country was 94% traditional religionist and 6% Muslim. By 2020, traditional religionists had declined to 32%, while Christianity increased to 62%, with Muslims remaining steady at 6%.

Indicators & Demographic Data

Population (2020)	13,610,000
% under 15 years	41%
Capital city (pop.)	Juba 403,000
% urban dwellers	20% (4.12% p.a.)
Official language	English
Largest language	Dinka (36%)
Largest people	Western Dinka (Rek) (15%)
Largest culture	Dinka (36%)
Development	39
Physicians	0.8
Gender gap	17%

Bible Translations		Churches		Missionaries		Gospel Access	
Languages	80	Denominations	43	Received	480	1900	Very low
Full Bible	19	Congregations	4,800	Sent	70	2020	Very high

Facts to Consider

- Religious institutions help provide a tremendous amount of stability for South Sudan, particularly in peace-building and humanitarian aid, which is critical for a country still experiencing the ramifications of generations of war and conflict. South Sudan experienced a civil war from 2013 to 2020 in which an estimated 400,000 people died and 4 million displaced both internally and in Uganda and Sudan.
- Women face many types of discrimination in society, including high rates of illiteracy, rape as a weapon of war, no laws that prohibit domestic violence, and widespread attitudes that women's professional work conflicts with domestic duties. Female genital mutilation/cutting is still practiced in some areas, though it is considered a criminal offense.
- Many international Christian NGOs, across denominations and traditions, work in South Sudan to provide a wide range of services such as food relief, disease prevention, refugee services, and trauma counseling. The Sudanese Development and Relief Agency and other indigenous relief organizations are also at work.
- Upon independence, South Sudan became home to 75% of the former united Sudan's oil reserves and the third largest oil reserves in sub-Saharan Africa. The Abyei region is still disputed between Sudan and South Sudan.

Christian Traditions in South Sudan

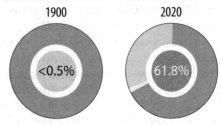

1900   2020

☐Independent ☐Protestant ■Catholic ■Orthodox ■Christian

There were hardly any Christians in South Sudan in 1900, limited perhaps to just a handful of European Catholics. Christianity grew over the 20th century to over 7.3 million affiliates—62% Catholic, 36% Protestant, and 2% Independent. Evangelicals make up 12% of South Sudan's population and Pentecostal/Charismatics make up 7%.

Christian Families in South Sudan

Family	Population 2020	%	Trend	Change
Latin-rite Catholic	7,350,000	54.0	↑	3.3
Anglican	1,922,000	14.1	↑	2.5
*Evangelicals	1,655,000	12.2	↑	2.2
Reformed, Presbyterian	1,033,000	7.6	↑	2.4
*Pentecostals/Charismatics	950,000	7.0	↑	3.1
Nondenominational	282,000	2.1	↑	2.7
Congregational	43,900	0.3	–	0.4
Baptist	18,700	0.1	↑	2.3
Oriental and other Orthodox	3,000	<0.1	–	0.0
Jehovah's Witnesses	2,900	<0.1	↑	0.7
Hidden believers in Christ	970	<0.1	↑	3.3

Catholics make up 54% of the country's population, and the country is home to 270 priests and around 200 sisters. Anglicans are the second largest Christian family and date to the work of the Church Missionary Society in 1899 among the Dinka, Malek, Nuer, Zande, and Bari peoples. Evangelicals are the third largest family and are found across all denominations, namely, the Anglican church, Africa Inland Church, Assemblies of God, Sudan Interior Church, and Evangelical Covenant Church. All of these denominations were started by American or British missionaries in the late 19th and early 20th centuries. The Pentecostal/Charismatic movement grew in the 1990s across the older Protestant churches. Newer Pentecostal churches have also been established, such as the Juba Christian Centre, Watoto Church (from Uganda), and the Full Gospel Church.

* These movements are found within Christian families	↑↑ extreme growth
	↑ growth
	↓↓ extreme decline
– no change	↓ decline

Christianity in Spain

Christianity has a long history in Spain, with some believing that the apostle Paul visited Spain on a missionary journey. Arian Visigoths overran the Iberian Peninsula in 409 CE, converted to Catholicism, and made it the state religion in 589. The region came under control of Muslim Berbers from north Africa in the 8th century and was recaptured by Christian rulers in 1249. By the 16th century, Spain was a vast overseas empire, sending Catholic missionary brothers to their new colonies in Latin America. The 16th-century Protestant Reformation encouraged a revival within Catholicism and resulted in the Inquisition that forced Spanish Jews and Moors to become Christians or leave Spain entirely. As a result, Spanish Catholicism was known for an ability to prevent the growth of any religious vitality outside the Catholic Church, including Protestantism. Protestantism was outlawed in Spain until 1868, when the first religious tolerance article was written into the constitution, and complete religious freedom was denied until 1967. Nevertheless, Protestantism began as a house church movement, working clandestinely.

Catholicism is still the majority religion in Spain today but changed significantly over the 20th century, moving from a national identity to an optional faith. Spain is also now the home to many immigrants from Latin America who have brought with them a charismatic form of the Catholic faith, a movement that also began in Barcelona in the 1970s. Catholic Charismatics sustain their faith through weekly prayer meetings, singing, Bible study, and retreats. Protestantism is still very small in Spain, comprising less than 1% of the population, and tends to attract people from marginalized populations in rural areas and villages.

One of the largest non-Catholic Christian movements in Spain is the Philadelphia Evangelical Church (Iglesia Evangélica Filadelfia), the Pentecostal movement among Roma people throughout the country. As a result, many Spaniards think that all *evangélicos* (non-Catholics) are *gitanos* (Roma). This church traces its origins to a revival among Roma in France in the 1950s that spread over the border into Spain. Independent and Pentecostal churches have been growing in major urban areas as well.

% Christian: 0 3 10 50 75 100

Religion in Spain

Spain has been a majority Christian country for many centuries and remains so today. The country was essentially 100% Christian in 1900, but the Christian share of the population dropped to 86% by 2020. Numerical increases were made primarily by Muslims (3%) and the nonreligious (11%). There are also small communities of Jews, Hindus, and Buddhists.

Indicators & Demographic Data

Population (2020) 46,459,000
% under 15 years 14%
Capital city (pop.) . . . . Madrid 6,618,000
% urban dwellers . . . . 81% (0.24% p.a.)
Official language . . . . Spanish
Largest language . . . . Spanish (43%)
Largest people . . . . Spaniard (36%)
Largest culture . . . . Spanish (45%)
Development 89
Physicians 39
Gender gap 2%

Bible Translations	Churches	Missionaries	Gospel Access
Languages 35	Denominations 340	Received 3,000	1900 . . . . Very high
Full Bible 23	Congregations 27,600	Sent 10,000	2020 . . . . Very high

Facts to Consider

- The government provides funding for Catholic education in public schools and will provide the same for Protestant and Muslim students if at least 10 students request it.
- In 2018, nearly 60 associations, educational unions, and political parties petitioned to end religious instruction in public schools, citing offenses to "religious indoctrination."
- The Catalan independence movement has roots in the 19th century. There have been several referendums for their independence from Spain (such as in 2014 and 2017), but they have not received 50% of the vote. The national government has tried to stop the votes, sometimes with violence.
- According to the Federation of Evangelical Religious Entities, over half of all Protestants in Spain are immigrants.
- Atheism and agnosticism are growing in Spain. Almost half of young people self-identify as "nonbeliever" or "atheist." Overall, 22% of survey respondents said religion is very important in their lives; 23% attend worship services at least monthly, and 25% believe in God with absolute certainty. Catalonia, Andalusia, and Madrid have the highest percentages of non-Christians.
- Islam has been growing in Spain, from zero in 1900 to 3% of the population in 2020 (1.4 million). Many have arrived from North Africa, in particular, Morocco.

Christian Traditions in Spain

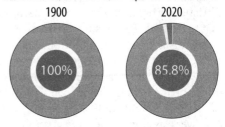

1900   2020

100%   85.8%

☐ Independent ☐ Protestant ■ Catholic ■ Orthodox ■ Christian

Christianity in Spain has historically been rather homogenous, and this is largely still true today. All Christians in Spain in 1900 were Catholic. Catholics were still the majority in 2020 (96% of Christians), followed by Orthodox (2%) and Protestant/Independents (2%). Evangelicals make less than 1% of Spain's population and Pentecostals/Charismatics make up 3%.

Christian Families in Spain

Family	Population 2020	%	Trend	Change
Latin-rite Catholic	38,970,000	83.9	–	-0.3
*Pentecostals/Charismatics	1,200,000	2.6	–	0.3
Eastern Orthodox	800,000	1.7	↑	1.0
*Evangelicals	400,000	0.9	↑	2.0
Jehovah's Witnesses	157,000	0.3	↓	-0.8
Latter-day Saints (Mormons)	63,200	0.1	↑	2.9
Adventist	19,600	<0.1	↑	1.1
Baptist	14,200	<0.1	↑	0.5
Christian Brethren	13,300	<0.1	–	-0.4
Anglican	11,900	<0.1	–	-0.1
Reformed, Presbyterian	9,900	<0.1	–	-0.1
Congregational	5,400	<0.1	–	0.2
Restorationist, Disciple	3,700	<0.1	↑	1.3
Holiness	2,400	<0.1	↑	2.0
Salvationist	950	<0.1	↑	1.3

Catholics make up 84% of the country's population, and Spain is home to over 20,000 priests, 2,900 brothers, and 40,000 sisters, but these vocations are all in decline.. Pentecostal/Charismatic Christianity is the second largest family, but represents only 3% of the country's population. The largest of these movements is among the Roma, numbering around 225,000. Other such denominations include the Assemblies of God (from the United States and United Kingdom) and the Christian Community of the Holy Spirit (from Brazil and Portugal). Eastern Orthodox include (in decreasing order) Romanians, Ukrainians, and Greeks. Found throughout many kinds of denominations, Evangelicals represent less than 1% of the population, of which the largest groups include the movement among the Roma, Assemblies of God, and many other Independents.

* These movements are found within Christian families

– no change

↑↑ extreme growth
↑ growth
↓↓ extreme decline
↓ decline

Christianity in Sri Lanka

Sri Lanka is an island nation in the Indian Ocean, off the southeastern coast of India. Christianity has a long history in the country, with the apostle Thomas allegedly arriving in the 1st century to spread the faith. Three forms of Christianity arrived with European colonial powers: the Portuguese brought Catholicism (16th century), the Dutch brought Reformed Christianity (17th century), and the British brought Anglicanism (19th century). Today, Sri Lanka is 9% Christian, and most Christians live on the west coast, with the highest concentration in Mannar. Most Christians are descendants of converts from the Portuguese colonial era, and Christianity is widely viewed as a Western, colonial religion. There is a close connection between Buddhism and national Sri Lankan identity.

Facts to Consider

- The Sri Lankan Civil War (1983–2009) was fought between the Sinhalese dominated government and the Tamil Tigers. An estimated 80,000 to 100,000 people died. Women and children suffered disproportionately during this time, subjected to starvation and rape. There are upward of 89,000 widows in the north and east.
- Conversions to Christianity from Buddhism, Hinduism, and Islam are rare, as Christians face persecution throughout the country. Attacks on churches and other Christian institutions have been rising, and Christians face increased legal restrictions on their activities.
- On Easter Sunday 2019, an estimated 270 people—many of them children—were killed in bomb attacks at three churches and three hotels.

Indicators & Demographic Data

Population (2020)	21,084,000
% under 15 years	23%
Capital city (pop.)	Colombo 613,000; Sri Jayewardenepura Kotte 96,600
% urban dwellers	19% (1.22% p.a.)
Official language	Sinhala, Tamil
Largest language	Sinhala (73%)
Largest people	Sinhalese (Singhalese) (73%)
Largest culture	Sinhalese (72%)
Development	77
Physicians	8.8
Gender gap	6%

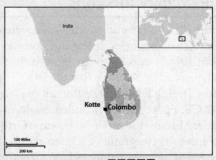

% Christian: 0 3 10 50 75 100

Christian Traditions in Sri Lanka

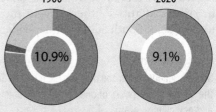

1900: 10.9% 2020: 9.1%

☐Independent ☐Protestant ■Catholic ■Orthodox ■Christian

The makeup of Christianity in Sri Lanka has changed little over time. In both 1900 and 2020, most Christians were Catholic (77%), followed by substantial minorities of Protestants and Independents. There is a small but growing Pentecostal/Charismatic movement.

Religion in Sri Lanka

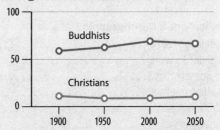

In 1900, Sri Lanka was 59% Buddhist, 23% Hindu, 11% Christian, and 7% Muslim. These percentages changed very little by 2020: 68% Buddhist, 13% Hindu, and 9% each for Muslims and Christians.

Bible Translations		Churches		Missionaries		Gospel Access	
Languages	17	Denominations	77	Received	1,700	1900	Low
Full Bible	11	Congregations	3,900	Sent	220	2020	High

Christianity in Sudan

Until 2011, Sudan and South Sudan were one country with intertwined histories. It was one country at independence from Britain and Egypt in 1956, until the south became independent in 2011. The first Christians in the country were those fleeing Egypt in the Roman persecutions of 250 and 297 CE. Egypt (which included modern-day Sudan) came under Muslim rule in the 7th century. Orthodox Christianity declined via emigration and conversion. Today, Christians are 5% of the population and most are Catholic. Anglicans are the second largest denomination. Most of the larger churches in the capital, Khartoum, consist of Christians from the south and those from the Nuba Mountains. Anti-Christian and anti-southerner sentiments have affected churches since South Sudan's independence in 2011.

Facts to Consider

- Sudan's leaders often speak of the Islamic identity of the nation under the "One Nation" policy of one language (Arabic), one religion (Islam), and one culture (Arab).
- President Omar al-Bashir was ousted in a coup in 2019 after 26 years in power. In 2020, he was handed over to the International Criminal Court under allegations of mass killing and rape of Christians in the Darfur region.
- Conversion from Islam (apostasy) and acts that encourage conversion from Islam are criminal offenses. Apostasy is punishable by death. Insulting religion, blasphemy, disturbing places of worship, and trespassing on burial sites can result in prison time, flogging, and/or fines.
- Muslim women are legally allowed to marry only Muslim men; a woman can be charged with adultery if she marries a non-Muslim man.

Indicators & Demographic Data

Population (2020)	43,541,000
% under 15 years	40%
Capital city (pop.)	Khartoum 5,829,000
% urban dwellers	35% (3.43% p.a.)
Official language	Arabic, English
Largest language	Arabic (74%)
Largest people	Sudanese Arab (14%)
Largest culture	Arab (Arabic) (65%)
Development	50
Physicians	31
Gender gap	17%

% Christian: 0 3 10 50 75 100

Christian Traditions in Sudan

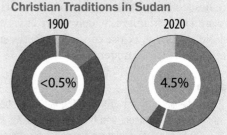

1900   2020

<0.5%   4.5%

☐Independent ☐Protestant ◼Catholic ◼Orthodox ◼Christian

The very small Christian community in Sudan in 1900 (2,400) were mostly Coptic Orthodox from Egypt (84%). By 2020, Christians in Sudan were 54% Catholic, 40% Protestant, and 5% Orthodox.

Religion in Sudan

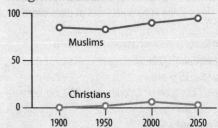

Sudan has historically been a Muslim-majority country. In 1900, the country was 85% Muslim and 15% followers of traditional religions. By 2020, Islam had grown to 92% with the decline of traditional religions to just under 3%. Christianity grew from less than 1% in 1900 to 5% in 2020.

Bible Translations		Churches		Missionaries		Gospel Access	
Languages	104	Denominations	19	Received	320	1900	Very low
Full Bible	18	Congregations	2,200	Sent	47	2020	Low

Christianity in Suriname

Suriname is located on the northeastern coast of South America, north of Brazil. Most of the population lives on the north coast in and around the capital city, Paramaribo. Indigenous peoples—mainly Arawak and Carib—have inhabited the region since at least 3000 BCE. The first European (and Christian) contact came via French, Spanish, and English explorers in the 16th century. The region was first colonized by the British until 1667, when the Dutch took over and ruled until independence in 1975. More than 80% of indigenous people have been baptized Catholic. The most significant Protestant work was carried out by Moravians, which became autonomous in 1963. The largest indigenous denomination is Gods Bazuin Ministries, a Charismatic group founded in 1963.

Facts to Consider

- Muslims in Suriname are comprised of Javanese, East Indians, Syro-Lebanese, and Afro-Surinamese. Hinduism is in two groups, the larger Sanatan Dharm, which emphasizes Brahmin priests and classical Hinduism, and the smaller Arya Samaj, that rejects Brahminical authority and Hindu gods.
- Interreligious relations are important in Suriname. Christian, Muslim, and Hindu holidays are celebrated nationally, clergy from all faiths are available to military personnel, and the Inter-Religious Council is active in promoting religious freedom and tolerance.
- Violence against women is common in Suriname, but various governmental and nongovernmental organizations combat it. Domestic violence became a heightened issue with the COVID-19 pandemic.

Indicators & Demographic Data

Population (2020)	578,000
% under 15 years	26%
Capital city (pop.)	Paramaribo 241,000
% urban dwellers	66% (0.88% p.a.)
Official language	Dutch
Largest language	Sranan Tongo (34%)
Largest people	Caribbean Hindi (27%)
Largest culture	Hindi (27%)
Development	72
Physicians	9.1
Gender gap	3%

% Christian: 0 3 10 50 75 100

Christian Traditions in Suriname

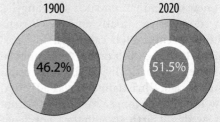

1900 — 46.2% 2020 — 51.5%

☐ Independent ☐ Protestant ■ Catholic ■ Orthodox ■ Christian

Christians in 1900 were largely Catholic (54%), with a sizeable Evangelical Protestant minority (46%). In 2020, Christians in Suriname were 60% Catholic, 30% Protestant, and 10% Independent.

Religion in Suriname

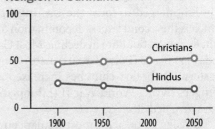

Christians

Hindus

In 1900, Suriname was 46% Christian, 26% Hindu, 10% Muslim, and 14% traditional religionist. By 2020, traditional religions had declined to just under 2%, while Christianity grew to 52%, Hinduism dropped to 21%, and Islam grew to 16%.

Bible Translations		Churches		Missionaries		Gospel Access	
Languages	24	Denominations	38	Received	440	1900	Medium
Full Bible	9	Congregations	510	Sent	25	2020	Very high

Christianity in Sweden

Most of the Swedish nobility converted to Christianity in the 9th century after the arrival of French monks. But Christianity largely lapsed until the arrival of English missionaries the following century, when the faith spread widely. A national church was organized in 1164 at the installation of the first bishop. The Swedish Reformation adopted the Lutheran Confession in 1527 and tied national Swedish identity with Lutheranism. It was illegal until 1860 to leave the Church of Sweden, despite the arrival of other denominations in the 18th and 19th centuries. The 19th century saw a revival of piety and growth of lay preaching, which spurred the creation of new denominations such as Evangelical Free churches. Sweden was essentially entirely Christian at the start of the 20th century. It became legal to leave Christianity only in 1951. In the 20th century, membership in the Church of Sweden drastically declined, as did the overall public influence of Christianity. It was only in the year 2000 that Swedes were no longer considered members of the Church of Sweden at birth, though the Church of Sweden is still the largest denomination. It has ordained women since 1959, and between 1998 and 2008, more women entered the ordination process than men. The first female archbishop was appointed in 2014. Eva Brunne, the former bishop of Stockholm, is the first openly lesbian bishop of a mainline denomination in the world and is married to a female Church of Sweden priest.

In 2011, Baptists, Methodists, and the Mission Covenant Church merged to form the Uniting Church of Sweden, which is the second largest denomination today. Most Protestant denominations are in decline. Most Catholics in Sweden today are Slavic (Poles, Croats), Latin American, or Middle Eastern. Orthodox churches increased after an influx of refugees during World War II (Ethiopians, Copts, Greeks, Russians, Serbs).

Sweden is one of the most secular countries in the world today. Only 8% of Swedes attend religious services regularly. Church-based weddings, baptisms, and funerals are on the decline, replaced by name-giving ceremonies and civil weddings. Religious belief is widely considered a private, individual affair.

% Christian: 0 3 10 50 75 100

Religion in Sweden

Sweden has been a majority Christian country for many centuries and remains so today—but differently from the past. The country was 99% Christian in 1900, but the Christian share of the population dropped to 58% by 2020. Numerical increases were made primarily by Muslims (9%) and the nonreligious (32%). There are also small communities of Buddhists, Jews, and Hindus.

Indicators & Demographic Data

Population (2020)	10,122,000
% under 15 years	18%
Capital city (pop.)	Stockholm 1,633,000
% urban dwellers	88% (0.89% p.a.)
Official language	Swedish
Largest language	Swedish (80%)
Largest people	Swedish (Swede) (62%)
Largest culture	Swedish (79%)
Development	93
Physicians	42
Gender gap	1%

Bible Translations		Churches		Missionaries		Gospel Access	
Languages	65	Denominations	100	Received	800	1900	Very high
Full Bible	49	Congregations	4,900	Sent	1,000	2020	Very high

Facts to Consider

- Sweden has the highest percentage of atheists in Europe (12%) and the second highest in the world (after North Korea, 15%).
- Sweden received more asylum seekers per capita than any other European country at the height of the refugee crisis in 2015. The rise in migrants also spurred a rise in nationalist groups. Christian refugees and refugees who convert to Christianity sometimes face persecution from Muslims.
- Because of the high number of people from other countries, the Swedish government has been addressing (and prohibits) female genital mutilation/cutting (40,000 victims of the practice live in Sweden) and honor-related violence such as retribution killings and sending children abroad for marriage.
- Muslims are now 9% of Sweden's population. The most recent arrivals have been from Iraq, Somalia, and Afghanistan. There are numerous Muslim organizations, such as the Islamic Association of Sweden, the Muslim Council of Sweden, and Islamic Relief.
- Sweden Democrats is the country's third largest political party, with roots in White supremacy and nationalism. Some members have made disparaging comments about religious minorities, advocate for national bans on the Islamic call to prayer, and have been charged with hate speech.

Christian Traditions in Sweden

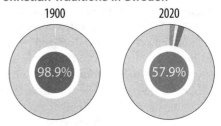

1900 2020

□Independent □Protestant ▨Catholic ■Orthodox ■Christian

Christianity in Sweden is historically majority Protestant (99%), and nearly the entire population was Lutheran in 1900. In 2020, Christianity was proportionally smaller but slightly more diverse, with Catholic and Orthodox each 2% of Christians. Evangelicals are 7% of Sweden's population and Pentecostals/Charismatics are 2%.

Christian Families in Sweden

Family	Population 2020	%	Trend	Change
Lutheran	5,305,000	52.4	–	0.0
*Evangelicals	684,000	6.8	–	-0.3
*Pentecostals/Charismatics	220,000	2.2	–	0.0
United church or joint mission	145,000	1.4	↓	-1.2
Latin-rite Catholic	120,000	1.2	↓	-1.6
Eastern Orthodox	102,000	1.0	–	0.1
Holiness	64,600	0.6	↑	1.8
Jehovah's Witnesses	35,400	0.3	–	0.5
Oriental and other Orthodox	33,100	0.3	–	0.1
Nondenominational	12,900	0.1	↓	-0.8
Latter-day Saints (Mormons)	10,800	0.1	↑	1.6
Salvationist	5,700	0.1	↓	-2.0
Anglican	3,600	<0.1	↑	0.9
Adventist	3,200	<0.1	–	0.0
Reformed, Presbyterian	3,000	<0.1	–	0.0

Lutherans make up 52% of the country's population (5.3 million). The Church of Sweden is still the largest denomination, but other Lutheran groups include Lutherans from Norway, Estonia, Finland, Denmark, and Latvia. Evangelicalism is the second largest Christian family in the country, with 7% of the population. There are some Evangelicals still in the Church of Sweden, but the Uniting Church of Sweden, Evangelical Free churches, and Pentecostal/Charismatic churches have a more robust Evangelical identity. The largest Pentecostal/Charismatic church is the Pentecostal Revival Movement of Sweden, with 85,000 members. The Pentecostal movement grew rapidly from 1930 to 1960 but then declined rapidly. The Uniting Church represents a 2011 merger of the Baptist Union, Methodist Church, and Mission Covenant Church.

* These movements are found within Christian families	↑↑ extreme growth
	↑ growth
	↓↓ extreme decline
– no change	↓ decline

Christianity in Switzerland

Christianity has a long history in Switzerland, arriving from Gaul (Celtic tribes) and Italy via merchants in the Roman era. The region was Christianized by the 7th century and was home to numerous Catholic monasteries. Switzerland is home to the longest continuously inhabited monastery in Europe, St. Maurice's Abbey in Valais (established in 515). In 1519, reformer Ulrich Zwingli began preaching reformation in the Catholic Church in Zurich, expounding on church corruption, clerical marriage, images in worship, and new kinds of expository preaching. He clashed with Catholics and Anabaptists, but his ideas spread from Switzerland throughout Europe. By 1536, there was a Protestant majority in Geneva under the leadership of John Calvin. From this point Switzerland was home to a substantial Catholic-Protestant rivalry that characterized Swiss political and religious life for many centuries. Today the country is 41% Catholic and 30% Protestant. The Catholic population has been largely sustained by immigrants from Italy, Spain, and Portugal, whereas Swiss citizens are majority Protestant. Protestant and Catholic communities are increasingly blended with the movement of people. The traditionally Protestant cities of Bern, Vaud, Zurich, and Basel are becoming increasingly Catholic, and the traditionally Catholic cantons of Valais, Tessin, and Fribourg are increasingly Protestant.

Switzerland consists of 26 cantons (member states of the Swiss Confederation). Seventeen of the cantons use German as the official language; four cantons have French co-official with German; the rest of the cantons speak Romansh or Italian. Latin is used on the Swiss franc (currency), stamps, and other national icons to avoid favoring one of the four official languages over the others.

The largest Protestant denomination is the Swiss Federation of Protestant Churches (Reformed/Presbyterian), with 26 member churches, 24 cantonal churches, and two free churches. The teachings of Zwingli have been more prominent in the German-speaking region, while the Calvinist teachings are more prominent in French-speaking regions. Switzerland is becoming more nonreligious. Only 9% of Swiss report that religion is important in their lives, 29% attend religious services at least monthly, 8% pray daily, and 11% believe in God with absolute certainty.

% Christian: 0 3 10 50 75 100

Religion in Switzerland

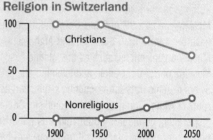

Switzerland has been a majority Christian country for many centuries and remains so today. The country was 99% Christian in 1900, but the Christian share of the population dropped to 74% by 2020. Numerical increases were made primarily by Muslims (7%) and the nonreligious (19%). There are also small communities of Buddhists, Hindus, and Jews.

Indicators & Demographic Data

Population (2020)	8,671,000
% under 15 years	15%
Capital city (pop.)	Bern 430,000
% urban dwellers	74% (0.79% p.a.)
Official language	French and 3 others
Largest language	Swiss German (50%)
Largest people	German Swiss (50%)
Largest culture	German (52%)
Development	94
Physicians	42
Gender gap	1%

Bible Translations		Churches		Missionaries		Gospel Access	
Languages	50	Denominations	160	Received	2,170	1900	Very high
Full Bible	40	Congregations	4,600	Sent	1,200	2020	Very high

Facts to Consider

- Islam grew from 5% in 2000 to 7% in 2020. Nearly 95% of Muslims are foreign-born (from 30 countries), and 80% live in urban areas. Most are from the former Yugoslavia, Albania, Turkey, North Africa, and the Middle East.
- A 2009 referendum made it illegal to construct new minarets in the country. Catholic, Protestant, Jewish, Evangelical Free, Evangelical, Old Catholics, and numerous other religious groups were against the ban, but it passed with 57.5% of the vote.
- Switzerland is home to the headquarters of the World Jewish Congress, founded in Geneva in 1936. Jews number around 18,000 (mostly in Zurich, Geneva, Basel, Lausanne, and Lugano), but anti-Semitic incidents are still common in the German-speaking part of the country.
- Domestic violence against migrant women is four times as high as against other women. There are numerous governmental, nongovernmental, and private entities to support survivors of violence.
- Women face unequal career opportunities, and women in the private sector earn 20% less than their male counterparts.
- Discrimination against LGBTQ individuals exists in Switzerland. Some Christian and political groups have advocated the repeal of a 2018 amendment to the antiracism law that criminalizes discrimination on the basis of sexual orientation, claiming it limits their freedom of expression.

Christian Traditions in Switzerland

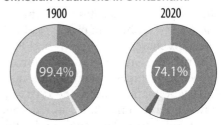

☐Independent ☐Protestant ■Catholic ■Orthodox ■Christian

Historically, Christianity in Switzerland was represented largely by both Protestant (58%) and Catholic (41%) populations. In 2020, Christianity was proportionally smaller but slightly more diverse: 54% Catholic, 40% Protestant, 4% Independent, and 2% Orthodox. Evangelicals and Pentecostals/Charismatics are small movements, each around 3% of the country's population.

Christian Families in Switzerland

Family	Population 2020	%	Trend	Change
Latin-rite Catholic	3,416,000	39.4	–	0.4
Reformed, Presbyterian	2,422,000	27.9	–	0.3
*Evangelicals	307,000	3.5	–	0.2
*Pentecostals/Charismatics	265,000	3.1	↑	0.6
Eastern Orthodox	140,000	1.6	↑	1.8
Jehovah's Witnesses	84,700	1.0	↓	-0.6
Nondenominational	22,300	0.3	↑	2.0
Exclusive Brethren	18,300	0.2	–	0.2
Anglican	14,400	0.2	–	0.4
Methodist	11,400	0.1	↓	-0.6
Old Catholic Church	10,600	0.1	↓	-0.9
Latter-day Saints (Mormons)	10,400	0.1	↑	2.5
Lutheran	6,800	0.1	↑	0.8
Congregational	6,100	0.1	↓	-2.9
Christian Brethren	5,700	0.1	↑	1.3
Adventist	5,400	0.1	↑	0.9
Salvationist	4,200	<0.1	↓	-1.8
Baptist	2,700	<0.1	↓	-2.1
Mennonite	2,300	<0.1	↓	-2.5
Holiness	2,100	<0.1	–	0.2

Catholics make up 40% of the country's population (3.4 million) and is the largest Christian family. Reformed/Presbyterian is the second largest (28%), represented largely by the Swiss Federation of Protestant Churches, the second largest denomination. Evangelicals and Pentecostals/Charismatics each make up 3% of the population. Evangelicals are found across many denominations, with the largest numbers in the Swiss Federation, the Assemblies of God, and the Swiss Pentecostal Mission. The largest Pentecostal/Charismatic groups include the Catholic Charismatic movement, the Swiss Federation, the New Apostolic Church, and the Assemblies of God. Eastern Orthodox includes Serbs, Greeks, Russians, and Romanians.

* These movements are found within Christian families
– no change
↑↑ extreme growth
↑ growth
↓↓ extreme decline
↓ decline

Christianity in Syria

Christianity in Syria dates to the time of the apostle Paul, who became a Christian on the road to Damascus. All the Orthodox churches in Syria trace their lineage to the time of Christ. The Greek Orthodox Church is, and historically has been, the largest denomination in the country. While Protestant missionaries in the 19th century attempted to draw converts from Islam and Judaism, most came from the historic Orthodox and Catholic churches. Christians unsuccessfully tried to avoid conflict in the 2011 Syrian Civil War. Minority religions tended to support the regime of President Bashar al-Assad, while Sunni Muslims stood with the revolution. An estimated 700,000 Christians were displaced in the conflict. Christians under the control of ISIS had four options: convert to Islam, pay the *jizya* tax (paid by non-Muslims) and accept *dhimmi* status (non-Muslims living in a Muslim country), leave the country, or die.

Facts to Consider

- At its height, ISIS held a third of Syria and 40% of Iraq but has since lost 95% of its territory. It is likely that most Christians who fled will never return.
- Countless Christians have been martyred since 2011, including indigenous Christians and humanitarian aid workers. Two archbishops of Aleppo, Boulos Yazigi and Gregorious Yohanna Ibrahim, were abducted in 2013, and their status is still unknown.
- Thousands of Yezidis (especially women) have been killed, kidnapped, or used as sex slaves since 2011 in what foreign observers have called a genocidal campaign.

Indicators & Demographic Data

Population (2020)	18,924,000
% under 15 years	34%
Capital city (pop.)	Damascus 2,392,000
% urban dwellers	55% (5.38% p.a.)
Official language	Arabic
Largest language	Arabic (89%)
Largest people	Syrian Arab (77%)
Largest culture	Arab (Arabic) (88%)
Development	54
Physicians	15
Gender gap	21%

% Christian: 0 3 10 50 75 100

Christian Traditions in Syria

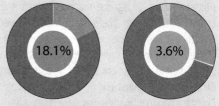

1900 — 18.1%   2020 — 3.6%

☐ Independent ☐ Protestant ◼ Catholic ◼ Orthodox ◼ Christian

Christians in Syria have always been majority Orthodox (82%), with a large Catholic minority (17%). By 2020, Christianity had declined substantially and was 67% Orthodox, 30% Catholic, and 3% Protestant.

Religion in Syria

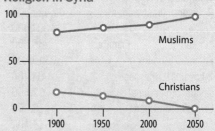

Muslims

Christians

Syria is historically a Muslim-majority country, and increasingly so. In 1900, the country was 81% Muslim, 18% Christian, and 1% Jewish. Islam grew to 94% with the decline of Christians (under 4%) and Jews (perhaps only 100).

Bible Translations		Churches		Missionaries		Gospel Access	
Languages	24	Denominations	47	Received	200	1900	Low
Full Bible	14	Congregations	540	Sent	100	2020	Medium

Christianity in Taiwan

Taiwan—also known as the Republic of China—is an island off the coast of China near Japan and the Philippines. Its status is controversial. Taiwan is not a member of the United Nations, and the People's Republic of China lays claim over it. There is significant political tension regarding Chinese unification, with opponents wanting complete Taiwanese independence, politically and otherwise. Hundreds of years of Western and Japanese colonization has influenced Christianity in Taiwan. Catholic missionaries arrived in the 17th century, and Protestants in the 19th century. Christianity grew under Japanese rule (1895–1945) and is found among the indigenous peoples of Taiwan, Taiwan islanders (largely Han Taiwanese), and Chinese from the mainland.

Facts to Consider

- Christianity grew in prestige with several Christian presidents: Sun Yat-sen, Chiang Kai-shek, Lee Teng-hui, and Ma Ying-jeou. But Taiwan is secularizing, and Christian growth has slowed since the 20th century. Cell groups are popular and effective ways to provide spiritual care.
- Catholics and Presbyterians are the largest Christian groups in Taiwan. The third largest is the Little Flock, or Assembly Hall Churches, which began on the mainland by Watchman Nee in 1926. They emphasize small house churches, personal evangelism, prayer, and home visitation.
- The fastest-growing churches are Independent groups that have formed since 1950. The fastest growth has been on the east coast.
- Upward of 80% of the population believes in some form of traditional folk religion, including shamanism, ancestor worship, and animism. These beliefs meld Christianity, Buddhism, Daoism, and Confucianism.

Indicators & Demographic Data

Population (2020)	23,818,000
% under 15 years	13%
Capital city (pop.)	Taibei 2,721,000
% urban dwellers	79% (0.65% p.a.)
Official language	Chinese (Mandarin)
Largest language	Chinese (97%)
Largest people	Taiwanese (Hoklo) (71%)
Largest culture	Han Chinese (97%)
Development	77
Physicians	35
Gender gap	4%

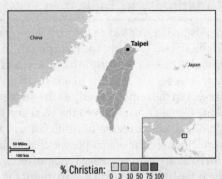

% Christian: 0 3 10 50 75 100

Christian Traditions in Taiwan

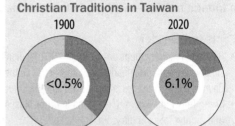

1900   2020

<0.5%   6.1%

☐Independent ☐Protestant ◼Catholic ◼Orthodox ◼Christian

The small Christian community in 1900 (9,000 Christians) consisted of Protestants (63%) and Catholics (37%). In 2020, Christianity was 43% Independent, 36% Protestant, and 20% Catholic.

Religion in Taiwan

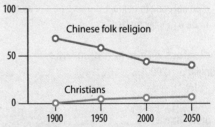

In 1900, Taiwan was 69% Chinese folk religionist, 18% Buddhist, 9% Daoist, and 3% traditional religionist. Today, the two largest religions are Chinese folk religion (42%) and Buddhism (27%).

Bible Translations		Churches		Missionaries		Gospel Access	
Languages	27	Denominations	170	Received	3,000	1900	Very low
Full Bible	14	Congregations	4,900	Sent	440	2020	High

Christianity in Tajikistan

Tajikistan is a landlocked country in central Asia, bordering Afghanistan, Uzbekistan, Kyrgyzstan, and China. Arabs brought Islam in the early 8th century, and ever since, Tajikistan has been a Muslim-majority area. Christianity was present in the region as early as the 4th century as it spread along the Silk Road between the West and China. The Soviet Union ruled the region until its fall in 1991. All churches were closed in the Soviet period of state-imposed atheism. Christianity is a minority religion today, less than 1% of the population. Generally, Christianity is seen by Tajiks as a foreign religion—a religion of the Russians.

Facts to Consider

- Several Christian groups arrived after 1991 to plant churches and start schools. Korean missionaries are active, such as the Korean Pentecostal Church, Grace Ministries International, and the Korean Methodist Church.
- Some Tajik Christians serve abroad in other Muslim-majority countries and among Tajiks in diaspora.
- Jehovah's Witnesses routinely experience roadblocks in registering with the government as a religious organization. They are frequently detained, interrogated by authorities, and are often jailed. They are typically accused of "inciting religious hatred."
- Out of fear of government harassment, people are often reluctant to discuss issues such as religious diversity. Religious topics are avoided, and religious minorities face significant social pressure.
- Domestic violence is widespread, but there are no specific laws in the criminal code to combat it. This type of violence is typically understood to be a "family matter."

Indicators & Demographic Data

Population (2020)	9,475,000
% under 15 years	35%
Capital city (pop.)	Dushanbe 916,000
% urban dwellers	28% (2.73% p.a.)
Official language	Tajik
Largest language	Tajik (68%)
Largest people	Tajik (Tadzhik) (67%)
Largest culture	Tadzhik (68%)
Development	65
Physicians	17
Gender gap	7%

% Christian: 0 3 10 50 75 100

Christian Traditions in Tajikistan

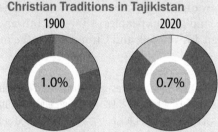

1900 — 1.0%
2020 — 0.7%

☐ Independent ☐ Protestant ■ Catholic ■ Orthodox ■ Christian

Christianity is a minority religion in Tajikistan and has historically been less than 1% of the population. In 2020, most of the small Christian population were Orthodox (80%) left from the Soviet period. Protestant Evangelical Christianity is small (around 2,000).

Religion in Tajikistan

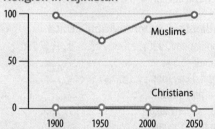

Islam dipped to 63% of the population during the Soviet period. It rebounded to 98% by 2020. The nonreligious peaked at 34% of the population in 1970, only to decline to 1% by 2020.

Bible Translations		Churches		Missionaries		Gospel Access	
Languages	40	Denominations	27	Received	40	1900	Very low
Full Bible	26	Congregations	190	Sent	5	2020	Medium

Christianity in Tanzania

The indigenous hunter-gatherer people of Tanzania arrived in the first wave of migration from Ethiopia and Somalia thousands of years ago. Subsequent peoples arrived from modern-day South Sudan and then from West Africa to the Lake Victoria and Lake Tanganyika areas. Zanzibar City was central to the African slave trade in the 19th century until it was abolished in the 1890s. The first European, and Christian, contacts were with the Portuguese in 1502. Germany conquered the region in the late 19th century and incorporated it into German East Africa. The United Kingdom seized it from Germany in 1916, renaming it Tanganyika until 1962, when the nation became independent as Tanzania. It is a deeply religious country with high rates of belief in God, miracles, angels, and evil spirits. Tanzania is 57% Christian, and the largest denominations are the Catholic Church, Evangelical Lutheran Church, and the Church of the Province of Tanzania (Anglican).

Indigenous Tanzanian priests, brothers, and sisters have an important role in the Catholic Church, more so than foreign missionaries. African bishops and leaders lead new diocese development, administrative expansion, and ecclesiastical life. Tanzanian Catholic sisters greatly outnumber missionary sisters. The Evangelical Lutheran Church is the largest Protestant group, formed in 1963 through a union of seven groups formed by German, American, and Scandinavian missionaries. Tanzania has a lower number of African Independent Churches (AICs) compared with other countries in Africa. The largest and most influential are from Kenya. The largest church indigenous to Tanzania is the Church of the Holy Spirit, a breakaway group from the Evangelical Lutheran Church (ELC), but most members returned to the ELC.

The Pentecostal/Charismatic movement arrived via missionaries from Sweden, Finland, and the United States in the 1930s. These efforts resulted in today's Pentecostal Churches Association in Tanzania and the Assemblies of God. Some of the most prominent Charismatic expressions of the faith are in the historic Evangelical Lutheran, Catholic, and Anglican churches.

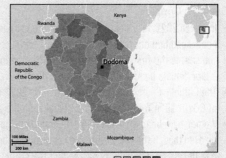

% Christian: 0 3 10 50 75 100

Religion in Tanzania

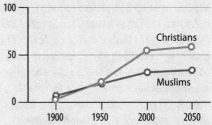

Tanzania's religious makeup changed dramatically over the 20th century. In 1900, the country was 91% followers of traditional religions, with smaller populations of Muslims and Christians. By 2020, Christianity had grown to 57% and Islam to 31%, followed by just 10% traditional religionists. There were also half a million Hindus.

Indicators & Demographic Data

Population (2020)	62,775,000
% under 15 years	44%
Capital city (pop.)	Dodoma 226,000
% urban dwellers	35% (4.89% p.a.)
Official language	Swahili, English
Largest language	Sukuma (16%)
Largest people	Sukuma (16%)
Largest culture	Tanganyika Bantu (48%)
Development	54
Physicians	0.2
Gender gap	7%

Bible Translations		Churches		Missionaries		Gospel Access	
Languages	144	Denominations	160	Received	5,000	1900	Very low
Full Bible	34	Congregations	47,100	Sent	340	2020	Very high

Facts to Consider

- In March 2021, President John Magufuli died at age 61, allegedly from a heart condition but rumored by COVID-19. His successor, Samia Suluhu Hassan, is the first female president of the country and Africa's first *hijabi* (female headscarf wearing) president.
- The Catholic Church was outspoken in early 2021 regarding the spread of COVID-19 in Tanzania, despite denial from the government.
- Women have been excluded from leadership positions in historic churches even though they constitute the majority of church membership. The rise of NGOs in the country has helped the status of women.
- Witchcraft related killings are common throughout the country, with women more often accused of witchcraft than men.
- Muslims make up 31% of the population, and Islam is most prominent in Zanzibar and Dar es Salaam. The Shirazi, Zaramo, Yao, Makonde, and Zigua are majority Muslim. Muslims in Zanzibar have the option of having legal cases covered by Islamic instead of national law.
- Although in decline as a primary affiliation, traditional ethnic religions are still followed, even alongside Christianity and Islam. The greatest number of practitioners are among the Iraqw people, followed by the Nyiha, Iramba, Maasai, and Arusha Maasai.

Christian Traditions in Tanzania

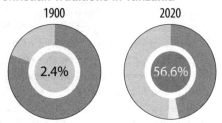

1900   2020

2.4%   56.6%

□ Independent □ Protestant ■ Catholic ■ Orthodox ■ Christian

The small Christian population in 1900 (92,000 Christians) were mostly Catholic (81%), with an Evangelical Protestant minority (19%). With the growth of Christianity also came increased Christian diversity. In 2020, Christians in Tanzania were 49% Protestant, 47% Catholic, and 4% Independent groups of various kinds. The country is also 11% Pentecostal/Charismatic.

Christian Families in Tanzania

Family	Population 2020	%	Trend	Change
Latin-rite Catholic	16,630,000	26.5	↑	2.6
*Evangelicals	9,400,000	15.0	↑	2.7
Lutheran	7,348,000	11.7	↑	2.8
*Pentecostals/Charismatics	6,400,000	10.2	↑	2.6
Anglican	4,234,000	6.7	↑	2.5
Baptist	1,252,000	2.0	↑	1.9
Nondenominational	767,000	1.2	↑	2.7
Adventist	594,000	0.9	–	-0.4
Moravian	581,000	0.9	↑	2.4
Mennonite	138,000	0.2	↑	2.3
Jehovah's Witnesses	47,800	0.1	↑	2.4
Holiness	47,000	0.1	↑	2.9
Restorationist, Disciple	34,000	0.1	↑↑	8.5
Friends (Quaker)	23,800	<0.1	↑	2.8
Salvationist	22,400	<0.1	↑↑	9.5
Christian Brethren	14,000	<0.1	↑	1.9
Eastern Orthodox	13,300	<0.1	–	0.2
Reformed, Presbyterian	11,000	<0.1	↑	2.9
Latter-day Saints (Mormons)	2,700	<0.1	↑↑	10.4
Methodist	1,400	<0.1	–	0.0

Catholics make up 27% of the country's population (16.6 million) and is the largest Christian family. Evangelicals are the second largest family (9.4 million, 15% of the population) and are found in many denominations: Evangelical Lutherans, Anglicans, Pentecostals, nondenominational Christians, Moravians, and others. Lutherans are the third largest family, largely due to the size of the Evangelical Lutheran Church as the second largest denomination in the country (after Catholics), which has 6.2 million members. Pentecostals/Charismatics include Evangelical Lutherans, the Pentecostal Churches in Tanzania, New Apostolic Church, Anglicans, Assemblies of God, and the Catholic Charismatic movement. Moravians have been in the country since 1879 and have around half a million members. The area east of Lake Victoria is served by Seventh-day Adventists, Mennonites, and African Inland churches.

* These movements are found within Christian families

– no change

↑↑ extreme growth
↑ growth
↓↓ extreme decline
↓ decline

Christianity in Thailand

Christianity has been present in Thailand since the establishment of a Portuguese community in Ayutthaya in the early 16th century. Protestant missionaries first arrived in 1828 from Dutch and British societies, followed by American Congregationalists, Baptists, and Presbyterians. Theravada Buddhism has been the primary religion of the Thai people since the 13th century and is an important marker for Thai identity. Thailand is 1% Christian today. The largest concentration of Protestants is in the north, along the border with Myanmar in Thailand's "Bible hat." Most Protestants are ethnic minorities, such as the Karen and Akha. Catholics are found throughout the country but are concentrated in the central and northeastern states.

Facts to Consider

- Thailand has seven major hill tribes, peoples who reside in the mountains in the northern and western regions. They are severely disadvantaged compared with the dominant Thai people. Treated as outsiders, hundreds of thousands of them are considered noncitizens, meaning that they cannot own land, move freely, or vote.
- Thailand is a popular destination for mission, humanitarian, and faith-based organizations. Northern Thailand (Chiang Mai, in particular) is well-poised to access peoples in China, Myanmar, India, Laos, and Vietnam.
- Many organizations work to assist women and children trapped in the national and regional sex trade. Thailand is a destination for child sex tourism, with migrant, ethnic minority, and poor children particularly vulnerable.
- Thailand is home to more than 40,000 Buddhist temples and 300,000 Buddhist monastics.

Indicators & Demographic Data

Population (2020). 69,411,000
% under 15 years 16%
Capital city (pop.) . . . . Bangkok 10,539,000
% urban dwellers. . . . . 51% (1.43% p.a.)
Official language. . . . . .Thai
Largest language. . . . . Thai (41%)
Largest people .Central Thai (Siamese) (33%)
Largest culture . . . . .Thai (43%)
Development. 75
Physicians. 4.7
Gender gap 0%

% Christian: 0 3 10 50 75 100

Christian Traditions in Thailand

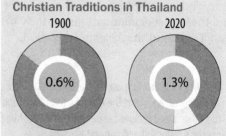

1900 — 0.6% 2020 — 1.3%

☐ Independent ☐ Protestant ▨ Catholic ▦ Orthodox ▪ Christian

The small Christian population in 1900 (35,000 Christians) was largely Catholic (85%), with a small Evangelical Protestant (15%) minority. Christianity diversified as it grew. In 2020, Christians were 50% Protestant, 41% Catholic, and 9% Independents of various kinds.

Religion in Thailand

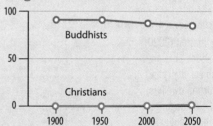

In 1900, Thailand was 91% Buddhist, 3% traditional religionist, and 2% Muslim. By 2020, it was 87% Buddhist, 6% Muslim, and 2% traditional religionist.

Bible Translations	Churches	Missionaries	Gospel Access
Languages. 87	Denominations 120	Received. 2,000	1900 . . . . Very low
Full Bible. 33	Congregations. 6,100	Sent 30	2020 . . . . Medium

Christianity in Timor-Leste

Timor-Leste (formerly known as East Timor) is a small island country located at the tip of Indonesia. In 1511, the Portuguese made the first Christian contact and claimed the island as a Portuguese colony until the Timorese people declared independence in 1975. Indonesia quickly invaded and occupied the country until 1999. Indonesian occupation was extremely violent, with over 100,000 deaths from conflict, hunger, and illness. Catholicism grew gradually over the centuries, and by the time of independence, the country was 81% Catholic. The Catholic Church supported Timorese independence. Protestants make up 5% of the population, and the largest denominations are the Christian Church of East Timor and the Assemblies of God.

Facts to Consider

- There is no state religion, but a concordat between the government and the Vatican allows the Catholic Church autonomy to establish and run schools and receive tax benefits. The government also protects the church's historical and cultural heritage.
- Violence against women, including domestic violence, is a persistent problem in Timor-Leste. Roughly 59% of women and girls ages 15 to 49 have experienced sexual or physical violence from an intimate partner. Because of staff shortages, the Ministry of Social Solidarity has had difficulty responding to cases.
- Overall, women and girls have lower levels of education than men and boys, with many girls dropping out as adolescents or becoming pregnant. There is strong cultural pressure for couples to marry if the woman becomes pregnant, despite their age. Around 19% of girls are married before age 18.

Indicators & Demographic Data

Population (2020). 1,381,000
% under 15 years 43%
Capital city (pop.) . . . . Dili 260,000
% urban dwellers. . . . . 31% (3.31% p.a.)
Official language. . . . . Portuguese, Tetun
Largest language. . . . . Tetun (31%)
Largest people . . . . Eastern Tetum (Belu) (31%)
Largest culture . . . . .Western Melanesian (37%)
Development. 62
Physicians. 0.8
Gender gap. 15%

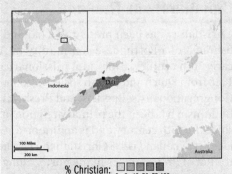

% Christian: 0 3 10 50 75 100

Christian Traditions in Timor-Leste

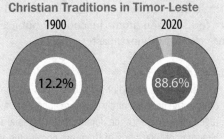

1900 — 12.2%

2020 — 88.6%

☐ Independent ☐ Protestant ■ Catholic ■ Orthodox ■ Christian

The small Christian population in 1900 (45,000 Christians) was entirely Catholic. Christianity diversified only slightly as it grew. In 2020, Christianity was 95% Catholic and 5% Protestant. Timor-Leste has the third highest percentage of Christians in Asia (after the Philippines and Armenia).

Religion in Timor-Leste

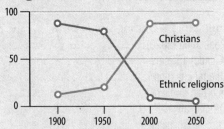

In 1900, Timor-Leste was 88% followers of traditional religions and 12% Christian. By 2020, Christianity had grown to 89%, while traditional religions declined to 7%.

Bible Translations		Churches		Missionaries		Gospel Access	
Languages.	23	Denominations	26	Received.	100	1900	Low
Full Bible.	4	Congregations.	410	Sent	40	2020	Very high

Christianity in Togo

Togo is a small nation in West Africa, neighboring Ghana, Benin, and Burkina Faso. The indigenous population of Ewe, Mina, and Gun peoples first encountered Christianity in the late 19th century via Catholics (1871) and Methodists from the Gold Coast (modern Ghana; 1860). Togo was part of the Atlantic slave trade for 200 years. Missionaries were restricted to work only in the southern regions under German (1905–1916) and French (1916–1959) occupation. Togo is 48% Christian today, comprised mostly of Catholics due to missionary efforts and Catholic work in health care, education, and rural development. The largest Protestant group is the Assemblies of God, which runs two Bible training schools for pastors and one for evangelists.

Facts to Consider

- Togo has many African Independent Churches (AICs), such as the Apostles Revelation Society, the Apostolic Church of Togo, and the White Cross Society.
- Many Pentecostal groups were banned from 1978 until religious freedom was declared in 1991. They have grown rapidly but also experience conflicts and divisions.
- Most Muslims (19% of the population) live in the central and northern regions, as well as in southern cities. They have a vision to build five to ten mosques a year throughout the country.
- Traditional ethnic religions have shown resilience against Christianity and Islam. People groups that are over 50% traditionalist include the Adele, Bassari, Gurma, Kabre, Kebu, Konkomba, Kpessi, Lamba, Moba, Naudeba, and Wachi.

Indicators & Demographic Data

Population (2020). 8,384,000
% under 15 years 41%
Capital city (pop.) . . . . Lomé 1,828,000
% urban dwellers. . . . . .43% (3.60% p.a.)
Official language. . . . . French
Largest language. . . . . Éwé (22%)
Largest people . . . . Ewe (Ahoulan, Ehve) (22%)
Largest culture . . . . Central Bantoid (Voltaic) (42%)
Development. 50
Physicians. 0.5
Gender gap 18%

% Christian: 0 3 10 50 75 100

Christian Traditions in Togo

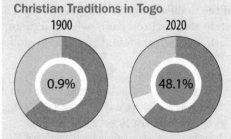

1900 — 0.9%

2020 — 48.1%

☐ Independent ☐ Protestant ▨ Catholic ■ Orthodox ▦ Christian

The small Christian population in 1900 (4,000 Christians) was a mixture of Catholics (64%) and Protestants (36%). Christianity diversified as it grew; in 2020, Christianity was 63% Catholic, 30% Protestant, and 7% Independent.

Religion in Togo

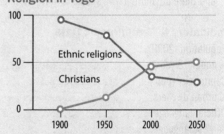

In 1900, Togo was 95% followers of traditional religions and 4% Muslim. By 2020, Christianity had grown from less than 1% to 48%, Islam grew to 19%, and traditional religions declined to 33%.

Bible Translations	Churches	Missionaries	Gospel Access
Languages. 54	Denominations 50	Received. 660	1900 . . . . Very low
Full Bible. 20	Congregations. 6,600	Sent 90	2020 . . . . Very high

Christianity in Tokelau

Tokelau is a very small island nation in the southern Pacific Ocean—home to only 1,400 people living on four square miles. It is a dependent territory of New Zealand. British seamen sighted Atafu in 1765, followed by Nukunonu in 1791 and Fakaofo in 1835. A British protectorate was proclaimed over all three atolls in 1877, and in 1925 the islands became territories of New Zealand. The last census revealed that 45% of the population was foreign-born, mostly from Samoa and New Zealand. Most of the country is Christian (94%), comprised of the Church in Tokelau (Congregationalist; 60% of the population) and Catholic (37%). The inhabitants of Atafu atoll are Protestants, while Nukunonu atoll is entirely Catholic; both are found on Fakaofo atoll.

Facts to Consider

- Most of Tokelau's national challenges stem from its geographical isolation. Climate change is also a pressing issue since the highest point in the country is just 16 feet above sea level.
- Tokelau is the first country in the world to use 100% renewable energy, switching entirely from diesel in 2012. The goal is 100% reduction in fossil fuels by 2030.
- The National Policy for Women and National Plan for Action are dedicated to addressing women's concerns in the country, including implementing the government's project to stop violence against women and young girls.
- Tokelauan is considered a "severely endangered" language by UNESCO, and there are more native speakers in New Zealand than in Tokelau.

Indicators & Demographic Data

Population (2020). 1,400
% under 15 years 36%
Capital city (pop.) . . . . Nukunonu 460
% urban dwellers. . . . . .0% (0.00% p.a.)
Official language. . . . . English, Tokelauan
Largest language. . . . . Tokelauan (96%)
Largest people . . . . Tokelauan (97%)
Largest culture . . . . other Polynesian (96%)
Development. 72
Physicians. 4.4
Gender gap. 5%

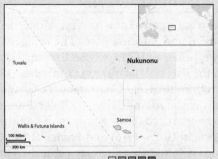

% Christian: | 0 3 10 50 75 100

Christian Traditions in Tokelau

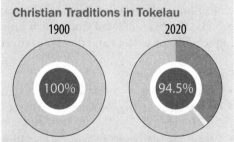

1900 — 100%

2020 — 94.5%

☐ Independent ☐ Protestant ■ Catholic ■ Orthodox ■ Christian

In 1900, Tokelau had a general population of only 900 people, all of whom were Protestant. By 2020, Christianity had diversified to 61% Protestant, 38% Catholic, and 2% Independent.

Religion in Tokelau

Christians

Baha'is

1900 1950 2000 2050

Tokelau has historically been a Christian country and remains so today. In 1900, the country was essentially 100% Christian. By 2020, Christianity had declined only slightly to 95% with a slight increase of the Baha'i population (less than 100 people).

Bible Translations	Churches	Missionaries	Gospel Access
Languages. 3	Denominations 6	Received. 2	1900 . . . . Very high
Full Bible. 1	Congregations. 14	Sent 1	2020 . . . . Very high

Christianity in Tonga

Tonga consists of 169 islands—36 inhabited—in the southern Pacific Ocean. Most inhabitants (70%) live on the main island, Tongatapu. Captain James Cook landed in Tonga in 1773. The London Missionary Society sent personnel in 1797, but three missionaries were killed in 1799. Christianity spread only after the conversion of some Tongan chiefs who led their people into the churches. Christianity became the nation's religion in 1845, and by 1853 all Tongans were Christian. Tonga is one of the few countries in the world where over half the population (55%) is affiliated with the Church of Jesus Christ of Latter-day Saints (Mormons). The Book of Mormon was translated by 1939 and revised in 1946. Their extensive school system has contributed to their growth.

Facts to Consider

- The nation's constitution requires Sabbath observance on Sundays, prohibiting commercial transactions (with some exceptions for hotels and resorts for tourists).
- In December 2021 and January 2022, an undersea volcanic eruption caused tsunamis in Tonga and across the region. It caused substantial damage to many of Tonga's islands.
- Many groups, both governmental and Christian, provide training programs to address human rights, child abuse, sexual harassment, and violence against women.
- Education until the age of 18 is compulsory, but many school buildings are not accessible to students with physical disabilities. As a result, attendance rates and educational levels are lower for students with physical disabilities than those without.

Indicators & Demographic Data

Population (2020)	111,000
% under 15 years	34%
Capital city (pop.)	Nuku'alofa 23,300
% urban dwellers	23% (0.99% p.a.)
Official language	Tongan, English
Largest language	Tongan (97%)
Largest people	Tongan (95%)
Largest culture	Tongan (97%)
Development	73
Physicians	5.6
Gender gap	4%

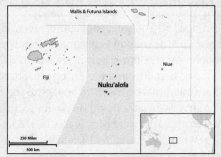

% Christian: 0 3 10 50 75 100

Christian Traditions in Tonga

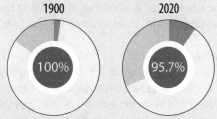

1900 — 100%
2020 — 95.7%

☐ Independent ☐ Protestant ☐ Catholic ■ Orthodox ■ Christian

In 1900, Tonga was entirely Christian, mostly Independents (82% of Christians), followed by Protestants (16%). In 2020, Christians were 59% Independent, 32% Protestant, and 10% Catholic.

Religion in Tonga

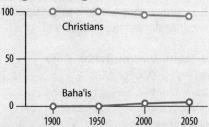

Tonga has historically been, and is still, a Christian country. In 1900, the country was 100% Christian. By 2020, Christianity had declined only slightly to 96% with a small increase of the Baha'i population to 4% (around 4,000 people).

Bible Translations		Churches		Missionaries		Gospel Access	
Languages	8	Denominations	26	Received	400	1900	Very high
Full Bible	5	Congregations	640	Sent	60	2020	Very high

Christianity in Trinidad and Tobago

Trinidad and Tobago is the southernmost country in the Caribbean, off the coast of Venezuela. The indigenous Amerindian people—Arawakan-speaking groups and Cariban-speaking groups—first encountered European Christians via Christopher Columbus on his third voyage to the Americas in 1498. The first two Catholic missionaries in 1513 were killed; the first Protestants were Moravians in 1783. Christianity is the largest religion today (64%). Spiritual Baptists are the largest indigenous Christian group; founded in 1860 by enslaved Africans, they incorporate elements of African Traditional Religions with Christianity. The largest Protestant group is the Pentecostal Assemblies of the West Indies, which sends missionaries to Montserrat, Barbados, and Martinique.

Facts to Consider

- Trinidad is home to 95% of the country's population, mostly Christian. People of African descent make up 32% of its population. Another 37% are of East Indian descent, half of whom are Hindu, and the other half are Muslim or Christian. Tobago is 85% of African descent and largely Christian.
- The Inter-Religious Organizations of Trinidad and Tobago includes members from different Christian churches, Hindus, Muslims, and Baha'i (25 members total). For the last 140 years on Good Friday, Hindus and Catholics share a Catholic Church in Siparia that has a dark-skinned statue of the Virgin Mary, whom Hindus worship as the goddess Kali.
- The government limits the number of long-term foreign missionaries in the country to 35 missionaries per registered religious group. Missionaries may stay for three years per visit.

Indicators & Demographic Data

Population (2020)................................1,378,000
% under 15 years 20%
Capital city (pop.).........................Port of Spain 544,000
% urban dwellers...........................53% (0.23% p.a.)
Official language......................................English
Largest language................. Trinidadian Creole English (53%)
Largest people .... Trinidad Black (37%)
Largest culture .... Hindi (41%)
Development..78
Physicians..18
Gender gap...-1%

% Christian: 0 3 10 50 75 100

Christian Traditions in Trinidad and Tobago

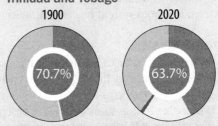

1900 — 70.7%   2020 — 63.7%

☐Independent ☐Protestant ■Catholic ■Orthodox ■Christian

In 1900, Christians in Trinidad and Tobago were largely Protestants (52%) and Catholics (47%). In 2020, Christians were more diverse: 42% Catholic, 39% Protestant, and 17% Independent. The largest Independent group is Spiritual Baptists.

Religion in Trinidad and Tobago

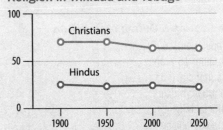

In 1900, the country was 71% Christian, 25% Hindu, and 4% Muslim. By 2020, Christianity had declined to 64% and Hindus to 24%, while Muslims slightly increased to 7%.

Bible Translations		Churches		Missionaries		Gospel Access	
Languages	12	Denominations	100	Received	560	1900	Very high
Full Bible	7	Congregations	1,900	Sent	170	2020	Very high

Christianity in Tunisia

Christianity has a long history in Tunisia, dating to the 1st century. As Arab Muslims took over the region in the 7th to 8th centuries, the region slowly transitioned from Latin-speaking Christian Berbers to Arabic-speaking Arab Muslims. Christianity disappeared by the 12th to 13th centuries. Tunisia was part of the Ottoman Empire before the French colonized it from 1881 until its independence in 1956. The 2011 Tunisian Revolution and the ousting of President Zine El Abidine Ben Ali caused a ripple effect across the region (the Arab Spring). Tunisia is 0.2% Christian today, and most Christians are foreigners (French and Italians). A few Christian leaders are indigenous.

Facts to Consider

- The constitution requires the president to be Muslim. There are technically no laws against proselytism, but religious services are permitted only in houses of worship or other nonpublic settings. Mosques are subsidized by the government.
- Arriving in 1991, the North Africa Mission launched an extensive Bible correspondence course that reached 20,000 Muslims before being banned by the government. All Protestant churches today are small and have limited influence in society.
- There is a very small movement of underground congregations consisting of Muslim converts to Christianity. Converts face strong social opposition and are often accused of bringing shame to their families.
- Jews had been present in Tunisia since antiquity but left the country en masse beginning in the 1950s because of regional conflicts related to the founding of the State of Israel in 1948. Fewer than 100 remain today.

Indicators & Demographic Data

Population (2020)	11,903,000
% under 15 years	24%
Capital city (pop.)	Tunis 2,365,000
% urban dwellers	70% (1.34% p.a.)
Official language	Arabic
Largest language	Arabic (98%)
Largest people	Tunisian Arab (89%)
Largest culture	Arab (Arabic) (98%)
Development	73
Physicians	13
Gender gap	10%

% Christian: 0 3 10 50 75 100

Christian Traditions in Tunisia

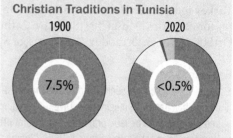

1900 — 7.5% | 2020 — <0.5%

☐Independent ☐Protestant ▨Catholic ◼Orthodox ◼Christian

Because of European colonization, essentially all Christians in Tunisia in 1900 were Catholic. The small Christian population in 2020 (23,000) was 83% Catholic, 11% Independent, and 5% Protestant.

Religion in Tunisia

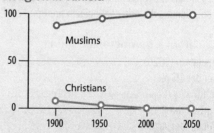

In 1900, Tunisia was 88% Muslim, 8% Christian (120,000), and 5% Jewish. Most Jews left the country, and Christianity declined to around 23,000 by 2020 due to emigration. Tunisia is nearly 100% Muslim today.

Bible Translations		Churches		Missionaries		Gospel Access	
Languages	14	Denominations	23	Received	220	1900	Very low
Full Bible	7	Congregations	140	Sent	4	2020	Low

Christianity in Turkey

Christianity in Turkey dates to the missionary journey of the apostle Paul to Asia Minor. The book of Revelation was written to the seven churches of Asia Minor, all of which are in modern-day Turkey. Christian history in Turkey is extremely rich, even though the country is only 0.2% Christian today. Islam's influence grew during the Ottoman Empire (1299–1922), despite that the country was 22% Christian in 1900. In the 20th century, Christian rights were systematically denied; as their property was confiscated, many Christians fled the country. Christians are generally considered foreigners in Turkey today, even if their families have lived in the country for centuries. Most Christians are Catholics, Armenian Orthodox, Greek Orthodox, Anglicans, or Syrian Orthodox.

Facts to Consider

- Turkey is technically a secular state, and the constitution prohibits discrimination based on religion. The Diyanet coordinates Islamic matters and promotes the beliefs, practices, and moral principles of Islam.
- Numerous monitoring organizations, both Christian and secular, report discrimination against Christians (primarily Protestants) related to residency permits. Deportations are common. Establishing viable Protestant churches is extremely difficult, and most Christian groups struggle to train leaders within the country.
- Converts from Islam are often shunned by their families, friends, and workplaces. Although spreading religious beliefs is not illegal, it is viewed with suspicion.
- The number of Jews declined from 80,000 in 1900 to 16,000 in 2020; anti-Semitic rhetoric continues in print and social media.

Indicators & Demographic Data

Population (2020)	83,836,000
% under 15 years	24%
Capital city (pop.)	Ankara 5,118,000
% urban dwellers	76% (1.11% p.a.)
Official language	Turkish
Largest language	Turkish (80%)
Largest people	Turk (62%)
Largest culture	Turkish (63%)
Development	79
Physicians	17
Gender gap	8%

% Christian: 0 3 10 50 75 100

Christian Traditions in Turkey

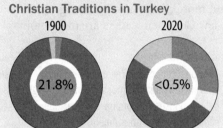

1900 — 21.8%   2020 — <0.5%

☐ Independent ☐ Protestant ▨ Catholic ■ Orthodox ▨ Christian

There were far more Christians in Turkey in 1900 (3 million) than in 2020 (171,000). Most Christians in 1900 were Orthodox. In 2020, the small community was a mixture of all traditions: 51% Orthodox, 27% Catholic, 15% Protestant, and 7% Independent.

Religion in Turkey

In 1900, Turkey was 77% Muslim and 22% Christian. Christianity declined to only 0.2%, while the Muslim population increased to 98%.

Bible Translations		Churches		Missionaries		Gospel Access	
Languages	51	Denominations	46	Received	560	1900	Medium
Full Bible	31	Congregations	530	Sent	30	2020	Medium

Christianity in Turkmenistan

Turkmenistan is a majority Muslim country (97%) in central Asia. Despite a long history of Christianity dating to the 5th century, Christianity died out by the 14th to 15th centuries and makes up only 1% of the population today. Turkmenistan was part of the Soviet Union from 1925 to 1991. As a result, most Christians in the country are ethnic Russians, and the Russian Orthodox Church is the largest denomination. The small Protestant and Catholic communities are largely underground. Christians in Turkmenistan face persecution both in society and by the government.

Facts to Consider

- After decades of religious suppression under the Soviet government, a renewed interest in Islam arose in the 1990s after independence.
- Survival is the main priority for Christians in Turkmenistan. Proselytism is illegal, and unregistered groups are not permitted to hold public religious services. Foreign missionaries are prohibited.
- Some Christian groups face harassment, and house churches attempting to gather for communal worship risk raids. Muslim converts to Christianity—especially ethnic Turkmen—face extreme social duress and discrimination by way of losing their jobs and being pressured to return to Islam.

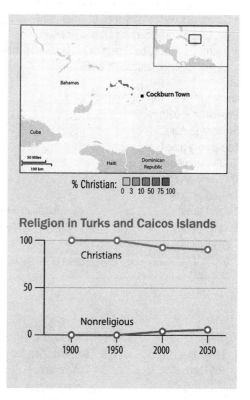

% Christian: 0 3 10 50 75 100

Religion in Turkmenistan

Christianity in Turks and Caicos Islands

Turks and Caicos Islands is a British Overseas Territory in the Caribbean, known for tourism and offshore financing. The islands were uninhabited when visited by the first European explorer in 1512, and the country is 91% Christian today. Baptists are the largest denomination, and most are related to the Jamaica Baptist Union. Seventh-day Adventists have three missions, in Grand Turk, Kew (North Caicos), and Blue Hills (Providenciales). There are five Anglican churches throughout the islands, and Anglican Church Women assists the work of the diocese and are active in outreach efforts from their parishes.

Facts to Consider

- Turks and Caicos Islands is a dependent territory of the United Kingdom, and as such the UK legal system protects human rights. There are no church-operated schools or medical institutions on the islands. There is no established church.
- The Turks and Caicos Islands Human Rights Commission was formed by constitutional order in 2011. It works on issues related to freedom of conscience and religion, assembly and association, property, and other fundamental rights and freedoms.

% Christian: 0 3 10 50 75 100

Religion in Turks and Caicos Islands

Christianity in Tuvalu

Tuvalu is an island nation in Polynesia where 11,500 people live on nine square miles of land. It is one of the world's smallest countries and is 95% Christian. European explorers visited the islands beginning in the mid-16th century. Then known as the Ellice Islands, the islands were colonized by the British from 1892 until 1975, then achieved full independence in 1978. Christianity is pervasive in the public sphere, and pastors are considered pillars of society, along with elders and chiefs. The Tuvalu Christian Church (Congregational) is the largest denomination, representing 77% of the country's population.

Facts to Consider

- Climate change is one of the most pressing issues for Tuvalu. Since 2000, the country has lost four islands to rising sea levels, mostly because of industrialization in other countries around the world.
- The church works closely with the government to raise awareness of climate change. Crops and drinking water are consistently threatened, but some Tuvaluans connect these kinds of environmental challenges to theological, not scientific, ideas.
- Tuvalu is one of the few countries in the world that reported zero cases of COVID-19 during the global pandemic. Its borders were entirely closed, and nearly the entire population has been vaccinated.
- Tuvalu has one congregation of Jehovah's Witnesses, with a monthly *Watchtower* magazine available in Tuvaluan.
- There is a small Baha'i presence in the country, mostly in Funafuti (the capital) and on Nanumea Island.

Indicators & Demographic Data

Population (2020)................................. 11,500
% under 15 years 36%
Capital city (pop.)............................Funafuti 6,300
% urban dwellers...........................64% (2.08% p.a.)
Official language...................................... none
Largest language............................. Tuvaluan (96%)
Largest people .... Tuvaluan (Ellice Islander) (66%)
Largest culture ....other Polynesian (97%)
Development.. 72
Physicians... 11
Gender gap..5%

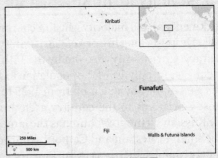

% Christian: 0 3 10 50 75 100

Christian Traditions in Tuvalu

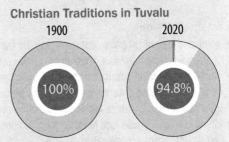

1900 — 100%
2020 — 94.8%

☐Independent ☐Protestant ▨Catholic ◼Orthodox ◼Christian

All Christians in Tuvalu in 1900 were Protestant. This was still largely the case in 2020, though there are now small populations of Catholics and Independents.

Religion in Tuvalu

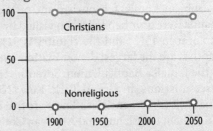

Tuvalu is a historically majority Christian country and remains so today. In 1900, the country was 100% Christian—but was home to only 2,500 people. Christianity declined slightly to 95% with small increases of Baha'i and the nonreligious.

Bible Translations	Churches	Missionaries	Gospel Access	
Languages............6	Denominations 10	Received.............5	1900	Very high
Full Bible.............5	Congregations........28	Sent 2	2020	Very high

Christianity in Uganda

Modern day Uganda forms part of the historical kingdom of Buganda, whose power increased during the 18th and 19th centuries (and still exists today). The first resident Christian evangelist in Uganda was an African—Scopion Dallington Maftaa, a freed slave from Nyasaland (today part of Malawi) who shared Christianity with Kabaka (King) Mutesa I of Buganda in 1875 (though he never converted). Maftaa labored alone for two years until the arrival of missionaries from the Church Missionary Society (Anglican). Catholic missionaries first arrived in 1879 and worked in the court of the king. Arab traders from Zanzibar (Tanzania) had also recently arrived and introduced Islam. The Uganda Martyrs—23 Anglican and 23 Catholic converts to Christianity—were killed by order of Kabaka Mwanga II from 1885 to 1887 during the three-way struggle for religious influence (Catholic, Anglican, Muslim) over the kingdom. This was also the period of the European Scramble for Africa, during which the British colonized Uganda from 1894 to 1962. Uganda was a majority Christian country by the time of its independence. After independence, however, Uganda suffered under the dictatorship of Idi Amin (1971–1979), with upward of half a million people killed and various attacks on religious life, including the ban of several Christian denominations and the Baha'i Faith. Many Christians were killed in 1977 after the murder of Anglican Archbishop Janani Luwum, a critic of the regime.

Over 136,000 Catholics were baptized in Uganda by 1912. Catholicism continued to grow quickly, in part because of the early development of indigenous clergy, the opening of a local sisterhood (1908), and the first ordained Ugandans in 1913. Pope Francis visited Uganda in November 2015 and preached on the theme of social justice at the Namugongo shrine in honor of the Uganda Martyrs.

Anglicans make up more than 35% of Uganda's population, and they continue to grow. The East African Revival swept through the churches in Uganda and Rwanda beginning in the 1920s and helped to culturally contextualize Anglicanism. The revival also resulted in two schisms, one from the African Inland Mission in 1955 and another from Anglicans in 1967. Uganda is also home to many African Independent Churches from neighboring Kenya.

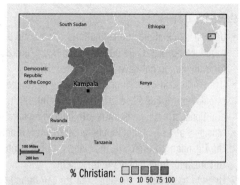

% Christian: 0 3 10 50 75 100

Religion in Uganda

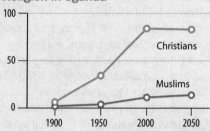

Uganda's religious makeup changed dramatically over the 20th century. In 1900, the country was 91% followers of traditional religions, with smaller populations of Christians (7%) and Muslims (2%). By 2020, Christianity had grown to 85% and Islam to 12%, followed by just 2% primarily traditional religionists. Just under 1% of the population is Hindu.

Indicators & Demographic Data

Population (2020)	47,188,000
% under 15 years	47%
Capital city (pop.)	Kampala 3,298,000
% urban dwellers	25% (5.41% p.a.)
Official language	English, Swahili
Largest language	Ganda (19%)
Largest people	Ganda (19%)
Largest culture	Interlacustrine Bantu (64%)
Development	52
Physicians	0.9
Gender gap	14%

Bible Translations		Churches		Missionaries		Gospel Access	
Languages	63	Denominations	110	Received	2,500	1900	Low
Full Bible	36	Congregations	45,600	Sent	600	2020	Very high

Facts to Consider

- Uganda is one of the poorest nations in the world despite active efforts to reduce poverty. Child education rates are low; 83% of 10-year-olds, for example, do not have basic literacy skills.
- Uganda has an open-door policy regarding refugees, with its refugee population tripling since 2016 (1.4 million). But this increase has put additional strain on a country with limited resources.
- Muslims, at 12% of the population, frequently report discrimination by the Ugandan government, including profiling, detention without trial, torture, and other inhumane treatment.
- Uganda has been a mission area for the Baha'i Faith, home to one of the world's seven Baha'i temples, in Kampala. The country has an estimated 140,000 Baha'i.
- Rape is punishable by life imprisonment or death, but it is a common problem throughout the country, and laws are inconsistently applied. Most victims do not report, as they are often accused of causing their own trauma. Lockdowns related to the COVID-19 pandemic exacerbated domestic violence against women.
- The government does not effectively enforce laws that provide the same legal status and rights between men and women. Women are regularly discriminated against in employment, education, owning property, and gaining custody of their children after divorce.

Christian Traditions in Uganda

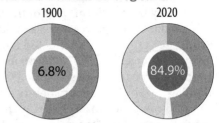

1900   2020

6.8%   84.9%

☐ Independent ☐ Protestant ■ Catholic ■ Orthodox ■ Christian

The Christian population in 1900 was largely Catholic (54%) and Protestant (46%) due to historic missionary efforts from each. Christianity diversified slightly as it grew, particularly with the introduction of new African Independent Churches. In 2020, Christianity in Uganda was 49% Catholic, 49% Protestant, and 3% Independent. Many Protestants are Anglicans, and Uganda is home to the third largest Anglican population in the world (after the United Kingdom and Nigeria).

Christian Families in Uganda

Family	Population 2020	%	Trend	Change
Latin-rite Catholic	19,400,000	41.1	↑	3.6
Anglican	16,297,000	34.5	↑	2.8
*Pentecostals/Charismatics	10,000,000	21.2	↑	3.3
*Evangelicals	8,700,000	18.4	↑	3.0
Adventist	612,000	1.3	↑↑	6.0
Baptist	321,000	0.7	↑	4.9
Holiness	170,000	0.4	↑↑	6.5
Reformed, Presbyterian	69,900	0.1	↑	2.9
Eastern Orthodox	32,000	0.1	↑	1.4
Salvationist	31,500	0.1	↑	2.8
Latter-day Saints (Mormons)	28,900	0.1	↑↑	12.4
Jehovah's Witnesses	25,700	0.1	↑↑	6.9
Restorationist, Disciple	24,300	0.1	↑	5.0
Friends (Quaker)	19,200	<0.1	↑	4.8
Nondenominational	4,200	<0.1	↑	3.4
Oriental and other Orthodox	1,000	<0.1	–	0.0

Catholics make up 41% of the country's population (19.4 million) and is the largest Christian family. Anglicans are the second largest family (35%) largely due to the Church of Uganda, but there have been smaller breakaway Anglican groups. Pentecostals/Charismatics are 21% of the country's population and are found in a wide variety of denominations. Uganda is home to several denominations that are entirely Pentecostal, like the Pentecostal Assemblies of God, New Apostolic Church, Assemblies of God, and United Pentecostal Church. Charismatics are also found in the Church of Uganda, the Catholic Church, and among Baptists and other historic denominations. The same is true for Evangelicals, the fourth largest family (18% of the population). Most Pentecostal denominations are also 100% Evangelical.

* These movements are found within Christian families

− no change

↑↑ extreme growth
↑ growth
↓↓ extreme decline
↓ decline

Christianity in Ukraine

Orthodox Christianity has over 2,000 years of history in Ukraine. Tradition states that in the 1st century the apostle Andrew visited what is today Ukraine. Volodymyr I adopted Christianity as the state religion in 988 at the behest of his wife, Anna Porphyrogenita, and Byzantine (Eastern) Christianity grew quickly during the 10th and 11th centuries. Ukraine has had a turbulent political history, which includes the 13th-century Mongol invasion, the 14th-to-15th-century rule of Lithuania and Poland, and 20th-century imperialism from Russia. Ukraine was part of the Soviet Union from 1922 to 1991, a period marked by famine, class struggle, mass killings, and suppression of public religion. Orthodox Christianity was revived in the 1990s, but in two competing groups: one under Moscow and the other under Kyiv. The divide in the Ukrainian Orthodox Church has little to do with theology and much to do with history, national identity, and politics.

After the 2014 Ukrainian revolution, Russian military forces invaded Ukraine's Crimean Peninsula and illegally claimed it for Russia via a sham referendum. Pro-Russia and anti-government groups then demonstrated in the Donbas and Luhansk regions, where separatist forces declared independence. Russian president Vladimir Putin recognized their independence in February 2022 and subsequently invaded Ukraine. In the first month of the war, upward of 7,000 Ukrainians were killed and at least 10 million people were displaced.

Catholicism has had a difficult history in Ukraine, with forced elimination of Catholicism in 1839 and the stripping of Catholic civil rights and spiritual life in 1946. Persecuted alongside all religions under the Soviet state, Catholicism became the second largest denomination after the fall of the Soviet Union. Evangelical Christianity also grew rapidly after 1991, with Ukraine known as the "Bible belt" of Eastern Europe. The country is known for training and sending missionaries even though Protestant, Evangelical, and Pentecostal churches are comparatively small.

% Christian: 0 3 10 50 75 100

Religion in Ukraine

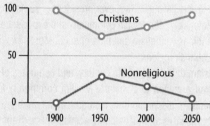

Ukraine has historically been a Christian country and remains so today, but Christianity experienced decline while the country was part of the Soviet Union. The country was 97% Christian in 1900, dropped to 60% by 1970, then rebounded to 86% by 2020. Likewise, the nonreligious grew from virtually zero in 1900 to a peak of 38% in 1970, only to drop to 12% today.

Indicators & Demographic Data

Population (2020)	43,579,000
% under 15 years	16%
Capital city (pop.)	Kyiv 2,988,000
% urban dwellers	70% (-0.27% p.a.)
Official language	Ukrainian
Largest language	Ukrainian (76%)
Largest people	Ukrainian (76%)
Largest culture	Ukrainian (76%)
Development	75
Physicians	30
Gender gap	1%

Bible Translations		Churches		Missionaries		Gospel Access	
Languages	67	Denominations	140	Received	6,000	1900	Very high
Full Bible	41	Congregations	45,600	Sent	440	2020	Very high

Facts to Consider

- Religious minorities are openly persecuted in Crimea, such as Jehovah's Witnesses, Orthodox Church of Ukraine (Kyiv), and especially Muslim Crimean Tatars.
- A recent report found that only 20% of Ukrainian Orthodox said religion was "very important" in their lives, yet 91% said they have religious icons in their homes.
- Domestic violence is a massive problem, with 101,000 complaints from January to June 2020 alone (a 40% increase from the prior year). Spousal abuse is common and was exacerbated by COVID-19 lockdowns.
- The number of Jews declined from 720,000 in 1900 to around 45,000 today, mostly because of the Holocaust and then emigration. Despite Ukraine having its first-ever president of Jewish background (Volodymyr Zelenskyy), the Jewish community still experiences anti-Semitic actions such as vandalism and hate speech. Most Jews live in the Donbas and Luhansk regions.
- Islam dates to the 15th century, and estimates of adherents range from half a million to 2 million. Muslim community leaders report various kinds of discrimination, including being unable to obtain more land for burial sites and often being accused of "extremism" and "terrorism."

Christian Traditions in Ukraine

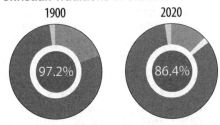

1900   2020

97.2%   86.4%

☐ Independent ☐ Protestant ▓ Catholic ▉ Orthodox ■ Christian

As has been the case historically, Christianity in Ukraine is primarily Orthodox. In 1900, Orthodox made up 78% of Christians, followed by Catholics at 20% and Protestants at just under 2%. By 2020, Orthodox had an even greater share of Christians (83%), followed by Catholics (13%). Protestants and Independents have both grown and each represent 2% of Christians. Jehovah's Witnesses are the largest Independent denomination, with over 280,000 members.

Christian Families in Ukraine

Family	Population 2020	%	Trend	Change
Eastern Orthodox	31,304,000	71.8	–	-0.2
Eastern-rite Catholic	3,707,000	8.5	–	-0.2
*Pentecostals/Charismatics	1,400,000	3.2	↑	0.8
Latin-rite Catholic	1,193,000	2.7	↑	2.2
*Evangelicals	520,000	1.2	↑	1.3
Oriental and other Orthodox	411,000	0.9	↓	-2.6
Jehovah's Witnesses	255,000	0.6	↓	-1.6
Baptist	179,000	0.4	–	-0.4
Reformed, Presbyterian	130,000	0.3	–	0.0
Adventist	48,100	0.1	↓	-3.5
Restorationist, Disciple	16,500	<0.1	↑	4.1
Hidden believers in Christ	11,300	<0.1	↑	2.9
Latter-day Saints (Mormons)	10,800	<0.1	–	-0.1
United church or joint mission	3,000	<0.1	–	0.0
Mennonite	2,500	<0.1	↓	-1.2

Eastern Orthodox make up 72% of the country's population (31.3 million) and is the largest Christian family. There are three large Ukrainian Orthodox churches: the Patriarchate of Moscow (13.5 million), the Patriarchate of Kyiv (16 million, which split from Moscow after the fall of the Soviet Union), and the Ukrainian Autocephalous Orthodox Church (800,000). Moscow only partially recognizes the Patriarchate of Kyiv. After Ukrainian Orthodox, the largest Orthodox traditions are Russian, Old Ritualist, Bulgarian, and Armenian. Catholics are the second largest Christian family and includes both Eastern- and Latin-rite. Pentecostals/Charismatics are mostly in Protestant or Independent denominations such as Christians of Evangelical Faith (which is a Pentecostal denomination), the Church of God of Prophecy, and Evangelical Christian Pentecostal Zionists.

* These movements are found within Christian families	↑↑ extreme growth
	↑ growth
	↓↓ extreme decline
– no change	↓ decline

Christianity in the United Arab Emirates

The United Arab Emirates (UAE) is in the eastern Arabian Peninsula, bordering Oman and Saudi Arabia. Islam spread to the region in the 7th century, and it has been Muslim-majority since. The UAE had protected status under the British through a variety of 19th century treaties until its full independence in 1971. Most churches in the UAE date only to the 20th century, largely from the oil boom of the 1960s and 1970s that demanded an increase of foreign workers. The largest denomination is the Catholic Church, with at least 30 congregations serving Catholics from around the world, especially Filipinos. Orthodox churches include the Syrian Orthodox Church (serving Indian Syrians), the Mar Thoma Syrian Church (Indians), Coptic Orthodox (Egyptians), and Greek Orthodox. Protestants are mostly Anglicans.

Facts to Consider

- Only 11% of the UAE's population are citizens of the country. The rest are noncitizen residents, most originating from South and Southeast Asia.
- Islam is the official religion of the country. The constitution does not technically prohibit Muslims from converting to another religion, but the law does stipulate up to five years imprisonment for preaching against Islam or proselytizing Muslims. Blasphemy (insulting God) is also illegal.
- It is illegal for Muslims to drink alcohol or eat pork. Both Muslims and non-Muslims are required to fast publicly during the holy month of Ramadan.
- People of religions other than Islam are generally permitted to worship and practice their religion within designated buildings and in private homes. There has been major growth of churches and congregations in the last 20 years.

Indicators & Demographic Data

Population (2020)	9,813,000
% under 15 years	14%
Capital city (pop.)	Abu Dhabi 1,483,000
% urban dwellers	87% (1.50% p.a.)
Official language	Arabic
Largest language	Arabic (52%)
Largest people	Gulf Arab (Emirian) (11%)
Largest culture	Arab (Arabic) (50%)
Development	86
Physicians	16
Gender gap	3%

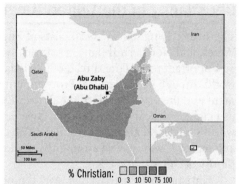

% Christian: 0 3 10 50 75 100

Christian Traditions in the United Arab Emirates

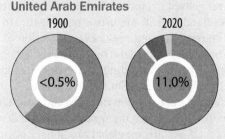

1900 — <0.5%

2020 — 11.0%

☐ Independent ☐ Protestant ▨ Catholic ▨ Orthodox ▮ Christian

The UAE had very few Christians in 1900 (less than 100). In 2020, Christianity in the country was 89% Catholic, largely due to migrant workers from overseas, 7% Orthodox, 3% Protestant, and 2% Independent.

Religion in the United Arab Emirates

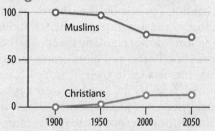

In 1900, the UAE was virtually entirely Muslim. But Islam declined to 79% with the increase of the Christian population to 11%, Hindus to 6%, and Buddhists to 2% due to migration.

Bible Translations		Churches		Missionaries		Gospel Access	
Languages	36	Denominations	81	Received	140	1900	Very low
Full Bible	21	Congregations	370	Sent	10	2020	Medium

Christianity in the United Kingdom

The United Kingdom (UK) consists of England, Scotland, Wales, and Northern Ireland. Historically, the UK played an important role in the spread of Christianity around the world through its Evangelical Protestant missionary movement and the broad reach of the British Empire, which, at its height in the early 20th century, covered a quarter of the world's total land area. As a result, British culture, religion, and legacy is widespread around the world, even as Christianity declines in the UK.

Christianity first arrived in what is now the UK when it was a part of the Roman Empire in the 1st century. St. Patrick evangelized Ireland, St. Columba established a monastery in Scotland, and St. Augustine became the first Bishop of Canterbury, all aiding in the evangelization of the British Isles. The Church of England split with the Catholic Church in 1534 and so began the tradition of the British monarch also serving as the head of the Church of England. Catholic-Protestant conflict was persistent from the 16th and 17th centuries, and in the 19th century, many new Protestant denominations were formed. Significant global missionary outreach efforts were also a main characteristic of historic British Protestantism, especially by female missionaries..

Most Catholic, Anglican, and other Protestant churches declined in the 20th century, especially from the 1960s. Many rural churches in particular are struggling. A recent survey found that there are around three times as many nonpracticing Christians (people who self-identify as Christian but only attend church a few times a year) as there are church-attending Christians. The Church of England (Anglican) is the largest denomination by far, though most baptized Anglicans do not regularly practice. Sunday church attendance is declining, and most people report that religion has little importance in their lives. Youth tend to be the most secular. Christianity in urban areas has been revived via the establishment of Black and other ethnic minority churches. Two-thirds of the population of London identifies as other than "White British." The arrival of migrants from around the world has contributed both to an increase in population and religious diversity. An estimated 40% of churchgoers are ethnically Black or Asian.

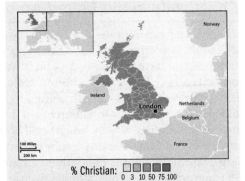

% Christian: 0 3 10 50 75 100

Religion in the United Kingdom

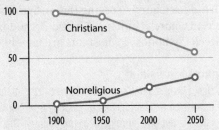

The United Kingdom has experienced a steep decline in its Christian population with the rise of other religions and the nonreligious. The country was 97% Christian in 1900 and dropped to 67% by 2020. Most gains were made by atheists and agnostics, who are now at least 23% of the country's population. The United Kingdom, now 7% Muslim, has large populations of Hindus, Sikhs, Jews, and Buddhists.

Indicators & Demographic Data

Population (2020)	67,334,000
% under 15 years	18%
Capital city (pop.)	London 9,304,000
% urban dwellers	84% (0.80% p.a.)
Official language	English
Largest language	English (86%)
Largest people	English (British) (68%)
Largest culture	English (British) (78%)
Development	92
Physicians	28
Gender gap	4%

Bible Translations		Churches		Missionaries		Gospel Access	
Languages	85	Denominations	820	Received	12,000	1900	Very high
Full Bible	64	Congregations	52,600	Sent	14,000	2020	Very high

Facts to Consider

- The Church of England is the state church, and the monarch must be a member of the church. It is also the mother church of the Anglican Communion, though Anglican belief and practice is far more widespread in the global South (particularly sub-Saharan Africa) than it is in the United Kingdom.
- Women make up the majority of British congregations, and denominations are split on the issue of women's ordination. Methodists have ordained female clergy since 1974, while Anglicans have done so since the 1990s. Catholics, Orthodox, and most Pentecostals, Independents, and many newer churches exclude women from ordained leadership.
- The United Kingdom is a religiously diverse country. Muslims include those from South Asia, the Middle East, and Southeast Asia, as well as some converts among the British. Hindus, Sikhs, Jews, and Buddhists are largely concentrated in London and other urban areas in England.
- The United Kingdom is home to one of the largest Jewish populations in the world (280,000), with most in England. Anti-Semitism has increased, especially among the political left.
- Among hate crimes, those that are racially motivated are the most commonly reported, particularly among Roma and people of African, Afro-Caribbean, South Asian, and Middle Eastern origin.

Christian Traditions in the United Kingdom

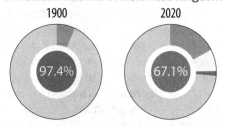

1900 — 97.4%   2020 — 67.1%

☐ Independent ☐ Protestant ▨ Catholic ▨ Orthodox ■ Christian

Christianity in the United Kingdom is historically Protestant (Anglican) and remains so today. In 1900, Protestants made up 93% of Christians, followed by Catholics at 7%. By 2020, the Protestant share had dropped to 74% with an increase of Catholics to 17% and newer Independent traditions to 7%. Jehovah's Witnesses are the largest Independent denomination, with over 260,000 members.

Christian Families in United Kingdom

Family	Population 2020	%	Trend	Change
Anglican	23,918,000	35.5	↓	-0.7
Latin-rite Catholic	6,388,000	9.5	↑	1.0
*Evangelicals	5,900,000	8.8	–	0.0
*Pentecostals/Charismatics	3,600,000	5.3	↑	0.9
Reformed, Presbyterian	1,343,000	2.0	↓	-1.1
Eastern Orthodox	539,000	0.8	↑	1.1
Methodist	421,000	0.6	↓	-2.8
Jehovah's Witnesses	265,000	0.4	–	-0.2
Lutheran	252,000	0.4	↑	4.2
Baptist	219,000	0.3	↓	-1.2
Latter-day Saints (Mormons)	183,000	0.3	–	-0.3
Christian Brethren	97,700	0.1	↓	-0.7
Nondenominational	80,400	0.1	↑	0.5
United church or joint mission	79,100	0.1	↑	0.8
Oriental and other Orthodox	60,600	0.1	↑	1.5
Salvationist	55,900	0.1	↓	-1.6
Congregational	52,400	0.1	↓	-0.7
Exclusive Brethren	47,600	0.1	–	-0.2
Adventist	45,400	0.1	↑	2.4
Friends (Quaker)	19,700	<0.1	↓	-0.9
Holiness	14,900	<0.1	↑	0.9
Eastern-rite Catholic	11,800	<0.1	↑	1.7
Hidden believers in Christ	4,300	<0.1	↑	1.9

Anglicans (23.9 million) make up 36% of the country's population and is the largest Christian family. This family includes the Anglican churches of England (23 million), Wales (1.1 million), and Northern Ireland (250,000), as well as several Anglican breakaway groups, though these are comparatively quite small. Catholics are the second largest family (10%) and again represents those in England and Wales (4.5 million), Northern Ireland (958,000), and Scotland (761,000). The United Kingdom is just under 9% Evangelical and 5% Pentecostal/Charismatic, both of which are found in the Anglican churches (though are small minorities). The largest Evangelical and Pentecostal/Charismatic denominations are the Elim Pentecostal Church, the New Testament Church of God, and the Assemblies of God.

---

* These movements are found within Christian families	↑↑ extreme growth
	↑ growth
	↓↓ extreme decline
– no change	↓ decline

Christianity in the United States

Christianity has played a central role in shaping the history and society of the United States (USA). The guarantee of religious freedom and lack of state-sponsored religion encouraged the development of an incredible diversity of Christian expression. Turtle Island—the indigenous name for North America—was home to an array of Native American peoples and advanced civilizations before the arrival of Europeans in the late 15th century. However, indigenous populations were soon decimated by disease and conflict and gradually dispossessed of their land. The first permanent Christian community was that of Catholics in Florida in 1565. English separatists arrived in the northeast and established the Massachusetts Bay Colony as a "city upon a hill" in 1630. The Great Awakening revivals of the 17th and 18th centuries shaped American Christianity in unique ways, flattening ecclesiastical hierarchies to allow new participation of enslaved Africans, freed Blacks, Native Americans, and women. Native Americans and Blacks contextualized Euro-American Christianity to their cultural contexts and continue to do so today. The United States was not necessarily founded as a "Christian nation," but it took on that identity in the 19th century.

The USA is often described as an exception to trends in being both highly religious and highly developed. It is a nation of immigrants from its founding to the arrival of millions of Irish and Italian Catholics in the 19th century and the arrival of millions of Asians after 1965. As membership in White churches declines, immigrants from Latin America maintain the USA's status as the country with the most Christians in the world. At the same time, 68% of White Evangelical Protestants say the nation does not have a responsibility to welcome refugees. Christianity is deeply divided along racial, ethnic, and political lines. Also, theological education is on the decline. And while the USA sends the most missionaries worldwide, it also receives the most from around the world. The USA is also the birthplace of the Church of Jesus Christ of Latter-day Saints (Mormons) and the Jehovah's Witnesses, both of which are now much larger outside the USA than within it due to highly organized missionary efforts.

% Christian: 0 3 10 50 75 100

Religion in the United States

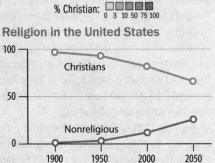

Christianity is in proportional decline, and today the USA is one of the most religiously diverse countries in the world. In 1900, the USA was 97% Christian, 1% Jewish, and 1% nonreligious. By 2020, Christianity had declined to 73% with a marked increase of the nonreligious (atheists and agnostics together) to 20%. There has also been an increase of Jews (2%), Muslims (2%), and Buddhists (1%).

Indicators & Demographic Data

Population (2020)............331,432,000
% under 15 years 19%
Capital city (pop.) . .Washington, DC 5,322,000
% urban dwellers..........83% (0.96% p.a.)
Official language..................... none
Largest language............English (69%)
Largest people ....USA White (38%)
Largest culture ....USA White (38%)
Development........................92
Physicians............................26
Gender gap...........................1%

Bible Translations		Churches		Missionaries		Gospel Access	
Languages..........273		Denominations 4,700		Received.........38,000		1900..........Very high	
Full Bible............86		Congregations....459,000		Sent...........135,000		2020..........Very high	

Facts to Consider

- American society is racially divided due to the ongoing legacy of slavery, segregation, and inequality. Multiethnic congregations are rare—86% of congregations are majority White, Black, Hispanic, or Asian only in ethnic makeup.
- Gun violence is endemic, with an estimated 390 million guns on the streets, far more than any other country. Research has found that between 39% and 65% of White Evangelicals own and regularly carry guns, even in church.
- Native American women are murdered and sexually assaulted at ten times the rate of other ethnicities. An estimated 84% of American Indian and Alaskan Native women have personally experienced violence.
- Many churches are divided over the inclusion of LGBTQ people, such as the United Methodist Church and the Evangelical Covenant Church. However, in May 2021, the Evangelical Lutheran Church elected the first openly transgender bishop of any major American denomination.
- Women make up at least 60% of church membership in the USA, but only 11% of congregations have a female lead pastor. The Catholic Church and many Evangelical churches, such as the Southern Baptist Convention, have struggled in recent years with scandals involving the sexual abuse of women and children.

Christian Traditions in the United States

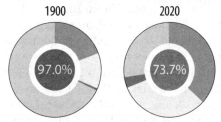

1900   2020

97.0%   73.7%

☐Independent ☐Protestant ☐Catholic ■Orthodox ■Christian

Christianity in the United States has always been diverse. In 1900, Christianity was 68% Protestant, 20% Catholic, and 12% Independent. Over the 20th century, mainline Protestant decline combined with immigration from Latin America contributed to an increase of the Catholic share to 37%. Independents are 32% of Christians, and Protestants dropped to 27%. The Orthodox are 4%. The USA is home to the largest unaffiliated Christian population in the world (47 million; 19% of Christians in the USA).

Christian Families in the United States

Family	Population 2020	%	Trend	Change
Latin-rite Catholic	72,194,000	21.8	↑	0.6
*Evangelicals	69,000,000	20.8	↑	1.1
*Pentecostals/Charismatics	65,000,000	19.6	↑	0.7
Baptist	39,235,000	11.8	↓	-0.6
Methodist	12,705,000	3.8	—	-0.1
Latter-day Saints (Mormons)	7,240,000	2.2	↑	1.4
Lutheran	6,588,000	2.0	↓	-1.2
Eastern Orthodox	5,460,000	1.6	↑	0.9
Restorationist, Disciple	3,342,000	1.0	↓	-0.6
Reformed, Presbyterian	3,310,000	1.0	↓	-2.7
Jehovah's Witnesses	2,934,000	0.9	↑	0.8
Holiness	2,467,000	0.7	↑	1.4
Anglican	2,042,000	0.6	—	0.3
Eastern-rite Catholic	1,706,000	0.5	↑	0.7
Oriental and other Orthodox	1,690,000	0.5	↑	1.7
Adventist	1,474,000	0.4	↑	1.4
Nondenominational	926,000	0.3	↑	0.7
United church or joint mission	744,000	0.2	↓	-3.7
Congregational	731,000	0.2	↑	0.7
Mennonite	488,000	0.1	↑	1.0
Salvationist	398,000	0.1	—	-0.5
Dunker	222,000	0.1	↓	-0.5
Old Catholic Church	172,000	0.1	—	-0.5

The Catholic Church is the largest Christian family in the United States, with 22% of the country's population. Evangelicalism is the second largest Christian family, even though the proportion of the US population that is Evangelical declined from 53% in 1900 to 21% in 2020. As a trans-denominational movement (like the Pentecostal/Charismatic movement), Evangelicalism is found throughout a number of denominations. The largest Evangelical denomination is the Southern Baptist Convention (18.8 million), followed by the Assemblies of God (3.5 million). Many Evangelicals are also found among unaffiliated Christians. Pentecostal/Charismatics grew from virtually zero in 1900 to nearly 20% of the US population in 2020. The largest movement in this family is the Catholic Charismatics, with an estimated 18 million members. The next largest is the Church of God in Christ (8 million), a Black denomination dating to 1895.

* These movements are found within Christian families	↑↑ extreme growth ↑ growth ↓↓ extreme decline
— no change	↓ decline

Christianity in the United States Virgin Islands

The United States Virgin Islands (USVI) is an unincorporated territory of the United States, consisting of 6 larger islands and 50 surrounding minor islands. The Arawak and Ciboney peoples historically inhabited the islands. Christopher Columbus sighted the islands in 1493, and they became Danish colonies in 1754. The United States bought them from Denmark in 1917. Danish Lutherans were the first Protestants, and the Frederick Lutheran Church in Charlotte Amalie (1666) is the second oldest Lutheran church in the Western Hemisphere. Other Protestant groups, in order of size, include the Episcopal Church, Seventh-day Adventists, and Methodists. The Catholic Church is the largest denomination (35% of the country's population).

Facts to Consider

- Freedom of religion is fully guaranteed, and there is separation of church and state.
- The USVI was struck by Category 5 Hurricane Irma in September 2017, causing extensive damage, especially in St. Thomas and St. John. Category 5 Hurricane Maria ravaged several islands just two weeks later. Ninety percent of buildings in the USVI were damaged in the storms.
- Tourism is the country's largest industry, with 2 to 3 million visitors annually, and makes up half of the islands' gross domestic product. COVID-19 related shutdowns and restrictions challenged the economy, and cases strained the already limited health care infrastructure.
- Blacks from the United States and Puerto Ricans have established many denominations on the islands, such as the African Methodist Episcopal Church and the Spanish-speaking Damascus Christian Church.

Indicators & Demographic Data

Population (2020)	105,000
% under 15 years	20%
Capital city (pop.)	Charlotte Amalie 51,700
% urban dwellers	96% (-0.11% p.a.)
Official language	English
Largest language	Virgin Islands Creole English (62%)
Largest people	Black (62%)
Largest culture	Black (African), English-speaking (62%)
Development	68
Physicians	39
Gender gap	3%

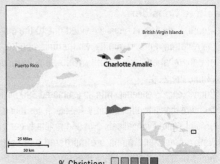

% Christian: 0 3 10 50 75 100

Christian Traditions in the USVI

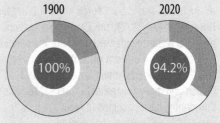

1900 — 100%
2020 — 94.2%

☐ Independent ☐ Protestant ☐ Catholic ■ Orthodox ■ Christian

Most of the Christians in 1900 were Protestant (80%) or Catholic (20%). In 2020, Christianity was slightly more diverse: 49% Protestant, 36% Catholic, and 15% Independent. Most Independents are Pentecostals/Charismatics.

Religion in the USVI

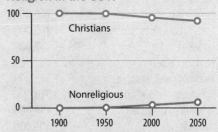

In 1900, the USVI was entirely Christian. Christianity declined only slightly to 94% by 2020 with an increase in the nonreligious population (4%).

Bible Translations	Churches	Missionaries	Gospel Access
Languages....7	Denominations 91	Received....170	1900...... Very high
Full Bible....4	Congregations....370	Sent 20	2020...... Very high

Christianity in Uruguay

Uruguay has always been a secular country, with Christianity at 63% of the country from 1900 to today. This contrasts with other Latin American countries, most of which were nearly 100% Christian at the start of the 20th century. Since colonial times, Catholic priests had less cultural influence here than elsewhere on the continent. Uruguay also had a much smaller indigenous population and was home to more European settlers who were already secularized. In the 20th century, the Catholic Church turned its attention toward problems of development in urban centers and other basic needs of society. The second largest denomination is the Church of Jesus Christ of Latter-day Saints, with over 100,000 members.

Facts to Consider

- About 94% of Uruguay's population today are Europeans or of European descent, mostly from Spain, Italy, and France.
- Religion does not have a prominent place in society. Christmas is called "Family Day," and Easter Week is known as "Tourism Week." A 2017 law called for an annual commemoration of secularism, celebrated on March 19.
- New Age religion is quite popular in Uruguay; for example, there are more registered New Age centers than Protestant churches.
- People from many religious traditions have expressed concern that the government discriminates against religious groups.
- Although Protestantism is small, some Evangelical and Pentecostal/Charismatic churches have grown in recent years. Most converts are former Catholics. Reasons for this growth include creative evangelistic outreach and use of popular media.

Indicators & Demographic Data

Population (2020)	3,494,000
% under 15 years	21%
Capital city (pop.)	Montevideo 1,752,000
% urban dwellers	96% (0.40% p.a.)
Official language	Spanish
Largest language	Spanish (91%)
Largest people	Uruguayan White (83%)
Largest culture	Latin-American White (84%)
Development	80
Physicians	37
Gender gap	-1%

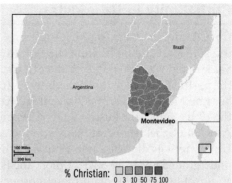

% Christian: 0 3 10 50 75 100

Christian Traditions in Uruguay

1900 — 62.7% 2020 — 62.2%

☐Independent ☐Protestant ▨Catholic ▪Orthodox ▪Christian

Most of the Christians in 1900 were Catholic (97%). In 2020, Christianity was only slightly more diverse: 83% Catholic, 10% Independent, and 5% Protestant. Many Independents are Pentecostals/Charismatics.

Religion in Uruguay

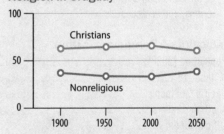

Uruguay has historically been the least religious country in Latin America. In 1900, the country was 63% Christian and 37% nonreligious. This changed very little over the 20th century: in 2020, these figures were nearly identical.

Bible Translations		Churches		Missionaries		Gospel Access	
Languages	22	Denominations	120	Received	2,500	1900	Very high
Full Bible	21	Congregations	2,300	Sent	500	2020	Very high

Christianity in Uzbekistan

Christianity in Uzbekistan dates to the 4th century with the spread of the faith along the Silk Road. A bishop of Samarkand was appointed in the 6th or 7th century and the position existed up until the 14th century. Most people became Muslims after the 7th century Arab conquest. In the 19th century, the Russian Empire expanded into central Asia, and Uzbekistan eventually became part of the Soviet Union until its dissolution in 1991. All religion was driven underground under the Soviet Union, and Islam experienced a revival in the 1990s, with more mosques in the country today than before Soviet rule. Christianity is a minority religion, only 1% of the population, and most are Russians.

Facts to Consider

- All religious groups must register with the Ministry of Justice, and unregistered groups are considered illegal. Many churches have unsuccessfully attempted to register. Proselytism and other missionary activities are illegal.
- The government frequently accuses some religious groups, both Muslim and non-Muslim, of "extremist" or "terrorist" activities. There are very few indigenous Christians.
- The state has control over all media coverage, including surveillance of social media. Bloggers have been arrested, and many report censorship by the government.
- Portions of Scripture were available in Uzbek since 1886, but the complete Uzbek language Bible was not completed until 2011.
- The largest churches outside the Orthodox tradition are among the country's Korean population, including Baptists, Methodists, Presbyterians, and Pentecostals.

Indicators & Demographic Data

Population (2020)	33,236,000
% under 15 years	28%
Capital city (pop.)	Tashkent 2,517,000
% urban dwellers	50% (1.25% p.a.)
Official language	Uzbek
Largest language	Uzbek (80%)
Largest people	Northern Uzbek (80%)
Largest culture	Uzbek (80%)
Development	71
Physicians	25
Gender gap	5%

% Christian: 0 3 10 50 75 100

Christian Traditions in Uzbekistan

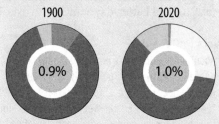

1900 — 0.9% 2020 — 1.0%

☐ Independent ☐ Protestant ■ Catholic ■ Orthodox ■ Christian

The Christian population in 1900 was mostly Orthodox (85%), with smaller communities of Catholics (10%) and Protestants (5%). In 2020, Orthodox dropped to 61% with the growth of Independents (27%) and Protestants (12%).

Religion in Uzbekistan

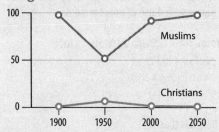

Muslims

Christians

Uzbekistan is a traditionally Muslim country (98% in 1900), but the Muslim share dropped to 50% during the Soviet era (42% nonreligious). In 2020, the country was 96% Muslim, 3% nonreligious, and 1% Christian.

Bible Translations		Churches		Missionaries		Gospel Access	
Languages	61	Denominations	91	Received	220	1900	Very low
Full Bible	35	Congregations	1,100	Sent	5	2020	Medium

Christianity in Vanuatu

Vanuatu is an island country (an archipelago of volcanic origin) in the South Pacific Ocean. Melanesian peoples were the first to inhabit the islands. Europeans (Spanish and Portuguese) arrived in the early 17th century. Missionaries in the 18th century were under constant threat of murder, warfare, and tropical disease. The French and British colonized the islands (known then as New Hebrides) together from 1906 until independence in 1980, when it was renamed Vanuatu. The country was majority Christian by 1970 and is 94% Christian today. The largest denominations are the Presbyterian Church, Assemblies of God, Catholic Church, and Anglican Church.

Facts to Consider

- As in other countries in Oceania, climate change is the most pressing issue related to sustainable development in Vanuatu, which experiences frequent earthquakes, tsunamis, and landslides. Awareness talks on climate change take place in churches, and church leaders partner with village chiefs and others to provide education on environmental justice.
- The Ministry of Health partners with several Christian churches to provide education, health resources, and disaster response to local communities.
- Most of the country is Christian, but theological issues remain on the roles of traditional beliefs and practices in Christian life. Traditional ethnic religion, known as Custom, is prominent on Tanna and Aniwa islands.
- There are three factions of John Frum (meaning "broom") cargo cults, a movement originating with a myth of a creature that would sweep away all Western influence and bring wealth to the indigenous population. Most John Frum followers are on Tanna Island.

Indicators & Demographic Data

Population (2020)................................. 294,000
% under 15 years 35%
Capital city (pop.)............................ Port Vila 52,000
% urban dwellers.............................26% (2.55% p.a.)
Official language........................Bislama, French, English
Largest language................................. Lenakel (6%)
Largest people ....Lenakel Tannese (6%)
Largest culture .... New Hebridean (89%)
Development...60
Physicians.. 1.9
Gender gap..13%

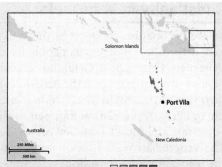

% Christian: 0 3 10 50 75 100

Christian Traditions in Vanuatu

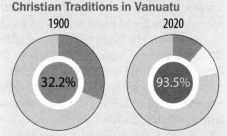

1900: 32.2% 2020: 93.5%

☐Independent ☐Protestant ▨Catholic ▨Orthodox ▪Christian

Christians in 1900 (14,500 total) were 69% Protestant (with many Evangelicals) and 31% Catholic. Christianity diversified slightly as it grew; in 2020, Christians were 79% Protestant, 11% Catholic, and 10% Independent.

Religion in Vanuatu

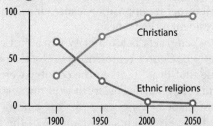

Vanuatu's religious makeup changed dramatically over the 20th century, from 32% Christian in 1900 to 94% Christian in 2020. Traditional religionists declined from 68% to 4% over the same period.

Bible Translations	Churches	Missionaries	Gospel Access
Languages..........115	Denominations 28	Received............340	1900 .... Low
Full Bible............15	Congregations...... 1,200	Sent 10	2020 .... Very high

Christianity in Venezuela

Before the Spanish conquest in the 16th century, an estimated 1 million indigenous people lived in what is now Venezuela. Christopher Columbus explored the region in 1498 on his third voyage to the Americas. Spain established their first settlement in what is today Cumaná in 1522, and the indigenous population dropped substantially because of warfare and the introduction of new European diseases. The Venezuelan War of Independence (1810–1823), under the leadership of Simón Bolívar, resulted in the nation's independence and the earliest democracies in Latin America. However, the country struggled with church-state relations, political turmoil, and dictatorships for much of the 19th and 20th centuries. The Catholic Church's relationship with the state became even more strained under the presidency of Hugo Chávez (1999–2013), who described the church hierarchy as a "cancer" and accused it of siding with the rich instead of the poor. His successor, Nicolás Maduro, also clashed with the church when it spoke out against Marxism and Communism. Maduro won a controversial reelection in 2018. Venezuelans have been suffering from high levels of crime, hyperinflation, and lack of basic necessities (food, water, shelter) under Maduro's dictatorship. The Catholic Church has been vocal in its opposition to Maduro and has helped in what has become the largest refugee crisis in the Americas. An estimated 5 million people fled the country between 1999 and 2020 to escape violence, poverty, and political instability. The United States and other countries still recognize opposition leader Juan Guaidó as the interim President of Venezuela.

Venezuela is a majority Christian country, with the Catholic Church representing 81% of the population in 2020. The first Protestants in the country were from the British and Foreign Bible Society in 1819, but sustained efforts were first made by Anglicans serving among British nationals in 1832. Protestants make up 7% of the population today, largest groups being the Assemblies of God, Seventh-day Adventists, and United Pentecostal Church. The country is home to at least 50 Independent denominations, many of which are Pentecostal/Charismatic in theology and worship. Pentecostal/Charismatic and Evangelical churches are growing across the country.

% Christian: 0 3 10 50 75 100

Religion in Venezuela

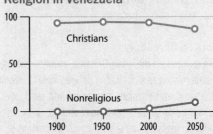

Venezuela has historically been a Christian country and remains so today. Christianity declined only 1% from 1900 to 2020, from 93% to 92%. In 1900, the second largest religion was traditional ethnic religions, which declined from 5% in 1900 to less than 1% in 2020. In 2020, the nonreligious (atheists and agnostics together) were 5% of the population and Spiritists were 1%.

Indicators & Demographic Data

Population (2020)	33,172,000
% under 15 years	27%
Capital city (pop.)	Caracas 2,939,000
% urban dwellers	88% (1.16% p.a.)
Official language	Spanish
Largest language	Spanish (95%)
Largest people	Venezuelan Mestizo (63%)
Largest culture	Mestizo (Spanish) (63%)
Development	76
Physicians	19
Gender gap	-1%

Bible Translations		Churches		Missionaries		Gospel Access	
Languages	58	Denominations	120	Received	6,000	1900	Very high
Full Bible	17	Congregations	30,700	Sent	1,000	2020	Very high

Facts to Consider

- Venezuela's political situation is unstable with continued conflict between Nicolás Maduro and Jean Guaidó. The military is responsible for keeping public order, though the government continues to carry out extrajudicial killings, arbitrary arrests (the majority from protests), and torture and abuse of detainees.
- The Maduro regime consistently represses basic human rights in the country, including peaceful assembly, freedom of expression, and freedom of the press. An increased number of children live on the streets, with an estimated 800,000 minors left behind as their parents fled the country. State-run facilities are inadequate to meet these needs.
- Clergy and other members of religious communities have been harassed by governmental officials for calling attention to the country's humanitarian and economic crises, which were compounded by the COVID-19 pandemic. Maduro's representatives have attacked churches and intimidated priests who criticized Maduro in their sermons.
- Venezuela has only roughly 7,500 Jews, but anti-Semitism is apparent in government media outlets, in statements linking the COVID-19 pandemic to Israel and Jews, and in Holocaust denial.

Christian Traditions in Venezuela

1900   2020

☐Independent ☐Protestant ▨Catholic ■Orthodox ■Christian

As in most Latin American countries, Christianity in Venezuela is historically majority Catholic. This was certainly the case in 1900, when 99% of Christians and 91% of the entire country was Catholic. This changed over the course of the 20th century. By 2020, Christians were 86% Catholic, 8% Protestant, and 6% Independent. The largest Independent denomination is the Jehovah's Witnesses, which grew from 20,000 members in 1970 to over 428,000 today.

Christian Families in Venezuela

Family	Population 2020	%	Trend	Change
Latin-rite Catholic	26,851,000	80.9	↑	1.0
*Pentecostals/Charismatics	6,300,000	19.0	↑	1.6
*Evangelicals	1,380,000	4.2	↑	2.4
Adventist	431,000	1.3	↑	3.8
Jehovah's Witnesses	428,000	1.3	↑	4.1
Nondenominational	210,000	0.6	↑	2.3
Latter-day Saints (Mormons)	193,000	0.6	↑	2.6
Baptist	132,000	0.4	↑	2.9
Eastern-rite Catholic	49,400	0.1	↑	4.9
Christian Brethren	44,600	0.1	↑	1.1
Congregational	32,600	0.1	↑	3.1
Eastern Orthodox	27,000	0.1	↑	1.0
Non-traditional, house, cell	18,300	0.1	↑	3.5
Holiness	15,200	<0.1	↑	3.1
Restorationist, Disciple	13,100	<0.1	↑	3.8
Lutheran	5,600	<0.1	–	0.0
Old Catholic Church	5,500	<0.1	↑	1.4
Oriental and other Orthodox	5,000	<0.1	–	0.1
Reformed, Presbyterian	4,700	<0.1	–	0.0
Anglican	1,300	<0.1	↑	3.6

The Catholic Church is the largest Christian family in Venezuela, with 81% of the country's population. There is significant overlap between Pentecostals/Charismatics and Evangelical churches, these being the second and third largest Christian families, respectively. The largest Charismatic movement is found among Catholics, with around 4 million affiliates. Other large Pentecostal groups are the Assemblies of God (695,000), the United Pentecostal Church (340,000), and the Light of the World Church (300,000). Large Evangelical groups also include the Assemblies of God, the National Baptist Convention (100,000), and the Organization of Evangelical Christian Churches (50,000). Arriving in 1920, Seventh-day Adventists make up the second largest denomination, with 359,000 members. Nondenominational churches include both indigenous-founded churches (Evangelical Missionary Union, Native Churches in Apure State) as well as churches from abroad (such as from Scandinavia and the United States).

* These movements are found within Christian families   ↑↑ extreme growth   ↑ growth   ↓↓ extreme decline

– no change   ↓ decline

Christianity in Vietnam

Vietnam is a very old country, tracing its history to at least the second century BC. Christianity dates to the arrival of the first Catholic missionaries in 1533, followed by Franciscan missionaries from the Philippines and then Jesuits. Jesuit Alexandre de Rhodes completed the first Vietnamese dictionary and catechism in a local script. Catholicism grew quickly, and there were 130,000 Catholics by 1639. Christians were persecuted in 1645, and the first Vietnamese priestly ordination was in 1668. Waves of persecution continued in the 17th and 18th centuries, resulting in upward of 30,000 martyrs. Foreign missionaries were banned in 1825, and France colonized the Indochina Peninsula (Vietnam, Cambodia, and Laos) in the late 19th century. The Catholic Church grew despite widespread persecution and the murder of one-third of the Christian population by indigenous guerrillas during the colonial period. All four Vietnamese bishops supported the independence movement in 1945, only for the country to become embroiled in the First Indochina War (1946–1954), followed by the American War (1955–1975). Tens of thousands of Christians fled to the south with the partition of the Communist north and democratic south. Church activities were severely limited in the north, and the clergy that remained were placed under house arrest.

National reunification in 1976 as the Socialist Republic of Vietnam expanded the setbacks that Christianity faced in the north into the south. The government took over all church properties and institutions, priests were sent to reeducation camps, and other Christians were imprisoned. Though restrictions on religion loosened in 1988, Christianity is still a minority religion (9%) in Vietnam. Most Christians are Catholics (77%). There are four main groups of Protestant/Independent (known as "Evangelical") churches: (1) ethnic Vietnamese who belong to the Evangelical Church of Vietnam South and the Evangelical Church of Vietnam North (split during the war), (2) ethnic Vietnamese who belong to unregistered house churches, (3) Montagnards of the Central Highlands (who are both in registered and unregistered churches), and (4) the Hmong and other ethnic minorities in the Northwest Mountainous Region (also in registered and unregistered churches).

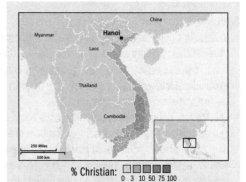

% Christian: 0 3 10 50 75 100

Religion in Vietnam

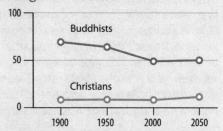

Buddhism has historically been the largest religion, but it declined from 69% to 50% between 1900 and 2020. Traditional religions have also declined (20% to 10%). Christianity grew only slightly in the 20th century, from 8% in 1900 to 9% in 2020. The increase of atheism and agnosticism (from zero in 1900 to 18% in 2020) is largely due to the Communist takeover.

Indicators & Demographic Data

Population (2020). 98,360,000
% under 15 years 23%
Capital city (pop.) . . . . Hanoi 4,678,000
% urban dwellers. . . . . 37% (2.70% p.a.)
Official language. . . . . Vietnamese
Largest language. . . . . Vietnamese (84%)
Largest people . . . . . Vietnamese (Kinh) (82%)
Largest culture . . . . Vietnamese (82%)
Development. 69
Physicians. 8.2
Gender gap . . . .-1%

Bible Translations		Churches		Missionaries		Gospel Access	
Languages.	97	Denominations	110	Received.	1,500	1900	Low
Full Bible.	19	Congregations.	18,100	Sent	.900	2020	High

Facts to Consider

- Vietnam is an authoritarian state under the sole control of the Communist Party. All religious groups must register with the government, but religious activities that are contrary to "national interest" or "public order" are banned.
- It is illegal to teach religion in public and private schools, including schools run by religious organizations. Authorities routinely monitor, interrupt, or disrupt house church meetings, especially among people who speak out against human rights abuses.
- Individuals from religious minority groups in the Central Highlands experience discrimination from the government, including monitoring, arbitrary detention, and interrogation. Most of those targeted belong to unregistered religious groups. Converts who leave their family's religion often face social ostracism and stigma.
- There is a close connection between religion and ethnicity. Ethnic minorities make up 14% of the country's population, and an estimated two-thirds of Protestants are from ethnic minority groups.
- There are approximately 100 New Religions in Vietnam, particularly ones that blend Buddhism and Christianity. Most are in the Northern and Central Highlands. The largest is the Cao Daist Missionary Church (Caodaism), founded in 1919, a mixture of popular Buddhism, Confucian ethics, and an ancestral cult with a Catholic-like organization. It is found mostly in the Mekong Delta.

Christian Traditions in Vietnam

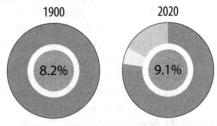

□Independent ▫Protestant ▪Catholic ◼Orthodox ◼Christian

Christians in Vietnam in 1900 were 100% Catholic due to French missions and colonization. An Evangelical Protestant movement emerged in the 20th century and in 2020 represented 19% of Christians. In 2020, most Christians in Vietnam were still Catholic (77%), followed by Protestants (17%) and Independents (6%). The largest Independent movement is unregistered house churches, with around 180,000 affiliates. Evangelicals and Pentecostal/Charismatics each make up around 1% of the country's population.

Christian Families in Vietnam

Family	Population 2020	%	Trend	Change
Latin-rite Catholic	7,221,000	7.3	↑	1.4
*Evangelicals	1,650,000	1.7	↑	1.8
Holiness	1,454,000	1.5	↑	2.8
*Pentecostals/Charismatics	800,000	0.8	↑	1.9
Non-traditional, house, cell	172,000	0.2	↑	0.7
Nondenominational	113,000	0.1	↑	4.4
Baptist	41,600	<0.1	↑	0.6
Media	38,700	<0.1	↑	1.0
Jehovah's Witnesses	20,500	<0.1	–	0.2
Adventist	15,900	<0.1	↑	2.6
Mennonite	14,300	<0.1	↑	1.2
United church or joint mission	10,000	<0.1	↑	2.9
Latter-day Saints (Mormons)	2,400	<0.1	↑↑	7.5
Anglican	130	<0.1	↓	-4.2

The Catholic Church is the largest Christian family in Vietnam, with 7% of the country's population. There is significant overlap between Evangelical and Pentecostal/Charismatic churches, these being the second and fourth largest Christian families, respectively. Large Evangelical denominations include the Evangelical Church of Vietnam (1.3 million), the Montagnard Evangelical Church (160,000), and Christian Fellowship Church (35,000). The house church movement in Vietnam is largely Pentecostal/Charismatic in worship and theology. There is also a small movement of Catholic Charismatics. Holiness churches include Vietnam Christ's Church (a split from the Christian & Missionary Alliance), the Evangelical Church of Vietnam (the largest Protestant group), and the Church of God (Cleveland), from the United States.

* These movements are found within Christian families
− no change
↑↑ extreme growth
↑ growth
↓↓ extreme decline
↓ decline

Christianity in Wallis and Futuna Islands

Wallis and Futuna Islands is an overseas French collectivity located two-thirds of the way from Hawaii to New Zealand in the South Pacific. It consists of three large tropical islands and several other tiny islands, some uninhabited. The country is home to just 11,600 people and is 97% Christian. The first Europeans to encounter the islands were the Dutch in 1616. France settled the islands in 1837, and subsequently most of the population became Catholic. In the 1960s, French Catholics transitioned leadership to indigenous national workers. St. Pierre Chanel Basilica in Poi is in honor of Polynesia's first Catholic saint, who worked on Futuna from 1837 until his martyrdom in 1841. He was canonized in 1954.

Facts to Consider

- Because Wallis and Futuna is a territory of France, all human rights and civil liberties are fully respected. But unlike in France, there is no real separation of church and state. Until 1970, the Catholic bishop had the title of "coprince" of the kingdom. Until the late 20th century, failure to attend Mass was punishable by a fine of one pig.
- Besides the Catholic Church, other denominations include Seventh-day Adventists, Futuna Evangelical Church, Jehovah's Witnesses, and Pentecostals. Seventh-day Adventists began work on Wallis in 2008.

% Christian: 0 3 10 50 75 100

Religion in Wallis and Futuna Islands

Christianity in Western Sahara

Western Sahara is a disputed area in northwest Africa, with 80% of the territory controlled by Morocco and the other 20% by the Popular Front for the Liberation of Saguia el-Hamra and Rio de Oro (POLISARIO), a Sahrawi movement that seeks Western Sahara's independence. Though Islam is the religion of the state, the constitution guarantees freedom of thought, expression, and assembly. Nevertheless, it is illegal to criticize Islam, and all educational institutions are required to teach Sunni Islam in accordance with the Maliki school.

Facts to Consider

- Western Sahara has perhaps only a dozen indigenous Christians. Likely there are more who practice their faith in secret, but it is impossible to know the size of the Christian community.
- Women have prominent roles in these "secret" Christian communities. Indigenous Christians tend to avoid association with expatriate Christians (mostly European Catholics). Christians face extreme social pressure to leave their religion, including social harassment.
- Violence against Sahrawis—including any indigenous Sahrawi Christians—is well documented by at least a dozen international human rights organizations.

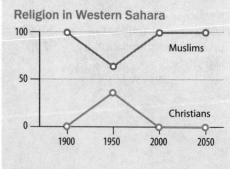

% Christian: 0 3 10 50 75 100

Religion in Western Sahara

Christianity in Yemen

Yemen is located on the southern end of the Arabian Peninsula, bordering Saudi Arabia and Oman. It was a part of the ancient kingdom of Sheba and perhaps had a small but growing Christian community in the 1st century. Islam displaced Christianity in the 8th century, and the country is 99% Muslim today. In 2004, fighting began between Houthis, a Zaydi Shia group, and government forces. Violence escalated with the Arab Spring in 2011, and the government was driven from power in 2014. ISIS, al-Qaeda, Houthis, and other forces continue to fight for control in a civil war, worsened by the Saudi Arabian–led military intervention to restore the ousted government.

Facts to Consider

- Islam is the state religion, and Sharia law is the source of all legislation. Conversion from Islam and proselytism are illegal.
- Houthis control an estimated 80% of the population and one-third of the territory; they are also known for persecuting religious minorities. Human Rights Watch has reported dozens of cases of Houthis responsible for arbitrary detentions and disappearances.
- The situation in Yemen is one of the largest humanitarian crises in the world, with 80% of people needing aid, especially millions of children. The COVID-19 pandemic exacerbated the continuing closures of schools and hospitals, widespread malnutrition, and economic decline.
- The head of the United Nations humanitarian program in Yemen called its plight "an impossible situation," citing a chronic lack of funding, workers, and resources.

Indicators & Demographic Data

Population (2020)	30,245,000
% under 15 years	39%
Capital city (pop.)	Sana'a 2,973,000
% urban dwellers	38% (3.71% p.a.)
Official language	Arabic
Largest language	Arabic (93%)
Largest people	Northern Yemeni Arab (46%)
Largest culture	Arab (Arabic) (94%)
Development	45
Physicians	3.1
Gender gap	57%

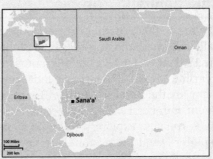

% Christian: 0 3 10 50 75 100

Christian Traditions in Yemen

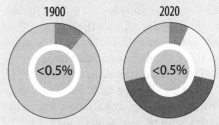

1900 — <0.5%
2020 — <0.5%

☐ Independent ☐ Protestant ■ Catholic ■ Orthodox ■ Christian

The small Christian population in 1900 (4,500) was mostly Protestant (89%). Christianity grew slightly in the 20th century but is still small today, with only 16,500 Christians (45% Orthodox, 28% Protestant, 21% Independent, and 7% Catholic).

Religion in Yemen

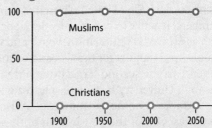

Yemen was 98% Muslim in 1900 and 99% in 2020. The country's Jewish population nearly disappeared over this period, dropping from over 33,000 in 1900 to under 100 today.

Bible Translations	Churches	Missionaries	Gospel Access
Languages............23	Denominations 21	Received............170	1900...........Very low
Full Bible.............9	Congregations........270	Sent 2	2020.............. Low

Christianity in Zambia

The region that is home to modern-day Zambia was originally inhabited by Khoisan peoples, followed by Bantus in the 13th century by way of migration from today's Cameroon and Nigeria. The largest people groups in the country today are the Bemba, Zambezi Tonga, Lozi, Nsenga, and Ngoni. European encounters began in the late 18th century via Portuguese explorers, followed by famous missionary explorer David Livingstone. Livingstone named the Victoria Falls (on the border between Zambia and Zimbabwe) after Queen Victoria. The British consolidated several areas into the protectorate of Northern Rhodesia and became a full-fledged colony in 1924. The British ruled Northern Rhodesia (today's Zambia), Southern Rhodesia (Zimbabwe), and Nyasaland (Malawi) as a semiautonomous region until Northern Rhodesia won independence in 1964 and renamed itself the Republic of Zambia.

The three largest umbrellas of churches in Zambia today are the Zambia Episcopal Conference, the main administrative body for the Catholic Church; the Christian Council of Zambia, which is linked to the World Council of Churches; and the Evangelical Fellowship of Zambia, which coordinates many local churches, missions, and para-church organizations in the country.

Catholicism arrived in 1879 but did not have a permanent presence until 1891. The first African bishop was consecrated in 1963. The first permanent Protestants arrived in 1884, and today dozens of Protestant denominations are in the country. The United Church of Zambia (1.2 million members) is active in community development in endeavors such as HIV/AIDS mitigation, youth and women's empowerment, and support for the sick and orphans. Seventh-day Adventists, the second largest denomination, established Rusangu University in Monze, a leading university.

Zambia is home to numerous African Independent Churches. One of the best-known of these churches is the Lumpa Church, founded by Alice Lenshina in 1953, which emphasized baptism, spiritual healing, and rejection of traditional religious practices. Pentecostal/Charismatic Christianity exploded starting in the 1970s, with the founding of several new denominations, the preaching of several foreign evangelists, and the declaration of Zambia as a Christian nation in 1990.

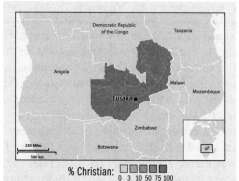

% Christian: 0 3 10 50 75 100

Religion in Zambia

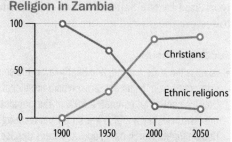

The religious makeup of Zambia changed dramatically over the 20th century. In 1900, the country was almost entirely followers of African Traditional Religions (99%). By 2020, Christianity had grown substantially to 86% of the country, followed by Baha'i, who grew to just under 2%, and Muslims to 1%. Traditional religions declined to 11%.

Indicators & Demographic Data

Population (2020). 18,679,000
% under 15 years 44%
Capital city (pop.) . . . . Lusaka 2,774,000
% urban dwellers. . . . . 45% (4.15% p.a.)
Official language. . . . . English
Largest language. . . . . Bemba (25%)
Largest people . . . . Bemba (22%)
Largest culture . . . . Central Bantu (68%)
Development. 59
Physicians. 0.9
Gender gap. 6%

Bible Translations	Churches	Missionaries	Gospel Access
Languages. 52	Denominations 200	Received. 3,500	1900 . . . . Very low
Full Bible. 28	Congregations. 32,700	Sent 270	2020 . . . . Very high

Facts to Consider

- Zambia is a Christian nation and upholds freedom of conscience, belief, and religion for all. All religious groups must register with a "mother body," and there are seven Christian bodies and seven non-Christian bodies. The government recently took steps to hold churches more financially accountable and regulate the conduct of clergy, including requiring theological education for some.
- Accusations of witchcraft are illegal and punishable by up to one year in prison. Accusations are often lodged against the elderly.
- Women in Zambia are held back from full political and economic participation because of a lack of education. Rape is also common, and laws against it are not regularly enforced. The Young Women's Christian Association works with the government and NGOs to address violence against women and gender-based discrimination. Sexual harassment and female genital mutilation are also common.
- Muslims are only 1% of the population but are very active in commerce. They primarily live in Lusaka, Eastern, and Copperbelt provinces and are immigrants from South Asia, Somalia, and the Middle East.
- African Traditional Religions are practiced by 11% of the population and are found largely among the Nyiha, Masi, Totela, and Mbowe peoples. However, many Christians hold traditional beliefs and practices in addition to Christianity.

Christian Traditions in Zambia

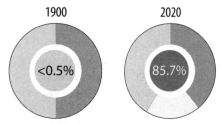

1900   2020

<0.5%   85.7%

☐Independent ☐Protestant ■Catholic ■Orthodox ■Christian

The very small Christian population in 1900 (only 2,000 Christians) was evenly split between Protestantism and Catholicism. Christianity became extremely diverse as it grew. In 2020, Christianity was 41% Protestant, 39% Catholic, and 20% Independent. The largest Independent denomination is the New Apostolic Church, which is the third largest community outside of the denomination's headquarters in Germany. Zambia is also home to one of the largest Jehovah's Witnesses populations in the world (over half a million).

Christian Families in Zambia

Family	Population 2020	%	Trend	Change
Latin-rite Catholic	6,000,000	32.1	↑	2.8
*Pentecostals/Charismatics	3,550,000	19.0	↑	2.3
*Evangelicals	2,900,000	15.5	↑	2.7
Adventist	2,319,000	12.4	↑↑	7.7
United church or joint mission	1,211,000	6.5	↑	0.5
Reformed, Presbyterian	771,000	4.1	↑	1.5
Jehovah's Witnesses	689,000	3.7	↑	2.6
Baptist	534,000	2.9	↑↑	6.2
Anglican	261,000	1.4	–	0.4
Holiness	223,000	1.2	↑	3.3
Restorationist, Disciple	157,000	0.8	↑	1.8
Nondenominational	137,000	0.7	↑	3.3
Christian Brethren	135,000	0.7	↑	1.5
Methodist	131,000	0.7	↑	1.4
Salvationist	62,100	0.3	↑	2.6
Mennonite	42,700	0.2	↑	4.8
Eastern Orthodox	7,700	<0.1	↑	0.8
Latter-day Saints (Mormons)	5,900	<0.1	↑↑	8.6
Moravian	4,500	<0.1	↑	3.0
Lutheran	3,900	<0.1	–	-0.3

The Catholic Church is the largest Christian family in Zambia, with 32% of the country's population. There is significant overlap between Pentecostal/Charismatic and Evangelical churches, these being the second and third largest Christian families, respectively. Large Pentecostal/Charismatic denominations include the New Apostolic Church (1.4 million), Pentecostal Assemblies of God (191,000), and the Pentecostal Holiness Association (185,000). There are hundreds of thousands of Evangelicals in the United Church and Reformed Church. The Baptist Convention, Baptist Union, Christian Brethren, and numerous Pentecostal churches are 100% Evangelical as well. Seventh-day Adventists are the second largest denomination (1.6 million members) and fourth largest family, representing 12% of the country's population.

* These movements are found within Christian families
– no change

↑↑ extreme growth
↑ growth
↓↓ extreme decline
↓ decline

Christianity in Zimbabwe

The region that is home to modern-day Zimbabwe was originally inhabited by San peoples, followed by Bantus in the 13th-century migration from today's Cameroon and Nigeria. The largest people groups in the country today are the Central Shona, Karanga, Ndebele, Zezuru, and Manyika. The first Christian contact with the Shona peoples was via Portuguese Jesuits in 1561, but no permanent Catholic presence was established until 1879. Robert Moffat, the pioneer Protestant missionary to Zimbabwe, opened a London Missionary Society station in 1859. No other groups entered until 1888. White Christian settlers—Anglicans, Methodists, Catholics, and Dutch Reformed—arrived in 1890 and formed separate settlements from Blacks. Black Christianity was mostly rural, with Whites presiding over their congregations, which led to the formation of many Independent Black churches. The British ruled Northern Rhodesia (today's Zambia), Southern Rhodesia (Zimbabwe), and Nyasaland (Malawi) as a semiautonomous region. Although Zambia achieved independence in 1964, Rhodesian independence was declared in 1965 but not recognized until 1980. The liberation struggle (known as *Chimurenga*) strained the churches during the wars for independence. After independence, 90% of the White population left the country. Zimbabwe is a majority Christian country today (83%), and churches serve as places of hope and healing.

Independent churches in Zimbabwe are classified either as Ethiopian or Zionist. Ethiopian churches were formed by evangelists unsatisfied with their lower-class position in mission-founded churches. The First Ethiopian Church was brought to Zimbabwe by a migrant laborer turned bishop in 1910. Zionist churches combine elements of African Traditional Religion, mission Christianity, and Charismatic Christianity. Their leaders claim to have revelations of God or angels and place significant emphasis on physical healing. The African Apostolic Church of Johane Maranke has over 1 million members after starting as a healing mission traveling through Zimbabwe, Zambia, Malawi, and the Democratic Republic of the Congo.

Pentecostal/Charismatic Christianity represents over 62% of the country's population (and 76% of Christians). Many Pentecostal churches have arrived from South Africa, such as the Apostolic Faith Mission, the country's largest denomination (2.3 million members).

% Christian: 0 3 10 50 75 100

Religion in Zimbabwe

Christians

Ethnic religions

1900   1950   2000   2050

The religious makeup of Zimbabwe changed dramatically over the 20th century. In 1900, the country was almost entirely followers of African Traditional Religions (96%). By 2020, Christianity had grown substantially, to 83% of the country, followed by Muslims to just under 1%. Traditional religions declined to 15%.

Indicators & Demographic Data

Population (2020). 17,680,000
% under 15 years 40%
Capital city (pop.) . . . . Harare 1,530,000
% urban dwellers. . . . . 32% (2.41% p.a.)
Official language English, Shona, and 12 others
Largest language. . . . . Shona (52%)
Largest people . . . . .Central Shona (22%)
Largest culture . . . . Shona (66%)
Development. 53
Physicians. 0.8
Gender gap 8%

Bible Translations		Churches		Missionaries		Gospel Access	
Languages.	36	Denominations	470	Received.	3,000	1900	Very low
Full Bible.	25	Congregations.	37,300	Sent	440	2020	Very high

Facts to Consider

- Many NGOs, domestic and international, have noted human rights abuses in Zimbabwe, such as violence against women and girls, restrictions on free expression, and widespread corruption. The government takes little action to investigate these claims or arrest or prosecute offenders.
- Freedom of religion is guaranteed in the constitution, and religious groups are not required to register with the government unless they want tax-exempt status. Christianity is taught in public schools but with an emphasis on religious tolerance.
- The Zimbabwe Gender Commission report in 2019 claimed that 22 women were raped every day in the country, a trend obscured by social stigma and fueled by a belief that rape is a "part of life." Domestic violence is also widespread and rarely prosecuted.
- The women's *manyano* ("prayer union") movement of the Methodist Church in Zimbabwe is a vital part of Christianity in the country, known for their prayer meetings, revivals, and casting out of spirits in the name of Jesus.
- African Traditional Religions are practiced by 15% of the population, mostly among the Ndau (Southeast Shona) and Hiechware San peoples. However, many Christians still associate with traditional beliefs and practices.

Christian Traditions in Zimbabwe

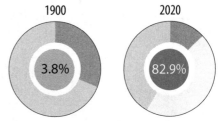

1900   2020

☐Independent ☐Protestant ▨Catholic ■Orthodox ■Christian

The small Christian population in 1900 were mostly Protestants (58%), followed by Catholics (31%). Christianity became extremely diverse as it grew. In 2020, Christians were 44% Independent, 43% Protestant, and 13% Catholic. The largest Independent denomination is the Zimbabwe Assemblies of God Africa (1.8 million members). Zimbabwe has exported many Independent denominations throughout Africa. In 2020, Evangelicals were 8% of the country's population and Pentecostal/Charismatics were 52%.

Christian Families in Zimbabwe

Family	Population 2020	%	Trend	Change
*Pentecostals/Charismatics	9,250,000	52.3	↑	1.9
Latin-rite Catholic	1,930,000	10.9	↑	1.0
Adventist	1,563,000	8.8	↑↑	5.1
*Evangelicals	1,380,000	7.8	↑	2.3
Methodist	569,000	3.2	↑	1.6
Anglican	485,000	2.7	↑	2.0
Baptist	335,000	1.9	↑	1.9
Restorationist, Disciple	323,000	1.8	↑	2.4
Lutheran	300,000	1.7	↑	3.6
Salvationist	210,000	1.2	↑	0.6
Reformed, Presbyterian	160,000	0.9	↑	1.0
Jehovah's Witnesses	139,000	0.8	↑	4.3
Mennonite	56,100	0.3	↑	4.3
Nondenominational	50,400	0.3	↑	1.5
Latter-day Saints (Mormons)	48,700	0.3	↑↑	10.1
Holiness	39,900	0.2	↑	2.6
United church or joint mission	38,400	0.2	↑	1.2
Congregational	16,100	0.1	–	0.1
Christian Brethren	9,500	0.1	↑	0.7
Eastern Orthodox	5,300	<0.1	↑	0.6

The Pentecostal/Charismatic family of churches is the largest in Zimbabwe, representing 62% of the country's population, and is expressed in a wide variety of church bodies. The largest of these churches originated in southern Africa, such as the Apostolic Faith Mission (South Africa, 2.3 million), Zimbabwe Assemblies of God Africa (1.8 million), African Apostolic Church of Johane Maranke (1.2 million), and Zion Apostolic Churches (1 million). There are also many Charismatics within the historic Protestant churches, such as Anglicans and Evangelical Lutherans, as well as a Catholic Charismatic movement. Catholics are the second largest family, with 11% of the population. Adventists, with 1.2 million members of the Seventh-day Adventist church, are the third. There are numerous Methodist groups, the largest of which are the United Methodist Church (200,000) and the Methodist Church in Zimbabwe (191,000).

* These movements are found within Christian families

– no change

↑↑ extreme growth
↑ growth
↓↓ extreme decline
↓ decline

Glossary

This glossary is designed to offer brief definitions of certain terms in this book that might be unusual or are used in specific ways in this book.

adherents: Followers, supporters, members, believers, devotees of a religion.

Adventists: Protestant tradition begun in 1844, emphasizing the imminent Second Advent of Christ.

affiliated: Followers of a religion enrolled and known to its leadership, usually with names written on rolls.

affiliated Christians: Church members; all people belonging to or connected with organized churches whose names are inscribed, written, or entered on the churches' books, records, or rolls.

African Independent Churches (AICs): Denominations indigenous to African peoples, begun without outside help; also termed African Indigenous Churches or African Initiated Churches.

agnostics: People who lack a religion or profess unbelief in a religion. The term includes (1) "classical" agnostics (who hold that it is impossible to know for certain whether God, or deity of any kind, exists), (2) those who profess uncertainty as to the existence of God, (3) other nonreligious people such as secularists and materialists, and (4) people who do not claim any religious affiliation but do not self-identify as atheists.

Anglicans: Christians related to the Anglican Communion, tracing their origin back to the ancient British (Celtic) and English churches; includes Anglican dissidents.

atheists: People professing atheism, the belief that there is no supernatural higher power; atheists might sometimes but not necessarily be hostile or militantly opposed to all religion (anti-religious).

Baha'is: Followers of the Baha'i World Faith, founded in 1844 by Baha'u'llah in what is now Iran.

Baptists: (1) In its widest meaning, all Christian traditions that baptize adults only, in contrast to paedobaptists, who baptize infants; (2) the specific tradition of Protestants and Independents calling themselves Baptists.

Bible: The whole or complete Bible of 66 books (sometimes plus Apocrypha).

Buddhists: Followers of the Buddha, mostly across Asia, including three main traditions: (1) Mahayana (Greater Vehicle); (2) Theravada (Teaching of the Elders); (3) Tibetan (Lamaists); plus (4) traditional Buddhist sects, but excluding neo-Buddhist New Religions or religious movements.

cargo cults: Religious movements in Oceania based on prophecies that if appropriate religious rites are performed, God will send ships and aircraft filled with cargo and goods.

Catholic Charismatics: Catholics who have come into an experience of baptism or renewal in the Holy Spirit.

Catholics: All Christians in communion with the Church of Rome, also known as Roman Catholics. Affiliated Catholics are defined here as baptized Catholics plus catechumens.

Catholics, non-Roman: Old Catholics and others in secessions from the Church of Rome since 1700 in the Western world, and other Catholic-type sacramentalist or hierarchical secessions from Protestantism.

Charismatic Renewal: The Pentecostal or neo-Pentecostal renewal or revival movement within the mainline Protestant, Catholic, and Orthodox churches characterized by healings, tongues, prophesyings, etc.

Charismatics: Baptized members affiliated to non-Pentecostal denominations who have entered into the experience of being filled with the Holy Spirit.

Christian Brethren: Independent Fundamentalist Protestant tradition begun in 1828 out of the Church of England; also called Open Brethren.

Christians: Followers of Jesus Christ of all kinds: all traditions and confessions and all degrees of commitment.

church: (1) A building set apart for Christian worship, or the services that go on in it; (2) a local congregation or worshiping body.

Confucianists: Followers of the teachings of Confucius and Confucianism. Sometimes spelled Confucians.

Congregation: (1) A local church or grouping of worshipers; (2) a religious order, society, or institute (mainly Roman Catholic usage).

Congregationalists: Protestant tradition with a system of church government in which the local congregation has full control and final authority over church matters within its own area.

continent: Any of the United Nations major areas of Africa, Asia, Europe, Latin America, and Oceania, along with the United Nations region of North America.

conversion: Change in a person's allegiance or membership in one religion to allegiance or membership in another.

converts: People who have become followers of a religion, leaving their former religion or nonreligion.

country: Term covering both (1) sovereign nations and (2) nonsovereign territories (dependencies or colonies) that are not integral parts of larger parent nations.

Daoists: Followers of the philosophical, ethical, and religious traditions of China, sometimes regarded as part of Chinese folk religion. Also spelled Taoists.

denomination: An organized Christian church, tradition, religious group, community of believers, aggregate of worship centers or congregations, usually within a specific country, whose component congregations and members are called by the same name in different areas.

Disciples: A Protestant tradition including the Disciples of Christ and Churches of Christ; also known as Restorationist, Restoration Baptist, Campbellite, or simply "Christian."

doubly affiliated Christians: People affiliated to or claimed by two denominations at once.

Eastern Orthodox: Refers to Chalcedonian Christians and their congregations and denominations that are in communion with the ecumenical patriarch of Constantinople. Excludes Oriental Orthodox.

Eastern-rite Catholics: All Catholics in communion with the Church of Rome who follow rites other than the Latin rite.

emigrant: A person who leaves a country or region to establish permanent residence elsewhere.

emigration: The movement of emigrants from one country to another.

ethnic religionists: Followers of a religion tied closely to a specific ethnic group, with membership restricted to that group; usually animists, polytheists, or shamanists. Also indigenous religionists or traditional religionists.

ethnolinguistic people: A distinct homogeneous ethnic or racial group within a single country, speaking its own language (one single mother tongue).

Evangelicals: Subdivision mainly of Protestants consisting of all affiliated church members calling themselves Evangelicals, or all people belonging to Evangelical congregations, churches, or denominations; characterized by commitment to personal religion (including new birth or personal conversion experience), reliance on Scripture as the only basis for faith and Christian living, emphasis on preaching and evangelism.

evangelism: The church's organized activity of spreading Christianity, in circumstances it can control, in contrast to witness, which is the normal term for the informal, spontaneous, unorganized sharing by individual Christians in circumstances they do not control.

evangelization: (1) The whole process of spreading Christianity, (2) the extent to which Christianity has been spread, (3) the extent of awareness of Christianity.

expatriate: Any person who has citizenship in one country but resides or lives in another country. In general usage, expatriate frequently connotes (1) temporary, often short-term, residence in the foreign country; and (2) higher socioeconomic status, with those of lower socioeconomic status being termed, e.g., "migrants."

faith-based organization (FBO): An activist organization whose values are based on faith, working to address social issues relevant to that faith.

folk religionists: Adherents of local traditions or religions, often rural, in which elements of major world religions are blended with local beliefs and customs.

foreign missionary: Full-time Christian workers who work in countries in which they are not citizens but foreigners, for at least two years.

foreign missions: Christian outreach carried out in any other countries than where a sending church or mission is based.

fundamentalist: Relating to or characterized by extreme conservatism, especially religious conservatism.

Hindus: Followers of the main Hindu traditions: Vaishnavism, Shaivism, Shaktism, neo-Hindu movements and modern sects, and other Hindu reform movements.

immigrant: A person who enters a country or region from elsewhere to establish permanent residence there.

immigration: The movement of immigrants to one country from another.

independency: The ecclesiastical position rejecting control of churches by centralized denominational headquarters; organizing churches and missions independent of historic Christianity.

Independents: Churches or individual Christians separated from, uninterested in, and independent of historic denominational Christianity.

indigenous: Originating or developing or produced naturally in a particular land or region or environment; not introduced directly or indirectly from the outside.

indigenous Christianity: In a particular region, that type of Christianity which, in contrast to imported or foreign types, is evolved or produced by populations indigenous to that region.

interreligious: Existing between two or more religions; used of activities or relationships between two or more of the major world religions (Judaism, Islam, Hinduism, Christianity, Buddhism).

Jains: Followers of the two Jain traditions, Svetambara and Digambara; originating in India as a reform movement from Hinduism in the 5th or 6th century BCE.

Jehovah's Witnesses: An Independent tradition begun in 1872; also called Russellites.

Jews: Followers of the various schools of Judaism; in the United States: Orthodox, Conservative, and Reform; in Israel: Haredi, Orthodox, Traditional, Observant, and secular; ethnically, Ashkenazi (Eastern Europe), Mizrahi (Middle Eastern), Sephardic (Iberian Peninsula).

Latin-rite Catholic: The part of the Roman Catholic Church that employs Latin liturgies (forms of Christian worship and liturgy utilizing or based on Latin).

Latter-day Saints: A generic term for followers of the Church of Jesus Christ of Latter-day Saints, an Independent Christian movement based in Salt Lake City, Utah, or of its break-off groups; also called Mormons.

LGBTQ: Acronym for lesbian, gay, bisexual, transgender, and queer (or questioning) people.

literacy: The ability to read and write, as measured by the percentage of the adult population who can read and write their own names and a simple statement. A higher level of competence is required for functional literacy.

Lutherans: Followers of Martin Luther and the original 16th-century German Protestant protesting tradition.

Mahayana: The Greater Vehicle school of Buddhism, or Northern Buddhism (China, Japan, etc.).

mainline Christianity: Relating to the historic Protestant churches of Northern and Western Europe (such as Methodist, Presbyterian, Lutheran).

martyr: Christian who loses their life prematurely in a situation of witness, as a result of human hostility.

megachurch: Very large local congregation or church; in a demographic sense, refers to a congregation or church with a membership over 2,000.

members: Affiliated (which usually means enrolled with names recorded) adherents of a religion.

Methodists: A tradition formed out of the Church of England in 1795. Many Methodist denominations are called "Wesleyan," "Holiness," or "United," although most belong to the World Methodist Council.

migration: Geographical or spatial mobility; physical movement by humans from one area to another with the declared intention to reside in or leave a country for at least a year.

mission: The dimension of Christian witness concerned with outreach to the world.

missionary societies: Local, denominational, national, or international religious organizations dedicated to starting and supporting missionary work. Also known as mission societies and mission agencies.

Muslims: Followers of Islam, in two primary branches: (1) Sunni and (2) Shia. Other, significantly smaller, branches include Kharijite, Sanusi, Mahdiya, Ahmadiya, Druzes, and Sabbateans.

New Religionists: Adherents of Hindu or Buddhist sects or offshoots, or new syncretistic religions combining Christianity with Eastern religions, mostly in Asia.

New Religions: The so-called Asiatic 20th-century New Religions, New Religious movements, or radical new crisis religions (new Far Eastern or Asiatic indigenous non-Christian syncretistic mass religions, founded since 1800 and mostly since 1945), including the Japanese neo-Buddhist and neo-Shinto New Religious movements, and Korean, Chinese, Vietnamese, and Indonesian syncretistic religions, among others.

nondenominational: Unrelated to any denomination or denominations, nor accountable to any.

nongovernmental organization (NGO): A nonprofit organization that operates independently of any government, usually in social work or politics.

nonreligious: People professing no religion, or professing unbelief or nonbelief, nonbelievers, agnostics, freethinkers, liberal thinkers, nonreligious humanists. In this book, typically used as an umbrella term for atheists and agnostics together.

Oriental Orthodox: Christians of Pre-Chalcedonian/Non-Chalcedonian/Monophysite tradition, of five major types: Armenian, Coptic, Ethiopian, Syrian, Syro-Malabarese.

Orthodox: In four traditions: Eastern (Chalcedonian), Oriental (Pre-Chalcedonian, Non-Chalcedonian, Monophysite), Assyrian, and nonhistorical Orthodox.

p.a.: Per annum, per year, each year, every year, annual, yearly, over the previous 12 months.

Pentecostals: Followers of Pentecostalism, a Christian movement originating around 1900.

poll: An opinion inquiry taken at a single point in time from a small carefully-constructed sample (usually around 1,500–2,500 adults) representative of the entire adult population, to solicit answers to carefully formulated questions to derive information applicable to that entire population.

population: For an area, the total of all inhabitants or residents of that area; or occasionally, the total number of persons who spend or spent the night in the area.

population census: A government survey to obtain information about the state of the population at a given time.

Presbyterian: See Reformed.

Protestants: Christians in churches originating in, or reformulated at the time of, or in communion with, the 16th-century Protestant Reformation. In European languages usually called Evangéliques (French), Evangelische (German), Evangélicos (Italian, Portuguese, Spanish), though not usually Evangelicals (in English).

quality of life: The effectiveness of social services in a country, measured by indexes such as the United Nations Human Development Index (HDI).

Reformed: A major Protestant tradition originating in continental Europe and including the term Presbyterian (originating in English-speaking countries).

refugees: People who have migrated because of strong pressures endangering their continued stay in their countries of origin and who are unable or unwilling to return; excludes labor and other migrants and also returnees.

region: In United Nations terminology, one of 21 areas into which the whole world is divided for purposes of analysis.

religion: An organized group of committed individuals that adhere to and propagate a specific interpretation of explanations of existence based on supernatural assumptions through statements about the nature and workings of the supernatural and about ultimate meaning. In this book, religion as used in a demographic sense includes the unaffiliated (i.e., agnostics and atheists).

religionists: People professing adherence to any religion, as contrasted with the nonreligious (i.e., agnostics or atheists).

religious change: Changes from one religion or religious system to another within a certain time period, e.g., in the course of a year.

religious demography: The scientific and statistical study of the demographic characteristics of religious populations, primarily with respect to their size, age-sex structure, density, growth, distribution, development, migration, and vital statistics, including the change of religious identity within human populations and how these characteristics relate to other social and economic indicators.

religious diversity: The degree to which a population comprises individuals with differing religious adherences. Inter-religious diversity describes the degree of over-all diversity of distinct religions (Islam, Hinduism, Judaism, and so on) within a population or geographic area, whereas intrareligious diversity encompasses the diversity found within a given world religion (for example, traditions such as Catholicism, Orthodoxy, and Protestantism within Christianity).

religious liberty: Freedom to practice one's religion with the full range of religious rights specified in the United Nations 1948 Universal Declaration of Human Rights.

religious men (brothers): Unordained male members of Catholic religious institutes or orders living a consecrated life of the Catholic Church. Vows of poverty, chastity, and obedience.

religious pluralism: The peaceful coexistence of different religions or denominations within a particular community.

Restoration Movement: (1) The Churches of Christ, or Disciples, a major USA group of denominations; (2) an Independent charismatic paradenomination splitting in 1974 from the Charismatic Renewal within the mainline Protestant churches in Britain and the USA.

Roman Catholics: All Christians in communion with the Church of Rome. Affiliated Roman Catholics are defined in this book as baptized Roman Catholics plus catechumens.

rural area: De facto areas classified as rural (that is, it is the difference between the total population of a country and its urban population); defined in many countries as an administrative district with a population of under 2,000.

secularism: A view of life or of any particular matter holding that religion and religious considerations should be ignored or purposely excluded.

secularization: The act or process of transferring matters under ecclesiastical or religious control to secular or civil or lay control; the process whereby religious thinking, practice, and institutions lose social significance.

shamanists: Ethnic religionists with a hierarchy of shamans and healers.

Shias: Shi'is Followers of the smaller of the two great divisions of Islam, rejecting the Sunna and holding that Muhammad's son-in-law Ali was the Prophet's successor and itself divided into the Ithna-Ashari Ismaili, Alawite, and Zaydi sects.

short-term missionaries: Persons serving as foreign missionary personnel for a single period between one week and 24 months only.

Sikhs: Followers of the Sikhism, founded by Guru Nanak in the 15th century in the Punjab region of the Indian subcontinent. Traditions include Akali, Khalsa, Nanapanthi, Nirmali, Sewapanthi, and Udasi.

Spiritists: Non-Christian spiritists or spiritualists, or thaumaturgicalists; high spiritists, as opposed to low spiritists (Afro-American syncretists), followers of medium-religions, medium-religionists.

Sunnis (Sunnites): Followers of the larger of the major branches of Islam, which adheres to the orthodox tradition of the *sunna*, acknowledges the first four caliphs, and recognizes four schools of jurisprudence: Hanafite, Hanbalite, Maliki, Shafiite.

socioeconomic status (SES): A measure of an individual's or group's position in society, based on factors including income, education, and occupation. Sometimes other factors—such as wealth, place of residence, race, ethnicity, and religion—are also used in determining SES.

state religion: An established religion; national religion recognized in law as the official religion of a country.

survey: A systematic method for gathering information from (a sample of) entities for the purposes of constructing quantitative descriptors of the larger population of which the entities are members.

switching (religious): When individuals leave a religion or religious body either to other religions or religious bodies or to no religion (agnosticism, atheism).

Theravada: The Teaching of the Elders or the Hinayana school of Buddhists, or Southern Buddhism (in Sri Lanka, India, Myanmar, Thailand, Cambodia, Laos).

tradition: An ecclesiastical family or type of denominations sharing historical and/or many common features.

traditional religion: Often used of the dominant pre-Christian religion in a country, sometimes described as ethnic or indigenous religion.

unaffiliated Christians: People professing allegiance and commitment to Christ but who have no church affiliation.

United churches: Churches formed from the union of various Protestant denominations (including Anglicans).

urban areas: De facto population living in areas classified as urban according to the criteria each area or country uses; often these are agglomerations of 2,500 or more inhabitants, generally having population densities of 1,000 people per square mile (391 people per square kilometer).

urbanization: The state or extent of urban areas or the process of becoming urbanized, in a particular country.

women religious (religious women): Female members of Catholic religious institutes or orders, working on behalf of the Catholic Church in a variety of settings, often social service and education. Vows of poverty, chastity, and obedience.

worldview: A general understanding of the nature of the universe and of one's place in it; outlook on the world, ideology, a cosmological conception of society and institutions.

Yezidis: Members of a monotheistic religion that has elements of ancient Mesopotamian religions and also combines aspects of Christianity, Judaism, and Islam.

Zoroastrians: Followers of a religion founded in Persia in BCE 1200 by the prophet Zoroaster teaching the worship of Ahura Mazda, now followed by Parsis in India and elsewhere.